Recent years have seen a revolution in our knowledge of how children learn to think and speak. In this volume, leading scholars from these rapidly evolving fields of research examine the relationship between child language acquisition and cognitive development. At first sight recent advances in the two areas seem to have moved in opposing directions: the study of language acquisition has been especially concerned with diversity, explaining how children learn languages of widely different types, while the study of cognitive development has focused on uniformity, clarifying how children build on fundamental, presumably universal, concepts. This book brings these two vital strands of investigation into close dialogue, suggesting a new synthesis in which the process of language acquisition may interact with early cognitive development. It provides original empirical contributions, based on a variety of languages, populations, and ages, and theoretical discussions that cut across the disciplines of psychology, linguistics, and anthropology.

MELISSA BOWERMAN is Senior Scientist at the Max Planck Institute for Psycholinguistics and Professor at the Free University of Amsterdam. Her work focuses on first language acquisition in children. She is author of *Early syntactic development: a cross-linguistic study with special reference to Finnish* (1973), and many articles and chapters on language development.

STEPHEN LEVINSON is Director of the Max Planck Institute for Psycholinguistics. He is editor of the Cambridge University Press series Language, Culture and Cognition. His previous books include *Pragmatics* (1983), *Politeness* (1987), and *Presumptive meanings* (2000), and he is co-editor of *Rethinking linguistic relativity* (1996).

Language, culture and cognition 3

Language acquisition and conceptual development

Language, culture and cognition

Editor
STEPHEN C. LEVINSON
Max Planck Institute for Psycholinguistics, Nijmegen

This new series looks at the role of language in human cognition – language in both its universal, psychological aspects and its variable, cultural aspects. Studies will focus on the relation between semantic and conceptual categories and processes, especially as these are illuminated by cross-linguistic and cross-cultural studies, the study of language acquisition and conceptual development, and the study of the relation of speech production and comprehension to other kinds of behavior in cultural context. Books come principally, though not exclusively, from research associated with the Max Planck Institute for Psycholinguistics in Nijmegen.

1. Jan Nuyts and Eric Pedersen (eds.) *Language and conceptualization*
2. David McNeill (ed.) *Language and gesture*
3. Melissa Bowerman and Stephen C. Levinson (eds.) *Language acquisition and conceptual development*

Language acquisition and conceptual development

Edited by

Melissa Bowerman and Stephen C. Levinson

Max Planck Institute for Psycholinguistics

PUBLISHED BY THE PRESS SYNDICATE OF THE UNIVERSITY OF CAMBRIDGE
The Pitt Building, Trumpington Street, Cambridge, United Kingdom

CAMBRIDGE UNIVERSITY PRESS
The Edinburgh Building, Cambridge CB2 2RU, UK www.cup.cam.ac.uk
40 West 20th Street, New York, NY 10011-4211, USA www.cup.org
10 Stamford Road, Oakleigh, Melbourne 3166, Australia
Ruiz de Alarcón 13, 28014 Madrid, Spain

First published 2001

Printed in the United Kingdom at the University Press, Cambridge

Typeface Monotype Times NR 10/12 pt *System* QuarkXpress™ [SE]

A catalogue record for this book is available from the British Library

Library of Congress Cataloguing in Publication data

Language acquisition and conceptual development / edited by Melissa Bowerman and Stephen C. Levinson.
p. cm – (Language, culture and cognition: 3)
Includes index.
ISBN 0 521 59358 1 – ISBN 0 521 59659 9 (paperback)
1. Language acquisition. 2. Cognition in children. I. Bowerman, Melissa. II. Levinson, Stephen C. III. Series.
P118.L2497 2000
401′.93 – dc21 99-42105 CIP

ISBN 0 521 59358 1 hardback
ISBN 0 521 59659 9 paperback

Contents

Preface

This volume has grown out of a conference on the theme "Language acquisition and conceptual development," which was held at the Max Planck Institute for Psycholinguistics in November 1995. The conference was an unusually stimulating and exciting meeting, where intellectual positions were on the brink of change. We hope that this volume captures some of that excitement about theory change in the making.

The program was devised by the editors of this volume in collaboration with Dan Slobin and Wolfgang Klein. All the papers delivered on that occasion are reprinted here, but with substantial revisions that take account of each other and the discussion at the conference. Part of that discussion was provided by commentators on each session, and we thank Shanley Allen, Martha Crago, Eve Danziger, Eric Pederson, and David Wilkins for their probing comments, comparisons, and substantial ideas, now partly woven into the fabric of the chapters. Differences in length between the chapters stem in part from the different roles of the papers in the original conference, and in part from constraints on the size of this volume.

We thank the Max Planck Society for sponsoring the conference, and the support staff of the Max Planck Institute for Psycholinguistics for their help. We especially thank Edith Sjoerdsma for her invaluable help in organizing the conference and collating the volume.

One of the participants at the conference was Martin Braine, who died a few months after the meeting. We would like to dedicate this volume to his memory. In the fields represented in this book, Marty was one of the great pioneers, whose intensity and enthusiasm was instrumental in making the area as intellectually stimulating as it is today. The chapter in this book by Marty and co-authors will give some idea of the probing questions he was in the midst of pursuing, and thus the extent of our loss. Those who were lucky enough to have known him will sorely miss the unique blend of acuity, curiosity, and breadth of learning which made a conversation with him always deeply profitable.

Melissa Bowerman and Stephen C. Levinson

Introduction

Melissa Bowerman and Stephen C. Levinson
Max Planck Institute for Psycholinguistics, The Netherlands

1 Background issues

1.1 Epistemology

This volume touches issues at the heart of Western thinking: how do we know what we know, and what are the mental prerequisites that make such knowledge possible? There is no better way to study these ancient epistemological questions than to examine carefully how children learn to think and speak. But the careful study of children's development dates back only to the end of the nineteenth century (see chapter by Deutsch, Wagner, Burchardt, Schulz, & Nakath, this volume), and indeed some of the most interesting techniques for investigation have only been devised in the last few years, in some cases by the contributors to this volume. Here then is a relatively new field of investigation which is rapidly evolving, but which, rather than being a narrow specialism like many modern branches of science, talks directly to the fundamental questions about why we think the way we do. It is a subject that every psychologist or cognitive scientist, every linguist or social scientist, every historian of ideas or philosopher, should keep an eye on. This volume should help to make accessible recent thought in the area, and give some sense of the intellectual ferment which characterizes it.

Two kinds of recent development have radically changed the way we think about this area. Since the mid-1980s, there has been a revolution in our knowledge of infant cognition: new techniques for exploring what infants know within the first year of life have revealed striking early abilities in the understanding of both the physical world and abstract concepts like number or animacy (see e.g. Carey 1985, Keil 1989, Wynn 1992, Spelke 1993). Over a similar period there have been parallel changes in the study of language acquisition. For example, new techniques provide increasingly sophisticated ways of probing linguistic knowledge even before production begins (e.g. Golinkoff, Hirsh-Pasek, Cauley, & Gorden 1987). In addition, the study of language acquisition in non-European languages and cultures (initiated on a comparative basis by Slobin 1967) has come at last to a point where we have a significant range of information (Slobin 1985, 1992), and these data have challenged many earlier theories and presumptions about universal processes. Both areas – the study of cognitive development and the study of language acquisition – are rich with hotly contested ideas about what might constitute adequate new theories to cover the new ground.

The study of both conceptual development and language acquisition in the child have been in large part conducted by psychologists (although of course there have been significant contributions from linguists, anthropologists, and others, especially in the field of language acquisition). But for historical reasons these two strands of investigation, one focused on nonlinguistic cognitive development and the other on the development of language, have often grown apart. One reason perhaps is that the methods of investigation sometimes diverge: cognitive development is now most often explored by careful experiments on children of different ages, whereas much language acquisition research, especially of languages other than English, is still based on long-term observation of naturally occurring behaviors. Another reason is that although many attempts were made (especially in the 1970s) to relate significant stages in language acquisition to the proposed (largely Piagetian) milestones in cognitive development, no close correlation could be established. A third reason for divergence has been the very success of theoretical linguistics, with rapidly changing, often dauntingly complex, theories about the structure of language; in consequence, many students of language acquisition have become linguistic specialists. Moreover, the more complex the nature of grammatical competence is seen to be, the less likely it seems that it could be acquired by general-purpose procedures for learning. This Chomskyan message suggests that language is a special cognitive capacity, which we acquire by virtue of special-purpose learning procedures that are part of our biological endowment, and that have their own distinctive constraints. Although many psychologists resist this conclusion (see e.g. Tomasello 1995), this kind of thinking, and the very technicality of linguistics, have driven a wedge between the study of general cognitive development and the study of how children learn language. This is so even though the Chomskyan (or latterly Fodorean) message has also come to inform the study of nonlinguistic cognitive development, suggesting that many special-purpose learning mechanisms may be involved there too (see Carey 1985, Keil 1989).

This volume brings these two strands of investigation, of the linguistic and nonlinguistic aspects of cognitive development, back into close connection with one another. It does so by focusing on conceptual content rather than on the structural properties of the underlying representations for language or thought. Here in the domain of ideas about space, time, number, logical quantifiers, physical objects, and their classification, and so on, it is clear that the formation of the same or similar concepts is crucial to both linguistic and nonlinguistic conceptual development. Words, and sub-word meaning elements like plural or tense morphemes, embody sophisticated concepts. How does a child master their meanings? Are such concepts essentially independent of language, such that language merely expresses them, or do children come to *construct* them through language, and under the catalytic effect of verbal interaction with their elders? If such concepts are at least partially independent of language, are they – or perhaps some of them – also independent of experience? These are obvious questions, and, together with finer-grained issues, these are the problems addressed in this volume.

It is clear that in principle such questions can have empirical answers: if children display knowledge of the relevant concepts long before they display a corresponding grasp of the language that expresses them, then the concepts would appear to be independent of language. Conversely, if languages differ and children's early concepts also differ in line with the language they are learning, then the concepts in question would appear to be language-induced. In practice, finding such answers can be difficult. For example, we would like to tap independently both the earliest understandings of language and the early nonlinguistic ideas in corresponding domains. The techniques for exploring these aspects of the infant's world are new and rather limited: in this volume Bowerman & Choi show how one can investigate language-specific semantic categories in the making even before infants can speak, and Carey, Spelke & Tsivkin, and others report on probes of early nonlinguistic cognition. But careful parallel studies of early semantics and early cognition across languages and cultures are yet to be done.

For this reason, for the moment at least, many different avenues of inquiry are necessary if we hope to get an understanding of the relevant processes. For example, we can look over the fence at our nearest primate relatives and get a sense of what conceptual development without language looks like, but to do so we need tools for estimating what concepts members of species without language can master (see the chapter by Langer in this volume). Alternatively, we can look at the concepts that children presume might make good meanings even though their particular language fails to encode them (Clark, this volume; see also Deutsch *et al.*, this volume, on the ephemeral forms invented by twins for dual self-reference). Or we can try to find methods for testing children's understandings of the world when they are only a few months old (again, see, for example, Carey, this volume). We can look across languages and see what concepts, if any, recurrently get encoded (see Slobin, this volume). We can try and find languages that differ radically in semantic structure and see how children come to terms with such different concepts (see e.g. the chapters by Brown, de León, and Bowerman & Choi, this volume). These and many other ways of approaching the issues are represented in this volume.

1.2 The child's innate biases: native constraints, learning mechanisms and "theories"

It will be useful to the reader to identify a number of the other themes that run through the chapters in this volume. Inevitably one of the leading questions is: just what is the child natively endowed with? When the enormity of the word learning task is considered, it is clear that the child must have *some* kind of head-start in terms of either conceptual content or learning principles, or at the very least in terms of constraints on likely meanings given by the nature of human predispositions and preoccupations with specific aspects of the physical and social environment. Consider Quine's (1960) well-known conundrum of "radical translation": we see a rabbit, the natives say *gavagai*, but how do we know whether they mean 'rabbit-stuff,' 'this instant of rabbit-experience,' or even just 'white tail'? Only because we *presume* they should have a word for rabbit, and we think they would expect us now to want to know *that* and not something else. Such thought experiments soon convince us that without all kinds of background assumptions, and clues from the structure of the language itself, languages would be unlearnable.

The question is: what exactly *are* these conceptual assumptions that the child natively brings to the word and morpheme learning task? Carey (this volume) explores the idea that there might be something as simple as a presumption of a commonsense notion of object, like that underlying our translation of *gavagai*. But she shows that very small infants don't seem to have such a notion: they have various proto-concepts of objects, which do not initially require even shape constancy, and even until right up towards the end of the first year they do not require size or color constancies. Indeed some aspects of our commonsense notion of object seem to be learnt simultaneously with, and thus perhaps partially through, the first words.

It appears, then, that only very primitive ontological assumptions are in place long before language, which makes it possible that the structure of specific languages may influence fundamental conceptual categories. These issues are explored further in a number of the chapters. Gopnik for example observes that in the 15–21-month period there is a very close interaction between language learning and conceptual development, with, for example, firm concepts of object permanence linked to the naming spurt. There is still likely to be an inevitability about certain concepts that are arrived at, despite crosslinguistic differences. Thus Gentner & Boroditsky show that the kind of mass-like noun semantics associated with classifier languages does makes a difference to presumptions underlying very early word learning, but prototype complex objects like artifacts are immune to this language-specific bias – the nouns describing them are assumed to name objects, not substances like other nouns. Lucy & Gaskins suggest that the language-specific bias perhaps only comes to dominate nonlinguistic classification much later in childhood. The emerging picture is complex, but it does suggest that language-specific patterns may have at least some influence on fundamental ontological categories.

If ontological assumptions are perhaps not fully fixed in advance of language learning, it could be that at least the learning mechanisms themselves are specified from the outset. Perhaps, then, there are highly specialized word learning mechanisms, as suggested by the sudden vocabulary spurt or "naming explosion" that occurs around the age of two, when children may learn up to ten new words a day (Clark 1993:13, 28). Is there a special "fast-mapping" process (Carey 1978), perhaps involving special faculties for the retention of words? Bloom (this volume) concludes that there is not: early memory for words is not markedly better than for other concepts, and all the special constraints and assumptions that have been proposed do not really seem to distinguish the learning of word meanings from the learning of other concepts, except in so far as they follow the grammatical distinctions in the language (like mass vs. count nouns). Similar conclusions are reached by Smith, who argues that the very most general processes of attentional learning can in fact account for the apparent biases and presumptions that have led scholars to think that there must be special-purpose word learning abilities. From a different angle, Tomasello (this volume) takes the position that once the interactional context, with its rich attentional and intentional cues, is taken properly into account, the mysteries of word learning seem to recede, and, again, no special mechanisms may need to be posited.

Ontology is fundamental to logic (Quine 1960) – for example, there can be no quantification without individuals or count nouns (see Carey, this volume). In fact, children have problems with quantification, and two rather different kinds of problem are analyzed in detail in the chapters by Brooks, Braine, Jia, & da Graca Dias and by Drozd in this volume. Braine (1994) has taken the view that logic in language is a reflection of the "syntax of thought." Children between four (the earliest point at which most such experiments have been done) and seven make well-known, repetitive logical errors. If logical reasoning is universal, and built in, why should such errors occur? Both Brooks & Braine and Drozd essentially argue that it is a mapping problem: children have the right underlying representations but map them to the wrong linguistic forms. What appears to be wonky thinking is just wonky speaking! The linguistic difficulties facing the child are analyzed rather differently in the two chapters. Brooks *et al.* assume simple canonical underlying forms, but with lexical quantifiers indicating or preferring certain scope distinctions; children may make the wrong associations between lexical quantifier and scope. Drozd argues that the lexical quantifiers belong to two very different, rather complex semantic classes, and children may assign a lexical quantifier to the wrong class. The claim that the problems are essentially linguistic would have as a corollary the tenet that logical structure is largely a native endowment, which might then be assumed to drive presumptions about language, for example about the kinds of reference that nouns may have if they are to be quantified over.

There are other kinds of conceptual bias and cognitive foundation that might underlie children's abilities to learn words so fast and, eventually at least, accurately. As mentioned above, the Chomskyan way of thinking has passed into the study of conceptual development, especially through the medium of Fodor's (1983) theory of the modular or compartmental nature of human thought. This theory posits that the mind consists of many innate specialized processing devices, interfacing with each of the sensory and motor systems, or input/output systems. An extension of Fodor's view is that the central thinking capacity, which he thought of as relatively undifferentiated, is itself composed of a collection of domain-specific theories. On this view, which is known affectionately as the "theory theory" (see Carey 1985; Gopnik, this volume), there are specific theories governing our ideas about such areas as naive physics (how objects behave), natural kinds, animals, other minds and their actions, perhaps also number, space, and so on. A "theory" in this sense is an articulated set of beliefs that allow the deduction of expectations. A first assumption might be that such theories have an innate basis, so that we might for example be born with these theories in some initial primitive state. Indeed, conceptual development is thought of as a series of theory replacements or reconstructions, as over-simple theories are replaced with ones more adequate to the data of experience (just as scientific theories are overthrown or revised). Such theory changes appear to be especially dramatic at just the time when language production begins to flourish (Gopnik, this volume), and these events may be closely linked, reciprocally feeding each other. Gopnik produces some novel comparisons across languages, which support the idea that language may play a leading role in such theory change.

The "theory theory" is an attractive way of reconstruing what conceptual development essentially consists of. Instead of some kind of seamless unfolding of predispositions under experience, or instead of the Piagetian picture of a stage-like progression across all domains, we are offered a picture of the child theorizer trying to make sense of specific domains, and radically restructuring the domain-specific theory in the light of growing experience (see Keil 1989 for exposition). Biases, classifications, and inferences are all guided by these specialized theories, which should impinge on language learning as assumptions about what words in specific domains can mean. One attraction of this kind of theory is that it might offer us a way of thinking about the transformative role of language in cognition as a systematic series of bridges linking the conceptual islands of each domain (as explored in this volume by Spelke & Tsivkin), a point returned to below.

But perhaps the "theory theory" overemphasizes both the amount of innate endowment (for example, the carving out of specific domains, with initial assumptions in each) and the degree of higher-level cognition involved. Smith (this volume) argues that we should turn back to biological models of development: after all, during the development of the embryo we get elaborate differentiation of organisms from the operation of entirely general processes, coupled with a specific history or trajectory of development (if you surgically switch a left-hand wing-bud on a chick embryo with a right-hand one, you still get a normal chick). She argues that, in the same way, we should explore the possibility that the simplest associative learning, coupled with attentional biases from initial stages of learning, can give us all the rich domain-specific effects we observe in children's cognitive and linguistic development. Another dissenting line is represented by the chapter by Tomasello. He argues that the whole line of argument for the necessity of innate biases, from the Quinean start to the "theory theory" finish, only arises because we underdescribe the situation of learning. Instead of treating the child as a passive observer, trying to map labels to objects or events, we should focus on the interactional situation in all its richness. It is the adult's intentions that the child is trying to decode, not inscrutable words, and the child uses all the clues provided by the nuances of the adult's actions, from gesture to attention to signs of distraction, to decide what the intentions are likely to be. By manipulating the adult's actions, one can test just what effect this over-arching communicative situation has on the child's assumptions.

1.3 Comparative perspectives

To sort out issues of these kinds we desperately need comparative perspectives: we need to have a sense for how variable the outcomes of learning can be. On the one hand, we have comparisons across primate species, of the kind that Langer offers in this volume. Such comparisons hint at the kinds of factors that may be the foundations or preconditions for language. Langer points out that the relative timing of certain cognitive developments may be crucial, because only if they are simultaneous can they feed one another. In this respect, the delay of language for a whole year or more after the beginning of other cognitive development clearly suggests that a core cognitive foundation must be in place before language production can begin. That foundation may be the formation of hierarchical sets, and it is noteworthy that even our nearest primate cousins, the chimpanzees, do not achieve this, at least in childhood, and even when they are intensively trained in protolanguage they have corresponding problems with grammar. There are almost certainly other cognitive preconditions to the learning of complex communication systems, for example specific kinds of social learning (see Tomasello, Kruger, & Ratner 1993). But these foundations for language found in general cognition are of course of a very much wider, less specific kind than the sort of specific innate language-acquisition device hypothesized by Chomsky (which may of course also be a precondition to language).

On the other hand, we can compare across human languages and consider what kind of cognitive endowment would be required to handle the diversity of meaning structures in different languages. Many of the chapters in this volume exploit language difference as a fundamental means of obtaining insight into the relationship between linguistic development and cognitive development. Thus for example the chapters by Gopnik and Gentner & Boroditsky both try to assess whether the "naming explosion" around the age of two is fundamentally associated with the naming of objects, or whether the emphasis can be shifted by particular languages towards the acquisition of verbs rather than nouns (they reach rather different conclusions). Clark explores whether the kinds of categories that get grammaticalized in languages other than the one the child is actually learning turn up momentarily as working hypotheses about the meaning of morphemes, and concludes that they do. Slobin, following a similar line of reasoning, looks across languages to see whether children might come equipped with an *a priori* sense of what concepts form natural grammaticalizable categories, but he concludes that they do not. Lucy & Gaskins explore whether different grammatical patterns across languages might actually influence nonlinguistic classification. They attempt to control carefully across two languages, doing exactly the same cognitive tasks in both cultures with children of different ages. They do find language-specific effects on nonlinguistic categorization, but they find them emerging years after children have mastered the relevant syntactic structures in language. Bowerman & Choi are likewise concerned with careful comparison across learners of two languages, but they apply in part techniques developed for the experimental study of pre-linguistic cognition in young infants to explore the beginnings of language comprehension. Perhaps if one can plumb the infant's understanding of linguistic expressions before he or she can actually speak, one will find misconstruals that directly reflect universal cognitive assumptions, later overridden by linguistic diversity. Although it is difficult to push far enough back into early infancy, comprehension before production does not so far seem to reveal universal cognitive bedrock. Studies of early production also seem to show very early language-specific assumptions. The cluster of chapters by Levinson, Brown, and de León are concentrated on one phenomenon: the contrast between the familiar European spatial concepts and descriptions, and those of Mayan speakers of two related languages in highland Chiapas, Mexico, who utilize very different spatial language and concepts. The study of adult language and cognition, and child comprehension and production, shows that major differences exist between those languages and say English- or Dutch-speaking communities, and that these differences surface surprisingly early.

What is the influence of differential experience on the conceptualization that underlies early language? Children growing up in different cultures experience worlds that differ not only in language, but in just about every facet of physical, social, and emotional experience. Clearly, it is difficult here to isolate out single contrasting features. One would like to have controlled experiments in which children are exposed to different experiences and later tested, but – except in the limited way explored in this volume, for example, in the chapter by Bloom on memory for novel words vs. information of other kinds – such experiments are of course ethically unthinkable (where they have accidentally occurred, as with feral children, they have exercised both popular and scientific imagination – see Candland 1993). However, there is at least one such natural experiment: children growing up even in the very same family can have a radically different exposure to experiences underlying the notion of person.[1] Some children are first or only children, others have older siblings, and some are born with a twin, identical or otherwise. The chapter by Deutsch and his collaborators in this volume exploits this natural experiment in detail. They show that whereas with first- vs. second-born children the effect may be primarily an effect on linguistic experience, so that second children are quicker to master the concept of shifting reference associated with pronouns, with twins one has a glimpse of a conceptual difference at a deeper level: some twins refer first to themselves as a dual entity – their names for themselves initially encompass them both. These findings from such natural "controlled experiments" can then help us unpick some of the tangled web of factors underlying cross-cultural differences. In many non-Western cultures, language acquisition does seem somewhat delayed (at least in production; see e.g. Bavin 1992, or Brown, this volume), and it is observable that the "input" (directed speech) to the children is often very different in character, infants sometimes being carried rather than interacted with, and later often being cared for by just-older siblings.

2 The major themes of the volume

As mentioned earlier, the two strands of investigation, of the development of language and of other aspects of cognition, have at times grown far apart. The recent revolution in our understanding of infant cognition has yet to have its full impact on the study of language acquisition. Similarly, the great increase in our understanding of how children learn languages that differ radically in structure and underlying categorization has yet to be fully exploited as a source of information about the processes of cognitive development. In this volume the reader will find that many of the chapters are concerned with trying to work out how best to reconcile these two rather different recent trends.

At first sight at least, the two trends appear to point in rather opposite directions. On the cognitive side, the more we learn about infant cognition, the earlier we often seem to be able to trace back quite complex cognitive assumptions that children make. In fact, there was at one time a kind of minor academic industry involved in showing that the benchmarks established by Piaget as an ordered sequence with expected achievement times are all much too conservative. The further back we can trace cognitive assumptions, the more they look as if they were there all along. For example, if we can show that five-month-old infants can do simple arithmetic (Wynn 1992), then they are unlikely to have learnt *that* from experience in the world. A rich set of innate presumptions looks inescapable. On the other hand, if we imagine the child endowed from the outset with *too* much in the way of specific assumptions and knowledge, we can hardly explain the existence of major steps in cognitive development at all. The "theory theory," described above (and see Gopnik, this volume), is one way to conceive of how children start with a definite foundation of presumptions and constraints but end up somewhere else under the influence of experience. Nevertheless, the presumption in all this work has been, as it was for Piaget, that cognitive development is essentially *convergent*: by and large, failing genetic or experiential deprivation (and sometimes even despite that – see e.g. Landau & Gleitman 1985), infants seem to arrive at a similar level of cognitive attainment by early childhood.

Now against this background, the recent developments in the study of language acquisition seem problematic. The central problem here is how do children, from an initially equivalent base, end up controlling often very differently structured languages? In other words, how do children successfully *diverge* in order to control the local language, whatever its idiosyncrasies? The Chomskyan tradition, with its emphasis on an innate syntactic ability, has led us to seriously underplay the extent and depth of *semantic* variation across languages. The concepts that underly words and grammatical morphemes can vary in fundamental ways across languages. For example, only some languages have tense, and different systems of tense interact with very variable notions of aspect in different languages (Behrens, this volume). On the one hand, such complex temporal notions are surely not given to us by the world at all, suggesting an essential role for innate predisposition, but, on the other hand, they are so variably constructed and expressed in languages that the influence of language on cognition in this domain seems inescapable. But even when, from a naive realist point of view, distinctions might seem to be just "out there" waiting to be conceived and named, we can get surprises in the way languages treat them. One such initially surprising variation explored in this book is the reference of nouns that pick out physical properties of the world. In some languages nouns prototypically seem to denote individuated physical objects, in line with a naive realist view. But in other languages nouns seem to have substances rather than individuals as primary reference, a bit like English mass nouns like *water* or *flour*. Thus in some Mayan languages the word for "tree" is also the word for wood, or the bench or other article manufactured from it. The chapters by Gentner & Boroditsky and Lucy & Gaskins debate the significance of this pattern.

Yet another area of significant variation is found in the domain of spatial semantics (see Bowerman & Choi, Brown, de León, Levinson, this volume), an area where variation might be least expected on the grounds that spatial cognition is just the kind of thing that has been demonstrated to be essentially innate in other species. Yet another kind of unexpected variation, if Slobin (this volume) is correct, is the kind of category that gets encoded in grammatical morphemes. These had long been suspected to have a strongly constrained universal basis, but they turn out in fact to be much more language-specific than expected. This range of documented semantic variation – which we can only expect to increase when we know something about the 80–90% of languages that are still not scientifically described – makes it clear that children cannot be armed in advance with just the right semantic categories or dimensions for the language they will have to learn. They will have to construct them, and in doing so they will develop semantic concepts potentially unique to that language group.

How then is one to reconcile these two perspectives, one pointing to convergence in cognitive development and the other to divergence in linguistic development? Perhaps it is essential to step back and ask a more general question: what exactly is the role of language in human cognition? Consider the classical Fodorean (1983) assumption: language is a mere (albeit somewhat variable) input/output device to a central area of thinking. As Pinker

(1994:82) has put it, "knowing a language, then, is knowing how to translate mentalese into a string of words and vice versa. People without a language would still have mentalese, and babies and many nonhuman animals presumably have simpler dialects." There has to be something essentially wrong with this view: as any scholar knows, acquiring a new representation can radically alter the way one *thinks* about a problem (the limiting effects of Roman numerical notation on the simplest mathematical procedures are well known, but think also of the power of diagrams, graphs, and special symbols). Being human is partly about having one's thoughts restructured by virtue of shared representations, communicated by semiotic systems "which have the potential to contribute remarkable design-enhancements to the underlying machinery of the brain" (Dennett 1991:208). For one thing, complex concepts can be packaged or recoded in such a way that higher levels of thinking are possible. As Miller (1956:95) put it in a paper that is one of the foundations of modern cognitive science: "the process of recoding is a very important one in human psychology. . . . In particular, the kind of linguistic recoding that people do seems to me to be the very lifeblood of the thought processes." What he had in mind was that a lexical package of complex semantic material is not only a convenience for communication, but also enhances thinking: it makes it possible to circumvent the extreme limitations of human working memory, limitations that are specified in terms of the number of chunks or packages, not the complexity of their content.

A number of the chapters in this volume wrestle with the implications of this renewed realization of the power of language to transform our thinking. Gopnik argues that it is language that is responsible for some of the quantum changes observable in children's "theories" of various domains. Carey wonders whether it is the very practice of naming that might introduce the kind of assumptions about physical objects that lie behind nominal reference. Spelke & Tsivkin argue that language may play a role linking more primitive, specialized cognitive modules: suppose we take the Fodorean view that the mind consists in part of specialized processing devices – how then are these to talk to one another? For example, if the specialized spatial module tells me where I am by representing only abstract geometric shapes and angles, and I know that what I am looking for is under a big green tree, how can I get there? Somehow, the information has to be shared between the colour, landmark, and spatial modules. Rats have serious limitations here. Humans do too – but only until they begin to learn language. Does then the cognitive advantage that language brings to thinking inhere in the way language allows us to represent different aspects of experience not only to others, but also to ourselves?

These chapters mark substantial changes in perspective within developmental psychology. Instead of language merely reflecting the cognitive development which permits and constrains its acquisition, language is being thought of as potentially catalytic and transformative of cognition. However, the chapters still do not fully bridge the gap between the differing views, from nonlinguistic and linguistic vantage points, of convergence and divergence in child development. If language does transform our thinking, do specific languages transform it in different ways? This question was the focus of the notorious Sapir–Whorf Hypothesis, or the doctrine of linguistic relativity, whereby it was supposed that "users of markedly different grammars are pointed by their grammars toward different types of observations . . . and hence are not equivalent as observers, but must arrive at somewhat different views of the world" (Whorf 1956:221). This view, perennially attractive to the layman, has been decidedly out of favor since the rise of the cognitive sciences, with their emphasis on universals in cognitive structure and processing. As Pinker (1994:58) has put it, "the discussions that assume that language determines thought carry on only by a collective suspension of disbelief." But in fact they cannot be so easily dismissed. Lucy (1992, and with Gaskins, this volume) has documented classification preferences varying with language. Levinson (1996, and this volume) has demonstrated correlations between different kinds of spatial description and different kinds of spatial thinking, measured in many different ways. Indeed, quite a bit of recent fact and theory, both inside and outside the study of human development (Gumperz & Levinson 1996), suggests that some very moderate form of "Whorfianism" may be unavoidable. The implications for human development are potentially far-reaching: not only language but also cognition may diverge – not so very much, perhaps, but enough to remove the anomaly of linguistic and nonlinguistic development heading in different directions. The conclusion could be, then, that the kinds of transformation of thinking by language that Carey, Gopnik, and Spelke & Tsivkin are entertaining may be subject to language-specific biases.

What specific evidence can we find for this in child development? On the linguistic side, it is easy to show that languages diverge in the way they classify various domains, and it has been shown that, from their very earliest speech, children are closer to their adult targets than to children speaking other contrasting languages (Bowerman 1996; see also Bowerman & Choi, and Gentner & Boroditsky, this volume). Similar early use of language-specific semantic categories is detailed in the chapters by Brown and de León in this volume. A problem with the analysis of children's early language is that we often cannot be sure that we understand *their* own immature semantics: perhaps the early language usage is less in line with adult targets than it seems. The chapter by Bowerman & Choi (this volume) attempts to address this by directly studying comprehension even before language production. The results are in line with the findings from early production: infants seem to have arrived at the language-specific classifications at a remarkably early age.

Now on the nonlinguistic side, we would like to know whether this very early internalization of language-specific classifications correlates with categories formed in nonlinguistic cognition – in the classification of perceptions or memories for states and events, and so on. Work here has hardly begun. The chapter by Lucy & Gaskins in this volume reports that such correlations between language-specific and nonlinguistic categories can definitely be found in middle childhood, but suggests that this may reflect a later reorganization (or in Miller's terms, "recoding') of cognition, long after initial language learning. But clues to earlier effects, at least on children's assumptions about what novel words might mean, are documented in other chapters in this volume (see Gentner & Boroditsky, Brown, de León).[2] At this point we still have little evidence about early culture-specific cognitive trends, since nearly all investigations in cross-cultural psychology have been conducted on school-age children and have not been closely tied to studies of language acquisition. The intriguing thing is that the methods now exist for the study of early cognition, and there is little doubt that in the next few years there will be increasing interest and evidence in this area.

In conclusion, the reader will find in this volume a range of new approaches to, and new perspectives on, the ancient epistemological questions with which we began this introduction. Earlier attempts to relate cognitive and linguistic development, for example by correlating milestones of linguistic competence with Piagetian stages, were not successful. Since then there have been major advances in the understanding of both linguistic and cognitive development, with new emphases on the semantic and crosslinguistic aspects of language acquisition, and on the early domain-specific cognitive abilities of infants. But for various reasons these advances have not been brought into close relation. What is unusual about the present volume is that it constitutes for the first time in recent years a serious, sustained engagement of the study of language acquisition with the study of cognitive development, with individual scholars currently working in both domains, and attempting to assess the interplay between the cognitive preconditions to language learning and the linguistic preconditions to advanced conceptual development. Out of this kind of interaction will likely emerge in the next few years a revolution in our understanding of how we come to be ourselves.

A note on the organization of this volume

As will be clear from the introduction, there are many cross-cutting themes linking the chapters in this volume. No linear organization can do justice to this, but we have organized the chapters into four parts. The first part addresses foundational issues about the nature of cognition in humans vs. other primates, and about how language might play a role in transforming human conceptual life. The second part examines contemporary claims about whether children come to the language-learning task with built-in constraints guiding their hypotheses about what new words could mean. All three authors argue "no," but for different reasons. The last chapter in this part introduces the importance of the concept of "an individual" for word learning, and this provides a natural transition to the third part, which examines questions about ontology, about what kinds of entities infants assume there are, and about how children quantify over and reason about them. The fourth and final part is devoted to relational concepts, e.g. notions of time and especially space. Chapters here examine whether the concepts encoded in relational words and grammatical markers are available to the child independently of language – either through nonlinguistic cognitive development or as a set of innately specified semantic universals – or must be constructed on the basis of linguistic experience. Although there are close connections between many of the chapters, they may be read independently. The reader will find many cross-references in the volume, and may prefer to follow that trail according to interest.

NOTES

1 Another is the insight afforded by comparing the linguistic development of sighted vs. sight-deprived children (Landau & Gleitman 1985). The language development of deaf children of hearing parents is another revealing kind of case (see Goldin-Meadow 1985).

2 An interesting study that builds on the distinction between spatial systems described in Levinson, this volume, has found systematic differences between populations by the age of four (see Wassmann & Dasen 1998).

REFERENCES

Bavin, E. 1992. The acquisition of Warlpiri. In D. I. Slobin (ed.), *The crosslinguistic study of language acquisition*, vol. 3. Hillsdale, NJ: Lawrence Erlbaum, 309–372.

Bowerman, M. 1996. The origins of children's spatial semantic categories: cognitive versus linguistic determinants. In J. J. Gumperz & S. C. Levinson (eds.), *Rethinking linguistic relativity*. Cambridge: Cambridge University Press, 145–176.

Braine, M. 1994. Mental logic and how to discover it. In J. Macnamara & G. E. Reyes (eds.), *The logical foundations of cognition.* Oxford: Oxford University Press, 241–263.

Candland, D. G. 1993. *Feral children and clever animals*. Oxford: Oxford University Press.

Carey, S. 1978. The child as word learner. In M. Halle, J. Bresnan, & G. A. Miller (eds.), *Linguistic theory and psychological reality*. Cambridge, MA: Bradford/MIT Press, 264–293.

1985. *Conceptual change in childhood*. Cambridge, MA: Bradford/MIT Press.

Clark, E. V. 1993. *The lexicon in acquisition*. Cambridge: Cambridge University Press.

Dennett, D. 1991. *Consciousness explained*. Boston: Little, Brown.

Fodor, J. 1983. *The modularity of mind: an essay on faculty psychology*. Cambridge, MA: MIT Press.

Goldin-Meadow, S. 1985. Language development under atypical learning conditions: replication and implications of a study of deaf children of hearing parents. In K. E. Nelson (ed.), *Children's language*, vol. 5. Hillsdale, NJ: Lawrence Erlbaum, 197–245.

Golinkoff, R., K. Hirsh-Pasek, K. M. Cauley, & L. Gorden, 1987. The eyes have it: lexical and syntactic comprehension in a new paradigm. *Journal of Child Language* 14: 23–45.

Gumperz, J. J., & S. C. Levinson (eds.). 1996. *Rethinking linguistic relativity.* Cambridge: Cambridge University Press.

Keil, F. C. 1989. *Concepts, kinds, and cognitive development*. Cambridge, MA: Bradford/MIT Press.

Landau, B., & L. R. Gleitman. 1985. *Language and experience: evidence from the blind child.* Cambridge, MA: Harvard University Press.

Levinson, S. C. 1996. Relativity in spatial conception and description. In Gumperz & Levinson, 1996, 177–202.

Lucy, J. 1992. *Grammatical categories and cognition: a case study of the linguistic relativity hypothesis*. Cambridge: Cambridge University Press.

Miller, G. A. 1956. The magical number seven, plus or minus two: some limits on our capacity for processing information. *Psychological Review* 63: 81–97.

Pinker, S. 1994. *The language instinct*. New York: William Morrow.

Quine, W. V. O. 1960. *Word and object*. Cambridge, MA: MIT Press.

Slobin, D. I. 1967. *A field manual for cross-cultural study of the acquisition of communicative competence*. Berkeley, CA: ASUC Bookstore.

(ed.). 1985. *The crosslinguistic study of language acquisition*, vols. 1 & 2. Hillsdale, NJ: Lawrence Erlbaum.

(ed.). 1992. *The crosslinguistic study of language acquisition*, vol. 3, Hillsdale, NJ: Lawrence Erlbaum.

Spelke, E. S. 1993. Physical knowledge in infancy: reflections of Piaget's theory. In S. Carey & R. Gelman (eds.), *The epigenesis of mind: essays on biology and cognition*. Hillsdale, NJ: Lawrence Erlbaum, 133–170.

Tomasello, M. 1995. Language is not an instinct. *Cognitive Development* 10: 131–156.

Tomasello, M., A. C. Kruger, & H. H. Ratner. 1993. Cultural learning. *Behavioral and Brain Sciences* 16: 495–552.

Wassmann, J., & P. Dasen, 1998. Balinese spatial orientation: some empirical evidence of moderate linguistic relativity. *Journal of the Royal Anthropological Institute* 4: 689–711.

Whorf, B. L. 1956. *Language, thought, and reality: selected writings of Benjamin Lee Whorf* (ed. J. B. Carroll). Cambridge, MA: MIT Press.

Wynn, K. 1992. Addition and subtraction by human infants. *Nature* 358: 749–750.

Part 1

Foundational issues

1 The mosaic evolution of cognitive and linguistic ontogeny

Jonas Langer

University of California at Berkeley

Before we can properly consider the relations between language and cognition from the perspective of a comparative primatology, we will need to establish some fundamental points about the similarities and differences of cognitive development in the different species. Towards the end of the chapter I shall then return to the central issue, and show that the comparative developmental data demonstrate that there can be no very intimate interaction between language and cognition in early ontogenesis – cognition leads.

A popular evolutionary theory of human cognition, neoteny, has it that we are developmentally retarded, allowing a greater period of plasticity for the acquisition of culture (e.g. Gould 1977; Montagu 1981). The comparative data, we shall see, do not support the neoteny theory. If anything, humans' cognitive development is precocious as compared to that of other primate species. Of course, this in no way denies that "changes in the relative time of appearances and rate of development for characters already present in ancestors" (the modern neo-Haeckelian definition of heterochrony proposed by Gould 1977:2) is a valid biogenetic law of the evolution of cognitive development (see McKinney & McNamara 1991; Mayr 1994; Langer & Killen 1998; and Parker, Langer, & McKinney 2000, for updated analyses). One product of such timing changes is mosaic organizational heterochrony of ancestral characters, whether morphological such as the body or behavioral such as cognition. That is, the evolution of organized characteristics is produced by a mix of changes in developmental timing of their constituent structures (see Levinton 1988, and Shea 1989, for data on and discussions of mosaic evolution). Organizational heterochrony, I have proposed, characterizes primate cognitive phylogeny and, as such, is a structural evolutionary mechanism of development (Langer 1989, 1993, 1994a, 1996, 1998, 2000; see also Parker 2000).

While Gould's definition of heterochrony focuses on phylogenetic changes in developmental onset ages and velocity, the present comparative analyses extend to changes in offset ages, extent, sequencing, and organization of primates' cognitive development. Primates' cognitive development comprises foundational physical cognition (e.g., knowledge about causality and objects), logical cognition (e.g., classificatory categorizing), and arithmetic cognition (e.g., exchange operations such as substituting to preserve a quantitative relation) reviewed in Langer, Rivera, Schlesinger, & Wakeley (in press). For expository convenience I will conflate logical and arithmetic cognition into logicomathematical cognition (while stipulating that the structures and processing of these two domains differ in important respects).

Since much of the relevant primate data comes from comparisons with my findings on young human children, I will first sketch essential features of the research methods I devised to generate them. Then I will turn to key invariant and variant features of primates' cognitive development, such as its sequencing. Most attention will be paid to the comparative extent (section 8) and organization (section 9) of the early development of different species of primate. These key features are central to my proposal of mosaic organizational heterochrony as an evolutionary mechanism of cognitive ontogeny. Also, I have already provided more details on other key features, such as the comparative developmental velocity of different primate species, elsewhere (especially in Langer 1998, 2000). The comparisons of primates' cognitive development will also provide the empirical base for hypothesizing evolutionary and developmental relations between primates' cognitive and linguistic ontogenies in the concluding section.

1 Research method

The research method was developed in the study of 6- to 60-month-old children's spontaneous constructive interactions with four to twelve objects (see the appendix of Langer 1980, for detailed description). The range of objects spans geometric shapes to realistic things such as cups (as illustrated in Figures 1.1–1.4). Some of the object sets presented embodied class structures (e.g., multiplicative classes that intersect form and color such as a yellow and green cylinder and a yellow and a green triangular column, shown in figure 1.1). However, nothing in the procedures required subjects to do anything about the objects' class structures. No instructions, training, or reinforcement were given and no problems were presented. Children played freely with the objects as they wished because my goal was to study their developing spontaneous constructive intelligence and to develop tests that could be applied across species.

With human children, this initial nonverbal and nondirective procedure was followed by progressively provoked probes. To illustrate, in one condition designed to provoke classifying, children were presented with two alignments of four objects. One alignment might comprise three rectangular rings and one circular ring while the other alignment comprised three

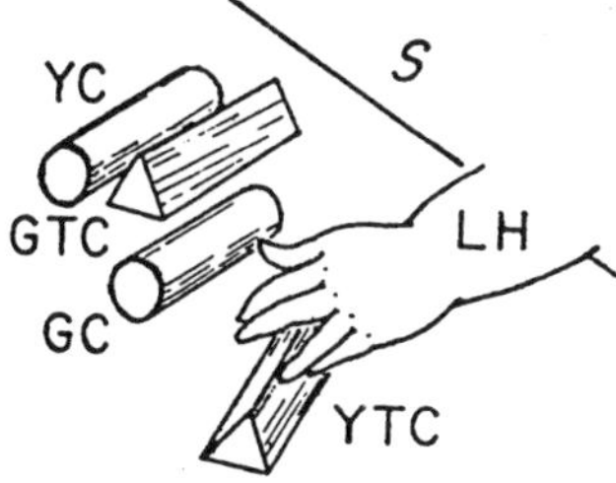

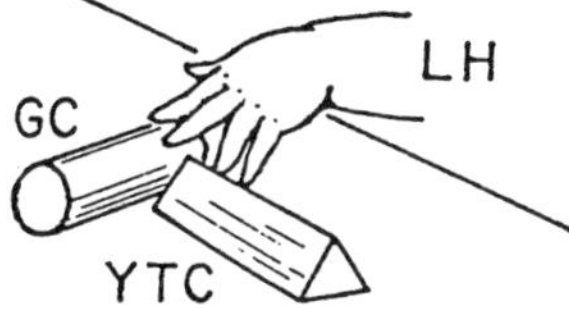

Fig. 1.1 6-month-old subject composing a set comprising a green cylinder (GC) with a yellow triangular column (YTC) using left hand (LH). S = subject.

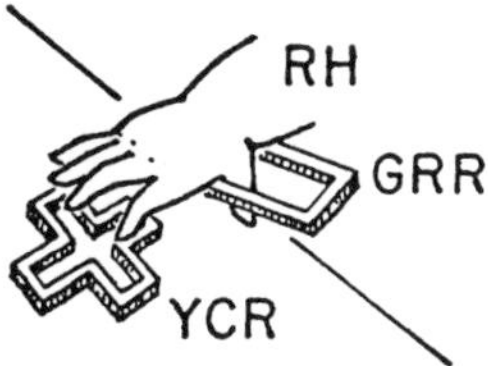

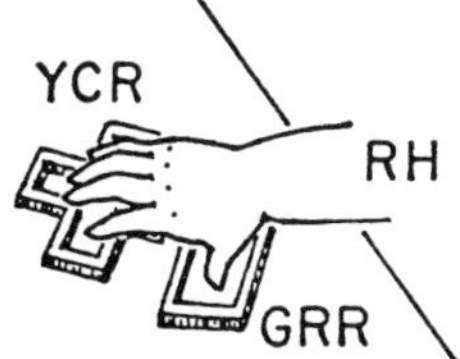

Fig. 1.2 6-month-old subject composing a set comprising a green rectangular ring (GRR) with a yellow cross ring (YCR) using right hand (RH).

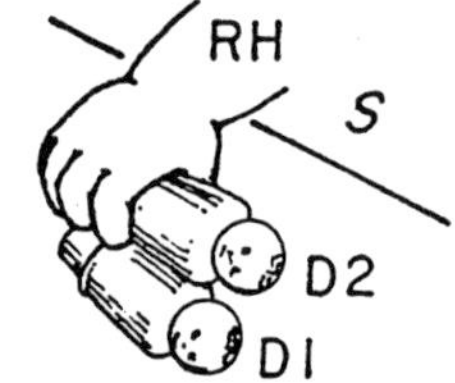

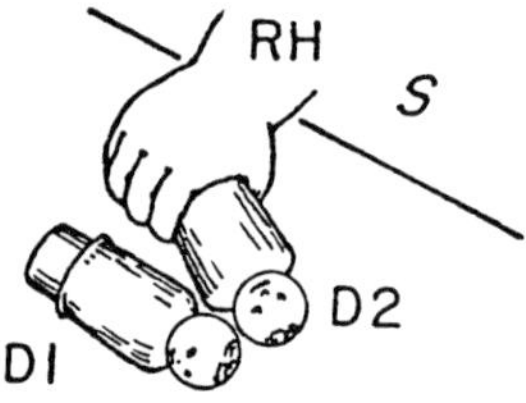

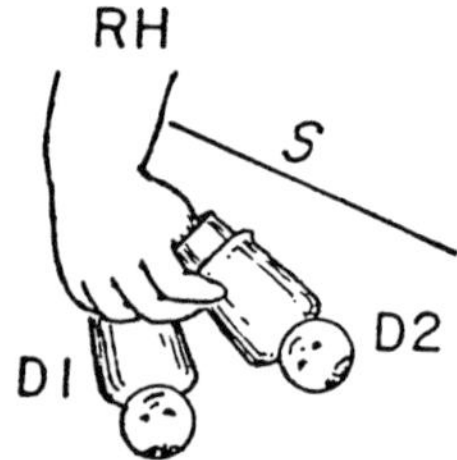

Fig. 1.3 6-month-old subject composing a set comprising two dolls (D1 and D2) using right hand (RH). S = subject.

circular rings and one rectangular ring. By age 21 months, some infants begin to correct the classificatory "mistakes" presented to them (Langer 1986); by age 36 months all children do (Sugarman 1983; Langer, in preparation). Some subjects even rebuke the tester. Thus, one 30-month-old (subject 30AP) remarked "No belongs this way" as she corrected the classificatory misplacements.

Many of the findings on humans that I will review have been replicated with 8- to 21-month-old Aymara and Quecha Indian children in Peru (Jacobsen 1984), and 6- to 30-month-old infants exposed *in utero* to crack cocaine (Ahl 1993). The Indian children were raised in impoverished conditions as compared to the mainly Caucasian middle-class San Francisco Bay Area children in my samples. Nevertheless, no differences were found in

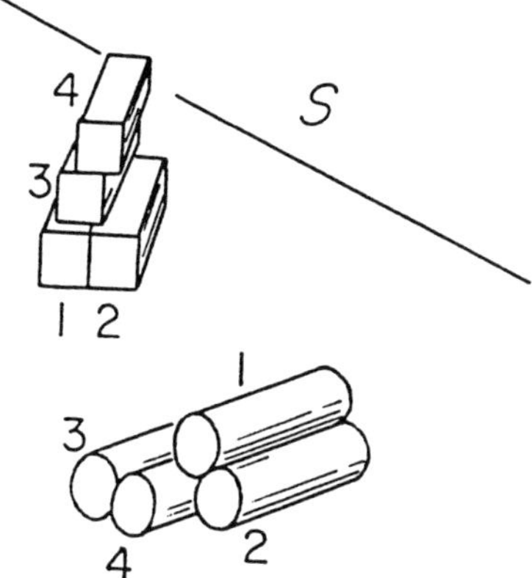

Fig. 1.4 Second-order classifying by a 21-month-old subject.

onset age, velocity, sequence, extent, or organization of cognitive development during infancy in these different human samples; though the crack cocaine babies, of course, manifest many other behavioral, especially emotional, dysfunctions.

Most of the comparisons of primates' cognitive development in the next sections are based on these studies of human children (Langer 1980, 1986, in preparation); and on parallel studies (Antinucci 1989; Spinozzi 1993; Poti 1996, 1997; Poti, Langer, Savage-Rumbaugh, & Brakke 1999; Spinozzi, Natale, Langer, & Brakke 1999) on cebus (*Cebus apella*), macaques (*Macaca fascicularis*) and common and bonobo chimpanzees (*Pan troglodytes and Pan paniscus*) using the nonverbal and nondirective methods developed to study human children's spontaneous cognitive constructions. We have yet to use provoked methods with nonhuman primates.

2 Invariant initial elements of cognition

Perhaps the most important foundational similarity (and difference, as we shall see in section 7) in primate cognition is in their composition of sets. All primates we have studied so far compose sets of objects as elements for their cognition (such as those illustrated in figures 1.1–1.4). They compose sets of objects by bringing two or more objects into contact or close proximity with each other (i.e., no more than 5 centimeters apart).

This is a fundamental similarity since combinativity structures, including especially composing sets, are foundational to constructing cognition and language, as elaborated in section 8. Thus, combinativity is a central general-purpose structure. Combinativity includes composing, decomposing, and recomposing operations (Langer 1980). (Here I focus only on composing for the sake of brevity.) These operations construct fundamental elements, such as sets and series.

Combinativity operations are foundational and fundamental because without them little if any cognition and language is possible (Langer 1980, 1986, 1993). To illustrate the generality of these combinativity structures, consider an aspect of composing. At least two objects must be composed with each other if: (a) they are to be classified as identical or different; and (b) a tool is to be used as a causal instrument to an end (e.g., one object is used to hit another). So, too, at least two symbols must be composed with each other if they are to form a minimal grammatical expression. Note, however, that the form of composing differs by domain. To illustrate, causal tool construction requires spatial composition of the objects involved (at the level of development we are dealing with here). Classificatory construction does not. Contemporaneous manipulation of objects suffices for human infants and young chimpanzees to categorize them even when they do not group them together spatially (Langer, Schlesinger, Spinozzi, & Natale 1998; Spinozzi, Natale, Langer, & Schlesinger 1998; Spinozzi & Langer 1999).

3 Invariant elementary logicomathematical and physical cognitions

It has long been recognized that all primates develop foundational physical cognitions such as notions of object permanence and of causal instrumentality (e.g. Kohler 1926; Parker & Gibson 1979). We now have evidence that human infants and juvenile chimpanzees and monkeys also develop: (1) logical operations such as classifying by the identity of objects (Ricciuti 1965; Woodward & Hunt 1972; Nelson 1973; Roberts & Fischer 1979; Spinozzi & Natale 1979; Langer 1980, 1986; Starkey 1981; Sinclair, Stambak, Lezine, Rayna, & Verba 1982; Sugarman 1983; Spinozzi 1993; Spinozzi *et al.* 1999); and (2) arithmetic operations such as substituting objects in sets to produce quantitative equality (Langer 1980, 1986; Poti & Antinucci 1989; Poti 1997; Poti *et al.* 1999). Thus, all primate species we have studied so far develop foundational logicomathematical as well as physical cognition.

4 Invariant onset age of physical cognition

Developing foundational logicomathematical as well as physical cognition does not mean that the onset age is the same for both domains of knowledge in all primate species. As far as we know, the onset age is the same in all primate species for the development of physical cognition only, which I now sketch.

Human infants begin to construct knowledge about the existence and causal relations of objects in space and time. The earliest symptoms are newborns' sensorimotor activity (e.g. tracking objects and thumb sucking). These activities maintain contact with objects, thereby constituting stage 1 of Piaget's (1952, 1954) six-stage sequence of object permanence development during infancy. So, too, these activities require (a) exerting effort ("work" or energy) and (b) taking into account spatiotemporal contact in order to maintain effective causal relations, thereby constituting the stage 1 efficacy and phenomenalism of Piaget's (1952, 1954) six-stage sequence of causal means–ends development during infancy.

Little attention has been given in comparative research to the onset age of physical cognition. The most I have been able to find is that the earliest symptoms of stage 1 object permanence begin to be manifest during their first week by macaques (*Macaca fuscata* and *fascicularis*; Parker 1977; Poti 1989), the second week by *Cebus appela* (Spinozzi 1989), and the fifth week by *Gorilla gorilla* (Redshaw 1978; Spinozzi & Natale 1989). While limited, the data suggest no or very little difference between human and nonhuman primates in the onset age for developing physical cognition. A fairly secure estimate would put onset age in the neonatal to early infancy range in all primates.

5 Invariant sequencing

The developmental stage sequences are universal, with one partial exception detailed below. The order of stage development is conserved, including no stage skipping or reversal, in all primate species and in all cognitive domains studied so far.

Universal invariance has been found for the most extensively studied developmental stage sequence of physical cognition, Piaget's (1954) six stages of object permanence. Since it therefore provides the most reliable data, it will serve as my example. Sequential invariance has been found in at least a variety of monkey species (i.e. cebus, macaques, and squirrel), gorillas, chimpanzees, and humans (e.g. Piaget 1954; Uzgiris & Hunt 1975; Parker & Gibson 1979; Doré & Dumas 1987; Antinucci 1989). Indeed, the universality of the invariant object permanence stage sequence extends to the mammal species that have been studied so far: cats and dogs (e.g. Gruber, Girgus, & Banuazizi 1971; Traina & Pasnak 1981; see Doré & Goulet 1998 for a review).

Our research has begun investigating whether within-domain stage sequences in logicomathematical cognitions are also universal in primate species. So far we are finding universality with one partial exception, Langer's (1980, 1986) five-stage sequence of logical classification in infancy.

The sequence of classifying is invariant in humans (Langer 1980, 1986) and chimpanzees (Spinozzi 1993; Spinozzi *et al.*, 1999) but not monkeys (Spinozzi & Natale 1989).

6 Variant velocity

The rate of cognitive development is accelerated in human ontogeny as compared to that of other primates. The development of classification is typical. For instance, cebus monkeys do not complete their development of first-order classifying – limited to constructing single categories of objects – until age 4 years (Spinozzi & Natale 1989). In comparison, it is already developed by age 15 months in humans (Langer 1986). So too, while chimpanzees develop rudimentary second-order classifying that extends to constructing two categories of objects, it does not originate until age 4½ years (Spinozzi 1993). In comparison, it originates at age 1½ years in humans.

This pattern of relatively precocious and accelerated cognitive development in humans supports heterochronic theories of progressive terminal extension (peramorphosis or "overdevelopment") in the evolution of primate cognitive ontogeny, and not neoteny (paedomorphosis or "underdevelopment"), as detailed in Langer (1998, 2000). Support for theories of progressive terminal extension is reinforced by findings of increasingly extended cognitive development in the primate lineage that I review in the next two sections. Fully understanding the evolutionary significance of humans' precocial, accelerated and extended cognitive development requires placing it in its full developmental context. I have already endeavored to do so in Langer (1998, 2000) and, therefore, will only allude to the core components here: relatively precocial brain maturation coupled with decelerated nonbrain physiological maturation and decelerated noncognitive behavioral development in humans. Thus, the comparative model of human development that is emerging in this proposal couples (a) nonbrain physiological and noncognitive behavioral immaturity with (b) brain and cognitive precocity.

7 Variant extent of developing elements of cognition

During their first three years, human infants already construct ever more powerful elements of cognition (Langer 1980, 1986, in preparation). Two measures permit central comparisons with the elements composed by young nonhuman primates (Antinucci 1989; Spinozzi 1993; Poti 1996, 1997; Poti *et al.* 1999; Spinozzi *et al.* 1999). I will outline the findings in turn.

With age, human infants include more objects in the sets they compose. For example, 14 percent of their sets comprise eight objects at age 30 months. The number of objects composed into sets also increases with age in chimpanzees. Up to age 5 years, the limit is about five objects. Thus, while already breaking out of the limits of the law of small numbers (defined as no more than three or four units), young chimpanzees seem to be restricted to the smallest intermediate numbers. Minimal increases are found in cebus and macaques during their first 4 years. With age, the set sizes increase from compositions of two objects to no more than three objects. They do not exceed the limits of small numbers.

During their first year, human infants only construct one set at a time. By the end of their first year they begin to construct two sets at a time. By the end of their second year they begin to construct three or four contemporaneous sets. More than half of their compositions comprise multiple contemporaneous sets by age 36 months. Young chimpanzees also begin to construct contemporaneous sets. But, up till age 5 years, they are limited to constructing minimal contemporaneous sets, that is, no more than two sets at a time. And their rate of production is comparatively small. Contemporaneous sets account for only 20 percent of their compositions. In stark contrast, cebus and macaques rarely if ever compose contemporaneous sets in their first 4 years.

8 Variant extent of developing cognition

The elements of cognition primates construct constrain the level of intellectual operations they can attain. Up to at least age 4 years, cebus and macaques are limited to constructing single sets of no more than three objects. Human infants already begin to exceed these limits by constructing two contemporaneous sets of increasingly numerous objects in their second year. The comparative consequence is that cebus and macaques are locked into developing no more than relatively simple cognitions, while progressive possibilities open up for children to map new and more advanced cognitions. For instance, young cebus and macaques are limited to constructing single-category classifying (Spinozzi & Natale 1989) while human infants already begin to construct two-category classifying by age 18 months (Ricciuti 1965; Woodward & Hunt 1972; Nelson 1973; Roberts & Fischer 1979; Starkey 1981; Sinclair *et al.* 1982; Sugarman 1983; Langer 1986; Gopnik & Meltzoff 1992).

Young chimpanzees, like human infants and unlike young monkeys, construct two contemporaneous sets as elements of their cognition. Unlike young monkeys they are therefore not limited to developing first-order cognitions, such as single-category classifying. Instead, like human infants, young chimpanzees begin to develop second-order cognitions, such as two-category classifying, but not until their fifth year (Spinozzi 1993; Spinozzi *et al.* 1999).

Up to at least age 5 years and unlike human infants, we have also seen, chimpanzees are limited to composing two contemporaneous sets. In their second year, human infants already begin to compose multiple contemporaneous sets. As a consequence, only chimpanzees are constrained to constructing no more than two-category classifying (Spinozzi 1993; Spinozzi *et al.* 1999). Humans already begin to develop three-category classifying during early childhood (Langer, in preparation).

This is a vital difference in the cognitive development attainable by chimpanzees and humans. The ability to construct three simultaneous sets is a precondition to building hierarchies, although it is of course not direct evidence of hierarchical ability. It determines whether hierarchically integrated cognition is possible. For example, three-category classifying opens up the possibility of hierarchization while two-category classifying does not permit anything more than linear cognition. Minimally, hierarchic inclusion requires two complementary subordinate classes integrated by one superordinate class. The capability of human infants to compose three contemporaneous sets permits hierarchization. Chimpanzees as old as age 5 years still do not compose three contemporaneous sets. As a consequence they remain limited to linear cognition.

Another vital difference in their potential cognitive development is that, unlike chimpanzees, human infants already begin to map their cognitions recursively onto each other towards the end of the second year (Langer 1986). Young chimpanzees only construct transitional recursive mappings of cognitions onto cognitions (Poti 1997; Poti *et al.* 1999). This is the reason why I have claimed that only the cognition of human children among young primates becomes fully recursive; and that recursiveness is a key to changing the rules of cognitive development (Langer 1994a). It further opens up possibilities for transforming linear into hierarchic cognition.

The elements of cognitive development are limited to contents such as actual sets of objects in all young nonhuman primates we have studied. This is never exceeded by young monkeys. It is barely exceeded by young chimpanzees. By age five years (effectively early adolescence), chimpanzees' cognition just begins to be extended beyond contents such as sets of objects. In comparison, the elements of cognitive development are progressively liberated from contents such as actual sets of objects in humans. By late infancy, the elements begin to be expanded to include forms of cognition (e.g. classifications, correspondences, and exchanges) as well as objects, sets, series, etc. Towards the end of their second year human infants begin to map their cognitive constructions onto each other (Langer 1986). For example, some infants compose two sets of objects in spatial and numerical one-to-one correspondence. Then they exchange equal numbers of objects between the two sets such that they preserve the spatial and numerical correspondence between the two sets. These infants map substitutions onto their correspondence mappings. This recursive operation produces equivalence upon equivalence relations.

Thus, in their second year human infants begin to map their cognitions onto each other. By this recursive procedure, they generate the onset of more advanced (representational) cognitions where the elements of their cognitive mappings are as much other cognitive mappings as actual things. By mapping their cognitions onto each other as well as objects, infants begin to detach their intellectual constructions from their initial concrete objects of application. In comparison, even the cognitions of young chimpanzees as old as five years remain bound to concrete objects. Detaching cognitions from their initial concrete object referents and, instead, mapping them onto other cognitions is pivotal to the formation of representational intelligence.

Representational intelligence, on this view, begins with hierarchic mappings upon mappings (Langer 1982, 1986, 1994a). Its conceptual origins in human ontogenesis are two-year-olds' recursive mappings of cognitions onto cognitions mapped onto objects, as in the above illustration of infants mapping substitution onto correspondence mapped onto two sets of objects. The referents of the substitution operations are no longer limited to the concrete objects forming the two corresponding sets. The referents can become equivalence *relations*. But relations are more abstract than objects. So the referents are becoming abstract.

Recursive development drives progressive change in the relation between the forms and contents of cognition. This opens up the possibility of transforming forms (structures) into contents (elements) of cognition. Thus, initial simple linear cognitions (e.g. minimal classifying) become potential elements of more advanced hierarchic cognitions (e.g. comprehensive taxonomizing). On this view, recursion is a precondition for the formation of all reflective cognition which requires hierarchization, including abstract reflection (Piaget, Grize, Szeminska, & Vinh Bang 1977), cognizance or conscious understanding (Piaget 1976, 1978) and metacognition (e.g. Astington, Harris, & Olson 1989). Linear cognition is not sufficient to these attainments.

In general, with the formation of hierarchic cognition, the referents of human infants' intellectual operations are no longer limited to objects. Cognition is no longer limited to the concrete. Progressively, the referents of infants' cognitions are becoming relations, such as second-order numerical equivalence and causal dependency, that are the product of other intellectual operations mapped onto objects. By mapping cognitions onto relations, infants' intelligence is becoming abstract and reflective. Reasons why or explanations for phenomena can begin to be constructed.

Reasoned explanation is an advanced cognitive development that requires an extensive base of hierarchic conceptual integration. Conceptual integration is not truly possible without the hypotheticodeductive formal operations that are uniquely human and originate in early adolescence (Inhelder & Piaget 1958; see Langer 1969, 1994b, for reviews of the stages of human cognitive development including formal operations). Formal operational development continues through young adulthood up to about age 30 years (Kuhn, Langer, Kohlberg, & Haan 1977).

9 Evolution from asynchronic to synchronic cognitive development

Our comparative research is discovering striking divergences in the organization of cognitive development in primate species that suggest divergent evolution, specifically heterochrony in the organization of their physical and logicomathematical cognition. Figure 1.5 represents my best attempt to portray the phylogenetic evolution of early cognitive ontogeny in the primates we have studied. It tries to capture central "changes in the relative time of appearances and rate of development for [cognitive] characters already present in ancestors" found for humans as compared to chimpanzees and monkeys and for chimpanzees as compared to monkeys. (My sole addition to Gould's definition of heterochrony is to specify parenthetically that the characters under consideration here are cognitive.) Figure 1.5 should be read as part findings and part hypotheses since the research is ongoing.

Physical and logicomathematical cognition develop in parallel in human children. The onset age for constructing these cognitions is the same, very early infancy and probably the neonatal period, and they develop in synchrony. To illustrate, first-order classificatory and causal relations are constructed by infants during their first year (Langer 1980); and second-order classificatory and causal relations are constructed in their second year (Langer 1986). Neither type of cognition begins or ends before the other during childhood. Consequently, both forms of cognition are open to similar environmental influences and to each other's influence.

We find the other extreme in cebus and macaques, namely, almost total asynchrony between their development of physical and logicomathematical cognition. Since they are out of developmental phase with each other, they are not likely to be open to similar environmental influences and to each other's influence. To help grasp the significance this has for the ontogeny of cognition, it may help to sketch some representative findings.

Central physical cognitions (such as object permanence and causal rela-

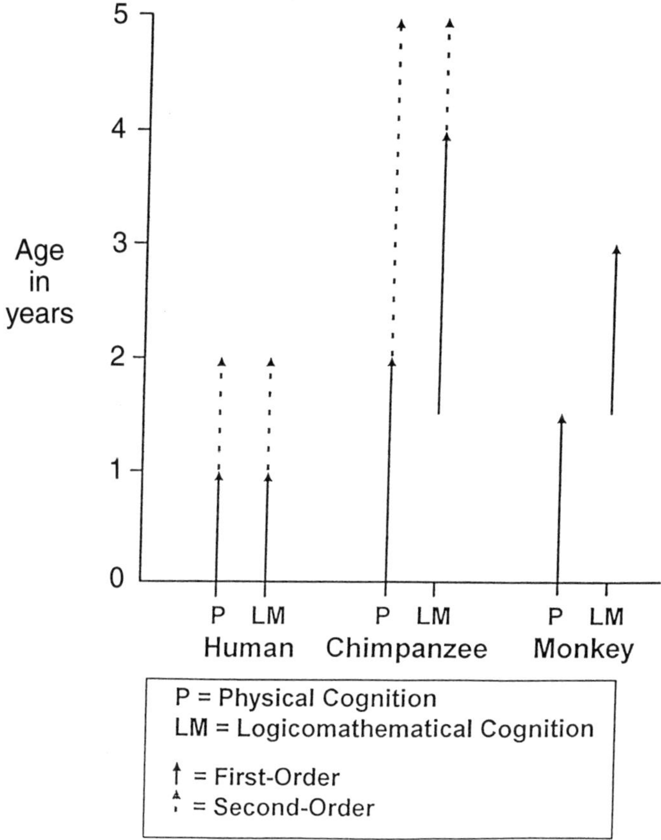

Fig. 1.5 Comparative cognitive development: vectorial trajectories of developmental onset age, velocity, sequence, and organization (but not extent or offset age).

tions) develop before central logicomathematical cognitions (such as classifying and substituting) in monkeys. The development of these physical cognitions is well underway or completed by the developmental onset of logicomathematical cognitions. To illustrate, cebus complete their development of object permanence (up to Piaget's stage 5) during their first year (Natale 1989) and only begin to develop logicomathematical cognition during their second year (Spinozzi & Natale 1989; Poti & Antinucci 1989).

The development of causal cognition also antedates logicomathematical cognition. Simple first-order causality (such as using a support as a tool to get a goal object) develops by age 9 months in cebus and 15 months in macaques (Spinozzi & Poti 1989). More advanced first-order causality (such as using a stick as an instrument to rake in a goal object) develops by age 18 to 20 months in cebus, and may never develop in macaques (Natale 1989). Thus, simple first-order causality is well developed by macaques or completely developed by cebus by the onset of their logicomathematical cognition. Advanced first-order causality is well developed by cebus or nonexistent in macaques by the onset of their logicomathematical cognition.

In chimpanzees' ontogeny, physical and logicomathematical cognition constitute partially overlapping developmental trajectories. While already well underway, chimpanzees' development of physical cognition (e.g. Spinozzi & Poti 1993) is not completed before the onset of logicomathematical cognition (Spinozzi 1993; Poti 1997). Physical and logicomathematical cognition constitute partially asynchronic developmental trajectories. We can therefore expect that these two cognitive domains may eventually begin to be partially open to similar environmental influences and to each other's influence, but beginning relatively late in chimpanzee ontogeny as compared with humans.

From the start of human ontogeny, physical and logicomathematical cognition constitute contemporaneous developmental trajectories that become progressively interdependent. Synchronic developmental trajectories permit direct interaction or information flow between cognitive domains. Mutual and reciprocal influence between logicomathematical and physical cognition is readily achievable since humans develop them simultaneously and in parallel. Thus, we have found that, even in infancy, logicomathematical cognition introduces elements of necessity and certainty into physical cognition (Langer 1985). At the same time, physical cognition introduces elements of contingency and uncertainty into logical cognition.

These findings of information exchange between *structural domains* indicate that physical and logicomathematical cognitions are not modular during human infancy; nor are they in later childhood under at least partially specifiable conditions (e.g. Inhelder, Sinclair, & Bovet 1974, chs. 7 and 8). Nor are they modular in much of the history of science (e.g. Bochner 1966). Different domains of knowledge can inform each other as long as they develop in parallel, as they do in much of human ontogeny.

The present expectation, then, that these different cognitive domains can only inform each other partially in chimpanzees is based upon their partially asynchronic development, not on the premise that they are modular structures that are mentally segregated from each other. If the domains were truly modular then they could not inform each other at all. Similarly, the present expectation that these cognitive domains can inform each other even less in monkeys is based upon their predominantly asynchronic development, not structural modularity.

On the other hand, aspects of cognitive *processes* are more prone to being modular in human ontogeny (see Langer 1998, for a fuller discussion). Accordingly, in the domain of logical cognition we have found that, in the main, infants' action construction of classes by composing objects does not influence their perceptual categorizing (in a standard habituation preparation); nor does their perceptual categorizing influence their action classifying (Schlesinger & Langer 1993). Insofar as there is any information exchange, it is one-way and age-dependent: action classifying enhances perceptual categorizing at age 6 months but no longer does so at ages 10 and 12 months. So too in the domain of physical cognition we are finding that, in the main, infants' action construction of causal relations does not influence their perception of causal relations, and vice versa (Schlesinger & Langer 1994; Schlesinger 1995).

In primate evolution, unilinear growth of physical *followed by* logicomathematical cognition evolved into multilinear growth of physical *at the same time as* logicomathematical cognition. The sequential pattern of physical followed by logicomathematical cognition in the ontogeny of cebus and macaques became "folded over" and, hence, concurrent developments: (a) first to form descendant partially multilinear development midway in chimpanzee ontogeny; and (b) eventually to form fully multilinear development from the start in human ontogeny (as illustrated in figure 1.5). The onset age for beginning to develop physical cognition is roughly the same in all primates studied so far (as noted in section 4). In cebus and macaque monkeys the onset age for logicomathematical cognition is retarded such that its development does not overlap with the development of physical cognition. In chimpanzees the onset age for logicomathematical cognition is accelerated such that its development partly overlaps with the development of physical cognition. In humans the onset age for logicomathematical cognition is further accelerated to the point that it becomes contemporaneous with the onset age of physical cognition.

Phylogenetic displacement in the ontogenetic onset or timing of one cognitive development relative to another within the same organism causes a disruption in the repetition of phylogeny in ontogeny. Such heterochronic displacement involves a dislocation of the phylogenetic order of succession. It produces a change in the velocity or timing of ancestral processes. Thus, heterochrony is an evolutionary mechanism by which ancestral correlations between growth, differentiation, centralization and hierarchic integration are disrupted and new descendent correlations are established. This entails cascading ontogenetic change, as proposed in Langer (1998, 2000).

The comparative organizations of primates' cognitive development are consistent with the hypothesis that heterochrony is a mechanism of its evolution. On this hypothesis, heterochronic displacement is a mechanism whereby consecutively developing ancestral cognitive structures were transformed in phylogenesis into simultaneously developing descendant cognitive structures in human ontogenesis. Heterochrony produced the reorganization of nonaligned ancestral cognitive structures in cebus and macaques into the partly aligned descendant structures in chimpanzees and the fully aligned descendant structural development of cognition in human infancy. Figure 1.5 depicts this phylogenetic trend towards a shift in intellectual dominance from physical cognition to equipotentiality between logicomathematical and physical cognition.

This heterochronic reorganization opened up the possibility for full information flow between logicomathematical (e.g. classificatory) and physical (e.g. causal) cognition in human infancy (making it possible, e.g., to form a "logic of experimentation"). These cognitive domains are predominantly segregated from each other in time and, therefore, in information flow in the early development of cebus and macaque monkeys. They are partially segregated from each other in time and, therefore, in information flow in the early development of chimpanzees.

The possibilities opened up for further development vary accordingly and, I propose, reciprocally constrain the "direction" of progressive cognitive ontogeny in primate phylogeny (with the stipulation that directional processes are probabilistic, not deterministic). As we have seen, cognitive development is already quite substantial in the youth of cebus and macaque monkeys. However, their asynchronic early cognitive development hampers much further progress with age. The partially synchronic and relatively advanced early cognitive development of chimpanzees multiplies the possibilities for substantial, if still limited, information exchange and further progress with age. Humans' synchronic and still more extensive early cognitive development opens up comparatively unlimited, permanent, and unique possibilities for further intellectual progress, such as a history of science (see Langer 1969: 178–180, for five criterial features of progressive cognitive development).

10 Cognition and language: phylogenetic dissociation, ontogenetic asynchrony

Unlike cognition, where the relation between developing domains in phylogeny evolves from asynchrony to synchrony, cognition and language are dissociated in phylogeny with one exception. Cognition and language only become associated developmentally in human ontogeny. But their ontogenetic trajectories are asynchronic (as illustrated in figure 1.6).

Cognition and language are dissociated in phylogeny until we get to human ontogeny, as was pointed out a long time ago (e.g. Vygotsky 1962).

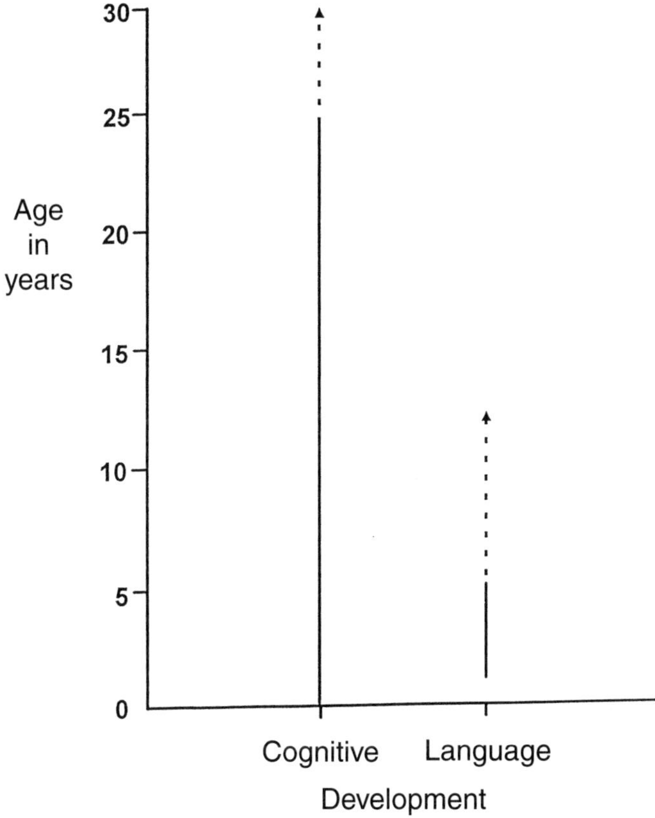

Fig. 1.6 Cognition and language: ontogenetic asynchrony.

In primates, we have seen, first-order cognition develops without the benefit of any language in young monkeys and chimpanzees. Young chimpanzees develop further, to at least rudimentary second-order cognition without the benefit of any language. In logicomathematical cognition this includes, for example, two-category classifying. In physical cognition this includes, for example, searching for nonvisibly displaced objects; thereby constituting stage 6 of Piaget's (1954) six-stage object permanence sequence.

In phylogeny, language does not originate until around the end of the first year of human ontogeny with the onset of the one-word stage (Brown 1973). By then, we have seen, humans are already in transition to second-order cognition. So, the ontogenetic onset and initial developmental stages of human cognition precede the onset of language by about a year.

On the other hand, the offset of language precedes the offset of human cognition by decades. The offset of cognitive development is around age 30 years in humans (Kuhn *et al.* 1977). The offset of language development is between age 5 years and puberty. (I use this large age spread because I don't know a consensually agreed-upon measure for determining the offset age of language development.) As compared to cognitive ontogeny, then, the velocity of language ontogeny is accelerated by a factor of 2 to 6. Thus, the initial lag in linguistic development is overcome rapidly.

In both phylogeny and ontogeny, then, cognition originates and develops prior to and without any language. Conversely, language does not originate prior to and without cognition. The phylogenetic dissociation proves that language is not a necessary condition for the origins of cognition and for its development up to at least second-order cognition. While it has long been recognized that language is not necessary for the evolution and development of elementary physical cognition (e.g. Kohler 1926; Vygotsky 1962; Parker & Gibson 1979), our research is showing that language is also not necessary for the evolution and development of elementary logicomathematical cognition such as classifying.

Language is not necessary for the *origins* of classifying. Single-category classes are constructed by monkeys, chimpanzees, and very young human infants (as outlined in section 8). Language is also not necessary for the subsequent *development* of logical classifying. Two-category classes are constructed by chimpanzees who have no language, as well as language-trained chimpanzees and older human infants. So it is not clear in what sense the foundations of concept formation might be related to language acquisition in evolution and development even if two-category classifying is correlated with a naming burst in American infants (Gopnik & Meltzoff 1992; Mervis & Bertrand 1994; but see Gershkoff-Stowe, Thal, Smith, & Namy 1997, for a nonreplication).

Cognitive operations generate knowledge. Symbols, including language, express meaning (a subset of the knowledge generated by cognition). Symbolic processes complement cognitive processes. Symbolic processes express or represent meaning based upon the knowledge generated by cognitive processes. The symbolic media used to express meaning range from gestural and iconic to linguistic and mathematical notation.

On the present view, cognition provides axiomatic properties necessary for any grammatical symbolic system, including language and mathematics. But symbolic systems also have special-purpose properties not found within cognition *per se*. For example, semantic rules of selection and representation are autonomous and vary from one symbolic medium to another, such as from language to mathematical notation (see Langer 1986, ch. 19, for a fuller discussion). Language and mathematical notation are powerful heuristic media that multiply new phenomena (i.e., possibilities, considerations, problems, contradictions, gaps, etc.) upon which cognition may operate.

Determining the relations between cognition and language is a central problem for all major theories of cognitive development (Piaget 1951; Vygotsky 1962; Werner & Kaplan 1963). Unlike these theories, however, our proposals are not based upon ontogenetic data that confound cognitive with linguistic data. They are based upon data on the development of cognitive operations that are independent of the data on the development of symbol formation, such as pretend routines and verbal utterances.

These data sets led us to conclude that the pace and depth of cognitive development is equal to or greater than linguistic development during most of human infancy. This proposition takes into account our data on cognitive development (Langer 1980, 1986) and the data on symbolic and linguistic development generated in our studies (Langer 1980, 1982, 1983, 1986) and that reported in the literature (e.g. Braine 1963; Bloom 1970; Brown 1973; Bowerman 1978; and Maratsos 1983). It is, of course, impossible to compare quantitatively cognitive with symbolic development since there is no common developmental metric that can measure both. Nevertheless, the data are rich enough to extract a set of qualitative generalizations:

1. First-order cognition is well developed during the second half of infants' first year when their symbolic behavior is extremely rudimentary. Symbolization involves little more than the transition between stages 3 and 4, signalling and indexing in Piaget's (1951) six-stage sequence of symbol formation.
2. Second-order cognition originates towards the end of infants' first year when their symbolic and linguistic productions begin to be substantial. Symbolizing progresses to well-articulated stage 5 indexing of nonvisible referents in Piaget's (1951) six-stage symbol-formation sequence.
3. Second-order cognition is well developed by the second half of infants' second year when their linguistic production is beginning to develop some power. Symbolizing is becoming protogrammatical, and includes initial forms of stage 6 arbitrary and conventional signing in Piaget's (1951) six-stage symbol-formation sequence.

To the extent that they may inform each other's development during human infancy when concept formation outstrips symbol formation, the predominant potential influence would therefore be from cognition to language. Since language lags behind ontogenetically during most of infancy, it is less possible for it to affect cognition. Indeed, infants develop second-order cognition before they begin to develop fully grammatical language marked by supple syntax and complex semantics towards the middle of their third year (Bickerton 1990; Lieberman 1991). Second-order cognition is a necessary condition for young children to produce and comprehend arbitrary but conventional rules by which symbols stand for and communicate referents in grammatical forms. Second-order cognitions may well be axiomatic to grammatical formations in which linguistic elements are progressively combinable and interchangeable yet meaningful. For example, this is not possible without the second-order operation of substituting elements within and between two compositions (or sets) that, as we have seen, develops towards the end of infants' second year. The hypothesis is that second-order operations (of composing, decomposing, matching, commuting, substituting, etc.) provide the rewrite rules without which grammatical constructions are not possible.

Infants' developing cognition provides the foundational grammatical abilities for generating progressive syntactic as well as semantic symbolic forms. In this way, they have implications for or provide the necessary developing parameters of and constraints upon the development of syntactic linguistic production, comprehension, and, for that matter, appreciation. The developing grammars governing the generation of syntactic forms within each symbolic medium are autonomous and unique (e.g. the generative grammar proposed for language by Chomsky 1965). As language catches up with cognition by late infancy and early childhood, the influences between cognition and language may become more mutual. Then, symbolic development may begin to have implications for concept formation. Symbolization may be exploited by young children to facilitate and expand the foundations of cognition once their construction is already well underway, perhaps beyond the level of second-order cognition. For instance, playful routines permit substitution of present and arbitrary (e.g. a wooden triangular column) for nonpresent and prototypic objects (e.g. a brush). Symbolization thereby extends the range of cognitive elements.

This begins to be particularly true of language around age 24 months. At this age, infants begin to use language as a notational medium in relatively powerful ways to symbolize the nonpresent, comparative values, amounts, etc. (see also the Bowerman & Choi, Gentner & Boroditsky, and Spelke & Tsivkin chapters, this volume). Thus, language begins to expand the range of thought in at least three ways: by multiplying the constant given elements of cognition; by increasing the problem space to which cognitions apply; and by providing cognition with a progressively abstract and flexible notational symbolic system of elements that are increasingly detached from their objects of reference.

Symbolic, including linguistic, development does not cause infants' concept formation. This is made plain by the ontogenetic facts, some of which I have reviewed here. During their first two years, infants' conceptual development generally outstrips their symbolic development (see Langer 1980, 1986, for a detailed presentation). Some symbolic productions are precocious, powerful, and complex for their age (e.g. "Broke it. I broke it," while decomposing Play-Doh objects, by an 18-month-old subject; and "He in boat. Sailing in boat," while placing a doll upright in a rectangular ring, by a 24-month-old subject). These precocious linguistic constructions are at least as advanced as any, and more advanced than most, utterances found at these early ages. Still, even these precocious linguistic productions do not exceed the power and complexity of infants' production of second-order cognition at the same ages.

The conceptual development of infants producing precocious language may be compared profitably with that of infants who do not produce precocious language. There is no difference in the respective conceptual production of these two groups that differ in their linguistic precocity. Infants producing precocious language do not produce precocious second-order cognition. Some subjects not producing precocious language do produce precocious second-order cognition – for example, true equivalences upon equivalences by substituting objects between corresponding compositions by age 24 months (Langer 1982, 1983, 1986).

It follows that this order of linguistic development is not even a necessary condition for conceptual development up to at least age 24 months, let alone a sufficient condition. Whether language development is necessary to the development of thought beyond second-order cognition is a subject of our ongoing cross-species primate research. Consider in this regard cebus and macaques who develop first-order but not second-order cognition. On the present view, they have therefore evolved the cognitive structures necessary for signalling. Cebus and macaques have not evolved the recursive hierarchical cognitive structures, necessary for grammatical language, that human infants begin to develop in their third year (for related discussions see Bickerton 1990, and Lieberman 1991).

Signal systems are rudimentary symbolic systems. They are very poor systems for generating new phenomena for cognitive consideration. If, as seems to be the case, cebus and macaques are limited to signalling, then their symbolizing can only play a minor role in expanding their cognitive development. In comparison, when human infants begin to develop advanced language their symbolizing can play a progressive role in fostering their continuing cognitive development. With continuing symbolic development, most especially in mathematical expressivity in childhood and adolescence, new and ever more powerful possibilities are increasingly opened up for cognitive development.

Second-order cognition, I have been hypothesizing, is a necessary condition for *developing* grammatical language in humans. It is also, I have hypothesized, a necessary condition for *learning* protogrammatical language by chimpanzees (Langer, 1996). While requiring much more research, support for the learning hypothesis is provided by the development of symbolic indexing (Savage-Rumbaugh 1998) and the acquisition of protogrammatical language by chimpanzees (Greenfield & Savage-Rumbaugh 1990; Savage-Rumbaugh, Murphy, Sevcik, Brakke, Williams, & Rumbaugh 1993), who develop second-order cognition, but not by monkeys, who only develop first-order cognition.

The further question we are currently investigating, I have already noted, is whether and to what extent learning protogrammatical language by chimpanzees in turn affects their cognitive development. This includes the central determination of whether they, unlike nonlanguage-trained chimpanzees, develop three-category classifying. The results are negative (Spinozzi *et al.* 1999). We are not finding any difference between language- and nonlanguage-trained chimpanzees up to at least age 11 years, effectively up to what is young adulthood in chimpanzees. This includes both common chimpanzees and bonobo chimpanzees. They do not progress beyond constructing two-category classifying to three-category classifying, which human children already begin to do in their third year (Langer, in preparation).

Protogrammatical language acquisition, then, does not seem to be a sufficient condition for the development of third-order logical classifying. Without the ability to construct three related categories, hierarchic concept formation is not possible, I argued in section 8. Whether and to what degree more advanced grammatical language development by children, aged 3 to 5 years, is implicated in the origins and development of hierarchic concepts remains an open question.

REFERENCES

Ahl, V. A. 1993. Cognitive development in infants prenatally exposed to cocaine. Unpublished doctoral dissertation, University of California at Berkeley.

Antinucci, F. (ed.). 1989. *Cognitive structure and development of nonhuman primates*. Hillsdale, NJ: Lawrence Erlbaum.

Astington, J. W., P. L. Harris, & D. Olson (eds.). 1989. *Developing Theories of Mind*. New York: Cambridge University Press.

Bickerton, D. 1990. *Language and species*. Chicago: University of Chicago Press.

Bloom, L. 1970. *Language development: form and function in emerging grammars*. Cambridge, MA: MIT Press.

Bochner, S. 1966. *The role of mathematics in the rise of science*. Princeton: Princeton University Press.

Bowerman, M. 1978. Structural relationships in children's utterances: syntactic or semantic? In T. E. Moore (ed.), *Cognitive development and the acquisition of language*. New York: Academic Press, 197–213.

Braine, M. D. S. 1963. The ontogeny of English phrase structure: the first phase. *Language* 39: 1–13.

Brown, R. 1973. *A first language: the early stages*. Cambridge, MA: Harvard University Press.

Chomsky, N. 1965. *Aspects of the theory of syntax*. Cambridge, MA: MIT Press.

Doré, F. Y., & C. Dumas. 1987. Psychology of animal cognition: Piagetian studies. *Psychological Bulletin* 102: 219–233.

Doré, F. Y., & S. Goulet. 1998. The comparative analysis of object knowledge. In Langer & Killen 1998, 55–72.

Gershkoff-Stowe, L., D. J. Thal, L. B. Smith, & L. L. Namy. 1997. Categorization and its developmental relation to early language. *Child Development* 68: 843–859.

Gopnik, A., & A. N. Meltzoff. 1992. Categorization and naming: basic-level sorting in eighteen-month-olds and its relation to language. *Child Development* 63: 1091–1103.

Gould, S. J. (1977). *Ontogeny and phylogeny*. Cambridge, MA: Harvard University Press.

Greenfield, P. M., & E. S. Savage-Rumbaugh. 1990. Grammatical combination in *Pan paniscus*: process of learning and invention in the evolution and development of language. In S. T. Parker & K. R. Gibson (eds.), *"Language" and intelligence in monkeys and apes: comparative developmental perspectives*. Cambridge: Cambridge University Press, 540–578.

Gruber, H. E., J. S. Girgus, & A. Banuazizi. 1971. The development of object permanence in the cat. *Developmental Psychology* 4: 9–15.

Inhelder, B., & J. Piaget. 1958 [1955]. *The growth of logical thinking from childhood to adolescence*. New York: Basic Books.

Inhelder, B., M. Sinclair, & M. Bovet. 1974. *Learning and the development of cognition*. Cambridge, MA: Harvard University Press.

Jacobsen, T. A. 1984. The construction and regulation of early structures of logic. A cross-cultural study of infant cognitive development. Unpublished doctoral dissertation, University of California at Berkeley.

Köhler, W. 1926. *The mentality of apes*. New York: Harcourt, Brace, and World.

Kuhn, D., J. Langer, L. Kohlberg, & N. S. Haan. 1977. The development of formal operations in logical and moral judgment. *Genetic Psychology Monographs* 95: 97–188.

Langer, J. 1969. *Theories of development*. New York: Holt, Rinehart & Winston.

1980. *The origins of logic: six to twelve months*. New York: Academic Press.

1982. From prerepresentational to representational cognition. In G. Forman (ed.), *Action and thought*. New York: Academic Press, 37–63.

1983. Concept and symbol formation by infants. In S. Wapner & B. Kaplan (eds.), *Toward a holistic developmental psychology*. Hillsdale, NJ: Lawrence Erlbaum, 221–234.

1985. Necessity and possibility during infancy. *Archives de Psychologie* 53: 61–75.

1986. *The origins of logic: one to two years*. New York: Academic Press.

1989. Comparison with the human child. In Antinucci 1989, 229–242.

1993. Comparative cognitive development. In K. Gibson & T. Ingold (eds.), *Tools, language and cognition in human evolution*. Cambridge: Cambridge University Press, 300–313.

1994a. From acting to understanding: the comparative development of meaning. In W. F. Overton & D. Palermo (eds.), *The nature and ontogenesis of meaning*. Hillsdale: Lawrence Erlbaum, 191–213.

1994b. Logic. In V. S. Ramachandren (ed.), *Encyclopedia of human behavior*. San Diego: Academic Press, 83–91.

1996. Heterochrony and the evolution of primate cognitive development. In A. Russon, K. A. Bard, & S. T. Parker (eds.), *Reaching into thought: the minds of the great apes*. Cambridge: Cambridge University Press, 257–277.

1998. Phylogenetic and ontogenetic origins of logic: classification. In Langer & Killen 1998, 33–54.

2000. The heterochronic evolution of primate cognitive development. In Parker, Langer, & McKinney 2000.

In preparation. *The origins and early development of cognition in comparative perspective*.

Langer, J., & M. Killen (eds.). 1998. *Piaget, evolution, and development*. Mahwah, NJ: Lawrence Erlbaum.

Langer, J., S. Rivera, M. Schlesinger, & A. Wakeley. In press. Early cognitive development: ontogeny and phylogeny. In J. Valsiner & K. Connolly (eds.), *Handbook of developmental psychology*. London: Sage.

Langer, J., M. Schlesinger, G. Spinozzi, & F. Natale. 1998. Developing classification in action. I. Human infants. *Human Evolution* 13: 107–124.

Levinton, J. S. 1988. *Genetics, paleontology, and macroevolution*. Cambridge: Cambridge University Press.

Lieberman, P. 1991. *Uniquely human*. Cambridge, MA: Harvard University Press.

Maratsos, M. 1983. Some current issues in the study of the acquisition of grammar. In P. H. Mussen (ed.), *Handbook of child psychology*. New York: John Wiley, 707–786.

Mayr, E. 1994. Recapitulation reinterpreted: the somatic program. *Quarterly Review of Biology* 69: 223–232.

McKinney, M. L., & J. K. McNamara. 1991. *Heterochrony: the evolution of ontogeny*. New York: Plenum.

Mervis, C. B., & J. Bertrand. 1994. Acquisition of the novel name – nameless category (N3C) principle. *Child Development* 65: 1646–1663.

Montagu, A, 1989. *Growing young.* Granby, MA: Bergin & Garvey.

Natale, F. 1989. Causality II: the stick problem. In Antinucci 1989, 121–133.

Nelson, K. 1973. Some evidence for the cognitive primacy of categorization and its functional basis. *Merrill-Palmer Quarterly* 19: 21–39.

Parker, S. T. 1977. Piaget's sensorimotor series in an infant macaque: a model of comparing unstereotyped behavior and intelligence in human and nonhuman primates. In S. Chevalier-Skolnikoff & F. E. Poirier (eds.), *Primate bio-social development: biological, social, and ecological determinants*. New York: Garland, 43–112.

2000. *Homo erectus* infancy and childhood, the turning point in the evolution of hominid behavioral ontogeny. In Parker, Langer, & McKinney 2000.

Parker, S. T., & K. R. Gibson. 1979. A developmental model for the evolution of language and intelligence in early hominids. *Behavioral and Brain Sciences* 2: 367–408.

Parker, S. T., J. Langer, & M. L. McKinney (eds.) 2000. *Biology, brain, and behavior: the evolution of human development*. Santa Fe, NM: School of American Research Press.

Piaget, J. 1951. *Play, dreams, and imitation in childhood.* New York: Norton.

1952 [1936]. *The origins of intelligence in children*. New York: International Universities Press.

1954. *The construction of reality in the child*. New York: Basic Books.

1976. *The grasp of consciousness*. Cambridge, MA: Harvard University Press.

1977. *Recherches sur l'abstraction réfléchissante*, vol. 1: *L'abstraction des relations logicoarithmetiques*. Paris: Presses Universitaires de France.

1978. *Success and understanding*. London: Routledge & Kegan Paul.

Piaget, J., J. B. Grize, A. Szeminska, & Vinh Bang. 1977. *Epistemology and psychology of functions*. Dordrecht: Reidel.

Poti, P. 1989. Early sensorimotor development in Macaques. In Antinucci 1989, 39–53.

1996. Spatial aspects of spontaneous object grouping by young chimpanzees (*Pan troglodytes*). *International Journal of Primatology* 17: 101–116.

1997. Logical structures in young chimpanzees' spontaneous object grouping. *International Journal of Primatology* 18: 33–59.

Poti, P., & F. Antinucci. 1989. Logical operations. In Antinucci 1989, 189–228.

Poti, P., J. Langer, S. Savage-Rumbaugh, & K. E. Brakke. 1999. Spontaneous logicomathematical constructions by chimpanzees (*Pan troglodytes, Pan paniscus*). *Animal Cognition* 2: 147–156.

Redshaw, M. 1978. Cognitive development in human and gorilla infants. *Journal of Human Evolution* 7: 133–141.

Ricciuti, H. N. 1965. Object grouping and selective ordering behavior in infants 12 to 24 months. *Merrill-Palmer Quarterly* 11: 129–148.

Roberts, R. J., & K. W. Fischer. 1979. A developmental sequence of classification skills. Paper presented at the Society for Research in Child Development meetings, San Francisco.

Savage-Rumbaugh, E. S. 1998. Scientific schizophrenia with regard to the language act. In Langer & Killen (ed.), 1998, 145–169.

Savage-Rumbaugh, E. S., J. Murphy, R. A. Sevcik, K. E. Brakke, S. L. Williams, & D. M. Rumbaugh. 1993. Language comprehension in ape and child. *Monographs of the Society for Research in Child Development* 58 [3–4, serial no. 233].

Schlesinger, M. 1995. Infants' developing knowledge about causality: perception, action, and perception–action relations. Unpublished doctoral dissertation, University of California at Berkeley.

Schlesinger, M., & J. Langer. 1993. The developmental relations between sensorimotor classification and perceptual categorization in early infancy. Paper presented at the Meeting of the Society for Research in Child Development, Chicago, IL, March.

1994. Perceptual and sensorimotor causality in 10-month-old infants. Poster presented at the Jean Piaget Society meeting, Philadelphia.

Shea, B. T. 1989. Heterochrony in human evolution: the case for neoteny reconsidered. *Yearbook of Physical Anthropology* 32: 69–101.

Sinclair, M., M. Stambak, I. Lezine, S. Rayna, & M. Verba. 1982. *Les bébés et les choses*. Paris: Presses Universitaires de France.

Spinozzi, G. 1989. Early sensorimotor development in Cebus. In Antinucci 1989, 55–66.

1993. The development of spontaneous classificatory behavior in chimpanzees (*Pan troglodytes*). *Journal of Comparative Psychology* 107: 193–200.

Spinozzi, G., & J. Langer. 1999. Spontaneous classification in action by a human-enculturated and language-reared bonobo (*Pan paniscus*) and common chimpanzees (*Pan troglodytes*). *Journal of Comparative Psychology* 113: 286–296.

Spinozzi, G., & F. Natale, F. 1989. Classification. In Antinucci 1989, 163–187.

Spinozzi, G., F. Natale, J. Langer, & K. E. Brakke. 1999. Spontaneous class grouping behavior by bonobos (*Pan paniscus*) and common chimpanzees (*P. troglodytes*). *Animal Cognition* 2: 157–170.

Spinozzi, G., F. Natale, J. Langer, & M. Schlesinger. 1998. Developing classification in action. II. Young chimpanzees (*Pan troglodytes*). *Human Evolution* 13: 125–139.

Spinozzi, G., & P. Poti. 1989. Causality I: the support problem. In Antinucci 1989, 113–119.

1993. Piagetian stage 5 in two infant chimpanzees (*Pan troglodytes*): the development of permanence of objects and the spatialization of causality. *International Journal of Primatology* 14: 905–917.

Starkey, D. 1981. The origins of concept formation: object sorting and object preference in early infancy. *Child Development* 52: 489–497.

Sugarman, S. 1983. *Children's early thought: developments in classification*. New York: Cambridge University Press.

Traina, E., & R. Pasnak. 1981. Object permanence in cats and dogs. *Animal Learning and Behavior* 9: 135–139.

Uzgiris, I.C., & J. M. Hunt. 1975. *Assessment in infancy: ordinal scales of psychological development*. Urbana: University of Illinois Press.

Vygotsky, L. S. 1962. *Thought and language*. New York: John Wiley and MIT Press.

Werner, H., & B. Kaplan. 1963. *Symbol formation*. New York: John Wiley.

Woodward, W. M., & M. R. Hunt. 1972. Exploratory studies of early cognitive development. *British Journal of Educational Psychology* 42: 248–259.

2 Theories, language, and culture: Whorf without wincing

Alison Gopnik

University of California at Berkeley

If there is one clear conclusion to be drawn from this volume it is that, after decades of obloquy, Benjamin Whorf is back. Of course, Whorf never really went away in the popular imagination or in the wilder reaches of the post-modern humanities. In serious cognitive psychology and cognitive science, though, that very fact reinforced the sense that Whorfian ideas were disreputable, not to say crackpot. In contrast to this scornful tradition, many of the chapters in this volume, both empirically and conceptually, seriously explore the possibility that the language we hear can have strong effects on the ways that we understand the world.

Aside from the sociology there were more serious reasons why cognitive science rejected Whorf. There were obvious empirical objections to his work. More broadly, Whorf presupposed a relativist, indeed a wildly relativist, and anti-realist ontology. In contrast, cognitive science is realist and anti-relativist almost by definition. "Cognition" refers to the way that we learn about the world around us in an at least roughly veridical way, and the assumption of cognitive science is that there are general procedures all human beings use to do so. Since the late 1960s psycholinguistics has built on this cognitive foundation.

In this chapter, I will outline an approach to the idea that language restructures cognition that is congruent with the wider insights of cognitive science rather than in conflict with them. I will suggest that one recently influential theory of cognitive development, what I will call the "theory theory", offers an interesting and novel account of the relation between language and thought. The theory proposes that cognitive development is analogous to processes of theory formation and change in science. The analogy to science suggests an interactive relation between language and cognition that is not like either the classical Whorfian or anti-Whorfian views. I will also present data from extensive empirical studies of the relation between language and cognition that support this view. In particular, I will present data from cross-linguistic studies comparing English and Korean which show that particular kinds of linguistic input can influence cognitive development. I will suggest that the analogy to conceptual change in science gives us a new way of characterizing these effects of language on cognition. We can combine Whorfian ideas with the insights of contemporary cognitive science.

1 The theory theory

Recently, an increasing number of cognitive developmentalists have employed the model of scientific theory change to explain cognitive development. The idea is both that the types of knowledge that are acquired in childhood are theory-like, and that the processes by which they are acquired are analogous to processes of theory formation and revision in science. This model of development has been applied to a wide range of areas of children's knowledge, including their understanding of the physical world, the biological world, and the psychological world (Karmiloff-Smith & Inhelder 1974; Karmiloff-Smith 1988; Gopnik 1984, 1988; Carey 1985, 1988; Wellman 1985, 1990; Keil 1987, 1989; Perner 1990; Gelman & Wellman 1991; Gopnik & Wellman 1992, 1994; Wellman & Gelman 1992). We have argued that these theory formation processes are deep and fundamental. There may be innate theories and the process of theory change and revision begins even in infancy (Gopnik & Meltzoff 1997).

We might think of the theory-formation view as a view about the characteristic representations that children employ in understanding the world and the characteristic rules they use to manipulate those representations. The thesis of the "theory theory" is that the rules and representations of infancy and childhood are similar to the rules and representations that are involved in scientific progress. There are several features, on this view, that are characteristic of theories and that differentiate theories from other types of cognitive structures.

First, theories have distinctive structural characteristics. Theories postulate abstract entities related to one another in complex and coherent ways. Causal attribution plays an important role in theories: theories are essentially accounts of the underlying causal structure of the world. As a consequence theories have distinctive functional features as well. They generate characteristically wide-ranging and unexpected predictions about evidence. Theories support both deductive and inductive inferences. They allow you to make constrained predictions about new events. Knowing that two animals are members of the same species, for example, allows you to make quite specific and new predictions about the properties of those animals. Theories also have strong interpretive effects. They lead to selections, interpretations, and sometimes misinterpretations of evidence. Finally, theories provide explanations of evidence.

Perhaps most importantly and distinctively of all, however, theories change. These changes are caused by external evidence, particularly, though not exclusively, counter-evidence to the theory. Often the initial reaction to evidence is simply a kind of denial – the theorizer ignores the counter-evidence. Eventually, however, enough counter-evidence accumulates to force revisions, and, eventually, even more radical changes in the theory. Simple falsification, however, is often not itself enough to generate theory change. An alternative theory must be available. The alternative theory often seems to come by borrowing ideas from other parts of the theory or from theories of other domains. For example, Darwin takes the idea of artificial selection, which was widely appreciated and understood, and applies it to natural processes of species change. (For detailed discussion see Gopnik & Wellman 1994; Gopnik & Meltzoff 1997). These dynamic aspects of theories will be most important in considering the relation between language and thought.

Historically, the theory theory has largely emerged out of the ashes of Piagetian theory. It might be seen as a way of continuing the general constructivist project while acknowledging that the principal substantive tenets of Piaget's theory have turned out to be wrong. Certainly, the theory theory shares several broad emphases with Piagetian constructivism. Like constructivism it proposes a kind of middle way, an alternative to either nativist or empiricist theories. Also like constructivism it emphasizes the interaction between cognitive structures that have already been developed, earlier theories, and new input. Qualitatively new types of conceptual structure emerge from this interaction. Finally, like constructivism, it stresses the increasing veridicality of new theories. The fundamental driving force of cognitive development, in this view, is the search for truth. It is the greater veridicality of new theories, reflected in their predictive and explanatory success, that ultimately leads to their successful overthrow of earlier theories.

At the same time, the theory theory also contrasts with Piagetian theory in almost all its substantive claims. Theory formation is specific to particular domains of knowledge. Theories of different kinds of events might develop quite independently of one another. A theory of the way that the mind works might proceed quite independently of a theory of the way that physical objects work. Thus the theory theory predicts domain-specific changes rather than the domain-general stage changes of Piagetian theory. More significantly, perhaps, the theory theory, as we have articulated it, presupposes that very young children and even infants have much more sophisticated capacities for causal inference, induction, and logical reasoning than Piaget proposed. Moreover, the theory proposes that very young children and even infants have abstract representations of the world that are removed from direct perceptual experience or action schemas.

The theory theory has been applied productively to several areas of cognitive development. First, psychologists have looked at our everyday categorizations of objects. Earlier theories tried to explain these categorizations in terms of the perceptual features of the objects. More recent research suggests that categorization is best understood in terms of our everyday theories about the underlying causal structure of objects (Murphy & Medin 1985). These theories allow us to make powerful and novel inductive inferences about those objects. If we look at young children's categorization, in both language and behavior, we see a very similar pattern. Even two- and three-year-old children appear to categorize objects in terms of "natural kinds," underlying essences with causal efficacy. They use those categorizations to generate new inductive inferences. Moreover, their decisions about which objects belong to these natural kinds appear to be rooted in naive theories of physics and biology. These very young children have coherent, abstract accounts of objects and animals and use those accounts to generate predictions and explanations (Carey 1985; Gelman & Markman 1986; Keil 1989; Gelman & Wellman 1991). Most significantly, it is possible to chart qualitative conceptual changes in children's categorization as their theories are constructed, modified, and revised. Thus, in Carey's work, for example, the child's categorization of an object as an "animal" or as "alive" changes as the child's "folk biology" changes (Carey 1985).

Second, the renewed interest in "folk psychology" has raised the possibility that our everyday understanding of the mind is analogous to a scientific theory. Empirical investigations of the child's developing understanding of the mind have tended to confirm this view – in fact, "theory of mind" has become the catch-phrase for research on children's folk psychology. The majority of investigators in the field have argued that the child's early understanding of the mind can be usefully construed as a theory and that changes in that understanding can be thought of as theory changes (Wellman 1990; Perner 1991; Gopnik 1993; Gopnik & Wellman 1994; Flavell, Green & Flavell, 1995; though see Harris 1991, and Leslie 1991, for opposing views). In the course of developing an account of the mind children postulate such mental entities as perceptions, beliefs, and desires as a way of explaining ordinary human action. Moreover, there are significant and far-reaching conceptual changes in the child's understanding of the mind, much like theory changes.

In my work, I have also applied the theory theory to cognitive developments in infancy, particularly to several striking cognitive changes that take place in late infancy (Gopnik 1988; Gopnik & Meltzoff 1997). During the period between about fifteen and twenty-one months, there appear to be significant changes in children's understanding of several basic domains, including their understanding of object appearances, of actions and goals, and of object categories. These changes are reflected in changes in the ways that these infants solve problems and act on objects.

Piaget originally observed some of these changes. He characterized them as manifestations of a single stage change, from early sensorimotor representations to a new "symbolic" type of representation. This new type of representation was a prerequisite for the emergence of language. Piaget's account of this transition is plainly incorrect. Many of the "symbolic capacities" Piaget identified, such as language use and deferred imitation, turn out, empirically, to be in place well before these other cognitive changes take place. Moreover, and more generally, recent work on infancy suggests that such abstract representations must be in place much earlier in infancy to underpin a variety of kinds of early knowledge. Finally, many studies suggest that the various types of changes in the broad period of late infancy are not correlated with one another. Although, on average, the abilities emerge at around the same age, there can be considerable independence among them.

I have argued that these changes can be more helpfully construed as theory changes. They involve fundamental and yet quite abstract and complex aspects of children's understanding of the world. These include children's understanding of the way that we perceive (or fail to perceive) objects, the way that our actions fulfill (or fail to fulfill) our goals, and the way that we divide the world into "natural kind" categories. These changes are manifested in changes in the ways that children search for hidden objects (in "object permanence" tasks), design solutions to problems (in "means–ends" tasks), and spontaneously sort and classify objects.

Changes in infants' underlying conceptions of these domains have quite wide-reaching implications: a variety of the infant's predictions and interpretations of evidence seem to shift together in a theory-like way. For example, at about eighteen months infants make a new set of predictions about a wide range of object disappearances, disappearances about which they made inaccurate predictions at fifteen months. These predictions seem to depend on a quite general conception of the way that objects can be perceived or can fail to be perceived. Similarly, infants begin consistently to make a wide range of new predictions about the causal properties of objects in this period, and use these predictions to guide their actions on the objects. Finally, children at this age develop new classification and categorization behaviors which may be the first sign of some understanding of "natural kinds." (See Gopnik & Meltzoff 1997, for detailed discussion.) Moreover, these changes are reflected in children's language. Early words do not just pick out some set of perceptual or functional features, nor do they simply encode social routines. Instead, they may, and often do, pick out events with quite different superficial features but similar underlying causal structure.

These changes also have some of the characteristic dynamic features of theory change. The two-year-old's conception of these domains appears to be qualitatively different from that of the one-year-old, and yet at the same time seems to follow logically from the failures of the earlier account. Children also seem to engage in extensive experimentation in these problem domains in this period.

2 Language, culture, and theorizing

How do language and culture fit into this picture of the child as theorizer? What role would the child's linguistic and cultural experience, and social life more generally, play in cognitive development on this view?

There is a classic opposition between two contrasting views of the relation between language and thought. On the one hand there is the Piagetian view which argues that cognitive and conceptual development are the driving force behind language development. On this account semantic development depends upon and reflects earlier conceptual development.

In spite of the ideological divides between Chomskyans and Piagetians, a similar view has been widespread in the Chomskyan tradition. The neo-Chomskyan position differs from the classical Piagetian position in two important respects. First, neo-Chomskyans tend to see cognitive structure itself as innate rather than constructed or developed. Second, and more significantly, they see cognition as a necessary but not sufficient condition for semantic development. On this position merely having a cognitive representation of the world does not determine one's semantic representations. Further rules are necessary to determine which aspects of the cognitive representation should be encoded linguistically.

For example, Pinker argues that children learn the semantic structure of their particular language by linking the cognitive representations of relevant contexts to the relevant syntactic structures, a process he calls "semantic bootstrapping" (Pinker 1989). Landau & Jackendoff (1993) suggest that semantic structures encode innate and universal representations that are determined by the perceptual system. Perhaps the most influential view of this sort in the literature on lexical acquisition comes from the work of Markman and her colleagues. Markman has proposed that there are quite general linguistic constraints on children's interpretation of early words. These constraints influence, even determine, children's decisions about which concepts those words encode (Markman 1989). The assumption behind the "constraints" view, however, is that these constraints are additions to basic conceptual structure. The child's conceptual system is capable of multiple construals of the world, and the constraints determine which of those construals will be encoded linguistically.

In contrast, Whorf (1956) and Vygotsky (1962) both advanced a view that was closer to what we might now call "social constructivism." On their view, much of cognitive development could be seen as the internalization of concepts that were provided by relevant adults in the society, particularly through the medium of language. Whorf emphasized the role of the particular syntactic structures of particular languages. The implication was that these structures embodied particular conceptual structures which were transmitted to speakers of the language. Vygotsky emphasized the particular distinctive pragmatic characteristics of the language parents produced in the course of their interaction with children, what we might now call "motherese." Again, however, the implication was that these linguistic interactions shaped children's cognitive development as well as their semantic development. More recently a number of researchers have been reviving both neo-Whorfian and neo-Vygotskyan ideas about this sort of influence of language on cognition.

The theory theory is often perceived as a theory that deemphasizes the role of language, culture, and social life in cognitive development, and so as a theory that would endorse the idea that cognition precedes language. Critiques of the theory theory often make the assumption that seeing the child as "little scientist" means seeing the child as a cognitive isolate, a recluse. This is not, of course, what children really are like, but then it is also not what scientists really are like. Both theoretically and empirically, the theory theory is very congruent with a stronger, more interactionist view of the relation between language and thought. In fact, we have argued that the model of theory change in science provides us with a particularly perspicuous way of understanding such interactions between cognitive and linguistic development. The view that emerges is different from either of the classical opposing views.

On this view, we can think of the child as analogous to a physics student, or perhaps to a "normal" scientist hearing about a new theoretical possibility from a scientific innovator. Consider the acquisition of scientific terms like *entropy* in these circumstances. Developing an understanding of such words and the ability to use them appropriately is one sign, often the most relevant sign, of theory formation. We pay attention to words like *entropy* because they are relevant to the scientific problems we are trying to solve. At the same time, however, learning the words is an important part of learning the concepts. At the simplest level, hearing the same word across a variety of contexts may lead us to see similarities in those contexts that we might not otherwise have considered. Hearing the professor say *entropy* both when she discusses randomness and when she discusses heat may lead us to link these otherwise disparate phenomena, and this linkage itself has implications for other aspects of our understanding of physics.

At a more sophisticated level, *entropy* gains its meaning from its connections to a number of other concepts in a complex, coherent theoretical structure. Most of us acquire this structure largely through the medium of language.

Neither the Piagetian/Chomskyan prerequisites view nor the classical Whorf/Vygotsky interactionist view seem to capture the character of this sort of semantic change in science. In such cases we do not say either that conceptual development precedes semantic development or vice versa. It is not simply that we have an innate repertoire of concepts, including "entropy," and are merely waiting to map the correct term onto that concept. But it is also not that we are simply mindlessly matching our linguistic behavior to that of our teacher, and that our cognition is shaped accordingly. Rather the two types of developments, learning the word and learning the related concept, appear to go hand in hand, with each type facilitating the other.

3 Developmental relations between language and cognition

Starting in the late 1980s, we have conducted a series of studies examining the empirical relations between linguistic and cognitive development in 15- to 21-month-old children. The results of these studies support the "theory-like" interactionist approach I have just outlined. Particular cognitive developments and related semantic developments appear to be closely linked, but one area does not seem to be a prerequisite for the other. Our earliest studies looked at the cognitive developments between 15 and 21 months that we described earlier as theory changes: object permanence and means–ends developments. These changes in problem-solving behavior turn out to be related to the emergence of "relational" words like *gone* and *uh-oh.* More recently we have examined the relations between children's spontaneous categorization and their development of a naming spurt. In a series of intensive longitudinal studies, we recorded children's spontaneous language development in detail using both a maternal questionnaire and video recordings, and also recorded children's performance on a variety of nonlinguistic cognitive tasks.

We found a relation between the development of words for disappearance, like *gone*, and the development of high-level object permanence abilities, a finding also replicated in other studies (Corrigan 1978; McCune-Nicolich 1981; Gopnik 1982, 1984; Gopnik & Meltzoff 1984, 1986; Tomasello & Farrar 1984, 1986). Within a week or two of the time children showed the highest-level object search behaviors in the laboratory, their mothers, quite independently, recorded that they had begun to say words like *allgone*.

We discovered another independent relation between words encoding success and failure, such as *there* and *uh-oh*, and the development of means–ends abilities, in particular the ability to solve certain problems with "insight," immediately and without a period of trial and error (Gopnik & Meltzoff 1984, 1986). Again within a week or two of our first observation of these behaviors in the laboratory, mothers independently reported the emergence of these words.

Finally, we found a relation between the naming spurt and children's spontaneous classification – in particular, the ability to sort objects exhaustively into many categories. This finding has been replicated by Mervis & Bertrand, both in normally developing children and in children with Down's syndrome (Gopnik & Meltzoff 1987, 1992; Mervis & Bertrand 1994). In addition, we have replicated and confirmed all these longitudinal studies with data from cross-sectional studies with a larger number of subjects (Gopnik & Meltzoff 1986, 1992).

All three of these specific relations between semantic and cognitive developments have some similar characteristics. All three take place on average at about the same time, around 18 months. All three involve particular semantic developments, the development of words with specific types of meanings, rather than involving structural developments, such as the ability to use words or combine them. Most significantly, in all three cases, the linguistic developments and the nonlinguistic cognitive abilities appear to emerge at about the same time, within a few weeks of one another in our longitudinal studies.

However, the three conceptual domains – knowledge about our perception of objects, reflected in "object permanence," knowledge about desires and actions, and knowledge about object categories – are strikingly independent of each other. Some individual children acquire *gone* and related nonlinguistic object permanence abilities months before they acquire "success/failure" words and related means–ends abilities. Other children reverse this pattern. Moreover, while there are strong relations between the ages at which the semantic developments emerge and those at which the related cognitive developments emerge, the cross-relations do not hold: object permanence is not linked to success/failure words and means–ends development is not linked to disappearance words. The same pattern holds for means–ends development and the naming spurt. Specifically, there are relatively small temporal gaps between the related cognitive and semantic developments, the two developments literally appearing at almost the same time in longitudinal studies. There are much larger gaps between the unrelated developments. Individual children begin to say the words and develop the related abilities at about the same time.

Similarly, in cross-sectional studies, eighteen-month-olds who solve object permanence tasks are more likely to say *gone* than children who do not solve these tasks. They are not more likely to say *uh-oh*. Eighteen-month-old children who solve means–ends tasks are not more likely to say *gone* than children who do not (Gopnik & Meltzoff 1986). Thus there are also specific correlations between linguistic and cognitive abilities in cross-sectional samples.

Rather than being the result of some more general relation between linguistic and cognitive abilities, these relations appear to involve quite specific links between particular conceptual developments and related semantic developments. These results are among very few empirical demonstrations of a close and specific relation between language and nonlinguistic cognition in this period (or in any other).

The specificity of these results strongly suggests that a conceptual change underlies both types of development, the nonlinguistic cognitive changes and the emergence of new words. By themselves either the linguistic or the cognitive changes might be due to many general developmental changes. For example, the words might emerge because of changes in general linguistic or phonological abilities, or the changes in problem-solving behavior might be the result of increased mnemonic or motor abilities. Indeed such proposals have been made in the literature. The close and specific relations between the semantic and cognitive developments are, however, very difficult to explain on these views. To explain these developments we need to postulate some underlying causal factor, some change in the child's mind, that is common to both the emergence of *gone* and the development of object permanence problem-solving, but is not common to either the emergence of *uh-oh* or the development of means–ends skill. A conceptual change, of the sort we see in theory change, seems the best candidate.

Notice that the fact that the two developments emerge at the same time provides particularly strong evidence for a causal relation between these particular linguistic and cognitive abilities. The correlational cross-sectional evidence shows that children who had developed the linguistic abilities tended to have developed the related cognitive ability. However, it might be that some earlier linguistic or cognitive development was responsible for the later developments, and the apparent relation between the specific cognitive and linguistic developments at eighteen months was due to these earlier relations. Of course, this would still imply that there were specific links between cognitive and linguistic developments, but they might not be the links we have identified. However, the fact that the two developments emerge at almost the same time would be difficult to explain on this view.

These relations don't fit neatly with either of the classical pictures of the relations between language and thought. Eighteen-month-olds do not simply encode every aspect of their cognitive representation of a context. They also do not encode the aspects of cognitive representation that are most fundamental to the grammar of the adult language, as the neo-Chomskyan views would suggest.

On the other hand, children also do not simply match the patterns in the speech they hear. The children's uses of such relational words as *gone* and *uh-oh* to encode concepts of disappearance and failure are often strikingly different from the uses of these words in the language the children hear. Children apply *gone*, for example, to a very wide range of cases in which an object is not visible to them, from turning over a piece of paper, to putting a block in a box, to turning away from an object. However, they never use *gone* to refer to the fact that an object is invisible to someone else. In fact, in some of our studies children would select a word to encode these concepts on the basis of just one or two salient uses. For example, one little girl used *come off* to refer to all cases of failure and Bowerman reports a similar use of *heavy* (Bowerman 1978).

These children choose to encode the concepts that are at the frontiers of their cognitive development, the concepts that are central to the theories that are currently under construction. In fact, there are interesting parallels between the kinds of cognitive developments that seem to occur between fifteen and twenty-one months and the kinds of concepts expressed most frequently in early language in the same period. Object appearances, actions, and kinds, as well as spatial relations, are all areas of great cognitive significance to children of this age. These are also the notions that are most likely to be encoded in early language.

So we have shown that linguistic development and related conceptual changes are closely linked. This concurrent development suggests a picture like the picture of our acquisition of scientific terms like *entropy*, where semantic and conceptual changes also seem to be closely linked. But we also said that hearing about "entropy" might itself be a cause of the conceptual change. Is this also true in childhood? Could linguistic input itself be a factor in theory change?

The fact that, in our longitudinal studies, the semantic and conceptual developments occurred in close temporal concert suggested that the interaction might go in both directions. The changes in problem-solving occurred at about the same time as the linked linguistic changes, and sometimes the linguistic changes preceded the changes in problem-solving. This temporal pattern raises the possibility that language was causally implicated in the conceptual change. Moreover, some studies suggest that providing infants with linguistic (or nonlinguistic) labels for objects in the laboratory makes them more likely to categorize those objects (Roberts & Jacob 1991; Waxman 1991; Baldwin & Moses 1994). Neither of these findings by itself demonstrates, however, that language is implicated in the kinds of theory changes we have described here.

4 Crosslinguistic studies

How could we further test the interactionist hypothesis that language may restructure and influence cognition? As always in developmental psychology, the crucial experiments are immoral or impossible: we could not experimentally alter children's linguistic environment and observe the effects on their problem-solving. We could, however, see whether naturally occurring variations in linguistic input are related to different patterns of cognitive development. Both Bowerman (1989) and Slobin (1982) have suggested that morphological and syntactic differences in different languages might make certain conceptual distinctions particularly salient. In collaboration with Professor Soonja Choi at San Diego State University, I have been investigating the relations between language and cognition in Korean-speakers (Gopnik & Choi 1990, 1995; Choi & Gopnik 1995; Gopnik, Choi, & Baumberger 1996).

English has a highly analytic structure, with relatively little reliance on morphological variation. Moreover, nouns are generally obligatory in English sentences. In contrast, Korean and Japanese, languages with similar structures, have a very rich verb morphology, depend on different verb endings to make important semantic distinctions, and are verb-final. Pragmatic rules in Korean and Japanese allow massive noun ellipsis, particularly in informal conversation where the objects that are referred to are present (Clancy 1985). Parental speech in these languages, which occurs in precisely such a setting, often consists of highly inflected verbs with few nouns, very much in contrast to North American English parental speech. As will be shown, we have found that Korean-speaking mothers consistently used fewer nouns than English-speaking mothers, and Fernald & Morikawa (1993) report a similar pattern for Japanese-speaking mothers.

There is also some evidence that there are differences in the very early language of Korean- and Japanese- vs. English-speaking children. A number of investigators have noted that Korean- and Japanese-speaking children use verb morphology productively earlier than English-speaking children, but use fewer and less varied names (Tanouye 1979; Clancy 1985; Choi 1986, 1991; Rispoli 1987; Fernald & Morikawa 1993; Choi & Gopnik 1995. Au *et al.* 1994 did not detect such a difference but there are a number of methodological reasons for this (see Gopnik *et al.* 1996)). Given the relations between language and cognition in English speakers we might predict that Korean speakers would be advanced in their understanding of actions, concepts encoded by verbs, and delayed in their understanding of object kinds, concepts encoded by nouns. These both seem to be important areas of conceptual change between fifteen and twenty-one months.

Gopnik & Choi (1990) studied the linguistic and cognitive development of five Korean-speaking children in an intensive longitudinal study. The results suggested that both the emergence of a naming explosion and the development of exhaustive categorization were indeed particularly delayed in Korean-speaking children relative to the children in a comparable English-speaking sample. In a second longitudinal study (Gopnik & Choi 1995; Gopnik *et al.* 1996), we tested a larger sample of Korean-speaking children. In each testing session children received both the cognitive tasks that we used in our earlier studies of English-speakers and an extensive language questionnaire specifically designed for Korean. Children received means–ends tasks that required the use of insight (such as using a rake to pull a distant object towards them), and spontaneous categorization tasks (such as sorting a set of different objects into groups). There was a significant difference between the Korean and English speakers' performance on the categorization tasks. The Korean speakers were significantly delayed on this measure compared to the English speakers. Similarly, there was a significant difference between Korean and English speakers' performance in the development of a naming explosion: Korean speakers were also delayed on this measure.

Importantly, however, the opposite pattern held for the development of means–ends abilities and success/failure words. Korean-speaking children were significantly advanced in both these areas of development compared to the English speakers.

In a second cross-sectional study we again compared the cognitive performance of eighteen Korean-speaking children and thirty English speakers (Gopnik *et al.* 1996). The results confirmed those in the longitudinal studies. The Korean speakers were significantly worse on categorization tasks than the English speakers: only 11% of the Korean children passed the task while 47% of the English speakers did. In contrast, 89% of the Korean speakers passed the means–ends task while only 60% of the English speakers did.

Moreover, we also collected data comparing the speech of these Korean-speaking mothers to the speech of English-speaking mothers. At the start and end of each testing session in the cross-sectional study, the mothers were asked to play and talk with their children for five minutes in one of two semi-structured sessions, either "reading" picture books or playing with a toy house. We then analyzed the mothers' use of nouns and verbs. Korean-speaking mothers consistently used more words that were relevant to actions than English speakers, they used more referential verbs – that is, verbs that refer clearly to actions – and in a pragmatic analysis they also used more activity-oriented utterances than English speakers. In contrast, English-speaking mothers used more nouns, more referential nouns and more naming-oriented utterances. The specific patterns of relations suggest that these differences in linguistic input may be responsible for the children's different patterns of cognitive development.

Precisely which aspects of the input are influential is still unclear. Cross-linguistic studies suggest that some languages which syntactically permit noun omission, like Italian, pattern differently than other languages, like Mandarin Chinese. Mandarin children, like Korean children, use verbs as early and as frequently as nouns, while Italian children do not. Our findings also suggest that it is not simply the presence or absence of nouns and verbs in the input that is important but the way that they are used in speech to children (see Caselli, Bates, Casadio, & Fenson 1996; Gopnik *et al.* 1996, Tardif 1996; Tardif, Gelman, & Xu 1999, for discussion).

5 Language as evidence

How might we conceptualize these effects of linguistic input on cognitive development? The classic Whorfian interpretation of these findings might be that the syntactic differences between English and Korean determine a basic difference, a kind of incommensurability, in the ways that English and Korean speakers conceptualize actions and objects. The behaviors of the children reflect this type of incommensurability. The English-speaking children conceive of the world in fundamentally different ways than the Korean speakers.

This view seems to us far too strong, both too strong in general, and too strong, in particular, when applied to our data. After all, in our studies both Korean and English children eventually seemed to converge on similar understandings of both actions and objects. At least, both groups of children came to share the same problem-solving abilities, and presumably the same conceptions of the world underlying those abilities, by the time they were two or three. On the theory view, the reason they did so was because these conceptions were accurate, or, at least, they accounted for the vast majority of the evidence that was available to the children in the most economical way. The differences lay more in the timing and the route by which children converged on the solutions than in the solutions themselves.

An alternative way of understanding these differences is that the different patterns of linguistic input in the two languages provided children with different patterns of evidence that were relevant to the cognitive problems the children attempted to solve. Recall that a crucial aspect of the theory theory is the idea that patterns of evidence cause theory formation and change. In principle, quite different patterns of cognitive development could take place, and quite different theories could be developed, if children were exposed to different patterns of evidence. The usual common, even universal, patterns of development stem from the fact that, for the problems children try to solve, the patterns of evidence are not typically very variable. The disappearances of objects or the relations between means and ends will generally be apparent in all the evidence the infant collects, and that evidence will be ubiquitous.

But once language enters the picture this uniformity and ubiquity will change. In infancy children are always acquiring evidence directly from their observations of the environment. Cultural patterns may have some effect, even at this point: children who are exposed to different types of objects may develop certain theories before others. Still, these cultural effects will largely be swamped by the uniform and ubiquitous behavior of objects, behavior that infants can easily observe.

At about eighteen months, however, children have a powerful new source of evidence about the structure of the world. As soon as children become members of the linguistic community they will acquire much, indeed most, of the evidence they use in theory formation through the medium of language. By the time they reach the stage of adult science, only a tiny portion of evidence will come from direct observation. The use of linguistic evidence is a double-edged sword. On the one hand, it gives children access to a vast store of information that has been accumulated by other people at other times. This includes information about far-off times and places that the child could not directly observe. On the other hand, it also raises the possibility that there will be wide variation in the kinds of evidence that individual children will receive. In fact, different children might receive conflicting evidence through the medium of language, depending on the beliefs of their adult informants. At the stage of adult science, this becomes a thorny problem, which requires a great deal of social infrastructure for its solution.

These effects of linguistic evidence on theory formation may range from relatively weak to quite strong. Simply using language at all in a context can be a powerful way of drawing children's attention to that context. At 18 months, or even earlier, infants already seem to recognize that language can be an important source of information about the world and to attend to events that are linguistically marked. In the case of Korean more language seems to be produced in action contexts than in object contexts, while the opposite pattern holds for English. At the simplest level a child who is paying more attention to actions than to objects might well have a more advanced understanding of that domain.

Moreover, the patterns of lexical use across contexts can draw children's attention to particular evidential patterns. The use of a single common name for a wide variety of objects, for example, may present the child with *prima facie* evidence that there is some common underlying nature to those objects. Moreover, such behaviors may suggest to the children that other inductive predictions about the objects will follow from their common name. Objects with the same name will also share other properties. In fact, there is good evidence that by 2½ or 3 children do make these assumptions. Linguistic similarities lead children to assume that there will be other similarities between objects. In fact, linguistic similarities play a more powerful role in determining children's inductions than other perceptual similarities between objects (Gelman & Markman 1986; Gelman & Coley 1991).

More generally, the very fact of naming itself, the fact that all objects are named, might lead children to notice, in general, that objects belong in categories. I have suggested that this may be the explanation for the link between the naming spurt and exhaustive categorization. The relevant fact about both these behaviors is that *all* objects, not just particularly salient or important objects, are named or classified. In the naming spurt, children provide, and search for, names for everything they see. In exhaustive categorization they spontaneously place all the objects they see into groups. The naming behaviors of mothers may prompt the children to make this more general inference that all objects have names and belong in kinds, as well as to make the particular inference that objects with the same name belong to the same kind. This may be particularly likely when mothers themselves are constantly naming a wide variety of objects, often for no apparent reason. This was the sort of behavior we saw particularly frequently in our English-speaking mothers.

Conversely, Korean mothers' emphasis on verbs may lead infants to attend to actions and relations. We know much less about children's developing understanding of actions and relations than about their understanding of objects (perhaps partly because most psychologists speak English!). The Korean mothers are also more likely to mark similarities between actions and relations than the English mothers, and this behavior may lead children to make further inferences about these events. Some suggestive evidence along these lines comes from the work of Choi & Bowerman (1991) on early spatial verbs in Korean. Korean spatial verbs mark different distinctions than spatial prepositions in English. For example, Korean verbs make distinctions between loose and tight fit rather than between containment and support. The Korean children show similar patterns in their use of these words from an early age. The theory theory would suggest that these children might also show distinctive nonlinguistic patterns of inference about spatial relations that reflect these linguistic patterns. If such effects do exist they might be analogous to the effects that

Gelman found in the domain of objects. Just as children assume that giving the same name to two objects means that they share a common nature, so they may make similar assumptions about marking two spatial events with the same verb.

More general effects might also be found. Just as the English-speaking children may have been prompted to the discovery that *all* objects belong in kinds, so Korean-speaking children may be prompted to similarly general discoveries about actions and relations, such as the fact that *all* actions may succeed or fail. Korean verbs mark the success or failure of actions in a particularly clear and perspicuous way. We have argued that this more general understanding of the nature of actions is reflected in the changes in children's performance on means–ends tasks, particularly the emergence of "insightful" problem-solving. These changes involve a very wide variety of particular actions and events. The cognitive changes appear to have less to do with the child's understanding of particular events (such as their understanding of tight and loose fit or support and containment) than with their understanding of how actions lead to events, in general (see Gopnik & Meltzoff 1997). In our studies, these linguistic and cognitive developments are closely related.

Our studies have been concerned with lexical rather than syntactic and morphological acquisition. We might speculate, however, that as children come to understand syntax and morphology, and begin to appreciate the propositional structure of language, language might play another and still stronger role in theory formation. One important element in theory change is the accumulation of patterns of evidence and counter-evidence. The kinds of linguistic effects I have discussed so far seem to reflect the way that children use language as a source of evidence. But another important factor in theory change is the availability of alternative theoretical models to the currently held models. As I mentioned earlier these alternative models may come from many sources.

Once we have complex syntax and morphology, language itself may be an important medium for passing on alternative theoretical models to children. Adults may not only pass on the relevant evidence to children, they may also provide the child with alternative theoretical models more directly, by representing them syntactically. Again, the fact that the theory the child will converge on is available in the adult language in this way may partly explain why the child's cognitive development is relatively swift – at least, in comparison to the slow and painful development of theories in science. As I mentioned earlier, in this regard the child may be more like a science student than a scientist *per se.*

This last possibility begins to sound more like the strong Whorfian alternative I initially rejected. The important difference, however, is that I think that the child is driven by considerations of veridicality, of predictive accuracy and explanatory adequacy, throughout development. Children will only consider novel patterns of evidence if they are congruent with other information in the world. The fact that objects have the same name *does*, in fact, correlate with other inductive generalizations about the objects. It is a good inductive strategy to predict that a new object that is described as a *cat* will have the same properties as familiar objects that are also called *cat*. Similarly, the general fact that all objects have names does correlate with the nonlinguistic fact that all objects belong in kinds, and so that this inductive strategy can be applied quite generally and productively. On my view purely arbitrary linguistic generalizations, generalizations that did not lead to good predictions or explanations in this way, would be rejected or reshaped.

Similarly, on this view, an alternative theory that was presented linguistically would only be accepted if it was relatively congruent with the child's previous theories and current evidence. If this is not the case the child may simply fail to make the new theory his own. (At one point I asked my six-year-old if he knew why the moon changed its shape. He replied with a surprisingly polished recital of the scientific story, only to add at the end: "Actually, I don't know why it changes at all, this is just what my big brother told me." Further discussion showed that this was quite true.)

More frequently, the theory the adults present will be modified and restructured to be more explanatorily adequate from the child's point of view. I mentioned examples of this kind of restructuring of input in our own work on children's use of "relational" words – for example, the use of *come off* to mean failure. Similar examples abound and many are offered in other chapters in this book, particularly in the work of Eve Clark and Melissa Bowerman. A particularly elegant example comes from Carolyn Mervis' work on child-basic categories (Mervis, Mervis, Johnson, & Bertrand 1992). In her studies, for example, young children used *money* only to refer to coins rather than bills. The adult use points to the underlying theoretical similarity of these objects in our "folk" (and for that matter our scientific) economics. But young children have no way of beginning to understand or evaluate this type of theoretical structure. Instead they restructure the adult usage to fit their own theories of the world more closely.

One might, in this way, be a kind of Whorfian in one's recognition of a strong effect of language on cognition and yet reject the anti-realism and relativism that seems to accompany the Whorfian position. Children do pay attention to the particularities of the adult language, and these particularities do affect the child's conception of the world. They do so, however, because they feed into universal mechanisms for understanding the world, particularly mechanisms for theory formation and change.

6 Theories, language, and relativity in adults

The kind of defanged Whorfianism I have been advocating so far seems particularly appropriate in the developmental context. The children in our studies do, after all, eventually converge on similar theories. It may seem more difficult to apply these ideas to the adult differences in language and cognition that have been charted by the cognitive anthropologists in this volume and elsewhere. I will argue that the theory theory itself suggests a hypothesis about the circumstances in which we will see something like linguistic relativity in adults.

The hypothesis is that we will see such effects when alternative linguistic or cognitive construals are equally congruent with the relevant evidence that is available to us about the structure of the world. One implication of work in the philosophy of science is that scientific theories may be, and indeed generally are, underdetermined by evidence. Two genuinely alternative theories may be equally well supported by the evidence, equally powerful in their explanatory structure and so on, at a given time. I suggest that this may well be the case in some of the more striking instances of linguistic and cognitive relativity that have been presented in this volume.

For example, something like this seems to be true of the material-kind-centered systems of nominal classification in Mayan vs. the object-kind-centered systems in languages like English (Lucy & Gaskins, ch. 9 of this volume). Both knowing something's material kind and knowing its shape or object kind are important and powerful sources of inference and prediction. To know that my desk is wood allows me to make one important set of predictions about it: it will burn in a fire, and stain if I place unprotected tea-cups on it. To know that it is a desk allows other predictions: that it will support a certain amount of weight, or that paper and envelopes can be found in its drawers, but not bananas or tomatoes. There seems to be no general advantage of making one type of prediction rather than another, though there may, of course, be advantages for each type of prediction in particular settings. The particular syntax of a language, we might imagine, can give one or the other type of prediction special weight. The Mayan speakers seem to classify objects nonlinguistically on the basis of their material kind, and they might also turn first to material kind in formulating inductive inferences.

The same picture might also account for the difference in systems of spatial reference in different languages – the body-centered system in English versus the landmark-centered system in Mayan, for example (Levinson & Haviland 1994; Levinson, ch. 19 of this volume). These alternative systems might indeed have genuine nonlinguistic consequences – the evidence suggests that English and Mayan speakers sort, solve problems and draw inferences in ways that reflect these linguistic differences. Nevertheless, there does not seem to be any obvious superiority of one system over another in terms of the weight of predictions and explanations. The two systems may genuinely not be equivalent, notational variants of one another; they may lead to genuinely different inferences. Still, neither seems to have a striking cognitive advantage, as, say, the two-year-old's object theory seems to do compared to the one-year-old's theory.

The same is true of the alternative Korean and English systems of spatial classification (Choi & Bowerman 1991; Bowerman & Choi, ch. 16 of this volume). Both organizing the world in terms of tight and loose fit and in terms of attachment and containment have cognitive consequences and advantages. Placing together objects with tight-fitting relations to their supports will call attention to one important set of inductive similarities among those relations, while organizing them in terms of containment will support another set. Both sets, however, seem overall to be roughly equal in predictive and explanatory power, given our ordinary cognitive projects.

We might want to predict that we would not see linguistic effects on cognition if those effects led to plainly non-veridical predictions and classifications. For example, color notoriously fails to support many interesting inferences: knowing the color of an object, by itself, tells us little about its other properties (though we may, of course, use color as a cue to the kind of an object). It certainly supports far fewer inferences than material or natural kind. We might predict that no language would give color the same syntactic weight that Mayan languages give to material kinds. Similarly, we might predict that no language would give the same locative term to spatial relations with radically different predictive consequences, say one word for objects falling and objects being to the left of other objects and another word for loose fit and objects being to the right of other objects. Or, at least, we would not expect to see cognitive consequences of such arbitrary classifications.

Of course, determining if two linguistic systems are roughly equivalent in their cognitive power will also depend on the particular purposes and projects of speakers. In fact, the adult Mayan system may well be superior for the purpose of the navigational and geographic projects that are particularly important in Mayan culture, but, in our culture, where such projects are less important, we make do with the inferior English system. Similarly, within the English-speaking culture, scientific languages or notational systems may be veridically superior to "natural" English, and yet the natural language system may be used for ordinary purposes. (Logic is, precisely, a language that has been invented to maximize veridical inferences, but it is not very suitable for everyday use). Determining the relative cognitive advantage of a linguistic system is a matter not just of counting up how many accurate inferences we can make with each system but also of deciding which inferences are important for what purposes. In fact, of course, this is also true in science itself where different levels of description or notational systems may be suitable for different predictive and explanatory purposes.

There is another type of case that might, on the theory theory, also be likely to lead to Whorfian effects in adulthood. The cases we have just considered involved alternative, but equally well-supported, theories of the external world. It is possible that for some normative and conventional practices there may also be genuinely alternative conceptual schemes, genuinely conflicting theories between cultural groups, and these may be caused by and reflected in linguistic differences. These cases would, however, have a rather different cognitive basis than those I just discussed.

Normative or conventional behaviors and practices notoriously have a self-constitutive quality. Given the flexibility of human behavior, there will be complex interactions between believing that people do act a particular way, believing that they should act that way, and actually making it the case that they act that way. My own favorite example of this is La Rochefoucauld's dictum that no one would fall in love if they hadn't read about it first. This is not a problem when we create theories of the physical world: no object ever fell at 32 feet per second squared because it had read that that was a wonderful way to fall, but lots of objects fall head over heels for a pair of blue eyes in just that way.

In the moral or social realm it may be difficult to separate injunctions to action and descriptions of action. The syntactically deep kinship terminology of the Australian Arrernte group may be a good example of this kind of effect.To be a member of a kinship system depends on understanding a certain set of somewhat arbitrary relations, and acting on that basis. Language is an important way of learning those relations, perhaps the only way, since they have little "objective" basis (unlike, say, spatial relations of containment or support). However, if you are in a community that, in fact, embodies those relations, and you yourself and everyone else acts in accordance with them, mastering the system will actually also give you considerable inferential, predictive, and explanatory power. It will help you to regulate your own behavior but it will also help you to explain the behavior of others.

Moreover these effects may not only involve straightforwardly normative and conventional practices, like kinship relations. They may extend to domains like folk psychology, as in the La Rochefoucauld example. One might speculate that learning terms for complex emotions and understanding those emotions, in particular, would be subject to these sorts of Whorfian effects. In the La Rochefoucauld example, my language may classify together as "love" a set of emotions – intense manic-depressive phenomenology, sexual attraction, intimacy, common understanding, jealousy, etc. – that would not be so grouped by another culture, or by our culture at another historical period. Once I and others have interpreted my behavior and feelings in accord with this classification, however, usually through the medium of language, then the classification will have genuine predictive and explanatory power (as in the old song that lists a set of typical erotic symptoms and concludes with the inference "You're not sick, you're just in love").

Human beings have two highly distinctive evolutionary traits. Both these traits are subsumed in the classical description of us as the rational animal and both seem deeply bound up with our linguistic capacities. More than any other animal, we search for causal regularities in the world around us. We are perpetually driven to look for deeper explanations of our experience, and broader and more reliable predictions about it. Cognitive science tries to explain how and why we can do this. But, also more than any other animal, we can change our behavior to suit the world we find ourselves in. We perpetually invent new ways of behaving. The variety of cultures is a tribute to this behavioral flexibility, and understanding it is the project of anthropology. Children seem, quite literally, to be born with both these traits: the desire to understand the world and the desire to discover how to behave in it. Inevitably, of course, both children and scientists eventually turn this explanatory drive on our own protean natures, and try to find stable explanations for our unstable and inconstant behavior. Inevitably, also, we run into paradoxes and difficulties when we do so. It appears, however, that this impulse to understand ourselves is itself a firmly rooted and deep part of our nature. Language plays a crucial role in allowing us to succeed in all of these distinctively human projects.

NOTE

This research was supported by National Science Foundation Grant DBS9213959. I am grateful to Andrew Meltzoff, Dan Slobin, and the contributors to this volume for ideas and comments.

REFERENCES

Au, T. K., M. Dapretto, & Y. K. Song. 1994. Input vs. constraints: early word acquisition in Korean and English. *Journal of Memory and Language* 33: 567–582.

Baldwin, D. A., & L. J. Moses. 1994. Early understanding of referential intent and attentional focus: evidence from language and emotion. In C. Lewis & P. Mitchell (eds.), *Origins of a theory of mind*. Hillsdale, NJ: Lawrence Erlbaum, 133–156.

Bowerman, M. 1978. The acquisition of word meaning: an investigation into some current conflicts. In N. Waterson & C. Snow (eds.), *The development of communication*. New York: John Wiley, 263–287.

1989. Learning a semantic system: what role do cognitive predispositions play? In M. L. Rice & R. L. Schieffelbusch (eds.), *The teachability of language.* Baltimore, MD: Paul H. Brookes, 133–169.

Carey, S. 1985. *Conceptual change in childhood.* Cambridge, MA: Bradford/MIT Press.

1988. Conceptual differences between children and adults. *Mind and Language* 3: 167–181.

Caselli, M. C., E. Bates, P. Casadio, & J. Fenson. 1995. A cross-linguistic study of early lexical development. *Cognitive Development* 10: 159–199.

Choi, S. 1986. A pragmatic analysis of sentence-ending morphemes in Korean children. Paper presented at the Linguistic Society of America, New York, December.

1991. Early acquisition of epistemic meanings in Korean: a study of sentence-ending suffixes in the spontaneous speech of three children. *First Language* 11: 93–119.

Choi, S., & M. Bowerman. 1991. Learning to express motion events in English and Korean: the influence of language-specific lexicalization patterns. *Cognition* 41: 83–121.

Choi, S., & A. Gopnik. 1995. Early acquisition of verbs in Korean: a crosslinguistic study. *Journal of Child Language* 22: 497–529.

Clancy, P. 1985. The acquisition of Japanese. In D. I. Slobin (ed.), *The crosslinguistic study of language acquisition*, vol. 1: *The data.* Hillsdale, NJ: Lawrence Erlbaum, 373–524.

Corrigan, R. 1978. Language development as related to stage 6 object permanence development. *Journal of Child Language* 5: 173–189.

Fernald, A., & H. Morikawa. 1993. Common themes and cultural variations in Japanese and American mother's speech to infants. *Child Development* 64: 637–656.

Flavell, J. H., F. L. Green, & E. R. Flavell. 1995. Young children's knowledge about thinking. *Monographs of the Society for Research in Child Development* 60 [1, serial no. 243].

Gelman, S. A., & J. D. Coley. 1991. Language and categorization: the acquisition of natural kind terms. In S. A. Gelman & J. P. Byrnes (eds.), *Perspectives on language and thought: interrelations in development.* Cambridge: Cambridge University Press, 146–196.

Gelman, S. A., & E. Markman. 1986. Categories and induction in young children. *Cognition* 23: 183–209.

Gelman, S. A., & H. M. Wellman. 1991. Insides and essence: early understandings of the non-obvious. *Cognition* 38: 213–244.

Gopnik, A. 1982. Words and plans: early language and the development of intelligent action. *Journal of Child Language* 9: 303–8.

1984. Conceptual and semantic change in scientists and children: why there are no semantic universals. *Linguistics* 20: 163–179.

1988. Conceptual and semantic development as theory change. *Mind and Language* 3: 197–217.

1993. How we know our minds: the illusion of first-person knowledge of intentionality. *Behavioral and Brain Sciences* 16: 1–14.

Gopnik, A., & S. Choi. 1990. Do linguistic differences lead to cognitive differences?

A cross-linguistic study of semantic and cognitive development. *First Language* 10: 199–215.

1995. Names, relational words, and cognitive development in English and Korean speakers: nouns are not always learned before verbs. In M. Tomasello & W. E. Merriman (eds.), *Beyond names for things: young children's acquisition of verbs.* Hillsdale, NJ/Hove: Lawrence Erlbaum, 63–80.

Gopnik, A., S. Choi, & T. Baumberger. 1996. Cross-linguistic differences in early semantic and cognitive development. *Cognitive Development* 11: 197–227.

Gopnik, A., & A. Meltzoff. 1984. Semantic and cognitive development in 15- to 21-month-old children. *Journal of Child Language* 11: 495–513.

1986. Relations between semantic and cognitive development in the one-word stage: the specificity hypothesis. *Child Development* 57: 1040–1053.

1987. The development of categorization in the second year and its relation to other cognitive and linguistic developments. *Child Development* 58: 1523–1531.

1992. Categorization and naming: basic-level sorting in eighteen-month-olds and its relation to language. *Child Development* 63: 1091–1103.

1997. *Words, thoughts, and theories.* Cambridge, MA: Bradford/MIT Press.

Gopnik, A., & H. Wellman. 1992. Why the child's theory of mind really is a theory. *Mind and Language* 7: 145–172.

1994. The "theory theory." In L. Hirschfield & S. Gelman (eds.), *Mapping the mind: domain specificity in culture and cognition.* New York: Cambridge University Press, 257–293.

Harris, P. 1991. The work of the imagination. In A. Whiten (ed.), *Natural theories of mind: the evolution, development and simulation of everyday mindreading.* Oxford: Basil Blackwell, 283–304.

Karmiloff-Smith, A. 1988. The child is a theoretician, not an inductivist. *Mind and Language* 3: 183–197.

Karmiloff-Smith, A., & B. Inhelder. 1974. If you want to get ahead, get a theory. *Cognition* 3: 195–212.

Keil, F. C. 1987. Conceptual development and category structure. In U. Neisser (ed.), *Concepts and conceptual development.* New York: Cambridge University Press, 175–201.

1989. *Concepts, kinds, and cognitive development.* Cambridge, MA: Bradford/ MIT Press.

Landau, B., & Jackendoff, R. 1993. "What" and "where" in spatial language and spatial cognition. *Behavioral and Brain Sciences* 16: 217–255.

Leslie, A. M. 1991. The theory of mind impairment in autism: evidence for a modular mechanism of development? In A. Whiten (ed.), *Natural theories of mind: evolution, development and simulation of everyday mindreading.* Oxford: Basil Blackwell, 63–78.

Levinson, S., & J. Haviland (eds.). 1994. Spatial conceptualization in Mayan languages. (Special issue) *Linguistics* 32: 613–907.

Markman, E. M. 1989. *Categorization and naming in children: problems of induction.* Cambridge, MA: MIT Press.

McCune-Nicolich, L. 1981. The cognitive bases of relational words in the single-word period. *Journal of Child Language* 8: 15–34.

Mervis, C. B., & J. Bertrand. 1994. Acquisition of the novel name – nameless category (N3C) principle. *Child Development* 65: 1646–1663.

Mervis, C. B., C. A. Mervis, K. Johnson, & J. Bertrand. 1992. Studying early lexical development: the value of the systematic diary method. In C. Rovee-Collier & L. Lipsitt (eds.), *Advances in infancy research*, vol. 7. Norwood, NJ: Ablex, 290–344.

Murphy, G., & D. Medin. 1985. The role of theories in conceptual coherence. *Psychological Review* 92: 289–316.

Perner, J. 1991. *Understanding the representational mind.* Cambridge, MA: Bradford/MIT Press.

Pinker, S. 1989. *Learnability and cognition: the acquisition of argument structure.* Cambridge, MA: MIT Press.

Rispoli, M. 1987. The acquisition of the transitive and intransitive action verb categories in Japanese. *First Language* 7: 183–200.

Roberts, K., & M. Jacob. 1991. Linguistic vs. attentional influences on nonlinguistic categorization in 15-month-old infants. *Cognitive Development* 6: 355–375.

Slobin, D. I. 1982. Universal and particular in the acquisition of language. In E. Wanner & L. R. Gleitman (eds.), *Language acquisition: the state of the art.* New York: Cambridge University Press, 128–149.

Tanouye, E. K. 1979. The acquisition of verbs in Japanese children. *Papers and Reports on Child Language Development* 17: 49–56.

Tardif, T. 1996. Nouns are not always learned before verbs: evidence from Mandarin speakers' early vocabularies. *Developmental Psychology* 32: 492–504.

Tardif, T., S. A. Gelman, & F. Xu. 1999. Putting the "noun bias" in context: a comparison of English and Mandarin. *Child Development* 70: 620–635.

Tomasello, M., & J. Farrar. 1984. Cognitive bases of lexical development: object permanence and relational words. *Journal of Child Language* 11: 477–493.

1986. Object permanence and relational words: a lexical training study. *Journal of Child Language* 13: 495–505.

Vygotsky, L. S. 1962. *Thought and language.* New York: John Wiley and MIT Press.

Waxman, S. R. 1991. Convergences between semantic and conceptual organization in the preschool years. In J. P. Byrnes & S. A. Gelman (eds.), *Perspectives on language and thought: interrelations in development.* Cambridge: Cambridge University Press, 107–145.

Wellman, H. M. 1985. The child's theory of mind: the development of conceptions of cognition. In S. R. Yussen (ed.), *The growth of reflection in children.* Orlando: Academic Press, 169–205.

1990. *The child's theory of mind.* Cambridge, MA: Bradford/MIT Press.

Wellman, H. M., & S. A. Gelman. 1992. Cognitive development: foundational theories of core domains. *Annual Review of Psychology* 43: 337–375.

Whorf, B. L. 1956. *Language, thought, and reality: selected writings of Benjamin Lee Whorf* (ed. J. B. Carroll). Cambridge, MA: MIT Press.

3 Initial knowledge and conceptual change: space and number

Elizabeth S. Spelke and Sanna Tsivkin
Massachusetts Institute of Technology

How do humans build the rich and intricate systems of knowledge that are characteristic of our species? How variable are these knowledge systems across human cultures, and what are their universal properties? What accounts for the flexibility, adaptability, and open-endedness of human knowledge systems on the one hand, and the ease of acquisition of some systems on the other? Finally, what differences between humans and other animals, even our closest primate relatives, lead only humans to develop highly elaborated knowledge systems?

Traditional answers to these questions are incomplete at best. On one view, humans are endowed with a powerful capacity for learning, shaping new concepts and beliefs to fit the environment. This view might account for the flexibility and adaptability of human knowledge systems but cannot readily explain why humans develop knowledge rapidly in some domains but slowly, with great difficulty, in others (see Chomsky 1975, and Keil 1981). On a second view, humans are endowed with domain-specific, core cognitive systems around which elaborated knowledge grows. This view might account for the ease of acquisition of certain knowledge systems but not for humans' ability to develop systematic knowledge in genuinely new domains or to change conceptions in radical ways (see Carey 1985; Hatfield 1990).

In this chapter, we explore a third answer to our opening questions. Humans, we suggest, are endowed with a set of core systems of knowledge, but the systems have critical limitations. Initial knowledge systems are domain-specific (each applies to a subset of the entities that infants perceive and act upon), task-specific (each serves to solve a limited set of problems), informationally encapsulated (each operates on only part of the information that perceivers detect and remember), autonomous (one system cannot change its operation to accord with the states of other systems), and isolated (each system gives rise to distinct representations of the environment). Because these properties are hallmarks of modular cognitive systems, humans' initial systems of knowledge are, to a first approximation, modules (see Fodor 1983[1]; Karmiloff-Smith 1992).

Humans overcome some of the limits of their initial knowledge systems, we suggest, by conjoining the separate representations that those systems deliver to create new concepts of greater scope and power. Whereas the initial systems of knowledge may underlie children's rapid learning in specific domains, the processes for conjoining domain-specific representations may underlie humans' ability to extend their knowledge into novel territory. Many core knowledge systems may be found in other animals, moreover, but the ability to conjoin representations rapidly and flexibly so as to yield new representations may be uniquely human. This ability may account in large part for the richness and diversity of mature human belief systems.

Although the ability to conjoin distinct representations remains obscure, the research to be described suggests that it involves language. Language might serve as a medium for conceptual change because of two of its central features. First, a natural language allows the expression of thoughts in any area of knowledge. Natural languages therefore provide a domain-general medium in which separate, domain-specific representations can be brought together. Second, a natural language is a combinatorial system, allowing distinct concepts to be juxtaposed and conjoined. Once children have mapped representations in different domains to expressions of their language, therefore, they can combine those representations. Through these combinations, language allows the expression of new concepts: concepts whose elements were present in the prelinguistic child's knowledge systems but whose conjunction was not expressible, because of the isolation of these systems. *Pace* Fodor (1975), children who learn a natural language may gain a more powerful system of representation than any they possessed before.

We will not argue here that this picture of cognitive development is true; indeed, experiments have hardly begun to test it. Rather, we hope to show that the picture is plausible, and that Fodor's (1975) compelling arguments for the impossibility of genuine conceptual enrichment through learning, particularly language learning, deserve another look. We discuss these issues in two concrete cases, describing studies of developing representations of space and developing representations of number. Finally, we consider the implications of this view for questions of linguistic relativity: might speakers of different languages think incommensurable thoughts?

1 Spatial representation

The ideas explored in this chapter were suggested by the thinking and research of Linda Hermer-Vazquez (Hermer 1994; Hermer & Spelke 1994, 1996; Hermer-Vazquez, Spelke, & Katsnelson 1999). Hermer-Vazquez's research began with a question that seems far removed from the study of language or cognitive development, concerning the spatial abilities of humans and other animals. Comparative studies of navigation and spatial localization present a striking puzzle. Research in behavioral ecology, experimental psychology, and cognitive neuroscience provides evidence that a wide variety of animal species, from insects to mammals, maintain an exquisitely precise sense of their own position in relation to significant places in the environment. Animals update their spatial representations as they move around, and they draw on those representations in navigating through the layout, reorienting themselves, and locating objects (see Gallistel 1990, and McNaughton, Knierim, & Wilson 1994, for reviews and discussion). Evidence for spatial representations is so ubiquitous in animals that Gallistel captures this evidence with striking simplicity: "There is no creature so lowly that it does not know, at all times, where it is."

In contrast, even casual observation suggests that one species is an exception to Gallistel's rule: *Homo sapiens*. Many people living in modern, technological societies appear to retain very little sense of their position or orientation, or of the egocentric directions of significant objects and places, as they move. Perhaps as a consequence, people often navigate on strikingly inefficient paths, even through familiar environments. To be sure, some people do remain aware of their egocentric orientation, but this fact raises a further question: why are human spatial abilities so variable, compared to those of other species?

Hermer-Vazquez's initial approach to these questions was based on the hunch that the unique weaknesses of human spatial representations would be counterbalanced by unique strengths. In particular, perhaps the inaccuracies and errors of human navigators are compensated by their flexibility. To explore this possibility, her research focused on a situation in which other mammals have been found to form and use spatial representations *inflexibly*: when they are disoriented and must call on memories of their surroundings in order to reorient themselves.

Cheng (1986) and Margules & Gallistel (1988) investigated rats' reorientation abilities by exposing hungry rats to partially buried food in a testing chamber, removing the rats and disorienting them, and then returning them to the chamber where the food was now fully buried. The investigators assumed that on first exposure to the food, the rats would record its geocentric position: for example, a rat might represent the food as buried in the northeast corner of the chamber. In order for a disoriented rat to retrieve the food on its return to the chamber, therefore, it first had to reorient itself: in this example, it would determine its current heading and then compute the egocentric direction of Northeast. A wealth of information was provided to specify the rats' geocentric orientation, including the presence of distinctive odors and patterns in different corners and, in some studies, the relative brightness of different walls. Rats' search patterns suggested, however, that they used only one property of the chamber to reorient themselves: its shape. Because the chamber was rectangular, its shape specified the rats' orientation up to a 180° ambiguity. Disoriented rats betrayed their strong reliance on geometric information by searching for the food with high frequency at its true location and at the geometrically equivalent, but featurally quite different, opposite location. Indeed, rats that were fully disoriented searched these two locations with equal frequency, despite the wealth of nongeometric information that distinguished the locations (Margules & Gallistel 1988).

In further studies, Cheng and Gallistel showed that rats' failure to distinguish between featurally distinct but geometrically equivalent locations was not attributable to a failure to attend to or remember the room's nongeometric properties (see Cheng 1986, and Gallistel 1990, for discussion). Rather, rats appeared specifically unable to use their memory for nongeometric properties of the room in order to reorient themselves. These findings led the investigators to conclude that the rat's reorientation process was task-specific and informationally encapsulated: "a geometric module" (Cheng 1986).

In contrast to rats, humans' spatial representations appear to be more flexible: a disoriented person may use a wealth of nongeometric information to determine where she is. Emerging from a subway, for example, a person may determine her heading by searching for the names of streets or the numbers on buildings, by looking for shops or other landmarks, or even by asking directions. These evident abilities to use nongeometric information might testify to just the sort of flexibility that distinguishes humans from other animals.

To address this possibility, Hermer-Vazquez adapted Cheng's task for use with human children and adults, and she focused on the reorientation processes of very young children. In her first experiment (Hermer & Spelke 1994), 18- to 24-month-old toddlers were introduced into a rectangular room that was either entirely white or had one nongeometric directional cue: a bright blue wall. After a toy was hidden in one of the four corners of the room, the children's eyes were covered, they were lifted and rotated several turns, and then they were placed on the floor and urged to find the toy. If children, like rats, can reorient by the shape of the room, then they should have searched the two geometrically appropriate corners of the white room more than the other corners. Moreover, if children can reorient by the distinctive coloring of one wall, they should have searched the correct corner of the room with the blue wall more than any other corner.

The findings of this experiment were both clear and surprising. First, children searched the two geometrically appropriate corners of the entirely

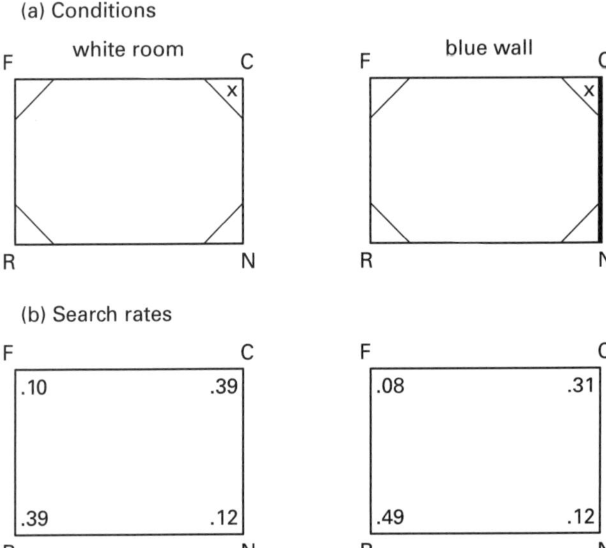

Fig. 3.1 (a) Overhead view of the chamber used in two conditions of a reorientation experiment. Although the object (indicated by x) was hidden in different corners for different subjects, the corner locations are rotated in this figure so that the correct search location is always depicted as the northeast corner (C) and the rotationally equivalent opposite location is always depicted as the southwest corner (R). The incorrect locations near and far from the correct corner are indicated by N and F. (b) The proportion of young children's search in corners C, R, N, and F in each condition of the experiment (after Hermer & Spelke 1996).

white room with high and equal frequency. This search pattern indicates that the children truly were disoriented, could not use any subtle, uncontrolled cues to locate the object, and reoriented in accord with the shape of the environment. Second, children utterly failed to use the blue wall to reorient themselves. In the room with one blue wall, children continued to search in geometrically appropriate locations, but they searched equally at the corners with appropriate vs. inappropriate coloring. Both qualitatively and quantitatively, children's performance closely resembled that of rats.

Because children's failure to use such a large and (to adults) salient landmark begged for explanation, subsequent analyses and experiments tested for a variety of possible sources of this failure. First, might children have searched only the corners that were visible when a trial began? A comparison of children's performance on trials which began with the correct corner in view vs. out of view ruled out this possibility, for children were almost equally likely to search initially visible and invisible corners.[2] Second, might children have failed to notice the blue wall? In a follow-up experiment (Hermer & Spelke 1994), either the experimenter pointed to the blue and white short walls of the room until the child looked at them before the object was hidden, or the experimenter and child played with the blue fabric before the test began and together placed it on the wall. Neither manipulation affected search performance, which closely resembled that of the first study.

Third, would children reorient by the distinctive color of a wall if the geometric information for reorientation were reduced? To address this question, children were tested in a square room that contained one very bright, red satin wall (Wang, Hermer-Vazquez, & Spelke 1999). Interestingly, children's performance differed in the square room in one respect: this was the only experiment in which children tended to search in a constant egocentric direction relative to their facing position at the end of the disorientation procedure. This finding suggested that disorientated children did not attempt to reorient themselves in this geometrically impoverished environment and instead relied on an egocentric strategy for finding the object. Nevertheless, the use of a square room did not enhance children's ability to reorient themselves in accord with a nongeometric landmark. Search was no more accurate in the room with the red satin wall than in the room that was entirely white, even though the satin wall drew children's attention quite strongly at the start of the search session.

Since these findings suggest that children's reorientation process is quite impervious to wall coloring, further experiments investigated whether the reorientation process could take account of information specifying the categorical identity and properties of objects. In one study (Hermer, unpublished), a large multicolored plastic statue of a person was placed directly against one of the short walls in the rectangular room, and a blue trash can of similar global proportions was placed against the opposite wall. Children reliably confined their search to the two geometrically appropriate corners, indicating that they were sensitive to the lengths of the two short walls. Nevertheless, they failed to distinguish the correct from the opposite corner, suggesting that their reorientation process was insensitive to the identities of the objects at the center of those walls (see also Hermer & Spelke 1994: Exp. 3).

In the next study, the color and patterning of the object's hiding location served as the nongeometric information for reorientation. Disoriented children searched for an object that was hidden inside one of two containers with distinctive coloring and patterning but identical shapes, placed in geometrically indistinguishable, opposite corners of the rectangular room. Although children searched for the object by passing their hand directly into the distinctive container, they searched the correct and incorrect containers with equal frequency. Nongeometric information again failed to serve as a basis for reorientation (Hermer & Spelke 1994).

Why was children's reorientation impervious to nongeometric information? One possible explanation roots children's difficulty in a general failure to perceive, attend to, or remember nongeometric information: perhaps children are inattentive to colors, textures, and patterns in an enclosed environment, fail to retain this information during a disorientation procedure, or fail to access this information during an object search task. These possibilities were tested by allowing children to watch as a toy was hidden in one of two distinctive containers in the rectangular room, disorienting the children as in the previous experiments, moving both the children and the containers into a larger, geometrically distinctive space, and encouraging children to find the toy. This search required that children use the nongeometric properties of the containers to track the location of a displaced object but not to reorient themselves. For the first time, children succeeded in searching the box with the appropriate nongeometric properties, suggesting that children's previous failures to reorient by these properties did not stem from limits on attention, memory, or the perceptual guidance of action (Hermer & Spelke 1996; see also Hermer & Spelke 1994, Exp. 4).

A final experiment tested directly whether children, like rats, reorient by virtue of a task-specific, encapsulated process (Hermer & Spelke 1996, fig. 3.2). Children first watched as a toy was hidden in one of two distinctively colored and patterned containers, placed in adjacent corners of the room, and then their eyes were closed and the containers were quietly moved to the opposite two corners of the room such that their geometric and nongeometric properties were dissociated (i.e., if pink and green boxes originally appeared to the left and right of a short wall, respectively, the boxes subsequently appeared on the opposite wall in reversed left/right relations). In one condition, children were disoriented while the containers were moved; in the other condition, they were not disoriented. Note that in both conditions, children saw exactly the same environment and events throughout the study and were asked to engage in the same actions. Nevertheless, the tasks faced by children in the two conditions were deeply different. The disoriented children needed to relocate *themselves*, so that they could determine the egocentric direction of the hidden object. In contrast, the oriented children knew where they were and therefore could determine, by computing the hidden object's expected egocentric direction and encountering an empty corner, that the object had moved. Their task was to relocate the *object*.

Search patterns were quite different in the two conditions. Whereas the disoriented children searched primarily the container with the appropriate geometry, the oriented children searched primarily the container with the

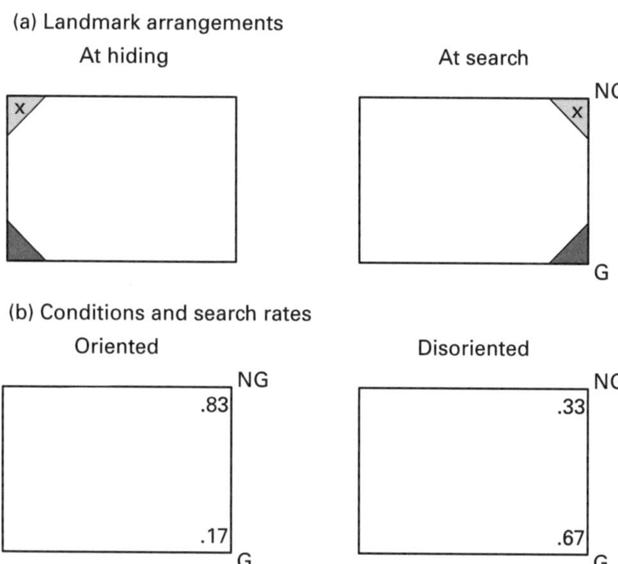

Fig. 3.2 (a) Overhead view of the chamber at the beginning (left) and end (right) of each search trial. For half the children, the geometrically correct location (G) was in the southeast corner as depicted; for the other children, the locations of that corner and of the nongeometrically correct corner (NG) were reversed. (b) The proportion of children's search in corners G and NG under conditions of orientation or disorientation (after Hermer & Spelke 1996).

appropriate color and markings. Importantly, the differing patterns were observed on the first search trial, before children could know what task they would face and what information they would need to remember. These findings provide evidence that young children perceive and remember both geometric and nongeometric properties of the environment, and that a task-specific, encapsulated reorientation process makes use only of a subset of these properties. Like rats, young children appear to reorient by a modular system sensitive only to geometry.

2 Developmental changes in spatial representation

Hermer-Vazquez's studies suggest a close correspondence between the reorientation systems of rats and humans, but they bring us no closer to answering the question with which we began: why are many people so bad at maintaining their orientation and navigating on efficient paths? To address this question, Hermer turned to studies of developmental changes in reorientation.

Her first study focused on adults (Hermer & Spelke 1994). College students were given the same reorientation and object search task as the children in the first study: they searched for an object hidden in a corner of a rectangular room that was entirely white or had one blue wall. Like children and rats, the adults confined their search to the two geometrically appropriate corners and searched those corners of the white room with equal frequency. These findings indicate that the adults were disoriented and were sensitive to the room's geometry. Unlike children or rats, however, adults confined their search to the single correct corner of the room with the blue wall, using nongeometric information to locate the object.

Adults' comments after the experiment were intriguing. Asked how they decided where to search for the object in the white room, few subjects mentioned any aspect of the room's shape, even after probing. Many subjects said they simply guessed a corner. Although the subjects used room geometry flawlessly in this study, they did not appear to be aware of what they were doing. In contrast, almost all subjects mentioned the wall coloring when asked how they located the object in the room with one blue wall. Many subjects described the direct relation of the hidden object to the wall: e.g. "I saw you hide it left of the blue wall."

These comments suggested that adults might have used the wall as a landmark for locating the object, rather than as a cue for reorienting themselves. A developmental experiment supported this suggestion. Three- to seven-year-old children were tested in the rectangular room with one blue wall (Hermer 1997). In one condition (an indirect task), the toy was hidden in a corner as in the previous studies: e.g., to the left of the blue wall. In the other condition (a direct task), the toy was hidden directly behind the center of a short wall: e.g., behind the blue wall. At six–seven years of age, children successfully located the object in both conditions. At three–four years of age, in contrast, children succeeded at the direct hiding task but not the indirect task. Because the blue wall provided the same information about the child's orientation in the two conditions, the younger children's performance suggests that they were not using the blue wall to reorient themselves but rather to specify the position of the hidden object. Such a specification would allow children and adults to locate the object while remaining in a state of disorientation.

Hermer's studies suggested that developmental changes in object localization were roughly correlated with changes in spatial language. Recall that adults both encoded and readily described the object's relation to the blue wall. In addition, young children's ability to encode the object's relation to the blue wall approximately coincided with the development of relevant spatial expressions: three- to four-year-old children command a variety of expressions, such as *in X* or *at X*, that could serve to specify the location of an object hidden directly behind a blue wall, and, six- to seven-year-old children are beginning to command the relevant left/right terminology to specify the object's location in the original studies (Hermer 1997). Although many explanations for these developmental relations could be offered, they raise the possibility that the development of spatial language contributes in some way to developmental changes in children's performance on these tasks.

Hermer-Vazquez's last series of experiments begins to test this possibility with adults, using a dual-task method (Hermer-Vazquez, Spelke, & Katsnelson 1999). College students participated in a reorientation experiment while performing a task designed to interfere with language production: verbal shadowing. As they spoke aloud continuously, repeating a prose passage to which they listened over a centrally located loudspeaker, they underwent the disorientation procedure and object search task in the room with one blue wall. Different subjects, moreover, were tested with a different attention-demanding task that involved no language: a task in which subjects continuously shadowed a rhythmic sequence by clapping. The results were striking: verbally shadowing adults reoriented in accord with the shape of the room but not its coloring, searching equally at the two geometrically appropriate corners. In contrast, adults who engaged in the rhythmic shadowing task or in no shadowing located the object successfully at the single, correct corner. A task that interfered with language production also interfered with the adults' ability to localize the object in relation to the blue wall.

Hermer-Vazquez's findings encourage us to speculate how the development of language might lead to developmental changes in her tasks. Before the development of spatial language, children evidently form both representations of the geometry of the stable environmental layout (used for reorientation) and representations of the nongeometric properties of objects and surfaces in the layout (used for finding displaced, hidden objects). Because these representations are constructed by autonomous and encapsulated systems, they cannot be conjoined. The inability to conjoin geometric with nongeometric descriptions of the environment precludes children's representing an object's location as being in a certain geometric relation to a certain nongeometric environmental property: e.g., left of a blue wall. Nevertheless, children's modular systems permit them to represent all the ingredients of relations such as "left of blue". The geometric system preserves information about sense relations, allowing children to differentiate between corners of the room which differ only with respect to the left/right relation of the short and long walls. Other systems preserve information about nongeometric properties of the environment, allowing children to confine their search for a displaced object to a container with appropriate coloring and patterning.

Because both geometric and nongeometric relations are represented prelinguistically, children could learn to use language to conjoin these relations in either of two ways. First, children might learn terms such as *left* and *near* by mapping the terms directly to representations constructed by the geometric system, and they might learn terms such as *blue* or *toy* by mapping the terms to appropriate nongeometric representations. Once these mappings are learned, the domain-general, combinatorial properties of language would allow the child to interpret expressions such as *left of the blue wall* or *near the toy*.

A second way of using language to conjoin information from distinct, modular systems assumes that complex spatial expressions conjoining geometric and nongeometric information are learned as wholes. In this case, terms such as *left* and *near* would derive their meanings not from mappings to a single system of representation, but from simultaneous mappings to several distinct systems. For example, children might first learn the meanings of expressions such as *your left hand* or *the picture near the window*. Learning these expressions would require the simultaneous activation of (a) representations of token objects (i.e. "there's an object x and an object y"), (b) nongeometric representations of each object (e.g. "x is a window," "y is a picture"), and (c) geometric representations of the relation between the objects ("y is near x"). If spatial terms are learned only in the context of expressions that require multiple, simultaneously active representations for their satisfaction, each term will connect to both geometric and nongeometric representations and therefore will link these representations to one another.[3]

Both of these processes exploit two central properties of language. First, language is a domain-general system of representation, containing terms that refer to objects and relations whose primary representations are constructed by a diverse collection of modular systems. Second, language is a combinatorial system, allowing terms to be conjoined irrespective of their (domain-specific) content. Language therefore can expand the range of a child's concepts by conjoining terms that map to elements in distinct, nonverbal representations.

Returning to the case at hand, we suggest that the acquisition of spatial language allows the child to represent the position of a hidden object in new ways. The use of spatial language also might underlie the marked differences between the spatial behavior of humans and other species. People, we have noted, represent space more flexibly than other animals, capturing properties of the environment with words and maps (which conjoin both information about the shape of the environment and nongeometric information such as the names of streets and other landmarks and the nature of the terrain). Language may provide an important medium in which such information is organized, allowing people to use a wide range of representational resources to encode and remember routes through the environment and the location of objects and places.

On the negative side, western adults often make their way through environments with little sense of their geocentric orientation, traveling on inefficient paths. These limitations may stem from two properties of the way language represents space. First, languages such as English represent space independently of the geocentric positions of the self or objects. As a consequence, speakers of these languages do not need to maintain a sense of geocentric direction in order to talk (see Levinson 1996a).[4] Second, all natural languages appear to represent spatial relations crudely, with terms that capture schematic, categorical relations among objects irrespective of their metrical structure (Talmy 1983; Landau & Jackendoff 1993). Linguistic descriptions of the layout therefore lack the precision of nonverbal, metric representations.

Finally, the use of spatial language could account, in part, for individual differences in spatial performance within a single language community. Because language in principle allows for a multiplicity of conjunctions of information, it allows for a variety of representations of the environment. People may differ both in their degree of dependence on language-based conjunctions, and in the specific conjunctions that they use to guide their actions. If this possibility is correct, then we would expect substantial individual variation in spatial performance that relies on conjunctions of information and less variation in spatial performance that relies on purely geometric information. This prediction has not been tested.

3 Number

In the domain of space, uniquely human representational abilities appear to entail costs in precision and accuracy but yield gains in representational power. In other domains, the ability to conjoin distinct representations may lead both to gains in representational power and to increased precision. Here we consider one domain where both advances may occur.

Starting again from a comparative perspective, research on a wide variety of animals suggests that representations of numerosity are ubiquitous among vertebrates. Fish, birds, and mammals respond systematically to the rate at which food is provisioned in natural settings, and pigeons and rats have been trained in laboratory experiments to respond to the number of events (light flashes, sounds) in a sequence or the number of actions they have performed (for reviews, see Gallistel 1990; Boysen & Capaldi 1993; and Dehaene 1997). There is no obvious upper bound to the size of sets that animals represent. Nevertheless, animals' number representations are imprecise and their accuracy declines with increases in set size, in accord with Weber's law.

A number of mammals also have been shown to represent exact numerosity and to take account of effects of simple addition and subtraction. For example, a raccoon was trained to respond positively to a box displaying exactly three objects (Davis 1984), and both a parrot and a chimpanzee have been trained to give unique responses to sets of objects of numerosities varying from one to six or more (Matsuzawa 1985; Pepperberg 1987). Most interestingly, untrained monkeys and tamarins have been shown to compute exact additions and subtractions on small sets: if two objects are placed in succession behind an occluder, the subjects look longer if the screen is raised to reveal one or three objects than if it reveals two objects, suggesting that the monkeys anticipated seeing the correct number (Hauser, MacNeilage, & Ware 1996; Hauser, Carey, & Hauser 2000). For these representations, however, there appears to be a limit on set size. As set size increases, learning labels for a set of a given numerosity requires more and more training. Moreover, number encoding does not appear to be a readily accessible process for animals. If a chimpanzee has learned to respond with a distinct Arabic symbol for each of the set sizes 1–4 and then a new symbol (*5*) and a new set size (five items) is introduced, the chimp appears to infer that *5* means "any set size that isn't 1–4," rather than one specific numerosity (Matsuzawa 1985). As sets get larger, the encoding of exact number therefore appears to become a last resort for many animals (see Davis & Perusse 1988).

Many experiments provide evidence that prelinguistic human infants represent number as well. Newborn infants discriminate between small sets of dots varying in number (Antell & Keating 1983), as do older infants (Starkey & Cooper 1980; Strauss & Curtis 1981; Starkey, Spelke, & Gelman 1990). Infants respond to the invariant number of elements in a set over changes in spatial patterning (e.g. Starkey & Cooper 1980), over motion and occlusion (van Loosbroek & Smitsman 1990), and over changes in a variety of properties of the elements in a set including size, shape, coloring, and categorical identity (Strauss & Curtis 1981; Starkey *et al.* 1990). Finally, infants pass the same addition and subtraction tasks as monkeys and tamarins (Wynn 1992a; Hauser *et al.* 2000), and they are sensitive to the correctness or incorrectness of simple addition even if the elements move (Koechlin, Dehaene, & Mehler 1996) or change properties (Simon, Hespos, & Rochat 1995). Evidence for exact, small-number representations also has been obtained with adults, who apprehend the exact numerosity of small sets rapidly and track small numbers of objects in parallel (Trick & Pylyshyn 1993). All these findings suggest that the capacity for representing the exact numerosity of small sets is common to humans and other animals and emerges early in human development.

What of the capacity to represent larger sets? Although early studies suggested that infants discriminate between large sets of elements exhibiting large differences in numerosity (Fantz, Fagan, & Miranda 1975), a later reanalysis of this work suggested that infants' discriminations depended on the spatial distribution of contrast in the displays (Banks & Ginsburg 1983). Nevertheless, there is ample evidence for approximate representations of large sets in adults, who can rapidly determine which of two large sets is more numerous if the sets are sufficiently different in number, and who can rapidly estimate the approximate answers to certain large-number arithmetic problems (see Dehaene 1997; Gallistel & Gelman 1992). There is also some evidence for these representations in infants (Xu & Spelke, 2000) and toddlers (Sophian, Harley, & Martin 1995). In particular, 6-month-old infants discriminated between sets of 8 vs. 16 visual elements, even when controls within the experiment insured that discrimination could not be based on the sizes, spacing, or arrangement of the elements, or on continuous variables such as the spatial extent that the set of elements occupies. In contrast, infants failed to discriminate sets with a smaller difference ratio: sets of 4 vs. 6 or 8 vs. 12 elements (Starkey & Cooper 1980; Xu & Spelke 2000). The representations of the approximate numerosity of large sets found in a variety of animals appear to exist in young children.

These findings suggest that both animals and preverbal infants have two systems for representing number. The first system serves to represent small numerosities exactly. It underlies animals' and infants' abilities to keep track of up to four objects in number discrimination and addition/subtraction tasks, and adults' rapid apprehension of small numbers of objects (see also Kahneman, Treisman, & Gibbs 1992; Trick & Pylyshyn 1993). These representations appear to be robust over variations in the properties of their elements such as shape and location. The second system serves to represent large sets. It also persists over development and underlies animals', infants', and adults' rapid apprehensions of the relative numerosity of large sets of entities, and underlies adults' abilities to give approximate answers to large-number arithmetic problems (see Dahaene 1997). These representations do not appear to be limited as to set size beyond the limits of sensory acuity, but their accuracy decreases with increasing set size in accord with Weber's Law.

In contrast to infants and to other animals, human adults have a third system for representing numbers, which typically involves verbal counting. Like the small-number system, this system allows the representation of exact numerosity, independently of other quantitative variables, and the computation of the exact effects of addition and subtraction. Like the large-number system, it has no upper bound on set size, beyond that imposed by limits on time and patience, and it allows comparisons of the relative numerosity of two sets.

It is widely believed that children develop the ability to use this new, uniquely human system of number representation when they learn verbal counting (e.g. Gallistel & Gelman 1992). But how does verbal counting develop, and how does its development give rise to a new system of number representation? Number is arguably our most abstract system of knowledge – why is this system tied to the child's developing understanding of a verbal activity like counting? How can children ever come to understand counting if they do not already understand the entities that counting singles out? Moreover, how does learning to count allow children to form representations, such as "exactly seven," that exceed the limits of their preverbal systems of number representation, circumventing Fodor's (1975) dictum that one can learn words only for concepts that one can already represent?

The most ambitious attempt to answer these questions may be found in Gelman & Gallistel's thesis that the system of knowledge underlying verbal counting is innate and inherent in the large-number representational system, and that children learn to count by gaining access to the principles that define the nonverbal system (Gelman & Gallistel 1978; Gallistel & Gelman 1992; see also Wynn 1990; Sophian, Harley, & Martin 1995, and Dehaene 1997 for further discussion of Gelman & Gallistel's thesis). A different account (Bloom 1994) builds on Chomsky's (1986) thesis that the conception of discrete infinity that grounds knowledge of the natural numbers stems from the generativity of language: children learn to count by gaining access to the grammatical principles giving rise to this generativity. One problem with both these accounts, however, is that it is not clear how the *principles* governing the operation of any modular representational system become accessible to other systems. In many cases, such access plainly does not occur: speaking a language does not give one knowledge of linguistics, and experiencing brightness contrast does not give one knowledge of calculus (Fodor 1983; Gallistel 1990; cf. Rozin 1976). Why and how might the principles underlying nonverbal counting or language generativity become accessible to the child?

The foregoing analysis of spatial orientation prompts a different account of number development. Children may attain the mature system of knowledge of the natural numbers by conjoining together the representations delivered by their two preverbal systems. Language may serve as a medium for this conjunction, moreover, because it is a domain-general, combinatorial system to which the representations delivered by the child's two nonverbal systems can be mapped.

More specifically, consider the precounting child's representation of "two." By our hypothesis, the child has two systems for representing arrays containing two objects: a small-number system of object representation (which represents this array, roughly, as "an object x and an object y, such that y ≠ x"; see Wynn 1992a) and a large-number system of representation (which, as in Gelman & Gallistel's account, represents this array as "a blur on the number line indicating a very small set"). Because of the modularity of initial knowledge systems, these representations are independent. When younger children hear the word *two*, therefore, they have two distinct representations to which the word could map and no expectation that the word will map to both of them.

Because all the number words appear in the same syntactic contexts (see Bloom & Wynn 1997) and occur together in the counting routine, experience with the ambient language may lead children to seek a common representational system for these terms. Thus, children may discover that all the terms map to representations constructed by the large-number system (although specific terms do not map to specific large-number representations, because of the inaccuracy of that system). This possibility is consistent with Wynn's (1992b) evidence that young children pass through a stage when they interpret all number words above *one* as referring to any display containing more than one object. In addition, because the terms *one*, *two*, and *three* map to specific representations delivered by the small-number system, children may discover these mappings. This possibility is consistent with evidence that young children typically learn the meanings of *one*, *two*, and *three* individually, in that order (Wynn 1992b).

With these advances, how do children learn the meanings of words such as *seven*? Unlike *two*, *seven* does not map to any representation in either the small-number system (which can only represent arrays of seven objects as "arrays of too many things to keep track of") or the large-number system (whose inaccuracy will often lead the child to confuse arrays of seven objects with arrays of six or eight objects). Nevertheless, learning the meanings of *one*, *two*, and *three* may provide the seeds of a solution to the problem of learning *seven*. First, because the words for small numbers map to representations in both the small-number system and the large-number system, learning these words may indicate to the child that these two sets of representations pick out a common set of entities, whose properties are the union of those picked out by each system alone. This union of properties may be sufficient to define the set of natural numbers. Second, because the words *two* and *three* are members of a larger set of terms that behave alike in the different linguistic contexts, learning the terms *two* and *three* may open the way to the insight that terms such as *seven* also refer to sets of objects with the same union of properties. Third, because the terms *one*, *two* and *three* form a sequence in the counting routine, children may discover that each of these number words picks out a set with one more individual than the previous word in the sequence, and they may generalize this learning to all the words in the counting sequence.

In summary, knowledge of the natural numbers may be constructed through the conjunction of representations delivered by two distinct, modular systems, with language providing the medium for this conjunction. Once the child learns that a single set of words maps to both these systems, she may gain the ability to conjoin information that the two representational systems deliver, capturing the strengths of both systems and overcoming limitations specific to one or the other system. From the small-number system may come the realization that each number word corresponds to an exact number of objects, that adding or subtracting exactly one object changes number, and that changing the shape or spatial distribution of objects does not change number. From the large-number system may come the realization that these sets of exact numerosity can increase without limit, and that a given symbol represents the set as a unit, not just as an array of distinct objects. The union of these properties may allow not only the learning of words such as *seven* but also the representation of concepts such as "seven", and of beliefs such as "seven plus seven is fourteen." In the domain of number as in the domain of space, the acquisition of language may lead to the development of concepts that were not expressible in the cognitive systems of the preverbal child.

The most direct tests of this possibility would focus on young children and probe for developmental changes in number representations that are consequences of the child's developing understanding of counting. Unfortunately, such studies have not been conducted. Nevertheless, studies of adults with arithmetic impairment and of adults who speak two languages offer suggestive support for this view.

First, studies in cognitive neuropsychology have focused on the number representations and arithmetic abilities of patients with disorders in arithmetic processing, or "acalculia" (see Dehaene 1997 for review). Interestingly, these patients tend to have both impaired language and impaired abilities to give the exact answers to arithmetic problems. In contrast, many are able to provide an approximate answer to a mathematical problem. For example, Warrington (1982) studied a patient who correctly supplied approximate answers to addition problems with fairly large numbers but often was unable to state the exact answer. The patient himself said that he felt that he knew the approximate, but not exact, answers to all the mathematical problems presented. Similarly, Dehaene & Cohen (1991) discussed the case of an aphasic and acalculic patient who failed to identify the errors in mathematical statements such as $7+3=11$ but was able to reject statements such as

$7+3=17$. These findings suggested that the patient's representations of approximate numerosity were intact, but exact calculations were impaired.

Further suggestive evidence in favor of the thesis that language underlies the representation of exact large numerosities comes from research on bilingualism. There are many anecdotal reports of bilinguals who perform arithmetic in their first language, even if that language is hardly used for other purposes: a person who has learned to do arithmetic in one language (L1) during childhood and then moves to a different country and becomes dominant in that country's language (L2) is apt to perform arithmetic calculations in L1.

A number of studies have bolstered these anecdotal reports by showing that bilingual subjects are faster at verifying or producing the correct answer to arithmetic problems in L1 than in L2 (Marsh & Maki 1976; McClain & Huang 1982; Frenck-Mestre & Vaid 1993). These findings do not show, however, that arithmetic is performed in a language-specific format because the L1 advantage may stem from processes that translate between an abstract language of numerical processing and a language of input and output (see McCloskey 1992). Bilinguals may habitually translate from and to L1, leading to their overpractice with L1 numerals and accounting for their faster performance in L1 (although see Gonzalez & Kolers 1982). To determine whether arithmetic truly requires language-specific representations, it would be desirable to conduct training experiments in which the exposure to numerals in L1 and L2 is controlled. If arithmetic calculations are language-specific, they should be performed faster in the language of training, even when practice with encoding and decoding is equalized across the two languages.

An additional limitation of existing bilingual studies is that they have failed to probe the limits of the L1 advantage. Are bilinguals faster and more accurate on all numerical problems when they perform in L1, or only on certain kinds of problems? The thesis that language serves as a medium for representing exact large numerosities leads to the prediction that language-specific effects will be obtained only for tasks requiring representations that are exact and large.

We have recently attempted to test these predictions (Dehaene, Spelke, Pinel, Stanescu, & Tsivkin 1999; Spelke & Tsivkin in press). In our first study, Russian–English bilinguals were trained to solve three sets of mathematical problems in each of their two languages. Half the subjects were trained in Russian on a set of tasks consisting of double-digit addition problems with addend 54, single-digit addition problems in base 6, and estimation of cube roots problems, and they were trained in English on double-digit addition problems with addend 63, single-digit addition problems in base 8, and estimation of logs base 2 problems. For the remaining subjects, the languages were reversed. After two days of training in each language, all the subjects were tested in two sessions, one administered in

Russian and one in English. In each session, the subjects were tested on all combinations of language and tasks, so that their performance on a given task could be compared across the two languages.

This design addresses a number of limitations of previous work on bilingual numerical processing. First, the introduction of training sessions allowed us to simulate the learning situation faced by children and to ensure that subjects spent an equal amount of time on each type of task across languages. Second, in order to test McCloskey's claim that language experience affects encoding and decoding processes but not the representation of numbers and arithmetic facts, we tested subjects on a subset of items requiring the same output across the two languages (e.g. $54+x=z$ in Russian and $63+y=z$ in English). Third, we assessed the language-specificity of training with both tasks calling for exact calculations and tasks calling for estimations.

The results were clear. First, there were improvements with practice across the two training sessions for all the tasks in this experiment. Training benefits of comparable magnitude were observed with both languages and all problem sets. Second, subjects' test performance in the language of training showed a clear advantage over their test performance in the untrained language for large-number addition and for addition in different bases. Language-specific training effects were observed both for the problems trained in L1 (Russian) and for those trained in L2. Importantly, there was no significant difference between performance on the items that shared the same output and those that did not, suggesting that training did not primarily influence the speed of encoding or decoding in a particular language. This finding suggests that there is a genuine language-specificity in the training effects with the tasks requiring exact calculation with large numbers.

The most important result from this study is that there was no advantage for the language of training on the estimation tasks. Subjects trained on cube roots in Russian, for example, were just as fast at estimating the cube roots in English. This finding indicates that language-specificity does not extend to all numerical processing tasks: only tasks requiring exact, large-number calculations appeared to be processed in a language-specific form. This result is especially striking in view of the design of the study. The experiment was set up to allow for identical conditions of training for all of the tasks involved: the number of training problems, repetitions, and other task factors were equated across all the tasks. The different patterns of transfer therefore suggest that there is something about exact, large-number arithmetic that involves language in ways that approximate arithmetic does not.

In a follow-up study, we extended this research in two directions

(Dehaene *et al.*, 1999; Spelke & Tsivkin in press). First, we investigated whether normal bilingual subjects, like acalculic patients, would show a dissociation between exact and approximate arithmetic within a single arithmetic operation. To this end, we trained separate groups of bilingual subjects on the same two sets of large-number addition problems, requiring one group to calculate the exact answer to each problem and the other group to calculate the approximate answer. If exact but not approximate addition requires a language-specific format, then only the subjects trained on the approximate answers should show a transfer of training to their second language.

Second, we attempted to address a conflict in the neuropsychological and animal literatures concerning the nonverbal estimation process. Gallistel (1990; Gallistel & Gelman 1992) has suggested that the large-number approximation system can be used to perform all arithmetic operations, including multiplication. In contrast, studies of at least one patient with impaired language and impaired exact calculation abilities but preserved approximation abilities suggest the patient can perform approximate addition but not approximate multiplication. Although the patient studied by Dehaene & Cohen (1991) correctly identified the errors in addition problems with answers that were distant from the correct answer (e.g. $7+3=17$), he was unable to identify errors in even the simplest multiplication problems (e.g. $3\times3=16$). In view of this conflict, we probed further for an approximate multiplication process by training the same two groups of subjects on a set of exact or approximate multiplication problems.

Each subject in this study was trained on two sets of problems, one in Russian and one in English. Subjects were administered one set of problems involving addition and one involving multiplication, with one task requiring exact calculation and one requiring approximate calculation. The pairings of languages, operations, and tasks (exact vs. approximate) were counterbalanced across the subjects.

Three findings are noteworthy. First, bilinguals showed no language-specific effects when trained on addition problems via estimation. This finding converges with those of Dehaene & Cohen (1991) and provides further evidence for a language-independent process for estimating approximate answers to addition problems. Second, we replicated our studies with bilinguals trained to solve addition problems via exact calculations. For the same items for which estimation-trained bilinguals failed to show any language-specificity, our exact calculation-trained bilinguals showed superior performance in the language of training.

Third, we found no evidence for approximate multiplication. Both the exact calculation-trained and the estimation-trained bilinguals were faster and more accurate when tested in the language of training, and they showed little transfer of training advantages across languages. This finding, like studies of patients with acalculia, suggests that adults can estimate large-number additions but not large-number multiplications in a language-independent manner.

In summary, there is a broad convergence between studies of number representation in children, brain-damaged patients, and bilingual adults. All these studies suggest that number representations and calculations are independent of language when the numbers involved are very small or answers required are imprecise. In contrast, number representations and arithmetic calculations appear to be language-specific when exact answers to large-number problems must be given. These findings are consistent with the thesis that human children and adults have one nonverbal system for representing small numerosities accurately and a second nonverbal system for representing large numerosities inaccurately. Language may serve to conjoin these two systems, allowing for the discovery of a third system of number representation that is both accurate and unbounded.[5]

4 Language, thought, and conceptual change

We have considered two domains in which children's conceptual resources appear to be enriched over development. In each case, we have suggested that this enrichment depends on a process of conjoining representations that were constructed by task-specific, encapsulated systems of knowledge, and that this process in turn depends on language. This puts us in the odd position of advocating a thesis that has been argued cogently to be absurd. Fodor's argument in *The language of thought* (1975) is intricate but its essence is simple: children can only learn the meaning of a term in a language if they can map the term to a preexisting expression in the language of thought. In that case, however, no language that children learn can go beyond the expressive power of the mental language they already possess.

The essential assumption that leads us to question Fodor's (1975) compelling argument comes again from Fodor, this time from *The modularity of mind* (1983). As every student of cognitive science knows, *The modularity of mind* develops the suggestion that an interesting subset of human cognitive systems are task-specific, informationally encapsulated, and autonomous. Recent research on early cognitive development provides considerable evidence, we believe, that the prelinguistic child's concepts and reasoning are subserved by cognitive systems with these central hallmarks of Fodor's modules. If that is true, however, then the infant might not have one language of thought, but many. If children have many languages of thought (or, as we prefer, systems of representation), then there may be thoughts that they cannot entertain, because the elements of which these thoughts are composed reside in different representational systems. These are the thoughts that a natural language (or some other domain-general, combinatorial system of representation) may make available.

We have considered two kinds of thoughts that may become expressible as children put together their domain-specific, modular representations: thoughts such as "left of the truck" and "five plus seven is twelve." In principle, the development of a domain-general, combinatorial system of representation could lead to a wide variety of new thoughts and concepts. If the present suggestions are correct, then human cognition would be limited only by three factors: the nature of the representations formed by initial, modular systems; the nature of the possible mappings from each of these systems to other domain-general representational systems such as a natural language; and the combinatorics of the latter representational systems.

Any domain-general, combinatorial system of representation in principle could serve to conjoin information from modular representations, but our evidence suggests that natural languages are the primary systems that play this role. The shadowing adults in Hermer-Vazquez's studies and the bilingual trainees in our studies did not appear to find a language-independent medium for representing that a toy was left of a blue wall or that 32 + 63 = exactly 95. Although language is not the only domain-general medium of representation that is available to humans, it does appear to provide a particularly powerful system for conjoining domain-specific representations into new concepts.

One research strategy for probing further the role of language in conceptual change is to investigate cognitive development and cognitive performance in speakers of different languages. In particular, the existence of languages lacking terms such as *left* and *right* (e.g. Levinson 1996a) raises the question of how speakers of these languages would perform in Hermer-Vazquez's reorientation tasks, and the existence of languages lacking counting words for all set sizes (e.g. Gordon 1994) raises the question of how children learning these languages develop number concepts and what concepts they develop.

Studies of linguistic variation also could address questions of linguistic relativity: if the acquisition of language allows the expression of new thoughts that conjoin information from domain-specific representations, do speakers of different languages develop different conjoint concepts? Note that, in principle, the present thesis leaves this question completely open. All conjoint, language-dependent concepts could turn out to be universal among speakers of any language, if (a) languages have strongly universal semantic properties, or (b) terms and expressions in a language can only map onto the representations delivered by the modular systems in a restricted set of ways. On the other hand, conjoint, language-dependent concepts could turn out to be highly variable, if the set of potential mappings across distinct languages is very large, relative to the number of mappings that any actual speaker realizes, and if different languages pick out different members of the set. A third, intermediate possibility now tempts us. It is possible that certain conjunctions of information across domains are especially natural for humans and therefore are found in most or all human cultures: the natural numbers are an example. Other conjunctions of information across domains may develop somewhat later and less universally and yet show only limited ranges of variation. Expressions like *left/east of the truck* or *in/loose-fitting against the bowl* may be such cases (see ch. 17 by Brown and ch. 16 by Bowerman & Choi, this volume). Still other conjunctions may be found later in development, be laborious to learn, and appear only in a small number of cultures. For example, when one uses natural numbers to represent the masses of objects, or the location of points in space, one opens the way to advances in physics and mathematics that may lead far beyond species-universal representations. The present thesis therefore does not presuppose linguistic relativity but leaves this possibility as a question for research.

As we have noted, the thesis that language serves as a medium for conjoining domain-specific systems of representation is only a suggestion, but we may close on firmer ground. First, studies of young children provide evidence that children's initial knowledge of space and number derives from cognitive systems that are domain-specific, task-specific, and encapsulated: cognitive modules. These initial knowledge systems appear to be shared by other animals: humans are not the only creatures that represent the shape of the layout, the identity and distinctness of objects, or the approximate numerosity of sets. Second, the studies provide evidence that human cognition extends beyond the limits of these modular knowledge systems, into domains of knowledge that only humans attain, and that this extension depends in part on processes that conjoin together the representations constructed by distinct knowledge systems.

The processes that underlie these conjunctions are still obscure and subject to debate. Nevertheless, the research efforts described in this volume suggest how one can begin to investigate these processes.

Developmental psychologists can study the emergence of these combinatorial processes through a systematic, two-pronged investigation, focusing both on the content and structure of the initial knowledge systems and on the changes that occur over cognitive development. Cognitive anthropologists can study the same processes through a complementary two-pronged investigation, focusing both on the content and structure of universal knowledge systems and on the variability in knowledge across different cultures. Through such studies, we may hope to shed light on what is perhaps the most intriguing aspect of human cognition: our ability to use our special-purpose systems of knowledge in order to extend our knowledge beyond those purposes, into novel territory.

NOTES

We thank Jerry Fodor, Lila Gleitman, and Steve Levinson for insightful comments on a draft of this chapter and Susan Carey and Linda Hermer-Vazquez for clarifying discussion of the issues it raises. Supported by NIH grant HD23103 to Elizabeth S. Spelke.

1 We depart from Fodor in arguing for the isolation of the modular cognitive systems. Fodor (1983) proposed that cognitive modules send their outputs to a single system of representation: the "language of thought" (see Fodor 1975). We propose that each module produces a separate set of representations that serve as inputs to other, specific modules but not to any central system of representation. On our view, therefore, the mind contains multiple, distinct mental languages, none of which is central or domain-general.

2 This pattern makes sense if one assumes that disoriented children have a representation of their geocentric heading, but that it has been rendered wholly inaccurate by the disorientation procedure. For example, a child who is set down facing North might represent her heading erroneously as southwesterly. If disoriented children, like rats, prefer to use the shape of the environment to make small rather than large corrections in perceived heading, then the child will correct her estimated heading from Southwest to South. Remembering that the toy was hidden in the northeastern corner, the child will then turn away from the two corners she is facing and search the geometrically correct corner behind her.

3 It may appear that a central question about conceptual enrichment has been begged: if the prelinguistic child can represent (a) through (c), don't these representations constitute a preexisting translation, in mentalese, of the English expression, *the picture near the window*? We submit that the prelinguistic child has no such translation, because (a)–(c) are not expressions in a single language of thought but expressions in three distinct systems of representation. Because of the modularity of these systems, these expressions cannot be combined directly with one another, although each can be mapped to language. Our account does beg a different question: if (a)–(c) are not expressions in a single mental language, what processes assure that the entity picked out by "x" in (b) is the same individ-

ual as that picked out by "x" in (c)? See Kahneman, Treisman, & Gibbs (1992) and Pylyshyn (1988) for ideas.

4 This observation raises the possibility that speakers of languages that encode spatial relations geocentrically will maintain a better sense of their own orientation as they navigate. Research discussed elsewhere in this volume is consistent with this expectation (see also Levinson 1996b).

5 Further evidence for these conclusions comes from neuroimaging studies of adults performing exact and approximate arithmetic under conditions that are similar to those in our bilingual experiments (Dehaene *et al.* 1999).

REFERENCES

Antell, S. E., & D. P. Keating. 1983. Perception of numerical invariance in neonates. *Child Development* 54: 695–701.

Ashcraft, M. H., T. S. Yamashita, & D. M. Aram. 1992. Mathematics performance in left and right brain-lesioned children and adolescents. *Brain and Cognition* 19: 208–252.

Banks, M. S., & A. P. Ginsburg. 1983. Early visual preferences: a review and a new theoretical treatment. In H. W. Reese (ed.), *Advances in child development and behavior*. New York: Academic Press.

Bloom, P. 1994. Generativity within language and other cognitive domains. *Cognition* 51: 177–189.

Bloom, P., & K. Wynn. 1997. Linguistic cues in the acquisition of number words. *Journal of Child Language* 24: 511–533.

Boysen, S. T., & E. J. Capaldi. 1993. *The development of numerical competence: animal and human models*. Hillsdale, NJ: Lawrence Erlbaum.

Carey, S. 1985. *Conceptual change in childhood.* Cambridge, MA: Bradford/MIT Press.

Cheng, K. 1986. A purely geometric module in the rat's spatial representation. *Cognition* 23: 149–178.

Chomsky, N. 1975. *Reflections on language*. New York: Pantheon.

1986. *Knowledge of language: its nature, origin, and use*. New York: Praeger.

Davis, H. 1984. Discrimination of the number three by a raccoon (*Procyon lotor*). *Animal Learning and Behavior* 12: 409–413.

Davis, H., & R. Perusse. 1988. Numerical competence in animals: definitional issues, current evidence, and a new research agenda. *Behavioral and Brain Sciences* 11: 561–615.

Dehaene, S. 1997. *The nunber sense.* New York: Oxford University Press.

Dehaene, S., & L. Cohen. 1991. Two mental calculation systems: a case study of severe acalculia with preserved approximation. *Neuropsychologia* 29: 1045–1074.

Dehaene, S., E. Spelke, P. Pinel, R. Stanescu, & S. Tsivkin. 1999. Sources of mathematical thinking: behavioral and brain-imaging evidence. *Science* 284: 970–974.

Fantz, R. L., J. F. Fagan, & S. B. Miranda. 1975. Early visual selectivity. In L. B. Cohen & P. Salapatek (eds.), *Infant perception: from sensation to cognition*. New York: Academic Press.

Fodor, J. A. 1975. *The language of thought.* New York: Thomas Y. Crowell.

1983. *The modularity of mind: an essay on faculty psychology.* Cambridge, MA: MIT Press.

Frenck-Mestre, C., & J. Vaid. 1993. Activation of number facts in bilinguals. *Memory and Cognition* 21: 809–818.

Fuson, K. C., G. G. Pergament, B. G. Lyons, & J. W. Hall. 1985. Children's conformity to the cardinality rule as a function of set size and counting accuracy. *Child Development* 56: 1429–1436.

Gallistel, C. R. 1990. *The organization of learning.* Cambridge, MA: MIT Press.

Gallistel, C. R., & R. Gelman. 1992. Preverbal and verbal counting and computation. *Cognition* 44: 43–74.

Gelman, R., & C. R. Gallistel. 1978. *The child's understanding of number.* Cambridge, MA: Harvard University Press.

Gonzalez, E. G., & P. A. Kolers. 1982. Mental manipulation of arithmetic symbols. *Journal of Experimental Psychology: Learning, Memory, and Cognition* 8: 308–319.

Gordon, P. 1994. Innumerate Amazonians and Kronecker's theism: one-two-many systems and the artificialism of number. Paper presented at the European Society for Philosophy and Psychology, Paris, June.

Hatfield, G. 1990. *The natural and the normative: theories of spatial perception from Kant to Helmholtz.* Cambridge, MA: MIT Press.

Hauser, M. D., S. Carey, & L. B. Hauser. 2000. Spontaneous number representation in semi-free-ranging rhesus monkeys. *Proceedings of the Royal Society of London B* 267: 829–833.

Hauser, M. D., P. MacNeilage, & M. Ware. 1996. Numerical representations in primates. *Proceedings of the National Academy of Sciences* 93: 1514–1517.

Hermer, L. 1997. Cognitive flexibility as it emerges over development and evolution: the case of two navigational tasks in humans. Unpublished doctoral dissertation, Cornell University.

Hermer, L., & E. S. Spelke. 1994. A geometric process for spatial reorientation in young children. *Nature* 370: 57–59.

1996. Modularity and development: the case of spatial reorientation. *Cognition* 61: 195–232.

Hermer-Vazquez, L., E. S. Spelke, & A. S. Katsnelson. 1999. Sources of flexibility in human cognition: dual-task studies of space and language. *Cognitive Psychology* 39: 3–36.

Kahneman, D., A. Treisman, & B. J. Gibbs. 1992. The reviewing of object files: object-specific integration of information. *Cognitive Psychology* 24: 175–219.

Karmiloff-Smith, A. 1992. *Beyond modularity: a developmental perspective on cognitive science.* Cambridge, MA: MIT Press.

Keil, F. C. 1981. Constraints on knowledge and cognitive development. *Psychological Review* 88: 197–227.

Koechlin, E., S. Dehaene, & J. Mehler. 1997. Numerical transformations in five-month-old human infants. *Mathematical Cognition* 3: 89-104.

Landau, B., & R. Jackendoff. 1993. "What" and "where" in spatial language and spatial cognition. *Behavioral and Brain Sciences* 16: 217–265.

Levinson, S. C. 1996a. Frames of reference and Molyneux's question: cross-linguistic evidence. In P. Bloom, M. A. Peterson, L. Nadel, & M. F. Garrett (eds.), *Language and space*. Cambridge, MA: MIT Press, 109–169.

Levinson, S. 1996b. The role of language in everyday human navigation. *Working Paper 38.* Nijmegen, The Netherlands: Cognitive Anthropology Research Group, Max Planck Institute for Psycholinguistics.

Margules, J., & C. R. Gallistel. 1988. Heading in the rat: determination by environmental shape. *Animal Learning and Behavior* 16: 404–410.

Marsh, L. G., & R. H. Maki. 1976. Efficiency of arithmetic operations in bilinguals as a function of language. *Memory and Cognition* 4: 459–464.

Matsuzawa, T. 1985. Use of numbers by a chimpanzee. *Nature* 315: 57–59.

McClain, L., & J. Y. S. Huang. 1982. Speed of simple arithmetic in bilinguals. *Memory and Cognition* 10: 591–596.

McCloskey, M. 1992. Cognitive mechanisms in numerical processing: evidence from acquired *dyscalculia. Cognition* 44: 107–157.

McNaughton, B. L., J. J. Knierim, & M. A. Wilson 1994. Vector encoding and the vestibular foundations of spatial cognition: neurophysiological and computational mechanisms. In M. S. Gazzaniga (ed.), *The cognitive neurosciences.* Cambridge, MA: Bradford/MIT Press.

Pepperberg, I. M. 1987. Evidence for conceptual quantitative abilities in the African Gray Parrot: labeling of cardinal sets. *Ethology* 75: 37–61.

Pylyshyn, Z. W. 1988. Here and there in the visual field. In Z. Pylyshyn (ed.), *Computational processing in human vision.* Norwood, NJ: Ablex.

Rozin, P. 1976. The evolution of intelligence and access to the cognitive unconscious. In J. M. Sprague & A. M. Epstein (eds.), *Progress in psychobiology and physiological psychology.* New York: Academic Press.

Simon, T., S. Hespos, & P. Rochat. 1995. Do infants understand simple arithmetic? A replication of Wynn (1992). *Cognitive Development* 10: 253–269.

Sophian C., H. Harley, & C. S. M. Martin. 1995. Relational and representational aspects of early number development. *Cognition and Instruction* 13: 253–268.

Spelke, E. S., & S. Tsivkin. In press. Language and number: a bilingual training study. *Cognition.*

Starkey, P., & R. G. Cooper. 1980. Perception of numbers by human infants. *Science* 210: 133–135.

Starkey, P., E. S. Spelke, & R. Gelman. 1990. Numerical abstraction by human infants. *Cognition* 36: 97–127.

Strauss, M. S., & L. E. Curtis. 1981. Infant perception of numerosity. *Child Development* 52: 1146–1152.

Talmy, L. 1983. How language structures space. In H. Pick & L. Acredolo (eds.), *Spatial orientation: theory, research, and application.* New York: Plenum Press, 225–282.

Trick, L. M., & Z. W. Pylyshyn. 1993. What enumeration studies can show us about spatial attention: evidence for limited capacity preattentive processing. *Journal of Experimental Psychology: Human Perception and Performance* 19: 331–351.

van Loosbroek, E., & A. W. Smitsman. 1990. Visual perception of numerosity in infancy. *Developmental Psychology* 26: 911–922.

Wang, R. F., L. Hermer-Vazquez, & E. S. Spelke. 1999. Mechanisms of reorientation and object localization by children: a comparison with rats. *Behavioral Neuroscience* 113: 475–485.

Warrington, E. K. 1982. The fractionation of arithmetical skills: a single case study. *Quarterly Journal of Experimental Psychology* 34A: 31–51.

Wynn, K. 1990. Children's understanding of counting. *Cognition* 36: 155–193.
1992a. Addition and subtraction by human infants. *Nature* 358: 749–750.
1992b. Children's acquisition of the number words and the counting system. *Cognitive Psychology* 24: 220–251.
Xu, F., & E. S. Spelke. 2000. Large number discrimination by 6-month-old infants. *Cognition* 74: B1–B11.

Part 2

Constraints on word learning?

4 How domain-general processes may create domain-specific biases

Linda B. Smith

Indiana University

How do we come to understand the world so that we can act in it, so that we talk about it? Where do our rich understandings – of causality and intention, of number and objects, of space and time, of language – come from? Many have looked at the diversity of human knowledge and at the certainty with which children acquire it all and concluded that the diversity is there to begin with. They have suggested that knowledge acquisition is driven by special mechanisms dedicated to specific domains (e.g. Fodor 1975, 1983; Chomsky 1980; Gleitman 1986; Keil 1989; Gelman 1990; Spelke, Breinlinger, Macomber, & Jacobson 1992; Leslie 1994).

The argument for the domain-specificity of cognitive development is easy to make along four lines.

1. What needs to be acquired is unique to each domain. Thus, nothing beyond the most superficial metaphors are likely to exist across domains.
2. One cannot get something from nothing. In cognitive development, this idea is often presented in terms of the problem of induction and the need for constraints. Briefly, there are an infinite number of objectively correct generalizations from any data set. Therefore, learning cannot happen without prior content-specific constraints on the generalizations that are formed.
3. The empirical evidence on children's learning strongly implicates domain-specific constraints on what is learned. Children exhibit learning biases specific to the content being learned.
4. The smartness of young children's domain-specific learning stands in stark contrast to the inadequacies of their general problem-solving skills. The general cognitive processes of infants and very young children just do not seem smart enough on their own to yield the diverse competence evident in human cognition.

Despite the coherence of this line of reasoning, the present chapter offers an opposing view. The larger idea, borrowed from development as it is understood in modern biology and embryology, is that specificity is constructed out of processes of great generality, that one can get something much more from something much less through a *history* of activity.

This view is presented in the context of what is known about children's initial generalizations of newly learned nouns. Children are very smart learners of object names; so smart that they seem to learn a lexical category from hearing just one object named once. This chapter presents evidence that this smart and domain-specific learning is made in the history of activity of quite general and dumb processes. The central idea is this: domain-general processes when at work in particular learning contexts self-organize to form context-specific learning biases. They do so by creating contexts for new learning that feed on themselves, propelling development to a seemingly certain end and creating destiny.

1 Novel word generalizations

Consider a commonplace example: a 24-month-old child sees a tractor for the very first time. This particular tractor is big, red, snorting, and pulling machinery. The child is told "That's a tractor." The referent of *tractor* is clearly underdetermined from this one naming episode. Nonetheless, evidence from experiments and observations indicate that, after seeing this one tractor and hearing it named, the child will in the future correctly recognize and name other tractors, even tractors different from the original in size or color, in not snorting, in not pulling machinery (e.g. Clark 1973; Mervis 1987). How can a young child know before learning the lexical category that being tractor-*shaped* is what is critical to being called *tractor*?

In an effort to understand the smartness of children's early word learning, many researchers have used an artificial word learning task (e.g. Gentner 1978; Landau, Smith, & Jones 1988). In these experimental studies, children are presented with a novel object, it is named with a novel pseudoword, and then the children are asked what other objects have the same name. For example, in one study, Landau, Smith, and Jones (1988) showed two- and three-year-old children the novel wooden object shown at the top of figure 4.1. The object was named with a novel count noun, for example, "This is a *dax*." The children were then presented with the test objects also depicted in figure 4.1 and asked about each, "Is this a dax?"

The children in this study extended the novel name to test objects that were the same shape as the exemplar regardless of variations in texture or size. The degree of their selective attention to shape was remarkable. In one case, the original exemplar object was 2 cubic inches in area and made of wood. Children extended the name *dax* to same-shaped test objects even when those objects were 100 times the exemplar in size, and to objects made of sponge or chicken wire. This systematic selective attention to shape in the context of learning a novel count noun has now been demonstrated in many different studies and by many different experimenters (e.g.

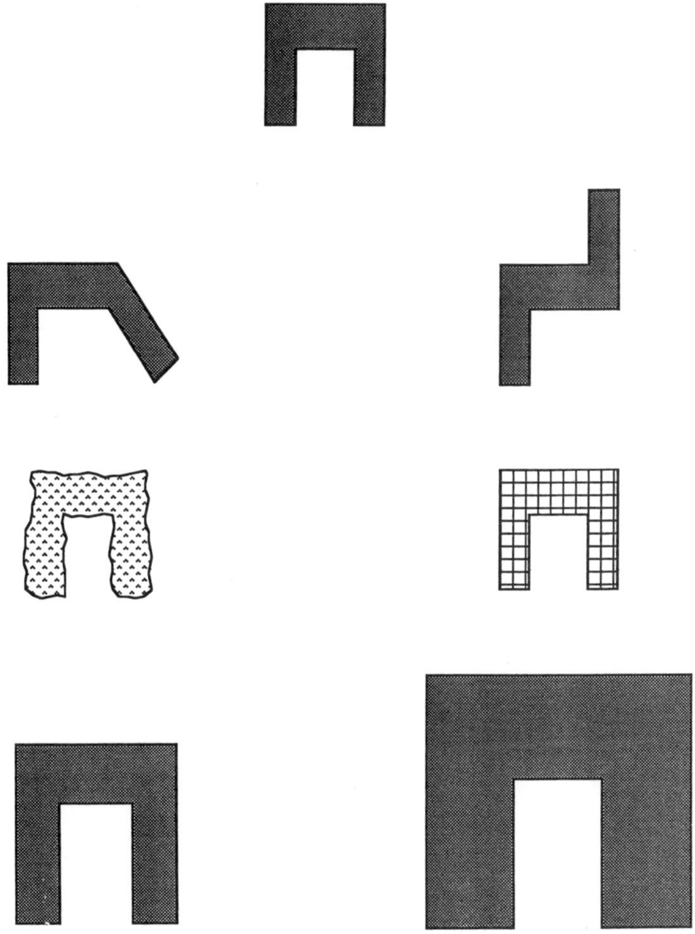

Fig. 4.1 Sample stimuli from Landau, Smith, & Jones (1988). All stimuli were three-dimensional objects made of wood, wire, or sponge.

Soja 1992; Imai, Gentner, & Uchida 1994; Keil 1994). It is a useful attentional bias: it promotes the learning of common nouns, lexical categories that typically refer to objects of similar shape (Rosch 1978; Biederman 1987).

Critically, in their study, Landau, Smith, & Jones contrasted children's attention to shape in the naming task with that in a nonnaming task. In the nonnaming task, they used the same stimuli depicted in figure 4.1 but asked two- and three-year old children to make similarity classifications, to pick out test objects that were "like" the exemplar. In this task, children did not attend selectively to shape but based their judgments on the wholistic similarity of the test object to the exemplar. That is, they picked out as "like" the exemplar test objects that were not too different from it overall, regardless of the dimension of difference. Apparently, young children do not go around in their everyday lives always attending selectively to the shape of things. Rather, they attend to shape when learning object names.

The selectivity of children's attention in the naming task and their nonselectivity in the nonnaming task illustrate well the idea of exceptional competence in special domains amidst the inadequacies of general cognitive skills. There is much evidence that young children consistently fare poorly in selective attention tasks, in tasks such as speeded and nonspeeded classification, discriminative learning, same/different judgments. In these tasks, young children seem unable to respond to only one attribute of an object while ignoring other attributes (see Aslin & Smith 1988, for a review). But the evidence from artificial word learning tasks indicates that same-aged children attend quite selectively to shape in the service of learning an object name. These facts are consistent with the idea of a domain-specific mechanism that is set apart from general attentional processes.

Other facts, however, suggest that if such a mechanism exists, it is complex and malleable. As research on children's artificial word learning has continued, it has become clear that children do not simply attend to the shape of things in the context of naming. Rather, the properties to which children attend are exquisitely tailored to the specific properties of the named object and the linguistic context. Moreover, these attentional biases change with age. The evidence for each of these conclusions is reviewed in turn.

1.1 The properties of the named object

1.1.1 Eyes Jones, Smith, & Landau (1991) examined the effect of the property of eyes on 36-month-old children's generalization of a novel noun. They reasoned that for many-eyed objects, texture (that is, being furry, or scaly, or feathered), as well as shape, is crucial for lexical categorization. A further impetus for the study was Massey & Gelman's (1988) finding that young children pay particular attention to texture when making judgments about which kinds of eyed objects (statues vs. living things) can move on their own.

The stimuli used by Jones *et al.* are shown in figure 4.2. In both conditions, the exemplar objects were made of painted wood; the only difference between the two conditions was that in one the exemplar and test objects were eyeless and in the other, they had eyes. Thus, in both conditions, the experimenter named the exemplar, "This is a dax," and asked about each

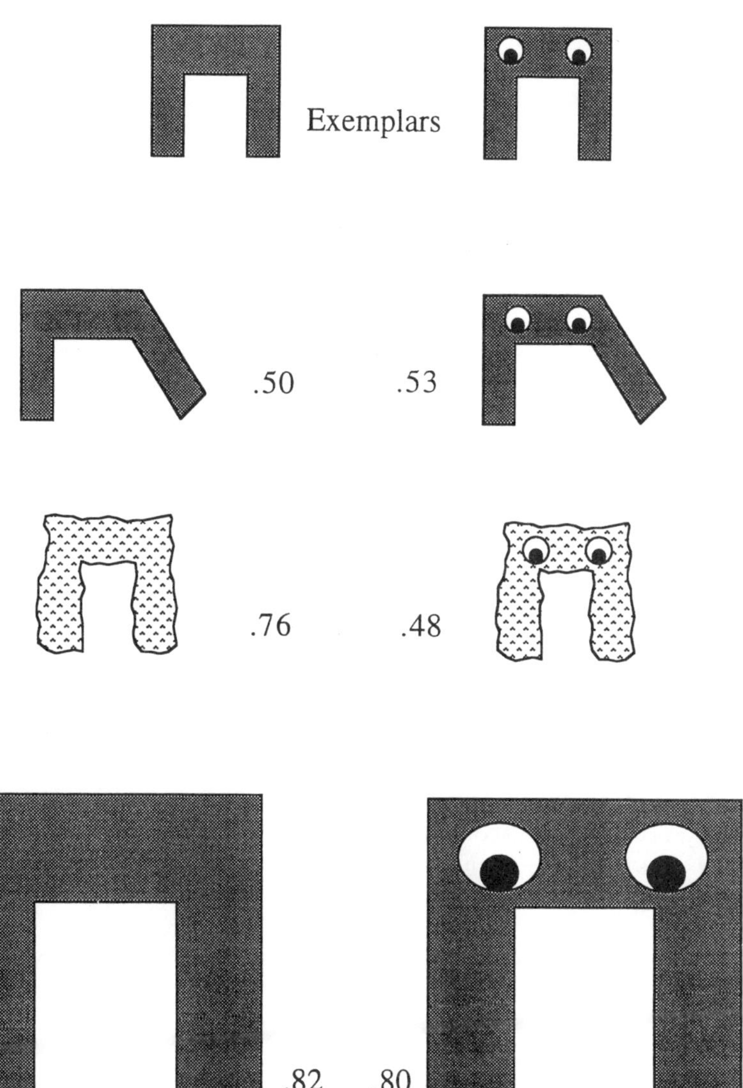

Fig. 4.2 Sample stimuli from Jones, Smith, & Landau (1991) and the proportion of times 3-year-old children extended the name of the exemplar to each of three kinds of test object.

test object, "Is this a dax?" The key results are summarized in the figure; next to each test object is the proportion of times children agreed that the novel noun named that test object. As is apparent, when the objects were eyeless, the children extended the name to same-shape objects. But when the objects had eyes, the children extended the name primarily to the same-shaped-and-same-textured test object. Thus, there is a shape bias for eyeless objects and shape-plus-texture bias for eyed objects.

Additional experiments showed that the presence of eyes affected children's attention only in a naming task. In a similarity judgment task, children attended wholistically both when the objects had eyes and when they did not. Thus, while it is naming that triggers selective attention, the trigger is not just to one property. Indeed, children's smart word learning biases are *context sensitive*.

1.1.2 Rigidity Eyes are not the only contextual cue that causes the form of the learning bias to change. Soja and her colleagues (Soja, Carey, & Spelke 1991; Soja 1992) examined children's novel word generalizations when the named objects were rigid things and when they were nonrigid substances. In the Rigid-object condition, the exemplar and two test items were made of substances that held their shape, for example hardened clay or wood. In the Substance condition, the stimuli were formed from nonrigid materials such as shaving cream mixed with gravel. The rigid and nonrigid stimulus sets were formed to present the same shapes as illustrated in figure 4.3. Also shown in the figure are the two test objects – one which matched the exemplar in shape and one which matched the exemplar in material. The procedure in both conditions was the same. Children aged from 2 to 2½ years old heard the exemplar named: "This is my mell." They were then asked to pick "the mell" from the two test objects.

Soja *et al.* found that the children formed different lexical categories when the exemplar was rigid than when it was nonrigid stuff. Specifically, *mell* was generalized to the same-shape test object when the named exemplar was rigid but to the same-material test object when the exemplar was nonrigid. Thus, there is a bias to attend to shape when learning names for rigid things, but a bias to attend to material when learning names for nonrigid substances.

Soja *et al.* also found that this systematic attention to shape in the one case and to material in the other was specific to the task of generalizing a novel name. Children did not show systematic attentional biases with either the rigid objects nor the nonrigid substances in a nonnaming similarity-judgment task. Again, it is specifically the task of naming that triggers selective attention, but the precise properties attended to depend on the perceptible properties of the named object.

Fig. 4.3 Sample stimuli from Soja (1992). On object trials, the exemplar and test objects were made of rigid substances such as wood. On substance trials, the exemplar and test objects were made of nonrigid substances such as foam.

1.1.3 Sneakers Eyes and rigidity are properties that signal biologically important distinctions and thus children's special sensitivity to these properties in the context of naming could be interpreted in terms of an evolved mechanism that incorporates specific content. Jones & Smith (1998) reported evidence that suggests that the object properties that modulate naming may be an open rather than closed set. They replicated the original Eyes study, but instead of using eyes, they used sneakers. Examples of the sneakered stimuli are shown in figure 4.4. The mean proportion of times 36-month-olds extended the novel name to each test object or said that each test object was "like" the exemplar is also given in the figure. As is apparent, in the naming task only, children attended principally to texture when the stimuli had sneakers. It is unlikely that children are specially prepared to learn how sneakered things are named. Rather, it seems that children have

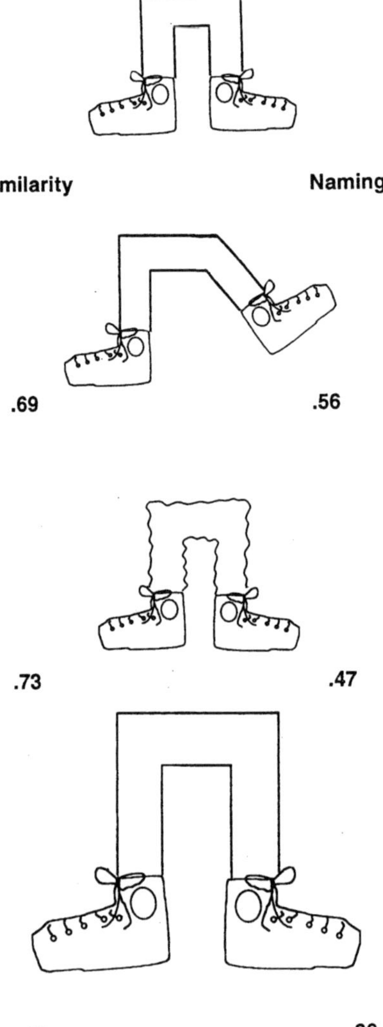

Fig. 4.4 Sample stimuli from a replication of Jones *et al.* that put sneakers rather than eyes on the stimuli and the mean proportion of times that 3-year-old children judged the test object to be "like" the exemplar in the Similarity judgment task and judged the test object to have the same name as the exemplar in the Naming task.

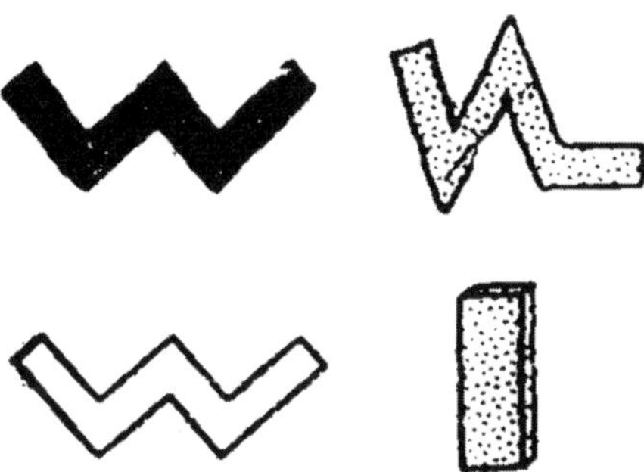

Fig. 4.5 Stimuli used in Smith, Jones, & Landau (1992). The colors of the exemplar and test objects were realized with glitter.

learned something about the correlation between sneakered things, eyes, and the relevance of texture to lexical categorization. These results suggest that children will learn and make use of any regularity when naming an object. Children's smart attention in the service of naming derives from mechanisms apparently open to arbitrary influence.

1.2 The role of syntax

The form of the word learning bias also depends on the syntactic frame in which the novel word is placed. One relevant contrast is that between the syntactic frame associated with count nouns, "this is a dax," and one associated with adjectives, "this is a dax one." A number of investigators have shown that children attend to different object properties in these two linguistic contexts (Smith, Jones, & Landau 1992; Landau, Smith, & Jones 1992; Waxman & Markow 1998; see also Au & Laframboise 1990). One relevant study (Smith, Jones, & Landau 1992) investigated 36-month-olds' shifting attention to color and shape when asked to interpret a novel word presented in the two syntactic contexts. The stimuli, shown in figure 4.5, varied in shape and color. The colors were realized by putting glitter in paint. In two separate experiments, these stimuli were presented either

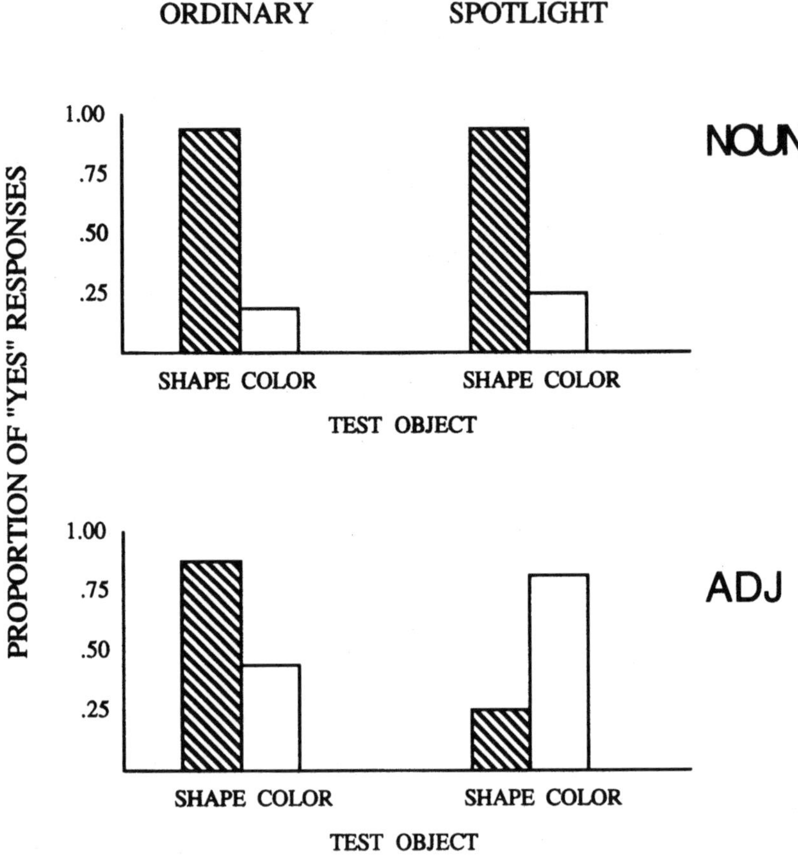

Fig. 4.6 Mean proportion of times the novel word in either a count noun or adjectival frame was extended to test objects that matched the exemplar in either color only or shape only under ordinary illumination or under a spotlight.

under ordinary illumination or in a darkened chamber with a spotlight. The effect of the spotlight was to make the glitter sparkle.

The results are shown in figure 4.6. The spotlight had little effect when the novel word was in a noun frame but controlled attention when the novel word was in an adjective frame. Children understood the novel noun as referring to objects the same shape as the exemplar under both ordinary and spotlight illumination. But children understood the novel adjective differently in the two lighting conditions: as referring to particularly shaped objects under ordinary illumination and as referring to the sparkling color under the spotlight. In other words, attention to shape in the context of a novel noun withstands the challenge of sparkling glitter but attention in the context of a novel adjective is organized differently when there is a sparkling color vs. when there is not. These results show that children's attentional biases in the service of word learning depend on *both* the properties of the labelled object and the linguistic context.

Soja's (1992) findings about two-year-old children's interpretation of novel words in count- and mass-noun frames makes the same point. In these experiments, she used the rigid and nonrigid stimulus sets depicted in figure 4.3 but named the exemplar either with a count noun, "This is a mell," or with a mass noun, "This is some mell." She found that children's novel word generalizations were different in the two contexts. Children were more likely to attend to shape in the context of a count noun than a mass noun. Moreover, syntactic frame interacted with object properties. Shape choices dominated given rigid objects in both syntactic contexts but substance choices dominated only in the context of a mass-noun frame *and* a nonrigid substance. Soja concluded that children possessed knowledge about both count/mass syntax and the perceptual properties critical to distinguishing objects and substances.

These findings about object properties and syntactic frames constitute quite strong evidence that children know a great deal about how words map to categories. Their attentional biases in the context of word learning are intelligently dependent on the kind of object and the kind of word.

1.3 Attentional biases change with development

Where does this knowledge about how words map to different kinds of categories come from? Figure 4.7 summarizes the many developmental experiments that have been conducted on children's biased word learning (Landau *et al.* 1988; Soja *et al.* 1991; Landau *et al.* 1992; Smith *et al.* 1992; Soja 1992; Waxman 1994). Each curve summarizes the developmental pattern given specific stimulus properties and/or syntactic context. Briefly, the evidence suggests that by twenty-four months there is an early tendency in naming tasks to attend to shape that gets both stronger with development and more specific to specific contexts. Descriptively, other biases seem to grow out of, differentiate out of, this earlier less-articulated shape bias.

The data summarized in figure 4.7 all derive from children learning English. If I were to add the growing evidence from children learning other languages – Korean, Japanese, Spanish, or Yucatec Mayan – I would have to add other curves. The work of Bowerman & Choi, Gentner & Imai, Gaskins & Lucy summarized in this volume, as well as studies by Waxman (1994), strongly indicate that children learning different languages develop different attentional biases. In all these languages, children seem to have domain-specific attentional biases that are smartly specific to the language being learned. How can this be?

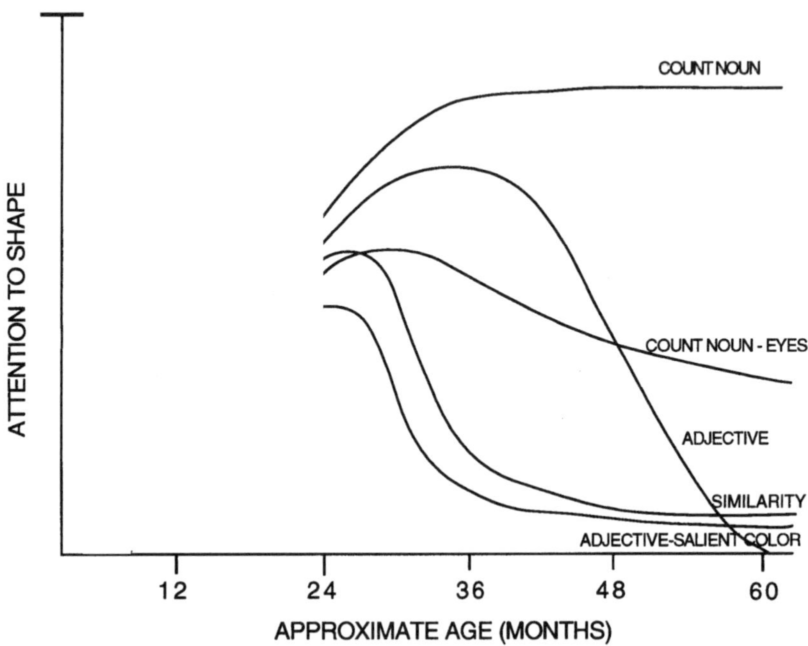

Fig. 4.7 Theoretical developmental trajectories summarizing findings across experiments.

2 An attentional learning account

One hundred years of research provides an answer in the most basic and universal processes of attentional learning (James 1890; Rescorla & Wagner 1972). When one perceptual cue is regularly associated with another, attention to the first mandatorily recruits attention to the second. The automatic control of selective attention by associative learning is one of the most widespread and well-documented phenomena in all of psychology. It is a fundamental process, evident in infants, children, adults, and nonhuman animals (e.g. MacIntosh 1965; Medin & Wattenmaker 1987; Lewicki, Hill, & Sasak 1989; Younger, 1990; Kruschke 1992). It is a process that may also be sufficient to explain young children's selective generalizations of a novel word to new instances.

The viability of this idea is suggested by the strong resemblance between the contextual control of children's attention in novel word learning tasks and the contextual control of selective attention that emerges in well-controlled studies of attentional learning. In such studies, some cue is regularly associated with attending to some property; and the presence of that cue comes to recruit attention to the associated property (e.g. MacIntosh 1965; Rescorla & Wagner 1972; Lewicki *et al.* 1989; Younger 1990). In learning language, children repeatedly experience specific linguistic contexts (e.g. "This is a ____" or "This is some ____") with attention to specific object properties and clusters of properties (e.g. shape or color plus texture). By hypothesis, then, these linguistic contexts come to serve as cues that automatically control attention. In so doing, they make attention in the context of language learning different from attention in other contexts and they push word learning in certain directions that will depend on the language being learned. This account affirms that children know a lot about how words map to categories. But it implements this knowledge in very general learning and attentional processes, associative connections, and attention weights, which themselves have no domain-specific content.

There are three points in favor of this account that merit recognition.

(1) The posited processes are nondeliberative, nonthoughtful, nearly reflexive. This is advantageous because young children, two- and three-year-olds, are not typically deliberative and reflective. They are particularly poor testers of explicit hypotheses (e.g. Kemler 1978) and particularly poor at strategically controlling their attention (see Aslin & Smith 1988). Thus, it is to the advantage of this account that the proposed mechanisms are also dumb and take no conscious thought.

(2) The posited processes are known to exist. Although some might question whether associative processes are sufficient to account for much in human cognition (e.g. Keil 1994), their existence is not in question. Associative processes of attentional learning *are* part of children's biology and thus could be the mechanism behind children's smart interpretations of novel nouns.

(3) These processes can be demonstrated to create attentional biases. The hypothesized mechanisms can be shown to work. For example, simulating learned attentional biases specific to specific contexts is easily achieved by connectionist networks of the most generic sort (e.g. Gasser & Smith 1991, 1998; Smith 1993, 1995).

These three points indicate the plausibility of the idea that children's domain-specific word learning biases originate in domain-general processes. In the next section, I present data from an ongoing series of experiments that provide further support for this account.

3 Tests of an attentional learning account

The proposal is that learned cues that automatically shift attention underlie the entire pattern of results summarized by the changing curves in figure

4.7. The idea is that early in word learning, the linguistic context "This is a ____" becomes associated with attention to the shape of rigid things *because* many of the words that children learn refer to categories of rigid objects similar in shape. A learned shape bias may be first among learned attentional biases because the correlation between shape similarity and lexical category is the broadest and most general in language to children (see Smith 1995). Other more local attentional biases will develop from more local statistical regulations as more words are learned. Attention will become modulated by the presence of eyes, or nonrigidity, or a mass-noun frame. The long-range theoretical goal is to explain all of this and especially the emerging complexity of attentional biases. However, our initial tests concentrate on the origins of children's attention to shape in the context of naming a rigid thing.

3.1 A longitudinal study

Many of the first nouns that children learn, nouns like *table*, *cat*, *bottle*, and *truck*, name objects similar in shape. The hypothesis is that learning enough nouns like this causes the act of naming to become a contextual cue that automatically recruits attention to shape. The key prediction that follows from this hypothesis is that a lexically specific shape bias should not be evident prior to language but should emerge only after some number of nouns has been acquired.

Susan Jones, Barbara Landau, and I tested this prediction in a longitudinal study of eight children from fifteen to twenty months of age. We tracked the children's vocabulary growth by having parents keep diaries of all new words spoken by their child. We measured the emergence of a shape bias by having the children come into the laboratory every three weeks to participate in an artificial word generalization task. At the beginning of the study, the children had very few words in their productive vocabulary (less than 15). At the end of the study, each child had over 150 words and for each child more than half of these were nouns that named concrete objects. Thus, if the shape bias is learned from learning words, children should not show a shape bias at the beginning of the study but should show one at the end – after they had learned a number of object names.

The stimuli used in the laboratory task are shown in figure 4.8. They include an exemplar object made of wood and three test objects that matched the exemplar in either color, shape, or texture. Because our subjects were so young at the start of the study, we modified the novel word generalization tasks used in our previous experiments as follows: the task began with the experimenter putting the exemplar and three test objects on the table in front of the child. The experimenter picked up the exemplar and said "This is a dax. Look, this is a dax." Then while still holding the exem-

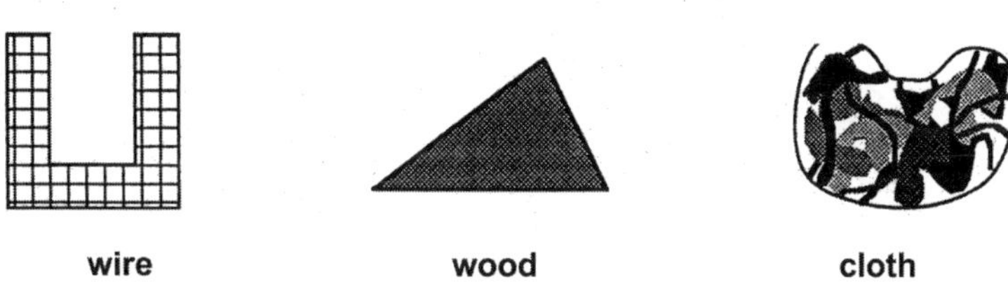

Fig. 4.8 Stimuli used in the longitudinal study of the development of the shape bias.

plar, the experimenter held out her other hand, palm up, and said, "Give me a dax. Give me another dax."

The results are shown in figure 4.9. As is apparent, shape choices did not predominate early in the study but did by the end. More specifically, all eight children began to systematically extend the novel word *dax* to the same-shape test object *after* they had fifty object names (and about eighty total words) in their productive vocabulary. This point (fifty object names) in the word learning trajectory is *after* the spurt in noun acquisitions commonly known as the "naming explosion" as defined by Gopnik & Meltzoff (1987; see also Dromi 1987; Gershkoff-Stowe & Smith 1997). The developmental timing of biased attention to shape thus suggests that it may be the consequence of word learning – the consequence of learning some number of names for shape-based categories.

3.2 A cross-sectional study

We conducted a cross-sectional replication of the longitudinal study for two reasons. The first purpose was to ensure that the repeated laboratory visits had not somehow created a shape bias. The second purpose of the cross-sectional study was to determine whether the shape bias was lexically specific when it first emerged. It should be if it is the product of an associative link between naming and attending to shape.

Sixty-four children between the ages of eighteen and twenty-four

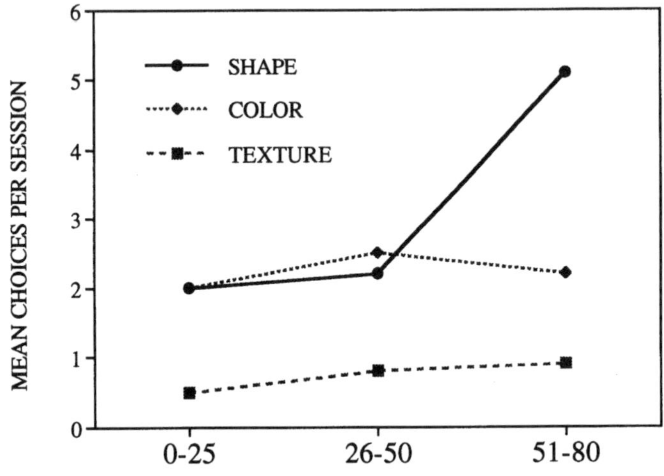

Fig. 4.9 Mean number of selections of test objects that matched the exemplar in shape, color, or texture as a function of the mean number of object names in the child's productive vocabulary.

months participated in the cross-sectional study. They came to the laboratory just once. Productive vocabulary was measured by having parents complete the MacArthur Toddler Communicative Development Inventory. This is a parent report measure which catalogues 625 of the most common early words and for which there is extensive normative and reliability data (Fenson, Dale, Reznick, *et al.* 1993). From this measure, children were assigned to four groups according to the number of nouns in their productive vocabulary: 0–25 nouns, 25–50 nouns, 50–75 nouns, and 75 and more nouns. Half the children at each level of productive vocabulary participated in a novel word generalization task. This Naming task was structured similarly to that used in the longitudinal study. Half the children participated in a Nonnaming task. All aspects of this task were the same as in the Naming task except the exemplar was not named. The experimenter merely held up the exemplar and said "Look, look at this" and then held out her hand and said "Get me one."

The key questions of this experiment are whether children systematically select test objects the same shape as the exemplar, whether they do so only in the Naming task and not in the Nonnaming task, and whether their selective attention to shape emerges only after they have acquired some number of nouns. The data are shown in figure 4.10 and, as can be seen, the

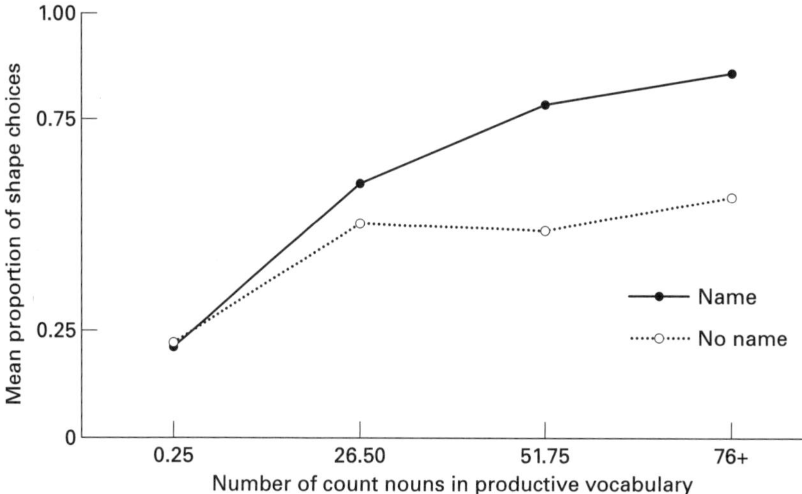

Fig. 4.10 Mean number of selections of test objects that matched the exemplar in shape in the Nonnaming and Naming tasks for children grouped according to the number of nouns in their productive vocabulary.

answer to each of these questions is "yes." There is a rise in shape choices as a function of vocabulary growth and it is specific to the Naming task. After children have acquired more than 50 nouns, it is the linguistic context of naming a novel object that recruits attention to shape. These results along with those of the longitudinal study fit the idea that learning words *creates* a shape bias by creating a contextual cue so regularly associated with attention to shape that the presence of that cue automatically shifts attention to shape.

3.3 A training study

Correlation, of course, is not causation. In order to provide stronger evidence that a lexically specific shape bias is the *consequence* of learning names for rigid things, we attempted a training experiment. The goal was to create biased attention to shape by teaching lexical categories well-organized by shape to children who did not yet know many words. The subjects were seventeen months of age and produced an average of 12 nouns at the start of the study. These children came to the laboratory for seven weeks and were given extensive training on four different novel categories – all well-organized by shape. The top of figure 4.11 illustrates the training stimuli for one lexical category.

Each lexical category was trained as follows: the two exemplars for a

Training set

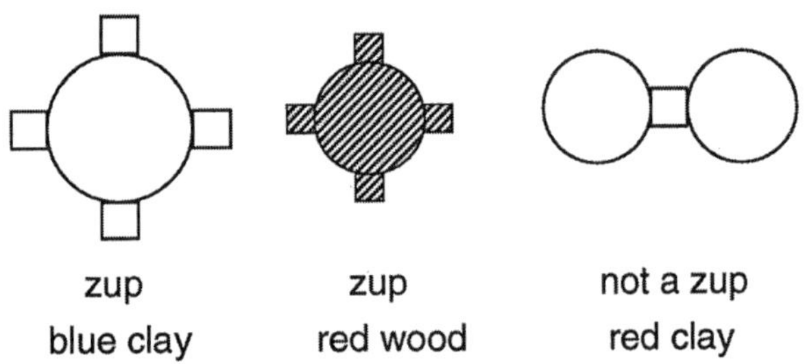

Test set

Week 8: trained lexical categories

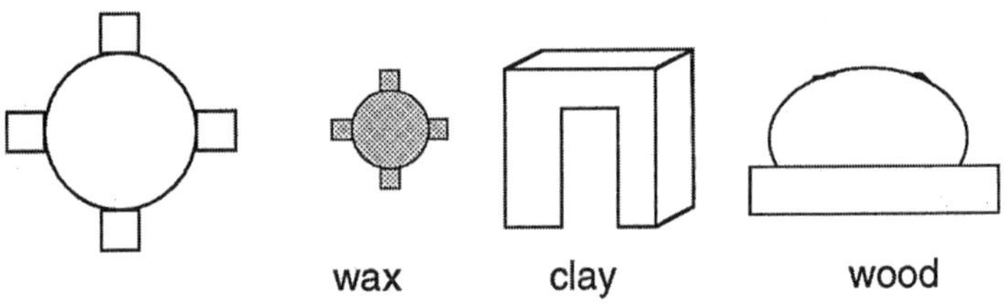

Week 9: novel lexical categories

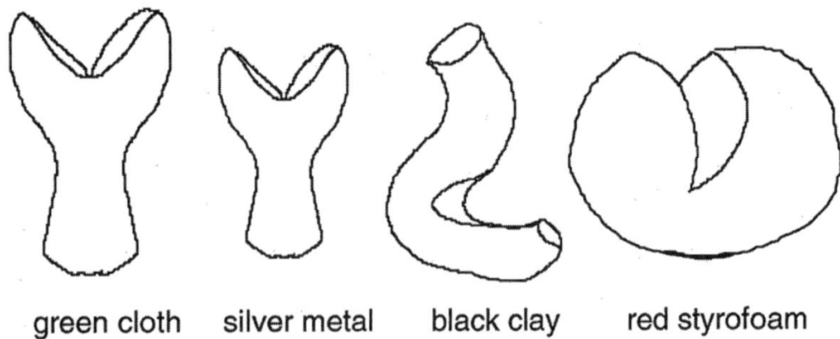

Fig. 4.11 Sample stimuli from the Training experiment: top – training stimuli; middle – stimuli for the test of generalization of the trained object name (week 8); bottom – stimuli for the test of generalization of novel names (week 9).

category were placed on the table and named (e.g. "This is a *zup*. Here is another *zup*.") As illustrated in figure 4.11, these two exemplars differed in many ways but were identical in shape. The experimenter and child played with these two objects for five minutes during which time the experimenter repeatedly named the objects (e.g. "Put the zup in the box. Can you put the zup in the wagon?"). Midway in a play session with one pair of exemplars, a nonexemplar for that category (see figure 4.11) was briefly placed on the table. The experimenter announced that this just-introduced object was not a member of the category (e.g. "*That's* not a zup!") and then removed it. This nonexemplar matched each exemplar in one nonshape attribute but differed from both exemplars in shape. This nonexemplar thus provides the child with negative evidence as to the kinds of things that are *not* in the lexical category.

For the first seven weeks of the experiment, the children were trained as described above on each of four lexical categories. In weeks 8 and 9 of the experiment, the children participated in two test sessions that asked them to generalize what had been learned over the first seven weeks. The first test session, in week 8, measured children's generalizations of the trained lexical categories to new instances. The structure of this task was identical to the novel word generalization task used in the longitudinal and cross-sectional studies described earlier. The stimuli used to test generalization of the *zup* category are illustrated in the middle section of figure 4.11. The test began with the experimenter placing one of the trained exemplars on the table along with three novel objects: one which matched the exemplar in material, one in color, and one in shape. The experimenter picked up the exemplar and said "This is a zup," then asked, "Get me a zup." For these children after their seven weeks of training, the exemplar is not a novel object and the label provided is not a novel name. Thus, if the children have learned that the specifically trained names refer to objects of a particular shape, they should generalize these already-learned names to the novel object that is the same as the exemplar in shape.

At week 9, the children were tested in a novel word generalization task structured in the same way as the generalization task at week 8. However, as illustrated by the sample stimulus set at the bottom of figure 4.11, all the objects and names were new. This generalization task thus tests the critical prediction that learning specific categories well-organized by shape transforms the task of naming into a contextual cue that automatically shifts attention to shape. If the seven weeks of intensive training on shape-based categories has caused the linguistic context of naming to cue attention to shape automatically, then these children should form and generalize *novel* names on the basis of shape.

This experiment also included ten Control children. These children did

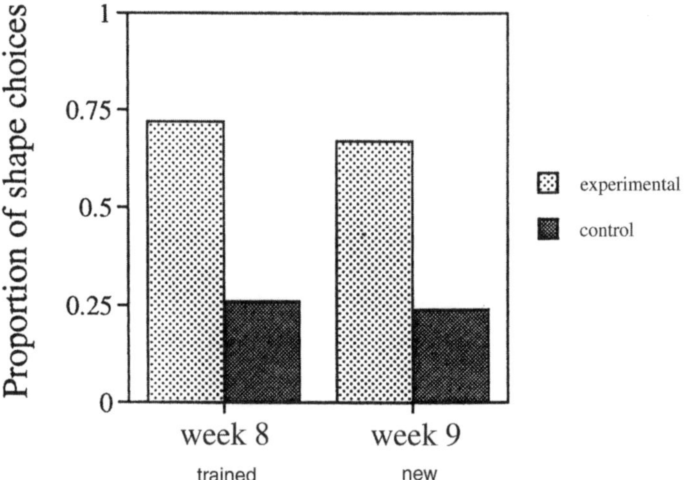

Fig. 4.12 Proportion of choices of test object the same shape as the named exemplar on the two generalization tests: week 8 – trained name and exemplar; week 9 – novel name and exemplar.

not participate in the seven weeks of training but were tested in the generalization tasks of weeks 8 and 9. The Control children were matched to the Experimental children in the number of nouns in their productive vocabulary at week 8 (mean = 26 for both groups). Since the Control children have learned few nouns and have not received intensive training on shape-based lexical categories, the expectation is that these children will not selectively attend to shape in the generalization tasks.

The main results are shown in figure 4.12. At week 8, when the Experimental children were asked to generalize the trained names to new objects, they did so on the basis of shape. These children have clearly learned that the words we taught them refer to objects of a particular shape. The Control children, for whom this is a *novel* word interpretation task, did not systematically attend to shape.

At week 9, both the Experimental and Control children heard novel objects named by novel nouns. However, the Experimental children, but not the Control children, systematically generalized these newly learned names to other novel objects by shape. In brief, we taught the Experimental children four categories organized by shape but they learned more than just these categories. They learned to attend to shape when novel rigid objects are named. This generalized attentional shift *is* a learning bias. These children are now biased to learn about shape when a novel object is named.

3.4 *Summary*

I proposed that, in the course of early word learning, children learn contextual cues (linguistic context, object properties) that automatically shift attention to specific object properties in that context. Three preliminary experiments in an ongoing research project were presented. The results support the attentional learning account by showing (1) that the shape bias in early naming does not precede language learning, (2) that it is lexically specific when it first emerges, and (3) that its emergence is accelerated by training on lexical categories well-organized by shape.

Clearly, more evidence is needed. Accelerating a bias by training is not as powerful evidence for learning as, for example, teaching a new and arbitrary bias. We are attempting such a stronger test of our attentional learning account. However, the evidence to date on the origins of the shape bias are encouraging. They suggest that at least in this case of word learning, young children's domain-specific smartness may originate in domain-general processes – in ordinary associative learning and the general mechanisms of selective attention.

4 Self-organizing biases

Several theorists in cognitive development have expressed doubt that the smartness of children's early word learning could emerge from general processes such as associative connections and the automatic control of attention weights (see e.g. Markman 1989; S. A. Gelman & Medin 1993; Keil 1994). In these views, the directedness of early word learning is too smart, too constrained, to be based on unconstrained associative processes. There is, however, much power in a single learned attentional bias, the power to start learning in directions that will build on themselves, the power to *create* a destiny. This point can be made by considering the cascading effects of learning just one context cue that automatically shifts attention.

Consider a two-year-old – say one of the children in the Experimental condition of the training study – who has learned enough for "That's a ____" in the context of a rigidly shaped object to cue attention to shape automatically. Imagine further that this is the *only* linguistically relevant attentional cue that the child has learned. From all that is known about associative learning, one would expect, as illustrated in figure 4.13, a generalization gradient around the original learning: the child's attention to shape should be maximal in contexts most similar to the original learning and should decrease in word learning situations as those situations become increasingly dissimilar to the context of original learning.

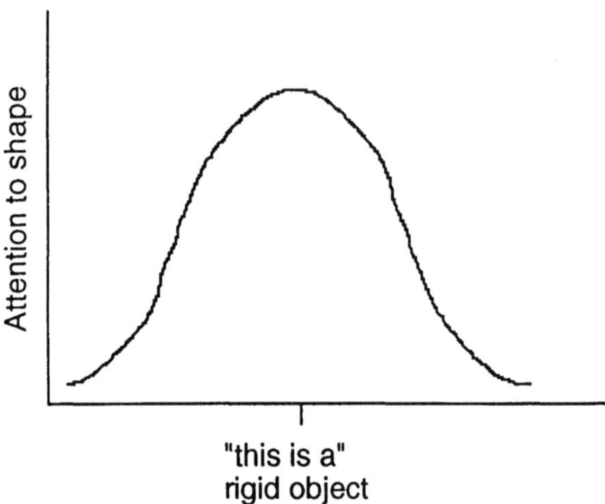

Fig. 4.13 A hypothetical generalization gradient.

By this account, given only a learned association between the count-noun frame, object rigidity, and attention to shape, one would expect the pull of shape to be less if the novel word were embedded in an adjectival rather than a count-noun frame. Because the pull to shape of the utterance "This is a dax one" is less than "This is a dax," the child will be likely to learn something different about a novel word in the two different frames. The child might, for example, learn that the word refers to sparkling colors in one frame but shape in the other. In this way, "knowing" only about count nouns means learning differently about nouns and adjectives.

The purpose of this account is not to "explain away" children's knowledge about adjectives. Rather, the proposed explanation is interesting because it shows what might be the mechanism through which an understanding of the semantic forces of nouns and adjectives develops. If children are less likely to attend to shape in the context of an adjective – whatever the reason for this decreased likelihood – then they are more likely to learn differently about adjectives and nouns. Put another way, *because* the generalized association to shape is weaker and more easily challenged in the context of a novel adjective than a novel noun, children with just a learned association between count nouns and shape will be already *biased* to learn differently about adjectives and nouns. In this sense, they do "know" something about adjectives but that knowledge is implemented through a single association that is not, strictly speaking, "about" adjectives at all. Nonetheless, such a "dumb" mechanism may start the development process in the right direction just as well as specific knowledge about adjectives. A simple generalization gradient creates an opportunity for learning differently in different contexts – learning that may culminate in the sophisticated use of lexical contrast (e.g. Au & Markman 1987; Au & Laframboise 1990) and in crosslinguistic differences in learning about nouns and adjectives (see Waxman 1994).

A similar account may be the right one for young children's differential interpretations of mass and count nouns. Recall that Soja (1992; Soja, Carey, & Spelke 1991) found that children's generalizations of a novel noun were modulated by both count/mass syntax and the rigidity of the labeled object: children attended to shape more in the context of a count noun and a rigid object but attended to material more in the context of a mass noun and a nonsolid substance. Soja concluded that children possessed knowledge both about count/mass syntax and the perceptual properties critical to distinguishing objects and substances.

This knowledge, however, could be implemented only by a strong association between a count-noun frame, rigidity, and attention to shape. Figure 4.14 shows a redrawing of Soja's data. The proportion of shape choices are shown as a function of the hypothesized dissimilarity of each kind of test trial from the context of hypothesized original learning: a count-noun naming a shape-based category of rigid objects. Children's shape choices in Soja's experiments clearly suggest a generalization gradient; shape choices decrease as similarity from the prototypical naming context decreases. But this generalization gradient means that these children are effectively biased to learn differently about how rigid and nonrigid objects are named and to learn differently about novel words in mass- and count-noun frames. Again, knowledge about one kind of word creates – by its very existence – biases for learning about other kinds of words.

Notice also what is happening with development. The differences between younger and older children in Soja's experiments suggest discriminative learning; the generalization gradient is steeper for older than for younger children just as would be expected if older children now have two contrasting associations – the original count-noun–rigid–shape association and the newer mass-noun–nonrigid–material association.

Such changes in the generalization gradients with development are predicted by the attentional learning account. Learning creates context cues that shape future learning; this future learning in turn creates new contexts for new learning. Each new word the child learns will change what the child knows about learning words – adding to, strengthening, weakening associations among linguistic contexts and attention to object properties. The history of these events will be laid on top of one another, making development. And thus, when we look back from adulthood at the developmental

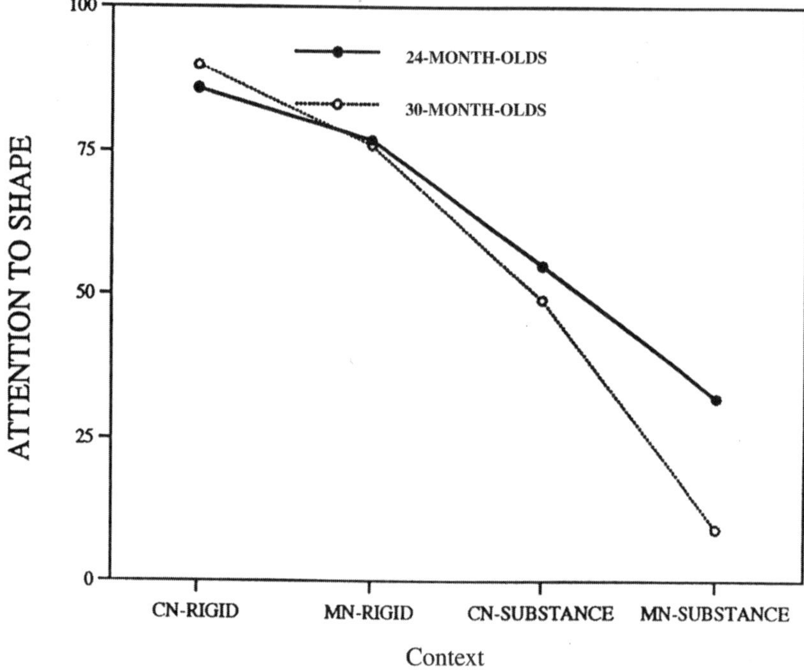

Fig. 4.14 Mean percentage choice of the test object that matched the exemplar in shape in Soja (1992) as a function of the hypothesized dissimilarity of the testing condition from the context of original learning. Chance equals 50 percent. Redrawn from the data reported in Soja (1992).

trajectory that brought us to maturity, it will look predestined. In fact, however, it will have been made in a history of possibilities.

5 Developmental process

When we look at development, it seems directed – so directed that it is hard to imagine how it is not predetermined and prescribed from within. Since this directedness is obvious in so many content-specific domains, it would also seem that there must be domain-specific mechanisms and processes that direct that development. The evidence presented in this chapter suggests how specialized developmental mechanisms could themselves be a product of development, the outgrowth of the history of activity of more fundamental and universal processes.

This idea, that specialization emerges from general processes, is the very idea of biological development and one whose truth can be seen at multiple levels of analysis. Consider, as one example, how animals get their basic body parts – the parts and organs that emerge in orderly fashion in the first weeks of life after conception (for more detail, see Wolpert 1971; Gierer 1981; Marx 1984a, b; Cooke 1988). The initial state from which these parts emerge is a seemingly homogenous and formless single cell. It makes copies of itself that are all the same. Formation of body parts occurs when there are about 10,000 of these cells amassed in an undifferentiated heap. But at this point, cells are already marked by their position in the mass to become distinct body parts. They are so marked by gradients of substances. These gradients are the consequence of pervasive processes not specific to these cells or this kind of organism; they arise, for example, from the "mundane" effects of gravity and the mechanical effects of molecular structure in the cell and at its surface. These gradients emerge out of the geography of this amorphous mass of cells. Remarkably, the effect of these gradients is to switch on and off the regulating genes in the nucleus of individual cells. These genes have their effects by making proteins; in so doing, they change the activity of once-identical cells into different kinds. They also change the environment of those cells, thus creating the context for more changes. In one probabilistic event after another, arms and legs and stomachs and lungs are created with seeming certainty. It happens because each event creates the context for, and thus constrains, what can happen next.

There are two points to note from this example: (1) it is the specific *history* of events and the contexts they create that makes specificity, that makes some cells destined to be of one kind and others to be of another kind; and (2) the processes that make development, that make the special parts of the body – protein synthesis, gravity, and the mechanical and biomechanical actions of cells – are very general processes. They are what all life is made of.

A similar story at the psychological level has been offered by O'Reilly & Johnson (1994) in their recurrent network model of imprinting in precocial birds. Their account presents a parallel case to embryology in that the specialized process of imprinting is a consequence of a pervasive external reality and the most general processes known to make up intelligence. The external regularity is the fact that objects tend to persist across space and time. The general processes are Hebbian learning, excitatory connections, and lateral inhibition. None of these is a prescription for imprinting or its sensitive period. But together in a particular history of events, O'Reilly & Johnson have shown they are enough to create a bias to fixate on the first conspicuous object seen after hatching.

The architecture of O'Reilly's & Johnson's model, illustrated in figure 4.15, is explicitly based on what is known about the patterns of connectivity in the chick brain. The network consists of three layers of units; each unit is

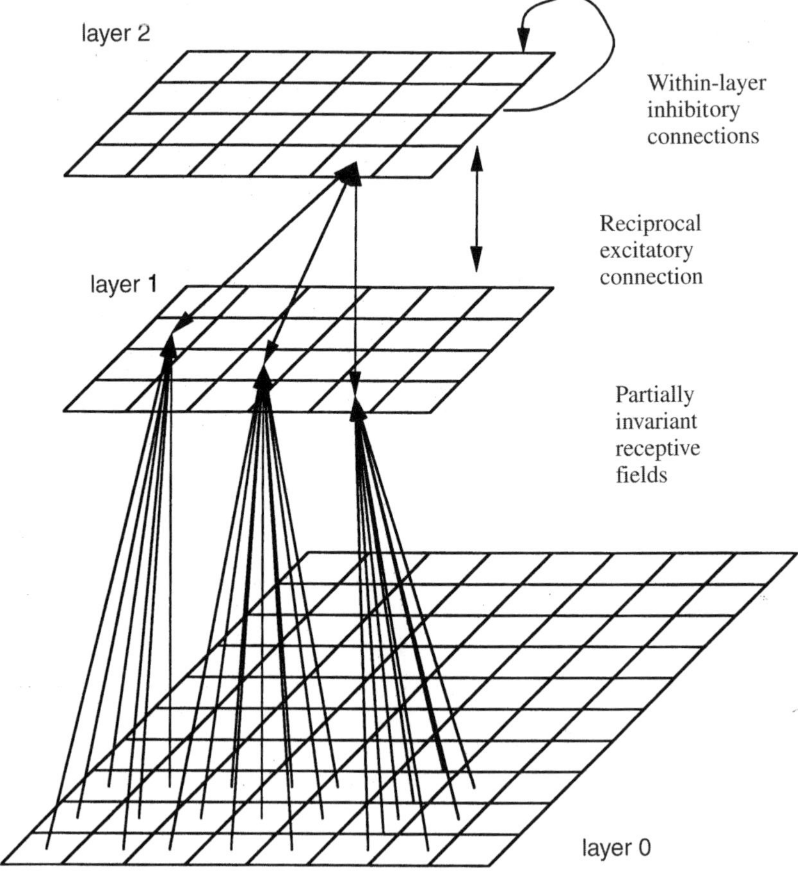

Fig. 4.15 The architecture of O'Reilly & Johnson's network.

represented by an individual rectangle in the grid. Spatially close units in the input layer (Layer 0) connect to the same units in Layer 1, creating spatially organized receptive fields, a common pattern of connection in many regions of the brains of many different kinds of animals. In the network, the connection weights between these two layers can change through Hebbian learning; thus the receptive fields on Layer 1 can vary within limits. The units on Layer 1, in contrast, project in an invariant fashion to those on Layer 2, but again in a manner that is common throughout sensory systems. Lateral inhibition is present in each layer of the model in the form of relatively large negative weights between all units in layer. Reciprocal (bidirectional) excitatory connections exist between Layers 1 and 2. Finally, there are recurrent connections. The activity in a unit depends not just on its immediate input from below but also on its own past activity and the past activity of the network as a whole. These building blocks are all the common stuff of brains and networks.

The experience O'Reilly & Johnson gave the network is also common stuff – looking at individual objects presented one at a time for varying durations, experiences that might correspond to ten minutes or one hour of viewing the same object. That is all there is to the model. But the outcome of these experiences is preferential recognition of the first object seen and the emergence of a self-terminating sensitive period. Quite simply, if early experience consists of an object that persists for sufficient duration, the strength of that bias cannot ever be overcome; through lateral inhibition and recurrent connections, it maintains itself. If, in contrast, early experience consists of sufficiently many different nonpersisting objects, no preference emerges and the possibility of developing such a preference is lost. The point of this example, like the one from embryology, like the attentional learning account of children's word learning biases, is that something special can *develop* out of the history of activity of general, indeed mundane, processes that subserve many other specializations.

Some readers may be questioning how this approach can explain what seems to be truly special about human cognition and truly smart – systematic belief systems and conscious, self-reflective thought. Could these possibly develop out of mundane, generic cognitive processes such as those considered here? The answer seems inescapable to me. If human cognition is a biological process, if it has a material cause, then it is made of processes, of bits of matter and connections, that are themselves *much less than what they yield.*

It is commonplace in psychological theorizing to impute to internal workings a "copy" of externally observed behavior (Smith & Thelen 1993). Thus, sucking in infants is explained by a sucking reflex, statements of beliefs by internally represented beliefs, categorization by represented categories, and syntax by an innate grammar. In each case, an abstract and sometimes truly elegant icon of the behavior to be explained is proposed as the mechanism that produces the behavior. There is a failure of imagination here that evokes the preformationism of eighteenth-century embryology (see Ausabel 1957).

It was once seriously believed that a miniature but fully formed little human being existed in the sperm and when implanted in the uterus, this little being fed off the egg and grew in bulk until it was big enough to be born. This preformationist theory eschews the complex developmental processes that we now know drive the formation of new structures in embryology. The eighteenth-century proponents of a preformationist embryology did not, of course, explicitly deny developmental process; the truth is, they could not imagine it. They could not imagine that the organism at conception is undifferentiated and *develops* its structure through a series of complex and cascading interactions, through a series of small steps that are each mundane and ordinary.

As students of cognitive development, we are like the early preformationists. It is hard for us to imagine how beliefs, conscious thought, theories about space and time could emerge from anything *less* than beliefs, conscious thought, or theories. This is perhaps a failure of imagination to be replaced by scientific fact.

6 Conclusion

The phenomena considered in this chapter, attentional biases that are specific to and promote word learning, are themselves much simpler than the phenomena usually interpreted in terms of domain-specific belief systems (see, for example, ch. 7 by Carey, ch. 3 by Spelke & Tsivkin, and ch. 2 by Gopnik in this volume). Still, the evidence suggests that these word learning biases may emerge out of processes both more general and simpler than the conceptual and linguistic knowledge embodied in these biases. These simple attentional biases, once created, may then help to create more thoughtful beliefs and belief systems about kinds of categories and about language (see Smith & Heise 1992; Thelen & Smith 1994, for further discussion).

Evidence from several other chapters in this volume also points to a created rather than predetermined developmental destiny: Slobin's arguments against predetermined biases in favor of associations among semantic concepts and closed-class words; Bowerman's & Choi's evidence on the diversity of spatial concepts; and the considerable evidence in many chapters on crosslinguistic variation. All of these point to domain-specific knowledge first as a product of development and then as a cause that shapes development further.

In conclusion, development and cognition may be more wonderful than a diversity of mechanisms that is there to begin with. Children's initial generalizations of novel words present an intriguing case. These generalizations are smart; they are domain-specific, embodying knowledge about how kinds of words are mapped to kinds of objects. But the processes that make this domain-specific smartness may themselves be general and dumb.

NOTE

The research program reported in this chapter was supported by NIH grant HD28675.

REFERENCES

Aslin, R. N., & L. B. Smith. 1988. Perceptual development. In M. R. Rosenweig & L. W. Porter (eds.), *Annual Review of Psychology* 39: 435–474.

Au, T. K., & D. E. Laframboise. 1990. Acquiring color names via linguistic contrast: the influence of contrasting terms. *Child Development* 61: 1808–1823.

Au, T. K., & E. M. Markman. 1987. Acquiring word meaning via linguistic contrast. *Cognitive Development* 2: 217–236.

Ausabel, D. 1957. *Theories and problems of child development*. New York: Grune and Stratton.

Biederman, I. 1987. Recognition-by-components: a theory of human image understanding. *Psychological Review* 94: 115–147.

Chomsky, N. 1980. *Rules and representations*. New York: Columbia University Press.

Clark, E. V. 1973. What's in a word? On the child's acquisition of semantics in his first language. In T. E. Moore (ed.), *Cognitive development and the acquisition of language*. New York: Academic Press, 65-110.

Cooke, J. 1988. The early embryo and the formation of body pattern. *American Scientist* 76: 35–41.

Dromi, E. 1987. *Early lexical development*. New York: Cambridge University Press.

Fenson, L., P. Dale, J. S. Reznick, E. Bates, J. Hartung, S. Pethick, & J. Reilly. 1993. *MacArthur Communicative Development Inventories*. San Diego: Singular.

Fodor, J. A. 1975. *The language of thought*. New York: Thomas Y. Crowell.

1983. *The modularity of mind: an essay on faculty psychology*. Cambridge, MA: MIT Press.

Gasser, M., & L. B. Smith. 1991. The development of a notion of sameness: a connectionist model. In *Proceedings of the 13th Annual Conference of the Cognitive Science Society*. Hillsdale, NJ: Lawrence Erlbaum, 719–723.

1998. Learning nouns and adjectives: a connectionist account. *Language and Cognitive Processes* 13: 269–306.

Gelman, R. 1990. First principles organize attention to and learning about relevant data: number and the animate–inanimate distinction as examples. *Cognitive Science* 14: 79–106.

Gelman, S. A., & D. L. Medin. 1993. What's so essential about essentialism? A different perspective on the interaction of perception, language, and concrete knowledge. *Cognitive Development* 8: 113–139.

Gentner, D. 1978. What looks like a jiggy but acts like a zimbo?: a study of early word meaning using artificial objects. *Papers and Reports on Child Language Development* 15: 1–6.

Gershkoff-Stowe, L., & L. B. Smith. 1997. A curvilinear trend in naming errors as a function of early vocabulary growth. *Cognitive Psychology* 34: 37–71.

Gierer, A. 1981. Generation of biological patterns and form: some physical, mathematical, and logical aspects. *Progress in Biophysics and Molecular Biology* 37: 1–47.

Gleitman, L. 1986. Biological disposition to learn language. In W. Demopoulos & A. Marras (eds.), *Language learning and concept acquisition: foundational issues*. Norwood, NJ: Ablex, 3–28.

Gopnik, A., & A. N. Meltzoff. 1987. The development of categorization in the second year and its relation to other cognitive and linguistic developments. *Child Development* 58: 1523–1531.

Imai, M., D. Gentner, & N. Uchida. 1994. Children's theories of word meaning: the role of shape similarity in early acquisition. *Cognitive Development* 9: 45–76.

James, W. 1890. *The principles of psychology,* vol. 1. New York: Dover Publications, Inc.

Jones, S. S., & L.B. Smith. 1998. How children name objects with shoes. *Cognitive Development* 13: 323–334.

Jones, S. S., L. B. Smith, & B. Landau. 1991. Object properties and knowledge in early lexical learning. *Child Development* 62: 499–516.

Keil, F. C. 1989. *Concepts, kinds, and cognitive development.* Cambridge, MA: Bradford/MIT Press.

1994. Explanation, association, and the acquisition of word meaning. In L. R. Gleitman & B. Landau (eds.), *The acquisition of the lexicon.* Cambridge, MA: MIT Press, 169–196.

Kemler, D. G. 1978. Patterns of hypothesis testing in children's discriminative learning: a study of the development of problem-solving strategies. *Developmental Psychology* 14: 653–673.

Kruschke, J. K. 1992. ALCOVE: an exemplar-based connectionist model of category learning. *Psychological Review* 99: 22–44.

Landau, B., S. S. Jones, & L. B. Smith. 1992. Syntactic context and the shape bias in children's and adult's lexical learning. *Journal of Memory and Language* 31: 807–825.

Landau, B., L. B. Smith, & S. S. Jones. 1988. The importance of shape in early lexical learning. *Cognitive Development* 3: 299–321.

Leslie, A. M. 1994. ToMM, ToBY and Agency: core architecture and domain specificity. In L. A. Hirschfeld & S. A. Gelman (eds.), *Mapping the mind: domain specificity in cognition and culture.* Cambridge: Cambridge University Press, 119–148.

Lewicki, P., T. Hill, & I. Sasak. 1989. Self-perpetuating development of encoding biases. *Journal of Experimental Psychology: General* 118: 323–338.

MacIntosh, N. J. 1965. Selective attention in animal discrimination learning. *Psychological Bulletin* 64: 125–150.

Markman, E. M. 1989. *Categorization and naming in children: problems of induction.* Cambridge, MA: Bradford/MIT Press.

Marx, J. L. 1984a. New clues to developmental timing. *Science* 226: 425–426.

1984b. The riddle of development. *Science* 226: 1406–1408.

Massey, C., & R. Gelman. 1988. Preschoolers' ability to decide whether pictured unfamiliar objects can move themselves. *Developmental Psychology* 24: 307–317.

Medin, D. L., & W. D. Wattenmaker. 1987. Category cohesiveness, theories, and cognitive archeology. In U. Neisser (ed.), *Concepts and conceptual development.* Cambridge: Cambridge University Press, 25–62.

Mervis, C. B. 1987. Child-basic object categories and early lexical development. In U. Neisser (ed.), *Concepts and conceptual development: ecological and intellectual factors in categorization.* New York: Cambridge University Press, 201–233.

O'Reilly, R. C., & M. H. Johnson. 1994. Object recognition and sensitive periods: a computational analysis of visual imprinting. *Neural Computation* 6: 357–389.

Rescorla, R. A., & A. R. Wagner. 1972. A theory of Pavlovian conditioning: variations in the effectiveness of reinforcement and nonreinforcement. In A. H. Black & W. F. Prokasy (eds.), *Classical conditioning*, vol. 2. New York: Appleton-Century-Crofts.

Rosch, E. 1978. Principles of categorization. In E. Rosch & B. B. Lloyd (eds.), *Cognition and categorization*. Hillsdale, NJ: Lawrence Erlbaum, 28–46.

Smith, L. B. 1993. The concept of same. *Advances in Child Development and Behavior* 24: 216–253.

1995. Self-organizing processes in learning to learn words: development is not induction. *The Minnesota Symposia on Child Psychology*, vol. 28: *Basic and applied perspectives on learning, cognition, and development*. Mahwah, NJ: Lawrence Erlbaum, 1–32.

Smith, L. B., & D. Heise. 1992. Perceptual similarity and conceptual structure. In B. Burns (ed.), *Percepts, concepts, and categories*. Amsterdam: Elsevier, 233–272.

Smith, L. B., S. S. Jones, & B. Landau. 1992. Count nouns, adjectives, and perceptual properties in children's novel word interpretations. *Developmental Psychology* 28: 273–289.

Smith, L. B., & E. Thelen. 1993. *A dynamics system approach to development: applications*. Cambridge, MA: MIT Press.

Soja, N. N. 1992. Inferences about the meanings of nouns: the relationship between perception and syntax. *Cognitive Development* 7: 29–46.

Soja, N. N., S. Carey, & E. S. Spelke. 1991. Ontological categories guide young children's inductions of word meanings: object terms and substance terms. *Cognition* 38: 179–211.

Spelke, E. S., K. Breinlinger, J. Macomber, & K. Jacobson. 1992. Origins of knowledge. *Psychological Review* 99: 605–632.

Thelen, E., & L. B. Smith. 1994. *A dynamic systems approach to the development of cognition and action*. Cambridge, MA: MIT Press.

Waxman, S. R. 1994. The development of an appreciation of specific linkages between linguistic and conceptual organization. In L. R. Gleitman & B. Landau (eds.), *The acquisition of the lexicon*. Cambridge, MA: MIT Press, 229–250.

Waxman, S. R., & D. Markow. 1998. Object properties and object kind: twenty-one-month-old infants' extension of novel adjectives. *Child Development* 69: 1313–1329.

Wolpert, L. 1971. Positional information and pattern formation. *Current Topics in Developmental Biology* 6: 183–223.

Younger, B. 1990. Infants' detection of correlations among feature categories. *Child Development* 61: 614–621.

5 Perceiving intentions and learning words in the second year of life

Michael Tomasello

Emory University

Most studies of the cognitive bases of language acquisition are concerned with semantic content: how young children conceptualize the referents of particular linguistic items and expressions. But being able to conceive of all the possible referents another person might intend to indicate is not enough. To acquire the conventional use of a new linguistic item a learner must also be able to identify which of these conceivable referents another person is attempting to single out when using that item in a particular communicative circumstance. This raises issues of *social* cognition and how young children understand the intentional actions, including communicative actions, of other persons.

The process is never totally straightforward. The philosopher Wittgenstein (1953) noted that even an ostensive definition – the seemingly simplest case of language acquisition in which one person "shows" another what a word means – is problematic because it assumes that both teacher and learner know what "showing" is and precisely how it serves to pick out individual referents in some language-independent way. The point was crystalized by Quine (1960) in his parable of a native who utters the expression "Gavagai!" and "shows" a foreigner the intended referent by pointing out a salient event as it unfolds. Given the stipulation that native and foreigner have no way to establish a common view of the event nonlinguistically, however, there is basically no way that the foreigner can know whether the native's novel expression is being used to refer to the event, to some participant in the event, to some part of the participant's body, to the color of the participant's hair, or to any of an infinite number of aspects of the situation. This is the basic problem of referential indeterminacy.

In the modern study of language acquisition there are essentially two approaches to this fundamental problem of language acquisition: the constraints approach and the social-pragmatic approach. In this chapter my intention is to provide evidence for the social-pragmatic approach, and in particular for the view that to acquire linguistic conventions in the situations in which they encounter them, young children must have more powerful skills of social cognition than is generally recognized. In all cases the key social cognitive skill is children's ability to perceive the intentions of the adult as she acts and speaks to the child. In making my case I first outline the two predominant views of early word learning; I then summarize seven experimental studies in which 18- to 24-month-old children try to determine adults' referential intentions in complex interactive situations; and I conclude by arguing more generally that the understanding of intentions – specifically, the understanding that other persons have intentions towards my intentional states – is the very foundation on which language acquisition is built.

1 Two views of word learning

One approach to the problem of referential indeterminacy in the study of lexical acquisition is the so-called "constraints" approach (e.g. Markman 1989, 1992; Gleitman 1990). In this view a learner, who knows already what words are, attempts to acquire a new word by: (1) creating a list of possible hypotheses about how the new word "maps" onto the real world, and (2) eliminating incorrect hypotheses in a semi-scientific manner. In all cases the learner's goal is to perform the task correctly and so to acquire accurately the mapping between word and world. The problem is that, as the philosophers have pointed out, there are simply too many possible hypotheses to be tested in a given case. Therefore, the child must be given a headstart on the process. This headstart takes the form of word learning "constraints" that eliminate certain hypotheses before they are seriously entertained.

One possible constraint on the process is that young children may be biased to pay attention to only some things in the environment, and they may know prior to any language learning that these will be the first referents of adult words addressed to them. For example, in Markman's (1992) account, young children attend to whole objects more than to their parts, properties, or activities, and so they assume initially that novel words refer to whole objects. In this theory, children also know prior to language acquisition that two different words do not map onto the same real world object (mutual exclusivity); therefore, if an adult uses a new word in the presence of an object whose name they already know, children assume that something other than the name of that whole object is the word's referent. The theory does not specify how children determine precisely which other aspect of a situation is being referred to by a word that is not the name of a whole object (although see Golinkoff, Hirsh-Pasek, Mervis, *et al.* 1995, for some suggestions). Other constraints theorists believe that for some classes of linguistic item, especially verbs and other predicative terms, the key to lexical acquisition is information provided by children's *a priori* knowledge of syntax (syntactic bootstrapping; Gleitman 1990). In this view, the syntactic structures surrounding words, verbs in particular, provide additional constraints on their possible mappings to the world of events and states of affairs. Although no one has to my knowledge proposed a conjoining of the two theories, it is perhaps possible that children use both word learning biases and syntactic information to help constrain their hypotheses about the meaning of novel linguistic items and expressions.

By all accounts – including those of Markman and Gleitman – these word learning constraints cannot solve the problem of referential indeterminacy by themselves. They only work if used in conjunction with social-pragmatic information about another person's specific referential intentions in specific contexts. That is, even if the child knows that an adult is using a new piece of language to refer to a whole object or a certain type of event, there is still the problem that in many word learning situations there are multiple referents in the immediate context that fit within these specifications. One way to supplement the constraints account is thus to add a few very specific pragmatic cues that, in combination with the various word learning constraints, would be sufficient to enable the child to determine the referential significance of novel words. One obvious candidate is something like eye gaze direction. For example, in this account a child might know *a priori* that an adult is referring to a whole object, but would use gaze direction to specify which of several possible candidates is the intended referent (as in the studies of Baldwin 1991, 1993a). The problem with this supplemental account is simply that gaze direction is itself insufficient in many cases of word learning, as adults quite often talk to children about referents that are not visually accessible at all – for example, in referring to an absent object or in requesting actions that the child may or may not actually perform. And children do learn words in these contexts as several empirical studies demonstrate (Tomasello 1992a; Tomasello & Kruger 1992; and all of the studies to be reported in this chapter).

The social-pragmatic approach to the problem of referential indeterminacy takes a very different perspective on lexical acquisition. It begins by rejecting truth-conditional semantics in the form of the mapping metaphor (the child maps word onto world), adopting instead an experientialist and conceptualist view of language in which linguistic symbols are used by human beings to invite others to experience situations in particular ways. Thus, attempting to map word to world will not help in situations in which the very same piece of real estate, for example, may be called: *the shore* (by a sailor), *the coast* (by a hiker), *the ground* (by a skydiver), and *the beach* (by a sunbather) (Fillmore 1982; Langacker 1986; Lakoff 1987). In the social-pragmatic view, each of the world's natural languages has its own set of communicative conventions, in the form of linguistic symbols created over thousands of years of human history, by means of which its speakers attempt to influence the interest and attention of other members of their speech communities (Talmy 1996). There are also universals in the way symbols are created, learned, and used across languages, of course, reflecting universals both in the way human beings experience the world and in the ways they interact and communicate with one another socially. There is nothing in human languages other than these symbols – which include grammatical symbols and categories of symbols – and the experiences they symbolize (Langacker 1987, 1991).

In the social-pragmatic approach to language acquisition in general, and to referential indeterminacy in particular, the focus is on two aspects of the process: (1) the structured social world into which the child is born – full of scripts, routines, social games, and other patterned cultural interactions; and (2) the child's capacities for tuning into and participating in that structured social world (Tomasello 1992b). Language is one means by which adults exhort children to attend to certain aspects of a shared social situation. In attempting to comply with these exhortations – that is, in attempting to comprehend adult use of these symbols and so to have the requested experiences – children use all kinds of interpretive strategies based on the pragmatic assumption that adult linguistic symbols are somehow *relevant* to the ongoing social interaction (Bruner 1983; Sperber & Wilson 1986; Bloom 1993). In the social-pragmatic view, young children are not engaged in a reflective cognitive task in which they are attempting to make correct mappings of word to world based on adult input, but rather they are engaged in social interactions in which they are attempting to understand and interpret adult communicative intentions – so as to make sense of the current situation (Nelson 1985). Having complied with adult instructions to experience a situation in a particular way in a given instance, children may then learn to produce the appropriate symbols for themselves when they wish for others to experience a situation in that same way – thus entering into the world of bidirectionally (intersubjectively) understood linguistic symbols (Tomasello 1996).

In the social-pragmatic view, then, children acquire linguistic symbols as a kind of by-product of social interaction with adults, in much the same way they learn many other cultural conventions (Tomasello, Kruger, & Ratner 1993). The acquisition of linguistic symbols does not need external linguistic constraints in this theory because children are always participating in and experiencing particular social contexts, and it is these social contexts that serve to "constrain" the interpretive possibilities. The child who knows that his mother wishes him to eat his peas (she is holding them up to his mouth and gesturing) assumes that her utterance is relevant to that intention, and this is what guides his interpretations of any novel language in the utterance. All of the philosophically possible hypotheses that Quine and others may create are simply not a part of the child's experience in this particular social context – assuming of course that by the time language acquisition begins young children do indeed have a reasonably adult-like understanding of at least some aspects of the social activities in which they participate. And of course a prerequisite for word learning is the child's ability to conceptualize referents in a manner similar to adults; it is just that in the social-pragmatic view these conceptualizations are not tied to language *a priori*, as they are in the constraints view, but rather the child must learn the connections from participating in meaningful communicative interactions.

Some early studies in the social-pragmatic perspective focused on the role of the adult in the acquisition process. Thus, it was found that when adults name new objects for young children by following into their already-established focus of attention, as opposed to using the new language to direct their attention to something new, word learning is made easier (Tomasello & Farrar 1986; Dunham, Dunham, & Curwin 1993). But this does not mean that the child is a passive participant in the word learning process. Subsequent studies have shown that when there is a discrepancy between the focus of attention of adult and child – when young children hear a novel word in situations in which their focus of visual attention differs from that of an adult – learners nevertheless are able to do the extra work to determine the adult's referential intentions, almost never assuming that the new word is being used for whatever is their current focus of attention irrespective of what the adult is attempting to do (Baldwin 1991, 1993a). In all cases of word learning, children make active attempts to understand adult referential intentions; it is just that some situations make it easier or harder for them to do so.

My own biases, as alluded to above, are towards the social-pragmatic view. It seems to me that children do not learn words by employing mechanical mapping procedures or testing hypotheses, but rather that they learn them in the same basic way they learn other cultural skills and conventions: in the flow of naturally occurring social interaction in which both they and their interlocutors have various pragmatic goals towards the world and towards one another. Adults may do things that facilitate the learning process, but the child must always do some social cognitive work to determine the adult's referential intentions. Children learn words as an integral part of their social interactions with other persons, an important part of which are their attempts to understand what adults are trying to get them to do and their own attempts to get adults to do things (Bruner 1983; Nelson 1985; Tomasello 1992b).

2 Learning words "in the flow" of social interaction

In my view, one of the main reasons that researchers have been drawn to at least some aspects of the constraints view is that the prototypical case of word learning is assumed to be the learning of an object label in an ostensive context: an adult intends that a child learn a word and so "shows" her its referent (e.g. by holding up or pointing) in temporal contiguity with the utterance. In this case, the pragmatic understanding involved – that the adult intends to indicate the object held up or pointed to – is so basic and seemingly simple that it is often overlooked completely. However, when we turn our attention to the acquisition of words with more relational meanings – for example, verbs and prepositions in English – this picture of the basic word learning situation changes. Western middle-class adults use verbs to children most often to regulate or anticipate their behavior, not to name actions for them (Tomasello & Kruger 1992). In such cases, the pragmatic cues that might indicate the adult's intended referent are less straightforward than in the ostensive context, and indeed they change in fundamental ways from situation to situation: the adult requests for the child to eat her peas by directing the spoon at her face, but requests that the child give her something by holding out her hand. That is to say, there is no standardized "original naming game" for actions/verbs, as there is for some children learning object labels (Tomasello 1995a). In other cultures, the prototypical word learning situation is even more dramatically divergent from the classic ostensive context, as adults rarely stop what they are doing to name things for children at all, and in some cases speak directly to them only infrequently (Brown and de León, chs. 17 and 18, this volume).

It would thus seem from casual observation that young children are able to learn words in a wide variety of social-interactive situations that differ significantly from the ostensive context. In the studies that follow I attempt to demonstrate experimentally that this is indeed the case for children in their second year of life – that is, for children who have just caught on to the process of word learning and have begun to build their initial vocabularies. Moreover, by establishing something of the wide variety of situations in which these nascent language learners can acquire new words, I attempt to undermine any attempt to characterize the process as wedded to any specific pragmatic cues such as gaze direction. Instead, I argue that learning new words is dependent on young children's ability to perceive and comprehend adult intentions in a very flexible manner using many different types of social-pragmatic information. A result of this line of argumentation is that the process of word learning comes to be seen as, in essence, just another manifestation of processes of cultural learning in general, and, like other manifestations of cultural learning, it depends on children's basic skills of social cognition (Tomasello *et al.* 1993).

The experimental studies my collaborators and I have recently performed share a number of features. The basic idea in all cases is to set up situations in which adults talk to children as they engage in various games, with novel

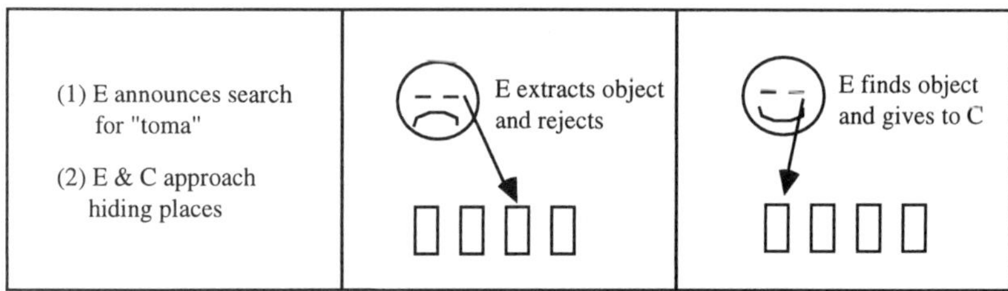

Fig. 5.1 The With Search condition in Tomasello & Barton (1994: Study 4).

words being introduced as naturally as possible into the ongoing flow of the game. In all cases there are multiple potential referents available; that is, there are multiple novel referents for which the child has no existing means of linguistic expression (this is checked before each study begins), and the novel word is introduced in a single type of linguistic context. Various pragmatic cues to the adult's intended referent are provided in different studies to see if children are indeed sensitive to them. The studies are designed so that none of the well-known word learning constraints that various investigators have proposed (e.g. whole object, mutual exclusivity, syntactic bootstrapping) will be helpful to the child in distinguishing among possible referents. The studies are also designed so that eye gaze direction is never diagnostic of the adult's referential intentions.

2.1 Determining which object the adult intends to find

In our first study of this type, Tomasello & Barton (1994, Study 4) had a female experimenter say to 24-month-old children, "Let's go find the toma," while looking directly into the child's eyes. The two of them then approached a row of five buckets. Each bucket contained a novel object, none of whose names the child knew beforehand, with the target object designated randomly across children. There were two experimental conditions. In the Without Search condition the adult went immediately to a bucket and excitedly found the target object and handed it to the child. In the With Search condition the adult went to the buckets, first extracted and rejected (by scowling at and replacing) two objects, and only then excitedly found and handed the child the target object (see figure 5.1). In both conditions the finding event was followed by the excited extraction of each of the other objects as the adult said "Let's see what's in this one." After several rounds of this procedure, comprehension and elicited production testing were conducted. The comprehension test consisted of the adult motioning in the general direction of all five objects (laid out in random order by a research assistant) and asking the child to bring her the toma. The elicited production task consisted of the adult holding up the target object and asking the child for its name (spontaneous productions at other times during the experiment were also recorded).

The outcome was that children learned the new word equally well in the two experimental conditions, both in comprehension and in production. Our interpretation of this result was as follows. Children could not have used a word learning cue such as "the object at which the adult is looking while saying the new word" because the adult was always looking into the child's eyes at this time. Nor could they have used some simple extension of this cue such as "the first object the adult looks at after uttering the new word" (or "first object the child sees"), because then they would have have performed better in the Without Search condition in which the target object was the first one extracted from the buckets; moreover, if they had used this cue in the With Search condition, they would have thought that the first object extracted and rejected was the toma (since the same object was always the first rejected object in all models for a given child) – which they did not, as they did not in a similar study by Baldwin (1993b). Because children performed equally well in the two conditions, our assumptions were that: (1) the children understood from the beginning that the adult's intention was to find a particular object called a toma; and (2) they tracked the adult's behavior and emotional expression until she seemed to fulfill that intention by expressing excitement and terminating the search (i.e, with the first object extracted in the Without Search condition and the third object extracted in the With Search condition). We do not know precisely which aspect of the adult's behavior was critical for the children – her excited demeanor or the termination of the search, for example – but in either case the adult's behavior was a meaningful cue precisely because it was an indication that she had fulfilled her intention to find the toma.

Akhtar & Tomasello (1996, Study 1) had 24-month-old children participate in a variation of this game. There were two main differences. The first was that one of the buckets in the row of five was actually a very distinctive toy barn (again there was a novel, nameless object hidden in each container). The second was that there were some initial rounds of a finding game (in which the adult used no new words), so that the child would come to know which object was in the toy barn (randomized across children). The procedure was thus as follows. The adult and child went through the buckets and barn several times extracting the objects, with the adult saying things like "Let's see what's in here." After these initial extractions, the language models began, with the locations of all objects remaining constant for a given child and the object in the barn always serving as the target object. In the language modeling rounds, the experimenter announced her

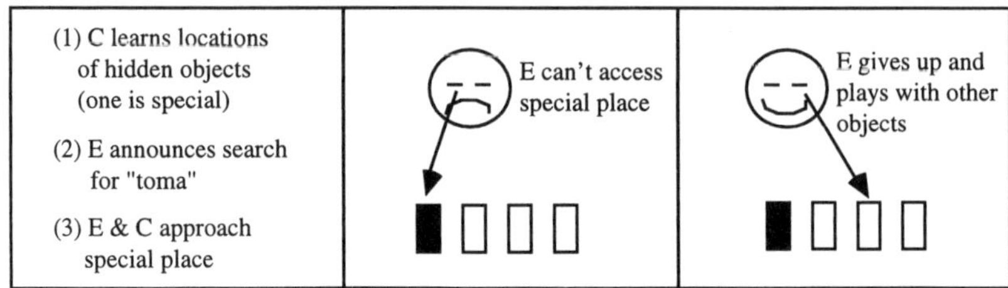

Fig. 5.2 The Absent Referent condition in Akhtar & Tomasello (1996: Study 1).

intention to find a specific object: "Now let's find the toma!" There were two experimental conditions. In the Referent condition, the experimenter proceeded directly to the barn and extracted the target object (then followed by extraction of the other objects). In the Absent Referent condition, she proceeded to the barn and attempted to open it, but after being unsuccessful (and looking disappointed) had to inform the child "It's locked. I can't open it" (followed by extraction of the other objects; see figure 5.2). Thus, children in the Absent Referent condition never saw the target object after hearing the novel word. Language modeling was followed in both conditions by comprehension testing and elicited production.

Once again the outcome was that children learned the new word equally well in the two experimental conditions. (As an additional control to make sure that children were actually learning the word additional subjects also participated in versions of the experimental conditions without the target language – the adult simply said of each container "Let's see what's in here" – and children performed at chance in the comprehension test.) As in the Tomasello & Barton study, this pattern of results indicated to us that (1) the children understood that the adult's intention was to find the toma, and (2) they then tracked her behavior and emotional expression in an attempt to determine when she had succeeded in doing so. In the Absent Referent condition, however, the adult did not succeed and thus never showed excitement in finding the target object – indeed she expressed her disappointment explicitly. Therefore, not only could children not have been using adult gaze direction, or "next object the adult sees," in this condition, they also could not have been using the adult's excitement as a cue; when the barn was locked the adult showed nothing but disappointment. Indeed, if they had used adult excitement as a cue, children would have inferred that the toma was the object extracted excitedly from the adjacent hiding place right after the failure, and almost no children did this. In this study children understood the adult's finding intention and used as a word learning cue her disappointment at her failure, remembering or imagining in the process what it was she had intended to find.

Taken together these two studies demonstrate that children have multiple ways of understanding adult intentions in finding games. Children come to the experiment knowing about finding as an intentional activity. They soon come to understand that the adult intends to find this thing called a toma. They then monitor the adult's behavior to see when she has fulfilled her intention. Across the two studies they must do this in different ways: in one study understanding that the object the adult is excited about is the toma, while in the other study understanding that the object never seen – the one the adult is disappointed in not finding – is the toma. The implication is thus that in both of these studies children are employing a very flexible social understanding of adults' actional and communicative intentions and how they play themselves out in different circumstances. Recently Tomasello, Strosberg, & Akhtar (1995) have extended these two findings to children eighteen months of age, demonstrating that these intentional understandings are not some late-developing word learning strategy, but rather are an integral aspect of children's word learning skills from very early in language development.

2.2 *Determining which action the adult intends to perform*

From the beginning of our thinking about the role of intentional understanding in word learning, the acquisition of verbs was seen as especially important. This is because many verbs (especially change-of-state verbs such as *give*, *put*, *make*, etc.) are only heard by young children as the adult requests an action of the child, anticipates the child's or her own impending action, or comments on a completed action – basically never using them in ostensive naming contexts (Tomasello & Kruger 1992). Verbs are thus the prototype of words that are experienced by children in the ongoing flow of social interaction with others.

In our first experimental study along these lines, Tomasello & Barton (1994, Study 3) exposed 24-month-old children to two novel verbs, one in each of two experimental conditions, both involving an impending action on an apparatus affording two actions. In the Target First condition an adult experimenter used a novel verb to announce her intention to perform a novel action on the apparatus, saying, for example, "I'm going to plunk Big Bird!" She then performed the target action intentionally, saying "There!", followed immediately by another action on that same apparatus performed "accidentally," in an awkward fashion, saying "Woops!" In the Target Last condition, the accidental action was performed first and the intentional action was performed second (see figure 5.3). (Because there

Fig. 5.3 The Target Last condition in Tomasello & Barton (1994: Study 3).

were two apparatuses, each with two possible actions, which actions were intentional and which were accidental – as well as the order of intentional and accidental actions – was totally counterbalanced across children.) After several models of this type, the child was given a new character and asked "Can you go plunk Mickey Mouse?", with both apparatuses present. There were also attempts to get the children to produce the new word as the adult performed the action.

Results demonstrated that the children quite readily associated the new action word with the adult's intentional action, regardless of whether it occurred immediately after the novel word or later, after an intervening accidental action. As in the previous studies, the exact cues the children might have been using to distinguish intentional and accidental actions were not identified precisely; the adult both acted differently and used a different vocal marker for the two types of action. But again, as in the previous studies, whatever cues they might have used, the children in this study apparently understood that the adult intended to plunk Big Bird, and they then tracked her behavior and emotional expressions to discover precisely what this plunking action might be.

Related to this finding is a study in which Akhtar & Tomasello (1996, Study 2) had an experimenter expose 24-month-old children to four novel actions using no new words. Each of these actions was uniquely associated with one and only one toy character and one and only one prop (e.g. catapulting was associated only with Ernie and only with a device for catapulting). Then came several language modeling rounds using a novel verb (the target) associated with one of the four actions (counterbalanced across children). There were two experimental conditions. For subjects in the Referent condition, the experimenter set out the target action prop and announced her intention to perform an action – for example "Let's pud Ernie!" She then proceeded to perform the target action (then followed by the other actions with their appropriate props and characters). For subjects in the Absent Referent condition, the experimenter also set out the target action prop and announced the same intention but, after searching, told the

Fig. 5.4 Absent Referent condition in Akhtar & Tomasello (1996: Study 2).

child she was unable to find Ernie and so she could not pud him (so she then went on to bring out the other props and characters and perform their respective actions; see figure 5.4). Children in this condition thus never saw the referent action after hearing the novel verb. Language modeling was followed in both conditions by comprehension testing and elicited production.

As in the very similar study with objects (see above), the outcome was that children learned the new word equally well in the two experimental conditions. (As an additional control to make sure that children were actually learning the word, additional subjects also participated in versions of the experimental conditions without the target language – the adult simply continued to say "Let's do this" – and they performed at chance in the comprehension test.) As in the similar study with objects, this pattern of results indicated to us that (1) the children understood that the adult's intention was to pud Ernie, and (2) they then tracked her behavior in an attempt to determine when she had done so. In the key condition, however, the adult never actually performed the action. Indeed, in the Absent Referent condition the next action the adult performed (after the disappointment of not being able to perform the target action) was one of the non-target actions. Thus, as in the similar study with objects, children in this study were able to understand in this highly scripted situation what the adult intended to do from her disappointment, without ever seeing the referent action paired with the novel verb.

These two studies with novel verbs thus demonstrate rather directly the role of children's understanding of intentional action in early word learning. Children know that adults use words to announce their intended actions, not their accidental actions (which would, of course, make no sense), and they have some ability in highly scripted situations to anticipate the adult's intended action even when it never actually happens and the adult shows disappointment – again evidencing a very flexible social understanding. We have not attempted these studies with younger children. However, two recent studies in which 16- and 18-month-old infants were asked to imitate novel actions on objects suggest that even at this younger age the ability to understand intentional action is present. In perfect parallel to the two verb-learning studies just reported: (1) Carpenter, Akhtar, & Tomasello (1998) found that 16-month-old infants were much more likely to imitate an adult's intentional than her accidental actions (cued mainly with the words "Woops!" and "There!" said with their appropriate intonations); and (2) Meltzoff (1995) found that 18-month-old infants were able to "imitate" full actions that the adult only initiated but did not complete (and thus the intention was never actually fulfilled). It is thus possible that children this young could learn novel verbs in our two experimental paradigms as well.

2.3 *Determining what is new for the adult*

In each of the studies just reported there was some set of pragmatic cues indicating which object or action the adult intended to indicate with her novel word. In a fifth study attempting to demonstrate the role of children's intentional understanding in the word learning process, Akhtar, Carpenter, & Tomasello (1996) set up a situation in which no special cues were associated with any one referent. In this study, 24-month-old children first played with three novel, nameless objects with two experimenters and a parent. The adults drew attention to each of the objects, handing them to the child and to one another excitedly, commenting on their characteristics, and in general playing with the objects enthusiastically. No language models were given during this initial play period. One experimenter and the parent then left the room while the child and the other experimenter played with a fourth object (the target) for an amount of time equal to that for which they had played with the other objects. The experimenter then set all four of the objects in a row, in random order. The other adults then returned. What they then did constituted the two experimental conditions. In the Language condition the adults looked at the group of objects (none singled out by gaze) and said: "Look, I see a gazzer! A gazzer!" (see figure 5.5). In the No Language condition the adults behaved the same but said: "Look, I see a toy! A toy!" (There was also another control study in which the novel object was not the last one the child played with.) In both conditions, the language model was later followed by a comprehension test in which the experimenter who had left the room asked the child to bring her the gazzer, and there was an elicited production question as well.

The main result of this study was that children learned the word for the target object in the Language condition, but they behaved randomly in the No Language condition. This result means that the children: (1) knew which object was novel for the adults who had left the room; and (2) knew

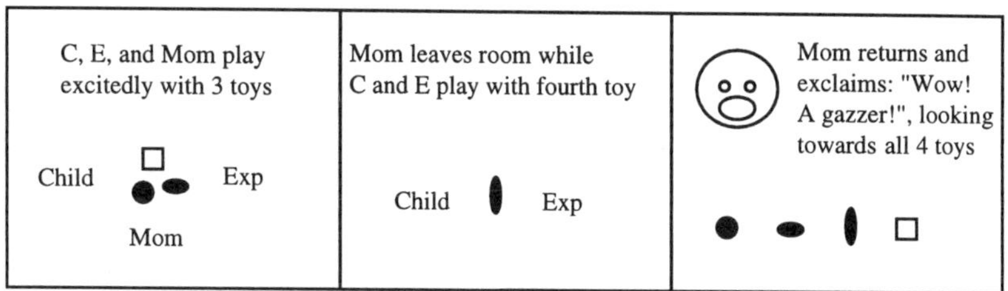

Fig. 5.5 The Language condition in Akhtar, Carpenter, & Tomasello (1996).

that adults only get excited about, and thus only use new language to talk about, things that are new to the discourse context. (Another way of expressing this second point is to say that the children knew that the adult had played with the other toys repeatedly previously and so it did not make sense for her to be excited about seeing them now, thus eliminating them as possible referents – analogous to the process of elimination in so-called "fast mapping" studies.) The important point is that the children in this study were able to single out the target object not on the basis of its being treated differently by the adults giving the language model; the pragmatic "cue" in this case was something much more distributed in terms of the child's understanding of the adults' experience during the entire experimental situation.

The power of this kind of understanding is underscored by another of our recent studies. Tomasello & Akhtar (1995, Study 1) were interested in whether children in this same general age range (24–26 months) could use their understanding of novelty from the adult point of view to help them determine to which ontological category a novel word might belong. The basic idea was that the language model would be given identically for all children – that is, using exactly the same language in exactly the same referential situation. What would differ across experimental conditions would be the experiences children had leading into that language model. There were two experimental conditions. In both conditions, children heard a novel word modeled as a one-word utterance ("Modi!") just as a nameless target object was engaging in a nameless target action. What preceded this model defined the experimental conditions. In the Action Novel condition, children initially performed several actions on the target object, so that when the language model was presented the target action was the novel element in the discourse context. (The "feel" was supposed to be something like: first we do this with it, then we do that with it, now we "modi".) In the Object Novel condition, children performed the target action on several objects so that when the language model was presented the target object

Fig. 5.6 Both experimental conditions in Tomasello & Akhtar (1995: Study 1).

was the novel element in the discourse context. (The "feel" was supposed to be something like: first we do it with this, then we do it with that, now we do it with "modi".) Figure 5.6 depicts both experimental situations.

There was an elicited production question and a comprehension test. The comprehension test was preceded by a pre-test (which actually took place at the very beginning of the experiment) in which children were given a cup, a spoon, and a ball. They were then asked to "Show me ball," "Show me bounce," and so forth, as a way of letting them know that with this one sentence frame ("Show me ____") we might be asking for either an object or an action. Most children showed clearly from the beginning a tendency to hold up or give objects when they were requested, and to perform actions when they were requested. (Any children who did not were trained to do so, or, in a few cases, dropped from the study.) The target comprehension test was thus "Show me modi" addressed to the child in the presence of multiple objects (all of which had been played with equally) and multiple possible actions (all of which had been performed equally). Results indicated that the children associated the word *modi* with the element that was new to the discourse context at the time of the model: children in the Action Novel condition associated *modi* with the target action, whereas children in the Object Novel condition associated *modi* with the target object. This finding is especially significant because it indicates for the first time that children's intentional understanding can even take them across ontological categories. That is, in all of the previous studies reported, children have understood from the outset that the adult was referring to either an object or an action and their task was to determine *which one*; in this study the child's task was to determine *what kind* of entity the adult intended to indicate with her novel language.

These two studies thus show that young children can use something like novelty to the discourse situation to determine adult referential intentions. In the first study children had to determine which one of a number of objects was new, and they had to do this totally from the adult's point of view. In the

<table>
<tr><td rowspan="2">E and C play with target object engaged in target action (no language)</td><td>Action Biasing: E prepares apparatus for C, alternates gaze between apparatus and C</td><td>Action Biasing: E says: "Your turn, Jason. Wigit!"</td></tr>
<tr><td>Object Biasing: E ignores apparatus, alternates gaze between object and C</td><td>Object Biasing: E says: "Wigit, Jason! Your turn."</td></tr>
</table>

Fig. 5.7 Both experimental conditions in Tomasello & Akhtar (1995: Study 1).

second study novelty was equal for both child and adult, but children had to use this novelty to determine what kind of entity, object or action, the adult intended to indicate. The ability to determine what is new in a situation for a potential communicative partner is of course not only an important skill in early word learning, it is also a crucially important skill in all aspects of language development as children learn to comprehend and produce utterances that are pragmatically appropriate to specific communicative contexts (e.g. for all kinds of topic-maintenance operations in discourse).

2.4 *Determining what the adult intends for me to do*

The final study in this series is Tomasello & Akhtar (1995, Study 2). The basic design is similar to that of the study just described: children saw a novel word modeled in a situation in which the adult might potentially be referring to either an object or an action. In this case, however, the adult behaved in a number of ways that differed between the two experimental conditions. To begin, all children saw an adult perform a novel and nameless action (target action) with a novel and nameless object (target object) on a special apparatus, and then they had the opportunity to perform the action with the object themselves – with no new words used at this time. Children in the Action Highlighted condition then watched as the adult prepared the apparatus so that the child could perform it again (by orienting the apparatus correctly for him). She then held out the object to the child and said "Your turn, Jason. Wigit!", while alternating her gaze between the child and the apparatus – as if requesting that the child perform the action. The experimenter behaved differently for children in the Object Highlighted condition. In this condition the experimenter did not prepare the apparatus for the child, and simply held out the object to the child and said "Wigit, Jason! Your turn," while alternating her gaze between the child and the object (never looking at the apparatus at all). Figure 5.7 depicts both of these conditions.

Elicited production and comprehension tests were then given, with the "Show me wigit" test, prepared by a pre-test, used to test comprehension as reported above (i.e. as in Tomasello & Akhtar, 1995, Study 1). The outcome was that children in the Action Highlighted condition learned the new word for the target action, whereas children in the Object Highlighted condition learned the new word for the target object. Once again a key aspect of this study was the fact that children did not know ahead of time whether we would be talking about a novel object or a novel action; it was only during the modeling itself that they learned the experimenter's referential intentions with respect to ontological category. The experimenter in this study did several things that differed in the two conditions: either prepared or did not prepare the apparatus, alternated gaze between the child and either the apparatus or the object, and said either "Your turn, Jason. Wigit!" or "Wigit, Jason! Your turn." Again in this case, therefore, we do not know the precise cue or cues used by children to determine the adult's referential intentions, but we do know that they used some aspects of the presented cue complex to distinguish situations in which the adult intended for them to perform an action from situations in which the adult intended to name an object for them.

It would also be interesting to perform this study, or something like it, with younger children. We have no experimental evidence that they could learn new words in this situation, but in Tomasello (1992a) I reported my daughter's acquisition of several verbs that seemingly were used by adults only in requestive situations (she sometimes complied and sometimes did not). A reasonable hypothesis is thus that even younger children could also learn novel verbs (at least in comprehension) from utterances in which adults request behaviors of them even if the actions are never actually performed – so long as the appropriate intention cues are present.

2.5 *Summary*

The fact that children can learn words in all of these different interactive situations – none of which consists of the adult stopping what she is doing to name something for the child – is a very important fact for theories of word learning (see table 5.1 for a summary). There are at least two possible explanations for this fact. On the one hand, it is possible that young children learn to deal with each of these learning situations separately – that is, they learn in each situation separately how the adult's new word "maps" onto one of the potential referents available: for example, through some kind of hypothesis-testing procedure with general *a priori* constraints, individual cue learning, and subsequent feedback. On the other hand, it is also possible that word learning is not a hypothesis-testing procedure needing to be

Table 5.1. *Some of the different sources of information by means of which children determine adult referential intentions in the second year of life – as evidenced by studies of word learning using experimental techniques*

Information from adult	Study
1. Directedness to an Object (including eyes, body, and voice)	Baldwin (1991, 1993a)
2. Expression of Intent and its Satisfaction (both objects and actions)	Tomasello & Barton (1994)
3. Expression of Intent + Event Knowledge (both objects and actions)	Akhtar & Tomasello (1996)
4. Expression of Surprise (new element for adult)	Akhtar *et al.* (1996)
5. Expression of Surprise (new element for adult across object–action boundary)	Tomasello & Akhtar (1995)
6. Expression of Intent Towards Child's Actions (across object–action boundary)	Tomasello & Akhtar (1995)

constrained at all, but rather it is a process of skill learning that builds upon a deep and pervasive understanding of other persons and their intentional actions (i.e., social cognition in general) that is available to children by the time language acquisition begins. This is the hypothesis to which we now turn.

3 Learning the first word

All of the studies just reported concern children in the 18- to 24-month age range. This is the period during which many children have a "vocabulary spurt" and thus would seem to be the period during which they have become skillful at learning new words – to the tune of several new words per day for many children. It is thus possible that what these studies represent is a set of acquired strategies for word learning that only become operative after a certain developmental period. In this scenario children's acquisition of their first words in the first half of the second year of life might not depend on an understanding of the intentional actions of others in the same way as does their word learning later in the second year. The other possibility is that, perhaps with some minor twists, the basic process of word learning is the same throughout early development. Indeed, in this view, the creation of linguistic conventions/symbols in the first place can only occur in organisms who understand their communicative partners as intentional agents. Children's learning of their first words is thus of a piece with their other social cognitive and cultural learning skills at this same developmental period early in the second year. This does not mean that word learning does not involve some additional complexities, only that it is not a completely modularized process in early development.

The story goes something like this. Human infants are social creatures from birth and so they clearly understand many things about other persons early in development. But they do not seem to understand other persons in terms of their intentional relations to the world. Five-month-old infants, for instance, do not do such things as following the gaze of others to outside entities or imitating their behavior on outside objects, preferring instead to focus on their own face-to-face interactions with others. All of this changes, however, at around the first birthday. Infants at this age begin for the first time to do such things as looking towards objects at which adults are looking (gaze following), monitoring adult emotional reactions to novel objects (social referencing), and acting on objects in the way adults act on them (imitative learning). All of these skills emerge in rough developmental synchrony because all of them reflect the infant's emerging ability to understand other persons as intentional agents whose attention, emotion, and behavior to outside objects may be actively followed into and shared (Tomasello 1995b). Experimental support for this view has recently been provided by the studies of Gergeley, Nádasdy, Csibra, & Biró (1995).

This social cognitive revolution at the infant's first birthday sets the stage for the second year of life in which it begins to learn imitatively the use of all kinds of tools and artifacts, with linguistic symbols being one special case. In all of these cases the imitative learning involved is not just a mimicking of adult body movements, and not just a reproducing of interesting environmental effects by whatever means imaginable, but rather it is an actual reproduction of the adult's intentional relations to the world. In these interactions the infant perceives the adult's overt actions as composed of both a goal and a means for attaining that goal, and then actively chooses the adult's means of goal attainment in contrast to others it might have chosen. For example, in a study by Meltzoff (1988) 14-month-old children observed an adult bend at the waist and touch her head to a panel, thus turning on a light. Most of them imitatively learned this somewhat awkward behavior, even though it would have been easier and more natural for them simply to push the panel with their hands. The supposition is that the infants understood that (1) the adult had the goal of illuminating the light, (2) chose one means for doing so, from among other possible means, and (3) if they had the same goal they could choose the same means. Imitative learning of this type thus relies fundamentally on infants' tendency to identify with adults, and on their ability to distinguish in the actions of others the underlying goal or intention and the different means that might be used to achieve it.

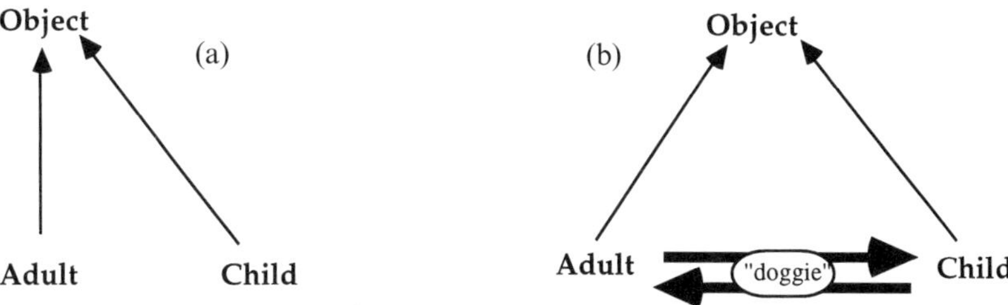

Fig. 5.8 (a) Adult acts on object and child imitatively learns that action. (b) Adult uses word to express intention (thick line) towards child's attention (thin line to object), and child imitatively learns that word with role reversal, thus creating a bidirectional linguistic convention/symbol.

This interpretation is supported by the recent finding of Meltzoff (1995) that 18-month-old infants also imitatively learn actions on objects that adults intend to perform, even if the adult is unsuccessful in actually performing them. It is likewise supported by Carpenter *et al.* (1998), who document that 16-month-old infants imitate adults' intentional actions on objects (indicated by "There!") and ignore their accidental actions (indicated by "Woops!") – in perfect parallel to the study of Tomasello & Barton (1994, Study 3 – as reported above).

The acquisition of linguistic symbols begins during this same developmental period quite simply because comprehending and producing language rely on the same basic understanding of persons as intentional agents as all of the other social cognitive and cultural learning skills that emerge at this same age. Nevertheless, linguistic symbols do have a special property. Unlike actions on objects, words are communicative actions directed to other persons; that is, words are social conventions and so involve a special application of social cognitive and cultural learning skills. This can be made clear by comparing the process by which infants imitatively learn an action on an object and the process by which they imitatively learn a linguistic convention.

Let us suppose that an infant observes an adult performing an intentional action on an object, and then imitatively learns that action herself. The process may be depicted as in figure 5.8a. Now suppose that an adult addresses a novel expression to a child, perhaps while pointing to an interesting event – for example, "A doggie!" The key is that the adult's intentional action in this case is not directed to the object, but rather to the child or, more specifically, to the child's intentions or attention. The child's comprehension of the adult's communicative act, therefore, requires an understanding that the adult is making this unfamiliar noise with the goal of getting me to do something intentional (i.e. focus my attention on some aspect of the ongoing event; see Gibson & Rader 1979, for the argument that attention is intentional perception). Once the child understands this communicative intention, a linguistic convention is created when she then acquires appropriate use of that communicative act herself. This process is similar to other acts of cultural learning in that the child understands and reproduces the adult's intentional act. It is different, however, in that the imitative learning of communicative acts involves a role reversal. If the child understands the adult's act as "She is making that sound in order to get me to attend to the doggie," then imitatively learning this act means that the child must reverse the roles: if *I* wish *others* to focus on the doggie *I* must use the sound "doggie" towards *them* (see figure 5.8b). As the child identifies with the adult and adopts her linguistic expression, of course, she retains the understanding that the adult also comprehends and uses it. The child's use of the expression thus creates a communicative convention, or symbol, whose essence is its bidirectionality or intersubjectivity (Saussure 1916), which constitutes the quality of being socially "shared" (Akhtar & Tomasello, in press).

It is important to note that not all communicative behaviors are bidirectional and shared in this same way. Thus, prelinguistic infants use a number of communicative gestures that are ritualized from noncommunicative behaviors; for example the "hands-up" gesture as a request to be picked up may be a ritualization of the infant trying to pull its way up to the parent's arms. There is no evidence that prelinguistic infants learn this gesture by imitative learning, or even that they comprehend these early gestures when they are produced by another person; if they do not, they cannot be viewed as bidirectional communicative conventions. The same may even be true of some of children's earliest "words," which may be learned through ritualization as well. That is, children may have some early "words" that they have acquired by simply mimicking an adult sound and then the adult responds in some predictable and interesting way. These so-called pre-symbolic forms are often characterized as being simply a part of an activity, not a symbol standing for anything else in the activity (Bates 1979). If they are of this nature, and they are not truly conventional (the child does not understand the adult's understanding of them), they are best called vocal signals.

The argument is thus that the child's earliest words depend in fundamental ways on her ability to perceive and understand the actions of other persons as intentional, and especially her ability to understand that other persons act intentionally towards her intentional states. It could be argued, of course, that this account does not solve the mystery of referential indeterminacy, but simply shifts it to a new domain: how does the child understand the intentions of others when they can be interpreted in many ways as well (Levinson 1995)? There are a number of different views of this problem, but my own view is that the process must get started by the infant recognizing in other persons intentions that are in some sense "the same" as intentions that she has experienced herself in her own intentional actions (Tomasello 1995b). In any case, even if the process of intention reading is at this point as mysterious as the process of linguistic reference that it is supposed to solve, at least the mystery is localized appropriately, in my view, so that future investigators will know where to look for more definitive answers. I should add that although some constraints theorists have discussed the problem of how children initially come to understand linguistic reference (e.g. Markman 1989; see also the Golinkoff *et al.* 1993 proposal for word learning principles), none has provided a satisfactory account beyond the proposal of Macnamara (1982) that reference is an ontogenetic "given."

A final question is whether, in addition to social-pragmatic information, children need word learning constraints (Woodward & Markman 1998). It could reasonably be argued that the child's understanding of adult communicative intentions presupposes a bias in making certain ontological distinctions – for example, a bias towards whole objects when the child understands the adult to be directing her attention to a doggie. But we must be very clear that what distinguishes the constraints position is not the claim that children are biased to conceptualize the world in certain ways – that is a claim that no theory of intersubjective communication can do without – but the claim that certain conceptualizations are tied to language in specific ways *a priori.* The social-pragmatic approach recognizes explicitly that the process of word learning depends fundamentally on the child being biased to conceptualize the world in certain ways (similar to adults' conceptualizations), it is just that the connection of conceptualizations to language must be learned in communicative interactions with others.

4 Conclusion

My argument may be summarized in an ontogenetically forward direction as follows. In the first half of the second year of life young children begin to learn language. The major social cognitive skill that underlies their ability to do this is their understanding of the intentional actions of others, especially their understanding that other persons have intentions towards their intentional states. Children's ability to reproduce these intentional communicative actions via some form of cultural or imitative learning involves a role reversal – the child has intentions towards the other person's intentional states – which leads to the creation of linguistic conventions. Linguistic conventions are most clearly distinguished from other forms of communication precisely by virtue of their bidirectional or "shared" nature. Then, in the second half of the second year of life, young children go on to become more and more skilled at determining precisely what are the referential intentions of others in particular situations. They learn to do this in all kinds of ongoing social interactions, whose complexity and diversity preclude the possibility that this learning is of a straightforward mechanical variety in which word is mapped to world – either with or without *a priori* constraints.

Perhaps due in part to the attention paid to children's so-called "theories of mind" at four years of age (involving their understanding of the beliefs of others), the importance of infant understanding of other persons' intentions as a social cognitive skill is only now being fully realized. Its great importance can perhaps best be appreciated when human children are compared with other organisms who do not possess this skill. Thus, the naturally occurring gestures of our nearest primate relative, the chimpanzee, resemble human gestures and words in a number of ways, but they are also different in a number of important ways as well. Most importantly for current purposes, chimpanzees in their natural habitats do not seem to acquire their skills of gestural communication via any form of cultural or imitative learning, but rather by ritualization, and so they do not develop any communicative conventions that are bidirectionally shared (Tomasello & Camaioni, 1997). There are various lines of evidence that chimpanzees do not understand others as intentional agents and that this is why they do not form such conventions, although chimpanzees raised and treated intentionally by humans may move some distance in this direction (Tomasello 1998). The same general point may be made about severely autistic children who, because of their biological deficit, do not seem to be skilled at understanding others as intentional agents with whom they may share attention, and so many of them learn little conventional language as a result (Landry & Loveland 1986).

Children's amazing skills at determining the specific referential intentions of adults in specific communicative circumstances are only now being fully appreciated. Indeed, in addition to the many and varied word learning contexts represented by the experimental studies summarized in this chapter, there is also observational evidence that children in some, perhaps many, of the world's cultures even tune into the flow of social interaction between third parties and learn some linguistic conventions from *their* linguistic interactions (Brown and de León, chs. 17 and 18, this volume). Acquisition in this circumstance also depends on children's ability to perceive and understand the communicative intentions of others, but the specific social information used may be different. And we should not neglect, in all of this concern with understanding nonlinguistic intentions, that, as children learn more language, language itself provides additional information for understanding the intentions of others. For example, as children learn a number of words in a particular semantic domain, acquiring new words in that domain becomes easier as a new word's communicative significance may be contrasted with that of the known words – perhaps on the pragmatic inference that people use new terms for new communicative intentions (Clark 1988). In addition, as children become grammatically more sophisticated, the linguistic context within which they hear new words becomes an increasingly important source of information as well (Brown 1973; Gleitman 1990).

Although there is no room to make the argument fully here, it is also important that children's later development in the more grammatical aspects of language may also be seen in these same intentional terms if grammatical competence is viewed in functional terms. In this case the process may be seen again as adults using linguistic forms with communicative functions, which children then appropriate for their own use by means of some form of cultural or imitative learning (Tomasello & Brooks 1999). It is just that in this case the linguistic forms they are learning are relatively abstract (e.g. tense markers), or else they are whole linguistic constructions, many of which are only categorically and schematically specified. The communicative function of linguistic constructions that guides the learning process is the symbolization of whole events with their participants, providing specific perspectives on those events and participants given the particularities of the current discourse context (Clark 1990). This process is especially clear in children's earliest linguistic constructions, which remain tied very concretely to specific events and the words used to talk about them (Tomasello 1992a).

To conclude, I will simply reiterate my view that the cognitive foundations for language acquisition are two: (1) children's growing ability to conceptualize the world in something like the same way as adults, and (2) children's growing ability to understand adults' communicative intentions towards particular aspects of that world in particular communicative circumstances. Future research on the cognitive bases of language acquisition should pursue the ontogeny of both of these cognitive foundations with equal vigor.

NOTE

Thanks to Steve Levinson and Melissa Bowerman for very helpful comments on an earlier version of this chapter.

REFERENCES

Akhtar, N., M. Carpenter, & M. Tomasello. 1996. The role of discourse novelty in children's early word learning. *Child Development* 67: 635–645.

Akhtar, N., & M. Tomasello. 1996. Twenty-four-month-old children learn words for absent objects and actions. *British Journal of Developmental Psychology* 14: 79–93.

1999. Intersubjectivity in early language learning and use. In S. Braaten (ed.), *Intersubjective communication and emotion in ontogeny*. Cambridge: Cambridge University Press, 316–335.

Baldwin, D. A. 1991. Infants' contribution to the achievement of joint reference. *Child Development* 62: 875–890.

1993a. Infants' ability to consult the speaker for clues to word reference. *Journal of Child Language* 20: 395–418.

1993b. Early referential understanding: young children's ability to recognize referential acts for what they are. *Developmental Psychology* 29: 1–12.

Bates, E. 1979. *The emergence of symbols: cognition and communication in infancy.* New York: Academic Press.

Bloom, L. 1993. *The transition from infancy to language: acquiring the power of expression.* Cambridge: Cambridge University Press.

Brown, R. 1973. *A first language: the early stages.* Cambridge, MA: Harvard University Press.

Bruner, J. S. 1983. *Child's talk: learning to use language*. New York: Norton.

Carpenter, M., N. Akhtar, & M. Tomasello. 1998. Sixteen-month-old infants differentially imitate intentional and accidental actions. *Infant Behavior and Development* 21: 315–320.

Clark, E. 1988. On the logic of contrast. *Journal of Child Language* 15: 317–336.

1990. Speaker perspective in language acquisition. *Linguistics* 28: 1201–1220.

Dunham, P. J., F. S. Dunham, & A. Curwin. 1993. Joint attentional states and lexical acquisition at 18 months. *Developmental Psychology* 29: 827–831.

Fillmore, C. 1982. Frame semantics. In Linguistic Society of Korea (ed.), *Linguistics in the morning calm.* Seoul: Hanshin, 111–138.

Gergely, G., Z. Nádasdy, G. Csibra, & S. Biró. 1995. Taking the intentional stance at 12 months of age. *Cognition* 56: 165–193.

Gibson, E., & N. Rader. 1979. Attention: the perceiver as performer. In G. Hale & M. Lewis (eds.), *Attention and cognitive development.* New York: Plenum Press, 6–36.

Gleitman, L. R. 1990. The structural sources of verb meanings. *Language Acquisition* 1: 3–55.

Golinkoff, R., K. Hirsh-Pasek, C. B. Mervis, W. Frawley, & M. Parillo. 1995. Lexical principles can be extended to the acquisition of verbs. In M. Tomasello & W. E. Merriman (eds.), *Beyond names for things: young children's acquisition of verbs*. Hillsdale, NJ/Hove: Lawrence Erlbaum, 185–221.

Golinkoff, R. M., C. B. Mervis, & K. Hirsh-Pasek. 1994. Early object labels: the case for a developmental lexical principles framework. *Journal of Child Language* 21: 125–155.

Lakoff, G. 1987. *Women, fire, and dangerous things: what categories reveal about the mind.* Chicago: University of Chicago Press.

Landry, S., & K. Loveland. 1986. Joint attention in autism and developmental language delay. *Journal of Autism and Developmental Disorders* 16: 335–349.

Langacker, R. W. 1986. An introduction to cognitive grammar. *Cognitive Science* 10: 1–40.

1987. *Foundations of cognitive grammar*, vol. 1. Stanford, CA: Stanford University Press.

1991. *Foundations of cognitive grammar*, vol. 2. Stanford, CA: Stanford University Press.

Levinson, S. 1995. Interactional biases in human thinking. In E. Goody (ed.), *Social intelligence and interaction.* Cambridge: Cambridge University Press, 221–260.

Macnamara, J. 1982. *Names for things: a study of human learning.* Cambridge, MA: MIT Press.

Markman, E. M. 1989. *Categorization and naming in children: problems of induction.* Cambridge, MA: Bradford/MIT Press.

1992. Constraints on word learning: speculations about their nature, origins, and word specificity. In M. Gunnar & M. Maratsos (eds.), *Modularity and constraints in language and cognition.* Hillsdale, NJ: Lawrence Erlbaum, 59–102.

Meltzoff, A. 1988. Infant imitation after a 1-week delay: long term memory for novel acts and multiple stimuli. *Developmental Psychology* 24: 470–476.

1995. Understanding the intentions of others: re-enactment of intended acts by 18-month-old children. *Developmental Psychology* 31: 838–850.

Nelson, K. 1985. *Making sense: the acquisition of shared meaning.* New York: Academic Press.

Quine, W. V. O. 1960. *Word and object*. Cambridge, MA: MIT Press.

Saussure, F. de. 1916. *Course in general linguistics.* New York: Philosophical Library.

Sperber, D., & D. Wilson. 1986. *Relevance: communication and cognition.* Cambridge, MA: Harvard University Press.

Talmy, L. 1996. The windowing of attention in language. In M. Shibatani & S. Thompson (eds.), *Grammatical constructions: their form and meaning.* Oxford: Oxford University Press, 235–238.

Tomasello, M. 1992a. *First verbs: a case study of early grammatical development.* Cambridge: Cambridge University Press.

1992b. The social bases of language acquisition. *Social Development* 1: 67–87.

1995a. Pragmatic contexts for early verb learning. In M. Tomasello & W. E. Merriman (eds.), *Beyond names for things: young children's acquisition of verbs.* Hillsdale, NJ/Hove: Lawrence Erlbaum, 115–146.

1995b. Joint attention as social cognition. In C. Moore & P. Dunham (eds.), *Joint attention: its origins and role in development*. Hillsdale, NJ/Hove: Lawrence Erlbaum, 103–141.

1996. The cultural roots of language. In B. Velichkovsky & D. Rumbaugh (eds.), *Communicating meaning: the evolution and development of language.* Mahwah, NJ: Lawrence Erlbaum.

1998. Social cognition and the evolution of culture. In J. Langer & M. Killen (eds.), *Piaget, evolution, and development.* Mahwah, NJ: Lawrence Erlbaum, 221–246.

Tomasello, M., & N. Akhtar. 1995. Two-year-olds use pragmatic cues to differentiate reference to objects and actions. *Cognitive Development* 10: 201–224.

Tomasello, M., & M. Barton. 1994. Learning words in non-ostensive contexts. *Developmental Psychology* 30: 639–650.

Tomasello, M., & P. J. Brooks. 1999. Early syntactic development: a construction grammar approach. In M. Barrett (ed.), *The development of language.* Hove: Psychology Press, 161–190.

Tomasello, M., & L. Camaioni. 1997. A comparison of the gestural communication of apes and human infants. *Human Development* 40: 7–24.
Tomasello, M., & J. Farrar. 1986. Joint attention and early language. *Child Development* 57: 1454–1463.
Tomasello, M., & A. Kruger. 1992. Joint attention on actions: acquiring verbs in ostensive and non-ostensive contexts. *Journal of Child Language* 19: 311–334.
Tomasello, M., A. C. Kruger, & H. H. Ratner. 1993. Cultural learning. *Behavioral and Brain Sciences* 16: 495–552.
Tomasello, M., R. Strosberg, & N. Akhtar. 1995. Eighteen-month-old children learn words in non-ostensive contexts. *Journal of Child Language* 22: 1–20.
Wittgenstein, L. 1953. *Philosophical investigations.* New York: MacMillan.
Woodward, A. L., & E. M. Markman. 1998. Early word learning. In W. Damon, D. Kuhn, & R. S. Siegler (eds.), *Handbook of child psychology*, vol. 2: *Cognition, perception, and language.* New York: John Wiley, 371–420.

6 Roots of word learning

Paul Bloom

Yale University

1 Introduction

What aspects of the child's mind are devoted to solving the problem of word learning? That is, what biases or constraints exist solely for the purpose of lexical acquisition?

In this chapter, I will argue that there are none. This is in contrast to two related proposals. The first is that there exist innate constraints on word learning that are part of a specialized language faculty. This is a natural extension of nativist theories of the acquisition of syntax. It is admittedly hard to find scholars who will explicitly endorse this position in its strongest form. But it is an idea that is in the air, so much so that even though nobody defends it, there are attacks on it – by Nelson (1988, 1990) for instance, who argues that certain constraint proposals, such as those developed by Markman and her colleagues (e.g. Markman & Hutchinson, 1984), entail an unrealistically nativist perspective on lexical development. Tomasello (ch. 5 of this volume) argues against these proposals on similar grounds.

In contrast, the second type of constraint proposal is very influential within developmental psychology, and is often endorsed by the same scholars who reject the nativist proposal. This view asserts that there do exist special constraints (or "biases," or "assumptions"; in this chapter I will use the terms interchangeably) on word learning, but that these are learned by the child. Under one intriguing version of this proposal, they are learned through a connectionist architecture that captures correlations between linguistic and perceptual input (Smith, ch. 4 of this volume).

Why posit special constraints on word learning? Under a nativist perspective, the child is assumed to need such constraints to solve the problem of indeterminacy inherent in learning any novel word – a problem outlined in different ways by Quine (1960) and Goodman (1983). This argument is plainly not available to those who would argue that special constraints are not innate, since these theorists claim it is through the acquisition of at least some words that the constraints are learned in the first place (e.g. Landau,

Smith, & Jones 1988). Instead a learning theorist might propose that although constraints are not necessary for word learning, they facilitate the process once acquired. Based on this theory, one could posit the following pattern of development: before children have much experience with words, lexical acquisition is slow and laborious and then, once they have learned the constraints, it becomes rapid and efficient. Some scholars argue that this is precisely what happens (e.g. Nelson 1988; but see Huttenlocher & Smiley 1987, for a different view).

This chapter will defend an alternative to both the nativist and the learning versions of the special constraints view. I will propose that children and adults learn the meanings of words through more general cognitive capacities. These include a rich system of conceptual representations, the capacity to infer the intentions of others, and a sensitivity to syntactic cues to word meaning. But there are no such things as constraints, assumptions, biases, etc., that are special to the problem of word learning. This is not to deny that word learning is by necessity constrained; of course any successful inductive process must be constrained. But the fact that the learning of a domain is constrained does not entail that there exist constraints special to this domain. After all, the learning of chess is also by necessity constrained, but nobody would suggest that there are (innate or learned) constraints that are special to the problem of chess acquisition. I will suggest that the same holds for word learning. Such a position entails that the systems underlying word learning (conceptual, intentional, and syntactic) have considerable richness, even at an early age, and one of the burdens of this chapter is showing why that is a reasonable claim to make.

I will discuss three phenomena from the domain of word learning: children's ability to acquire aspects of the meaning of a word rapidly on the basis of only a few exposures ("fast mapping"); their tendency to treat a new word as referring to a kind of whole object; and their tendency to generalize a new object name on the basis of shape. The argument in each of these domains is identical – one can explain more of the data, and can do so in a less *ad hoc* manner, by giving up the idea of special constraints and instead viewing the developmental phenomena as resulting from more general aspects of human learning and cognition.

2 Fast mapping

One motivation for suggesting that people have special cognitive mechanisms for learning words, either innate or learned, is how good we are at this sort of learning. Putting aside worries about how we cope with the infinity of logically possible meanings that any new word can have, the difficulty of parsing the speech stream, and the puzzle of how we learn to establish the correct mappings between sound and meaning, the sheer *numbers* are impressive. The average adult speaker of English knows over 60,000 distinct morphological forms (Anglin 1993). Children start to learn words at about the age of twelve months, and so this entails that they they learn an average of ten new words a day – a new word every waking ninety minutes (Anglin 1993; Pinker 1994).

Children not only learn many words, they learn them quickly and efficiently. Both experimental and anecdotal evidence suggest that they can come to grasp aspects of the meaning of a new word on the basis of only a few incidental exposures, without any explicit training or feedback – even without ostensive naming. This process has been dubbed "fast mapping" by Carey (1978). In the first study to explore this phenomenon systematically, Carey & Bartlett (1978) casually introduced a new color word to three- and four-year-old children who were involved in another, unrelated, activity. The children were asked by the experimenter to walk over to two trays, a blue one and an olive one, and to "Get me the chromium tray, not the blue one, the chromium one." All of the children retrieved the olive tray, correctly inferring that the experimenter intended *chromium* to refer to this new color. Furthermore, most of the children remembered some of the meaning of *chromium* when tested six weeks later, either the precise color which the new word described (olive) or, more often, just that the new word was a color term, forgetting precisely which color it picked out.

How does fast mapping work? What are its limits; under what circumstances does it work best? Oddly, despite the prominence of the Carey & Bartlett study, and even though there have been countless subsequent studies in which children have been taught new words and then tested for what they think these words mean, nobody has yet attempted to replicate the most central feature of the original study – the long delay between exposure to the new word and testing for its retention. Giving a child a new word and then immediately exploring how she extends the word, as is done in virtually all word learning studies, is a fine way of exploring the nature of children's conceptual and linguistic biases. But it is a poor way to learn about the retention capacity so manifest in normal word learning. As it stands, then, certain basic questions about word learning remain unanswered.

For one thing, color names constitute a relatively narrow domain, with universal constraints on the terms that exist and the order in which they are acquired (Berlin & Kay 1969). In contrast, there are thousands of object names, and these show more variability across cultures, as their referents include foods (*apple*, *bagel*), animals (*dog*, *snake*), artifacts (*clock*, *car*), and so on. It is a natural question whether fast mapping applies in this less constrained domain. If so, there is the further question of whether – after a suitably long interval following the initial exposure – children will be able to learn the correct and complete meaning of the object label or whether they will remember that a new word refers to an object, but not remember precisely which object, analogous to the results from Carey & Bartlett's study with color words.

Also, is there any difference between children's and adults' abilities to fast map? One might expect adults to be better, since they have had more experience acquiring words and are typically superior at learning and memory tasks. Nevertheless, young children are notably superior to adults at successful acquisition in the linguistic domains of phonology, morphology, and syntax (Newport 1990), and it is conceivable that a similar "critical period" might exist in lexical acquisition.

Finally, and most relevant to the topic of this chapter, it is an open question whether the ability to fast map is the result of a distinct capacity specialized for this purpose. Children's capacity to learn new words quickly on the basis of limited experience is sometimes cited as a demonstration of their impressive ability in the domain of language (e.g. Pinker 1994) – a position congenial to both nativist and learning proponents of the special constraints view. But it is also possible that children's abilities emerge through general capacities of human learning and memory. This issue can be addressed by exploring whether fast mapping of arbitrary information occurs with equal force in contexts other than word learning.

Lori Markson and I (Markson & Bloom, 1997) addressed these issues in an experiment similar to the original fast mapping study. Forty-eight three-year-olds, forty-seven four-year-olds and forty-eight adults first participated in a sequence of activities in which they measured different objects in a variety of ways. There were ten kinds of objects, six of them novel (in the sense that children and adults would find them unfamiliar and not be able to name them), and four of them familiar, such as pennies. Subjects were asked to use some of these objects to measure other objects. For instance, in one of the tasks, subjects were requested to use pennies to measure the circumference of a plastic disk. Children were told that this was a game, and adults were told that this was a game designed to teach young children how to measure objects.

In the course of this training phase, all subjects were exposed to a new word – *koba* – which referred to either one unfamiliar object or several identical unfamiliar objects. The word was presented in contexts such as the following: "Let's use the kobas to measure which is longer. Line up the kobas so we can count them. We can put the kobas away now." In addition to the new word, half of the subjects were given a linguistically presented fact. They were told that one or more of the novel objects was given to the experimenter by her uncle: "We can use the things my uncle gave to me to measure which is longer. My uncle gave these to me. We can put the things my uncle gave to me away now." The other half of the subjects were given a visually presented fact. They watched as a sticker was placed on one of the unfamiliar objects, and were told: "Watch where this goes. This goes here [placing the sticker onto one of the objects]. That's where this goes."

One-third of the subjects were tested immediately after this training phase, one-third after a one-week delay, and one-third after a one-month delay. During this test phase, subjects were presented with the original array of ten items (six novel and four familiar; only one object from each kind) used during the training phase. All subjects were asked to recall which object was the koba ("Is there a koba here? Can you show me a koba?"). Those subjects originally taught the linguistically presented fact were also asked: "Is there something here that my uncle gave to me? Can you show me something that my uncle gave to me?" Subjects originally exposed to the visually presented fact were handed a small sticker and requested to: "Put this where it goes. Can you show me where this goes?"

The main results were as follows (see Markson & Bloom 1997, for full analyses and discussion).

- In the new word task, children and adults in all three delay conditions performed significantly above chance. Even after one month, three-year-olds and four-year-olds were doing as well as adults, and all age groups remembered which object corresponded to *koba* over half of the time. Fast mapping for words thus extends to object names; it is not limited to color terms.
- In the linguistically presented fact task, all age groups again performed significantly better than chance in all delay conditions. There were no age differences and no significant declines across delay conditions. Thus fast mapping is not limited to words.
- In contrast, in the visually presented fact task, adult performance was considerably diminished after any delay, and the three-year-olds and four-year-olds, taken together, showed a significant decline over time, and did significantly worse than in the other two conditions. Also, unlike the other two tasks, only the adults performed significantly better than chance after a one-month delay; the children's performance was indistinguishable from guessing.

We can now return to the three questions raised earlier. First, the long-term retention of information via fast mapping does apply in the domain of object names. Even after a one-month interval, most children and adults retained the meaning of a novel object label that was presented to them in an incidental context. Second, there does not appear to be a critical period for fast mapping. There is no long-term advantage in word learning for either adults or children, at least for the time intervals used here. Finally, fast mapping is not limited to word learning. Children and adults were as good at remembering an arbitrary linguistically presented fact about an entity as they were at remembering its name. Nevertheless, fast mapping does not apply to any arbitrary memorization task, as illustrated by the children who, after a one-month delay, were unable to recall which object a sticker was applied to. (It is unclear why there was no fast mapping in the visually presented fact task; see Bloom 2000 for discussion.)

These findings do not refute the claim that there is a dedicated mechanism for word learning, as it is possible that there are *two* distinct mechanisms explaining our findings, one underlying the new word task, the other underlying the non-lexical "Uncle" task. But why would we possess such a word-specific mechanism if more general mechanisms suffice? That is, since children and adults seem to have a general ability to fast map, there is no motivation to posit a separate mechanism that applies just in the domain of word learning. The lack of a critical period for word learning also suggests a more parsimonious conclusion: the capacity to learn and retain new word meanings is the result of more general mechanisms of learning and memory that both children and adults possess.

3 The bias to treat new words as referring to object kinds

3.1 Arguments for and against special constraints

What about the actual constraints on children's hypothesis space that dictate precisely how they construe the meaning of a new word? The act of interpreting the meanings of new words is perhaps where special constraints are most likely to apply.

In particular, scholars of language acquisition have long known that names for kinds of whole objects have a special status in word learning. There is a wealth of evidence that children and adults tend to interpret new words as referring to kinds of whole objects – not to parts of objects, properties of objects, or the stuff that objects are made out of (e.g. Gentner 1982; Macnamara 1982; Markman & Hutchinson 1984; Soja, Carey, & Spelke 1991; Waxman & Markow 1995).

One explanation for this phenomenon is that children possess a "whole object assumption" (biasing in favor of the whole object interpretation) and a "taxonomic assumption" (biasing in favor of the "kind" interpretation). These are specific to the process of word learning and not the result of more general principles of sorting or categorization (e.g. Markman & Hutchinson 1984; Markman 1990).

What about words that are not object labels? Markman & Wachtel (1988) posit a further constraint stipulating that two distinct words cannot have overlapping extensions ("Mutual Exclusivity"). This is false as a property of natural language since there are words such as *dog* and *animal* that have overlapping extensions. It could nevertheless exist as a probabilistic bias that sometimes serves to override the whole object and taxonomic constraints. In particular, once a child has already acquired a name for a kind of object (such as *dog*), Mutual Exclusivity would bias her to infer that any further words describing the same object are probably not names for the object kind, but might instead refer to a property of the object ("brown"), the action the object is performing ("barking"), and so on (for a different perspective, based on the Principle of Contrast, see Clark 1987).

There is considerable evidence for this constraint proposal. Even two-year-olds are drawn to take novel words as object names under a variety of circumstances, and they shun words that overlap in extension. Moreover, there is a sense in which the taxonomic constraint is word-specific. Markman & Hutchinson (1984) found that when shown a novel object and told "See this dax. Find another dax," children tend to pick out another object of the same kind. If shown one novel animal, for instance, they will tend to choose another animal of a similar appearance. But if they are simply told "See this. Find another one," they are less likely to choose something of the same kind, tending to focus more on non-taxonomic relations, such as that between a dog and a bone, or a man and a truck. This finding, which has been replicated several times, has led many to the conclusion that the bias to favor object kinds is somehow special to lexical development.

Nevertheless there are problems with the special constraint theory. Most notably, while children are biased to learn names for object kinds, they have little problem learning other sorts of words. Consider, for example, the findings of Nelson, Hampson, & Shaw (1993), who examined the speech of forty-five children who were an average age of twenty months. These children knew many names for object kinds, but they also possessed verbs (*eat*), adjectives (*nice*), and many nominals that were not names for kinds of objects, such as pronouns (*it*), names for specific people (*Fred*), names for substances (*water*), names for events (*nap*), and names for temporal entities (*minute*). In fact, more than half of the words that these children knew were not names for object kinds. Other studies looking at younger children's very first words (e.g. Nelson 1973; Bates, Bretherton, & Snyder 1988; Bloom 1990), have obtained similar results.

Could this be explained in terms of Mutual Exclusivity? Only in some cases. For instance, it might be the case that a child can only learn a name for a part (like *handle*) after learning a name for the whole (like *cup*). But it is unlikely that this sort of analysis can be extended to the other types of nominals that appear in children's lexicons. Pronouns and proper names are used to refer to objects, but they do not name *kinds* of whole objects, instead they refer to specific individuals. Nevertheless, children are capable of linguistic reference to specific individuals before they show any sign of learning common nouns that refer to the kinds that the individuals belong to, like *person*, *man*, or *woman* (Nelson, 1973). This suggests that the acquisition of words like *this* and *she* and *Fred* cannot be explained through Mutual Exclusivity.

Other nominals fall outside the scope of the proposed constraints, since they do not refer to whole objects at all. For instance, the acquisition of substance names (which occurs very early in lexical development) is unaccounted for by the constraint theory, as is the acquisition of more abstract nominals that children learn (like *nap*). In fact, even for the acquisition of part names such as *handle*, Mutual Exclusivity only explains why these words are not mistaken for names of whole objects – it does not explain how children actually learn what they mean.

3.2 An alternative proposal

How could the bias to construe new words as names for kinds of whole objects emerge without special constraints?[1] One possibility is that it emerges from two more general facts about language and cognition, as follows:

- whole objects are highly salient individuals;
- count nouns – words that appear with quantifiers such as *a* and *another* and can be pluralized – refer to kinds of individuals.

These suffice. When a child hears a new word that describes an object and assumes that it refers to that kind of whole object, she is *not* doing so because she has one constraint that words refer to objects and another constraint that words refer to kinds. Instead she is doing so because, first, whole objects are naturally thought of as individuals and, second, it is a fact about English that count nouns, and not prepositions or adjectives or mass nouns, refer to kinds of individuals.

This presupposes considerable sophistication on the part of young children. It assumes that they possess a notion of individuation that is broader than their notion of whole object. This is in contrast to the view that children are initially restricted to construing complex cohesive objects, as suggested by Imai & Gentner (1997), and animate entities, as suggested by Gentner & Boroditsky (ch. 8 of this volume), as discrete individuals. And it assumes that they appreciate the relationship between a syntactic category (count noun) and a semantic category (kind of individual), which is in contrast to the view that this grasp of linguistic semantics is a relatively late accomplishment, as suggested by Gathercole (1986) and Levy (1988), among others.

It is clear that older children and adults can individuate entities other than whole objects. We track, categorize, count, and refer to objects, but we do the same for non-object entities such as shadows, jokes, parties, stories, holes, fingers, and songs – and most of the count nouns we use in our speech refer to entities other than objects. What about pre-linguistic infants? Surprisingly, there is some evidence that they have similar capacities. The relevant experiments explore their capacity to determine numerosities, to "count" the number of items in a display. The logic behind this is that there is no enumeration without individuation. If you can look at a scene and judge that it contains three objects, for instance, this presupposes the ability to parse the scene into distinct objects; there is no other way to do it. Infants can count small arrays of linearly arranged dots (Antell & Keating 1983), randomly arranged household objects depicted in photographs (Starkey, Spelke, & Gelman 1990), and computer-generated displays of moving random checkerboard patterns (van Loosbroek & Smitsman 1990). They can also count *sounds* – six-month-olds are capable of matching the number of objects they are shown with the number of sounds they hear (Starkey *et al.* 1990). Finally, they can count actions such as jumps. They can do so both when the jumps are bounded by periods of stillness (as when a puppet jumps, stops for a moment, and jumps again) and when they are defined by patterns of motion (as when a puppet jumps, wiggles for a moment, and then jumps again) (Wynn 1996). Ongoing experiments that Karen Wynn and I are conducting explore whether they can also count collections of objects and, if so, whether the factors underlying this capacity are the same as those found in studies of adults (Bloom 1996a, 2000).

These capacities pose some intriguing questions. What (if anything) do objects and patterns and sounds and actions have in common that makes the child construe them all as individuals? How does the intuitive notion of individual (or, equivalently, of "countable entity") relate to perceptual principles of grouping, and to more abstract "naive theories"? What is the nature of the difference between infants and children, and children and adults (for discussion, see Bloom 2000)? In any case, for the purposes here the evidence is decisive – prior to language acquisition, infants do have a notion of "individual" that includes, but is not limited to, whole objects.

Even though whole objects are not the only sorts of individuals that children can think about, there is little doubt that objects are special. Object names make up a higher proportion of the vocabularies of children than of those of adults (Gentner 1982; Macnamara 1982; Gentner & Boroditsky, ch. 8 of this volume). They are also salient individuals outside the domain of word learning. Shipley & Shepperson (1990), for instance, found that when children are shown an array of objects and explicitly asked to count colors or parts or kinds, they show a strong tendency to ignore the instructions and count the objects. It is not that children are limited to counting objects – it is that they find it hard to override their bias to treat objects as individuals. If there are no objects available, children have no problem counting non-object individuals. In fact, at roughly the same age that they are first able to count objects linguistically, they can also count sounds and actions (Wynn 1990).

Do children know that count nouns correspond to kinds of individuals? The classic study was done by Brown (1957), who showed preschoolers a picture of a strange action performed on a novel substance with a novel object. One group of children was told "Do you know what a sib is? In this picture, you can see a sib" (count-noun syntax) and another was told "Have you seen any sib? In this picture, you can see sib" (mass-noun syntax). Brown found that the preschoolers tended to construe the count noun as referring to the object, and the mass noun as referring to the substance. Katz, Baker, & Macnamara (1974) find that even children younger than two are sensitive to the contrast between words used with noun phrase syntax ("This is ____") and words used with count-noun syntax ("This is a ____") in word learning; they tend to take noun phrases as referring to specific individuals (as in "This is Fred") and count nouns as names for kinds (as in "This is a doll").

Other studies have explored the role of count/mass syntax in the acquisition of names for kinds of individuals that are not objects. Soja (1992) found that once two-year-olds show productive command of the count/mass distinction, they can use this syntactic cue to infer whether a word refers to a non-solid substance (such as the mass noun *water*) or to a bounded individual composed of that non-solid substance (such as the count noun *puddle*). Bloom (1994a) found that three- and four-year-olds will construe a plural count noun that describes a series of actions as referring to the individual actions, and a mass noun describing the same series as referring to the undifferentiated activity, and Bloom & Kelemen (1995) found that adults and older children can use count-noun syntax to learn names for novel collections, words such as *family* and *flock* that refer to groups of distinct physical entities. Finally, Gordon (1992) reports that as soon as two-year-olds start to use words with count-noun syntax in their speech, they do so with both names for objects and names for other sorts of individuals, such as names for parts and events (see also Nelson *et al.* 1993). All of this suggests that children's initial appreciation of count-noun semantics emerges very early, and that it corresponds to their conceptual notion "kind of individual," not "kind of whole object."

What about word learning in the absence of syntactic cues (see Bloom 1996b)? Although knowing that a word is a count noun is an excellent cue that it refers to a kind of individual, other cues can lead the child to the same interpretation (see Tomasello, ch. 5 of this volume). The mere presence of a salient object under the right discourse conditions is sometimes enough to motivate children to treat a novel word as referring to the object kind, even if the syntax of the word they hear is *not* that of a count noun, showing that syntactic cues can be overridden (e.g. Markman & Wachtel 1988; Waxman & Markow 1995). Note, however, that, under different circumstances, children who are exposed to a word that is not syntactically marked will interpret the word as a name for substance kind (Soja *et al.* 1991), a specific individual (Hall 1996), or an action (Tomasello, ch. 5 of this volume) – showing that "object kind" is *not* a universal default when a child is exposed to a new word. And although syntax is not essential, children's bias to treat words as referring to object kinds is strongest when the words are presented with count-noun syntax, suggesting that their sensitivity to this cue partially explains why this bias exists.

There is evidence, then, that children do possess the requisite syntactic and conceptual capacities to account for their bias to treat new words as names for object kinds, without having to appeal to any additional special constraints.

3.3 Comparison with the constraint theory

But isn't it *simpler* just to propose that children believe that new words refer to kinds of objects and be done with it? What justifies this more complex analysis?

First, the special constraint proposal is redundant. *If* two-year-olds know that count nouns correspond to kinds of individuals, and *if* they are prone to treat whole objects as individuals, then there is no role left for special constraints, either innate or learned, and hence no reason to assume that they exist.

Second, the theory defended here captures the fact that the preference for kinds of whole objects is not word-general, but only applies to count nouns. When a child is exposed to a novel word with the syntax of a noun phrase (like *he*, which cannot be used with quantifiers), the default assumption is that it is a pronoun or proper name, not a name for a kind; when they hear a new mass noun (like *water*, which cannot be pluralized and appears with *much* and *some*), they assume that it is a name for a kind of non-individuated stuff, such as a substance; when they hear a new adjective, they take it as a property name; when they hear a preposition, they take it as denoting a spatial relationship, and so on (Bloom 1996b).

Third, unlike the special constraint proposal, a theory that draws on the more abstract notion of "individual" allows for the fact that children learn count nouns that do not refer to kinds of whole objects, such as *finger* or *family* or *hole*. One can debate the extent to which such names for non-object individuals are fully understood by two-year-olds (though names for parts, like *finger*, are among the very earliest words children know, and these are typically used correctly) – but there is no doubt that three- and four-year-olds know many such nouns and as they get older such words come to occupy an ever-increasing proportion of their lexicons.

Fourth, the account here explains certain patterns of development that are otherwise mysterious. Why are pronouns and proper names, which violate the taxonomic bias, relatively easy to learn? Answer: because they are not count nouns, they are lexical noun phrases, and children are sensitive to syntactic class. Why is a solid substance name like *wood* more difficult to acquire than a non-solid substance name like *water* (Dickinson 1988; Prasada 1993)? Answer: *water* and *wood* are both mass nouns, and hence do not refer to kinds of individuals; they refer to kinds of non-individuated entities, to stuff. But while water is easily construed as stuff, wood is not. Unlike water, any instance of wood is also an instance of a whole object, and thinking of a block of wood as a portion of non-individuated stuff runs afoul of the bias to think of objects as distinct individuals (Bloom 1994b).

Finally, there is the issue of generality. Children's focus on whole objects is not limited to words. It is found in domains as diverse as linguistic counting (Shipley & Shepperson 1990), tracking and categorization (Spelke 1994), and addition and subtraction (Wynn 1992). What about the focus on kinds? Consider again the evidence for the position that this is limited to words, as part of the taxonomic constraint. Children generalize on the basis of object kinds when given a new word ("This is a zav. Find another zav") but not when simply told something like "See this. Find another one." Studies that purport to demonstrate a shape bias (see below) provide a similar result – children generalize on the basis of shape when exposed to a new word, but not when asked something like "Which one goes with this?" (Landau *et al.* 1988; Smith, ch. 4 of this volume).

These findings are typically taken as showing that the constraints are word-specific, but there is a simpler explanation (Nancy Soja, personal communication). The focus on kinds might be specific to *categorization*, which is, after all, the act of putting together items that belong to the same kind. Nouns motivate categorization because nouns refer to kinds. If one is shown something, told it is a zav, and asked to "Find another zav," it is natural to look for something of the same kind, because this is what it means for something to be another zav. General statements like "Find another one" or "Which one goes with this?" do not focus children on kinds because they are not explicit requests to categorize; they are so vague that they do not lead to any sort of systematic behavior.

There is evidence for this alternative. In one experiment, we showed adults a novel object, gave them a new word to describe it, and then saw how they extended the word. They tended to extend the word to another object of the same kind, where kind was generalized on the basis of shape. So if they were shown a backwards-S-shaped piece of copper, they would extend the name for this piece to a different backwards-S-shaped piece of rubber, but not to a twisted V-shaped piece of copper. This just replicates all other studies of the shape bias. But we also ran a variant in which we simply asked subjects to "Find something of the same kind." Even without a new word, they again focused on shape, showing that *any* cue to categorization does just as well. We have not yet run children on this experiment, but Lucy & Gaskins (ch. 9, this volume) report a series of studies in which children were shown a target object and two alternatives, one which was of the same shape but of a different material and the other which was of a different shape and the same material. When simply asked which of the alternatives was most similar to the target – without the introduction of any novel word – the dominant response by the children was to choose the object of the same shape. This result held both for children acquiring English and for children acquiring Yucatec, which is a classifier language. In light of these findings, the fact that children do not generalize by kind when asked a question such as "Which one goes with this?" provides no support for the claim that the child's focus on kinds (or shape) is strictly a lexical phenomenon.

In general, the problem with the special constraints proposal is that it applies a specific lexical solution to a broad conceptual problem. Golinkoff, Mervis, & Hirsh-Pasek (1994), for instance, introduce their own theory of "lexical principles" by stating that these "enable the child to avoid the Quinean (1960) conundrum of generating limitless, equally logical possibilities, for a word's meaning" (126). Quine's conundrum, as they see it, is that any act of naming is consistent with a logical infinity of possibilities, most of them incorrect as the target meaning of the word. The child hears *cup* used to describe a cup, and has to somehow exclude the possibility that the word means "undetached cup parts" or "cup, but only until the year 2000" or "cup or prime number." Perhaps it is the lexical principles that guide the child to the correct interpretation – that *cup* refers to cups.

This cannot be entirely right, however. Any animal capable of learning – a human infant, a chimpanzee, a dog – must be disposed to prefer some concepts over others. As Goodman (1983) points out, the problem of "limitless, equally logical possibilities" exists for any act of induction – and successful induction is the stuff of life. If a dog jumps onto a stove and gets burned, she is likely to infer that stoves are hot – not that undetached stove parts are hot, or that stoves until the year 2000 are hot, or that stoves or prime numbers are hot, even though these alternatives are logically consistent with her experience. Such constraints on the dog's inference have nothing to do with lexical principles, since dogs do not have any lexical principles. In general, problems of induction are not going to have specifically *lexical* solutions; they must instead be solved, at least in part, through nonlinguistic aspects of the human and animal mind.

4 The bias to generalize object names on the basis of shape

Once the child knows that a word refers to a kind of object, what dictates her intuitions as to the boundaries of the kind? Suppose she hears *dog* used to describe a dog and infers that *dog* refers to that kind of object. What tells her what other objects belong to this kind?

There is considerable evidence that children are prone to generalize new object names on the basis of shape, with other perceptual properties being less relevant. Landau *et al.* (1988) suggest that children possess a "shape bias" causing them to map object names onto categories of objects that share a common shape, as opposed to a common size, color, or texture (see also Landau, Jones, & Smith 1992; Smith, ch. 4 of this volume). Just as with the whole object constraint, this is said to be limited to word learning; under one proposal, it is acquired through a connectionist network that is sensitive to correlations between linguistic and perceptual experience (Smith, ch. 4 of this volume).

Once again, however, there is evidence that the shape bias is the result of more general properties of language and cognition. In particular:

- some words refer to kinds of objects
- we often categorize objects on the basis of shape

The first claim is obvious; words *do* sometimes refer to object kinds and children must at some point come to know this. As for the second claim, the centrality of shape shows up in studies of categorization (e.g. Rosch, Mervis, Gray, Johnson, & Boyes-Braem 1976) and in psychological and neurophysiological studies of the visual representations of objects (e.g. Marr 1982; Hoffman & Richards 1984; Biederman 1987; see Landau & Jackendoff 1993, for review). Words like *fork* and *duck* are typically extended to entities that share a common shape because these words refer to forks and ducks, and – quite independent from language – people are disposed to categorize forks and ducks on the basis of their shape.

Object kinds are often categorized on the basis of shape because shape is the best cue to the kind to which an object belongs. This is especially true for artifacts, whose nature is related to properties such as the intent of the artifact's creator (Dennett 1987; Rips 1989; Hall 1995; Bloom 1996c, 2000). If you want to know if something was constructed with the intent that it should be a chair, shape is an excellent cue. For one thing, sameness of shape is seen as highly non-random (Leyton 1992). Something is unlikely to be shaped like a typical chair unless it was constructed with the intent to be shaped like a typical chair, and hence one can usually figure out what someone intended an object to be by focusing on its shape. Moreover, shape is relevant to why the artifact was created in the first place – to its function. Given the typical function of chairs and cups, their shape is quite constrained while, with the exception of traffic lights and camouflage, the color of an object is largely irrelevant to why one would create it and hence color is a poor cue to artifact kind (see Kelemen & Bloom 1994).

Shape is also relevant to the identification of animals and parts of animals since it is often the result of selectional processes establishing some fit between the animal's phenotype and properties of its environment. It is no accident, after all, that a cat's teeth are pointy or that fish are streamlined. Since animals can be reliably classified on the basis of shape (more so than on color, size, or texture), it is little surprise that the hominid mind (and likely the minds of other species) has evolved to exploit shape as a basis for categorization.

Under this proposal, shape is a *cue* to object kind – but object kind does not reduce to object shape. Object kind is instead related to deeper properties that entities share, such as the creator's intent for artifacts, and core biological, chemical, or physical properties for natural kinds. If young children know this, they should appreciate that objects of the same kind need not be of the same shape. They do. Preschoolers learn superordinate terms like *animal* and *furniture*, artifact names like *clock* and *telephone*, relationship terms like *brother* and *uncle* and so on, and they show little difficulty coming to grips with the fact that none of these object names are reliably generalized on the basis of shape (see Soja, Carey, & Spelke 1992). Similarly, even for basic-level categories that share a common shape, children know that something can belong to a kind even if it is not the same shape as typical members of that kind. For instance, if one modifies a porcupine so that it looks like (has the shape of) a cactus, children nonetheless believe that it remains a porcupine (Keil 1989). These findings suggest that shape is neither necessary nor sufficient for object-kind membership. Children use shape as a cue when categorizing (and naming) object kinds but they are never restricted to categorizing (and naming) members of these kinds on the basis of shape.

4.1 Shape and visual representations

Consider now an apparent counter-example. Landau *et al.* (1992) point out that there is a 60-foot metal statue of a clothespin in Philadelphia by Claes Oldenburg, which is called "the clothespin." One does not have to be told that this is the name; one can tell what it is called just by looking at it. It is called "the clothespin" because it is shaped like a clothespin. It plainly does not fulfill the function that clothespins typically fulfill, and it was not created with the intent underlying the creation of typical clothespins. This seems to pose a problem for the above proposal that shape is a cue to object kind, since it suggests that the English word *clothespin* really does refer to all and only entities that are clothespin-shaped, regardless of other properties that these entities may possess. If so, then shape is much more than a cue; shape is essential.

There is an alternative analysis of this sort of "clothespin" example, however. English (and perhaps all languages) allows people to use a name for a kind to refer to a visual representation of a member of that kind (Jackendoff 1992). Hence we call the statue of a clothespin "a clothespin" because it is a visual representation of a clothespin. Shape is relevant because if a statue is shaped like a clothespin, it is an excellent bet that it was intended to represent a clothespin, and we tend to categorize representations on the basis of what they were intended to represent. As with objects in general, shape is a cue (in this case, to what a statue was intended to represent) but it is not criterial.

Which explanation is right? Do we call the statue a clothespin because it is shaped like a clothespin or because we believe it was intended to represent a clothespin? Adults can plainly name representations that are not the same shape as what they depict. On a map, an "X" can depict treasure, even if it is not shaped like treasure. I can draw a picture of my friend Fred, and people will acknowledge that it is a picture of Fred, even if it is not Fred-shaped; a crude oval with dots for eyes will do just fine (Soja *et al.* 1992). But do children share these intuitions? It is possible that they do not. Perhaps shape is the sole factor in their interpretation of novel words, and the more abstract knowledge of representations is acquired later.

To address this, we are conducting a series of studies. These studies ask the following question: do children only individuate representations through their shape or is the creator's intention also relevant, sometimes sufficiently so that it can apply in the absence of shape cues? The results so far suggest the following (see Bloom & Markson 1996, 1998).

- Four-year-olds know that a picture is likely to be of whatever someone is looking at when they are drawing it. For instance, in one study the experimenter placed a fork and a spoon on either side of the child and stared at the fork intensely while pretending to draw a picture. Then the child was shown the picture and asked what it was. The picture was actually drawn prior to the experiment, and had been pretested to ensure that it looked equally like both of the objects; in this case, it looked equally like a fork and a spoon. We found that children named the picture in accord with what the experimenter was looking at when she drew it. If the experimenter was looking at a fork while she seemed to draw the picture, the child tended to describe the picture as "a fork"; if she was looking at the spoon, it would be described as "a spoon." Since the picture was always the same, the naming behavior of the child could not be based on appearance alone; her assumptions about the representational intent of the experimenter must have played some further role. More speculatively, the child might have reasoned: the experimenter was looking at the fork while she drew the picture, so she must have been intending to draw the fork, and so her drawing could legitimately be called a fork.

In a variant of this study, the experimenter would stare intently at the fork and then produce a picture that looked (according to pretesting) much more like the spoon than the fork. Here both children and adults tended to say it was a picture of the spoon, despite the experimenter's behavior. Our interpretation of this (supported by what our adult subjects told us) is that people found it unbelievable that someone would intend to draw a fork and then produce a picture that looked so much like a spoon; it is more natural to assume (correctly, in fact) that the experimenter was only pretending to draw the fork. In general, there are certain correspondences between appearance and intent that people expect. While it is plausible that someone might draw a picture that does not look much like what it is supposed to depict, it is very hard to imagine that someone could be intending to draw a picture of X and produce something that looks so much like Y. These issues are discussed in more detail in Bloom (1996c).

- Three- and four-year-olds individuate their own pictures in terms of intent. In another study, they were asked to draw pairs of pictures that we believed would turn out to be of identical shape. They were asked to draw a lollipop and then, on a separate piece of paper and with a different color crayon, were asked to draw a balloon. Children of this age typically draw the same form in both pictures – a circle with a line descending from the bottom. They were also asked to draw a picture of themselves and, on a different piece of paper, to draw a picture of the experimenter. Again, the appearance of the drawings would typically be indistinguishable – one could not tell by looking at the drawings that one of them was of the child and the other was of the experimenter. After a pause of about twenty minutes, the children were shown their own pictures and asked to identify them. Some examples of four-year-old's drawings are shown in figure 6.1.

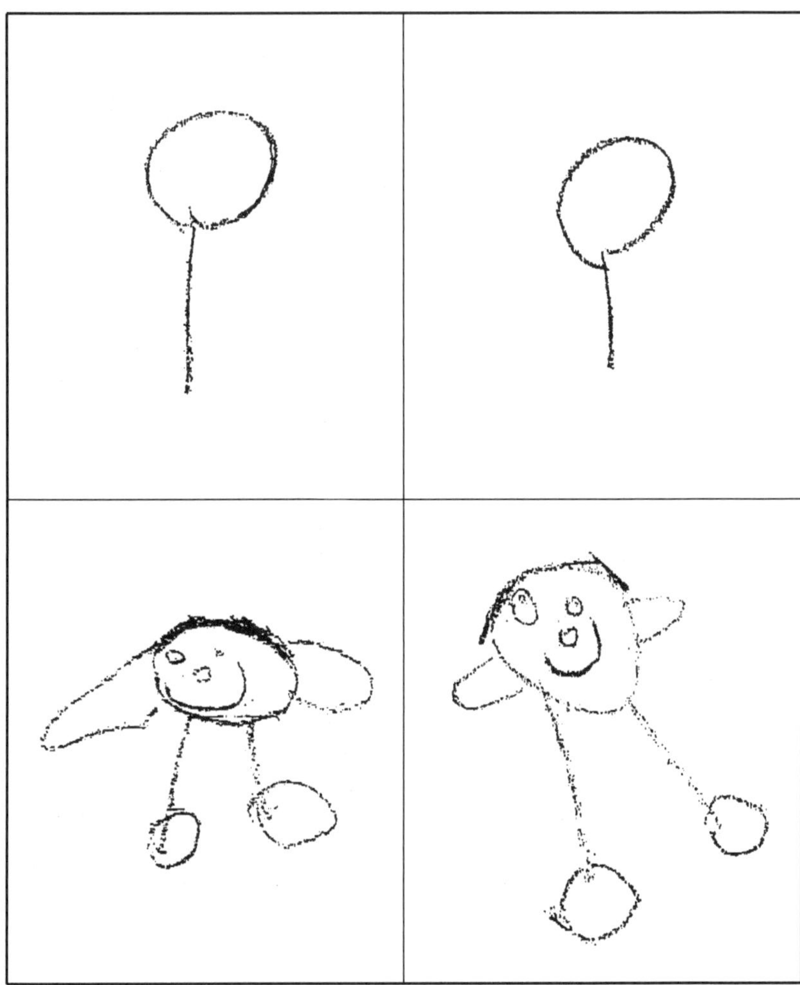

Fig. 6.1 A sample drawing by a 4-year-old of a balloon, a lollipop, the experimenter, and herself.

We found that children tended to name the picture in terms of their intent at the time it was drawn. For instance, a child would point to the picture on the top left and insist it was "a balloon," to the top right and insist that it was "a lollipop," to the bottom left and insist that it was the experimenter, and to the bottom right and insist that it was the child herself. This could not have been done on the basis of what the pictures looked like. Instead it suggests that the children remembered what they had intended each of the pictures to depict and assumed that this intention individuated the pictures; the picture on the top left is a balloon, and not a lollipop, just because the child has *intended* it to depict a balloon and not a lollipop.

This phenomenon is not subtle. Children will *insist* that the picture on the top left is a lollipop and not a balloon; if the experimenter describes it as a balloon, they will often rigorously correct her. The same effect shows up outside the laboratory. Children younger than those we tested frequently describe their drawings as "a cat," "my house," or "Mommy," even though they rarely look much like cats, houses, or specific people. If a child who draws something with the intent that it be a cat hears an adult describe it as a dog, she will often correct the adult – the fact that it looks just as much like a dog will not convince a child that it is permissible to call it "a dog."[2]

- Finally, three- and four-year-olds can productively name representations of arbitrary shape. In one study, they were told that the drawings they were about to see were drawn by a child with a broken arm, but who had nonetheless intended to draw certain things and was trying her best to do so. In one condition of this study, they were shown two blobs of different sizes and told that the child intended to draw a flower and a house. Most children easily grasped that the representations should be individuated by size, and described the smaller blob as "a flower" and the larger blob as "a house."

  It is unclear how children succeeded at the task. They might have been doing so through a sophisticated act of intentional interpretation, reasoning: "The girl with the broken arm intended to distinguish the pictures and could only do so through size differences, hence size will distinguish them." Or they might have succeeded though a simpler appreciation of analogy (see Gentner 1983): the flower is smaller than the house; this blob is smaller than that blob; hence this blob refers to the flower and that blob refers to the house. The above study does not distinguish these possibilities – but it does show that the naming of pictures does not require sameness of shape.

The proposal for the shape bias is that it emerges in part through our knowledge of language (some words refer to object kinds) and in part through our understanding of kinds in the world (shape is an excellent way to determine the extension of some kinds). This supports the same moral that was drawn for fast mapping and the whole object and taxonomic biases: even young children possess linguistic and conceptual resources that underlie their acquisition and use of words; these resources explain how they can so quickly fast map new words, and why they tend to construe new words as naming object kinds, some of which are generalized on the basis of shape. These are the roots of word learning; nothing else is needed.

The above conclusion – that there is nothing in the child's mind special to the task of word learning – is unlikely to hold for language acquisition in general. There is evidence that phonology, morphology, and syntax *are* acquired through dedicated neural mechanisms. The acquisition of these aspects of language follows a strict maturational timetable and shows strong critical period effects. It can be selectively impaired through injury or disease (including disorders that are genetically transmitted) and dissociated from more general learning abilities in normal children. It is linked to characteristic regions of the human brain; and is constrained by structural principles that cannot be derived from other cognitive systems (Pinker 1994). But none of this is true for word learning. These considerations suggest that the sort of reductive theory proposed above for word learning cannot be extended to other aspects of language acquisition. More speculatively, this difference between words and other aspects of language might have some relevance to more general questions about the nature of human language, how it is realized in the human brain, and how it has evolved.

NOTES

I am grateful to Melissa Bowerman, Steven Levinson, Lori Markson, and Karen Wynn for helpful comments on an earlier version of this chapter. The research discussed here was supported by grants from the Spencer Foundation and the Sloan Foundation.

1 See also Markman (1991) for a different proposal as to how these assumptions can be explained in terms of more general properties of the child's cognitive systems.

2 This is one way in which representation differs from pretense. If the child draws a picture of a sword and someone later says "Oh, what a nice telephone," the child will object. This fits the adult intuition; if I draw something with the intention to depict X, it remains a representation of X no matter what someone else thinks it is or wishes it to be. But if I spend a few minutes pretending a banana is a sword, this pretense does not *stick*; you are free to pick it up later, and pretend it is a telephone, and, if you did so, I would not normally say that you are mistaken. Ongoing experiments are testing whether children distinguish representation from pretense in this regard.

REFERENCES

Anglin, J. 1993. Vocabulary development: a morphological analysis. *Monographs of the Society for Research in Child Development* 10 [serial no. 238].

Antell, S. E., & D. P. Keating. 1983. Perception of numerical invariance in neonates. *Child Development* 54: 695–701.

Bates, E., I. Bretherton, & L. Snyder. 1988. *From first words to grammar: individual differences and dissociable mechanisms.* Cambridge: Cambridge University Press.

Berlin, B., & P. Kay. 1969. *Basic color terms*. Berkeley: University of California Press.

Biederman, I. 1987. Recognition-by-components: a theory of human image understanding. *Psychological Review* 94: 115–147.

Bloom, P. 1990. Syntactic distinctions in child language. *Journal of Child Language* 17: 343–355.

1994a. Syntax–semantics mappings as an explanation for some transitions in language development. In Y. Levy (ed.), *Other children, other languages: theoretical issues in language development*. Hillsdale, NJ: Lawrence Erlbaum, 41–75.

1994b. Possible names: the role of syntax–semantics mappings in the acquisition of nominals. *Lingua* 92: 297–329.

1996a. Possible individuals in language and cognition. *Current Directions in Psychological Science* 5: 90–94.

1996b. Word learning and the part of speech. In R. Gelman & T. Au (eds.), *Handbook of perceptual and cognitive development*. New York: Academic Press, 151–184.

1996c. Intention, history, and artifact concepts. *Cognition* 60: 1–29.

2000. *How children learn the meanings of words*. Cambridge, MA: MIT Press.

Bloom, P., & D. Kelemen. 1995. Syntactic cues in the acquisition of collective nouns. *Cognition* 56: 1–30.

Bloom, P., & L. Markson. 1996. The role of intentionality in children's naming of representations. Poster presented at the West Coast Theory of Mind Conference, University of California, Berkeley, May.

1998. Intentionality and analogy in children's naming of pictorial representations. *Psychological Science* 9: 200–204.

Brown, R. 1957. Linguistic determinism and the part of speech. *Journal of Abnormal and Social Psychology* 55: 1–5.

Carey, S. 1978. The child as word learner. In M. Halle, J. Bresnan, & G. A. Miller (eds.), *Linguistic theory and psychological reality*. Cambridge, MA: MIT Press, 264–293.

Carey, S., & E. Bartlett. 1978. Acquiring a single new word. *Papers and Reports on Child Language Development* 15: 17–29.

Clark, E. V. 1987. The principle of contrast: a constraint on language acquisition. In B. MacWhinney (ed.), *Mechanisms of language acquisition.* Hillsdale, NJ: Lawrence Erlbaum, 1-33.

Dennett, D. 1987. *The intentional stance*. Cambridge, MA: MIT Press.

Dickinson, D. K. 1988. Learning names for materials: factors constraining and limiting hypotheses about word meaning. *Cognitive Development* 3: 15–35.

Gathercole, V. 1986. Evaluating competing linguistic theories with child language data: the case of the mass–count distinction. *Linguistics and Philosophy* 9: 151–190.

Gentner, D. 1982. Why nouns are learned before verbs: linguistic relativity versus natural partitioning. In S. A. Kuczaj II (ed.), *Language development*, vol. 2: *Language, thought, and culture*. Hillsdale, NJ: Lawrence Erlbaum, 301–334.

1983. Structure-mapping: a theoretical framework for analogy. *Cognitive Science* 7: 155–170.

Golinkoff, R. M., C.B. Mervis, & K. Hirsh-Pasek. 1994. Early object labels: the case for a developmental lexical principles framework. *Journal of Child Language* 21: 125–155.

Goodman, N. 1983. *Fact, fiction, and forecast.* Cambridge, MA: Harvard University Press.

Gordon, P. 1992. Object, substance, and individuation: canonical vs. non-canonical count/mass nouns in children's speech. Unpublished ms., University of Pittsburgh.

Hall, D. G. 1995. Artifacts and origins. Unpublished ms., Department of Psychology, University of British Columbia.

1996. Preschoolers' default assumptions about word meaning: proper names designate unique individuals. *Developmental Psychology* 32: 177–186.

Hoffman, D., & W. Richards. 1984. Parts of recognition. *Cognition* 18: 65–96.

Huttenlocher, J., & P. Smiley. 1987. Early word meanings: the case of object names. *Cognitive Psychology* 19: 63–89.

Imai, M., & D. Gentner. 1997. A cross-linguistic study of early word meaning: universal ontology and linguistic influence. *Cognition* 62: 169–200.

Jackendoff, R. 1992. Mme Tussaud meets the binding theory. *Natural Language and Linguistic Theory* 10: 1–31.

Katz, N., E. Baker, & J. Macnamara. 1974. What's in a name? A study of how children learn common and proper names. *Child Development* 45: 469–473.

Keil, F. 1989. *Concepts, kinds, and cognitive development.* Cambridge, MA: Bradford/MIT Press.

Kelemen, D., & P. Bloom. 1994. Domain-specific knowledge in simple categorization tasks. *Psychonomic Bulletin and Review* 1: 390–395.

Landau, B., & R. Jackendoff. 1993. "What" and "where" in spatial language and spatial cognition. *Behavioral and Brain Sciences* 16: 217–265.

Landau, B., S. Jones, & L. B. Smith. 1992. Perception, ontology, and naming in young children: commentary on Soja, Carey, and Spelke. *Cognition* 43: 85–91.

Landau, B., L. B. Smith, & S. Jones. 1988. The importance of shape in early lexical learning. *Cognitive Development* 3: 299–321.

Levy, Y. 1988. On the early learning of formal grammatical systems: evidence from studies of the acquisition of gender and countability. *Journal of Child Language* 15: 179–186.

Leyton, M. 1992. *Symmetry, causality, mind.* Cambridge, MA: MIT Press.

Macnamara, J. 1982. *Names for things: a study of human learning.* Cambridge, MA: MIT Press.

Markman, E. M. 1990. Constraints children place on word meanings. *Cognitive Science* 14: 57–77.

1992. The whole-object, taxonomic, and mutual exclusivity assumptions as initial constraints on word meaning. In S. A. Gelman & J. P. Byrnes (eds.), *Perspectives on language and thought: interrelations in development.* Cambridge: Cambridge University Press, 72-106.

Markman, E. M., & J. E. Hutchinson. 1984. Children's sensitivity to constraints in word meaning: taxonomic versus thematic relations. *Cognitive Psychology* 16: 1–27.

Markman, E. M., & G. F. Wachtel. 1988. Children's use of mutual exclusivity to constrain the meaning of words. *Cognitive Psychology* 20: 121–157.

Markson, L., & P. Bloom. 1997. Evidence against a dedicated system for word learning in children. *Nature* 385: 813–815.

Marr, D. 1982. *Vision*. San Francisco: Freeman.

Nelson, K. 1973. Structure and strategy in learning to talk. *Monographs of the Society for Research in Child Development* 38 [1–2, serial no. 149].

1988. Constraints on word meaning? *Cognitive Development* 3: 221–246.

1990. Comment on Behrend's "Constraints and Development." *Cognitive Development* 5: 331–339.

Nelson, K., J. Hampson, & L. K. Shaw. 1993. Nouns in early lexicons: evidence, explanations, and extensions. *Journal of Child Language* 20: 61–84.

Newport, E. 1990. Maturational constraints on language learning. *Cognitive Science* 14: 11–28.

Pinker, S. 1994. *The language instinct*. New York: William Morrow.

Prasada, S. 1993. Learning names for solid substances: quantifying solid entities in terms of portions. *Cognitive Development* 8: 83–104.

Quine, W. V. O. 1960. *Word and object*. Cambridge, MA: MIT Press.

Rips, L. J. 1989. Similarity, typicality, and categorization. In S. Vosinadou & A. Ortony (eds.), *Similarity and analogical reasoning*. New York: Cambridge University Press, 21–49.

Rosch, E., C. B. Mervis, W. D. Gray, D. M. Johnson, & P. Boyes-Braem. 1976. Basic objects in natural categories. *Cognitive Psychology* 8: 382–439.

Shipley, E. F., & B. Shepperson. 1990. Countable entities: developmental changes. *Cognition* 34: 109–136.

Soja, N. N., S. Carey, & E. S. Spelke. 1991. Ontological categories guide young children's inductions of word meaning: object terms and substance terms. *Cognition* 38: 179–211.

1992. Perception, ontology, and word meaning. *Cognition* 45: 101–107.

Spelke, E. S. 1994. Initial knowledge: six suggestions. *Cognition* 50: 431–445.

Starkey, P., E. S. Spelke, & R. Gelman. 1990. Numerical abstraction by human infants. *Cognition* 36: 97–127.

van Loosbroek, E., & A. W. Smitsman. 1990. Visual perception of numerosity in infancy. *Developmental Psychology* 26: 916–922.

Waxman, S. R., & D. Markow. 1996. Words as invitations to form categories: evidence from 12- to 13-month-old infants. *Cognitive Psychology* 61: 1461–1473.

Wynn, K. 1990. Children's understanding of counting. *Cognition* 36: 155–193.

1992. Addition and subtraction by human infants. *Nature* 358: 749–750.

1996. Infants' individuation and enumeration of sequential actions. *Psychological Science* 7: 164–169.

Part 3

Entities, individuation, and quantification

7 Whorf versus continuity theorists: bringing data to bear on the debate

Susan Carey
New York University

1 Introduction

I take it as a given that the language we speak both reflects and shapes our conceptualization of the world. Theory changes, including changes in *intuitive* theories, often involve the construction of a new language for describing some domain of phenomena, a language incommensurable with that which preceded it. On this view, sometimes theory learning involves the construction of a new representational resource, a new language not expressible or definable in the terms of the old one (Kuhn 1962, 1982; Feyerabend 1962; Kitcher 1978; Hacking 1993; but see Davidson 1974, and Fodor 1998, on the very coherence of the notion of conceptual change; see Carey 1985, 1988, 1991, for a defense of the notion and its application to theories of cognitive development).

Accepting the existence of genuine conceptual change in the course of cognitive development is tantamount to accepting the Whorfian hypothesis. After Black, scientists used a different language for describing thermal phenomena, one which led them to see phenomena such as heating and cooling, thermal expansion, and thermal equilibrium totally differently from the ways earlier scientists in an Aristotelian or Galilean tradition did (Wiser & Carey 1983); after Levoisier, scientists saw phenomena such as burning, and entities such as chemical compounds and air, totally differently from the ways scientists who held the phlogiston theory did (Kitcher 1978; Kuhn 1982). Further, I believe that there are many changes of this sort in the course of normal cognitive development (intuitive physics, McCloskey 1983; intuitive astronomy, Vosniadou & Brewer 1992; intuitive biology, Carey 1985, 1995).

If we accept the coherence of a conceptual change framework for describing cognitive development, the question then becomes: what is the scope of conceptual change during development? What aspects of language are cultural constructions? The above literature concerns mainly the open-class lexicon; what is at issue in these discussions is theoretical vocabulary in scientific and folk theories. But there is nothing in principle that precludes the closed-class vocabulary, or the conceptual distinctions reflected in natural language syntax and morphology, from being in the scope of the conceptual change framework. It is, of course, an empirical question.

Many (e.g. Macnamara 1982; Pinker 1984; Gleitman 1990) have argued for a continuity/universality theory of the acquisition of the conceptual representations that underlie the closed-class vocabulary, and the conceptual distinctions marked in syntax/morphology (from now on I will use the loose term "grammaticized concepts" to refer to this domain of language). "Continuity" is the thesis that cognitive architecture does not change throughout development, that the infant's prelinguistic representations of the world are couched in the same vocabulary as later linguistic representations. "Universality" is the thesis that all natural languages draw on the same stock of grammaticized concepts. The argument for the continuity/universality thesis often begins with the observation that there is a distinction between concepts that are grammaticized in natural languages of the world (e.g. number), and those that are not (e.g. color). Languages express tens of thousands of concepts lexically, and a potentially infinite set propositionally, but only a small subset are grammaticized. On this view all languages draw on the same small set of grammaticized notions, although each exploits only a subset. Language learning is then a complex mapping problem – discovering which of the set of possible grammaticized notions are exploited in the language being learned and how. Semantic bootstrapping theories of the beginning stages of syntax acquisition (e.g. Pinker 1984) and syntactic bootstrapping theories of the beginning stages of the acquisition of lexical meanings (e.g. Gleitman 1990) each depend upon the continuity/universality position.

Continuity admits a certain degree of nonuniversality. In this theory, the language acquisition faculty includes antecedently the whole stock of grammaticized notions. Those grammatical distinctions not expressed in a given language might be lost (e.g. in the case study of Lucy 1992, and Lucy & Gaskins, ch. 9 of this volume, the fact that inanimate nouns in Yucatec Mayan are not marked for count/mass status leads the distinction between individuated and nonindividuated inanimate entities to be lost, or at least to become much less salient), just as those phonemic distinctions not expressed in a given language are lost early in infancy if a language does not exploit them (e.g. the r/l distinction in Japanese).

The continuity position differs from an extreme Whorfianism, in which the grammaticized categories of each language are cultural constructions mastered anew by each child as he/she masters the language which embodies them. On the Whorfian alternative, those conceptual categories that are syntactically marked are no different from other concepts as far as being cultural constructions is concerned, but they are particularly important, because they are marked with every use of relevant constructions – every noun phrase, every verb – and thus serve to entrench a cultural and language-specific experience of the world.

There is a long history of attempts to decide the debates between continuity and Whorfianism with *a priori* arguments. Often, learnability considerations are appealed to; there is no known computational mechanism which can achieve conceptual change. True, but this does not decide the issue. If one accepts the analysis of conceptual change in the course of theory development, then there is an existence proof for its possibility, even though the mechanisms underlying it are not fully understood. Further, many have sketched parts of a change mechanism (e.g. Nersessian 1992; Carey & Spelke 1994). In sum, I see no compelling *a priori* argument for the continuity/universality position. To repeat: ultimately, it is an empirical question.

Many chapters in this volume begin to bring data to bear on the debate, and are taken to support the Whorfian position. Slobin, ch. 14 of this volume, mounts an interesting challenge to there being a sharp distinction between grammaticized and nongrammaticized notions, and, consequently, to the idea that there is only a small set of grammaticized concepts. In addition, Slobin, along with many others, challenges the universality assumption, arguing there is marked linguistic variation in conceptual packaging underlying given domains of grammaticized notions (e.g. spatial prepositions, motion verbs, principles of individuation within the nominal system). Of course, for such considerations to be a successful challenge to continuity, it would have to be shown that these variations are not merely parameter settings within an antecedently specified space of possibilities. As we ponder this debate, we must remember that a possible outcome will be that the continuity thesis is true for some grammaticized notions, and the Whorfian hypothesis is true for others. Indeed, this is exactly the conclusion drawn here from a case study of certain aspects of noun semantics and the expression of numerical concepts in thought and language.

In this chapter, I sketch one approach to bringing empirical data to bear on these questions. The research program has several steps: first, identify candidates for universally grammaticized notions. Second, establish whether these articulate the mental representations of *prelinguistic* human infants. Insofar as they do, the continuity/universality position receives support. Third, for conceptual resources marked in languages that do *not* articulate infant representations of their world, establish when these conceptual resources become available to children, and explore the mechanisms by which they do so. These latter cases are candidates for Whorfian influences.

I illustrate this approach with a case study of the conceptual and linguistic representations of number. Of course, *some* representations of number are clearly cultural constructions (e.g. the decimal system, fractions, irrationals). I limit my attention to representations of number deeply entrenched in human languages.

2 The expression of number and sortal concepts in human language

Not all languages have a counting sequence that expresses natural numbers. Nonetheless, numerical concepts are universally reflected in grammaticized contrasts, the most important numerical primitive being the concept *one*. Number is typically grammatically marked on both nouns and verbs, usually reflecting the basic distinction between one/many (singular/plural), or sometimes reflecting three or more distinctions: singular/dual/many or singular/dual/trial(3)/many or singular/dual/paucal(few)/many (Croft 1990). In addition, noun quantifiers express numerical concepts (e.g. *an*, *another*, *few*, *many*). *An* expresses 'one,' *another* expresses 'numerically distinct individual,' and *few/many/some* all express subtly different contrasts from *one*.

One must be applied to an individuated entity. Thus, languages must represent concepts (called sortals) which pick out individuals. Sortals have been extensively studied in the philosophical literature on logic and semantics (Wiggins 1967, 1980; Hirsch 1982; see Macnamara 1987; Xu & Carey 1996, for a discussion of sortal concepts within the context of psychological studies of concepts). In languages with a count/mass distinction, sortal concepts are expressed by count nouns, naturally, which is why they are called "count nouns"; they provide the criteria for individuation and numerical identity that enable entities to be counted. Recently Lucy (1992) has argued for language variation in the dividing line between grammatically individuated material entities and nonindividuated material entities (i.e. some languages individuate only people, others only people and animals, and still others, such as English, people, animals, plus any objects that are bounded, coherent wholes which maintain their boundaries as they move through space). Note that this emphasis on crosslinguistic variation does not deny that all languages mark the distinction between individuated and nonindividuated entities, even if nouns are not marked for count/mass status. Lucy's proposal is for a parameterized system of language variation.

The final linguistic reflection of number I explore here is the contrast between the concepts that establish the individuals in the world (sortals) and the properties that can be attributed to them (predicates). This distinction is a logical one, reflected in the syntactic distinction between nouns and verbs/adjectives. Properties such as *red* differ from sortals such as *cup* in the role they play in logical form (see Macnamara 1987, for a summary of the argument against *bare particulars*, the argument that individuals must be specified by sortals which then bear predication). In this literature, the property of being a cup plays a very different semantic role from the property of being red (Wiggins 1967, 1980; Hirsch 1982; Macnamara 1987). This is not to deny that an entity's properties play important roles in the criteria for application, individuation, and numerical identity supplied by sortals.

Thus, number is reflected in language in five different but interrelated ways: explicitly in counting sequences (*one, two, three*...), grammatically in number markers on nouns and verbs and in quantifier systems; in the criteria for individuation and identity embodied in the sortal concepts the language lexicalizes; in the distinction between count and mass nouns; and in the distinction between count nouns and predicates. In the following sections, I ask which, if any, of these five representational resources that language makes use of in expressing numerical concepts are available to prelinguistic infants.

3 Object as a primitive sortal: the quantifier concepts "one," "another"

Piaget was the first to attempt to bring empirical data to bear on the question of whether human infants have a representation of objects as existing apart from themselves, apart from their own actions upon them, and apart from their perceptual contact with them. Studies of object permanence are, in part, studies of criteria for numerical identity, for they involve the capacity to establish a representation of an individual, and trace this individual through time and through loss of perceptual contact. When we use the term "object permanence" to describe the baby's knowledge, we presuppose that he/she recognizes that the object retrieved from behind the barrier is the *same one* as the one that was hidden.

Piaget, of course, did not believe that prelinguistic infants have the capacity to establish representations of permanent, individuated objects. In his celebrated studies of infants' reaching for hidden objects, he charted a protracted developmental sequence from failing to reach for hidden objects altogether, to perseverative errors (A, not B, errors), to finally being able to reason about invisible displacements, which he took as conclusive evidence for representations of object permanence (Piaget 1954). Piaget saw the achievement of this representational capacity as part of the transition to symbolic thought, intimately bound up with the early stages of language acquisition.

Since the late 1980s, massive evidence has become available revealing that Piaget's reaching studies underestimated infants' conceptual resources.

Babies as young as 2½ to 3 months represent the continued existence of objects that have gone behind barriers (Baillargeon & DeVos 1991) and have spatiotemporal criteria for individuation and numerical identity of objects (criteria such as one object cannot be in two places at once; objects trace spatiotemporally continuous paths – Spelke 1991; Spelke, Kestenbaum, Simons, & Wein 1995; Xu & Carey 1996). The research exploits a recently developed method for characterizing human infants' spontaneous cognitive capacities: the "violation of expectancy method," which measures visual preference for impossible events over possible events (Spelke 1985). Put simply, babies stare at the outcomes of magic tricks more than at the outcomes of ordinary events. This fact enables us to separate knowledge which they have from that which they don't have (after all, they must be sensitive to the impossibility of a given magic trick to respond to it). If we are clever we can design studies that constrain our theories of how that knowledge is represented.

Many experiments using the violation of expectancy method support the conclusion that very young babies represent object permanence. Here I briefly describe two, chosen because they illuminate the relation between object permanence, on the one hand, and spatiotemporal criteria for individuation and numerical identity of objects, on the other, and because they also show that prelinguistic infants' representations are quantified by "one" and "another."

Spelke *et al.* (1995) showed that babies of 4½ months do not merely expect objects to continue to exist through time, when out of view, but also that they interpret apparent evidence for spatiotemporal discontinuity as evidence for two numerically distinct objects. Infants were shown two screens on a stage, from which objects emerged as in figure 7.1. The objects were never visible together; their appearances were timed so that the movements would be consistent with a single object going back and forth behind the two screens, except that no object ever appeared in the space between the screens. Rather, one object emerged from the left edge of the left screen and then returned behind that screen, and, after a suitable delay, a second object emerged from the right edge of the right screen and then returned behind it. Babies were habituated to this event. Adults draw the inference that there must be two numerically distinct objects involved in this display, for objects trace spatiotemporally continuous paths – one object cannot get from point A to point B without tracing some continuous trajectory between the points. The babies in Spelke *et al.* made the same inference. If the screens were removed and only one object was revealed, they were surprised, as shown by longer looking at outcomes of one object than at the expected outcome of two objects. Control experiments established that infants were indeed analyzing the path of motion, and not, for example,

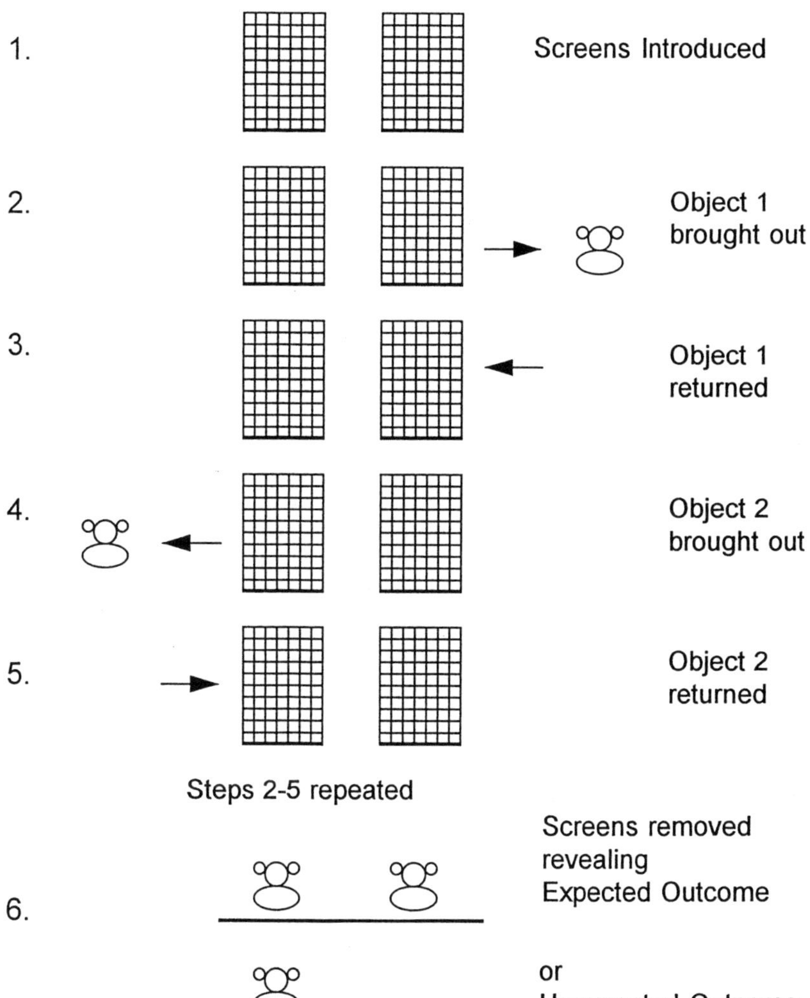

Fig. 7.1 Discontinuous condition in the procedure from Xu & Carey (1996) modeled after Spelke *et al.* (1995). In this condition, no object ever appears in the space between the screens as the objects emerge alternately from the left screen and the right screen.

expecting two objects just because there were two screens. That is, a different pattern of results obtains if an object appeared between the screens as it apparently went back and forth, emerging as before from either side. (See Xu & Carey 1996, for a replication with 10-month-olds.) These data show: infants know that objects continue to exist when they are invisible behind barriers; infants distinguish one object from two numerically distinct but physically similar objects (i.e. they have criteria for object individuation and numerical identity, and they distinguish "one object" from "one object, another object"; infants use spatiotemporal criteria for object individuation: if there is no spatiotemporally continuous path between successive appearances of what could be one or more than one object, they establish representations of at least two numerically distinct objects.

Additionally, Wynn's (1992a, 1995) studies of infants' abilities to add and subtract provide further conclusive evidence that infants represent object permanence, and that spatiotemporal criteria determine object individuation and numerical identity. Wynn (1992a) showed infants of 4½ months an object – a Mickey Mouse doll – placed on a stage. She then occluded the doll from the infant's view by raising a screen, introduced a second doll behind the screen, and then showed the infant an empty hand withdrawing from behind the screen. Then she lowered the screen, revealing either the possible outcome of two objects, or the impossible outcomes of one object or of three objects. Infants looked longer at the unexpected outcomes of one object or three objects than at the expected outcome of two objects. Wynn (1992a) also carried out a subtraction version of this study, beginning with two objects on the stage, occluding them with a screen, removing one from behind the screen, and upon lowering of the screen, revealing either the possible outcome of one object or the impossible outcome of two objects. Again, 4½-month-olds looked longer at the unexpected outcome. Wynn interpreted these studies as showing that infants can add $1 + 1$ to yield precisely 2, and that they can subtract 1 from 2 to yield 1. These studies have been widely replicated (Baillargeon, Miller, & Constantino 1994; Koechlin, Dehaene, & Mehler 1997; Simon, Hespos, & Rochat 1995; Uller, Carey, Huntley-Fenner, & Klatt 1999). Before considering exactly how infants represent number (section 9), here we emphasize the implications of these studies for infant representations of objects:

1. Infants represent objects as continuing to exist behind invisible barriers.
2. Infants distinguish two numerically distinct but physically similar dolls from one doll (i.e. infants have criteria for individuation and numerical identity, they distinguish "one object" from "one object, another object").
3. Infants' criteria for individuation and numerical identity of objects are spatiotemporal, including principles such as one object cannot be in two places at the same time.

These studies contradict Piaget's conclusion that the sortal concept, "object," is built up slowly over the first two years of human life. Rather, it is most likely an innate primitive of the human conceptual system that serves to guide how experience shapes the development of physical knowledge. Of course, these data raise the question of why infants do not exploit their knowledge of object permanence in the reaching tasks Piaget studied. There are several suggestions in the literature: (1) that representations of objects vary in robustness, and that reaching requires a more robust representation than does looking (Munakata, McClelland, Johnson, & Siegler 1997); (2) that the basic Piagetian object permanence task requires means–ends planning skills that are still developing in late infancy (Diamond 1991; Baillargeon 1993); (3) that the Piagetian A, not B paradigm requires the inhibition of a competing response, a capacity that depends upon late-maturing frontal systems (Diamond 1991). These possibilities are not mutually exclusive; they could all contribute to the earlier reflection of knowledge of objects in the looking-time paradigm.

But for our purposes here, the important lesson is the evidence that infants represent at least one concept that provides criteria of individuation and numerical identity: the sortal "object." It is available by 2½ to 3 months, way before it is expressed in natural languages. Also, the prelinguistic infant's representational resources include notions with the force of the basic quantifiers *one*, *another*. The capacity to represent sortals and at least some basic quantifiers, central to the syntax of human language, articulates infants' representations of the world prior to language production or comprehension. Thus, the continuity/universalist position receives strong support with respect to these grammaticized notions.

4 Do preverbal human infants represent the count/mass distinction?

As the above studies show, infants have criteria for the individuation of small, movable objects. They spontaneously establish representations of countable entities. But do they spontaneously establish conceptual representations of nonindividuated entities? And if so, do they quantify over such entities differently from over individuated entities such as objects? The nonindividuated end of Lucy's continuum consists of nonsolid substances, which are noncohesive and do not maintain boundaries as they move through space. We sought to open the question of whether infants represent a conceptual distinction between individuated and nonindividuated entities (the rudiments of the count/mass distinction) by exploring whether they would enumerate piles of sand.

In collaboration with Huntley-Fenner (1995), we carried out a series of studies comparing infant reasoning about sand with infant reasoning about objects that looked just like a pile of sand. The objects were pile-shaped and coated with sand, such that if they were resting on a table adults judged that they were piles of sand. However, they were suspended on a narrow thread and so could be moved through space as a coherent, separable movable object.

Huntley-Fenner's studies address two related questions: first, exactly what is being individuated in the studies cited in section 3? The objects on the stage are good perceptual individuals in the sense of figure/ground perception. They have clear boundaries and stand out against the blue tabletop. In this sense, a pile of sand is also a good perceptual individual. However, a pile of sand is not a canonical *conceptual* individual; it is not a canonical entity that is construed "one entity," as it can also be construed as "some sand" or "some stuff." If babies are enumerating perceptual individuals in these studies, they should also enumerate piles of sand. But if they are enumerating conceptual individuals, objects perhaps, they may fail to enumerate piles of sand. Second, and related, do babies represent the distinction between countable material entities, on the one hand, and uncountable material entities on the other? Failure at enumerating piles of sand would be consistent with the claim that they naturally encode sand as "some stuff" or "some sand," representations for which number of individuated portions is irrelevant.

In Huntley-Fenner's studies, babies were assigned either to the Object condition or the Sand condition. Infants in the Object condition were familiarized with a sand object before the experiment – they were shown it up close and allowed to handle it. Similarly, infants in the Sand condition were familiarized with sand before the experiment; they were shown sand being poured back and forth between containers, and then onto a plate right before them, and were allowed to handle it. The sand object was suspended by a thin black thread, and thus obviously maintained its boundaries as it moved through space. The sand was poured from a clear measuring cup. Thus, although the final appearance of a sand object resting on the stage was identical to that of a pile of sand resting on the stage, infants had ample evidence that the former was a bounded, coherent object whereas the latter was neither bounded nor coherent.

Our first study was a comparison of a $1 + 1 = 2$ or 1 procedure with our sand-pile objects, on the one hand, and piles of sand, on the other. Half of the infants (8-month-olds) were in the Object condition and half were in the Sand condition. The $1 + 1 = 2$ or 1 object condition (figure 7.2, left panel) was closely modelled on Wynn's procedure. The infants saw an object lowered onto the stage floor, after which a screen that hid it was raised. They then saw a second object lowered behind the screen, and the screen was removed, revealing either the expected outcome of two objects

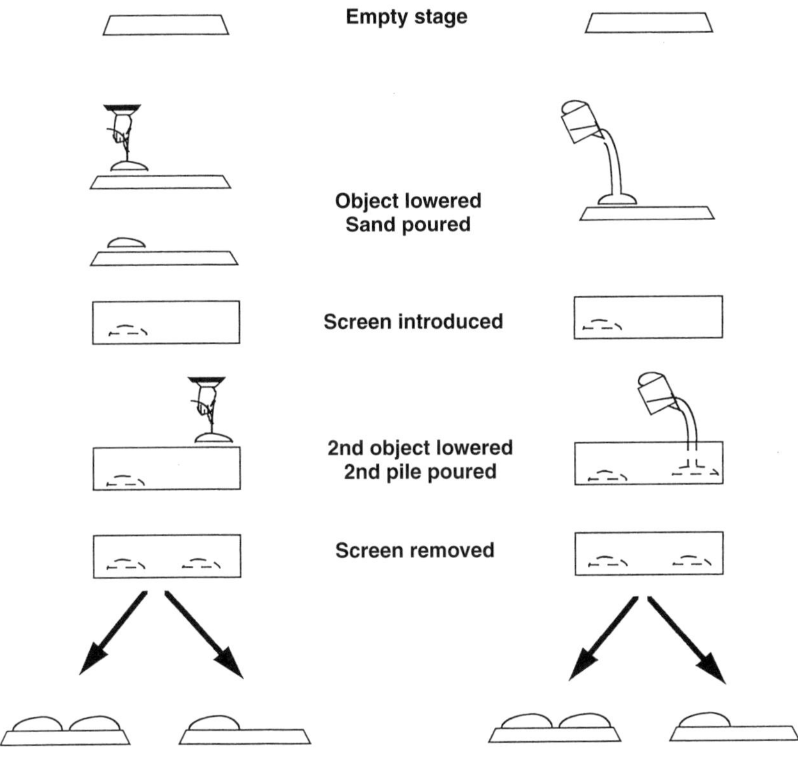

Fig. 7.2 Left panel: 1 + 1 addition paradigm with objects. Right panel:

or the unexpected outcome of one object. Given that 4-month-olds succeed on this task, it is not surprising that our 8-month-olds did; they looked longer at the unexpected outcome of one object than at the expected outcome of two objects. The important question in these studies is how the infants did in the Sand condition, which was made to be as parallel as possible (figure 7.2, right panel). A pile of sand was poured onto the empty stage, the screen hid it, a second pile of sand was poured, and the screen was then removed, revealing either the expected outcome of two piles of sand on the stage or the unexpected outcome of just one. Infants of 8 months failed at this task, showing absolutely no tendency to look longer at the unexpected outcome of one pile of sand; rather, they looked slightly longer at the expected outcome of two, which is also the baseline preference.

Infants' failure to enumerate piles of sand in this condition is consistent with a representational distinction between "some stuff," on the one hand,

and "an object, another object," on the other. However, it is also possible that infants did not notice that the two piles of sand were being poured in distinct positions behind the screen. If the second portion were poured on top of the first, then one pile of sand (albeit a larger pile) would be expected. To address the possibility that infants had not encoded the distinct locations of the two pourings, an easier $1 + 1 = 2$ or 1 sand pile problem was posed (see figure 7.3). In this version, a pile of sand was poured onto the stage, and then two separate screens were introduced and a second pile of sand was poured behind the second screen. Then, the screens both were removed, revealing either two piles of sand (possible outcome) or just one pile of sand (impossible outcome). Again, infants of 8 months failed to look longer at the impossible outcomes, and so did infants of 12 months. Thus, fully 8 months after infants succeed at $1 + 1 = 2$ or 1 object enumeration tasks (4 months; see Wynn 1992; Simon *et al.* 1995; Koechlin *et al.* 1997) infants fail to enumerate two piles of sand. Clearly they are enumerating individuated objects in these infant addition experiments, not perceptually defined individuals, as the outcomes in the Object conditions of this experiment are perceptually indistinguishable from the outcomes in the Sand conditions.

The failure in the two-screen version of this experiment (figure 7.3) underlines the conceptual relation between individuation and permanence. The two-screen task can be thought of as a sand permanence task: to succeed, all the baby needs to represent is sand which continues to exist when poured behind the second screen. But permanence is the continued existence of an individuated portion of sand (*same sand* means "same portion of sand" not "same kind of sand"). Apparently even 12-month-old babies cannot set up a representation of an individuated portion of sand under these circumstances.

These experiments admit of other interpretations. Perhaps the event of pouring sand is much more complex than the event of lowering a sand object. After all, the sand is in three different states during this event – in the cup, in a long thin stream, and gathered into a pile, whereas the object is always in its pile-like configuration. Maybe babies just have a harder time predicting the outcomes of the sand events, especially because they have much less experience with nonsolid substances than with solid objects. Ongoing studies in my laboratory will establish whether the *noncohesiveness* of the sand is crucial to the failure in the above studies. If so, it would seem that prelinguistic babies make a principled and spontaneous (there is no training in these studies) distinction between individuated and nonindividuated material entities. That is, prior to the acquisition of language, the conceptual system makes a rudimentary count/mass distinction.

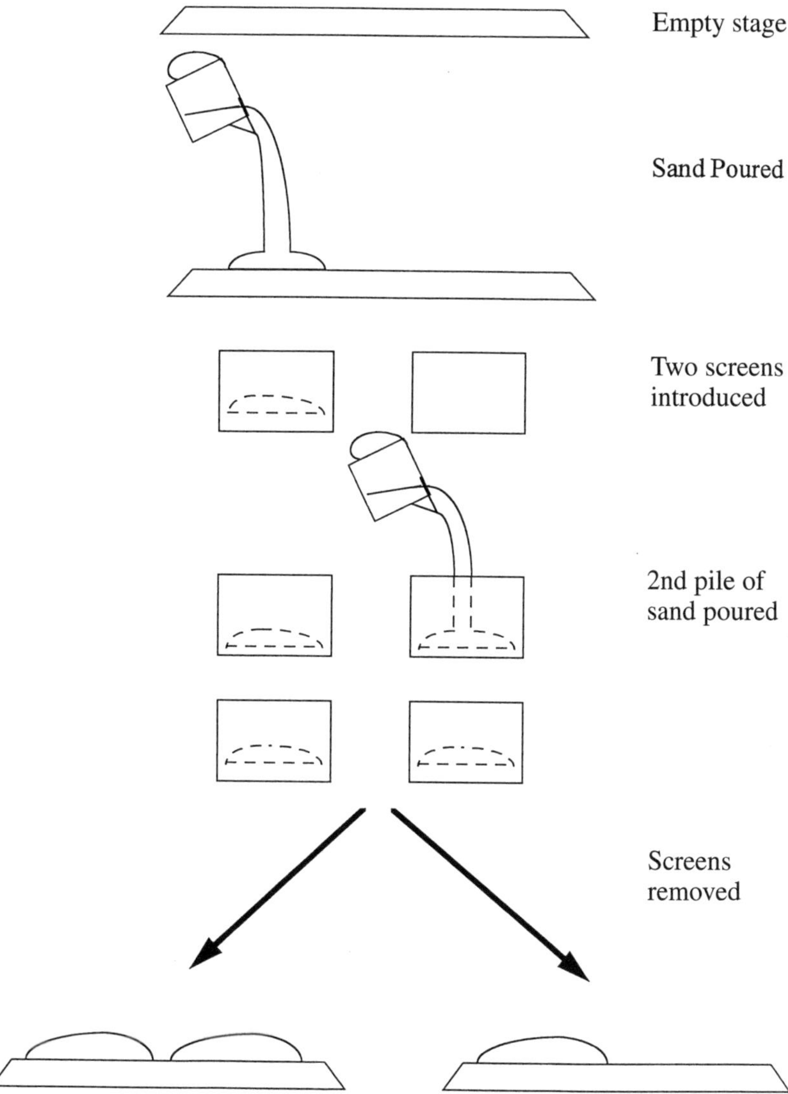

Fig. 7.3 1 + 1 addition paradigm with piles of sand poured behind separate screens.

5 Crosslinguistic variation in individuation?

Gentner & Boroditsky (ch. 8 of this volume) summarize evidence for two hypotheses: (1) what is easy to individuate should be early to name, and (2) crosslinguistic variation in syntactic individuation influences spontaneous naming patterns (Imai & Gentner 1997) and spontaneous categorization of entities (Lucy & Gaskins, ch. 9 of this volume).

In support of the first hypothesis, Gentner & Boroditsky cite the word learning studies of English speakers by Soja, Carey, & Spelke (1991), as well as those of Japanese speakers by Imai & Gentner (1997). These studies show that both Japanese- and English-speaking children as young as 2;0 project the meaning of a newly heard word that has been ostensively defined as referring to a novel artifact (e.g. a plumber's T, an apple corer, a honey dipper) to other objects of the same kind. Such stimuli are easy to individuate; small, mobile objects with complex functional shapes fall far to the individuatable end of their individuation continuum. And apparently such objects are easy to name, as the word learning studies of Soja *et al.* (1991) and Imai & Gentner (1997) attest.

In support of the second hypothesis, Gentner & Boroditsky cite crosslinguistic variation in the projection of word meanings for newly heard words ostensively defined as referring to novel simple objects (e.g. a pyramid made of clay). English speakers as young as age 2;0 project the meaning of the word to other similar pyramids; Japanese speakers of all ages are equally likely to project the word to other portions of clay as to other pyramids. They also cite the evidence of Lucy and Gaskins (ch. 9 of this volume) that speakers of Yucatec Maya spontaneously group as similar entities that share material, in marked contrast to speakers of English, who spontaneously group as similar entities that share membership in functionally defined object kinds.

The studies reviewed in sections 3 and 4 indicate that Hypothesis 1 of Gentner & Boroditsky is incorrect. There is no simple relationship between ease of individuation and patterns of object categorization and naming. In Wynn's studies, and in the replications by Simon *et al.* (1995) and by Koechlin *et al.* (1997), the objects were small human/animal figures (clothed Mickey Mouses, Bert/Ernie, etc.). In terms of Lucy's animacy continuum, or Gentner's & Boroditsky's individuation continuum, these stimuli indeed should be highly individuatable, being representations of animate beings, and being small, independently movable complex objects. However, the sand objects are paradigmatic simple shapes, exactly like those for which Imai & Gentner (1997) found different patterns of naming from that found by Soja *et al.* (1991). Yet the sand objects are every bit as *individuatable* in the studies of Huntley-Fenner (see section 4, above) as are the complex objects. Indeed we have systematically compared sand objects and dolls in two versions of the addition paradigm that are sensitive reflections of infant individuation ability. There was no difference: infants systematically failed in some conditions whether stimuli were simple or complex, and they systematically succeeded in other conditions whether the stimuli were simple or complex. Whereas it may be more difficult to learn a new word that applies to kinds of simple objects than to kinds of complex objects, simple objects are no less individuatable than are complex objects.

We shouldn't be surprised by this result. In terms of spatiotemporal criteria for individuation (objects trace spatiotemporally continuous paths), simple objects do not differ from more complex objects or even from animals and people. But these spatiotemporal criteria do not determine criteria for naming. Object classification and naming are determined by criteria more specific than these general criteria for individuation. Nouns name *kinds* of objects and *kinds* of nonindividuated entities. Here there appears to be scope for linguistic variation. But what exactly is this crosslinguistic variation?

In their summaries of the results of Imai & Gentner, Gentner & Boroditsky state that the difference between English and Japanese speakers is found in the ambiguous stimuli, the simple shapes. It is true that differences are found there. English speakers of all ages project words for such stimuli to other objects of the same kind, and not to other portions of material of the same kind, whereas Japanese speakers of all ages randomly project the words to other objects of the same kind or other materials of the same kind. But Imai & Gentner *equally* found crosslinguistic differences in the naming of nonsolid substances. Japanese speakers of all ages beyond 2;0 projected words for nonsolid substances to other substances of the same kind, not to other portions of different substances fashioned into identical shapes, whereas English speakers of all ages were random on these stimuli. Indeed, the ontological distinction between simple shapes and nonsolid substances was equally salient in both the Japanese data and the English data, even though subjects from the two languages differed in a bias to assume the newly heard word referred to material.

This is an interesting and systematic result, but it is not yet understood. The individuation continuum of Gentner & Boroditsky does not provide an explanation, for nonsolid substances are on the firmly nonindividuatable end of the continuum. According to the hypothesis derived from the individuation continuum, speakers in no language should project words ostensively defined for portions of nonsolid substances to other individuated portions of the same shape (irrespective of substance), but that is exactly what English speakers did in this experiment. These data do not replicate those of Soja *et al.* (1991; in which English-speaking subjects of all ages projected words for nonsolid substances to other materials of the same kind more often than would occur by chance).

Similarly, the data from Lucy & Gaskins (ch. 9 of this volume) are not fully understood. The Maya classifications are not systematically based on material; rather, they are usually at chance. It would be extremely interesting to see word learning studies in this population.

In sum, although there is clearly crosslinguistic variation in the salience of material and functionally/shape-based object kind for object classification and naming, these differences do not relate simply to the criteria that determine the ontological distinction between spontaneously individuatable and nonindividuatable entities.

6 Sortals more specific than "object"

In section 3 I argued that prelinguistic infants represent at least one sortal concept, "object," which provides spatiotemporal criteria for individuation and identity. In section 5 we saw that classification must be kept conceptually separate from individuation. But a moment's reflection shows that the relation between the two is complex. Human adults use other types of evidence besides spatiotemporal information in establishing individuals and tracing their identity through time: property information and membership in kinds more specific than physical object (sortal information). An example of use of property information: if we see a large red cup on a window sill, and later a small green cup there, we infer that two numerically distinct cups were on the sill, even though we have no spatiotemporal evidence to that effect (i.e. we didn't see both at once in different locations). With respect to kind information: adult individuation and numerical identity depends upon sortals more specific than physical object (Wiggins 1967, 1980; Hirsch 1982; Macnamara 1987). When a person, Joe Schmoe, dies, Joe ceases to exist, even though Joe's body still exists, at least for a while. The sortal "person" provides the criteria for identity of the entity referred to by the same *Joe Schmoe*; the sortal "body" provides different criteria for identity.

And it is these more specific sortals that are lexicalized as count nouns in human languages with a count/mass distinction. In this section we turn to the question of when infants represent sortals more specific than objects. Here we find a different result – a suggestion that the emergence of specific sortals is not independent of language learning. Recent data suggest that young infants (below 12 months of age) represent only the sortal "object" and no more specific sortals such as "book," "bottle," "car," "person," "dog," "ball." That is, they represent only spatiotemporal criteria for individuation and identity, and not criteria that specify more specific kinds.

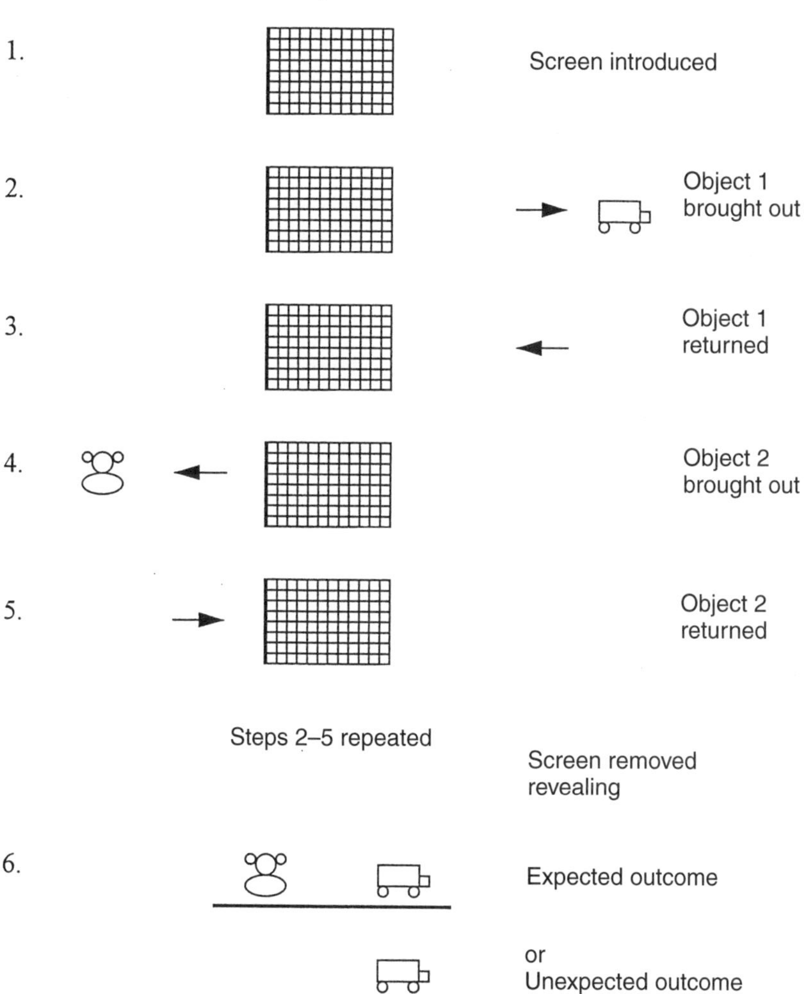

Fig. 7.4 Paradigm from Xu & Carey (1996) designed to test whether infants use the differences in kind between individuals (e.g., truck vs. bear) or the differences in properties between individuals (e.g. red, metal, truck-shaped vs. brown, cloth, bear-shaped) as a basis for individuation.

Consider the event depicted in figure 7.4. An adult witnessing a truck emerge from behind and then disappear back behind the screen and then witnessing a bear emerge from behind and then disappear behind the screen would infer that there are at least two objects behind the screen: a truck and a bear. That adult would make this inference in the absence of any spatio-temporal evidence for two distinct objects, not having seen two at once or any suggestion of a discontinuous path through space and time. Adults trace identity relative to sortals such as "truck" and "bear" and know that trucks do not turn into bears.

Xu & Carey (1996) carried out four experiments based on this design, and found that 10-month-old infants are not surprised at the unexpected outcome of only one object, even when the entities involved are highly familiar objects such as bottles, balls, cups, and books. By 12 months of age, infants make the adult inference, showing surprise at the unexpected outcome of a single object. Importantly, we found that if 10-month-old infants were given spatiotemporal evidence that there were two objects involved (that is, they saw the truck and the bear at the same time to each side of the screen for a few seconds before the series of emergences), they succeeded. The method is sensitive to enumeration ability; 10-month-olds use spatiotemporal evidence for individuation whereas 12-month-olds use kind information as well.

Xu and I have found convergent evidence that sortals more specific than "object" begin to articulate infants' representations of the world between 10 and 12 months of age. We habituated infants to the display of figure 7.5, which adults see as a duck standing on top of a car. That is, adults use the kind difference between a yellow rubber duck and a red metal car to parse this display into two distinct individual objects, even in the absence of spatiotemporal evidence of the two objects moving independently of each other. In the test trials, the hand reached down and picked up the duck by its head; in the unexpected outcomes the single duck/car came up as a piece; in the expected outcomes, just the duck was lifted by the hand. Infants of 10 months were not surprised at the unexpected outcome; 12-month-olds, like adults, revealed surprise by longer looking when the duck/car was raised as a single object. We replicated 10-month-olds' failure to use kind differences for individuation in this paradigm with a shoe and a cup, as well (Xu, Carey, & Welch 1999).

I interpret these results as showing that, before 12 months of age, infants use only the spatiotemporal criteria provided by the sortal "object" when establishing representations of distinct objects in their mental models of the world. By 12 months, infants have constructed more specific sortals, such as "cup," "bottle," "car," "ball," "book," "duck," and so on.

I am not claiming that young infants cannot represent properties of objects, or that they cannot recognize similarity among different objects with some of the same properties. Indeed, very young infants can be habituated to different exemplars of animals, or dogs, or tigers, or vehicles, and will dishabituate if shown an exemplar of a new category (e.g. Cohen & Younger 1983; Quinn & Eimas 1993; Eimas & Quinn 1994). Young infants clearly recognize bottles, cups, books, toy cars, toy ducks, and balls, for they

Fig. 7.5 Stimuli for duck/car individuation procedure. Top panel: habituation display. Bottom left: expected outcome. Bottom right: unexpected outcome.

know some object-specific functions for them (which ones to roll, which ones to drink from, etc.). Similarly, young infants clearly recognize examples of person, for they expect people to move by themselves and to be able to causally interact without contact. And very young infants recognize particular people, such as their mothers. But none of these phenomena show that infants represent concepts like "a bottle," "a book," "a cup," "Mama" – specific sortals or proper names that provide criteria of individuation and identity. One could recognize examples of objects which exemplify cuphood, or Mamaness, and have particular expectancies about objects with such properties, without representing Mama as a single enduring individual, or representing "cup" as a distinct sortal from "book." The results of Xu & Carey suggest that, prior to age 12 months or so, such is the human infant's representational system.

It is significant that babies begin to comprehend object names at about 10 to 12 months of age, the age at which they begin to use the differences between cups and elephants to individuate objects. In two different studies of highly familiar objects (bottle, ball, book, cup), Xu & Carey (1996) found that comprehension of the words for these objects predicted the small number of 10-month-olds who could use these contrasts for object individuation. That is, babies do not seem to learn words for bottle-shaped or bottleness; they begin to learn words such as *bottle* just when they show evidence for sortal concepts such as "bottle" that provide criteria for individuation and numerical identity.

The mastery of sortals more specific than "object" comes way before language production, and before the mastery of any of the syntactic reflexes of sortals in natural language. Thus, syntax acquisition plays no role in this mastery, contrary to Quine (1960; see Soja *et al.* 1991; Carey 1994). However, the correlation Xu and Carey found between word comprehension and success in the individuation task leaves open the possibility that word learning plays some role in the acquisition of specific sortals. It may be that infants expect object labels to map onto kinds, and thus can employ word usage as evidence for what property distinctions are correlated with kind distinctions. However, given that rhesus monkeys appear to resemble English-speaking 12-month-olds and adults on such a task (Hauser & Carey 1998), it seems unlikely that experience with language, let alone with a language that encodes sortals as count nouns, is necessary for the construction of sortals more specific than "object."

7 The sortal/predicate distinction

The studies outlined in section 6 provide good evidence that 10-month-olds do not represent sortals more specific than "object," but the successes at 12 months do not provide unambiguous evidence that older babies do. After all, as mentioned above, under the conditions of these experiments, adults would use property differences between objects as well as sortal differences as sufficient evidence for individuation. Shown a red cup emerging from one side of the screen and returning, followed by a green cup, adults would infer that there were at least two numerically distinct objects behind the screen. The successes of 12-month-olds in the above studies could be due to property differences between the objects (yellow vs. red; rubber vs. metallic). Xu and I have just carried out a series of four studies with 12-month-old babies, using the design of figure 7.4, except that the objects differed on the basis of properties that would be lexicalized in most languages as adjectives rather than as count nouns: big cup vs. small cup; red ball vs. blue ball; red and white fuzzy striped block vs. blue and green plaid vinyl block. We first showed that the infants are sensitive to the property differences under the conditions of these studies. For example, they take longer to habituate to the big cup and the small cup emerging alternately from the sides of the screen than to just a small cup emerging from the sides of the screen. But in no case did the 12-month-olds use these property differences to infer that there were two objects behind the screen. That is, when the screen was removed, revealing what for adults is the unexpected outcome of just one of the two objects, they did not look longer than when the expected outcome of both objects was present. Remember, at this age babies succeed at this task if the two objects differ in kind. It appears that prior to learning any words for adjectives, infants represent a distinction between sortal concepts, such as "cup," and property concepts, such as "red." Only the former provide criteria for individuation in the experiments of Xu & Carey.

Of course, it is also possible that shape is merely a more salient property than are color, size, and texture, and it is this property, shape, that is doing the work when infants succeed at these tasks. To address this issue, Xu & Carey tried one more contrast – two very differently shaped cups (a coffee mug and a sippy cup) within a single kind. Children of 12 months failed to use this difference as a basis for individuation. The data to date, then, are consistent with the possibility that prior to learning any syntax, infants distinguish between concepts that provide criteria for individuation and identity, i.e. sortals, and those that do not, i.e. property concepts.

8 Interim conclusions: the continuity hypothesis receives support

We have examined spontaneous infant representations of their world for four reflections of number that articulate syntactic distinctions in natural language: criteria of individuation and numerical identity; the quantifier concepts "one," "another"; the count/mass distinction; and the sortal/property distinction. In each case, we tentatively conclude that spontaneous infant representations are articulated in terms of the same conceptual contrasts that are marked syntactically in the world's languages. These aspects of conceptualization of the world are not learned through a process of mastering culturally constructed, language-specific syntactic devices. In these cases, at least, the continuity hypothesis receives support.

It is important to see, however, that the answer that emerges from empirical examination of a given set of cases need not necessarily generalize to the next case. That is, the Whorfian position may be true of other aspects of language. Indeed, I believe it is true of the fifth representational resource related to number considered here: the representation of integers.

9 The representation of integers by human infants

In section 3, I discussed the infant addition/subtraction studies as they bore on nonlinguistic representations of objects – object permanence, principles of individuation and numerical identity for objects – and on nonlinguistic representations of basic quantifier concepts such as "one," "another." Here I return to the infant addition/subtraction studies as they bear on the question of prelinguistic infants' representation of the first three natural integers: *1, 2, 3.*

Simple habituation experiments provide ample evidence that young infants, even neonates, are sensitive to numerical distinctions among sets of 1, 2, and 3 entities (e.g. dots: Antell & Keating 1983; sets of varied objects: Starkey & Cooper 1980; continuously moving figures: van Loosbroek & Smitsman 1990; jumps of a doll: Wynn 1996). In such studies, infants are habituated to arrays of a given set size (e.g. 2 entities), and are then shown to dishabituate to arrays of a different set size (e.g. 1 or 3 entities). Wynn's addition and subtraction studies confirm that prelinguistic infants discriminate among sets of 1, 2 and 3 objects, and, additionally, that they know some of the numerical relations among them, for they have been shown to succeed at 1 + 1, 2 – 1, 2 + 1, and 3 – 1 tasks (Wynn 1992a, 1995; Simon *et al.* 1995; Uller *et al.* 1999; Koechlin *et al.*, 1997).

The results presented so far leave open the nature of the representations underlying infants' performance. What these representations might be, and the senses in which they may or may not be "genuinely numerical," is a source of intense debate. In order to engage this debate, one must distinguish among classes of models that may underlie performance, and attempt to bring data to bear on which, if any, underlies infant performance. I know of three serious proposals for infant representation of number that could account for babies' successes in the studies cited above.

- *The numeron list proposal* (Gelman & Gallistel 1978)

Gelman & Gallistel proposed that infants establish numerical representations through a counting procedure that works as follows. There is an innate mentally represented list of symbols called "numerons": !, @, +, %, $ . . . (Of course, we do not know how such symbols would actually be written in the mind.) Entities to be counted are put in one-to-one correspondence with items on this list, always proceeding in the same order through the list. The number of items in the set being counted is represented by the last item on the list reached, its numerical values determined by the ordinal position of that item in the list. For example, in the above list, "@" represents the number 2, because "@" is the second item of the list.

- *The accumulator proposal* (Meck & Church 1983)

Meck & Church proposed that animals represent number with a magnitude that is an analog of number. The idea is simple. Suppose that the nervous system has the equivalent of a pulse generator that generates activity at a constant rate, and a gate that can open to allow energy through to an accumulator that registers how much energy has been let through. When the animal is in counting mode, the gate is opened for a fixed amount of time (say 200 ms) for each item to be counted. The total energy accumulated will then be an analog representation of number. This system works as if length were used to represent number, e.g. "__" being a representation of 1, "____" a representation of 2, "______" a representation of 3, and so on (see Gallistel 1990, for a summary of evidence for the accumulator model).

- *The object file proposal* (Uller *et al.* 1999; Simon *et al.* 1995)

Babies may be establishing a mental model of the objects in the array. That is, they may be constructing an imagistic representation of the stage floor, the screen, and the objects behind the screen, creating one object file (Kahneman, Treisman, & Gibbs 1992) for each object behind the screen. Such a model represents number, e.g. the number 2, in virtue of being an instantiation of: $(\exists x)(\exists y)((\text{object}(x)\ \&\ \text{object}(y))\ \&\ x \neq y\ \&\ \forall z(\text{object}(z)\ \text{-}{>}(z = x) \vee (z = y))$. In English this states that there is an entity and there is another entity numerically distinct from it, that each entity is an object, and there is no other object. This sentence is logically equivalent to "There are exactly two objects," but note that, in such a representation, there is no distinct symbol for the number 2 at all, not "2" or "@" or "____" or any other. This model exploits no representational resources other than those demonstrated in the previous sections: object sortals and the capacity to distinguish "one" from "another."

Besides differing in the nature of the representation of integers, the three models differ in the process underlying discrepancy detection between the representation formed as objects are introduced (or removed from, in subtraction) behind the screen and the representation of the resultant display after the screen is removed. Take an event of $1 + 1 = 2$ or 1 as an example. On the two symbolic models, the results of two counts are compared – the symbol for the number of objects resulting from the operation of adding (e.g. "@" or "____") is compared to the symbol resulting from a count of the objects in the outcome array ("@" or "____" in possible outcomes vs. "!" or "__" in impossible outcomes). According to the object file proposal, a representation consisting of two object files constructed during the addition portion of the event is compared to a representation of two object files (possible outcome) or one object file (impossible outcome) by a process that detects 1–1 correspondence between the object files in the two representations.

These three proposals for nonlinguistic representational systems for number are genuinely different from each other. The first two (the numeron list model and the accumulator model) embody distinct symbols for each integer, but differ in the nature of the symbols they use. In the numeron list model each symbol bears a discrete and arbitrary relation to the number it represents. In the accumulator model, in contrast, an analog representational system exploits the fact that the symbols are magnitudes linearly related to the numbers they represent. And, as previously noted, in the object file system, there is no distinct symbol that represents each integer at all. In this model, there is nothing that corresponds to counting in terms of a set of symbols, whether arbitrary (numerons) or analog (states of the accumulator).

Not all languages have an explicit system for representing integers, but those that do exploit the numeron list model (*one, two, three* . . ., *un, deux, trois* . . ., etc.). Thus, particularly relevant to our present concerns would be evidence that the numeron list model underlies the infant habituation and infant addition/subtraction results. If the numeron list system is available to infants, then learning to count in a natural language is simply a mapping problem – learning the list in the language that corresponds to the list in mentalese – and this state of affairs would be another case in support of the continuity position. However, as I read the available evidence, this state of affairs does not obtain.

Uller *et al.* (1999) present several arguments in favor of the object file model as that which underlies performance on the infant addition and subtraction experiments. The main argument is empirical: several experimental manipulations that might be expected to influence the robustness of mental models of the objects in the arrays, but not a symbolic representation of the number of individuals such as "@" or "____," are shown to affect performance of infants in the addition studies. To give just one example: the timing of the placement of the screen on the stage, relative to the placement of the objects behind it, determines success on a 1 + 1 = 2 or 1 addition study. The classic Wynn study (1992a), and most of the replications (Simon *et al.* 1995; Wynn 1995; Koechlin *et al.* 1997) use an "object-first design" (see figure 7.3). The first object (1) is placed on the stage, then the screen is introduced, and then the second object (+1) is introduced behind the screen. Infants as young as 4 months of age succeed in this design. Uller *et al.* (1999) contrasted this design with a "screen-first design," in which the screen is placed on an empty stage, and then one object (1) is introduced behind it, and then a second (+1) is introduced behind it. Note that on the symbolic models, both of these designs simply require incrementing the counting mechanism twice, yielding a representation of two ("@" or "____"), and holding this symbol in memory until the screen is removed, so these two experimental designs should be equivalent in difficulty. But if we make some reasonable assumptions about the factors that might influence the robustness of mental models, then it seems likely that the object-first design will be markedly easier than the screen-first design. These assumptions are: (1) a mental model of an object actually seen on the stage is more robust than one constructed in imagery, and (2) each update of a mental model in imagery decreases the robustness of the model. The object-first condition begins with a representation of one object on the stage constructed from perception and requires only one update in imagery; the screen-first condition requires that the representation of the first object on the stage be constructed in imagery, and requires two updates in imagery. And indeed, infants succeed in object-first tasks by 4–5 months of age, but in comparable screen-first tasks not until 10 months of age (Uller *et al.*, 1999).

Other considerations favor the object file model as well, not the least of which is the finding of a sharp limit on the numerosities infants represent. Simple habituation experiments with infants, as well as the addition/subtraction studies, have shown that infants represent the numerical values of 1, 2, and 3, but in general fail to discriminate among higher numerosities. There is no such limit on the accumulator model, or the numeron list model, but this limit is predicted by the object file model, on the assumption that there is a limit of parallel individuation of three object files in short-term memory (see Trick & Pylyshyn 1994).

In sum, we suggest that the weight of evidence currently available supports the proposal that the representation of number underlying infants' successes and failures in the addition/subtraction experiments, as well as habituation studies, consists of mental models of the objects in the arrays. These representations are numerical in that they require that the infant have criteria for numerical identity, because a representation that instantiates $(\exists x)(\exists y)((\text{object}(x) \,\&\, \text{object}(y)) \,\&\, x \neq y \,\&\, \forall z(\text{object}(z) \rightarrow (z = x) \vee (z = y))$ is logically equivalent to "There are exactly two objects," and because comparisons among models are on the basis of 1–1 correspondences among object files. However, they fall short of symbolic representations of integers, as there is no unique symbol for each integer, and because there is no counting process defined over them.

The upshot of this argument is that there is no evidence for a prelinguistic representational system of the same structure as natural-language count sequences, such as *1, 2, 3, 4, 5* . . . There is no evidence from the infant studies that such a system is an antecedent representational system, available to be exploited in the learning of language. The difficulty children experience learning the meanings of the words *two* and *three*, the process taking a whole year after they have learned the meaning of *one* and know how to recite the counting list, lends further credence to this conclusion (Wynn 1990, 1992b). It is likely that this symbolic representation of integers is a cultural construction, mastered anew by each child as he/she comes to understand natural-language counting systems. The Whorfian position is most likely correct in this case.

10 Conclusions

Early in the conceptual history of the child, before mastery of any specific natural language, spontaneous mental representations are articulated in terms of contrasts that become marked in natural-language syntax. Those discussed here include criteria for individuation and numerical identity (the sortal "object"; more specific sortals like "cup," "book"); quantifiers such as "one" and "another," the distinction between individuated entities and non-individuated entities; and the distinction between sortals and predicates. Apparently, these conceptual distinctions are not induced from experience with language; rather, they support language learning from the beginning. Hauser & Carey (1998) argue that the history of these distinctions articulating cognitive architecture is longer still, way back in evolutionary time. They show that the violation-of-expectancy method yields interpretable data both in the wild (rhesus macaques) and in the laboratory (cottontop tamarins). The spontaneous conceptual representations of rhesus macaques and cottontop tamarins are like those of human babies with respect to the representations of "object" as a sortal, the distinction between "one," "another," and in the case of rhesus, probably also the representation of more specific sortals such as "carrot," "squash" (Hauser & Carey 1998). These are some of the conceptual primitives from which language is built, both in phylogenesis and in ontogenesis. They are not language-specific cultural constructions.

Finally, there is no doubt that babies are sensitive to numerical distinctions among sets of objects; that is, they represent number as one dimension of their experience of the world. These include representations of small numerosities (perhaps in the form of one, two, or three object files held in parallel in short-term memory). All of these aspects of representations of number are prior to the linguistic expression of numerical concepts in the lexicon or syntax of natural languages.

However, the representation of the integers in terms of a list of numerals, or numerons (mentally represented numerals), is most likely a human cultural construction. Mastering it requires months, or years, of training, suggesting that it is importantly different from the prelinguistic representations of numbers available to both infants and animals. The object file and accumulator models are both candidate nonlinguistic representational systems for number, and both are importantly different from the numeron list model in ways that would explain why it is difficult to learn and not culturally universal. In the object file model there is no symbol for integers at all, and in the accumulator model there is no discrete symbol for each integer.

It is possible that this construction was made possible by human language, but also required a long history of cultural development. Human children learn the list of numerals, and the counting procedure, well before they map any of the numerals beyond *1* onto the numbers they represent. They then laboriously learn what *2* means, and then *3*. By the time they have learned what *4* means, they have induced the principle by which the whole list represents number, and they immediately know what all the numbers in their count sequence mean (Wynn 1992b). This occurs by around age 3½ years in normally developing children learning a language with a system of numerals. It can also be mastered by nonhuman animals – chimpanzees (Matsuzawa 1985; Boysen & Bernston 1989; Matsuzawa, Itakura, & Tomonaga 1991; Rumbaugh & Washburn 1993) and an African gray parrot (Pepperberg 1987, 1994) – and, as with children, extensive training (in the case of animals, years of daily training) is required. Humans and other animals have the capacity to build representational systems that transcend those that get cognition and language learning off the ground, systems that may be culturally constructed.

This case study makes clear the vast amount of work that remains to be done. We need to examine aspects of language case by case for their ontogenetic and phylogenetic history in creatures without language (human infants, nonhuman animals). Those grammaticized notions that articulate nonlinguistic spontaneous mental representations are candidates for nativist/universalist components of the human language faculty. And for those aspects of language for which we can find no evidence in these nonlinguistic creatures, we must provide detailed proposals for how such new representational resources might be culturally constructed, and how they are created anew by children as they master the language that embodies them.

REFERENCES

Antell, S. E., & D. P. Keating. 1983. Perception of numerical invariance in neonates. *Child Development* 54: 695–701.

Baillargeon, R. 1993. The object concept revisited: new directions in the investigation of infants' physical knowledge. In C. E. Granrud (ed.), *Carnegie Mellon Symposia on Cognition*, vol. 23: *Visual perception and cognition in infancy*. Hillsdale, NJ: Lawrence Erlbaum, 265–315.

Baillargeon, R., & J. DeVos. 1991. Object permanence in young infants: further evidence. *Child Development* 62: 1227–1246.

Baillargeon, R., K. Miller, & J. Constantino. 1994. Ten-month-old infants' intuitions about addition. Unpublished ms, University of Illinois.

Boysen, S. T., & G. G. Bernston. 1989. Numerical competence in a chimpanzee. *Journal of Comparative Psychology* 103: 23–31.

Carey, S. 1985. *Conceptual change in childhood.* Cambridge, MA: Bradford/MIT Press.

1988. Conceptual differences between children and adults. *Mind and Language* 3: 167–181.

1991. Knowledge acquisition: enrichment or conceptual change? In S. Carey & R. Gelman (eds.), *The epigenesis of mind: studies in biology and cognition.* Hillsdale, NJ: Lawrence Erlbaum, 257–291.

1994. Does learning a language require conceptual change? *Lingua* 92: 143–167.

1995. On the origins of causal understanding. In D. Sperber, D. Premack, & A. J. Premack (eds.), *Causal cognition*. Oxford: Clarendon Press, 268–308.

Carey, S., & E. Spelke. 1994. Domain-specific knowledge and conceptual change. In L. A. Hirschfeld & S. A. Gelman (eds.), *Mapping the mind: domain specificity in cognition and culture*. Cambridge: Cambridge University Press, 169–200.

Cohen, L. B. & B. Younger. 1983. Perceptual categorization in the infant. In E. K. Scholnick (ed.), *New trends in conceptual representation*. Hillsdale, NJ: Lawrence Erlbaum.

Croft, W. A. 1990. *Typology and universals*. Cambridge: Cambridge University Press.

Davidson, D. 1974. The very idea of a conceptual scheme. In *Proceedings and addresses of the American Philosophical Association*, vol. 47. Clinton, OH: American Philosophical Association, 5–20.

Diamond, A. 1991. Neuropsychological insights into the meaning of object concept development. In S. Carey & R. Gelman (eds.), *The epigenesis of mind: studies in biology and cognition*. Hillsdale, NJ: Lawrence Erlbaum, 67–110.

Eimas, P., & P. Quinn. 1994. Studies on the formation of perceptually-based basic-level categories in young infants. *Child Development* 65: 903–917.

Feyerabend, P. 1962. Explanation, reduction, empiricism. In H. Feigl & G. Maxwell (eds.), *Minnesota studies in the philosophy of science*, vol. 3. Minneapolis: University of Minnesota Press, 41–87.

Fodor, J. 1998. *Concepts: where cognitive science went wrong*. Oxford: Oxford University Press.

Gallistel, C. R. 1990. *The organization of learning*. Cambridge, MA: MIT Press.

Gelman, R., & C. R. Gallistel. 1978. *The child's understanding of number*. Cambridge, MA: Harvard University Press.

Gleitman, L. R. 1990. The structural sources of verb meanings. *Language Acquisition* 1: 3–55.

Hacking, I. 1993. Working in a new world: the taxonomic solution. In P. Horwich & J. Thomson (eds.), *World changes*. Cambridge, MA: MIT Press, 275–310.

Hauser, M. D., & S. Carey. 1998. Building a cognitive creature from a set of primitives: evolutionary and developmental insights. In D. Cummins & C. Allen (eds.), *The evolution of mind*. Oxford: Oxford University Press, 51–106.

Hirsch, E. 1982. *The concept of identity*. New York: Oxford University Press.

Huntley-Fenner, G. 1995. Infants' representations of non-solid substances. Unpublished doctoral dissertation, Massachusetts Institute of Technology, Cambridge, MA.

Imai, M., & D. Gentner. 1997. A crosslinguistic study of early word meaning: universal ontology and linguistic influence. *Cognition* 62: 169–200.

Kahneman, D., A. Treisman, & B. J. Gibbs. 1992. The reviewing of object files: object-specific integration of information. *Cognitive Psychology* 24: 175–219.

Kitcher, P. 1978. Theories, theorists and theoretical change. *Philosophical Review* 87: 519–547.

Koechlin, E., S. Dehaene, & J. Mehler. 1997. Numerical transformations in five-month-old infants. *Mathematical Cognition* 3: 89–104.

Kuhn, T. S. 1962. *The structure of scientific revolutions*. Chicago: University of Chicago Press.

1982. Commensurability, comparability, communicability. *PSA 1982*, vol. 2. East Lansing: Philosophy of Science Association, 669–688.

Lucy, J. A. 1992. *Language diversity and thought: a reformulation of the linguistic relativity hypothesis*. Cambridge: Cambridge University Press.

Macnamara, J. 1982. *Names for things: a study of human learning*. Cambridge, MA: MIT Press.

1987. *A border dispute: the place of logic in psychology*. Cambridge, MA: MIT Press.

Matsuzawa, T. 1985. Use of numbers by a chimpanzee. *Nature* 315: 57–59.

Matsuzawa, T., S. Itakura, & M. Tomonaga. 1991. Use of numbers by a chimpanzee: a further study. In A. Ehara, T. Kimura, O. Tokenaka, & M. Iwamoto (eds.), *Primatology Today*. Amsterdam: Elsevier, 317–320.

McCloskey, M. 1983. Intuitive physics. *Scientific American* 248: 114–128.

Meck, W. H., & R. M. Church. 1983. A mode control model of counting and timing processes. *Journal of Experimental Psychology: Animal Behaviour Processes* 9: 320–334.

Munakata, Y., J. McClelland, M. Johnson, & R. Siegler. 1997. Now you see it, now you don't: a gradualistic framework for understanding infants' successes and failures in object permanence tasks. *Psychological Review* 104: 686–713.

Nersessian, N. J. 1992. How do scientists think? Capturing the dynamics of conceptual change in science. In R. N. Giere (ed.), *Cognitive models of science*. Minnesota Studies in the Philosophy of Science 15. Minneapolis: University of Minnesota Press, 3–44.

Pepperberg, I. M. 1987. Evidence for conceptual quantitative abilities in the African gray parrot: labeling of cardinal sets. *Ethology* 75: 37–61.

Numerical competence in an African gray parrot (*Psittacus erithacus*). *Journal of Comparative Psychology* 108: 36–44.

Piaget, J. 1954. *The child's construction of reality*. New York: Basic Books.

Pinker, S. 1984. *Language learnability and language development*. Cambridge, MA: Harvard University Press.

Quine, W. V. O. 1960. *Word and object*. Cambridge, MA: MIT Press.

Quinn, P., & P. Eimas. 1993. Evidence for representations of perceptually similar natural categories by 3- and 4-month-old infants. *Perception* 22: 463–475.

Rumbaugh, D. M., & D. A. Washburn. 1993. Counting by chimpanzees and ordinality judgements by macaques in video-formatted tasks. In S. T. Boysen &

E. J. Capaldi (eds.), *The development of numerical competence: animal and human models*. Hillsdale, NJ: Lawrence Erlbaum, 56–91.

Simon, T., S. Hespos, & P. Rochat. 1995. Do infants understand simple arithmetic? A replication of Wynn (1992). *Cognitive Development* 10: 253–269.

Soja, N. N., S. Carey, & E. S. Spelke. 1991. Ontological categories guide young children's inductions of word meaning: object terms and substance terms. *Cognition* 38: 179–211.

Spelke, E. S. 1985. Preferential looking methods as tools for the study of cognition in infancy. In G. Gottlieb & N. Krasnegor (eds.), *Measurement of audition and vision in the first year of post-natal life*. Hillsdale, NJ: Lawrence Erlbaum, 323–364.

1991. Physical knowledge in infancy: reflections on Piaget's theory. In S. Carey & R. Gelman (eds.), *The epigenesis of mind: essays on biology and cognition*. Hillsdale, NJ: Lawrence Erlbaum, 37–61.

Spelke, E. S., R. Kestenbaum, D. J. Simons, & D. Wein. 1995. Spatio-temporal continuity, smoothness of motion and object identity in infancy. *British Journal of Developmental Psychology* 13: 113–142.

Starkey, P., & R. G. Cooper. 1980. Perception of numbers by human infants. *Science* 210: 1033–1035.

Trick, L., & Z. Pylyshyn. 1994. Why are small and large numbers enumerated differently? A limited capacity preattentive stage in vision. *Psychological Review* 101: 80–102.

Uller, C., S. Carey, G. Huntley-Fenner, & L. Klatt. 1999. What representations might underlie infant numerical knowledge? *Cognitive Development* 14: 1–36.

van Loosbroek, E., & A. W. Smitsman. 1990. Visual perception of numerosity in infancy. *Developmental Psychology* 26: 916–922.

Vosniadou, S., & W. F. Brewer. 1992. Mental models of the earth: a study of conceptual change in childhood. *Cognitive Psychology* 24: 535–585.

Wiggins, D. 1967. *Identity and spatio-temporal continuity*. Oxford: Basil Blackwell.

1980. *Sameness and substance*. Oxford: Basil Blackwell.

Wiser, M., & S. Carey. 1983. When heat and temperature were one. In D. Gentner & A. Stevens (eds.), *Mental models*. Hillsdale, NJ: Lawrence Erlbaum, 267–297.

Wynn, K. 1990. Children's understanding of counting. *Cognition* 36: 155–193.

1992a. Addition and subtraction by human infants. *Nature* 358: 749–750.

1992b. Children's acquisition of the number words and the counting system. *Cognitive Psychology* 24: 220–251.

1995. Origin of numerical knowledge. *Mathematical Cognition* 1: 36–60.

1996. Infants' individuation and enumeration of sequential actions. *Psychological Science* 7: 164–169.

Xu, F., & S. Carey. 1996. Infants' metaphysics: the case of numerical identity. *Cognitive Psychology* 30: 111–153.

Xu, F., S. Carey, & J. Welch. 1999. Infants' ability to use object kind information for object individuation. *Cognition* 70: 137–166.

8 Individuation, relativity, and early word learning

Dedre Gentner and Lera Boroditsky

Northwestern University and Stanford University

Which words do children learn earliest, and why? These questions bear on how humans organize the world into semantic concepts, and how children acquire this parsing. A useful perspective is to think of how bits of experience are conflated into the same concept. One possibility is that children are born with the set of conceptual conflations that figures in human language. But assuming (as we will) that most semantic concepts are learned, not innate, there remain two possibilities. First, aspects of perceptual experience could form inevitable conflations that are conceptualized and lexicalized as unified concepts. In this case, we would have *cognitive dominance*: concepts arise from the cognitive–perceptual sphere and are simply named by language. A second possibility is *linguistic dominance*: the world presents perceptual bits whose clumping is not pre-ordained, and language has a say in how the bits get conflated into concepts.

We propose that *both* cognitive and linguistic dominance apply, but to different degrees for different kinds of words (Gentner 1981, 1982). Some bits of experience naturally form themselves into inevitable (preindividuated) concepts, while other bits are able to enter into several different possible combinations.

1 Relational relativity and the division of dominance

Embracing both cognitive and linguistic dominance may seem to be a vague middle-of-the-road position. But we can make the distinction sharper by asking *which* applies *when*. We suggest a larger pattern, a *division of dominance* (Gentner 1988). This distinction takes off from the classic distinction between open- and closed-class words whereby an *open class* is a large lexical category that readily accepts new members – e.g. noun, verb, and adjective in English – and a *closed class* is a (typically small) lexical category to which new members are rarely added – for example, preposition, determiner, and conjunction in English. Whereas open-class words have denotational functions, closed-class words[1] serve grammatical or relational functions; their role is to provide linguistic connections among the more

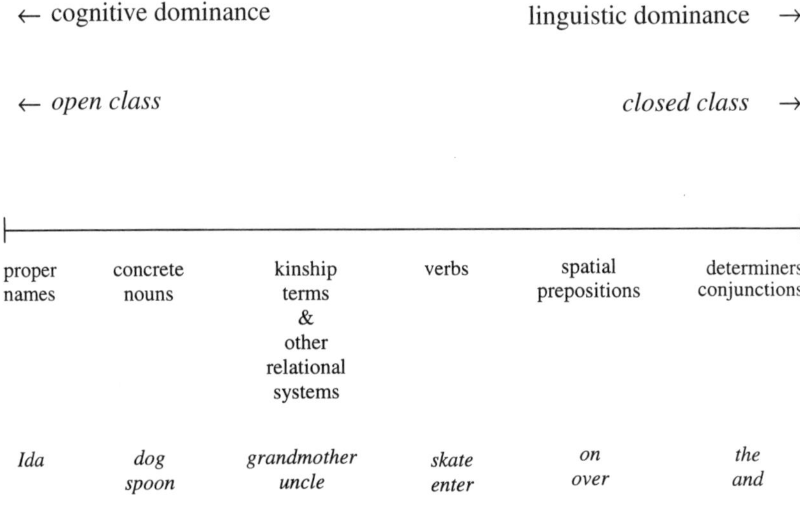

Fig. 8.1 The Division of Dominance.

referential open-class terms. Closed-class words have a number of interesting properties relative to open-class words: they are mostly of high frequency, they are not easily translated, they are rarely borrowed in language contact, their interpretation is context-sensitive, and they are often polysemous and even syncategorematic.

This distinction has traditionally been considered a dichotomy in English, with nouns, verbs, and other contentives in the open class. But, as Gentner (1981, 1988) reviewed, this division is better viewed as a continuum, with verbs and prepositions ranged between nouns and closed-class terms. Like closed-class terms, verbs and prepositions perform relational functions. Further, to return to our main issue, they are linguistically embedded: their meanings are invented or shaped by language to a greater degree than is the case for concrete nouns.

The Division of Dominance continuum is shown in figure 8.1. At one extreme, concrete nouns – terms for objects and animate beings – follow cognitive–perceptual dominance. They denote entities that can be individuated on the basis of perceptual experience. At the other extreme, closed-class terms – such as conjunctions and determiners – follow linguistic dominance. Their meanings do not exist independent of language. Verbs and preposi-

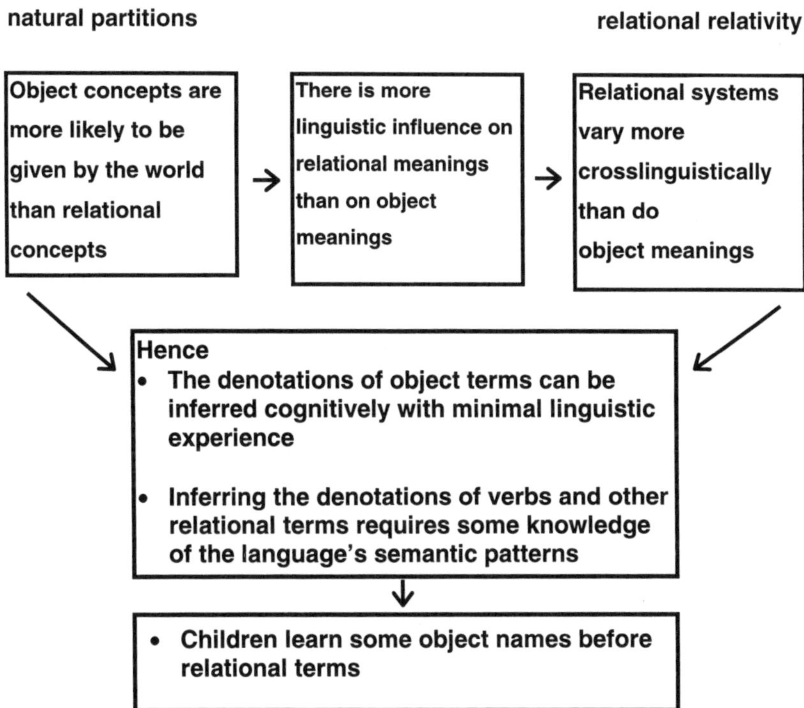

Fig. 8.2 Natural partitions and relational relativity.

tions – even "concrete" motion verbs and spatial prepositions – lie between. Unlike closed-class terms, they have a denotational function, but the composition of the events and relations they denote is negotiated via language.

1.1 Language acquisition and the Division of Dominance

How does all this connect with early word learning? Gentner's (1982) prediction that nouns should enter the vocabulary before verbs rests on two corollaries of the Division of Dominance: natural partitions and relational relativity (figure 8.2). Although the first has received more attention, the second is, to our thinking, more interesting:

1. *Natural partitions*: "there are in the experiential flow certain highly cohesive collections of percepts that are universally conceptualized as objects, and . . . these tend to be lexicalized as nouns across languages. Children learning language have already isolated these cohesive packages – the concrete objects and individuals – from their surroundings" (Gentner 1982: 324).

2. *Relational relativity*: "when we lexicalize the perceptual world, the assignment of relational terms is more variable crosslinguistically than that of nominal terms . . . Predicates show a more variable mapping from concepts to words. A language has more degrees of freedom in lexicalizing relations between coherent objects than in lexicalizing the objects themselves . . . Thus, for verbs and other relational terms, children must discover how their language combines and lexicalizes the elements of the perceptual field" (Gentner,1982: 323–325).

According to the natural partitions hypothesis, the first concepts to be lexicalized are cognitively preindividuated natural conflations – concepts whose representations are densely internally connected (Gentner 1981). The relational relativity hypothesis states that the meanings of relational terms – even "concrete" relational terms such as motion verbs and spatial prepositions – exist in linguistically defined systems and are therefore more variable crosslinguistically than those of concrete nouns. Thus cognitive dominance prevails at the first referential connection. Later, as the child enters the language, linguistic dominance becomes more important.

The relational relativity hypothesis drew on research by Talmy (1975), Bowerman (1976), Maratsos & Chalkley (1980), and Langacker (1987) showing crosslinguistic differences in characteristic patterns of meanings for verbs and other predicate terms.[2] Recent research has further demonstrated the crosslinguistic variability of relational terms (e.g. Choi & Bowerman 1991, ch. 16 of this volume; Bowerman & Pederson 1992; Levinson 1996, ch. 19 of this volume; Sinha, Thorseng, Hayashi, & Plunkett 1994; Slobin 1996; Waxman, Senghas, & Benveniste 1997). For example, in his classic treatise on motion verbs, Talmy (1975) noted differences in conflation patterns between English and the Romance languages. English verbs readily conflate manner of motion with change of location, leaving path as a separate element: e.g. *fly away*, *tiptoe across*. In contrast, French and Spanish motion verbs[3] tend to include path, with manner optionally added separately: e.g. *partir en volant*, *traverser sur la pointe des pieds*. The infant must learn which of these conflationary patterns applies in her language.

At one end of the Division of Dominance lie concrete nouns, whose referents are highly likely to be clumped into single units. These are likely to have crosslinguistically stable denotations (because all cultures can perceive them as wholes) and to be easily learned by children (because their referents are easy for a child to individuate). Verbs and prepositions lie further towards the linguistic pole, where semantic conflation patterns are linguistically specified. Learning the denotations of these terms requires some understanding of the language. Thus they will be acquired later, in part through bootstrapping from previously learned noun–object pairs.

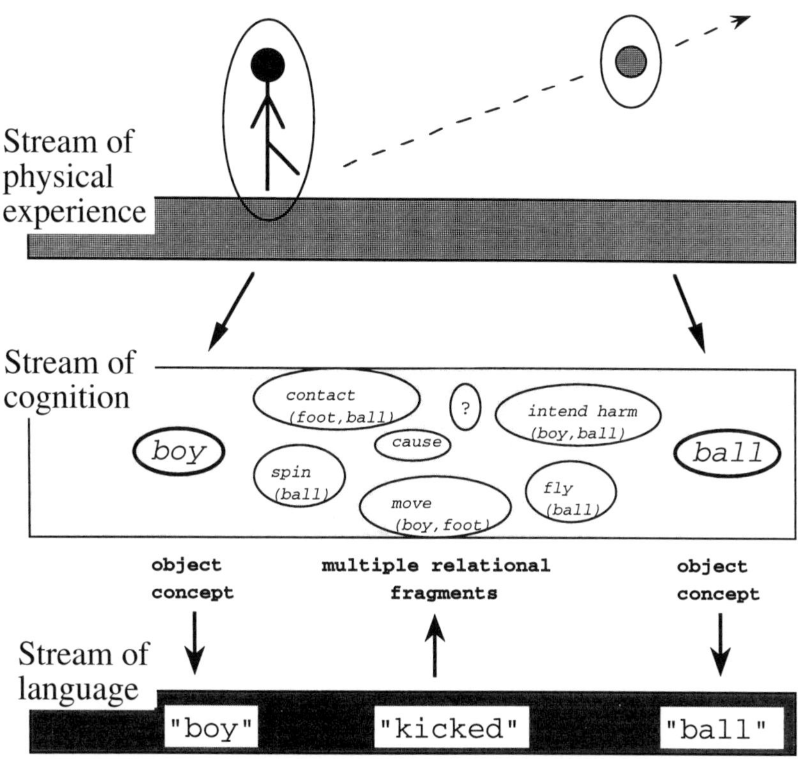

Fig. 8.3 Early interactions of language and experience.

We suggest that different word classes behave very differently in language acquisition. Consider the child's initial task in its simplest terms, as one of attaching words in the stream of speech to their referents in the stream of experience (figure 8.3). Concrete objects and entities have already been individuated prelinguistically (Spelke 1985, 1990; Baillargeon 1993). Given a salient potential referent, part of the child's task of finding word–referent connections is already solved; it remains only to find the correct linguistic label. In contrast, for verbs and other relational terms,[4] isolating the word is only part of the job. The child must also discover which conflation of the available conceptual elements serves as the verb's referent in her language. Not only the intensions but even the extensions of relational terms must be learned in part from language. This is not to suggest that young children fail to perceive relations, or that they are not interested in them. On the contrary, movement, change, agency, and causality are fascinating to infants. But although relational fragments are perceived from early on, there is no one best way in which they cohere into referential units.

There are other reasons to expect particular classes of verbs and prepositions to be learned late relative to nouns. Many concrete verbs have referents that exist only briefly; concrete nouns typically have referents that persist over time. There is also evidence that the instantiation of relational terms depends on their arguments (Gentner & France 1988). For example, in "The goose rode the horse" *goose* and *horse* can be imaged independently of the rest of the terms, but *rode* cannot.

Research by Gillette, Gleitman, Gleitman, & Lederer (1998) demonstrates the difficulty of picking out possible verb referents (see also Gleitman & Gleitman 1992; Gleitman 1994; Fisher, Hall, Rakowitz, & Gleitman 1994). These investigators showed adult subjects silent videos of mothers talking to young children, with beeps marking the instance of a particular noun or verb. The subject's task was to guess the word uttered at the beeps. After six different instances of a given word, subjects were able to guess correctly only 15% of the time for verbs (as compared to 45% of the time for nouns). If subjects were also given the nouns used by the mother, they were about twice as accurate, at 29%. Interestingly, if nonsense syntactic frames – e.g. "Gorp the fendex" – were also given, the percentage rose to 90% – evidence for the role of syntactic frames in selecting among possible verbs (but see also Pinker 1994).

Another line of evidence attesting to children's difficulties in learning relational meanings comes from their semantic errors during verb learning. For example, in Bowerman's (1974, 1976, 1978) studies of children's spontaneous semantic errors for verbs, she found that two- to four-year-olds, having previously used verbs like *eat* and *fall* correctly, began making errors like "But I can't eat her!" (meaning "I can't make her eat") and "I'm gonna just fall this on her" (meaning "make fall, drop"; Bowerman 1974). She suggested that the children were overextending a common English conflationary pattern by which a word denoting a state – e.g. "The door is *open*" – can also be used as a causative, as in "*Open* the door" (i.e. *Cause* the door to *become open*). These late errors suggest that children take a fair bit of time to discover the patterns of conflation in their language. L. Bloom's (1973) observations of children's speech also illustrate their difficulties in expressing relations between objects. For example, 3-year-old Gia, wishing to put a disc into her pocket, says "Button. Button. Button. Button" and "Pocket. Pocket," but "cannot express the relationship she wants to exist between the two objects she can name separately" (1973: 13). To say "*Put* the button *into* the pocket" seems trivial to an adult, but the child must learn that *put* does not contain a path element, that English uses *put* for inanimate destinations and *give* for animate destinations, and so on.

Of course, lexical acquisition should also be influenced by the input, as Gentner (1982) noted – both by typological factors like word order and morphology and by interactional factors such as patterns of child-directed speech. We suggest that when all the input factors are taken into account, there will remain a contribution from conceptual preindividuation. A full test of this prediction requires calibrating the various input factors across languages, and comparing them with observed patterns of vocabulary acquisition. Although this kind of research can and should be done, there is a "quick and dirty" shortcut that may be informative. If words with highly individuable referents – such as names for entities and objects – predominate in early vocabularies across a wide range of input variation, this would constitute evidence for conceptual factors in early word learning.

There is evidence in English for an early predominance of names for objects and individuals and a later increase in the proportion of relational terms (Woodward & Markman 1998). Nouns predominate in early production and comprehension (Macnamara 1972; Nelson 1973; Huttenlocher 1974; Goldin-Meadow, Seligman, & Gelman 1976; Gentner 1982; Huttenlocher & Smiley 1987). Further, children appear to take novel words as names for objects (Markman 1989, 1990; Waxman 1991; Waxman & Hall 1993; Landau, Smith, & Jones 1998), even as early as 13 months of age (Waxman & Markow 1995) and to learn object reference readily (Goldin-Meadow, Butcher, Mylander, & Dodge 1994).

Yet despite this support, the claim of an early noun bias has recently become the focus of intense controversy. A number of challenges have emerged, some of them based on new crosslinguistic findings. In section 3 of this chapter, we respond to these challenges in detail. First, however, we take a new tack. We explore a new prediction of the Division of Dominance framework that escapes certain difficulties by staying within one form class. In the next section we present this extension, which we call the *Individuability continuum*, and give new evidence.

2 Individuability and early word learning: predictions within the object class

We have argued that ease of individuation is a strong predictor of early naming, and that this is a factor in the advantage of concrete nouns over concrete verbs. But comparing across form classes risks confounding other differences along with individuability. We now look within the noun class as another way of testing this claim. If the conceptual naturalness of individuation is the source of the noun advantage, then there should be differential acquisition *within* the noun class, as well as between nouns and relational words. Specifically, (1) relational nouns that are acquired early should initially be taken as object reference terms; and (2) the names of highly individuable objects and entities should be acquired before those of less easily individuated objects.

There is evidence for the first prediction in the acquisition of relational nouns like *uncle* and *passenger.* Children at first tend to interpret these as object-reference terms and to extend them according to common object properties. For example, Keil (1989) found that preschoolers initially interpreted *uncle* as "a friendly man with a pipe" and later shifted to an interpretation in terms of kinship relations. Likewise, Waxman & Hall (1993) found that preschool children taught new relational terms, such as *passenger*, tended to interpret them as object-reference terms.

The second prediction, that ease of individuation is a strong predictor of initial learning, requires deciding which kinds of objects are highly individuable. One route is to ask what contributes to infants' sense of objecthood. Spelke's (1985, 1990) findings suggest that from a very early age children expect continued "objecthood" when they perceive a stable perceptual structure moving against a background (the Gestaltists' *common fate* principle). Later they come to use the perceptual *well-formedness* of an object as a predictor of its continued stability. If individuability is predictive of early word learning, then these patterns imply that the first words should include words for moving entities – animate beings and small movable objects – and words for objects that are perceptually coherent and well-formed.

We begin with perceptual coherence and return to animacy below. We suggest two related criteria for "perceptual coherence," both of which assume that objects can be represented in term of interrelated components such as geons (Biederman 1987) or object parts (Palmer 1978; Tversky & Hemenway 1984). The first is internal connectivity. Highly coherent objects have densely interconnected representations, in which the number of internal links between components is large relative to the number of components (Palmer 1978; Gentner 1981). The second contributor to perceived coherence is well-formed structure. Higher-order relations such as symmetry or monotonicity promote coherence (Garner 1978; Palmer 1978; Prasada 1996; Kotovsky & Gentner 1996).

Does object coherence affect early word learning? Research on Japanese and English conducted in collaboration with Mutsumi Imai suggests that the answer is "yes."

2.1 Individuation and the mass/count distinction

One way to approach the issue of early individuation is to ask what makes children treat something as an object rather than a substance in word learning. Object terms and substance terms have fundamentally different patterns of reference. While object terms like *chair* have discrete reference, substance terms like *flour* have "scattered" reference and can refer cumulatively. Any portion of flour is also flour, but the legs of a chair are not a chair. A child must realize that a term like *chair* can be extended to similarly shaped objects regardless of material, while a term like *flour* projects to stuff of the same material regardless of shape.

How might children learn the object–substance distinction? As before, there are three possibilities: the distinction could be innate; learned from experience of the world; or learned from language. The latter possibility was suggested by Quine (1969), who noted that in English the object–substance distinction is correlated with the grammatical distinction between count nouns and mass nouns. (See Gordon 1985; Gathercole 1986). Count and mass nouns take different determiners: *a chair* vs. *some flour*. Count nouns can be pluralized directly (as in *several chairs*), but mass nouns cannot (**several flours*). Finally, count nouns can be directly counted, but mass nouns require a unitizer before they can be counted (e.g. *two chairs* vs. *two cups of flour*).

Soja, Carey, & Spelke (1991) investigated children's understanding with an ingenious technique. They taught young children new words for either solid objects or nonsolid substances and then asked the children to extend the word, using phrasing that was neutral with respect to the count/mass distinction (e.g. "This is my blicket – show me your blicket"). They found that even 2-year-olds distinguished between objects and substances in their word extensions. When shown an object, they extended on the basis of common shape, indicating an object interpretation; when shown a substance, they extended on the basis of common material, indicating a substance interpretation. Soja *et al.* concluded that there is a prelinguistic, possibly innate ontological distinction between objects and substances that children use to constrain possible meanings of new words.

Despite the elegance of this reasoning, the conclusion rests on the problematic issue of when linguistic influences begin. English 2-year-olds lack productive competence in the count/mass distinction, but may nonetheless have been influenced by the syntactic distinction. Therefore, Imai & Gentner (1997) decided to undertake a stronger test by taking advantage of crosslinguistic differences. Many numeral classifier languages, such as Yucatec Maya and Japanese, lack a syntactic count/mass distinction (Lucy 1992b). All inanimate nouns, even nouns referring to concrete objects, are treated like English mass nouns: they cannot be pluralized and they require classifiers in order to be enumerated (much as in the English *three sheets of paper*). Since classifier languages provide no linguistic support for the object–substance distinction, they provide a natural arena in which to investigate the distinction in young children.

Imai & Gentner therefore replicated Soja *et al.*'s study, using monolingual Japanese children living in Tokyo and American children living near Chicago. These two groups receive highly comparable experience with the world, but differ in linguistic input. Following Soja *et al.*, the investigators used three types of standards: *substances*, *simple objects* (simple rigid entities such as a kidney-shaped piece of paraffin) and *complex objects*[5] (artifacts such as wire whisks with relatively complex, perceptually coherent, shapes). On each trial they were given a novel label for the standard, in syntax that was neutral as to count/mass: e.g. "This is my dax" in English or "This is dax" in Japanese[6] (the normal pattern in that language). They were then asked which of two alternatives – one alike in shape but not material, and the other alike in material but not shape – could also be called *dax*. (See figure 8.4.) Children (aged 2, 2½, and 4) and adults received four trials for each type of standard.

For our purposes, the key question concerns the youngest children, the 2-year-olds. If there is an innate ontological distinction, then both language groups will show it from the start. If the object–substance distinction is learned in part from count/mass syntax, then English children should show the distinction to a greater degree than Japanese children. Finally, if the individuation continuum is correct, then children should be more likely to show object-extension patterns for complex coherent objects than for simple objects.

The results, shown in figure 8.5, show two commonalities and one striking difference. In both languages, complex objects were treated as objects from the beginning. Regardless of language, children as young as 2 years extended words applied to complex objects according to shape. This finding accords with Soja *et al.*'s finding of 93% shape-responding in young American children and suggests that the complex, perceptually coherent objects were readily individuated regardless of language. The second commonality was that in both languages, words applied to substances tended to be extended according to material. Despite their language's lacking a count/mass distinction, Japanese infants nevertheless distinguish (complex) objects from substances. This is evidence for a prelinguistic conceptual distinction between objects and non-objects.

Where the languages differed was on the simple object trials. English children, whose grammar groups simple objects together with complex objects as individuated entities, showed a fairly pronounced shape bias even at 2 years old. In contrast, young Japanese children, whose language provides no guidance as to whether simple objects should be seen as objects or as substances, responded at the level of chance.

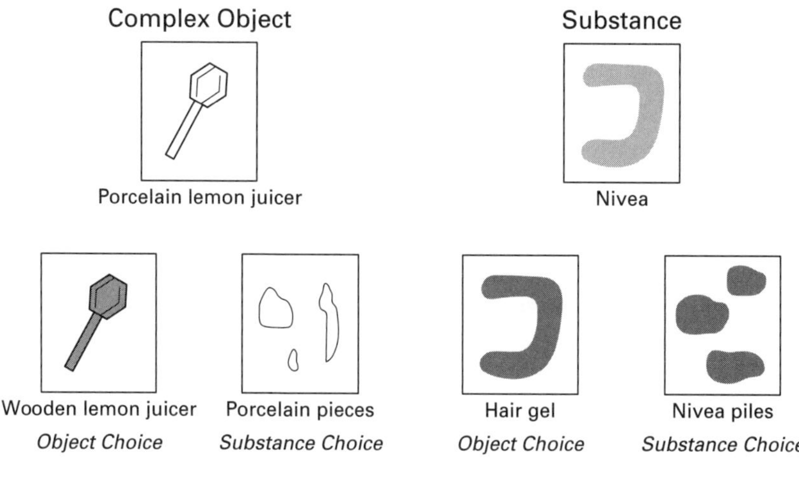

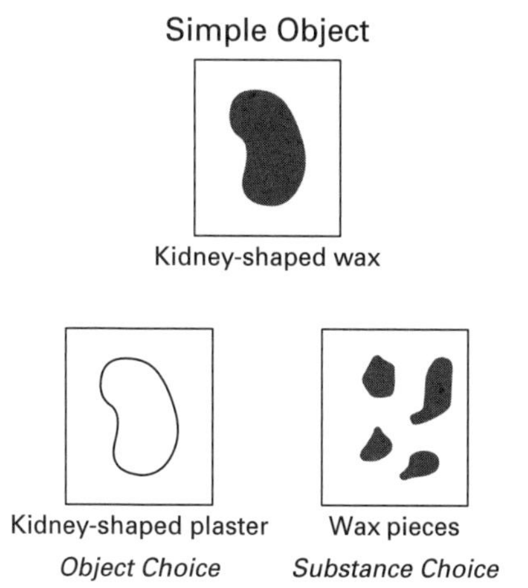

Fig. 8.4 Materials used in the Imai & Gentner experiment.

2.2 *Object complexity, individuation, and the object-naming bias*

The pattern of results is support for the individuation continuum. Irrespective of language, all children in our study treated complex objects as individual entities. The privileged status of complex objects was particularly striking for Japanese 2-year-olds: they consistently extended terms applied to complex objects according to shape, even though they performed at chance for simple objects and substances. Thus even among children

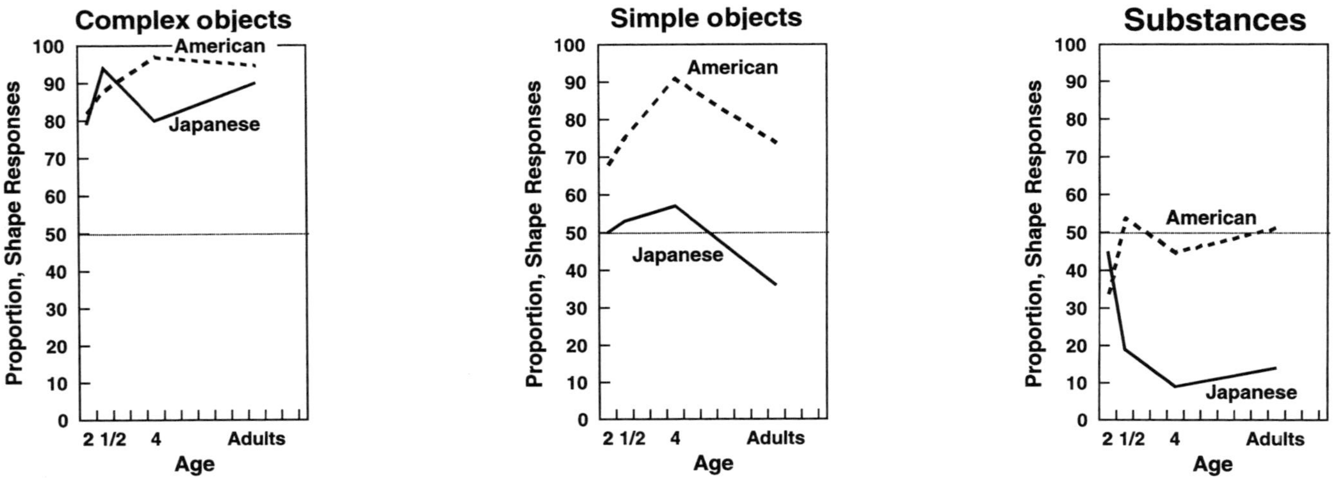

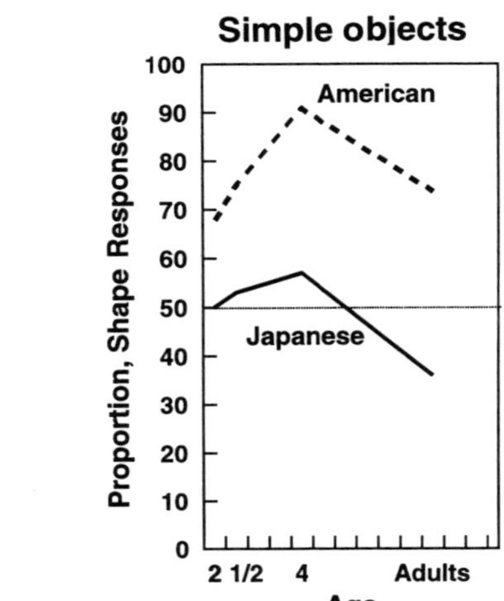

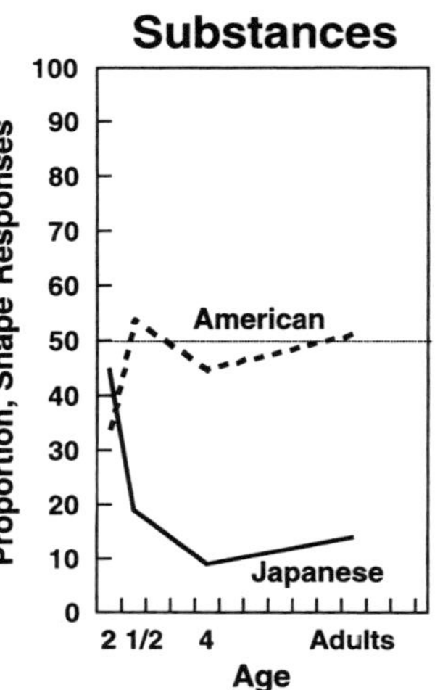

Fig. 8.5 Results of the Imai & Gentner experiment.

whose grammar provides no support for an object–substance distinction, complex objects were treated as individuals. This is consistent with the claim that perceptual coherence[7] contributes to the individuability of entities in the world, and that this in turn influences early word learning.

These findings have implications for theories of the early noun–object connection such as Markman's (1989, 1990) whole-object constraint, by which infants take a word applied to an object to apply to the whole object, not to any of its parts or qualities, and Waxman's (1991) noun-category linkage. The findings of Imai & Gentner suggest that the whole-object constraint may need to be graded to take account of differences in the coherence or individuability of objects. Further, the scope of these constraints may be learned from language.

2.3 *Effects of language*

The pattern for simple objects suggests very early effects of language. American 2-year-olds – whose language cuts the continuum into objects and substances – projected new words by shape for both simple and complex objects, showing an object-naming pattern for all solid bounded entities. In contrast, 2-year-old Japanese children treated the three categories as a continuum, from complex objects to simple objects to substances (see figure 8.6 below). It appears that even something as basic as the scope of early object naming is influenced very early by the language learned (see Smith 1996, ch. 4 of this volume). These findings accord with other reports suggesting that children learn some semantic patterns very early (e.g. Slobin 1987; Choi & Bowerman 1991, ch. 16 of this volume; but see Gentner & Bowerman 1996; Bowerman & Gentner, in preparation).

2.4 *Entrainment*

When asked to extend words for substances, the two language groups diverged with age. Japanese children shifted from chance responding (55% material responding) in 2-year-olds to a strong material bias (81%–91%) among older groups. American children started with a slight material bias which never increased; in fact, older groups showed chance responding. Japanese speakers became more likely to interpret novel terms for substances as referring to the material; English speakers did not.

These findings are consistent with Lucy's (1992) speculation that, whereas the grammar of languages like English invites attention to shape, the grammar of Yucatec Maya and other numeral-classifier languages invites attention to material. For example, Lucy (1992b: 74) notes that in Yucatec Maya, a single noun (*ha'as*, which we might translate as 'banana-stuff') is used to denote what in English are three different nouns: *banana* (i.e. the fruit), *banana leaf*, and *banana bunch*. The distinction is conveyed by the shape classifier used to unitize banana-stuff for individuation and enumeration: one-dimensional, two-dimensional, and three-dimensional, respectively. Lucy suggests that this linguistic pattern leads its speakers to focus on material even in nonlinguistic cognition.[8] He found that when given the same stimuli to sort or remember, English adults give extra weight to shape, and Mayans to material.

2.5 *Early ontology vs. individuality*

Our evidence is consistent with parts of Soja, Carey, & Spelke's proposal in suggesting a prelinguistic distinction between objects (at least, complex, cohesive objects) and substances. However, the results do not support a strong version of the universal early ontology view. First, the fact that complex objects are privileged but simple objects are not is difficult to reconcile with an ontological dichotomy between objects and substances. Second, the link between complex objects and an object interpretation is far stronger than the link between substances and a material interpretation. Japanese 2-year-olds were at chance on the substance trials, and American 2-year-olds showed only 66% material responses. In contrast, both groups showed about 80% shape responses for complex objects. Soja *et al.*'s American 2-year-olds showed a similar pattern. These findings don't appear consistent with the idea that infants possess an innate ontology commensurate with that of adults. Rather, they suggest that extremely clear cases of preindividuated objects – namely, complex objects – are prelinguistically distinguished from substances, but that the middle ground – simple objects – is malleable by language.[9] A sense of ontology may emerge out of the child's cognitive and linguistic experience, rather than predating it.

2.6 *The individuation continuum*

In the preceding sections, we invoked classifier languages to separate linguistic from experiential explanations. Now we propose to use these contrasts as typological clues to individuability. As noted above, classifier languages like Yucatec or Japanese differ from English in that they do not grammatically treat objects as naturally preindividuated. In English, substances must be unitized before they can be counted – e.g. "four teaspoons of sand." In Yucatan Maya, the same goes for concrete objects. One counts banana leaves by saying roughly "three sheets of banana" and bananas by saying "four rods of banana." English speakers may find it remarkable that

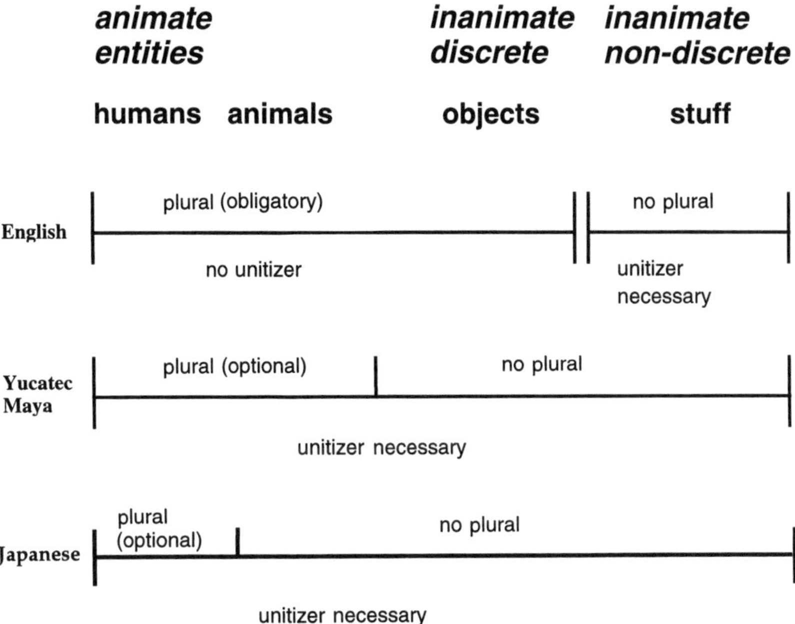

Fig. 8.6 The Animacy continuum (adapted from Lucy 1992b).

all languages do not take cups and bananas as automatically preindividuated, yet languages are clearly free to differ on this point.

Although languages differ in where they set the count/mass division, the pattern is not random. A useful way to compare languages is to use what is sometimes called the *Animacy continuum* (Allan 1980; Comrie 1981; Croft 1990; Lucy 1992b). A simplified version, shown in figure 8.6, extends from human to animal to concrete object to substance. It can be used to characterize where a given language draws the line between things that it considers to be preindividuated and those that must be unitized before being counted or pluralized.[10] As figure 8.6 shows, English has a generous individuation assumption – it grants individual status to concrete objects, whereas Yucatec Maya and Japanese reserve it for animate beings (or, even more exclusively, for humans).

This fundamental point – that languages differ in what they are willing to treat as automatically individuated in the grammar – suggests another clue to individuability. We suggest that patterns of grammatical individuation across languages can inform us about what constitutes a natural individual. Suppose those entities most likely to be treated as individuated across languages are just those that are most individuable in human

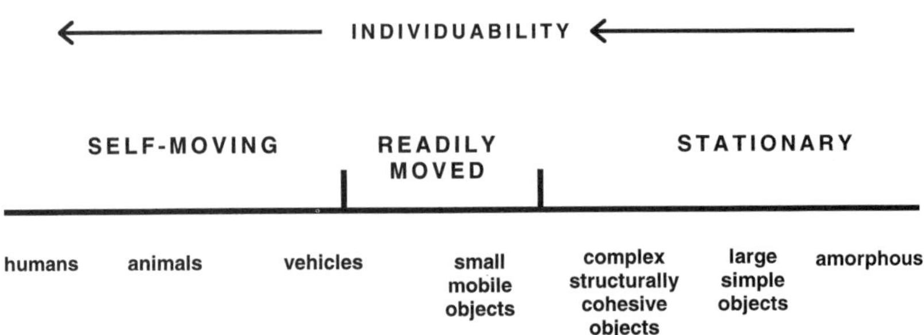

Fig. 8.7 The Individuation continuum: range of individuability across types.

cognitive–perceptual experience. On this assumption, animate beings are most likely to be inevitably individuated, followed by concrete objects.

We propose an Individuation continuum, inspired by the Animacy continuum, from animate beings through coherent, well-structured, and/or movable objects through simple objects to substances. The further we move rightward along the continuum, the more experience with language is necessary to individuate semantic entities. The Individuation continuum, shown in figure 8.7, is primarily a perceptual continuum. It both adds and omits distinctions found in the Animacy continuum. It adds a differentiation between complex, structurally coherent objects and simple objects. As Lucy (personal communication, approx. June 1994) points out, there is no linguistic justification for separating complex coherent objects from simple objects, nor for separating small movable objects from large immovable objects. Yet these distinctions, we suggest, are important to perceptual individuation. In the other direction, the Individuation continuum omits some differentiations that are relevant in the Animacy continuum (though not depicted here – see note 10): namely, differences in status, gender, etc., that seem unlikely to be reflected in young children's individuation patterns.

If perceptual ease of preindividuation influences the kinds of meanings that children learn first, then names for animate beings, which are self-individuating by virtue of their spontaneous motion, should be among the first words acquired. Applying this order to infant word learning, we would expect that animate beings would be the earliest preindividuated entities, and hence that their names would figure largely among children's first word meanings. Thus, words like *Mommy*, *Rover*, *Auntie*, and *kitty* are expected to be among the frequent early names. Many of these will be proper names,[11] the inclusion of which is thus essential to testing the natural partitions hypothesis.

There is evidence to support the claim of early learning of names for animate beings. Caselli, Bates, Casadio *et al.* (1995) used the MacArthur checklist to assess the early vocabularies of 659 English-speaking and 195 Italian-speaking infants. Words for animate beings constituted on average two of the first five words produced in English (*Daddy* and *Mommy*) and four of the first five in Italian (*Mamma*, *Papa*, *bau-bau* (for dogs), and *Nonna* (grandmother)). In Nelson's (1973) study of the first eight to ten words acquired by eight English-speaking infants, names for animate beings made up an average of 62% of the nominals and 41% of the total vocabulary. Nelson also noted names for moving vehicles and small manipulable objects whose motion against a background can be used to individuate them.

For the six children of six different languages whose early vocabularies are given in Gentner's (1982: table 5) corpus, names for animate beings – including both proper and common nouns – accounted for from 33% to 100% of the first nominals. Furthermore, as expected, the proportion of animates to total nouns drops as vocabulary size increases. Interestingly, the makeup of the early animates may differ cross-culturally. Children whose cultures emphasize extended sets of relatives tended to have large numbers of person names (proper names and kin terms). For example, a Kaluli girl at 1;8 (with 16 recorded words) had as her first 8 nominals 7 names for people and 1 animal term. Thus names for animate beings constituted 100% of her early nominals, with person names dominating. For Xiao-Jing, a Mandarin girl aged 1;6 with 37 recorded words (discussed below), animates constituted 50% of the early nominals and 30% of her total vocabulary, and most of these were person names. An English girl (age 1;2, vocabulary 39) and a German boy (age 1;8, vocabulary 33) also showed a fair proportion of animates (about 36%), but for these children, animal names were as prominent as person names.

3 The controversy: are object names learned before relational terms?

Over the last decade, a number of challenges to the natural partitions hypothesis have been lodged. Some – the first three listed below – question the noun dominance pattern in general. Others accept the pattern in English but question its cognitive basis, using crosslinguistic evidence to suggest that noun dominance, when it exists, can be traced to nonsemantic input factors. We present the challenges in boldface italics, followed by our replies.

(1) Children's early nouns may conceptually be verbs: that is, a child may say "door" meaning "open," so that scoring "door" as an object term is inaccurate.

Dromi (1987) investigated this question using her child's first words in Hebrew. She found remarkable stability: roughly 90% of her child's first nouns (by adult classification) were used for objects, and 87% of the first verbs were used for actions. Huttenlocher & Smiley (1987) carried out a detailed analysis of whether early object words co-occur with particular actions in children's early vocabularies. They found that early object words tended to be used for objects of a particular kind, but with a varied set of actions. They concluded that these object words refer to classes of objects, not to actions nor to object–action complexes. It appears that although object words may be pragmatically used to accomplish various goals, they retain a sturdy basis of object reference.

(2) Counts of early nominals should include only common nouns; the inclusion of proper nouns gives an inflated estimate of the noun advantage.

Many researchers who have argued against early noun dominance have counted only common nouns, omitting proper nouns (e.g. Gopnik & Choi 1990, 1995; Nelson, Hampson, & Shaw 1993; Bloom, Tinker, & Margulis 1993; Choi & Gopnik 1995; Tardif 1996). Tardif (1996) explicitly raised this concern and recounted Gentner's (1982) data omitting the proper nouns. But which terms should be counted depends on the theory under consideration. To test the natural partitions hypothesis, it is essential to include proper nouns.

(3) The noun advantage in English simply reflects the adult pattern: there are more noun types than verb types in the input language.

It is true that there are more nouns than verbs in English, as in most languages; in fact, nouns and verbs have altogether different patterns of occurrence (Gentner 1981). A large number of noun types is used, mostly with low frequency; and a small number of verb types is used, often with very high frequency. In this respect, as in many others, verbs behave more like closed-class terms than do nouns. Young English-speaking children show this same pattern: they use a greater variety of object names than relational words, but they use each of their relational words more often on average than their object names (Gopnik & Meltzoff 1982).

One might suggest, then, that there is nothing to explain: children's word distributions simply match those of adults, with many nouns and a few highly frequent relational words. But to say the patterns match does not provide a *mechanism* of learning. Although animals can match their response frequencies to the relative payoffs of two keys, we know of no learning mechanism that allows learners to match category frequency when – as is the case for nouns and verbs – the categories consist of distinct exemplar types. Indeed, classical learning theory would predict that the determining factor should be the relative numbers of *tokens* of each type: that is, children should learn those types experienced most frequently. But in this case verbs would be far more predominant in early vocabularies than they are. Gentner (1982) estimated that verbs compose about 20% of the 100 most frequent words used in English, while nouns compose only 6%. If input frequency were the sole governing factor, then many verbs would be learned before most nouns.

(4) There is a noun advantage in English, but it results purely from linguistic input features that make nouns more salient to young children, rather than from semantic and conceptual factors (Choi & Gopnik 1995; Gopnik & Choi 1995; Tardif 1996).

This issue is crucial in evaluating the natural partitions hypothesis, and since fresh evidence is available, we will delve into the issues a bit here. Gentner (1982) noted a number of linguistic input features of English that could account for the noun advantage without invoking semantic–conceptual factors: namely, *word frequency*, *word order*, *morphological transparency*, and *patterns of language teaching*. To these could be added *stress* and the presence of *verb-only utterances* (i.e., pro-drop sentences).

In considering these possibilities we must distinguish the claim that certain input factors *influence* children's rate of word acquisition from the stronger claim that these factors entirely *account for* the early noun advantage. To preview our conclusions, we will suggest (as in Gentner 1982) that the data support the first claim but not the second.

3.1 Word frequency

Could word frequency determine acquisition rate? Aside from the point mentioned above, that children fail to learn frequent verbs, evidence against word frequency as the sole determinant of acquisition rate comes from studies that have controlled the input to children. In a series of elegant studies, Leonard, Schwartz, Camerata, and their colleagues found that English-speaking infants were faster to learn and produce new names for objects than new names for actions, even when there were strict controls for number of exposures (frequency), position in the sentence (Schwartz & Leonard 1980), stress, and phonology (Camerata & Schwartz 1985; Camerata & Leonard 1986). Rice & Woodsmall (1988) found that 3- and 5-year-olds learned fewer action words than object and property words after viewing videotaped stories that included all three word types. Golinkoff and her colleagues found that children could fluently extend new verbs to new exemplars (using pictorial depictions) at 34 months (Golinkoff, Jacquet, Hirsh-Pasek, & Nandakumar 1996), 6 months after they could extend nouns to further exemplars in a similar task (at 28 months; Golinkoff, Hirsh-Pasek, Bailey, & Wenger 1992). Merriman, Marazita, & Jarvis (1993) found that 4-year-olds were faster to map new object words onto referents than new action words. Thus, word frequency must play a role, but it does not by itself account for the noun advantage.

3.2 *Nature of the input language*

The above studies have found that factors such as frequency and position do not account for the noun advantage. But they were conducted within English. Perhaps there are features of English that make nouns salient, and once this salience is established children can find nouns even in more difficult surroundings. Gentner (1982) suggested several input factors that could lead to a noun advantage in English acquisition, including word order, relative morphological transparency, and language teaching patterns. English SVO (subject–verb–object) word order places nouns in sentence-final position, known to be advantageous for word learning (Slobin 1973). Verbs typically occur in the least advantaged middle position. Morphological transparency – that is, how easily a root can be perceived within the surrounding word – is also a possibility. English verbs can take a greater variety of inflections than nouns; hence the sound–meaning relation may be more difficult to perceive for verbs. Finally, practices of linguistic interaction with infants, such as the object-naming routines used in American families, might lead to faster noun learning than, for example, the kinds of social-interaction routines practiced among the Kaluli (Schiefflin 1979). Gentner (1982) compared early vocabularies in English with those of five languages – Mandarin, Turkish, Kaluli, Japanese, and German – that varied in these key parameters in ways that should make them more "verb-friendly." While the *degree* of noun advantage varied with input factors, nouns (common and proper) were the most dominant class in all the studied languages. Gentner concluded that (1) input factors are important but (2) there is a persistent early noun advantage, supporting the natural partitions hypothesis.

However, these conclusions must be regarded as provisional, owing to the variability of the language samples. Recent studies of acquisition in languages that provide verb-oriented input to the child, such as Korean, Italian, and Mandarin Chinese have led some researchers to conclude that nouns are not always learned before verbs (Gopnik & Choi 1995; Tardif 1996).

3.3 *Mandarin*

Tardif (1996) studied acquisition in Mandarin Chinese. Mandarin is verb-friendly in that verbs and nouns have equivalent morphological transparency: neither nouns nor verbs are inflected. Mandarin is also a pro-drop language: the subject of a sentence can often be omitted. Since word order is SVO, subject-dropping creates verb-initial (VO) sentences, in which the verb occupies a more salient position than in the English SVO sentence (Slobin 1973). Tardif tabulated the vocabularies of ten Mandarin-speaking infants using transcriptions of hour-long tapes of their spontaneous interactions with caregivers. She reported a mean of 13.8 common nouns and 19.1 main verbs. With proper names included, the mean number of nouns rose to 19, making nouns and verbs roughly equal. Tardif concluded that the early noun advantage is not universal, and that the relative rates of acquisition of object and relational terms depend on linguistic factors.

However, a later more comprehensive study of Mandarin revealed a clear noun advantage (Gelman & Tardif 1998; Tardif, Gelman, & Xu 1999). Parents were asked for their children's full production vocabularies, using a Mandarin-adapted MacArthur checklist, for 24 Mandarin and 24 English children of about 20 months old. The results showed 2.4 times as many nouns as verbs for Mandarin children and 6.1 times as many for English children. To correct for the fact that the Mandarin children had larger vocabularies (with a mean of 316 types) than the English children (160 types),[12] Tardif *et al.* (1999) compared pairs of subjects with similar vocabularies. The noun–verb ratio remained significantly greater for English (4.6) than for Mandarin (2.8), supporting the prediction that verb-friendly features of the input language can make verbs easier to acquire. However, consistent with the natural partitions hypothesis, both groups showed a solid noun advantage.

The Tardif *et al.* study used rather advanced children. What about early acquisition? In both Mandarin and English, mothers reported that their children's first object word had preceded their first action word (Gelman & Tardif 1998). Gentner (1982) reported first vocabularies for 2 Mandarin-speaking children with vocabularies of under 50 words, using parental data collected by Mary Erbaugh (1980, personal communication) in Taiwan.[13] For both children, nominals (including proper nouns) were the dominant class (.65 and .59 of the total). For example, at age 1;6, the child Xiao-Jing had 37 words, of which 22 (.59) were nouns, 7 were relational terms (e.g. *go*, *come*, *pick-up*), and 2 were modifiers. Half the nominals referred to animate beings, including 8 (73%) person names – e.g. *Mommy*, *Grandfather*, *Cousin*, *Uncle*.

3.4 *Korean*

Another verb-friendly language is Korean (Gopnik & Choi 1990; Au, Dapretto, & Song 1994; Choi & Gopnik 1995). Korean follows SOV word order and is a pro-drop language, so verbs often appear alone or in the salient utterance-final position. Choi & Gopnik verified that in a sample of Korean adult speech to children, there were almost twice as many verbs as nouns (19.8 verbs vs. 11.9 nouns per 100 utterances). Thus if input factors dominate, Korean children should learn verbs earlier than nouns. Choi & Gopnik asked Korean parents to report on their children's vocabularies, using a modified version of Gopnik's relational inventory questionnaire and encouraging parents to list other words their children said. They found that the proportions of nouns and verbs in the first 50 words were 44% and 31% respectively. This proportion for nouns is substantially lower than the 60–70% range found in English.

However, other studies of Korean have reached different conclusions. Au *et al.* (1994) studied early vocabulary acquisition in Korean using a checklist method. They first confirmed Choi & Gopnik's finding that Korean input to children is verb-favored. Verbs were four times more likely than nouns to appear in the salient final position in Korean language to children (46% vs. 10%). In English, the reverse was found: verbs occupied 9% of the utterance-final positions, and nouns 30%. But despite this verb advantage in input, when Au and her colleagues examined early vocabularies of Korean children (using an adapted MacArthur CDI parental checklist) they found a sizable noun advantage. The median noun-to-verb ratio in very early Korean acquisition was about 4:1. This is a striking finding: children produced four times as many nouns as verbs despite hearing four times as many verbs in the final position.

Other findings on Korean have corroborated Au *et al.*'s results. Pae (1993) used a MacArthur checklist adapted for Korean to assess the vocabularies of 90 children living in Seoul between the ages of 12 and 23 months. She found a strong noun advantage throughout, comparable to that for English. Most children (87 of the 90) used a noun as their first word, and none had a verb as first word. Nouns increased rapidly from the stage of 1–5 words on; verbs did not appear until the 11–20-word stage. At 51–100 words, children's vocabularies contained 50–60% nouns and about 5% verbs.

3.5 Italian

Caselli *et al.* (1995) suggested that Italian has several verb-friendly features relative to English (but see Tardif, Shatz, & Naigles 1997). Italian has variable word order, including many verb-final constructions in speech to children; subject omission (pro-drop) constructions are common (e.g. *Piove* 'It is raining'); and unstressed (clitic) pronouns are often used for established referents, so that the child hears many sentences in which the verb is the only content word (as well as the final word in the sentence; e.g. *Lo voglio* 'It

(I) want'). Caselli *et al.* used parental MacArthur CDI checklist data to assess the early vocabularies of 195 Italian infants. They found that "verbs, adjectives, and grammatical function words are extremely rare until children have vocabularies of at least 100 words." Common nouns made up 28.8% of the early vocabulary, over ten times the proportion of verbs (2.3%). Caselli *et al.* concluded that "nouns predominate and grow sharply (in proportion to other items) across the first stages of lexical development."

3.6 *Comparing methods of assessment*

There is a striking convergence between the methodology used to assess vocabulary and the findings obtained. Studies that have used checklist data have found that nouns predominate in early vocabulary (e.g. Au *et al.* 1994; Caselli *et al.* 1995) while studies using taped sessions or interview tasks have often found that they do not (Bloom *et al.* 1993; Choi & Gopnik 1995; Tardif 1996).

The comparison of methods discussed above (Gelman & Tardif 1998; Tardif *et al.* 1999) bears on two important methodological issues: (1) how stable are vocabulary estimates derived from transcript data; and (2) how well do these estimates agree with vocabulary data obtained by the checklist method? As discussed above, parents were asked to provide vocabularies for 24 Mandarin and 24 English children aged about 20 months. The same children were also tape-recorded in naturalistic interactions with caregivers in three controlled contexts, which were designed to be either noun-favorable (reading a picture book together), verb-favorable (playing with a mechanical toy that offered several different activities), or neutral (playing with various toys). The findings are striking. First, the transcript results showed high variability across contexts. The noun–verb (N/V) ratios are 2.2, .62, and .51 for Mandarin and 3.3, 1.0, and .7 for English for noun-friendly, neutral, and verb-friendly contexts, respectively (Tardif *et al.* 1999). Depending on context, one could conclude that the Mandarin children had twice as many nouns as verbs, or half as many.[14] Even for English, two of the transcript findings would lead us to conclude that children know as many or more verbs as nouns.

The second striking methodological finding is that the checklist revealed higher ratios of nouns to verbs than did any of the transcripts. The N/V ratios revealed on the checklist were 6.1 and 2.4 for English and Mandarin children, respectively, as compared with N/V ratios of 2.1 for English and 1.4 for Mandarin across the transcribed sessions.[15] Pine, Lieven, & Rowland (1996) also found that checklists revealed a higher proportion of nouns than did transcribed sessions.

The third important finding concerns completeness. Apart from their extreme variability, the transcript results were also less comprehensive than the checklist results. The total number of words in the transcripts ranged from 13 to 38 types. The checklist revealed many times this number: 316 types (Mandarin) and 160 types (English). Of course, longer recording sessions could increase transcript coverage. But these figures make it clear that we cannot in general equate transcript results with the child's vocabulary.

The underestimate may be especially severe for nouns. As noted above, nouns are used in a more referentially specific manner than are verbs (Bates, Bretherton, & Snyder 1988). People use a large variety of noun types, each fairly infrequently, and a small number of relational types, each fairly frequently (Gentner 1981). For example, Gopnik & Meltzoff (1984) compared the results of multiple taped sessions of nine 1–2-year-olds and found that children used a small number of relational terms across multiple sessions, but used nominals in a more context-specific manner: 75% of the relational terms occurred in more than one session, compared to only 25% of the nominals. Thus the results of any given transcript session are likely to underestimate nouns relative to verbs.

This is not to say that checklists are perfect. Tardif *et al.* (1999) found that some words (more verbs than nouns) were spoken but not reported on the checklist (interestingly, this imbalance was stronger in English than in Mandarin). Further research is needed to assess the extent of this kind of underreporting. The checklist method may be the best single method, but its limitations need to be kept in mind: (1) it can discourage proper nouns, unless parents are encouraged to provide them; (2) its success depends on having an inclusive, language-appropriate list; (3) it asks first for nouns, possibly leading to fatigue factors in reporting verbs (this could be remedied); (4) it may underestimate phrases used as wholes; (5) for heavily morphologized languages it may be difficult to decide how to count words; and (6) the context of use is not provided. The best method, apart from exhaustive diaries, may be to combine checklist and observational lists (Pine, Lieven, & Rowland 1996).

3.7 *Navajo*

Along with Bill Nichols, we studied the acquisition of Navajo, another language that might be considered verb-friendly (Gentner, Boroditsky, & Nichols, in preparation). Navajo is a polysynthetic language of the Athapaskan family. It uses SOV word order (Young, Morgan, & Midgette 1992). Thus verbs occur in the salient utterance-final position, and because nouns are often omitted, verbs can stand as complete utterances. Another consideration is relative morphological transparency. Navajo verbs are heavily inflected – they can include up to 14–16 bound morphemes (as prefixes), and 11 is fairly typical – whereas nouns rarely have more than about 4–5 affixes and/or inflections. However, the verb morphology is considerably more transparent than the noun morphology. Navajo verbal affixes appear as prefixes before the verb stem, so that the verb stem itself appears in the salient word-final position. In contrast, nouns take affixes both before and after the noun stem. Thus the verb stem has the favored word-final position (in addition to its sentence-final position). Navajo forms a useful further point in our exploration of the determinants of early verb learning.

The study was conducted in the Navajo reservation near Shiprock, New Mexico. We first developed a checklist for Navajo, by translating, adapting, and augmenting the MacArthur CDI for Infants.[16] We tape-recorded this list for use with nonliterate families and interviewed the caretakers (all mothers or grandmothers) of 5 Navajo-speaking infants aged 18–26 months, with vocabulary sizes ranging from 31 to 187 words. The families were selected to be in remote parts of the reservation, where Navajo is likely to be the dominant or only language spoken in the homes.

We categorized the children's productive vocabularies according to the following categories: *nominals* (terms referring to concrete objects and entities, including proper names); *relational terms* (terms referring to spatial, temporal, or quantity relations – as in 'down,' 'later,' 'more' – or causal events – 'break'); *modifiers* (e.g. 'pretty'); *indeterminate terms* that are ambiguous as to noun–verb status (e.g. 'pee-pee'); *sound effects* (e.g. 'moo-moo'); and words associated with social games and routines (e.g. 'bye-bye').

Table 8.1 summarizes the results. Both predictions of the Division of Dominance hypothesis were supported. First, all 5 infants produced many more nominals than relational terms. Object terms made up an average of 44.8% of early Navajo vocabulary, compared to 17.1% for relational terms. The mean ratio of object terms to relational terms was 3.2. Consistent with the predictions of the Individuation continuum, the proportion of names for animate beings (including both concrete and proper nouns) was high in early vocabularies and declined as vocabulary increased. The average proportion of animates among nominals was 73% for the three children with the smallest vocabularies (31, 32, and 47), and 40.5% for the two children with the largest vocabularies (131 and 187).[17]

These findings also support the relational relativity claim that acquiring the meanings of verbs and other relational terms requires specific experience with the particular language being learned. With one exception, the proportion of relational terms increased with vocabulary size.

Table 8.1. *Early vocabularies of five Navajo children: mean percentages of nominals, relational words, and other classes*

Child Gender/ Age (mths.)	1 M/23	2[b] F/18	3 F/25	4[b] F/19	5 M/26	Mean percent	Mean number
Total nominals	51.6 (16)[a]	21.9 (7)	55.3 (26)	51.1 (67)	43.9 (82)	44.8	(39.6)
Animate beings	35.5 (11)	18.8 (6)	36.2 (17)	15.2 (20)	22.5 (42)	25.6	(19.2)
Other objects	16.1 (5)	3.1 (1)	19.1 (9)	35.9 (47)	21.4 (40)	19.1	(20.4)
Relations	9.7 (3)	15.6 (5)	10.6 (5)	20.6 (27)	28.9 (54)	17.1	(18.8)
Modifiers	1.0 (1)	0.0 (0)	2.1 (1)	5.3 (7)	4.3 (8)	2.5	(3.4)
Sounds/routines	35.5 (11)	40.6 (13)	27.7 (13)	16.0 (21)	12.3 (23)	26.4	(16.2)
Other	0.0 (0)	21.9 (7)	4.3 (2)	6.9 (9)	10.7 (20)	8.8	(7.7)
Total vocabulary[c]	**31.0 [5]**	**32.0**	**47.0**	**131.0 [7]**	**187.0 [43]**		
N/V	**5.3**	**1.4**	**5.2**	**2.48**	**1.52**	**3.2**	

Notes:

[a] Numbers in the table represent the percentages of total vocabulary. Numbers in parentheses represent the actual numbers of words.

[b] Proper names were not obtained for these two children's vocabularies, so their totals for animates and total nominals are probably underestimates.

[c] The entries for Total Vocabulary are the total number of Navajo words for each child, including both checklist counts and words added by parents. Numbers in square brackets represent words added by parents.

3.8 *Tzeltal*

Brown (1998) discusses another way a language can be verb-friendly. She notes that Tzeltal (along with other Mayan languages such as Tzotzil) has "heavy" verbs – that is, verbs that are specified as to the object properties of their arguments.[18] For example, the early verb *eat-tortilla* specifies both the event 'eating' and the object 'tortilla.' Brown studied Tzeltal acquisition in two children. Both started at around 15–17 months with a small set of nouns, mostly animates (caregivers), as well as deictics. This early noun advantage is also apparent in the early vocabulary of a child called X'anton, as recorded by the child's father (Brown, personal communication, November 1995). Nine of the child's eleven words are nominals, and, of those nine, four (36% of total vocabulary) are animates and a fifth, *car*, is another mobile object (see table 8.2).

However, later acquisition of verbs was rapid. For example, Xan[19] at 25 months had 52 words, of which 31 were nouns (including proper nouns) and 20 were verbs (Brown 1998: table 1). This is a comparatively high number of verbs: most studies have reported 10 or fewer verbs at the 50-word vocabulary level.[20] Likewise, de León (1999a, b, c) reports a large

Table 8.2. *First words of a Tzeltal child, according to her father (Reported by P. Brown)*

At 15 months, 5 days:
Mother
Father
At 15 months, 15 days:
cow [baby word for cow, used to mean 'dog']
car
tree/wood
At 15 months, 23 days:
tortilla
eat-tortilla (verb for eating tortillas)
At 16 months:
cat
At 17 months:
chili
potato
breast/suck

number of verbs in a 19-month-old Tzotzil child. We consider below the possibility that "heavy" verbs might be particularly easy to acquire.[21]

Taken together, the new crosslinguistic findings point to two conclusions. First, there is an early noun advantage across languages. Even in verb-friendly languages like Korean, Mandarin, and Italian, concrete nouns – especially names for animate beings – seem to serve as the entry-points to referential language. Second, there are clear effects of the input language. The accessibility of verbs in the input influences how early they are acquired.

4 Summary and implications

Are denotations formed nonlinguistically and simply named by language, or does language shape or even determine the denotations themselves? Both extremes are clearly wrong, and a bland compromise is unsatisfying. Our aim has been to present a specific proposal by which some parts of the semantic system are cognitively driven and others linguistically driven. Building on Gentner's (1982) proposal, we laid out a Division of Dominance continuum, according to which verbs, prepositions, and other relational predicates have denotations that are linguistically influenced, whereas concrete nouns are in many cases simply names for preexisting cognitively natural referents.

According to this framework, the denotations of concrete nouns tend to follow natural partitions – naturally preindividuated perceptual groupings.

For these noun-to-referent bindings, the cognitive parsing of the world is pre-solved, leaving only the linguistic parsing to be done. Relational terms, even concrete verbs and prepositions, are more linguistically influenced – the relational relativity claim. Their acquisition requires entry into the system of semantic distinctions that their language uses.

Our review of the current "nouns vs. verbs" debate leads us to conclude that the claim of an early noun advantage holds up well cross-linguistically.[22] The results indicate a strong early noun advantage even in languages with verb-friendly input characteristics, such as Mandarin and Korean. Even Tzeltal, which as a heavy-verb/light-noun language poses a strong contrast to English, seems to show an early noun advantage; however, further exploration of languages like Tzeltal and Tzotzil will be valuable. The evidence also suggests that input structure matters. The referential insight may be first established through a noun–object connection, but the subsequent rate of verb acquisition is affected by the input structure.[23]

4.1 *The nature of the early noun advantage*

The natural partitions hypothesis shares assumptions with other theories that have postulated an early noun–object link (Macnamara 1972; Maratsos 1991; Golinkoff *et al.* 1992), such as Markman's (1989, 1990) whole-object and taxonomic constraints and Waxman's (1991) early noun–category linkage. Although these constraints have sometimes been taken to be innate, the natural partitions hypothesis derives the noun–object connection from general learning principles (see also Smiley & Huttenlocher 1995; Bloom, ch. 6 of this volume; Smith, ch. 4 of this volume) and assumes that it is sensitive to the degree of preindividuation of the referent object.

4.2 *Noun dominance as counterintuitive*

The idea of early noun dominance runs contrary to the intuition that children, being interested in dynamic changes, motion, and causality, should want to talk about things usually conveyed by verbs (Nelson 1973; Gopnik & Meltzoff 1993). But children's word meanings are not a simple reflection of what is most interesting to them; they are also influenced by what is understandable within their system. For example, in Gentner's (1978b) *jiggy-zimbo* study of form vs. function in early noun meaning, young children labeled a new object according to its form, even though it shared an enthralling function – that of giving candy – with a different previously named object. Their language labeling was based not only on their interests

– which were clearly focused on the candy function – but also on their current understanding of how word meanings work. We suggest that the idea that "children's word learning is based on what they are interested in" is seriously incomplete. It misses the fact that language is a *system* of ways to codify experience and that children are learning that system. Children's propensity to learn nouns in no way impugns their interest in events and relations – merely their knowledge of how to lexicalize them.

4.3 *The paradox of verb centrality*

Another source of resistance to the idea of early noun dominance is that it seems to challenge the centrality of verbs in language processing. This is actually the tip of a much larger paradox. Linguistically and cognitively, the verb can be said to be the core of a sentence: it conveys the central set of events and relations in which the nouns participate. Chafe (1970: 97–98) analogized the verb and nouns to the sun and planets: "anything which happens to the sun affects the entire solar system," whereas "a noun is like a planet whose internal modifications affect it alone, and not the solar system as a whole." Yet verbs are harder to remember, both in recognition and in recall; more mutable in meaning under semantic strain; less prone to be borrowed in language contact; and less stable in translation between languages than nouns (Gentner 1981). How can verbs be so central and yet so elusive?

Such a paradox signals the need for a finer-grained analysis. We cannot simply assume that the verb's centrality confers some kind of generalized potency. For example, the verb's role as central connector requires it not only to link its noun arguments in the specified syntactic manner but to provide a set of relations that might meaningfully connect those objects, and this sometimes requires compromising the verb's default meaning (Gentner & France 1988). Thus the very centrality of verbs may contribute to their mutability under semantic strain and hence to their polysemy and fragility in sentence memory.

4.4 *The Individuation continuum in early acquisition*

Within the nominal class, we proposed an Individuation continuum and showed evidence for two implications. First, words applied to complex, well-structured objects are taken as object names (as evidenced by their being extended according to shape rather than substance) even very early in acquisition, and even by Japanese children who lack a syntactic marker for the object–substance distinction. Second, names for animate beings are learned early in many languages, as evidenced by findings from English, Italian, Navajo, and Tzeltal.

Crosslinguistically, words for animates are the most likely category to be treated linguistically as individuated (i.e. to be pluralizable and to be quantifiable without a unitizer – Croft 1990; Lucy 1992b). Developmentally, the extremely good cases of preindividuation within the nominal class – animate beings and complex movable objects – are already individuated either before or just at the onset of word learning. They thus provide natural candidates for the child's first forays into symbol–referent bindings.

These early referential bindings may provide natural entry points into language – "an initial set of fixed hooks with which children can bootstrap themselves into a position to learn the less transparent aspects of language" (Gentner 1982: 329; see also Maratsos 1990; Naigles 1990; Gleitman 1994). Noun–object bindings could provide a basis for working out the more variable aspects of language, including the binding of semantic relations to verb structures (Fisher 1996, 1999).

The early connection between nouns and highly individuable concrete referents may also lay the ground for the interpretation of other, more abstract nominals (but see P. Bloom 1994, ch. 6 of this volume). For example, as noted above, relational nouns like *uncle* or *passenger* are typically interpreted first as object-reference terms, and only later relationally (Keil 1989; Waxman & Hall 1993). We suggest that early referential concepts are highly concrete, and that the notion of an abstract individual arises as a later abstraction.

4.5 An Individuation continuum for relational terms?

Are there naturally cohesive relational concepts, analogous to preindividuated objects and animate beings, that children discover on their own and bring to language? One possibility is that the child's own goals could provide cohesion (Tomasello 1992; Gopnik & Meltzoff 1993). Indeed, Huttenlocher, Smiley, & Charney (1983) found that change-of-state verbs like *give* and *open* were more frequent in early production than action verbs like *run* and *jump*, and that they were produced initially only with the child as agent. However, a case could also be made for intransitive verbs denoting actions with distinctive motion patterns, such as *jump* and *bounce.* These might be individuated early for the same reasons as well-structured objects: they denote actions with high perceptual coherence and distinctiveness. Consistent with this possibility, Huttenlocher *et al.* (1983) found earlier *comprehension* of action verbs than of change-of-state verbs. (See also Gentner 1978a.)

Going further in the direction of coherence, we come to "heavy" verbs that specify object–action conflations. These form additional candidates for natural early verbs. We've suggested that one difficulty in learning verb denotation is learning what to extract, and in particular extracting relational elements away from the participants. As Brown (1998) notes, the rapid acquisition of verbs in Tzeltal suggests that heavy verbs, which allow a child to retain a cohesive event schema, are easier to learn than light verbs like English *make* and *go*.

Even in English, children may initially learn some relational terms in an overly conflationary manner, retaining the objects as well as the relational elements.[24] For example, in Gentner's (1982: 305–307) longitudinal vocabulary study, Tad's first relational words were *up* and *down*, at 19 months (8–9 months after his first nominals). He initially used *down* only when in his high chair, as a request to be taken out, and *up* while raising his arms, as a request to be picked up.[25] Olguin & Tomasello (1993) found that 25-month-olds who had been taught new verbs used them initially only with a highly restricted argument set.[26] As noted above, Huttenlocher *et al.* (1983) found that early verbs are understood first with the child as agent.

These patterns suggest that there may be something analogous to an Individuation continuum for verbs. Is the degree of cognitive preindividuation for heavy verbs comparable to that for "heavy nouns," such as names for animate beings? We suspect not. Brown's finding that names for animates are acquired before heavy verbs in Tzeltal suggests that more linguistic experience is required to learn verb meanings – even for heavy verbs – than to learn the meanings of nouns denoting animate beings.

4.6 *Relational relativity*

Relational relativity is, to us, the most interesting (and most overlooked) aspect of verb acquisition: "There is . . . variation in the way in which languages conflate relational components into the meanings of verbs and other predicates. Loosely speaking, noun meanings are given to us by the world; verb meanings are more free to vary across languages" (Gentner 1981: 169). The fact that languages vary widely in what constitutes the referents of their "concrete" verbs – far more so than for concrete nouns – has inescapable implications for word learning. No matter how important children find relations, they still must *learn* how to conflate them into word meanings.

For example, an English child and a French child standing side by side watching a duck float past a tree would need to lexicalize the event differently – *The duck floats past the tree* vs. *Le canard passe l'arbre en flottant.* The distribution of semantic components across the verb and satellite is different between the two languages (Talmy 1975, 1985). In contrast, *duck* (*le canard*) and *tree* (*l'arbre*) have essentially the same denotations. Examples like this show that children cannot possibly learn the denotations of verbs solely from perceptual experience. Some knowledge of linguistically influenced semantic systems is required to learn verb meanings. We suggest that this knowledge is typically bootstrapped by the noun–object referential connection.

4.7 Language and thought

The question of whether linguistic categories affect general cognitive categories has been (to put it mildly) relegated to the fringe for some time (although see Lucy & Shweder 1979; Kay & Kempton 1984). However, recently the issue of linguistic influences on cognition has returned to the research foreground in three ways. First, recent theorizing has explored subtler versions of the linguistic influence hypothesis (as did Whorf himself – 1956), such as Slobin's (1987) "thinking for speaking" and Hunt & Agnoli's (1991) review of evidence that language may make certain habitual distinctions extremely fluent. Second, recent research suggests influences of language on conceptual development (e.g. Gopnik & Meltzoff 1984, 1986; Gopnik & Choi 1990; Byrnes & Gelman 1991; Shatz 1991; Gentner & Medina 1997). For example, when given object labels, children shift their attention from thematic relations to likeness relations, promoting the formation of categories (Markman 1989; Waxman 1991). Third, as discussed below, recent research has explored domains that appear more likely to reveal linguistic influences than the color domain on which much prior work centered (e.g. Bowerman 1985, 1993, 1996; Shatz 1991; Gentner & Rattermann 1991; Lucy 1992a, b; Brown 1994; Levinson & Brown 1994; Levinson 1994, 1996, ch. 19 of this volume; Pederson 1995; but see Li, Gleitman, Landau, & Gleitman 1997). From what has been said, two promising arenas are the object–substance distinction and the linguistic partitioning of spatial relations.

As discussed above, Imai & Gentner (1997) found crosslinguistic differences between English and Japanese speakers in their patterns of extension for object words and substance words. First, while both language groups showed a shape focus (i.e. an object interpretation) for complex objects, Americans were far more likely throughout development to extend by shape for simple objects. Second, the two groups diverged across age on substances, with Japanese becoming more likely to make material-based extensions and Americans remaining neutral across development. These findings fit with Lucy's (1992b) analysis, which would suggest that Japanese should promote a substance focus and English a shape focus.

However, as noted above, these entrainment effects show only that grammar influences speakers' assumptions about word meanings, not that they influence the cognitive categories associated with the words. To investigate conceptual influences, Imai & Mazuka (1997) conducted a nonlinguistic similarity task. American and Japanese adults were shown the same triads used in Imai & Gentner's word-extension task, but were simply asked which of the two alternatives was most similar to the standard. For both languages, the similarity judgments closely mimicked the corresponding word-extension patterns[27] in Imai & Gentner's study, with English speakers focusing on common shape and Japanese speakers on common substance. These results parallel Lucy's (1992b) finding of shape-oriented classification for English speakers and substance-oriented classification for Yucatec Maya speakers.

Interestingly, the results for 4-year-olds on this similarity task did not mimic their patterns in the word-extension task. For example, the English 4-year-olds were less shape-oriented in the similarity task than in the word-extension task. This could suggest that such cognitive effects are manifest only after considerable experience with language. This interpretation fits with Lucy & Gaskin's (ch. 9, this volume) finding that Mayan semantic patterns find their way only rather late into perceptual classification patterns. Likewise, Smith & Sera (1992) found in their investigation of the development of dimensional terms that carrying out a correct polarity mapping between dimensions (e.g. *big/small* → *loud/soft*) occurs first in the context of word usage and only later in a purely perceptual context, suggesting that the linguistic distinction leads the perceptual distinction developmentally.

4.8 Relational relativity and the linguistic partitioning of space

Spatial relations are a promising arena in which to investigate possible effects of language on cognition, for three reasons. First, Whorfian effects are possible only for those aspects of language that are malleable crosslinguistically. Thus, returning to the Division of Dominance continuum (figure 8.1), we suggest that linguistic influences on thought are most likely to be found for relational terms. (Of course, purely grammatical terms are also highly malleable crosslinguistically, but since they operate chiefly at the grammatical level, their cognitive consequences are hard to test.) Second, verbs and other relational terms – including those concerned with spatial relations – provide framing structures for the encoding of events and experience; hence a linguistic effect on these categories could reasonably be expected to have cognitive consequences. Finally, *spatial* relations in particular offer the possibility of specific tests of the Whorfian claims, as in the work of Levinson and his colleagues (Pederson 1995). For example, Levinson (1996) found that Tzeltal speakers, whose language makes heavy use of absolute spatial terms (analogous to *North/South*), behave differently in a nonlinguistic spatial task from Dutch speakers, whose language uses a speaker-relative system of *right/left/front/back*. When shown a scene and asked to turn around and reconstruct it on a table behind them,

Dutch speakers preserve the left–right order of objects, but Tzeltal speakers preserve the north–south order.

In summary, we suggest that the relation between language and cognition is far more intricate than a one-way path. At one end of the Division of Dominance continuum, cognition calls the shots; language must adapt itself to cognitive–perceptual concepts. In the other direction, language influences our semantic categories. Children can most easily enter the lexicon at the cognitive end of the continuum. Once into the language, powerful mechanisms for learning regularities can come to grasp the semantic patterns that hold at the linguistically determined end of the continuum. This is the most interesting reason that children learn nouns before verbs.

NOTES

This research was supported in part by NSF grant SBR-95–11757. The Navajo study was conducted in collaboration with Bill Nichols. Oswald Werner and William Morgan provided invaluable advice on the Navajo language and culture. The Japanese research was conducted in collaboration with Mutsumi Imai. We thank Melissa Bowerman and Steve Levinson for extremely helpful comments on the chapter, and Susan Carey, Bill Croft, Eve Danziger, Nick Evans, Susan Goldin-Meadow, John Lucy, Sandeep Prasada, Marilyn Shatz, Linda Smith, Elizabeth Spelke, Gregory Ward, David Wilkins, and Phillip Wolff for discussions of the ideas.

1 The closed class is often extended to include grammatical morphemes such as plural *-s*. Also, although we have emphasized grammatical terms as purely linguistic terms, conveying relations internal to the language, they can also denote abstract conceptual relations (Talmy 1985).

2 Although these researchers have argued for the crosslinguistic variability of certain relational terms, they would not necessarily agree with the claim that relational terms are *more* crosslinguistically variable than object terms.

3 This difference holds for sentences with destination frames or boundary crossings (Slobin, 1996).

4 For brevity, we will often refer to this contrast as between nouns and verbs; however, many of the points made for verbs apply in varying degrees to prepositions and other relational predicate terms. As discussed below, there are also some relational systems that are lexicalized as nouns – e.g. kinship and cardinal directions in English.

5 Soja *et al.* compared simple objects and complex objects with substances in separate experiments, and found substantially the same results for both in English.

6 The instructions in Japanese were "Kono osara-wo mite. Kore-wa dax to iimasu. Dewa, kondowa kochirano osara-wo mite. Dochirano osara ni dax ga notte-imasuka?"

7 There is also the possibility that the complex objects were advantaged because children perceived their functional affordances (e.g. lemon-squeezing). However, we consider it unlikely that 2-year-olds knew these functions.

8 In contrast, Imai & Gentner's results do not entitle us to conclude an effect of

language on thought. They only show an influence of grammar on the child's assumptions about word meaning. We return to this issue in section 4.

9 Another possibility, pointed out by Sue Carey and Liz Spelke (personal communication, November 1995), is that children are universally endowed with an ontological distinction between objects and substances, but that (1) this distinction manifests itself more readily with complex objects than with simple objects, which are more ambiguous as to their ontological status, and (2) learning the English count/mass distinction may superimpose attention to shape over this ontological distinction.

10 This discussion is necessarily broad and omits many subtleties of classifier systems that are unlikely to bear on infants' perceptual individuation. Animacy distinctions enter into many other aspects of the grammar besides pluralization, including case markings; and they draw on other conceptual distinctions besides those discussed here, such as person (in pronouns), gender, and status (Comrie 1981: 187–193).

11 Comrie (1981: 179) notes that some languages treat proper names as being "higher in animacy" than common noun phrases: e.g. "William Shakespeare" vs. "the author of Hamlet."

12 Because any early noun advantage should diminish as vocabulary increases, language effects must be assessed on children of matched vocabulary size.

13 The data are based both on transcriptions of natural interaction sessions and on a parental vocabulary list.

14 The proportion of noun types to totals ranged from .44 to .21 to .16 in English and from .46 to .18 to .16 in Mandarin for the noun-favorable, neutral, and verb-favorable contexts, respectively.

15 Tardif *et al.* (1999) give their results in terms of N/N + V ratios; we have converted these to N/V ratios for comparability with other findings.

16 We thank Oswald Werner for his invaluable help and guidance. We also thank Ed Shorty, Anthony Yazzi, Larry King, and Begaye, and especially William Morgan, for assistance in preparing Navajo materials. Finally, we thank Terry Au, Mirella Dapretto, & Y. Song for giving us their Korean checklist, which helped to augment our starting list.

17 These figures are probably underestimates. For two of the children (child 2 and child 4) the experimenter failed to elicit terms beyond the checklist, and this resulted in a lack of proper nouns. If these two children are omitted, the figures become 27.5% for the two smallest vocabularies and 22.5% for the child with the largest vocabulary.

18 Tzeltal has other verb-friendly features: it uses VOS word order and allows noun-dropping, so that children hear sentences consisting of a verb with its associated morphology.

19 Xan's vocabulary was assessed with a combination of transcripts and parental lists.

20 For example, Pae's (1993) Korean children had a mean of 2 verbs (and 17 nouns) at 21–50 words and a mean of 4 verbs (and 49 nouns) at 51–100 words, comparable to English.

21 Another factor here may be the relative "lightness" of nonanimate nouns. As in Yucatec Maya, these specify substance and require a classifier to specify shape (Lucy 1992b).

22 There remain questions as to whether this framework will hold for languages in which the noun–verb distinction is disputed, such as Salish or Tagalog (Evans, in press). However, Croft (1990) offers encouragement for the claim that the categories of nouns and verbs have semantic/pragmatic correlates. In his universal-typological theory, the category *noun* expresses "reference to an object" in the typologically unmarked case.

23 We speculate that the more linguistically embedded a term is, the more its acquisition will be sensitive to frequency.

24 A possibly related point is the prevalence of bathroom terms like *pee-pee* in early language. These events are characterized by a nearly perfect correlation of action and associated object context.

25 However, Bowerman (personal communication, November 1995) noted rapid generalization of some early relational terms in her children.

26 In contrast, Tomasello & Olguin (1993) found that 23-month-olds readily generalize new nouns across different verb frames.

27 Using the neutral syntax version of the word task in English, which is the form most comparable to the Japanese word extension task.

REFERENCES

Allan, K. 1980. Nouns and countability. *Language* 56: 541–567.

Au, T. K., M. Dapretto, & Y. K. Song. 1994. Input vs. constraints: early word acquisition in Korean and English. *Journal of Memory and Language* 33: 567–582.

Baillargeon, R. 1993. The object concept revisited: new directions in the investigation of infants' physical knowledge. In C. E. Granrud (ed.), *Carnegie Mellon Symposia on Cognition*, vol. 23: *Visual perception and cognition in infancy.* Hillsdale, NJ: Lawrence Erlbaum, 265–315.

Bates, E., I. Bretherton, & L. Snyder. 1988. *From first words to grammar: individual differences and dissociable mechanisms.* Cambridge: Cambridge University Press.

Biederman, I. 1987. Recognition-by-components: a theory of human image understanding. *Psychological Review* 94: 115–147.

Bloom, L. 1973. *One word at a time: the use of single word utterances before syntax.* The Hague: Mouton.

Bloom, L., E. Tinker, & C. Margulis. 1993. The words children learn: evidence against a noun bias in early vocabularies. *Cognitive Development* 8: 431–450.

Bloom, P. 1994. Possible names: the role of syntax–semantics mappings in the acquisition of nominals. *Lingua* 92: 297–329.

Bowerman, M. 1974. Learning the structure of causative verbs: a study in the relationship of cognitive, semantic, and syntactic development. *Papers and Reports on Child Language Development* 8:142–178.

1976. Semantic factors in the acquisition of rules for word use and sentence construction. In D. M. Morehead & A. E. Morehead (eds.), *Normal and deficient child language*. Baltimore, MD: University Park Press, 99–179.

1978. The acquisition of word meaning: an investigation into some current conflicts. In N. Waterson & C. Snow (eds.), *The development of communication.* New York: John Wiley, 263–287.

1985. What shapes children's grammars? In D. I. Slobin (ed.), *The crosslinguistic study of language acquisition*, vol. 2. Hillsdale, NJ: Lawrence Erlbaum, 1257–1319.

1993. Typological prespectives on language acquisition: do crosslinguistic patterns predict development? In E. V. Clark (ed.), *The Proceedings of the 25th Annual Child Language Research Forum.* Stanford, CA: Center for the Study of Language and Information, 7–15.

1996. Learning how to structure space for language: a crosslinguistic perspective. In P. Bloom, M. A. Peterson, L. Nadel, & M. F. Garrett (eds.), *Language and space.* Cambridge, MA: MIT Press, 385–436.

Bowerman, M., & E. Pederson. 1992. Crosslinguistic perspectives on topological spatial relationships. Paper presented at the annual meeting of the American Anthropological Association, San Francisco, CA, December.

Brown, P. 1994. The INs and ONs of Tzeltal locative expressions: the semantics of static descriptions of location. *Linguistics* 32: 743–790.

1998. Children's first verbs in Tzeltal: evidence for an early verb category. *Linguistics* 36: 715–753.

Byrnes, J. P., & S. A. Gelman. 1991. Perspectives on thought and language: traditional and contemporary views. In S. A. Gelman & J. P. Byrnes (eds.), *Perspectives on language and thought: interrelations in development.* Cambridge: Cambridge University Press, 3–27.

Camarata, S., & L. B. Leonard. 1986. Young children pronounce object words more accurately than action words. *Journal of Child Language* 13: 51–65.

Camarata, S., & R. G. Schwartz. 1985. Production of object words and action words: evidence for a relationship between phonology and semantics. *Journal of Speech and Hearing Research* 28: 323–330.

Caselli, M. C., E. Bates, P. Casadio, J. Fenson, L. Fenson, L. Sanderl, & J. Weir. 1995. A cross-linguistic study of early lexical development. *Cognitive Development* 10: 159–199.

Chafe, W. L. 1970. *Meaning and the structure of language*. Chicago: University of Chicago Press.

Choi, S., & M. Bowerman. 1991. Learning to express motion events in English and Korean: the influence of language-specific lexicalization patterns. *Cognition* 42: 83–121.

Choi, S., & A. Gopnik. 1995. Early acquisition of verbs in Korean: a cross-linguistic study. *Journal of Child Language* 22: 497–529.

Clark, E. V. 1993. *The lexicon in acquisition.* Cambridge: Cambridge University Press.

Comrie, B. 1981. *Language universals and linguistic typology: syntax and morphology.* Chicago: University of Chicago Press.

Croft, W. A. 1990. *Typology and universals.* Cambridge: Cambridge University Press.

de León, L. 1999a. Verb roots and caregiver speech in early Tzotzil (Mayan) acquisition. In B. Fox, D. Jurafsky, & L. Michaelis (eds.), *Cognition and function in language.* Stanford, CA: Center for the Study of Language and Information, 99–119.

1999b. Verbs in Tzotzil early syntactic development. *International Journal of Bilingualism* 3: 219–240.

1999c. Why Tzotzil children prefer verbs over nouns? Paper presented at the Fourth International Conference for the Study of Child Language. San Sebastian, Spain, July 1999.

Dromi, E. 1987. *Early lexical development.* Cambridge: Cambridge University Press.

Evans, N. In press. Word classes in the world's languages. In G. Booij, C. Lehmann, & J. Mugdan (eds.), *Morphology/Morphologie: a handbook on inflection and word formation/ein Handbuch zur Flexion und Wortbildung*, vol. 1. Berlin: Walter de Gruyter.

Fisher, C. 1996. Structural limits on verb mapping: the role of alignment in children's interpretations of sentences. *Cognitive Psychology* 3: 41–81.

1999. From form to meaning: a role for structural alignment in the acquisition of language. In H. W. Reese (ed.), *Advances in child development and behavior*, vol. 27. New York: Academic Press, 1–53.

Fisher, C., D. G. Hall, S. Rakowitz, & L. R. Gleitman. 1994. When it is better to receive than to give: syntactic and conceptual constraints on vocabulary growth. In L. R. Gleitman & B. Landau (eds.), *The acquisition of the lexicon.* Cambridge, MA: MIT Press, 333–375.

Garner, W. R. 1978. Aspects of a stimulus: features, dimensions, and configurations. In E. Rosch & B. B. Lloyd (eds.), *Cognition and categorization.* Hillsdale, NJ: Lawrence Erlbaum, 99–133.

Gathercole, V. 1986. Evaluating competing linguistic theories with child language data: the case of the mass–count distinction. *Linguistics and Philosophy* 9: 151–190.

Gelman, S. A., & T. Tardif. 1998. Acquisition of nouns and verbs in Mandarin and English. In E. V. Clark (ed.), *The proceedings of the 29th Annual Child Language Research Forum.* Stanford, CA: Center for the Study of Language and Information, 27–36.

Gentner, D. 1978a. On relational meaning: the acquisition of verb meaning. *Child Development* 49: 988–998.

1978b. What looks like a jiggy but acts like a zimbo? A study of early word meaning using artificial objects. *Papers and Reports on Child Language Development* 15: 1–6.

1981. Some interesting differences between nouns and verbs. *Cognition and Brain Theory* 4: 161–178.

1982. Why nouns are learned before verbs: linguistic relativity versus natural partitioning. In S. A. Kuczaj II (ed.), *Language development*, vol. 2: *Language, thought, and culture.* Hillsdale, NJ: Lawrence Erlbaum, 301–334.

1988. Cognitive and linguistic determinism: object reference and relational reference. Paper presented at the Boston Child Language Conference, Boston, MA, November.

Gentner, D., L. Boroditsky, & B. Nichols. In preparation. Early acquisition of nouns vs. verbs: evidence from Navajo.

Gentner, D., & M. Bowerman. 1996. Crosslinguistic differences in the lexicalization of spatial relations and effects on acquisition. Paper presented at the 7th International Congress for the Study of Child Language, Istanbul, July.

Gentner, D., & I. M. France. 1988. The verb mutability effect: studies of the combinatorial semantics of nouns and verbs. In S. L. Small, G. W. Cottrell, & M. K. Tanenhaus (eds.), *Lexical ambiguity resolution: perspectives from psycholin-*

guistics, neuropsychology, and artificial intelligence. San Mateo, CA: Kaufmann, 343–382.

Gentner, D., & J. Medina. 1997. Comparison and the development of cognition and language. *Cognitive Studies: Bulletin of the Japanese Cognitive Science Society* 4: 112–149.

Gentner, D., & M. J. Rattermann. 1991. Language and the career of similarity. In S. A. Gelman & J. P. Byrnes (eds.), *Perspectives on language and thought: interrelations in development.* Cambridge: Cambridge University Press, 225–277.

Gillette, J., H. Gleitman, L. R. Gleitman, & A. Lederer. 1998. Human simulations of vocabulary learning. Unpublished ms., University of Pennsylvania.

Gleitman, L. R. 1994. The structural sources of verb meanings. *Language Acquisition* 1: 3–55.

Gleitman, L. R., & H. Gleitman. 1992. A picture is worth a thousand words, but that's the problem: the role of syntax in vocabulary acquisition. *Current Directions in Psychological Science* 1: 31–35.

Goldin-Meadow, S., C. Butcher, C. Mylander, & M. Dodge. 1994. Nouns and verbs in a self-styled gesture system: what's in a name? *Cognitive Psychology* 27: 259–319.

Goldin-Meadow, S., M. Seligman, & R. Gelman. 1976. Language in the two-year old. *Cognition* 4: 189–202.

Golinkoff, R. M., K. Hirsh-Pasek, L. M. Bailey, & N. R. Wenger. 1992. Young children and adults use lexical principles to learn new nouns. *Developmental Psychology* 28: 99–108.

Golinkoff, R. M., R. C. Jacquet, K. Hirsh-Pasek, & R. Nandakumar. 1996. Lexical principles may underlie the learning of verbs. *Child Development* 67: 3101–3119.

Gopnik, A., & S. Choi. 1990. Do linguistic differences lead to cognitive differences? A cross-linguistic study of semantic and cognitive development. *First Language* 10: 199–215.

1995. Names, relational words, and cognitive development in English and Korean speakers: nouns are not always learned before verbs. In M. Tomasello & W. E. Merriman (eds.), *Beyond names for things: young children's acquisition of verbs.* Hillsdale, NJ/Hove: Lawrence Erlbaum, 63–80.

Gopnik, A., & A. N. Meltzoff. 1986. Relations between semantic and cognitive development in the one-word stage: the specificity hypothesis. *Child Development* 57: 1040–1053.

Gordon, P. 1985. Evaluating the semantic categories hypothesis: the case of the count/mass distinction. *Cognition* 20: 209–242.

Hunt, E., & F. Agnoli. 1991. The Whorfian hypothesis: a cognitive psychology perspective. *Psychological Review* 98: 377–389.

Huttenlocher, J. 1974. The origins of language comprehension. In R. L. Solso (ed.), *Theories in cognitive psychology: the Loyola Symposium.* Potomac, MD: Lawrence Erlbaum, 331–368.

Huttenlocher, J., & P. Smiley. 1987. Early word meanings: the case of object names. *Cognitive Psychology* 19: 63–89.

Huttenlocher, J., P. Smiley, & R. Charney. 1983. Emergence of action categories in the child: evidence from verb meanings. *Psychological Review* 90: 72–93.

Imai, M., & D. Gentner. 1997. A crosslinguistic study of early word meaning: universal ontology and linguistic influence. *Cognition* 62: 169–200.

Imai, M., & R. Mazuka. 1997. A crosslinguistic study on the construal of individuation in linguistic and non-linguistic contexts. Poster presented at the Society for Research in Child Development, Washington, DC, April.

Kay, P., & W. Kempton. 1984. What is the Sapir–Whorf hypothesis? *American Anthropologist* 86: 65–79.

Keil, F. C. 1989. *Concepts, kinds, and cognitive development.* Cambridge, MA: Bradford/MIT Press.

Kotovsky, L., & D. Gentner. 1996. Comparison and categorization in the development of relational similarity. *Child Development* 67: 2797–2822.

Landau, B., L. Smith, & S. Jones. 1998. Object shape, object function, and object name. *Journal of Memory and Language* 38: 1–27.

Langacker, R. 1987. *Foundations of cognitive grammar*, vol. 1. Stanford, CA: Stanford University Press.

Levinson, S. C. 1994. Vision, shape and linguistic description: Tzeltal body-part terminology and object description. *Linguistics* 32: 791–855.

1996. Frames of reference and Molyneux's question: crosslinguistic evidence. In P. Bloom, M. A. Peterson, L. Nadel, & M. F. Garrett (eds.), *Language and space.* Cambridge: MIT Press, 109–169.

Levinson, S. C., & P. Brown. 1994. Immanuel Kant among the Tenejapans: anthropology as applied philosophy. *Ethos* 22: 3–41.

Li, P., L. Gleitman, B. Landau, & H. Gleitman. 1997. Space for thought. Paper presented at the 22nd Boston University Child Language Development Conference, Boston.

Lucy, J. A. 1992a. *Language diversity and thought: a reformulation of the linguistic relativity hypothesis.* Cambridge: Cambridge University Press.

1992b. *Grammatical categories and cognition: a case study of the linguistic relativity hypothesis.* Cambridge: Cambridge University Press.

Lucy, J. A., & R. A. Shweder. 1979. Whorf and his critics: linguistic and nonlinguistic influences on color memory. *American Anthropologist* 81: 581–618.

Macnamara, J. 1972. Cognitive basis of language learning in infants. *Psychological Review* 79: 1–13.

Maratsos, M. P. 1990. Are actions to verbs as objects are to nouns? On the differential semantic bases of form, class, category. *Linguistics* 28: 1351–1379.

1991. How the acquisition of nouns may be different from that of verbs. In N. Krasnegor, D. Rumbaugh, R. Schiefelbusch, & M. Studdert-Kennedy (eds.), *Biological and behavioral determinants of language development.* Hillsdale, NJ: Lawrence Erlbaum, 67–88.

Maratsos, M. P., & M. A. Chalkley. 1980. The internal language of children's syntax: the ontogenesis and representation of syntactic categories. In K. Nelson (ed.), *Children's language*, vol. 2. New York: Gardner, 127–214.

Markman, E. M. 1989. *Categorization and naming in children: problems of induction*. Cambridge, MA: Bradford/MIT Press.

1990. Constraints children place on word meanings. *Cognitive Science* 14: 57–77.

Merriman, W. E., J. Marazita, & L. H. Jarvis. 1993. Four-year-olds' disambiguation of action and object word reference. *Journal of Experimental Child Psychology* 56: 412–430.

Naigles, L. 1990. Children use syntax to learn verb meanings. *Journal of Child Language* 17: 357–374.

Nelson, K. 1973. Some evidence for the cognitive primacy of categorization and its functional basis. *Merrill-Palmer Quarterly* 19: 21–39.

Nelson, K., J. Hampson, & L. K. Shaw. 1993. Nouns in early lexicons: evidence, explanations, and implications. *Journal of Child Language* 20: 61–84.

Olguin, R., & M. Tomasello. 1993. Twenty-five-month-old children do not have a grammatical category of verb. *Cognitive Development* 8: 245–272.

Pae, S. 1993. Early vocabulary in Korean: are nouns easier to learn than verbs? Unpublished doctoral dissertation, University of Kansas, Lawrence.

Palmer, S. E. 1978. Structural aspects of visual similarity. *Memory and Cognition* 6: 91–97.

Pederson, E. 1995. Language as context, language as means: spatial cognition and habitual language use. *Cognitive Linguistics* 6: 333–362.

Pine, J. M., E. V. M. Lieven, & C. Rowland. 1996. Observational and checklist measures of vocabulary composition: what do they mean? *Journal of Child Language* 23: 573–590.

Pinker, S. 1994. How could a child use verb syntax to learn verb semantics? *Lingua* 92: 377–410.

Prasada, S. 1996. Knowledge of the count/mass distinction: the relation of syntactic, semantic, and conceptual structure. *Proceedings of the 12th Eastern States Conference on Linguistics.* Ithaca, NY: Cornell University Press, 256–266.

Quine, W. V. O. 1969. *Ontological relativity and other essays*. New York: Columbia University Press.

Rice, M. L., & L. Woodsmall. 1988. Lessons from television: children's word learning when viewing. *Child Development* 59: 420–424.

Rosch, E. 1978. Principles of categorization. In E. Rosch & B. B. Lloyd (eds.), *Cognition and categorization.* Hillsdale, NJ: Lawrence Erlbaum, 28–46.

Schieffelin, B. B. 1985. The acquisition of Kaluli. In D. I. Slobin (ed.), *The crosslinguistic study of language acquisition*, vol. 1. Hillsdale, NJ: Lawrence Erlbaum, 525–593.

Schwartz, R. G., & L. B. Leonard. 1980. Words, objects, and actions in early lexical acquisition. *Papers and Reports in Child Language Development* 19: 29–36.

Shatz, M. 1991. Using cross-cultural research to inform us about the role of language in development. In M. H. Bornstein (ed.), *Cultural approaches to parenting*. Hillsdale, NJ: Lawrence Erlbaum, 139–153.

Sinha, C., L. A. Thorseng, M. Hayashi, & K. Plunkett. 1994. Comparative spatial semantics and language acquisition: evidence from Danish, English, and Japanese. *Journal of Semantics* 11: 253–287.

Slobin, D. I. 1973. Cognitive prerequisites for the development of grammar. In C. A. Ferguson & D. I. Slobin (eds.), *Studies of child language development.* New York: Holt, Rinehart & Winston, 175–208.

1987. Thinking for speaking. In *Proceedings of the 13th Annual Meeting of the Berkeley Linguistic Society*. Berkeley, CA: Berkeley Linguistics Society, 487–505.

1996. Two ways to travel: verbs of motion in English and Spanish. In M. Shibatani & S. Thompson (eds.), *Essays in syntax and semantics*. Oxford: Oxford University Press, 195–220.

Smiley, P., & J. Huttenlocher. 1995. Conceptual development and the child's early words for events, objects, and persons. In M. Tomasello & W. E. Merriman (eds.), *Beyond names for things: young children's acquisition of verbs.* Hillsdale, NJ/Hove: Lawrence Erlbaum, 21–61.

Smith, L. B., & M. D. Sera. 1992. A developmental analysis of the polar structure of dimensions. *Cognitive Psychology* 24: 99–142.

Soja, N. N., S. Carey, & E. S. Spelke. 1991. Ontological categories guide young children's inductions of word meaning: object terms and substance terms. *Cognition* 38: 179–211.

Spelke, E. S. 1985. Perception of unity, persistence, and identity: thoughts on infants' conception of objects. In J. Mehler & R. Fox (eds.), *Neonate cognition: beyond the blooming buzzing confusion.* Hillsdale, NJ: Lawrence Erlbaum, 89–114.

1990. Principles of object perception. *Cognitive Science* 14: 29–56.

Talmy, L. 1975. Semantics and syntax of motion. In J. Kimball (ed.), *Syntax and semantics*, vol. 4. New York: Academic Press, 181–238.

1985. Lexicalization patterns: semantic structure in lexical form. In T. Shopen (ed.), *Language typology and syntactic description*, vol. 3: *Grammatical categories and the lexicon*. Cambridge: Cambridge University Press, 57–149.

Tardif, T. 1996. Nouns are not always learned before verbs: evidence from Mandarin speakers' early vocabularies. *Developmental Psychology* 32: 492–504.

Tardif, T., S. Gelman, & F. Xu, 1999. Putting the noun bias in context: a comparison of English and Mandarin. *Child Development* 70: 620–635.

Tardif, T., M. Shatz, & L. G. Naigles. 1997. Caregiver speech and children's use of nouns versus verbs: a comparison of English, Italian, and Mandarin. *Journal of Child Language* 24: 535–565.

Tomasello, M. 1992. *First verbs: a case study of early grammatical development.* New York: Cambridge University Press.

Tomasello, M., & R. Olguin. 1993. Twenty-three-month-old children have a grammatical category of noun. *Cognitive Development* 8: 451–464.

Tversky, B., & K. Hemenway. 1984. Objects, parts, and categories. *Journal of Experimental Psychology: General* 113: 169–191.

Waxman, S. R. 1991. Convergences between semantic and conceptual organization in the preschool years. In J. P. Byrnes & S. A. Gelman (eds.), *Perspectives on language and thought: interrelations in development*. Cambridge: Cambridge University Press, 107–145.

Waxman, S. R., & D. G. Hall. 1993. The development of a linkage between count nouns and object categories: evidence from fifteen- to twenty-month-old infants. *Child Development* 64: 1224–1241.

Waxman, S. R., & D. B. Markow. 1995. Words as invitations to form categories: evidence from 12- to 13-month-old infants. *Cognitive Psychology* 61: 1461–1473.

Waxman, S. R., A. Senghas, & S. Benveniste. 1997. A cross-linguistic examination of the noun-category bias: its existence and specificity in French- and Spanish-speaking preschool-aged children. *Cognitive Psychology* 32: 183–218.

Whorf, B. L. 1956. *Language, thought, and reality: selected writings of Benjamin Lee Whorf* (ed. J. B. Carroll). Cambridge, MA: MIT Press.

Woodward, A. L., & E. M. Markman. 1989. Early word learning. In W. Damon, D. Kuhn, & R. S. Siegler (eds.), *Handbook of child psychology*, vol. 2: *Cognition, perception, and language* (5th edn). New York: John Wiley, 371–420.

Young, R. W., W. Morgan, Sr., & S. Midgette, S. 1992. *Analytical lexicon of Navajo.* Albuquerque: University of New Mexico Press.

9 Grammatical categories and the development of classification preferences: a comparative approach

John A. Lucy and Suzanne Gaskins

University of Chicago and Northeastern Illinois University

1 Introduction

The defining characteristic of the human species is its culture-bearing capacity whereby very similar biological organisms develop and sustain extraordinarily diverse behavioral repertoires. Research on human behavior, then, must necessarily concern itself with the scope and significance of this diversity and the process of its development in childhood. However, contemporary psychological research often assumes instead a homogeneity of repertoire and of underlying psychological function – coupled with a concomitant assimilation of the psychological to the biological – and neglects the process of culture acquisition. Theories and methods developed from such a perspective neither incline their proponents to developmentally oriented comparative research nor provide a set of concepts and tools adequate to undertake it.

The reality of cultural diversity requires us to adopt a comparative perspective from the beginning as part of a coherent effort to account for the actual range of human psychological functioning and the process of its formation. Such a coherent effort demands more than simply testing whether our local findings generalize to other cultures or looking for a specific, naturally occurring equivalent for some odd manipulation we cannot perform within our own culture for one reason or another. Rather, it requires taking seriously the proposal that the human developmental process is designed to support diversity in behavioral outcome and that psychological research programs must take account of this from the outset if they are to produce adequate methods and theories. Taking a comparative perspective from the outset involves the following general steps: documenting ethnographically the range and patterning of behavioral diversity, formulating and testing for tangible psychological implications of the diversity manifest in various cultures, and then exploiting the diversity itself in order to uncover the nature of the psychological mechanisms and developmental processes at work. The ultimate objective is a body of psychological theory and method founded on an understanding of the range of cultural diversity and therefore adequate to the full range of human experience.

Nowhere is the neglect of diversity and need for a comparative perspective greater than in the study of the relationship between language and thought. Psychological research on this topic since the late 1950s has generally ignored the potential cognitive significance of language diversity in children and adults. Yet the diversity of the world's languages is obvious and compelling: no child or adult speaks a generic Language understood by all, but rather one or more particular languages shared within a community. Just as theories of language use and acquisition must account for this diversity, so too must theories of the relationship between language and cognition. We need to know not only how a single biological organism can sustain such a diversity of languages, but also whether and how that diversity has an impact on intellectual functioning and when and how that impact takes shape. These questions simply cannot be addressed within a single language group nor dismissed across the board because of the presence of some linguistic or cognitive universals at an early age.

At present we know little about whether the particular language we speak influences the way we think, despite the obvious bearing of this issue on our theoretical understanding of mind and culture, on research methodology, and on public policy. Direct empirical research on the topic scarcely existed until the early 1990s and what did exist had often been poorly done and yielded ambiguous results (Lucy 1992a). In place of empirical research, the literature has been filled with a wide variety of speculative answers that inevitably confirm the initial theoretical predilections of the analyst. Such speculation has flourished because it has never had to accommodate to an accepted body of rigorous empirical findings about the relevant cognitive performance of speakers of diverse languages. People have freely extrapolated from research data on our own language or some telling personal experience with another. Additional speculation of this type seems unlikely to resolve whether structural diversity among languages has a significant impact on cognition.

The remedy for this situation lies in developing a viable empirical approach to the issue and using it. An analytic review of existing empirical research (Lucy 1992a) yielded four requirements that should be met by such research: (1) it should be comparative from the outset, presenting contrastive data on two or more language communities; (2) the comparison should utilize an external "reality" as the metric or standard for calibrating the content of both linguistic and cognitive categories; (3) the language analysis should concern one or more categories of reference having general significance in the languages; and (4) language-based cognitive predictions should be evaluated in light of the actual nonverbal performance of individual speakers.[1] These requirements are not especially demanding given the nature and importance of the question, but at the time of the review no existing study met all four requirements.[2] Therefore it was necessary to take a second step, namely, illustrating the approach by developing a new concrete case study. A study meeting these requirements (Lucy 1992b) explored the relation between language and thought among adult speakers of American English and of Yucatec Maya, an indigenous language spoken in southeastern Mexico. The study compared grammatical number marking patterns in the two languages and then tested for associated cognitive differences on classification and memory tasks involving picture and object stimuli.

In this chapter, we draw on this previous research as well as more recent work on both adults and children to illustrate what psychological research on language and thought needs to include in order to meet the four criteria listed above. It begins with the reality of language diversity, explores its significance for adult functioning, and traces its development during childhood. The emphasis throughout will be on the general logic and broader relevance of adopting a comparative strategy, that is, how one moves from the account of behavioral diversity through the identification of psychological correlates to a more viable theory of human functioning and development. In the sections to follow we will show how the grammars of the two languages differ in fundamental ways, that these differences correspond to adult cognitive preferences (that is, that there are two distinct developmental outcomes depending on the language spoken), and, finally, when and how these distinct patterns emerge in development. We conclude by revisiting the arguments about comparative methodology in terms of the particular substantive findings of the study.

2 Cultural background and language contrast

The Maya who form the comparison group here are subsistence farmers living in a small community in the scrub jungle of the eastern Yucatan peninsula. Descendants of the peoples who built the well-known monumental architecture of the region, today they raise corn and a variety of other crops in a slash-and-burn agricultural regime. The material culture, social organization, and ritual life of the community can best be described as traditionally "Yucatecan" – that is, they derive from a long complex accommodation between pre-Columbian Mayan, Colonial Spanish, and modern Mexican influences. Isolation and poverty combined to ensure that the village remained very traditional even by local standards well into the 1970s at which time a road was built into the community. Thereafter the pace of change quickened both because of the arrival of new influences in the form of medical clinics, agricultural projects, packaged foods, electricity, and modern appliances such as TVs and refrigerators, and because of easier access to the outside world, in particular to the employment and market opportunities of the nearby tourist resort of Cancun.

Despite these recent cultural changes, Yucatec Maya remains the language of everyday life both within the community and in nearby trade towns. Most women and children are monolingual and a substantial number of men are too. Even the school curriculum is fully in Yucatec for the first three years with many children dropping out after this point. Spanish, the language of the outside world, is spoken increasingly often by young adults, especially men, but few individuals have anything like full fluency.

Yucatec and English differ in their nominal number marking patterns, the grammatical focus of the present study. First, the two languages contrast in the way they signal plural for nouns. English speakers *obligatorily* signal plural for a *large number* of their nouns whereas Yucatec speakers *optionally* signal plural for a comparatively *small number* of their nouns. Specifically, English speakers typically mark plural for nouns referring to animate entities and ordinary objects but not for amorphous substances (e.g. *sugar*, *mud*, etc.). Yucatec speakers sometimes mark plural for animate entities but only occasionally mark it for any other type of referent. These patterns of semantically contingent plural marking are consistent with well-attested crosslinguistic typological patterns (see Lucy 1992b: ch. 3).

Second, the two languages contrast in the way they enumerate nouns and this contrast derives from a deep underlying difference between the two languages. English numerals directly modify their associated nouns (e.g. *one candle*, *two candles*) whereas Yucatec numerals must be supplemented by a special form, usually referred to as a *numeral classifier*, which typically provides crucial information about the shape or material properties of the referent of the noun (e.g. *'un-tz'íit kib'* 'one long thin candle,' *ká'a-tz'íit kib'* 'two long thin candle'). Numeral classifiers of this type are a well-known grammatical phenomenon and occur in a wide variety of languages throughout the world, perhaps most notably in the languages of Asia – Chinese, Japanese, Thai, etc.

Since many classifiers have to do with shape or form, one common interpretation of them is that they represent a special emphasis on these concepts in a language's semantics. Such a view would be more plausible if the classifiers were optional, occurred in many morphosyntactic contexts, and appeared only in a few languages. But in fact they are obligatory, confined to a single morphosyntactic context, and are fairly common among the world's languages – all of which suggests that they represent an indispensable solution to a formal referential difficulty characteristic of languages of a certain morphosyntactical type.

So why have numeral classifiers? What problem do they solve? The need for them reflects the fact that *all nouns in Yucatec are semantically unspecified as to quantificational unit* almost as if they referred to unformed substances. So, for example, the semantic sense of the Yucatec word *kib'* in the example cited above is better translated into English as *wax* (i.e. glossed as 'one long thin wax') – even though, when occurring alone without a numeral modifier in conditions other than enumeration, the word *kib'* can routinely refer to objects with the form and function of objects that we would call candles (as well as to other wax things). Once one understands the quantificational neutrality of the noun it becomes obvious that one must specify a unit when counting – that is, provide a classifier, since expressions such as *one wax* wouldn't make quantificational sense. By contrast, many nouns in English include the notion of quantificational 'unit' (or 'form') as part of their basic meaning – so when we count these nouns, we can simply use the numeral directly without any classifier (e.g. *one candle*). Where our English nouns are quantificationally neutral like those of the Yucatec, we use the functional equivalent of a classifier construction ourselves: *one cube of sugar*, *one clump of dirt*, and so forth.

For those Yucatec lexical nouns with no close neutral analogue in English, it can be quite difficult to render the exact Yucatec sense. Actually, even for those cases where English has a somewhat equivalent neutral noun, the translation can only be approximate since in Yucatec such nouns are not in systematic contrast with a set of nonneutral nouns as they are in English. The substance reading we give *kib'* when we translate it as *wax* in order to try to make the syntactic neutrality clear isn't quite right semantically because there is no contrasting word for 'candle' in Yucatec. *Kib'* can mean either 'candle' or 'wax' and to choose either as the translation is to lose part of its regular referential meaning.

The patterns of plural marking and numeral modification just described are closely related and form part of a unified number-marking system. Hence, languages with rich, obligatory plural marking such as Hopi tend not to have numeral classifiers and those with a rich, obligatory use of numeral classifiers such as Chinese tend not to have plural marking. Moreover, for languages with both types of marking, the lexicon tends to be internally divided such that nouns requiring plural marking with multiple referents tend not to require classifiers for counting, and those requiring classifiers for counting tend not to require plurals when used with multiple referents (Lucy 1992b: ch. 2).

3 Cognitive correlates

3.1 Original triads study

To assess whether traces of these verbal behavior patterns appear in speakers' cognitive activities more generally, we need first to draw out the implications of these different grammatical patterns for the general interpretation of experience. We have seen that English encodes quantificational unit (or some equivalent) in a large number of its lexical nouns whereas Yucatec does not. But it is difficult to form a single generalization about the concrete denotational meaning value of such patterns because the kind of unit presupposed varies across the spectrum of lexical noun types both within and across languages. But for those lexical nouns where the contrast between the English and Yucatec is maximal – those referring to discrete objects[3] – certain regularities exist from which denotational implications can be drawn.

The quantificational unit presupposed by English nouns of this type is usually the shape of an object. Hence use of these English lexical items routinely draws attention to the shape of a referent insofar as this is the basis for incorporating it under some lexical label and assigning it a number value. Yucatec nouns of this type, lacking such a specification of quantificational unit, do not draw attention to shape and, in fact, fairly routinely draw attention to the material composition of a referent insofar as this is the basis for incorporating it under some lexical label. If these linguistic patterns translate into general cognitive sensitivity to these properties of referents of the discrete type, then *Yucatec speakers should attend relatively more to the material composition of objects (and less to their shape), whereas English speakers should attend relatively less to the material composition of such objects (and more to their shape).*

This prediction was tested with adult speakers from both languages (Lucy 1992b:136–141[4]). They were shown triads of naturally occurring objects familiar to both groups. Each triad consisted of an original *pivot* object and two *alternate* objects, one of the same shape as the pivot and one of the same material as the pivot. Informants were shown eight such triads and asked to decide for each pivot which of the two alternates was most like it. So, for example, speakers were shown a small cardboard box (of the type used for holding cassette tapes) as a pivot and asked whether it was more like a small plastic box of roughly the same size and shape or more like a small piece of cardboard about the size of a matchbook. The expectation was that English speakers would match the pivot to the box and Yucatec speakers would match it to the cardboard. This prediction was strongly borne out across the set of eight triads when shown to a sample of Yucatec and English speakers: eight out of ten Yucatec speakers favored the material alternates, and twelve out of thirteen of the English speakers favored the shape alternates ($p < .0007$, one-tailed Fisher exact test). Table 9.1 shows the results of this original study. Clearly the two groups classify these objects differently and in line with the expectations based on the underlying lexical structures of the two languages. Notice that both pat-

Table 9.1. *Number of English and Yucatec speakers preferring shape or material as a basis for object classification: original triad task*

	Classification preference	
Language group[a]	Shape	Material
English ($n = 13$)[b]	12	1
Yucatec ($n = 10$)[c]	2	8

Notes:
[a] English versus Yucatec: $p < .0007$, one-tailed Fisher exact.
[b] English versus Chance: $p < .005$, $n = 13$, one-tailed binomial test (P = .56 for Shape, Q = .44 for Material).
[c] Yucatec versus Chance: $p < .025$, $n = 10$, one-tailed binomial test (P = .56 for Shape, Q = .44 for Material).
Source: After Lucy 1992a:141, table 34.

terns of classification are reasonable and neither can rightly be described as superior to the other.

3.2 *Recent extensions*

Despite the positive results, the design of this task left open several issues. First and most importantly, a number of unintended responses are possible. For example, in the triad mentioned earlier, an apparent shape or "box" match might actually arise from attending to the similarity of function as closable containers or to their size in comparison to the small piece of cardboard or to their wholeness compared to the fragment of cardboard; likewise, an apparent material or "cardboard" match might actually arise from attending to similarity of color or the greater familiarity of the two cardboard objects in contrast to the somewhat novel plastic box. Some of these alternative readings can be seen as shape and material responses in disguise, and it is likely that across the entire set of triads such unintended responses did not greatly affect the results, but it seemed desirable to improve control over these factors.

Second, the same cognitive patterns might not appear with more complex reasoning and memory tasks. It seemed worth exploring the effect of increasing the task complexity and/or difficulty. Additionally, it is possible that the simple directness of the contrast presented in the triads elicits a lexical labeling strategy: so, for example, English speakers seeing the triad just described will say "box" to themselves when they see the pivot and so choose the box alternate.[5] Although there would still be a language effect under this interpretation, it would stem more from the immediate lexical label for the particular stimulus item rather than from the broader grammatical pattern. To guard against this, the original set of triads was counter-balanced for the presence of simple lexical labels at least in Yucatec (i.e. some of the probes shared lexical labels with the substance choice and some did not), but it seemed wise to control more carefully the possibility of immediate lexical influences. A more complex task where the contrast at stake might be less obvious and less subject to the influence of immediate item labeling seemed worth undertaking.

Thus, to improve control over the stimulus materials and increase task complexity, two new assessment procedures were undertaken. The first assessment procedure replicated the triads sorting study with a more rigorously controlled set of stimulus materials. The second assessment procedure used the same sorts of stimulus materials but involved a new, more complex classification task. Both procedures were presented to twelve English and twelve Yucatec adult speakers. For full details on these and related studies, see Lucy & Gaskins (in preparation).

3.2.1 Controlled stimulus materials Many new triad types were constructed to explore with greater precision the competing bases of classification. The focus here will be on the set of twenty-one triads that we used most extensively. Each triad consisted of three objects that were deliberately selected to be familiar to both language groups so as to insure cultural interpretability. The dimensions of control for the new triads are detailed below, along with the results of the choices that English and Yucatec speakers made for these triads.

3.2.1.1 Control of color and size

Color does not typically find its way into grammatical distinctions, and size does so only in relatively limited ways (e.g. diminutives), although many if not most languages have forms capable of referring to these qualities. Yet these two qualities can be very salient cognitively, so we wanted to assure ourselves that they were not affecting the results. However, it proved very difficult to control color and size with naturally occurring objects familiar to both groups since many such objects do not come in a variety of colors and sizes. In particular, there is a tight linkage between color and material as is readily suggested by the way we use material names such as *gold* and *copper* as color descriptors. Our solution was to be sure that in at least a third of the triads, the color of the pivot and the material choice were different. Likewise there seems to be a linkage between size and shape such that if size is identical it seems to facilitate a shape match, and if size varies dramatically enough it impedes a shape match: consider whether you would want to match a round wooden bead with a square wooden block of similar size or with a much larger beach ball – the larger the ball the less appealing the shape match. So we worked to assure that in at least a third of the shape matches, the size differential was greater than 10% although not vastly different. Looking at the choices that English and Yucatec speakers made across the entire set of twenty-one new triads, we found that the rate of material choices was unaffected by color redundancy and that the rate of shape choices was unaffected by an exact size match. In short, color and size cannot explain relative preference for shape or material in the results to be discussed below.

3.2.1.2 Control of function

The dimension of function, in the sense of the typical use of an object, does sometimes play a role in grammar – most notably in selection restrictions on predicate-argument agreement. Hence we took great pains to evaluate this as a basis of preference. The twenty-one triads were divided into seven sets of three, each set designed to treat the function dimension in a different way. The seven types are listed and illustrated in figure 9.1.

The two triad sets that controlled function most closely were sets 1 and 2. Set 1, the Unifunctional Wholes, consisted of three whole objects that all had a single function, thereby neutralizing function as a possible choice. Set 2, the Trifunctional Wholes, consisted of three whole objects that each had a different function thereby neutralizing function as a possible choice. The original finding was replicated: Yucatec speakers favored material choices in the triads 55.6% of the time whereas English speakers favored material choices only 23.6% of the time ($p < .009$, Kolmogorov–Smirnov two-sample test). These data are given in table 9.2, along with the data from the original triads task (recoded here by triad rather than by subject to facilitate comparison[6]) and data from the other functionally neutral triads that we turn to next. (Again, to facilitate comparison, we have reported all results here in terms of degree of material preference, but the degree of shape preference in any instance can easily be derived since shape and material preferences always add up to 100%. So, for example, English speakers' 23.6% preference for material on this task implies 76.4% preference for shape.)

Another three sets of triads (see figure 9.1) also controlled function by precluding a function match, but, in addition, one or more of the alternates had no function whatsoever. Lack of function was achieved by presenting a scrap or piece of a familiar object as an alternate where the scrap clearly had no customary function at all. (All of the pivots in these triad sets were still whole objects.) We undertook this manipulation because it appeared

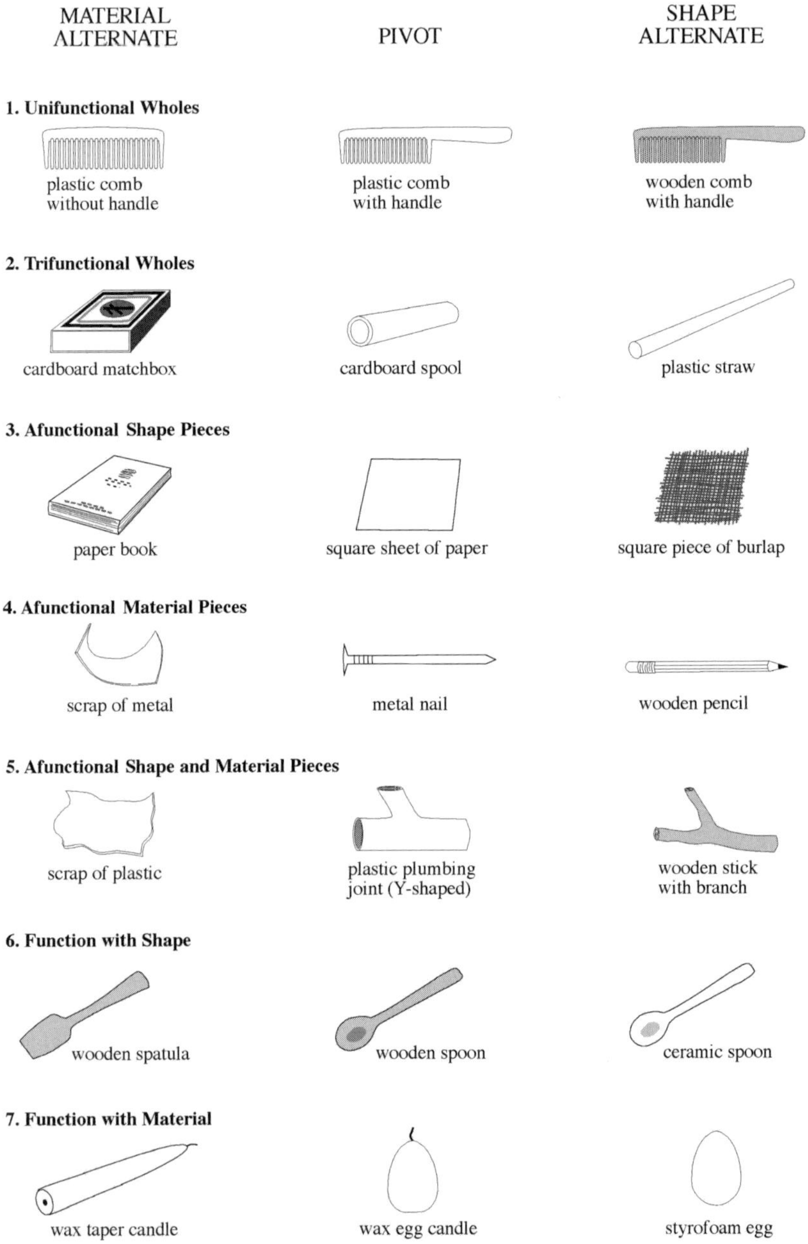

MATERIAL ALTERNATE	PIVOT	SHAPE ALTERNATE
1. Unifunctional Wholes		
plastic comb without handle	plastic comb with handle	wooden comb with handle
2. Trifunctional Wholes		
cardboard matchbox	cardboard spool	plastic straw
3. Afunctional Shape Pieces		
paper book	square sheet of paper	square piece of burlap
4. Afunctional Material Pieces		
scrap of metal	metal nail	wooden pencil
5. Afunctional Shape and Material Pieces		
scrap of plastic	plastic plumbing joint (Y-shaped)	wooden stick with branch
6. Function with Shape		
wooden spatula	wooden spoon	ceramic spoon
7. Function with Material		
wax taper candle	wax egg candle	styrofoam egg

Fig. 9.1 Examples of types of triad stimuli.

Table 9.2. *Percentage of English and Yucatec choices showing preferences for material as a basis for object classification: Function Neutral triad task*

	Preference for material (percent)	
Task type	English	Yucatec
Original Triads[a]	37.5	80.0
Function Neutral Triads		
Uni/Trifunctionals (1–2)[b]	23.6	55.6
Afunctional Pieces (3–5)[b]	22.2	64.8
All Function Neutral (1–5)[b]	22.8	61.1

Notes:

[a] Recoded from table 9.1 to facilitate comparison (see n. 6).

[b] English versus Yucatec: $p < .009$, $n = 12$, one-tailed Kolmogorov–Smirnov two-sample test.

that some of the strongest of the original triads used pieces of things, much like the piece of cardboard in the original example, and we wondered whether this enhanced substance choices.

Set 3, the Afunctional Shape Pieces set, consisted of three items without shared function wherein the pivot and the material alternate were recognizable objects but the shape alternate was clearly just a piece of something. Set 4, the Afunctional Material Pieces set, consisted of three items without shared function wherein the pivot and the shape alternate were recognizable objects but the material alternate was clearly just a piece of something. Set 5, the Afunctional Shape and Material Pieces set, consisted of three items without shared function wherein the pivot was a recognizable object but both the shape and material alternates were clearly just pieces of something. The results on these three sets of triads were essentially the same as those of the first two sets, but the contrast between the two groups was sharpened a bit: English preference for material fell to 22.2% and Yucatec rose to 64.8% ($p < .009$, one-tailed Kolmogorov–Smirnov two-sample test). The use of pieces rather than whole objects in triads otherwise controlled for function appears to have had no major effect on the pattern of preferences. Thus, for the purposes of further comparison, all five of these sets (fifteen triads in all) will be joined and termed the Function Neutral triads. Table 9.2 lists the composite results for the three Afunctional Pieces triad types as well as the values for the composite category of Function Neutral triads.

For all five sets of triads, the Yucatec preference for material choices was not as different from chance (50%) as the English one – which is to be expected. Strictly speaking, the Yucatec grammatical pattern is neutral: nouns referring to discrete objects do not code a quantificational unit as part of their semantics but neither do they code any particular substance quality at this grammatical level. Therefore, on grammatical grounds, the Yucatec cognitive preference for shape or material should, by rights, be fairly balanced and fall near to 50% on this task. Hence the Yucatec preference for material choices is a relative preference rather than an absolute one – relative, that is, to English speakers, who package quantificational unit into nouns of this type and show a strong inclination to classify objects by shape. To the extent that the Yucatec response rate rises significantly above 50%, it suggests that the grammatical neutrality has been intensionalized as a general substance orientation, perhaps because relatively more lexical elements incorporate substance semantics. Such increased response rates do in fact appear on some tasks, for example, the more complex classification task discussed below.

A final two sets of triads (see figure 9.1) controlled function in yet a third way by intentionally joining it systematically with one of the two alternates. Set 6, the Function with Shape set, consisted of three whole objects wherein the pivot and the shape alternate shared function thereby aligning shape with function. Set 7, the Function with Material set, consisted of three whole objects wherein the pivot and the material alternate shared function thereby aligning material with function.

This stimulus manipulation produced dramatic effects when function lined up *against* the dominant cultural preference, moving the response rate strongly towards that of the other group.[7] Hence the Yucatec preference for material dropped from 61.1% on the Function Neutral triads to 38.9% when function was aligned with shape and the English preference for material rose from 22.8% for the Functional Neutral triads to 72.2% when function was aligned with material (Yucatec change: $p < .021$; English change: $p < .003$, two-tailed Wilcoxon matched-pairs tests). However, when function lined up with the existing cultural preference, it did not produce statistically reliable changes. These patterns are shown in table 9.3.

Overall, it appears that when function matches are available, they can affect the results and need to be carefully controlled when assessing a relative shape versus material classification preference. The dramatic effect of function alignment on English speakers also suggests that function is relatively more important for English speakers than it is for Yucatec speakers. Indeed, for English speakers, joining material and function results in more material choices than the Yucatec speakers typically exhibit.

Taken together, these new triads bring an improved level of control to the assessment of Lucy's (1992b) original hypothesis. The relative shape and material preferences reported in the original study are not only replicated

Table 9.3. *Percentage of English and Yucatec choices showing preferences for material as a basis for object classification: Function Biased triad task*

	Preference for material (percent)	
Task type	English	Yucatec
Function Neutral Triads (1–5)[a]	22.8	61.1
Function Biased Triads		
Function with Shape (6)	8.3	38.9[b]
Function with Material (7)	72.2[c]	55.6

Notes:

[a] Drawn from table 9.2 to facilitate comparison.

[b] Function with Shape versus Function Neutral Triads: $p < .021$, $n = 12$, two-tailed Wilcoxon matched-pairs test.

[c] Function with Material versus Function Neutral Triads: $p < .003$, $n = 12$, two-tailed Wilcoxon matched-pairs test.

but also prove to be robust for stimuli of this type when the dimensions of function, color, and size are controlled.

3.2.2 Complex classification task In order to increase the complexity of the triad classification task, we developed a new task, called the nine-sort task, where we asked informants to sort sets of nine objects into two piles. Four objects were made of the same material but each in a different shape; these were the material alternates. Four others were all the same shape but each made of a different material; these were the shape alternates. A ninth, pivot item was made of the same material as the material alternates and in the same shape as the shape alternates. Five different sets of nine-sorts were used in the current assessment. An example of one such set is depicted in figure 9.2 wherein the material alternates are made of cardboard, the shape alternates are tubes, and the pivot is a cardboard tube.

The twelve informants from each language were each asked to sort the nine objects into two groups. The groups were begun by placing one material and one shape alternate onto plastic trays in front of the person.[8] Then the remaining alternates were handed to them one by one, and they were asked to make two piles so that everything in each pile was the same. The last item presented was always the pivot. If the informant had built one pile of things of the same material and another of things of the same shape, he or she was now forced to decide between material or shape in placing it. For the nine-sort set presented in figure 9.2, for example, if the informant sorted one pile of tube-shaped items and another of cardboard items, then

ALTERNATES

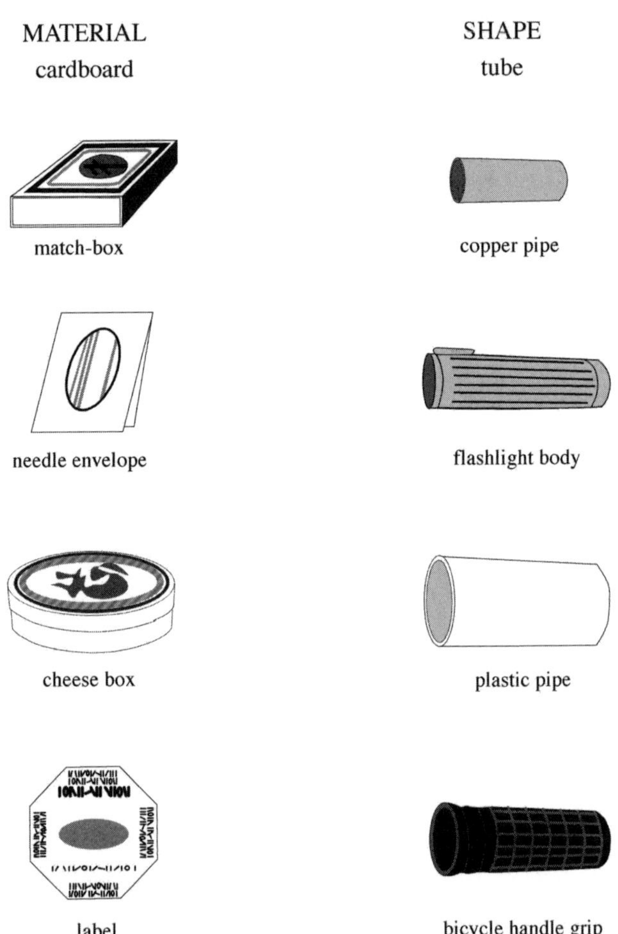

PIVOT

MATERIAL + SHAPE

cardboard + tube

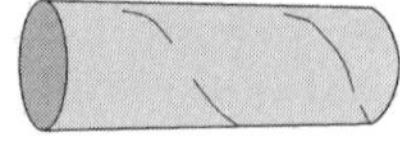

toilet paper core

Fig. 9.2 Examples of a set of nine-sort stimuli.

the pivot item, the cardboard tube, which was presented last, posed a problem for the informant, for it could be put into either pile according to the categories that had been constructed during the sorting of the piles. The assignment of the ninth object is taken to reveal the informant's bias in an ambiguous situation. The nine-sort sets were pretested, and modified as necessary, to ensure that the items could be reliably sorted according to the categories of interest, namely, material and shape.

In this nine-sort task the informant is forced to form a more complex judgment over a series of items. Furthermore, since a variety of objects must be grouped together before coming to the pivot, the verbal name for any one of those objects will not suffice to guide the grouping, so any possible use of this strategy should diminish. For example, if the cardboard group includes a container and a package label, then the only way to include the cardboard tube with that group is to extract the common dimension of cardboard.

This procedure also provided a rich variety of qualitative information about how informants were approaching the classification task. Respondent's answers unfolded in sequence so one could see what items gave them pause. Informants were allowed to rearrange their groups enroute if they wished, and many did so once they had seen a larger range of the items in a given sort. Their preliminary groupings gave important clues to their other classification strategies, even though their final piles ended up being based on material and shape. And the range of grouping strategies, incidental remarks, and follow-up discussions revealed much about how they were approaching the task, particularly in the Yucatec case.

When one looks at how informants chose to place the pivot, the same group differences in preference for material and shape seen in the triads tasks emerge once again, but with a somewhat *stronger* material preference now among the Yucatec. As shown in table 9.4, adult English speakers assign the pivot item on the basis of material only 23.6% of the time, compared to 73.6% for the adult Yucatec speakers ($p < .001$, one-tailed Kolmogorov–Smirnov two-sample test). This suggests that the effects found in the earlier triad studies will be replicated (and may even be stronger) on more complicated tasks and that immediate lexical labeling with respect to a single probe is unlikely to account for the previous triad results.

The qualitative information provided by this task cannot be described in full here, but it supports the interpretation we have given to the quantitative data. The Yucatec speakers were constantly evaluating the material composition of the test items before sorting them: feeling how heavy they were, poking their nails into them to test for malleability, scraping the surface to see what the material under the paint was, smelling and tasting the objects,

Table 9.4. *Percentage of English and Yucatec choices showing preferences for material as a basis for object classification: nine-sort task*

	Preference for material (percent)	
Task type	English	Yucatec
Function Neutral Triads (1–5)[a]	22.8	61.1
Nine-Sorts[b]	23.6	73.6

Notes:
[a] Drawn from table 9.2 to facilitate comparison.
[b] English versus Yucatec: $p < .001$, $n = 12$, one-tailed Kolmogorov–Smirnov two-sample test.

and generally questioning or commenting on their material properties – and all this with familiar objects. The English-speaking Americans showed none of this sort of reaction – they could get all the information they needed by sight alone. A particularly striking example of an alternative sorting occurred with one Yucatec woman during pilot work, where we could not make sense of the principle she was using. When we asked her about her reasons during the follow-up discussion, she replied that the things on one tray would melt if they were burned whereas the ones on the other tray would turn to ash. This was a level of attention to material properties that went much deeper than we had originally imagined.

3.3 *Summary*

On the basis of these results, we can draw three conclusions about the relationship between language spoken and classification preference. First, classification preferences differ in these two language groups. English speakers consistently exhibit a relative preference for shape-based classifications, and Yucatec speakers consistently exhibit a relative preference for material-based classifications. Gentner & Boroditsky (ch. 8, this volume) report a similar pattern of classification differences between speakers of English and Japanese (a classifier language), suggesting that the results reported here will not prove unique.

Second, the findings are robust. They have proven replicable across many years, samples, stimulus configurations, and task types (not all of which have been reported here). It remains to be seen how widely this pattern generalizes, but the various controlled manipulations described here make it unlikely that the basic differences in shape and material preference result from artifacts of the stimuli (i.e. color, size, or function) or task design (i.e. lexical labeling, task simplicity, task directness).

Third, these relative classification preferences were predicted on the basis of the semantic patterns implicit in the grammatical categories of the two languages. Similar sorts of correspondences between number-marking patterns and cognitive performance have been found in a number of other tasks using quite different stimuli (Lucy 1992b: 93–136). All these factors converge to suggest that the cognitive differences stem at least in part from the grammatical patterns.

4 Developmental issues

Next we want to consider the formation of these language-related preferences in childhood: at what age and in what manner do they arise? The adult cognitive contrast not only gives rise to these questions, it also provides part of the key to their solution. By testing for the presence of the known adult contrast at various ages, we can locate the point in development when language and thought begin to interact in this way. Similarly, comparative work can help illuminate the developmental process itself by separating the constant from the variable, the crucial from the less relevant.[9]

Pilot work (Lucy & Gaskins 1989) indicated that the onset of these changes was between 7 and 9 years of age, so we undertook a more extensive study of these two ages using the classification tasks described above. Twelve English-speaking and twelve Yucatec-speaking children at each age were presented with the same triad materials used in the adult samples. On the Function Neutral triads (i.e. sets 1–5), both English-speaking and Yucatec-speaking 7-year-olds showed an identical early bias towards shape – choosing material alternates only 11.7% of the time. By age 9, the English-speaking children continued to favor shape, choosing material alternates only 17.8% of the time. But by this age, the Yucatec-speaking children were choosing material alternates 41.7% of the time, much like adult Yucatec speakers. Thus, the same kind of language-group difference found among adult speakers is also found in children by age 9 ($p < .033$, one-tailed Kolmogorov–Smirnov two-sample test). The group comparison as a function of age is shown graphically in figure 9.3 (adults are labeled "15+").[10]

Results for the two Function Biased triad sets, where function was alternately aligned with shape or material (i.e. sets 6 and 7) did not produce the big deflections characteristic of the adult groups.[11] The Yucatec children's responses on these triad types were virtually identical to their responses with the Function Neutral triads. The English children's responses showed some small effects in the expected directions as early as age 7, but they were not statistically reliable. These results are shown graphically in figures 9.4 and 9.5.

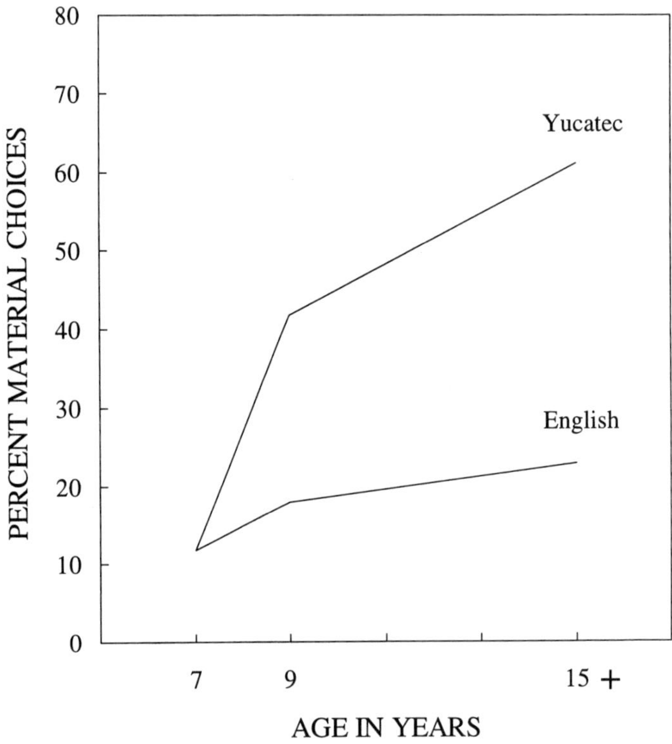

Fig. 9.3 Developmental pattern for English and Yucatec classification preferences: material vs. shape using Function Neutral triad types.

A modified version of the nine-sorts task was also administered to the same groups of children. The modified procedure was developed because children were much more likely to generate bizarre groupings with the first few objects, groupings they would then doggedly stick with rather than revise in light of subsequent objects appearing in the set. To minimize this tendency, all the alternates and the pivot were made visible to the children from the outset. In the modified procedure a paper cross (or "X") with four points was placed on the table and was encircled by an array of the eight alternate items. Then the pivot item was put in the middle of the cross, and the children were asked to pick from the array of alternates one item for each point of the cross such that the five items ending up on the cross would all be the same. This allowed the children to scan the total array of items before forming a group, and they usually had no trouble forming a plausible grouping under this arrangement. Indeed, one striking fact about both 7- and 9-year-olds

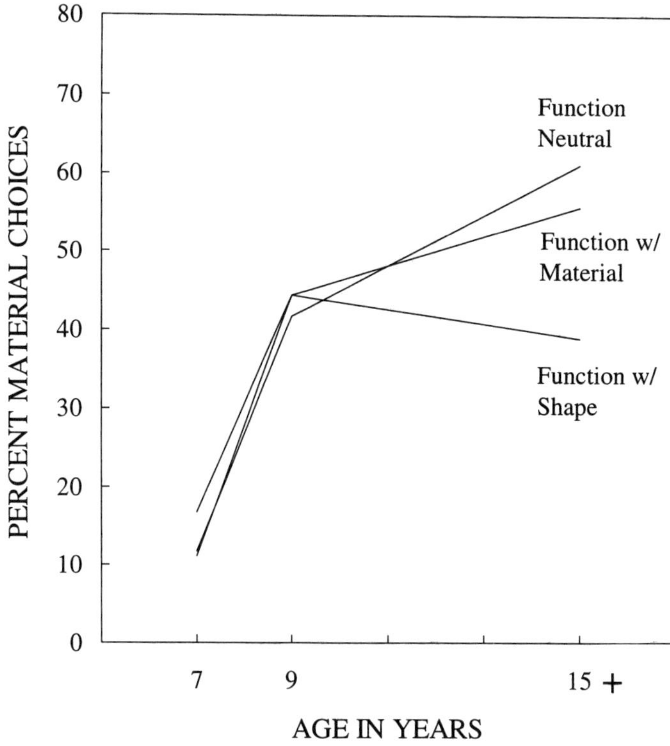

Fig. 9.4 Developmental pattern for Yucatec classification preferences: effect of joining function with shape and material.

was that they responded very decisively to the task in this form: they were sure there was a "right answer," and that they had sorted according to it. They often didn't even see the alternative classification possibility.

The same general pattern of Yucatec speakers showing relatively greater preference for material emerges on this task, but with one significant difference. Although the 7-year-old children in both groups favor shape as a basis of classification, the Yucatec-speaking children already demonstrate a tendency towards the adult Yucatec pattern. English-speaking children choose on the basis of material only 2.8% of the time whereas the Yucatec do so 20.8% of the time ($p < .033$, one-tailed Kolmogorov–Smirnov two-sample test). By age 9, the English-speaking children continued to favor shape, choosing material alternates only 8.3% of the time, but the Yucatec-speaking children have shifted dramatically, choosing material alternates 48.6% of the time, approaching the adult pattern, as they did on the triads

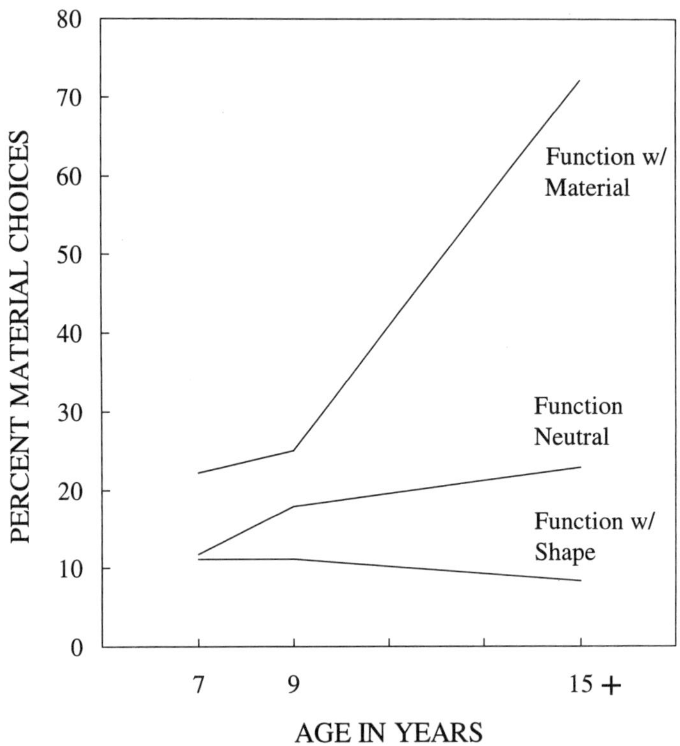

Fig. 9.5 Developmental pattern for English classification preferences: effect of joining function with shape and material.

task (p < .009, one-tailed Kolmogorov–Smirnov two-sample test). The group comparison as a function of age is shown graphically in figure 9.6.

Overall, the more complex nine-sort task appears to be more sensitive than the triads task to the Yucatec material bias in that the bias is stronger at all ages. The task even reveals a bias at age 7, suggesting that there may be some grammatical-category-related effects as early as this age. Nonetheless, as the graph makes clear, the major move in this direction occurs after age 7 with the Yucatec bias and the group differences becoming larger with age.

Taken as a whole, these developmental data suggest that there is a major shift towards the culturally specific adult cognitive pattern by age 9. On the basis of these results, we can draw three conclusions about the development of language-related classification preferences for these kinds of objects. First, the early tendency at age 7 is to prefer shape over material as a basis of classification for these kinds of objects regardless of language affiliation. This preference is unaffected by the introduction of function as an alterna-

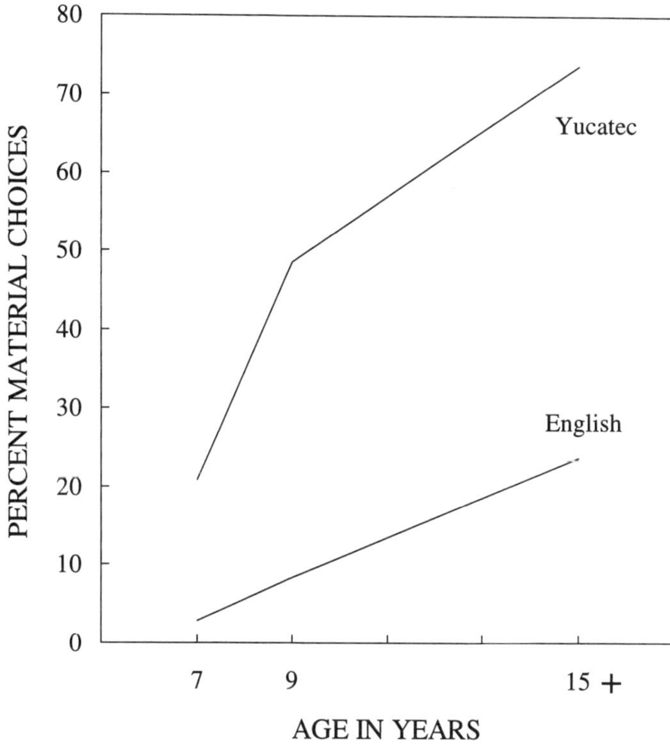

Fig. 9.6 Developmental pattern for English and Yucatec classification preferences: material vs. shape using nine-sorts.

tive basis of classification. Although Yucatec-speaking children already show some early relative inclination towards material choices, their overwhelming absolute preference is for shape.[12]

It is perhaps worth emphasizing that just as the English-speaking children have substantial command of the plural by age 7, so too do the Yucatec-speaking children have substantial command of the numeral classifier system by this age. Seven-year-old Yucatec-speaking children reliably use classifiers when counting, draw appropriate semantic distinctions among them in comprehension tasks, and will judge a number construction lacking them as faulty. However, they fall far short of having command of the full range of classifiers in comprehension and their range in production is narrower still. In short, they have the basic structural implications straight but do not yet have the full lexical range of an adult (Lucy & Gaskins, in preparation). Hence, to the extent these cognitive results derive from these basic structural characteristics of the language rather than mastery of specific lexical items, there is no reason they could not appear at age 7. That they do not do so suggests that some rather specific reorganizations in the relation between language and thought take place between ages 7 and 9.

Second, Yucatec-speaking children at age 9 show a strong relative preference for material as a basis of classification and appear well on their way towards the adult Yucatec pattern. Although English-speaking children also show a very slight increased sensitivity to material bases of classification by age 9, their overwhelming preference continues to be for shape, in line with the adult English pattern. Because the adult preference for English speakers agrees with that shared by young children, there is little evidence for overt change in classification preference by age for the English-speaking sample. Indeed, it would be difficult to identify this age period as the crucial one without the comparative Yucatec data. But the English-speaking adults are not quite so shape-biased as the 7-year-olds, and the 9-year-olds typically show an intermediate pattern suggesting that they are beginning to respond to the same factors as English-speaking adults. In time it should be possible to design further tests to assess whether the same underlying psychological mechanisms are operating for the English samples to produce the shape preference during the various age periods, or whether there is in fact a developmental change in the basis for classification in the English sample as well, even though the overt preference for shape is uniformly expressed at all ages. More generally, additional work will be necessary to determine whether other language-related shifts occur during this age range.

Third, the results indicate that children are more rigid than adults in their responses on these classification tasks. Children in both groups begin with a strong preference for shape and shape alone. By age 9, there is a greater sensitivity to material in both groups, but its potency is heavily conditioned by language group membership. By adulthood, function plays a significant role, deflecting the baseline preference for shape versus material; but, again, the potency of these shifts depends heavily on language group membership, with function only having a significant effect when it runs counter to the baseline preference in the language. The effects of these changes appear clearly in figures 9.4 and 9.5: with increasing age for both groups there is a move away from shape (revealed by greater vertical displacement) and towards greater impact of functional manipulations (revealed by greater absolute spread in the degree of material preference across various triad types). What we see then is a shared decline in rigidity and the growth of greater classification flexibility across both language groups, but a flexibility markedly deflected by differing group norms and differentially sensitive to displacement by other factors, again as a function of those norms.

5 Conclusion

These empirical findings provide an excellent illustration of the importance of adopting a comparative approach in the study of the relation between language and thought (cf. Byrnes & Gelman 1991). By extension we would argue that such comparative work is essential in human psychology more generally because of its deeply cultural nature. A comparative approach was adopted from the outset here and it is worth reviewing exactly how this was important for the research process.

First, by documenting the range and patterning of behavioral diversity, an important set of problems and hypotheses was opened up. In particular, close study of a non-European language revealed basic differences in morphosyntactic structuring that were then interpreted in terms of the different verbal construals of experience implicit in them. We have gone on to explore the possible broader cognitive consequences of these differences – in particular, how speakers of the two languages might be interpreting reality differently beyond the act of speaking, but it is worth noting that the same contrast raises many other important questions. For example, the differences raise questions about the viability of certain proposals about how languages are structured and how children learn them. A large number of studies have appeared in recent years attempting to show that young children have an early bias towards drawing a sortal–object distinction, that is, towards believing that words refer to discrete or bounded solid objects (e.g. Markman 1990, 1991; Soja, Carey, & Spelke 1991; Clark, ch. 13 of this volume). Researchers differ on whether they think the sources of this bias are more cognitive (e.g. Bloom, ch. 6 of this volume) or more specific to language learning (e.g. Waxman 1994), but they are in accord about the utility of such a bias because they believe all languages are structured this way. Yet when we consider the many languages that differ dramatically in both their number marking systems and the relative importance of such a distinction for the language, we can immediately see that such proposals need to be tempered. What good is an early bias that has to be systematically undone by a quarter or more of the world's people in order to speak properly? Clearly some rethinking is required here.

Second, the descriptive linguistic work was used as a platform for formulating and testing for tangible psychological implications of the linguistic differences. The work with adults indicates that language-specific grammatical patterns are indeed correlated with classification preferences. Whether or not one believes that the language patterns give rise to the differences, the comparative cognitive data alone compel a rethinking of the notion of a unified developmental outcome for cognition. To the extent language does give rise to these cognitive differences, the study casts doubt on the notion, widely held, that cognition enables and influences language but not vice versa (e.g. Fodor 1975). What is especially important to note is that the contrast between languages both gives rise to the cognitive prediction in the first place and then indicates exactly what difference we need to look for. Without the comparative contrast, the harmony of language and thought in English would both obscure the existence of the cognitive differences and make detecting them nearly impossible. (Spelke & Tsivkin, ch. 3, this volume, make a similar argument.)

Third, the study exploits the diversity in adult response in order to uncover the nature of the psychological mechanisms and developmental processes at work. The contrast between the two groups is essential to establishing when the language-linked cognitive patterns arise, what the qualitative nature of the classification preference is before the differences arise, and how responses differ in flexibility from subsequent adult forms. In short, by exploiting known differences among adults we have a powerful way to diagnose both the timing and the qualitative nature of important developmental shifts.

Regarding the changes in middle childhood, there already exists, of course, substantial evidence suggesting that thought and language are changing in new and important ways during this period. Cognitive developmentalists (Piaget & Inhelder 1969; Vygotsky 1987 [1934]) have long recognized this as the period in which the child completes a shift from dependence on more spontaneous, perceptual strategies to reliance on more systematically organized, conceptual ones. In the realm of language development, there is during this period a general reorganization of grammar along adult lines, increasing sensitivity to the syntactic and semantic presuppositions of prior discourse, and increasingly hierarchical organization of narratives (Chomsky 1969; Bowerman 1982; Karmiloff-Smith 1984; Hickmann 1993; Berman & Slobin 1994). What has not been obvious before is the degree to which these two sets of transformations may be linked in language-specific ways. Children may well draw on their increasingly sophisticated grammatical and discursive skills to reconfigure existing cognitive competencies into more stable, shared conceptual systems, systems that can then be relied on to correct or supplement interpretations of the world that have heretofore been partial and highly susceptible to perceptual and immediate contextual factors. In short, the child now enters the world of the adult, which is more heavily guided by systems of shared cultural meaning (Lucy & Gaskins 1994).

Both the recognition of such developmental linkages and their detailed exploration profit enormously from adopting a comparative approach. More generally, we cannot ever hope to reach an adequate understanding of human beings by ignoring behavioral diversity, nor through assimilating it to our own norms as advanced or deficient, nor through regarding it as incomprehensible. Rather, such understanding will only come through the careful study of that diversity for what it can tell us about how people's experience of the world is mediated (developed and sustained) through languages and cultures and, in turn, how those languages and cultures are mediated (developed and sustained) by psychological processes.

NOTES

The new research reported here has been supported by the Spencer Foundation (Chicago, USA) and the Max Planck Institute for Psycholinguistics (Nijmegen, The Netherlands). Christine Kray assisted with the Yucatec sample. Kathryn Mason assisted with the English sample. We thank the volume editors Stephen Levinson and Melissa Bowerman for detailed comments on the original draft. Inge Doehring helped with the figures.

1 For a fuller discussion of these four requirements, see Lucy (1992a: 263–275; also 1992b: 1–2). In particular, the characterization of "reality" must not favor any one language and yet be consistent with how reality "appears through the window of language."

2 The two closest candidates, after Whorf's (1956 [1939]) pioneering effort comparing Hopi and English, were Carroll's comparison of Hopi and English (Carroll & Casagrande 1958) and Heider's comparison of Dani and English (Heider 1972). Both are weak on criterion (3) in that they dealt with contrasts between small lexical sets without reference to a general structural or functional analysis of the two languages. For a full discussion, see Lucy (1992a). Since that review, an important body of new work has been produced by Steve Levinson and his colleagues (Levinson 1992, 1996; Brown and Levinson 1993; Pederson 1995; Pederson, Danziger, Wilkins *et al.* 1998). For a review, see Lucy (1997).

3 The term *discrete* here is being used to designate a common characteristic of referents of lexical nouns falling into a category defined by formal comparison of the two languages as discussed in Lucy (1992b: 56–83). The focus here will be entirely on this type of lexical noun. Other noun types and their referents are dealt with in separate studies (Lucy 1992b: 93–136; Lucy & Gaskins, in preparation; cf. Gentner & Boroditsky, ch. 8 of this volume).

4 The example described here is only one of a range of studies reported in Lucy (1992b: ch. 3) testing for various cognitive correlates of linguistic patterns.

5 For an example of another indirect test that eliminates this possibility and reveals the same preference pattern, see Lucy (1992b: 136–144).

6 Subject coding was used in the original study where the aim was to characterize individual sorting tendencies as a function of language spoken. In the present study, where the focus is on the effect of different triad types within and across languages, item coding was used instead. Since each subject contributes equally to the results and they have been expressed as percentages for the group comparisons, the statistical sample size ($n = 12$ for each group) has not been artificially inflated.

7 Some differences among referent types in word learning tasks as reported by Gentner & Boroditsky (ch. 8 of this volume) may have their origins in the shift-

ing alignment of function with other features of reference. However, in the developmental studies reported below, this adult effect does not appear.

8 The order of presentation of alternates, including which ones were presented first, and the right–left presentation of shape and material alternates were counterbalanced within and across subjects.

9 Full demonstration of the utility of the comparative approach for illuminating the developmental process itself cannot be undertaken here because it would require the introduction of several additional studies (see Lucy & Gaskins, in preparation).

10 Figure 9.3 is misleading in one respect. Preliminary assessments at ages 11 and 13 among Yucatec-speaking children suggest that the 9-year-old level of performance persists and a further rise to the adult level of performance does not occur until after age 13. However, because these data are incomplete and we lack any comparable English data, we have omitted them from figure 9.3.

11 See n. 7.

12 The early preference for shape classification with objects of this type should not be interpreted as a general bias towards all referents. In experiments with stimuli that both languages would treat as materials, both groups show similar material preferences across this age range (Lucy & Gaskins, in preparation).

REFERENCES

Berman, R. A., & D. I. Slobin. (eds.). 1994. *Relating events in narrative: a cross-linguistic developmental study*. Hillsdale, NJ: Lawrence Erlbaum.

Bowerman, M. 1982. Reorganizational processes in lexical and syntactic development. In E. Wanner & L. R. Gleitman (eds.), *Language acquisition: the state of the art*. Cambridge: Cambridge University Press, 319–346.

Brown, P., & S. C. Levinson. 1993. Linguistic and nonlinguistic coding of spatial arrays: explorations in Mayan cognition. *Working Paper 24*. Nijmegen, The Netherlands: Cognitive Anthropology Research Group, Max Planck Institute for Psycholinguistics.

Byrnes, J. P., & S. A. Gelman. 1991. Perspectives on thought and language: traditional and contemporary views. In S. A. Gelman & J. P. Byrnes (eds.), *Perspectives on language and thought: interrelations in development*. Cambridge: Cambridge University Press, 3–27.

Carroll, J., & J. Casagrande. 1958. The function of language classifications in behavior. In E. Maccoby, T. Newcomb, & E. Hartley (eds.), *Readings in social psychology*. New York: Henry Holt, 18–31.

Chomsky, C. 1969. *The acquisition of syntax in children from 5 to 10*. Cambridge, MA: MIT Press.

Fodor, J. A. 1975. *The language of thought*. New York: Thomas Y. Crowell.

Heider, E. 1972. Universals in color naming and memory. *Journal of Experimental Psychology* 93: 10–20.

Hickmann, M. 1993. The boundaries of reported speech in narrative discourse: some developmental aspects. In J. A. Lucy (ed.), *Reflexive language: reported speech and metapragmatics*. Cambridge: Cambridge University Press, 63–90.

Karmiloff-Smith, A. 1983. Language development as a problem-solving process. *Papers and Reports on Child Language Development* 22: 1–23.

Levinson, S. C. 1997. Language and cognition: the cognitive consequences of spatial description in Guugu Yimithirr. *Journal of Linguistic Anthropology* 7: 98–131.

1996. The role of language in everyday human navigation. *Working Paper 38.* Nijmegen, The Netherlands: Cognitive Anthropology Research Group, Max Planck Institute for Psycholinguistics.

Lucy, J. A. 1992a. *Language diversity and thought: a reformulation of the linguistic relativity hypothesis.* Cambridge: Cambridge University Press.

1992b. *Grammatical categories and cognition: a case study of the linguistic relativity hypothesis.* Cambridge: Cambridge University Press.

1997. Linguistic relativity. *Annual Review of Anthropology* 26: 291–312.

Lucy, J. A., & S. Gaskins. 1989. Language diversity and the development of thought. Paper presented at the 88th Annual Meeting of the American Anthropological Association, Washington, DC, November.

1994. The role of language in shaping the child's transition from perceptual to conceptual classification. Paper presented at the 93rd Annual Meeting of the American Anthropological Association, Atlanta, GA, December.

In preparation. Grammatical categories and cognitive development.

Markman, E. M. 1990. Constraints children place on word meanings. *Cognitive Science* 14: 57–77.

1991. The whole object, taxonomic, and mutual exclusivity assumptions as initial constraints on word meaning. In S. A. Gelman & J. P. Byrnes (eds.), *Perspectives on language and thought: interrelations in development.* Cambridge: Cambridge University Press, 72–106.

Pederson, E. 1995. Language as context, language as means: spatial cognition and habitual language use. *Cognitive Linguistics* 6: 333–362.

Pederson, E., E. Danziger, D. Wilkins, S. C. Levinson, S. Kita, & G. Senft. 1998. Semantic typology and spatial conceptualization. *Language* 74: 557–589.

Piaget, J., & B. Inhelder. 1969. *The psychology of the child.* New York: Basic Books.

Soja, N. N., S. Carey, & E. S. Spelke. 1991. Ontological categories guide young children's inductions of word meaning: object terms and substance terms. *Cognition* 38: 179–211.

Vygotsky, L. S. 1987 [1934]. Thinking and speech. In R. W. Rieber & A. S. Carton (eds.), *The collected works of L. S. Vygotsky*, vol. 1: *Problems of general psychology* (trans. N. Minnick). New York: Plenum Press, 37–285.

Waxman, S. R. 1994. The development of an appreciation of specific linkages between linguistic and conceptual organization. In L. Gleitman & B. Landau (eds.), *The acquisition of the lexicon.* Cambridge, MA: MIT Press, 229–258.

Whorf, B. L. 1956 [1939]. The relation of habitual thought and behavior to language. In J. Carroll (ed.), *Language, thought, and reality: selected writings of Benjamin Lee Whorf.* Cambridge, MA: MIT Press, 134–159.

10 Person in the language of singletons, siblings, and twins

Werner Deutsch, Angela Wagner, Renate Burchardt, Nina Schulz, and Jörg Nakath

Technische Universität Braunschweig

1 Introduction

Many of the chapters in this book are concerned with the child's grappling with concepts of the nature of countable objects, or the very mechanisms of counting themselves or of the logical and spatial relations between objects: naive physics, geometry, logic and maths. But in this chapter we turn to an area of much greater concern to the child him- or herself: the realm of person identification. Clearly person identification is the precondition to socio-emotional attachment, and indeed meaningful human social life.

What can we learn about children's conceptions of the person by looking at early language? At first sight perhaps not much. Person identification is in place long before the beginnings of language. Moreover, there are some particular, intrinsically linguistic difficulties with person reference – namely the fact that proper names are replaced by pronouns in first and second persons (at least in the familiar European languages). The tendency for children's first references to self to use their own names or nicknames has been well documented (see e.g. Tanz 1980: ch. 4 for review; Chiat 1986), and their difficulties with pronouns are natural given the way in which their reference shifts according to who is speaking. But the data in this chapter suggest that more can be at stake than mere linguistic difficulty: this becomes especially evident in a special kind of self-reference to be found occasionally among twins. Here the resistance to conceiving of the pair of twins as distinct individuals seems to have a deeper cognitive significance as we shall see.

In this chapter, there are two theoretical issues at stake.

1. What is the effect of a special kind of context on children's acquisition of pronominal reference to self and addressee – namely the context of the immediate siblings? An infant growing up as a single child has a fundamentally different cognitive and linguistic experience. An infant who has older siblings naturally has linguistic input from them which is more

advanced. But in the case of twins we have a control: the twin is a conceptual other of equal linguistic ability.

2. What is the conceptual effect of the special experience of having a twin on the very essence of the idea of person? We will examine these questions by looking at a range of children at the moments just before and after they make the transition from nominal to pronominal forms – children who have no siblings, older siblings, and twin siblings.

But first we need to establish some historical background about ideas concerning the pronominal breakthrough.

2 A tribute to Clara and William Stern

At the beginning of the twentieth century the German philosopher and psychologist William Stern (1871–1938) and his wife Clara Stern started a project which became a classic study in developmental psychology. Over a period of eighteen years they documented the development of their three children in twenty-four diaries (Behrens & Deutsch 1991). Since then the computerized version of the diaries has become accessible via CHILDES (a child language database). For the most part, Clara Stern made entries in the Stern diaries. In contrast to Preyer, who saw young fathers – preferably doctors of medicine – as the best-suited observers (Preyer 1882: XI), William Stern emphasized the capacity of mothers for this task. Because the mother spends most of her time with the children, she is able to follow their development regularly and inconspicuously. She is also able to integrate the observed facts into the natural course of development of the child.

Notes were taken at irregular time intervals, at times daily, at other times with intervals ranging from several days to weeks. Since no technology for the recording of pictures and sounds was available to the Sterns, Clara Stern kept small notes on the behavior and utterances of the children during the course of the day, so that she could enter them into the diary in the evenings, and, together with William Stern, evaluate and comment on them. Often the diary entries are summaries of particular aspects of development. At certain intervals, e.g. on their children's birthdays, they made listings of the children's vocabulary and the grammatical structures being mastered. Therefore the diaries contain much more than mere raw data. However, the Sterns emphasized the point that observation had to be strictly distinguished from interpretation (C. Stern & Stern 1909: 316). If the parents wanted to record longer language sequences, e.g. picture descriptions, story tellings, or experiments on testimony, Clara Stern busied herself with the child, so that, together with the child, she looked at a picture, posed questions, or let the child tell a story, while William Stern sat alongside and acted as if he were at work writing letters. In fact he was keeping a running record of what the child was saying. The children were so used to seeing their father working that it never occurred to them that the father's writings pertained to them (cf. Stern-Anders 1950; Graf-Nold 1989: 61). Stern stressed that modern technical development could be of great help to this kind of research, once the "phonograph" and photography were developed to the point where it would be possible to make concealed recordings (C. Stern & Stern 1909: 318f.).

Due to the nature of the data collection, the Stern diaries can be described as "portraits from the nursery," intended to characterize just that which is routine and normal to child development. The goal of this was to grasp as fully as possible the entire psychological development of the child, which in the Sterns' view included: language, play, intentionality, character, intelligence, emotion, perception, and creativity (cf. C. Stern & Stern 1907/1928: III). The focal point of the entries in the Stern diaries changed over the years, from the motor and language development of the small child through the development of memory to the influence of schooling on the older child.

What can we learn from the Stern diaries about children's conceptual and linguistic development of the notion of person? Quite a lot! Let's for example look into the diary entry of November 20, 1901, when Hilde, the first daughter of the Sterns, was aged 1;07.13.

> Yesterday evening I showed Hilde her own picture on a calling card and asked "Who is that?" Answer: "Hilde." Hilde had hardly ever seen this little picture, but we often show her our cabinet picture, in which she is photographed with us, and have her point to "Papa" and "Mama," something which she has long since done correctly, but up to now she has not reacted correctly to her own likeness in spite of our repeated pointing and naming. That happened yesterday for the first time.

This entry is interesting for various reasons. First of all, it indicates that Hilde has had a difficult time recognizing and identifying herself in photographs specifically and perhaps mirror images in general. These difficulties are quite common among children until a certain point in development, as contemporary research on self-identification, using, for example, the Rouge-task (Lewis & Brookes 1979; Bischof-Köhler 1989), has shown. Clara Stern was able to repeat this observation for her two later-born children, Günther and Eva, too. As a matter of fact, the correct identification of other persons in pictures precedes correct self-identification in development. So, this diary observation concerning a single child from the beginning of the century is in accordance with well-established facts from old and new studies.

The diary entry also provides a fact about linguistic development which is not limited to Hilde Stern. Children growing up in various cultures and languages use nominal forms of self-reference like proper names or nicknames when they successfully recognize themselves in photographs, drawings, and mirror images. This situation may provide candidates for person references that are universally expressed with nominals in early linguistic development. Let's now move on to Günther Stern's first ever instance of linguistic self-reference, when he was aged 1;06.30.

When something happens with others, when, e.g. Hilde receives a little treat, or when her nose is wiped, the funny little fellow immediately pipes up "Me too, me too." [in German: "I au, i au" meaning "Ich auch, ich auch"]. Here the pronoun "I" ["Ich"] is appearing for the first time, albeit not altogether distinctly, something all the more remarkable because, prior to this, there is no record of Günther referring to himself with his own name. Normally, the use of "I" is something that happens much later.

The difference between the two Stern children is remarkable. Günther's start into self-reference is connected with a pronoun. Interestingly enough, as an adult Günther actually called himself "Günther Anders" (*anders* in German means "different" in English). His linguistic development regarding person reference is not unique at all, even in the context of the Stern diaries. Clara Stern was able to observe that her third child, Eva, likewise used first pronouns and then her own name. By this stage her mother was less surprised at this reversal of the initially expected pattern than she had been in Günther's case.

Among the three Stern children, the development of person reference is different and similar at the same time. It is different, in that the first-born daughter starts with a nominal form for self-reference, whereas her later-born brother and sister begin with a pronoun. The functions of these very first utterances and the situations in which they occur are also different: Hilde describes a state when identifying herself in a photograph, while her younger siblings refer with first person pronouns to a (desired) change of state. It is similar in that, later on, all three children use nominal as well as pronominal self-references side by side for several months, and construct similar form–function relations.

The Stern children use possessive and personal pronouns to express their claim on certain objects. Utterances such as Hilde's *mein brot* 'my bread' (Hilde, 1;10.29) are not meant as confirmatory descriptions of ownership, as in adult language, but are instead demands, hence volitional. In this context, Hilde is watching her mother buttering bread and demands a piece. The meaning is thus "I want some bread!" and not "This is my bread." This particular form–function relationship as it relates to possessive constructions not only holds for the Stern children, but also has been found in a previous study of two American children (Deutsch & Budwig 1983; Deutsch 1984). These children use constructions of the type *proper name + object name* (e.g. *Adam truck* 'This is Adam's truck') in indicative function. That is, children characterize themselves as owner of an object by using a declarative utterance. In contrast, they express wishes and requests, i.e. the volitional function, by the construction type *my + object name* (e.g. *My truck* 'I want this truck'), quite independently of whether the child in fact owns the object. A similar functional contrast was found in studies by Budwig (1985, 1989) and in an experimental investigation of early self-reference in German. Young children used their proper name for self-reference in response to a mirror image of themselves, while the personal pronoun *ich* 'I' served the volitional function. That is, children tend to respond with their proper name to the question "Who is this," whereas they respond "I" or "Mine" to the question "Who wants this?" (Kolodziej, Deutsch, & Bittner 1991).

By the age of 4 all three Stern children have given up their system of form–function relations in personal reference and closely approximate the target language system of person deixis, contrasting individuals in speaker and addressee roles by the appropriate use of the respective possessive and personal pronouns.

3 The sibling effect extended

Traditionally, early language development has also been called the acquisition of the mother tongue. The expression "mother tongue" suggests that children learn to speak through contact with their mother. Surely this contact plays a significant role in early linguistic and also prelinguistic development. Nevertheless, can we conclude that the speech of other persons is of but secondary significance for linguistic development? If, for example, a German family with a 3-year-old child moves from Braunschweig to Berlin, the parents will scarcely adjust to the new speech environment; the child, in contrast, will give up its "mother" ("father") tongue in favor of the speech of its new friends. In language development, children use many-faceted linguistic "offerings," not just those stemming from the parents (Dunn 1983; Tomasello & Mannle 1985; Tomasello, Mannle, & Kruger 1986). As regards the development of person reference, we are even inclined to assume that older siblings set the tone, especially in the early period of development. While parents perhaps use baby talk with younger children, and in the interests of simplicity replace pronouns with names, the older child will pointedly use pronouns, especially in the first person, so as to articulate its will and gets its own way in competitive situations. The younger child has a living, breathing example of pronominal person reference that is missing from the family environment of the only child. In addition, younger siblings are more favorably situated to observe reference changes on the part of others, e.g. during an interaction between a parent and an older sibling. We think that both advantages result in an earlier transition from nominal to pronominal person references among siblings than among singletons, even in situations where nominal references are at first generally dominant, as in naming pictures or other images of oneself. It is just this hypothesis that has its origins in the observations by Clara and William Stern (1907/1928) regarding the (differential) linguistic development of their own three children, Hilde, Günther, and Eva.

Presumably, the Sterns were the first to notice this between-person difference among children raised in one and the same family. For the sake of simplicity, we have called the difference in the development of person reference the *sibling effect*. The Stern diary entries are, throughout, helpful for purposes of establishing the chronology of the sibling effect. Yet broader conclusions are hardly possible. The data reflect observations of single cases and not comparisons of samples of children who, for example, are raised either alone or with only one older sibling. Even more important is that the situations to which the diary entries refer are not comparable. In Hilde's case, the first self-reference had a descriptive function. She names her own photographic image. In Günther's case, the first self-reference had a volitional function. He wants to effect a change of state.

Ninety years after the Sterns' study, we have attempted to examine the scope of the sibling effect, by constituting samples of siblings and singletons in which as many factors as possible, such as time of investigation, family constellation, etc., are controlled. How and when do children begin to replace names with pronouns in the naming of photographs of persons and of objects possessed by persons? Can the Sterns' sibling effect be observed in the transition from child language to mature language? Do siblings approximate the target stage faster than singletons? Are singletons more prone to qualitative problems such as pronoun reversals?

3.1 Sample

The purpose of this study required a careful selection of the sample in terms of completeness of the family, age and sex of the children, age differences between siblings, and willingness to participate. We were able to engage forty-seven suitable research families, among them twenty-seven families with single children and twenty families with siblings of the same sex differing in age by not more than two years. Table 10.1 provides a more detailed description of the sample. It is worth mentioning that all the families participated from beginning to end. For a longitudinal investigation this exceptional participation rate amounts to a "blessing from heaven."

Table 10.1. *The sample of the singletons and siblings study*

Experimental session		Singletons			Siblings		
		all	male	female	all	male	female
	N	27	16	11	20	9	11
T1	Age (average)	**1;10.13**	1;10.10	1;10.18	**1;11.18**	1;11.07	1;11.26
	Range		1;08.11–2;00.29	1;08.19–2;03.06		1;07.21–2;02.20	1;08.14–2;07.12
T2	Age (average)	**2;02.09**	2;02.07	2;02.12	**2;03.13**	2;03.11	2;03.15
	Range		1;11.28–2;05.22	2;00.27–2;06.23		2;00.15–2;07.06	1;11.17–2;10.11
T3	Age (average)	**2;06.19**	2;06.20	2;06.19	**2;07.11**	2;07.01	2;07.19
	Range		2;04.24–2;09.15	2;05.00–2;11.24		2;02.20–2;11.10	2;02.23–3;02.02

3.2 Tasks, procedure, and data analysis

We used two tasks: Task A, person-naming, and Task B, possessor-naming. Neither task presents the child with new or unfamiliar problems. For children between the ages of 2 and 3 years, the naming of persons and objects shown in photographs is a daily routine. Whether and how children name pictures depends not only on their own interests, but also on the promptings provided by the people with whom they look at the pictures. In our studies, we sought the participation of the very people with whom the child normally looks at pictures: the mother and, in exceptional cases, the father. To make the procedure as similar as possible across children, we asked all the participating adults to take part in a training exercise in which standardized questions were embedded (Task A: Who is that? Task B: What is that? To whom does that belong?). With these questions, children were prompted to initiate person references in dialogue. The child was thus assigned the role of speaker, while the mother (or father) was the person addressed. This constraint was necessary first of all to achieve the appropriate preconditions for pronominal deixis, and secondly to enable us to pinpoint, under constant conditions across various measurement occasions, the transition from nominal to pronominal person references. Further standardization seemed ill-advised; we did not wish to impose any interaction style on the adults which did not fit with their other behavior.

The research team made at least seven house visits to each of the participating families. The first visit involved introductions and the exchange of information about the planned course of the project. The following six visits were grouped into three pairs, with the two sessions of a pair always scheduled close together and the three pairs spaced about three months apart. During the first visit of a pair, an up-to-date picture was taken of the child and his or her mother/father (frontal view) and possessions. Possessions were chosen which, in the parent's judgment, the child would certainly be able to recognize as his or her own, or as belonging to Mom or Dad. During the second visit of a pair, the photographs were presented in Tasks A and B, with person references prompted by means of the standardized questions on which the parents had been trained. In both tasks, pictures calling for references to self vs. reference to the addressee were sequenced randomly.

For both tasks in each of the three sessions for all children, the interaction was recorded in picture and sound; the total number of protocols is 279. The speech portions of the video recording were transcribed according to the CHILDES system (MacWhinney 1991). We developed a comprehensive coding system for person references that has proven quite reliable. Among trained coders who analyzed six randomly selected transcripts, agreement levels were in the 91% range; for the categories of own name, role name, personal pronoun, and possessive pronoun, which were of primary significance in the statistical analyses, the agreement rate even reached a perfect 100%.

For every question that was designed to elicit a person reference, we investigated first of all whether the child in fact produced a person reference; secondly, whether any person reference correctly identified the appropriate person or possessor; and third, whether a semantically correct person reference was expressed in the appropriate form of the target language, namely, as a pronoun. When the child produced more than one person reference, we selected the one that most closely approximated the target form, with the proviso that a semantically correct nominal form was given precedence over a semantically incorrect pronominal form. Beyond this, we analyzed the extent to which there were qualitatively peculiar forms of person reference such as pronominal reversals – utterances in which the speaker refers to him- or herself as "you" or to the addressee as "me" or "mine." With the help of log-linear models we tested statistically whether and how theoretically relevant variables like time of measurement (first, second, or third session), direction of reference (self or addressee), type of task (A or B), and sibling constellation (singleton or sibling) related to the coded person-reference categories.

3.3 *Results*

We limit ourselves to the main findings, since details have been published elsewhere (Wagner, Burchardt, Deutsch, Jahn, & Nakath 1996; Deutsch,

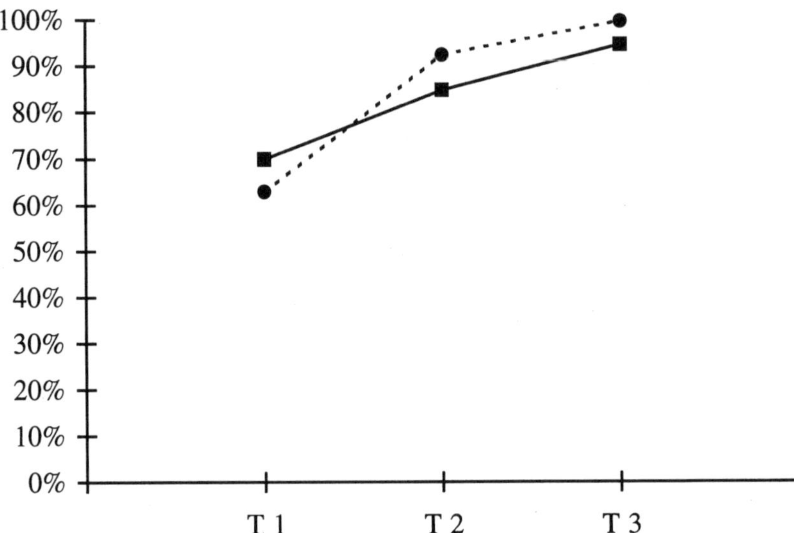

Fig. 10.1 Semantically correct speaker-reference at three consecutive sessions in Task A – for 27 singletons (broken line) and 20 siblings (solid line).

Jahn, Wagner, Burchardt, & Schulz, 1997). The results of the two tasks are described separately and discussed jointly.

3.3.1 Person naming in Task A We examined whether singletons and siblings differ in various perceptual and conceptual parameters underlying the production of personal reference in Task A, including how long the children looked at the photographs, articulation latencies in naming, smiling responses while looking at the photographs, etc. There were no statistically significant differences between the two groups on these parameters. There were also no significant differences in either the relative proportion of missing personal references, or – as shown in figures 10.1 and 10.2 – semantically correct references, with nominal and pronominal references taken together.

From T1 to T3 there is a clear developmental trend: children produce more semantically correct speaker- as well as addressee-references. Moreover, the initial difference between speaker- and addressee-reference gradually disappears with development. The direction of the difference is consistent with the well-known fact that children find it difficult to recognize themselves in pictures. Finally, figures 10.3 and 10.4 make clear that there is also a difference between groups. However, the difference is limited to the category of semantically correct pronominal reference.

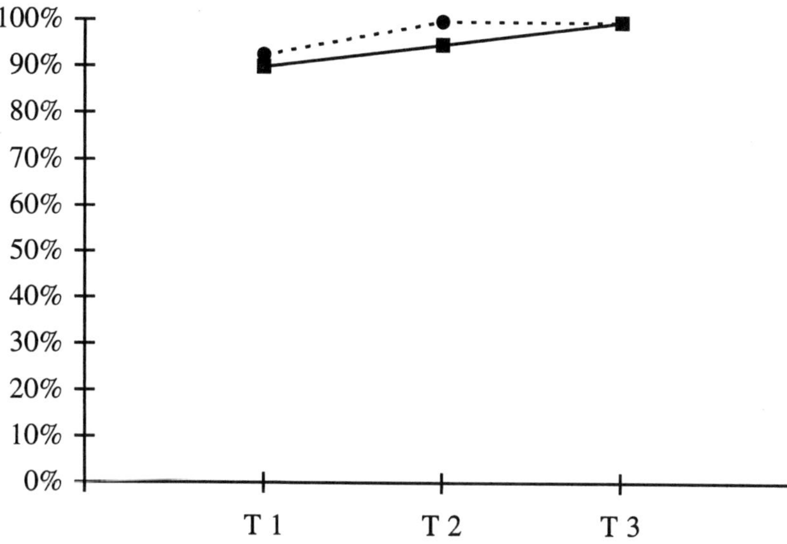

Fig. 10.2 Semantically correct addressee-reference at three consecutive sessions in Task A – for 27 singletons (broken line) and 20 siblings (solid line).

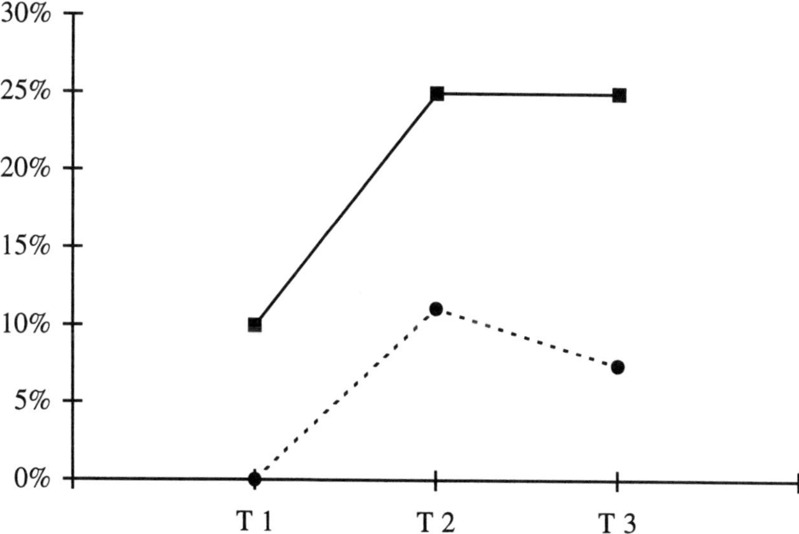

Fig. 10.3 Semantically correct pronoun speaker-reference at three consecutive sessions in Task A – for 27 singletons (broken line) and 20 siblings (solid line).

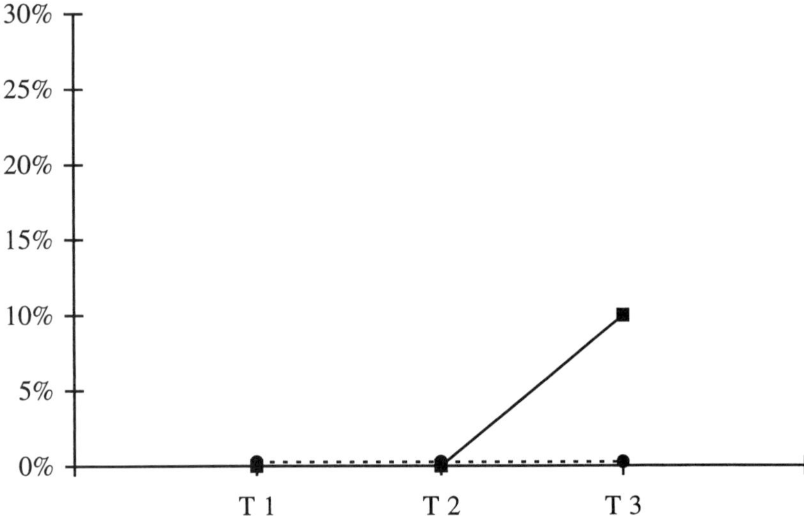

Fig. 10.4 Semantically correct pronoun addressee-reference at three consecutive sessions in Task A – for 27 singletons (broken line) and 20 siblings (solid line).

3.3.2 Possessor naming in Task B As with Task A, differences between singletons and siblings are hard to obtain. The cognitive processes underlying the identification and naming of the possessor of the depicted object appear to be highly similar. There is no hint that singletons or siblings inspect the depicted objects for a longer or shorter time. Figure 10.5 and figure 10.6 show how often singletons and siblings produced descriptions containing an appropriate reference to the possessor. Although singletons produced more semantically correct possessive reference than siblings in the first session of the study, neither this difference nor any other comparison reaches statistical significance.

However, there is one important exception which echoes a finding from Task A: pronouns appeared earlier and more often in siblings than in singletons, as figure 10.7 and figure 10.8 make clear. In the first session, T1, neither singletons nor siblings used (semantically correct) pronouns to indicate a possessive relation between the depicted possessum and the (to-be-inferred) possessor. This result supports the claim that possessive (or personal) pronouns are initially not used when children's utterances carry out a descriptive function, whereas the same children's volitional utterances may already contain pronominal references (see, for example, Deutsch & Budwig 1983; Kolodziej, Deutsch, & Bittner 1991). In contrast, at T2 both singletons and siblings had begun to refer to the possessors of the depicted

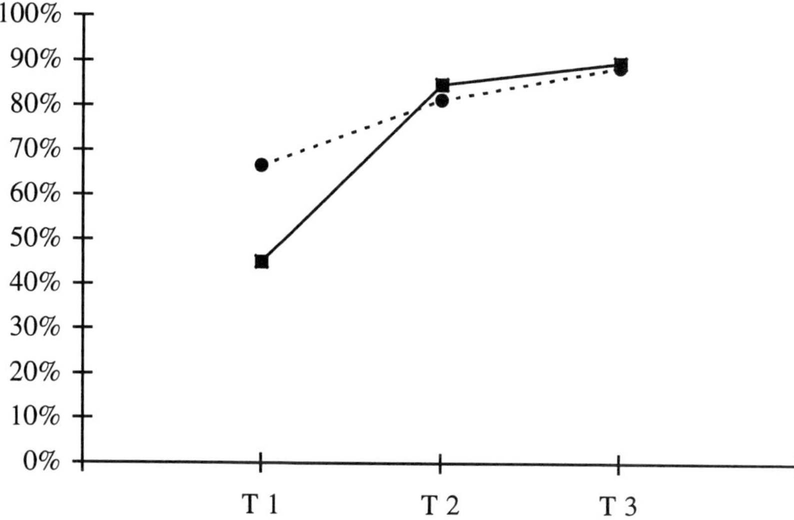

Fig. 10.5 Semantically correct speaker-reference at three consecutive sessions in Task B – for 27 singletons (broken line) and 20 siblings (solid line).

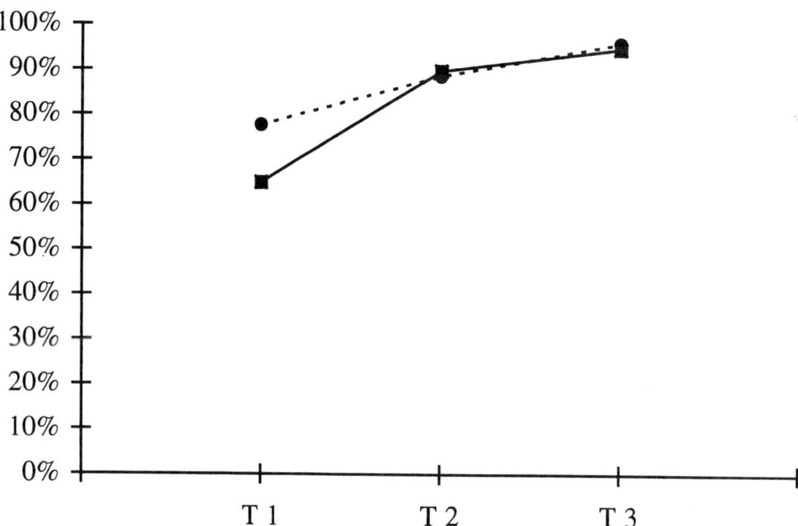

Fig. 10.6 Semantically correct addressee-reference at three consecutive sessions in Task B – for 27 singletons (broken line) and 20 siblings (solid line).

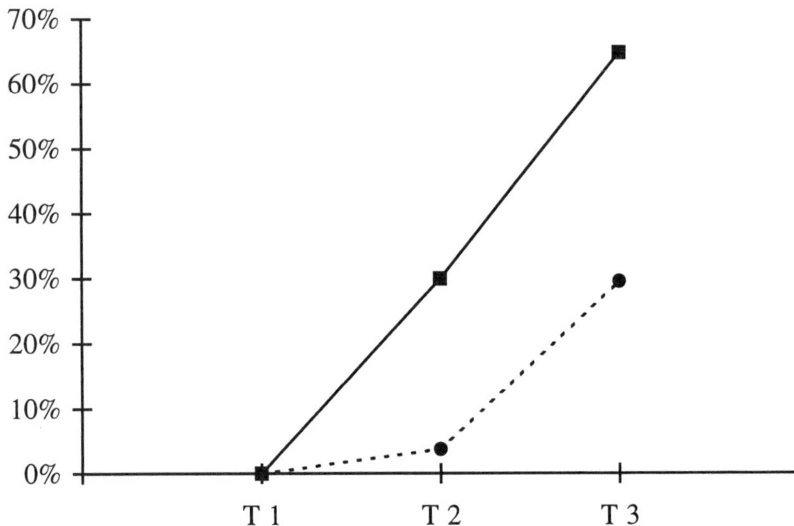

Fig. 10.7 Semantically correct pronoun speaker-reference at three consecutive sessions in Task B – for 27 singletons (broken line) and 20 siblings (solid line).

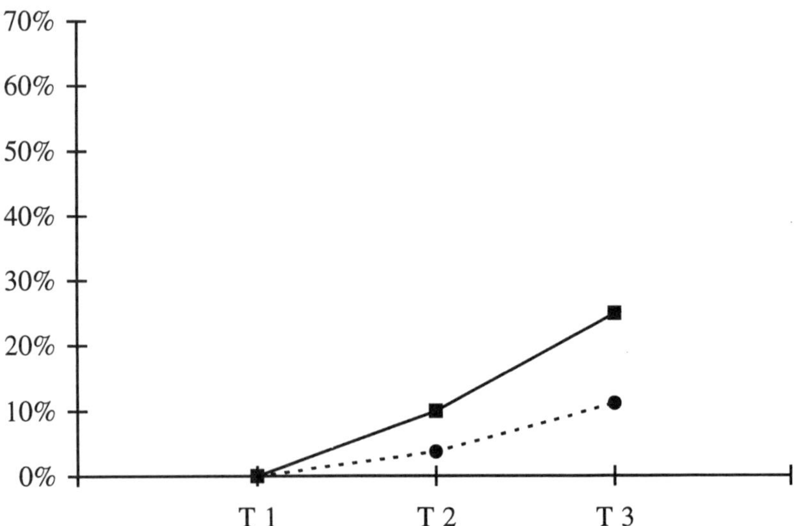

Fig. 10.8 Semantically correct pronoun addressee-reference at three consecutive sessions in Task B – for 27 singletons (broken line) and 20 siblings (solid line).

object with pronouns. There is a remarkable difference between the two groups of children: the approximation toward adult-like possessive references is much faster in siblings than in singletons. This "sibling effect" appears in both conditions of the task, reference to self as well as reference to other (mother). However, between the two conditions differences are evident: pronominal references are more frequent for "self" than "other."

3.4 Discussion

Both the sibling effect and the asymmetry between self and other are present in both tasks. However, the two tasks differ in that pronominal references are used more frequently by both siblings and singletons for possessors of depicted possessions (Task B) than for the persons shown in the pictures (Task A). This finding is consistent with a study by Deutsch & Budwig (1983) in which alienable possession appeared to be the first semantic domain in which pronominal expressions occurred in child language. The sibling effect appears to be relatively far-reaching, in that it is not limited to natural interactions centered around the volitional function of reference to persons, but is also present in tasks like these that elicit the descriptive function of personal references. Having said that the sibling effect is far-reaching, we must add here that it also has definite limits. It is tied to particular linguistic forms, i.e. pronouns. Our results thus suggest that progress in the transition from child language to target language is domain-specific. Obviously children do not suddenly discover the rules inherent in a target language at some point in development, but they grow stepwise into an adult-like use of personal deixis from an egocentric, speaker-based vantage point (cf. Clark 1978).

Our project on the origins of pronominal reference in child language is of course (and happily) not the only one currently concerned with the sibling effect on the development of personal reference. The methods and the languages used in the available studies are complementary, so that the results fit together like the pieces of a jigsaw puzzle to provide a more complete picture of the whole. While our project is chiefly concerned with determining the range of the sibling effect under controlled conditions, other investigations – for example the studies by Oshima-Takane (1988), Oshima-Takane, Cole, & Yarembo (1993), and Oshima-Takane & Derat (1996) – have analyzed the differences in the way children with and without older siblings interact in natural circumstances. Under these conditions, singletons are disadvantaged in that they do not experience dyadic speech from the outside (as spectators) as often as siblings do. Such (observer) situations can provide a model of shifting reference in personal deixis, which could promote the use of pronouns in personal reference. The observation of shifting reference in interacting dyads may also reduce the tendency to treat pronouns as if they were nominals. Our data provide us with evidence for this interpretation: in our possessive and personal reference tasks, siblings were less prone to confuse pronouns semantically than singletons were.

The Sterns (1907) mention a further reason that siblings may find it easier to master pronominal reference, namely the occurrence of competitive situations in which older siblings resort to the use of pronouns such as *my* or *mine*; their behavior is soon copied by their younger sisters and brothers (see Clara Stern's diary entry pertaining to Günther). Children who interact with older siblings are exposed to a different speech input than singletons. The sibling effect makes it clear that this difference leaves traces that become apparent during the transition from child language to target language.

Our study examined only one of many possible sibling constellations. The evaluation of other sibling constellations might well provide answers to various questions like: does the sibling effect vanish if the age gap between the siblings is greater (than two years)? Does it make any difference if the siblings are of opposite sexes rather than the same sex? And so on. Our research group chose not to take up these and related issues, interesting as they are. Instead, we began a project to investigate the development of personal reference in a very special sibling constellation, pairs of (mono- and dizygotic) twins.

4 Twin effects in the development of personal reference

In developmental psychology, twins present a special sibling constellation. Often, they have a stronger relationship to one another than to any other person, including their parents. Hence they are not able to profit from the differences that separate the closest interaction partners in the family, and this is especially true in early childhood (cf. Rutter & Redshaw 1991; Deutsch, Fricke, & Wagner 1994). Not only in language development but also in other areas of development it has repeatedly been found that in comparison with non-twins, twins lag behind, or even follow a developmental course that deviates from, the normal variants. For example, twins score, on average, seven intelligence points below their same-age non-twin peers. This difference is constant across social classes (cf. Zazzo 1960). What is remarkable is the current paucity of twin research aimed at revealing the limiting (and, possibly, also enhancing) conditions that differentiate the developmental courses of twins and non-twins. The reason for this neglect is easy to discern. Since the time of the founding father of research on twins, Francis Galton (1822–1911), twin studies have been part of a behavioral genetic

Table 10.2. *Sample of the twin study*

Experimental session		Monozygotic twins			Dizygotic twins		
		all	male	female	all	male	female
	N	12	5	7	11	6	5
T1	Age (average)	**2;00.23**	1;11.24	2;01.13	**1;11.26**	1;11.06	2;00.20
	Range		1;09.12–2;01.22	1;10.20–2;02.21		1;09.14–2;00.19	1;11.09–2;02.05
T2	Age (average)	**2;03.27**	2;03.04	2;04.14	**2;03.11**	2;03.00	2;03.25
	Range		2;00.06–2;06.00	2;04.05–2;07.00		2;01.30–2;03.23	2;02.13–2;05.11
T3	Age (average)	**2;07.17**	2;06.24	2;08.03	**2;06.21**	2;06.07	2;07.07
	Range		2;05.21–2;08.22	2;06.08–2;09.19		2;05.12–2;07.27	2;05.14–2;08.27

research program. Such research, which in recent years has experienced a revival, is concerned with determining the heritability of characteristics through comparisons of monozygotic and dizygotic twins who have been reared either separately or together. The most sensational discovery is perhaps that the effects of genetic determination of differences between persons do not decline but instead increase with age (Plomin 1986). Compared with the behavioral genetics branch of twin research, research oriented towards the special influences on the development of twins is quite underdeveloped. In our research, we do not ignore the enormous progress in behavioral genetics (and, recently, also molecular genetics) that is of relevance for the study of twins.

The following questions are central to our twin study. Does the developmental course of person reference, as revealed in the person-naming and possessor-naming tasks, proceed differently among twins and non-twins? Are there forms of person-reference among twins that cannot be observed elsewhere? Some studies (Savic 1980; Waterman & Shatz 1982) have already suggested that twins refer to one another with a nominal "dual." Does such a dual also occur in the naming of photographs depicting single persons or single possessions? Finally, do twins make the transition to adult forms of pronomial reference more slowly than other children?

4.1 Twin sample

Our twin sample consisted of twenty-three twin pairs. These twins are the same age as the singletons and siblings we studied and are, like them, being reared in intact families. A special feature of our study is certainly the fact that at the beginning of the project we did not want to know – and because all pairs were same-sexed could not know – which pairs are monozygotic and which are dizygotic. We have used this initially unknown zygosity to create a central research question. During their visits to the twin families the members of the research team, as well as the parents, made their own independent subjective judgments of zygosity. These subjective or phenotypic judgments could then be compared with an objective determination of zygosity that was carried out at the Institute for Human Genetics of the Medical College of Hannover (Director Professor Dr. Schmidtke). The procedure used is that of genetic "fingerprinting" (cf. Krawczak & Schmidtke 1994). This involves a DNA analysis of cells of the mucous membrane of the mouth. The risk here of falsely classifying monozygotic twins as dizygotic, and vice versa, is extremely small, because the genetic fingerprint has proven itself as the most exact procedure since its introduction in 1989 by Jeffrey (cf. Krawczak & Schmidtke 1994).

The zygosity of only one twin pair was known at the beginning of the study. Of the other twenty-two twin pairs, half were mono- and half were dizygotic. The comparison between the genetic determination via the fingerprint method and phenotypic classification leads to a finding that in the context of twin studies might be considered a small sensation. While the phenotypic diagnoses of the research team agreed 100% with DNA determinations of zygosity, the agreement of the latter with the judgment of the parents was not so high. Parental judgments on the third and last occasion are incorrect in five cases. However, the errors are exclusively in one direction. Of the eleven monozygotic twins, five were incorrectly classified as dizygotic. There was not a single case in which a dizygotic twin-pair was falsely classified as monozygotic. How can this surprising finding be explained? The judgmental errors of the parents might have their origins in a refined sensibility for the phenotypic differences between their own genetically identical twin children, because in everyday life parents of twins are "forced" to recognize the respective identities of their offspring.

4.2 Task, procedure, and data analysis

The same tasks and procedures used in the sibling study were also used in the twin study. The twins were tested individually. Of course, this sometimes caused difficulties, since some twin pairs didn't want to be separated, but in these cases we were able to test individually by asking another family member to take care of the brother or sister of the twin while he or she was engaged in the two tasks. In Task A (person naming) twins received not only photographs of themselves and the parent acting as investigator, but also photographs of their twin brother or sister, and in Task B (possessor naming), they were shown a picture of an object owned by their twin.

4.3 *Results*

4.3.1 The nominal dual In the twin study literature, reports have occasionally surfaced of twins who established their own language or twin-dialect (cf. Mogford, 1988; Rutter & Redshaw 1991; Deutsch, Fricke, & Wagner 1994). As regards person reference, there are reports documenting the appearance of a special form: one that refers at times to the twins as a dyad and at other times to one or another member of the dyad.

In a pilot study for our twin project we were able to confirm this peculiar phenomenon. We had not encountered any instance at all of this peculiarity in our investigations of siblings and only children. Reported dual forms have a similar syllabic structure, consisting of reduplicated consonant–vowel or vowel–consonant–vowel syllables, e.g. *Gaga*, *Tata*. How often does such a form occur in our more comprehensive twin sample? Before answering this question, we would like to examine a single case or, more precisely, a single twin pair, more closely.

The following passages document how the interaction between the mother and her son Simon (twin brother to Jonas) unfolded during the first session of the study, when Simon was 1;09.12. The passages are transcribed according to the CHILDES method, but are translated here from German into English.

Let us begin with Task A, the naming of the pictures of three persons. In the case of his own photograph, the course of the interaction is as follows:

Participants: Simon B. (Target Child), Mrs. B. (Mother)
Sibling: Jonas B. (Twin)
Age of Simon: 1;09.12
Sex of Simon: male
Task A, Condition: Self
Mother: Let's look what's in it! Who is that? (showing photograph of Simon)
Simon: Enna.
Mother: Enna?
Simon: ezä (= unintelligible speech).
Mother: Please what is Enna's name?
Mother: I didn't hear it. Say it again.
Simon: einäeizä (= unintelligible speech).
Mother: Enna with trousers, yes indeed.
Mother: That was Simon, wasn't he . . . with trousers.

In naming the photographed person, Simon says the name *Enna*, which his mother repeats in the form of a question. When no understandable improvement follows, the mother asks once again, this time for the name of "Enna." Simon's answer to this is again unintelligible. Now the mother gives up. She takes up the name *Enna* produced by Simon as a question, and proceeds immediately to identify the photographed person with the conventional name *Simon*.

How does Simon name the photo that shows his twin brother Jonas?

Task A, Condition: Other (twin)

Mother:	And who is that? (showing photograph of Jonas)
Simon:	Enna.
Mother:	That's Jonas?
Simon:	Yes.
Mother:	Hmm, he has trousers on, too, hasn't he?

After the opening question, what follows is identical to that which occurred when Simon named his own photograph *Enna*. The mother follows with the correct (conventional) name of the twin brother, *Jonas*, although with a questioning intonation. Simon confirms with "Yes," to which the mother responds with an observation about an article of clothing (trousers) worn by the photographed person.

Simon had no problem naming the photograph of his mother:

Task A, Condition: Other (mother)

Mother:	And who is that?
Simon:	Mama.
Mother:	That's Mama, isn't she? You recognized that right away.
Mother:	Let's put that one right back.

Simon names his mother with the role name *Mama*, which the named person confirms through repetition and validates with quick acknowledgment.

In Task B (possessor naming) Simon is shown pictures of objects which, according to the parents, can be regarded as owned individually by either Jonas or Simon. In both cases he calls the owner *Enna*. He sticks to *Enna* even when his mother wants to get him to name photographed elements individually.

Does *Enna* belong only to the vocabulary of Simon, or do we also encounter it in Simon's twin brother Jonas? The following segments of the transcription of the session with Jonas shed light on this question.

Task A, Condition: Self (Jonas)

Mother:	Look. So, who is that? (showing photograph of Jonas)
Jonas:	Baby.
Mother:	A baby is that?
Jonas:	Yes.
Mother:	Yes. Who is that now?

Jonas: Enna.
Mother: Enna, and which Enna?
Jonas: Azizä (= unintelligible speech).
Mother: That's Jonas.
Jonas: Sisi (= Simon)
Mother: That is not Sisi; that's Jonas.

Task A, Condition: Other (twin)
Mother: Here we have another picture. Who is that? (showing photograph of Simon)
Jonas: Enna.
Mother: Enna?
Jonas: Yes.
Mother: Which Enna?
Jonas: xxx (= unintelligible speech).
Mother: Sisi?
Jonas: No.
Mother: No?
Jonas: Jojo (= Jonas).
Mother: It is Jojo. Is it Jonas?
Jonas: No.
Mother: That is Simon. I think it is Simon.

How similar the person references of Simon and Jonas are! Jonas, too, begins with the name *Enna*. At the urging of the mother, he gives up this name and replaces it with nicknames *Sisi* and *Jojo*, which are still different from the designations that the mother wishes. Jonas calls the photographic image of himself *Sisi* and that of Simon *Jojo*, a confusion that obviously does not please the mother. So she interjects to correct, but this has no effect on the boy. In the case of possessions, *Enna* is once again used to name both things owned by Jonas and things owned by Simon.

Who is "Enna"? From the perspective of the twin brothers, it could be both Jonas and Simon or else Jonas *or* Simon. Like the English word *either*, the twins' linguistic invention *Enna* can refer to both members of the twin pair and to one or the other member of the dyad. The word *Enna* and its application is something that the twins themselves have invented and maintained despite the rather different naming conventions in their social environment. *Enna* did not last for long, at least in the case of Jonas and Simon. They yielded to the linguistic pressure of their social surroundings, which insisted on the use of single-person references. The case of *Enna* fits with the non-extensive series of already documented individual cases showing that in the development of person reference among twins a special phenomenon can occur: the dual. As far as we know, this has not been observed among non-twins, at least in cultures and languages which stress the importance of being a single person. A term like *Enna*, however, could be useful in another culture which emphasizes the dyad as a psychological unit in its own right. What is odd in the context of one culture might be entirely normal in another. For example, *Enna* could make sense in Australian languages in which there are kinship terms that work just as *Enna* does to refer to both members of the dyad individually AND to the unit as a whole (Merlan & Heath 1982; McGregor 1996).

Is *Enna* a nominal or pronominal form of personal reference? We cannot completely rule out the possibility that twins use terms like *Enna* as a pronominal expression. However, there is some empirical evidence that *Enna* should not be taken as a dual equivalent to first-person pronouns like *I*, *me*, *my*, *mine*. When twins utter *Enna* as the subject in spontaneous utterances, they use the third person singular inflection for verbs. Is *Enna* then a third person pronoun? We find the interpretation of *Enna* as a dual nominal more parsimonious.

In this section we have introduced the phenomenon with a case-study example. It happens that the development of person reference can be qualitatively different in twins than in non-twins. This raises the question of whether the special phenomenon discussed above can be observed among many or perhaps even most twin pairs, or whether it is exceptional.

With our sample consisting of twenty-three twin pairs, we could achieve a rather clear answer to this question. Among the twenty-three twin pairs there were only three pairs of the "Enna" type, where such a term was used in both tasks and by both co-twins. In the linguistic development of twins, therefore, the sharing by co-twins of an innovative dual is a rarity rather than a broadly general phenomenon. Moreover, it is worth noting that in the three clear cases of this phenomenon in our investigation, the dual was not maintained, but rather disappeared relatively quickly, at least under the special conditions of our naming tasks. We cannot rule out the possibility that in everyday speech the dual would continue to be used, possibly in situations where twins express their "we" feeling. Unfortunately, we neglected in our study to make photographs of twin pairs, so as to check if this circumstance prompts naming expressions having the form and sense of the dual more strongly than do separate photographs of twins as single persons.

Apart from three clear cases, our twin sample also yielded two cases which speak less clearly for the presence of a dual. In these cases, only one member of the twin pair used such an expression. However, we discovered quite a number of twin pairs who used a weaker version of a dual nominal. They were not as innovative as the *Enna* cases since they expressed the meaning of a dual with the conventional name of one of the twins. We hope

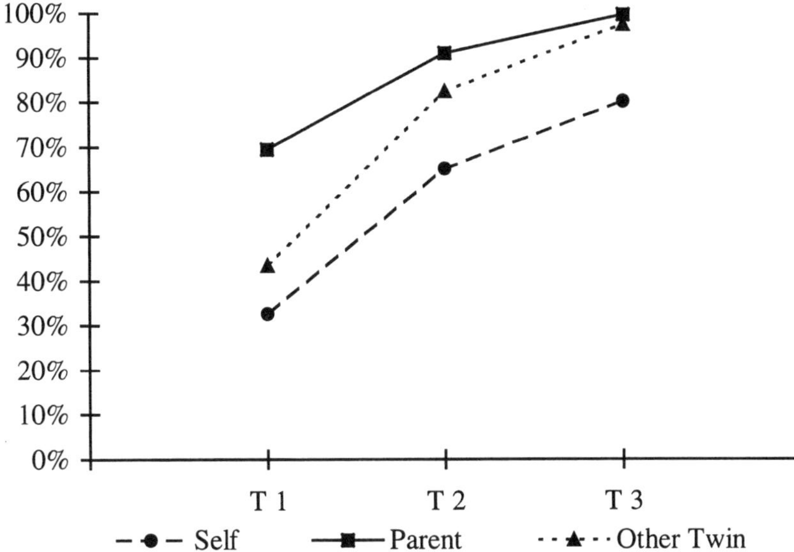

Fig. 10.9 Semantically correct reference at three consecutive sessions in Task A for 23 twins.

to finish a more detailed analysis of the origin and decline of duals in twins in the not-too-distant future.

4.3.2 The normal development of person reference among twins There are only a few studies which do not point to developmental deficits shown by twins in comparison with non-twins. Our results would harmonize with this widely held view if we limited ourselves only to the findings obtained in the early sessions of our study. From a longitudinal perspective, however, it is remarkable how quickly twins make up the delays and approximate the same target states as non-twins do.

4.3.2.1. Person naming in Task A

Semantically correct references reflect the recognition of oneself, one's parent, and the other twin in photographs. Figure 10.9 summarizes the results.

First, there is a clear developmental trend: the recognition of each of the three categories of person improves over time. At T1 twice as many semantically correct references have occurred for parent (mother) as for self. Within half a year, this difference becomes smaller due to a tendency towards a ceiling effect. At T3, however, still more than 20% of the photographs depicting self have not yet been correctly named, mainly due to missing or semantically incorrect references in monozygotic twins.

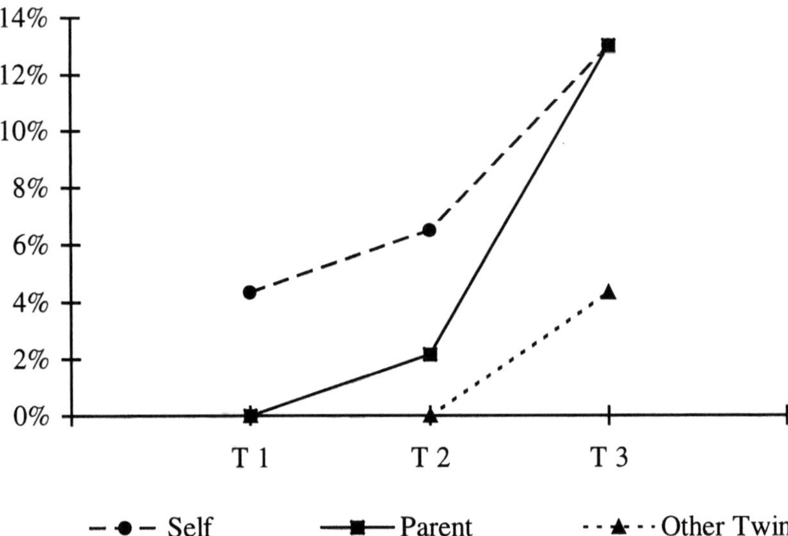

Fig. 10.10 Semantically correct pronoun reference at three consecutive sessions in Task A for 23 twins.

In Task A, semantically correct uses of pronouns are rare among twins (see figure 10.10). Unlike names, pronouns are used correctly more often for self than for parent.

4.3.2.2. Possessor-naming in Task B

As far as semantically correct references in Task B are concerned, twins begin at a lower level than non-twins. However, figure 10.11 makes evident how quickly twins make up initial delays in naming the correct possessor of an object depicted in a photograph. Differences among the three categories of possessor also disappear over time.

How do twins start out in using pronouns to name possessors? As in task A, they do best for the self in the speaker position, producing utterances like "My ball," "Mine," "Teddy belongs to me," etc. Correct pronominal references to the parent or the other twin as possessors are rare (see figure 10.12).

If one compares the person references of twins with those of the only children and siblings from our previous study, the twins clearly perform worse. However, they quickly make up the deficit. By the third measurement occasion, the difference between twins and non-twins has dissipated in both tasks. Where the twins are still functioning below the level of non-twins is when monozygotic twins have to name correctly a photograph of themselves. Nevertheless, we see here a noteworthy longitudinal improvement

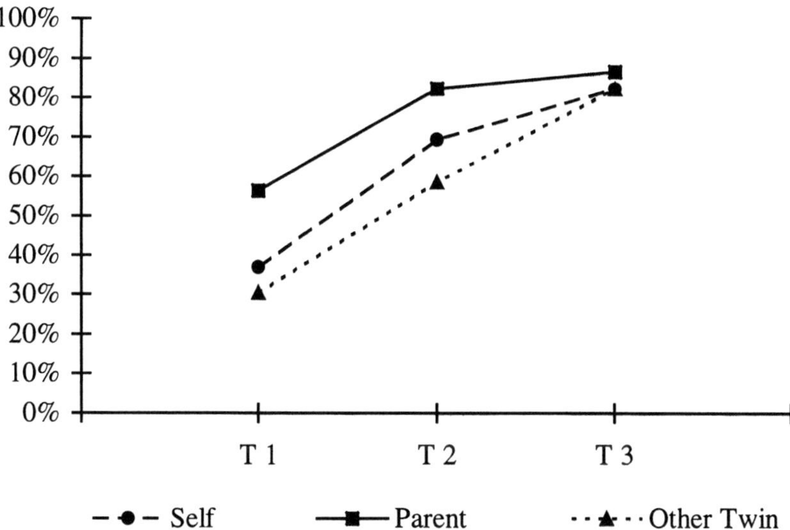

Fig. 10.11 Semantically correct reference at three consecutive sessions in Task B for 23 twins.

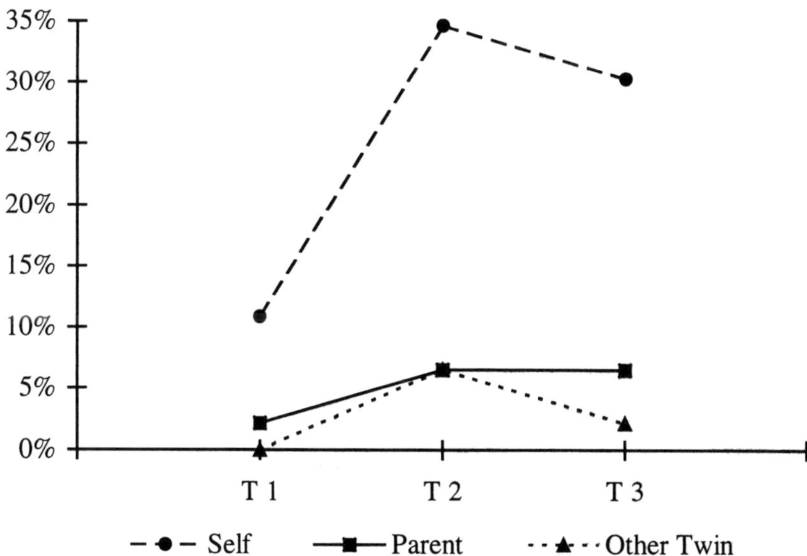

Fig. 10.12 Semantically correct pronoun reference at three consecutive sessions in Task B for 23 twins.

which could surely continue further in the direction of the ceiling effect. Semantically correct uses of pronouns are rare among both twins and non-twins. With respect to this criterion, the twins appear worse than siblings and better than singletons, according to what little data are available.

On the third occasion, the twins have nearly reached the level of non-twins. On both Task A and Task B, the proportion of correctly used pronouns falls close to that of singletons. We obtained the same task-specific findings in all of the populations we studied – only children, siblings, and twins: pronominal person references occur first in the domain of possessions and indeed are more likely in reference to what one owns oneself. Later on, pronominal expressions appear in naming persons in pictures where "Me first" is obviously the speaker-based vantage point.

5 Conclusions

5.1. The key issue

This book is about the relationship between conceptual and linguistic development in children. Is there anything we can learn about this key issue from the studies presented, even though our studies seem to focus on linguistic development and leave conceptual development aside?

When children enter the domain of personal reference during their second year of life, they are already experts at person perception, person recognition, and person-to-person interaction. There is one notable exception, and that is visual self-recognition. Many studies have shown that it is hard for children to recognize themselves in mirror-images, person-drawings, and photographs (see for example Berthenthal & Fischer 1978; Lewis & Brooks 1979; Bischof-Köhler 1989; Asendorpf & Baudonniere 1993). This milestone of cognitive development is achieved at around the same time that children start to use language to make person reference. Some of our results support the well-known observation that it is more difficult to recognize oneself in photographs than a familar other person such as one's mother: in Task A, there is clearly an asynchrony between self- and parent recognition in both singletons and siblings, and in both mono- and dizygotic twins. Semantically correct person references can be taken as a clear indication of correct person identification, but this measure may underestimate children's abilities, since it is possible of course to recognize people without being able to name them. Is the asynchrony between naming photographs of oneself and naming photographs of another thus a cognitive problem, a linguistic problem, or both?

Children acquire the linguistic means to refer to the self and other persons around the same time (cf. C. Stern & Stern 1907), so the asynchrony in visual person-recognition – other-recognition prior to self-recognition –

has no direct counterpart in linguistic development. Children's difficulty recognizing themselves in second-order representations such as pictures (cf. Perner 1991) is clearly a conceptual problem, since they know how to use self-referring expressions on other occasions – for example, when they try to initiate a change of state or provide an answer to the question "What's your name?" In other words, although naming persons in visual recognition tasks certainly presupposes the conceptual distinction between self and (highly familiar) others, its conceptual prerequisites go beyond this: visual self-recognition requires a mapping between a (partially unfamiliar) second-order representation – a picture of oneself – and a first-order representation – a conscious image of one's own appearance.

In the beginning, nominal expressions predominate for naming second-order representations of persons, even in the context of a discourse with the communicative roles of speaker and addressee clearly defined. Our studies indicate that the transition to personal deixis – use of pronouns – has its vantage point in the speaking child, after the conceptual problem of self-recognition has been solved. The "Me first" phenomenon highlights the asymmetry of linguistic progress in early development. Similar findings were obtained for possessor naming, where "Mine first" serves as the main entry to pronominal reference. At this point constructions of the form Noun (proper name, role name) + Noun (object name) are replaced by deictic constructions for self as possessor, and genitive constructions for other as possessor (cf. also Behrens & Deutsch 1991).

How widespread are these speaker-based, egocentric strategies in the developmental process of getting into personal deixis? They are obviously valid for singletons and siblings, but not for many twins. Twins seem to have a different conceptual approach to person recognition. A single person may be conceived of as a member of a closely related dyad whose members are as like as two peas in a pod. The conceptual difference between twins and non-twins is reflected in their early person naming. However, twins are capable of adjusting. They mostly give up their innovative approach and begin to follow the conventions of other single people. This result from an intracultural study may invite us to look at other cultures and languages – e.g. in Australia – where twin-like dyads are not the exception, but relatively common.

5.2 *The sibling issue*

First language acquisition depends crucially on natural input provided by speakers who are more proficient than the language-learning child. Without such a model, language acquisition cannot proceed towards its target state. How important is the social relationship between the child and his (or her) advanced interlocutor? Our studies show that progress is possible under different social settings. Even if linguistic input is limited to just one parent or older sibling, this may suffice for a child to become a native speaker in a natural language. However, our comparisons between singletons and siblings (i.e. children with an older brother or sister) point to qualitative and quantitative differences across children in the developmental course from child language to target language. Siblings were not only faster than singletons to replace nominals in favor of (adult-like) pronominals, but they were also less prone to make semantic errors by reversing pronouns. Within the population of siblings, twins form a special, but nonetheless heterogeneous, category. Certain phenomena such as the use of new nominals or proper names as duals were never observed in non-twins.

How specific are our findings? Can we conclude from our results that the process of acquiring a first language is generally speeded up in siblings compared with singletons on the one hand and twins on the other? Do siblings have better input conditions than singletons and twins? Does input from peers always improve learning? Oshima-Takane & Derat (1996) have recently shown that the sibling effect is domain-specific. Even in language acquisition, there are other areas in which siblings don't differ from singletons, or are even inferior to them; this is already known from birth-order studies using verbal test measures (Nelson 1973; Dunn 1983; Gibbs, Teti, & Bond 1987). The effects of different social contexts on first language acquisition are obviously not uniform. Conclusions such as "Input from other kids always speeds the learner up," or "Kids who spend more time with adults learn faster" (suggested by Harkness 1977), or "More interaction with older children than with adults slows learners down" (suggested by Bates 1975) are simplistic.

How can the specificity of the sibling effect on pronouns be explained? We have already mentioned that siblings may benefit from an interaction style which is more common in interactions between dyads of peers than child–adult dyads. Demuth (1992) described this difference as "confrontational" vs. "accommodational." Although older brothers and sisters may well be able to use "motherese" in interactions with their younger siblings (see among others Shatz & Gelman 1973; Dunn & Kendrick 1982; Tomasello & Mannle 1985), they know when and how to switch register, for example in conflicts about access to alienable possessions. In these situations it is most unlikely that the older siblings will replace pronouns with nominals – to the contrary, conflicts over possession in fact provoke the use of pronominal forms. In adult–child interactions (as Clara and William Stern showed at the beginning of the twentieth century) parents stick to motherese and avoid personal deixis to promote their child's comprehension of person reference, but siblings are likely, at least on some occasions, to produce a more advanced linguistic input with stressed and repeated pronominals like "Mine, mine, mine." This confrontational input is certainly not a necessary condition for acquiring personal deixis, but it is a facilitating factor: it directs the attention of the younger sibling to both the form *and* the function of personal deixis. There is another important input factor, namely the opportunity to observe shifting person reference in other dyads. Singletons have fewer opportunities than siblings to observe how other participants refer to themselves as speakers and others as addressees. While siblings have ready access from early on to dialogues in which personal deixis is used in a mature fashion, singletons are more often involved in accommodating child–adult interactions.

5.3 The person issue

Many contemporary scholars see children as processing machines. Linguistic input from any natural language can start the machine and keeps it running. Breakdowns are unlikely, as long as the machine's hardware is functioning, even if the linguistic input is far from perfect. For producing and comprehending utterances children develop software programs which within a couple of years approximate the standards of a competent native speaker.

Is the metaphor of a processing machine really a good one for children's role in the process of language development? Are children little linguists who are busy cracking the code of the language spoken around them? Do all children pursue a similar agenda in language development?

Our studies are grounded in a framework that dates back to the beginning of the twentieth century. For William Stern, the individual person serves as the basic unit in psychology. Stern's approach is not at all "modular" in the modern sense. To the contrary, he is convinced that development is a process of differentiating distinct domains out of a "psychophysical uniformity" (Stern 1927). This is why we started our research with a reanalysis of Clara and William Stern's meticulous case studies. Only in-depth case studies can provide a realistic account of processes ongoing in development. However, natural case studies should lead on to controlled and systematic studies in populations of children growing up under different circumstances. This research strategy allows us to pay attention to the general and the particular developmental processes at the same time.

Our studies on "Person" show that all the children investigated master major milestones in cognitive development within a certain amount of time. They become able to recognize themselves and others in pictures. Even twins can overcome initial confusions of the "Who is who?" type. In linguistic development, children are faced with new facets of "Person" as a fundamental category of social life. Persons bear different types of names, but persons can also be referred to with indexicals dependent on the social structure underlying language use. Children do not then simply map cognitive concepts of persons onto linguistic concepts of them (see among others Slobin 1973; Cromer 1974). For example, the notions of speech roles of speaker and addressee are essential for acquiring personal deixis. These notions are not stable characteristics, but potential functions of persons. Our studies demonstrate that experiencing different types of social upbringing influences the speed and smoothness by which personal deixis is learned in language production. Nonetheless, the acquisition process appears to tolerate a variety of (social) input conditions while the child continues to move towards the target language. Thus, the combination of robustness and sensitivity explains why common trends can go hand-in-hand with patterns of individual variation.

NOTE

We thank the German Research Foundation for generous financial support of our projects on "Person" (De 338/4-1/4-2); the seventy families in our longitudinal study for their most enjoyable cooperation; the photographer of our institute, Rolf Toch, for taking numerous pictures; our research assistants Thorsten Brants, Britt Bürgel, Barbara Flotho, Torsten Fricke, Christian Füllgrabe, Zorana Gavranovic, Claudia Goebel, Karen Jahn, Ingrid Kirchner, Ulrike Koch, Göran Kühne, Petra Lienau, Anne Lübke, Maria Malavé, Gowert Masche, Oliver Müller, Tobias Müller, Cornelius Pawlak, Claudia Ruff, Helge Schäfer, Thomas Schmidt, Stephanie Schreblowski, and Markus Wenglorz for their help with the collection, transcription, coding, and statistical analysis of the data; and last but not least Melissa Bowerman, James T. Lamiell, and Stephen C. Levinson for their invaluable help with the English text.

REFERENCES

Asendorpf, J., & P.-J. Baudonniere. 1993. Self-awareness and other-awareness: mirror self-recognition and synchronic imitation among unfamiliar peers. *Developmental Psychology* 29: 88–95.

Bates, E. 1975. Peer relations and the acquisition of language. In M. Lewis & L. Rosenblum (eds.), *The origins of behavior*, vol. 4: *Friendship and peer relations.* New York: John Wiley, 259–292.

Behrens, H., & W. Deutsch. 1991. Die Tagebücher von Clara und William Stern [The diaries of Clara and William Stern]. In H. E. Lück & R. Miller (eds.), *Theorien und Methoden psychologiegeschichtlicher Forschung* [Theories and methods of psychohistorical research]. Göttingen: Hogrefe, 66–76.

Berthenthal, B. I., & K. W. Fischer, 1978. Development of self-recognition in the infant. *Developmental Psychology* 14: 44–50.

Bischof-Köhler, D. 1989. *Spiegelbild und Empathie* [Mirror image and empathy]. Bern: Huber.

Budwig, N. 1985. I, my and "name": children's early systematizations of forms, meanings and functions in talk about the self. *Papers and Reports on Child Language Development* 24: 30–37.

1989. The linguistic marking of agentivity and control in child language. *Journal of Child Language* 16: 263–284.

Chiat, S. 1986. Personal pronouns. In P. Fletcher & M. Garman (eds.), *Language acquisition*. Cambridge: Cambridge University Press, 356–374.

Clark, E. V. 1978. From gesture to word: on the natural history of deixis in language acquisition. In J. S. Bruner & A. Garton (eds.), *Human growth and development: Wolfson College Lectures 1976*. Oxford: Oxford University Press, 85–120.

Cromer, R. F. 1974. The development of language and cognition: The Cognition Hypothesis. In B. Foss (ed.), *New perspectives in child development*, Harmondsworth: Penguin, 184–252. Reprinted in Cromer, R. F. 1991. *Language and thought in normal and handicapped children*. Oxford: Basil Blackwell, 1–54.

Demuth, K. 1992. The acquisition of Sesotho. In D. Slobin (ed.), *The crosslinguistic study of language acquisition*, vol. 3. Hillsdale, NJ: Lawrence Erlbaum, 557–638.

Deutsch, W. 1984. Language control processes in development. In H. Bouma & D. G. Bouwhuis (eds.), *Attention and performance*. Hillsdale, NJ: Lawrence Erlbaum, 395–416.

Deutsch, W., & N. Budwig. 1983. Form and function in the development of possessives. *Papers and Reports on Child Language Development* 22: 36–42.

Deutsch, W., T. Fricke, & A. Wagner. 1994. Ist die Sprachentwicklung von Zwillingen etwas Besonderes? [Is language development in twins a special case?]. In K.-F. Wessel & F. Naumann (eds.), *Kommunikation und Humanontogenese* [Communication and human ontogenesis]. Bielefeld: Kleine, 238–258.

Deutsch, W., A. Wagner, R. Burchardt, K. Jahn, & N. Schulz. 1997. From Adam('s) and Eve('s) to mine and yours in siblings and singletons. In E. V. Clark (ed.), *The proceedings of the 28th Annual Child Language Research Forum*. Stanford: Center for the Study of Language and Information, 85–94.

Dunn, J. 1983. Sibling relationships in early childhood. *Child Development* 54: 787–811.

Dunn, J., & C. Kendrick. 1982. *Siblings: love, envy, and understanding*. Cambridge, MA: Harvard University Press.

Gibbs, E.D., D. M. Teti, & L. A. Bond. 1987. Infant–sibling communication: relationship to birth-spacing and cognitive and linguistic development. *Infant Behaviour and Development* 10: 307–323.

Graf-Nold, A. 1989. Eva: Besonders resistent gegen Suggestionen. Interview mit Eva Michaelis-Stern [Eva: Especially resistant to suggestions. Interview with Eva Michaelis-Stern.] *Psychologie Heute* [*Psychology Today*] July: 60–67.

Harkness, S. 1977. Aspects of social environment and first language acquisition in rural Africa. In C. E. Snow & C. A. Ferguson (eds.), *Talking to children: language input and acquisition*. Cambridge: Cambridge University Press, 309–316.

Kolodziej, P., W. Deutsch, & C. Bittner. 1991. Das Selbst im Spiegel der Kindersprache [The self as reflected in child language]. *Zeitschrift für Entwicklungspsychologie und Pädagogische Psychologie* 23: 23–47.

Krawczak, M., & J. Schmidtke. 1994. *DNA-fingerprinting*. Heidelberg: Spektrum.

Lewis, M., & J. Brooks. 1979. Self-knowledge and emotional development. In M. Lewis & L. A. Rosenbaum (eds.), *The development of affect*. New York: Plenum Press, 205–226.

MacWhinney, B. 1991. *The CHILDES project: tools for analyzing talk*. Hillsdale, NJ: Lawrence Erlbaum.

McGregor, W. 1996. Dyadic and polyadic kin terms in Gooniyandi. *Anthropological Linguistics* 38: 216–247.

Merlan, F., & J. Heath. 1982. Dyadic kinship terms. In J. Heath, F. Merlan, & A. Rumsey (eds.), *Languages of kinship in Aboriginal Australia*. Sydney: Oceanic Linguistic Monographs, 107–140.

Mogford, K. 1988. Language development in twins. In D. Bishop & K. Mogford (eds.), *Language development in exceptional circumstances*. Edinburgh: Churchill Livingstone, 80–95.

Nelson, K. 1973. Structure and strategy in learning to talk. *Monographs of the Society for Research in Child Development* 38 [1–2, serial no. 149].

Oshima-Takane, Y. 1988. Children learn from speech not addressed to them: the case of personal pronouns. *Journal of Child Language* 15: 95–108.

Oshima-Takane, Y., E. Cole, & R. L. Yarembo. 1993. Pronominal semantic confusion in a hearing-impaired child: a case study. *First Language* 13: 148–168.

Oshima-Takane, Y., & L. Derat. 1996. Nominal and pronominal reference in maternal speech during the later stages of language acquisition: a longitudinal study. *First Language* 16: 319–338.

Perner, J. 1991. *Understanding the representational mind*. Cambridge, MA: Bradford/MIT Press.

Plomin, R. 1986. *Development, genetics, and psychology*. Hillsdale, NJ: Lawrence Erlbaum.

Preyer, W. 1882. Notes on the development of self-consciousness, from *Die Seele des Kindes* [The mind of the child] (trans. M. Talbot). *Education*. January: 290–300.

Rutter, M., & J. Redshaw. 1991. Annotation: Growing up as a twin: twin–singleton differences in psychological development. *Journal of Child Psychology and Psychiatry* 32: 885–895.

Savić, S. 1980. *How twins learn to talk. A study of the speech development of twins from 1 to 3*. London: Academic Press.

Shatz, M., & R. Gelman. 1973. The development of communication skills: modifications in the speech of young children as a function of listener. *Monographs of the Society for Research in Child Development* 38 [5, serial no. 153].

Slobin, D. I. 1973.Cognitive prerequisites for the development of grammar. In C. A. Ferguson & D. I. Slobin (eds.), *Studies of child language development*. New York: Holt, Rinehart and Winston, 175–208.

Stern, C., & W. Stern. 1900–1918. *Die Tagebücher*. Elektronische Abschrift der unveröffentlichten Tagebücher aus dem Nachlaß. [The diaries. Electronic copy of the unpublished diaries from the literary estate.] Nijmegen: Max Planck Institute for Psycholinguistics.

1907/1928. *Die Kindersprache* [Child language]. Leipzig: Barth.

1909a. Anleitung zur Beobachtung der Sprachentwicklung bei normalen, vollsinnigen kindern. [Guidance in the observation of language development of normal children without sensory deficits.] *Zeitschrift für angewandte Psychologie und Psychologische Sammelforschung* 2: 313–337.

1909b. *Erinnerung, Aussage und Lüge in der ersten Kindheit* [Remembrance, testimony and lies in early childhood]. Leipzig: Barth.

Stern, W. 1927. Selbstdarstellung [self-portrait]. In R. Schmidt (ed.), *Die Philosophie der Gegenwart in Selbstdarstellungen* [Contemporary philosophy in self-portraits]. Leipzig: Felix Meiner, 129–184.

Stern-Anders, G. 1950. Bild meines Vaters [A picture of my father]. In W. Stern, *Allgemeine Psychologie auf personalistischer Grundlage*, 2. Auflage. [General psychology from a personalistic standpoint, 2nd edn]. The Hague: Martinus Nijhoff, XXIII–XXXII.

Tanz, C. 1980. *Studies in the acquisition of deictic terms*. Cambridge: Cambridge University Press.

Tomasello, M., & S. Mannle. 1985. Pragmatics of sibling speech to one-year-olds. *Child Development* 56: 911–917.

Tomasello, M., S. Mannle, & A. C. Kruger. 1986. Linguistic environment of 1- to 2-year-old twins. *Developmental Psychology* 22: 169–176.

Wagner, A., R. Burchardt, W. Deutsch, K. Jahn, & J. Nakath. 1996. Der Geschwistereffekt in der Entwicklung der Personreferenz. Eine Längsschnittstudie mit 27 deutschsprachigen Einzel- und 20 Geschwisterkindern im zweiten und dritten Lebensjahr. [The sibling effect in the development of personal reference. A longitudinal study with 27 German singletons and 20 German siblings during their second and third year of life.] *Sprache und Kognition* 1/2: 3–22.

Waterman, P., & M. Shatz. 1982. The acquisition of personal pronouns and proper names by an identical twin pair. *Journal of Speech and Hearing Research* 25: 149–154.

Zazzo, R. 1960. *Les jumeaux. Le couple et la personne*. Paris: Presses Universitaires de France.

11 Early representations for *all*, *each*, and their counterparts in Mandarin Chinese and Portuguese

Patricia J. Brooks, Martin D. S. Braine, Gisela Jia, and Maria da Graca Dias

College of Staten Island and the Graduate School of City University of New York, New York University, Lehman College of City University of New York, Universidade Federal de Pernambuco

There were two points of departure for the work summarized here on the development of children's comprehension of universal quantifiers. One came from the claim that there is a mental logic (Braine 1978; Braine, Reiser, & Rumain 1984). The mental logic theory posits that some logical framework is available essentially innately. The child's task is to learn, through experience, associations between natural-language logical expressions and representations in the mental logic. Much of the theoretical work of Braine and colleagues in this area has been on reasoning at a propositional level with inferences that depend on the meanings of words like *and*, *or*, *if*, and *not* (e.g. Braine *et al.* 1984; Braine 1990; Braine, O'Brien, Noveck, *et al.* 1995). Expanding the work on reasoning to include inferences involving quantifiers has been on the agenda from the start and several years ago we became interested in the issue of the development of comprehension of universal quantifiers such as *all*, *each*, and *every*, in part because they give rise to an especially rich set of inferences.

Our initial framework for thinking about universal quantifiers and their development stemmed from the work of Vendler (1967) and Ioup (1975). Vendler suggested that there were at least two sorts of basic representations corresponding to the meanings of *all*, *each*, and *every*. First was a collective representation whereby a predicate applies to a whole set in a collective sense. This is illustrated by the sentence *All the boys are riding an elephant* if it is given the interpretation that all the boys are on the same elephant. The second representation was distributive whereby the predicate applies to the whole set one member at a time. The distributive representation is illustrated with the sentence *Each boy is riding an elephant* with the interpretation that each boy is alone on his elephant, with no elephant carrying more than one boy (i.e. with boys and elephants in one-to-one correspondence). Vendler argued that the collective representation was essentially canonical for *all* and the distributive representation for *each.* Ioup (1975) went on to suggest, based on an analysis of fourteen languages, that it was universal for languages to have a universal quantifier corresponding to the English quantifier *all* and another universal quantifier corresponding to English *each* or *every*. Ioup's analysis was basically a claim that all languages mark the distinction between collective and distributive representations, and that typically each representation is marked by its own quantifier.

Taken together, the work of Vendler (1967) and Ioup (1975) makes two interesting suggestions. First is the idea that the distinction between distributive and collective interpretations should be extremely primitive, on the general basis that what is universal is expected to be primitive and, perhaps, innate. The second interesting claim is that natural languages deal lexically with a scope distinction that standard logic deals with using parentheses – the parentheses indicate the order in which a universal quantifier is interpreted relative to an existential quantifier in the same sentence. For a collective interpretation, *All the boys are riding an elephant* would be interpreted in standard predicate logic as stating that there is an elephant such that every boy is riding it, with the existential, indefinite article interpreted prior to the universal quantifier. For the distributive interpretation of *Each boy is riding an elephant*, the standard treatment is for the universal quantifier to be interpreted first, such that for every boy there is some elephant that he is riding. Natural languages, in contrast to standard logic, often use distinct lexical items, in addition to word order, to signal scope differences.

The second point of departure for our work on children's comprehension of universal quantifiers was evidence for what Philip and his colleagues have called "quantifier spreading" (e.g. Philip 1991; Philip & Aurelio 1991; Philip & Takahashi 1991). Quantifier spreading refers to a type of error preschool-aged children routinely make when interpreting sentences containing universal quantification. In the literature there appear to be two kinds of quantifier-spreading errors which can be distinguished. One sort is associated with Philip's work on *every* and has been described as an over-exhaustive search error (see also Drozd, ch. 12, this volume). When presented with a picture of several boys, with each boy riding an elephant, along with one extra elephant, preschool-aged children typically deny that every boy is riding an elephant because nobody is riding one of the elephants. Philip (1991) has proposed the event quantification hypothesis to explain the occurrence of such errors. The event quantification hypothesis is that preschool-aged children interpret universal quantifiers as modifying entire events rather than specific noun phrases. The child does not restrict the universal quantifier to a particular noun phrase in the sentence. Philip argues that young children's representations of sentences containing universal quantification are symmetric: for the preschool child the sentence *Every boy is riding an elephant* is true only if every event, within a contextually defined minimal group of scenes or events, consists of a boy on an elephant. Thus, the sentence is correct only if there is perfect one-to-one correspondence between boys and elephants.

Now, the second type of quantifier spreading is the Piagetian error. In Inhelder & Piaget's work (1958, 1964) on the class inclusion task the error is associated with *all* rather than *every.* It occurs when the child is presented with a set of objects, for instance, three white circles, a white square, and a blue square, and is asked *Are all of the circles white?* Typically the preschool-aged child replies "no" incorrectly. Inhelder & Piaget provided evidence that the error occurred because the child interpreted the question as meaning "Are all the circles white and all the white ones circles?" Brooks & Braine (1996) assumed that the Philip quantifier spreading error and the Piagetian quantifier spreading error are the same error and potentially they are. Inhelder & Piaget interpreted the error as false quantification of the predicate, in other words, suggesting that not only is the quantifier taken as modifying the subject, but also as modifying the predicate. This is, quite literally, spreading of the quantifier. On the other hand, there is a question as to whether the Philip and Piagetian errors are the same, since in one case the error is associated with *every*, at least in the experimental work, and in the other it is associated with *all.* We will address this issue further as we report our experimental findings.

Our work was begun with basically two goals. One was to find out if the development of the understanding of universal quantifiers yields evidence for the early availability of canonical collective and distributive representations. We chose to study children's interpretations of the quantifiers *all* and *each*, rather than *all* and *every*, because these are the two poles according to Vendler (1967). It is plausible that the acquisition of the quantifiers *all* and *each* involves learning a mapping between specific lexical items and preexisting canonical representations. That would be the simplest hypothesis, however there is nothing in our work which could possibly prove this. Ideally, the experimental work would shed light on whether this hypothesis is plausible or not and would serve the preliminary function of clarifying the developmental relation between the quantifiers *all* and *each* and the collective and distributive representations.

Table 11.1. *Percentage of correct responses in Experiment 1*

	Age				
Sentence type	4	5–6	7–8	9–10	Adults
All of the Xs are (verb)ing a Y	83.3	98.3	100	100	100
There is an X (verb)ing all of the Ys	83.3	93.3	100	100	100
Each X is (verb)ing a Y	46.7	56.7	76.7	86.7	100
There is an X (verb)ing each of the Ys	43.3	40.0	38.3	75.0	100

A second goal was to examine quantifier spreading theories. In the work of Inhelder & Piaget and the recent work of Philip and colleagues there seems to be implied an early symmetric representation. Now, if the child's early representations of sentences containing universal quantification are symmetric, then children should not be sensitive to the location of the universal quantifier in the sentence. That is, there should be no difference in meaning assigned to pairs of sentences such as *Every girl is riding a horse* and *There is a girl riding every horse.* The event quantification hypothesis of Philip makes the prediction that children shouldn't be able to distinguish such pairs of sentences, and our first question was whether children would actually fail as predicted.

1 Can children restrict a universal quantifier to the noun it modifies?

Brooks & Braine (1996) assumed that the quantifier *all* would be biased towards a collective interpretation. Children were presented with a choice between two pictures and a sentence such as *All of the men are carrying a box* or *There is a man carrying all of the boxes.* The child's task was to select which of the two pictures went best with each sentence presented. One picture showed three actors acting on a single object along with two extra objects not acted upon, whereas the other depicted one actor acting on three objects along with two extra people not involved in the activity (see figures 11.1a and 11.1b). Children as young as 4 years of age had little difficulty associating the sentences with *all* with the correct pictures. Table 11.1 presents the mean percentages of correct picture choices for each age group.

For sentences with *each*, again following Vendler (1967), Brooks & Braine presented children with two distributive choices. Children heard a sentence such as *Each man is carrying a box* or *There is a man carrying each of the boxes* and selected between two pictures the one which best fit the sentence. One picture showed three actors each acting on a unique object

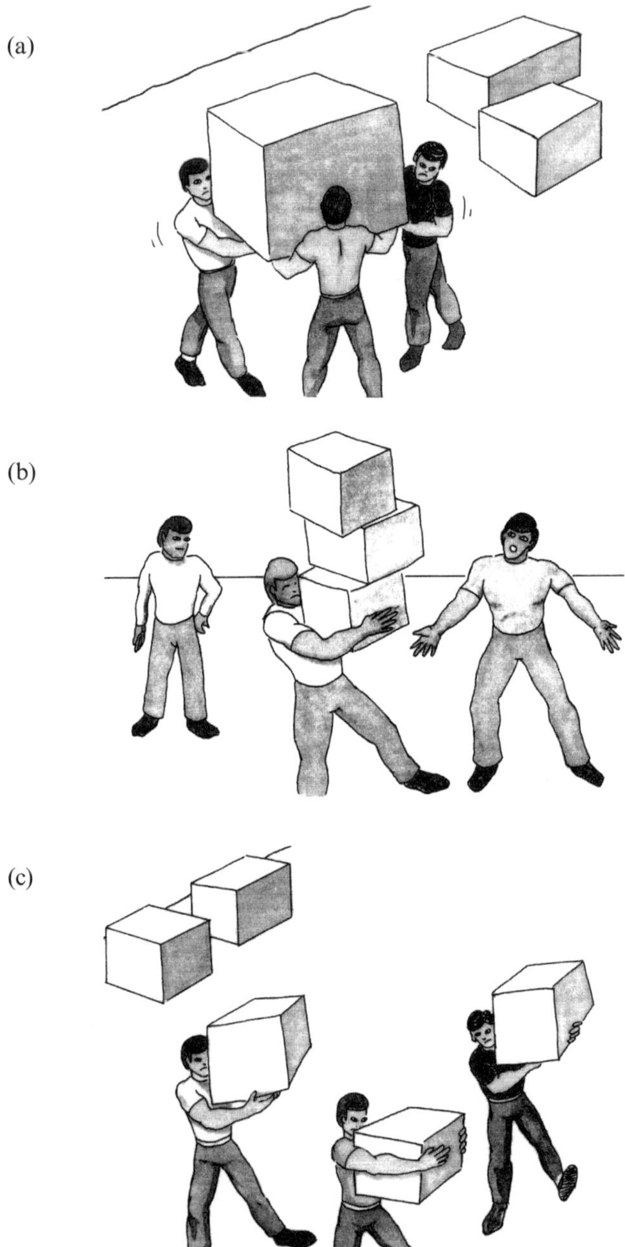

Fig. 11.1 Picture choices for Experiment 1: (a) collective subject-exhaustive, (b) collective object-exhaustive, (c) distributive subject-exhaustive, (d) distributive object-exhaustive.

(d)

along with two extra objects (see figure 11.1c). The second picture again showed three actors each acting on a unique object, but in this case two extra people were not involved in the activity (see figure 11.1d). When children were presented with distributive picture choices and sentences with *each*, an entirely different pattern of results emerged. For sentences with *each*, it was not until age 9–10 that children showed a sensitivity to the location of *each*. (See table 11.1 for mean percentages.) Clearly this result is consistent with the work of Philip and colleagues who make the prediction that children shouldn't be able to distinguish pairs of sentences such as *Each man is carrying a box* and *There is a man carrying each of the boxes* because their interpretations of such sentences are symmetric.

2 Is *all* canonically collective and *each* distributive?

One possible interpretation of the results of the experiment for sentences with *each* is that children know nothing about the meaning of *each*. The next experiment was designed to test whether children would preferentially associate *each* with a distributive interpretation and *all* with a collective one. If children were given a choice between three interpretations, that is, a collective one, a distributive one, and an exhaustive one, would children match sentences with *each* with the distributive picture and sentences with *all* with the collective one? Brooks & Braine selected an exhaustive interpretation as a foil for the experiment for several reasons. The exhaustive choice showed three actors and five objects associated exhaustively with one another, for instance, three women carrying five cakes with none left over. One could ultimately argue that the exhaustive picture is perfectly correct for sentences like *Each woman is carrying a cake* even though it does not match the hypothesized canonical representation. If young children show a preference for a distributive picture over an exhaustive one for sentences with *each*, this suggests that children know something about the canonical interpretation of *each*, even if they are unable to discriminate between cases in which there are extra objects versus extra actors left over, as in the previous experiment.

Second, there is another possible sentence, *The women are carrying the cakes*, that is typically associated with an exhaustive interpretation. Brooks & Braine suggested that an exhaustive representation might come from a representation of mass nouns, given that sentences like *The soup is in the bowls* would normally be interpreted as meaning that all of the soup has been put in the bowls and all of the bowls have some soup in them. Because plural nouns behave very much like mass nouns in many ways, children should interpret sentences like *The women are carrying the cakes* exhaustively. If children were drawing analogies, they might even select an exhaustive interpretation in cases where a collective or distributive one is more appropriate. The occurrence of the Piagetian type of quantifier-spreading error suggests that exhaustivity *per se* may be salient to young children. If children attempt to make a Piagetian quantifier-spreading error, then they should pick the exhaustive interpretation because both sets of entities are exhausted by the predicate.

In the experiment children were presented with collective, distributive, and exhaustive interpretations of actional events (see figure 11.2) and selected the picture that best fit each sentence. The sentences presented were of three types:

1. All of the (actors) are (verb)ing an (object).
2. Each (actor) is (verb)ing an (object).
3. The (actors) are (verb)ing an (object).

The results for each sentence type are presented in table 11.2. For sentences of the type *All of the women are carrying a cake* adults basically split their choices between collective and distributive interpretations, with some preference for the collective one. The results are much the same for children from age 5–6 on, although the youngest children do make some exhaustive choices. Nonetheless, in no case is the exhaustive choice above chance (33.3%). The results, in sum, show a slight preference for the *all* being associated with the collective interpretation over the distributive picture, but at no age is that preference particularly strong.

The sentence type *Each woman is carrying a cake*, in contrast, is clearly associated with the distributive interpretation by 5–6 years of age. This result indicates that children will pick a distributive over a collective interpretation for sentences with *each* at an age where they are not yet able to distinguish the two different distributive representations. The obvious interpretation is that the canonical distributive representation is one in which one-to-one correspondence is preserved. Children fail to show sensitivity to the sentence position of *each* until quite late in development

Fig. 11.2 Picture choices for the actional context: (a) non-exhaustive collective, (b) non-exhaustive distributive, (c) exhaustive.

Table 11.2. *Percentage of responses in which subjects selected collective, distributive, and exhaustive interpretations of sentences in Experiment 2*

	Interpretation selected		
Sentence type	Collective[a]	Distributive[b]	Exhaustive[c]
All Xs are (verb)ing a Y			
4-year-olds	33.3	44.4	22.2
5–6-year-olds	48.6	30.6	20.8
7–8-year-olds	52.8	40.3	6.9
9-year-olds	61.1	30.6	8.3
Adults	58.3	41.7	0
Each X is (verb)ing a Y			
4-year-olds	25.0	47.2	27.8
5–6-year-olds	9.7	57.0	33.3
7–8-year-olds	9.7	80.6	9.7
9-year-olds	2.8	77.8	19.4
Adults	0	97.2	2.8
The Xs are (verb)ing the Ys			
4-year-olds	25.0	30.6	44.4
5–6-year-olds	12.5	34.7	52.8
7–8-year-olds	0	38.9	61.1
9-year-olds	0	27.8	72.2
Adults	0	2.8	97.2

Notes:

[a] The collective pictures showed three actors engaged in an activity with a single object, with two objects left over.

[b] The distributive pictures showed three actors individually engaged in an activity with three distinct objects, with two objects left over.

[c] The exhaustive pictures showed three actors engaged in an activity with five objects, none left over.

because the canonical representation is symmetric, perfect one-to-one correspondence. In neither experiment were children given the option of selecting a picture with perfect one-to-one correspondence, because each picture showed extra objects or actors. Nonetheless, children opted for the distributive picture over an exhaustive choice for sentences with *each* because it is closer to the ideal.

As it turned out, the exhaustive picture wasn't much of a lure. There was little evidence that it was actually salient to the children or that it captured the children's attention as it was never associated with sentences with *all* or *each* at rates that exceeded chance (33.3%). Brooks & Braine (1996) concluded that in this task children do not appear to be susceptible to the Piagetian quantifier-spreading error. Hence the hypothesis that children make quantifier-spreading errors because they adopt an exhaustive interpretation of a sentence in cases where a collective or distributive interpretation is more appropriate was not confirmed. For the sentence type *The women are carrying the cakes* there was a marked developmental shift, with adults unanimously associating this sentence with an exhaustive interpretation. For younger children picture choices were by no means unanimous, with many children opting for the distributive picture.

3 A crosslinguistic comparison of universal quantifiers

The next experiment explored whether children learning other languages might also show early associations between universal quantifiers and collective and distributive interpretations. The languages examined were Portuguese and Chinese. Sentences were selected to be natural ways of expressing universal quantification in each language. Children were given the same task as the American children in the previous experiment. That is, children selected from sets of collective, distributive, and exhaustive pictures the one which best fit each sentence presented. In addition to the actional pictures of the previous experiment, locative pictures were constructed (see figure 11.3). Including sentences with locative predicates along with the sentences with action verbs enabled us to examine children's comprehension of a wider variety of sentence types.[1]

3.1 Portuguese

In Portuguese, the sentences targeted for the collective interpretation contained the universal quantifier *todos* and the sentences targeted for the distributive interpretation contained the quantifier *cada.* Four Portuguese sentence types were presented and are illustrated below.

(1) *Todas as flores estão em um vaso.*
all the flowers are in a/one vase
'All of the flowers are in a/one vase.'

(2) *Todos os homens estão carregando uma caixa.*
all the men are carrying a/one box
'All of the men are carrying a/one box.'

(3) *Cada flor está em um vaso.*
each flower is in a/one vase
'Each flower is in a/one vase.'

(4) *Cada homen está carregando uma caixa.*
each man is carrying a/one box
'Each man is carrying a/one box.'

Fig. 11.3 Picture choices for the locative context: (a) non-exhaustive collective, (b) non-exhaustive distributive, (c) exhaustive.

Figure 11.4 presents the results for the Portuguese sentences targeted for the collective and distributive pictures. For sentences with *todos*, there was essentially unanimity in picture selections from age 4 onwards. *Todos* was strongly associated with the collective interpretation. For sentences with *cada* there was the same high degree of unanimity of association between *cada* and the distributive interpretation for the locative context. For the actional sentences, the youngest children split their responses primarily between distributive and collective choices. It is noteworthy that children at all ages rarely selected the exhaustive pictures for sentences containing either *todos* or *cada.*

3.2 *Mandarin Chinese*

In Mandarin Chinese, two of the sentences targeted for the collective interpretation contained the universal quantifier *suo3you3* and the scope adverb *dou1* (numerals 1–4 designate tones). *Dou1* normally collocates with a wide variety of Mandarin universal quantifiers, and we found that it seems to have a collective-promoting effect on sentence interpretation. In addition to these two collective expressions, Mandarin has a colloquial quantifier-noun *da4jia1* that literally means "big family". This colloquial expression was included in a third sentence type targeted for the collective interpretation. *Da4jia1* is loosely translated as "everyone" and was applicable in the action context only because the locatives involved inanimate subjects. (NOM = nominative, CL = classifier, DUR = durative aspect.)

(5)

Suo3you3	*de*	*hua1*	*dou1*	*cha1*	*zai4*	*yi1-ge4*	*hua1-ping2*	*li3.*
all	NOM	flower	all	put	LOC	one-CL	vase	in

'All the flowers are in a/one vase.'

(6)

Suo3you3	*de*	*ren2*	*dou1*	*zai4*	*ban1*	*yi1-ge4*	*xiang1-zi.*
all	NOM	person	all	DUR	carry	one-CL	box

'All the men are carrying a/one box.'

(7)

Da4jia1	*zai4*	*ban1*	*yi1-ge4*	*xiang1-zi.*
everyone	DUR	carry	one-CL	box

'All the men are carrying a/one box.'

The Mandarin translation of *each* is *mei3*. Four sentence types were constructed which contained *mei3*. In sentences 8 and 9 *mei3* is collocated with the scope adverb *dou1*. These two sentences are very natural ways of expressing universal quantification in Mandarin. To evaluate the contribution of *dou1* to sentence interpretation, we constructed sentences with *dou1* omitted. Sentences 10 and 11 contain *mei3* without *dou1*. These sentences are less natural than their counterparts containing *dou1*, but they are still possible Mandarin sentences. In sentence 11 the pronoun *ta1men2* was

(a)

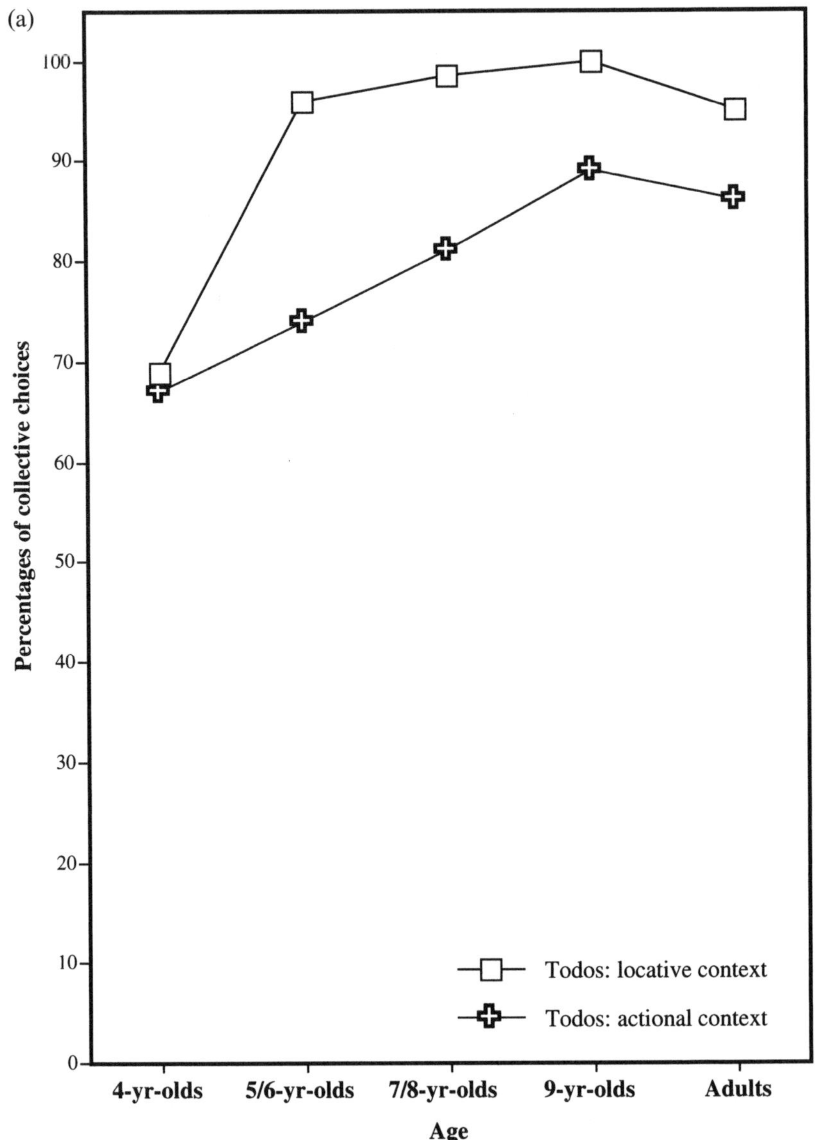

Fig. 11.4 Percentages of (a) collective picture choices and (b) distributive picture choices for Portuguese sentences; chance performance = 33.3%.

(b)

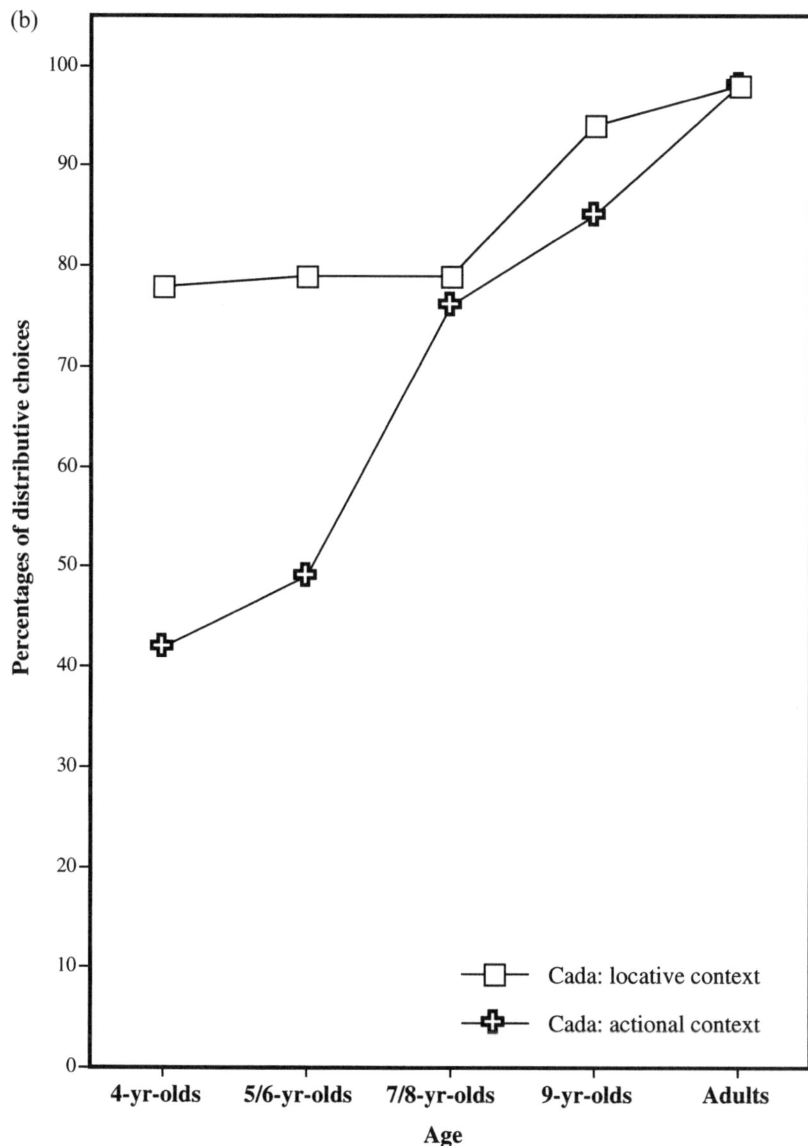
100
90
80
70
60
50
40
30
20
10
0
Percentages of distributive choices
4-yr-olds
5/6-yr-olds
7/8-yr-olds
9-yr-olds
Adults
Age
Cada: locative context
Cada: actional context

added at the beginning of the sentence and *mei3 yi1-ge4 ren2* was contracted to *mei3-ren2*; these changes make the sentence more colloquial. In addition to the universal quantifier *mei3*, Mandarin has another common way of talking about one-to-one correspondence. Because Mandarin doesn't mark a singular/plural distinction on nouns, it is possible to say something analogous to "one flower is in one vase" and have this sentence be ambiguous as to how many flowers and vases there actually are. What is emphasized by this construction is the fact that flowers and vases are in one-to-one correspondence. Sentences 12 and 13 present this construction in the locative and action contexts.

(8) *Mei3 yi4-zhi1 hua1 dou1 cha1 zai4 yi1-ge4 hua1-ping2 li.*
each one-CL flower all put LOC one-CL vase in
'Each flower is in a/one vase.'

(9) *Mei3 yi1-ge4 ren2 dou1 zai4 ban1 yi1-ge4 xiang1-zi.*
each one-CL person all DUR carry one-CL box
'Each man is carrying a/one box.'

(10) *Mei3 yi4-zhi1 hua1 cha1 zai4 yi1-ge4 hua1-ping2 li.*
each one-CL flower put LOC one-CL vase in
'Each flower is in a/one vase.'

(11) *Ta1men2 mei3-ren2 zai4 ban1 yi1-ge4 xiang1-zi.*
they each-person DUR carry one-CL box
'Each man is carrying a/one box.'

(12) *Yi4-zhi1 hua1 cha1 zai4 yi1-ge4 hua1-ping2 li.*
one-CL flower put LOC one-CL vase in
'Each flower is in a/one vase.'

(13) *Ta1men2 yi1-ren2 zai4 ban1 yi1-ge4 xiang1-zi.*
they one-person DUR carry one-CL box
'Each man is carrying a/one box.'

The results for the Mandarin sentences targeted for the collective and distributive interpretations are presented in figure 11.5. Children of all ages associated sentences with *suo3you3* and *dou1* with the collective interpretation, with children's picture selections becoming increasingly consistent with age. For the sentence type containing *da4jia1*, interpretations were even more unanimously collective. In sum, the results for the Mandarin sentences targeted for the collective interpretation closely parallel the results for the Portuguese and suggest that the collective representation is highly salient to the young children acquiring these languages.

For the sentences targeted for the distributive interpretation a more complicated pattern emerges. When *mei3* occurred in a sentence construction with *dou1* (as it typically does), children tended to split their choices between the collective and distributive interpretations. Only children older than 9 years of age and adults selected mostly distributive pictures and, in the locative context, even the adults were not unanimous. When *dou1* was omitted, children as young as 5–6 years of age consistently associated *mei3* with a distributive interpretation. This result provides support for the idea that *dou1* may function as a collective cue. *Dou1* functions as *mei3* when it occurs in the same sentence, especially if children may weigh the available cues differently than adults. For the sentences containing the "one flower is in one vase" collocation, there was a very strong association between this construction and the distributive interpretation from the ages of 3 to 4. In sum, the Chinese results again nicely parallel the Portuguese by indicating a clear association between natural language expressions and collective and distributive representations in young children.

3.3 English

In both Portuguese and Mandarin Chinese the indefinite article is homophonous with the numeral *one*, as is also the case in many other languages. We suspected that the stronger association between the Portuguese and Mandarin equivalents of *all* and the collective interpretation could conceivably be due to the conjoining of the indefinite article with the numeral *one* in the relevant sentences. If the article is interpreted as meaning "exactly one" by young speakers of these languages, this would be expected to bias the Portuguese and Chinese speakers towards a collective interpretation. To explore how the English indefinite article contributes to sentence interpretation in comparison to the numeral *one*, additional English data were collected. The following English sentence types were presented:

(14) All of the flowers are in a vase.
(15) All of the flowers are in one vase.
(16) All of the men are carrying a box.
(17) All of the men are carrying one box.
(18) Each flower is in a vase.
(19) Each flower is in one vase.
(20) Each man is carrying a box.
(21) Each man is carrying one box.

American children's performance on the sentences targeted for the collective and distributive interpretations are presented in figure 11.6. For sentences containing *all* in the locative context, the sentence with *one* is much more strongly associated with the collective interpretation than the sentence with *a*. For *all* sentences in the actional context, the collective-promoting effect of *one* is less pronounced, but, nonetheless, influences the children's performance.

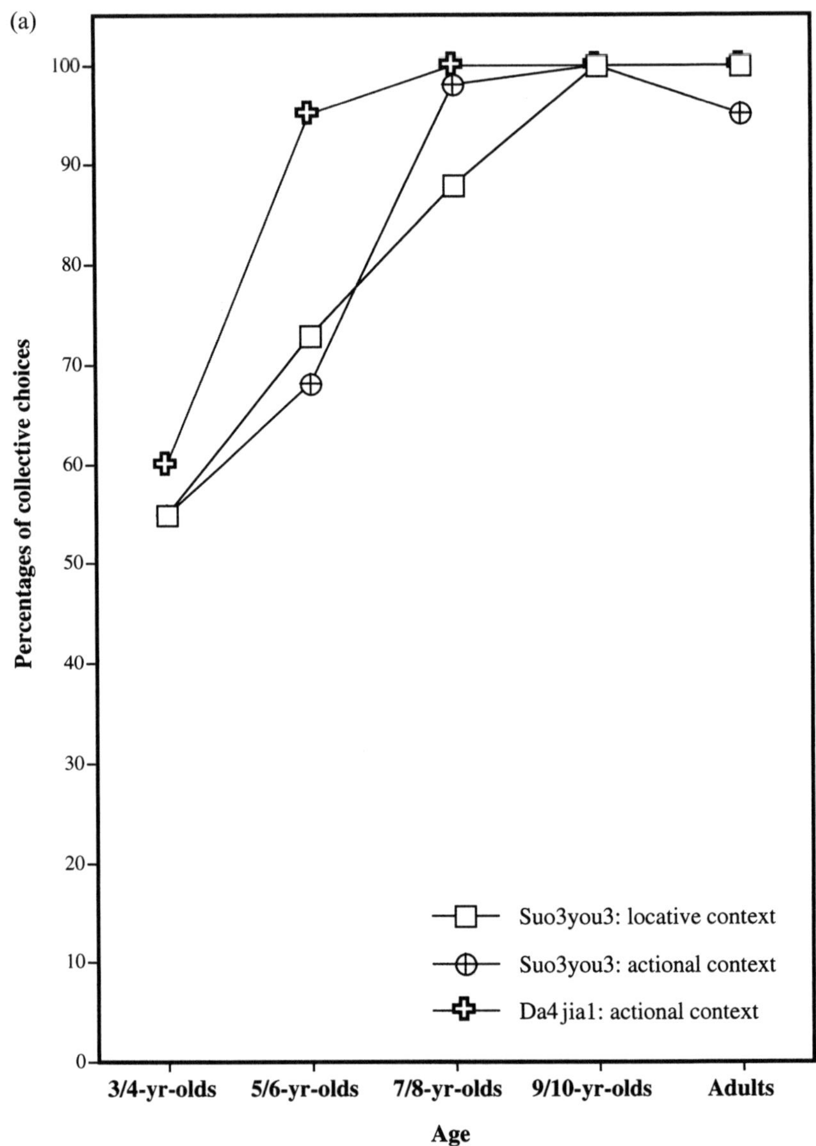

Fig. 11.5 Percentages of (a) collective picture choices and (b) distributive picture choices for Chinese sentences; chance performance = 33.3%.

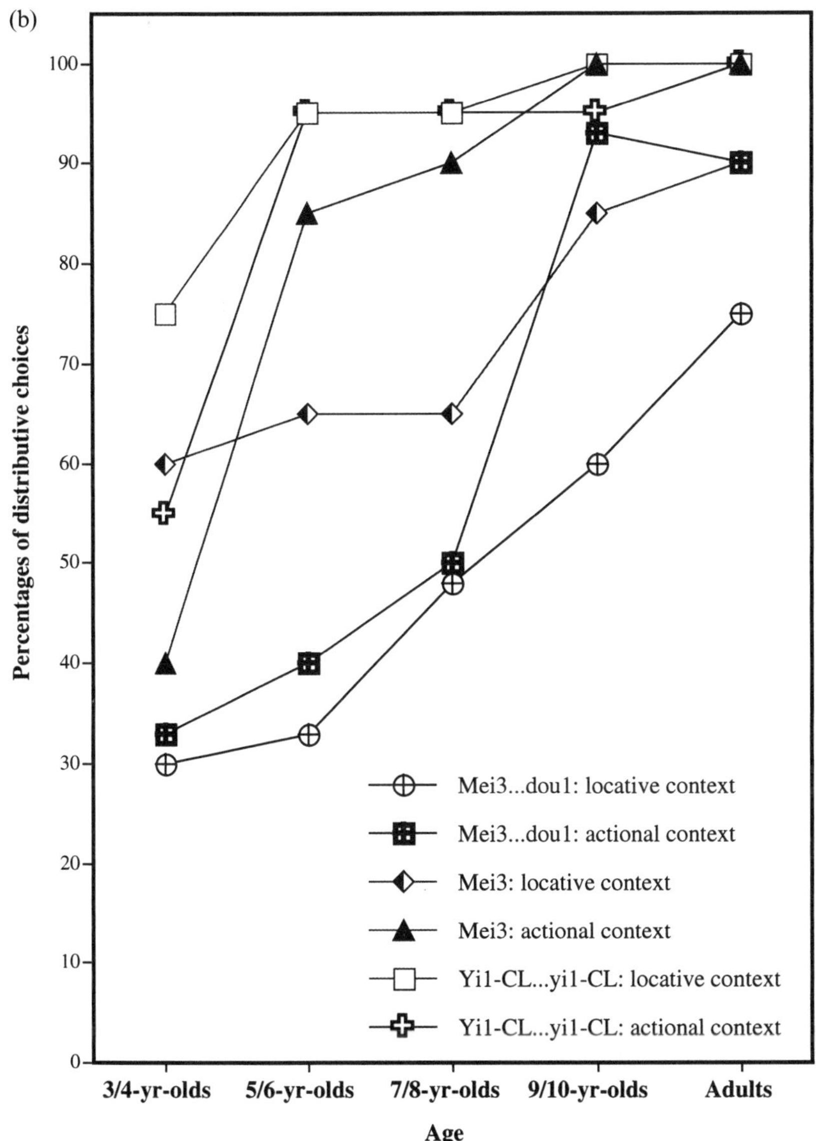
(b)
Percentages of distributive choices
100
90
80
70
60
50
40
30
20
10
0
3/4-yr-olds
5/6-yr-olds
7/8-yr-olds
9/10-yr-olds
Adults
Age
Mei3...dou1: locative context
Mei3...dou1: actional context
Mei3: locative context
Mei3: actional context
Yi1-CL...yi1-CL: locative context
Yi1-CL...yi1-CL: actional context

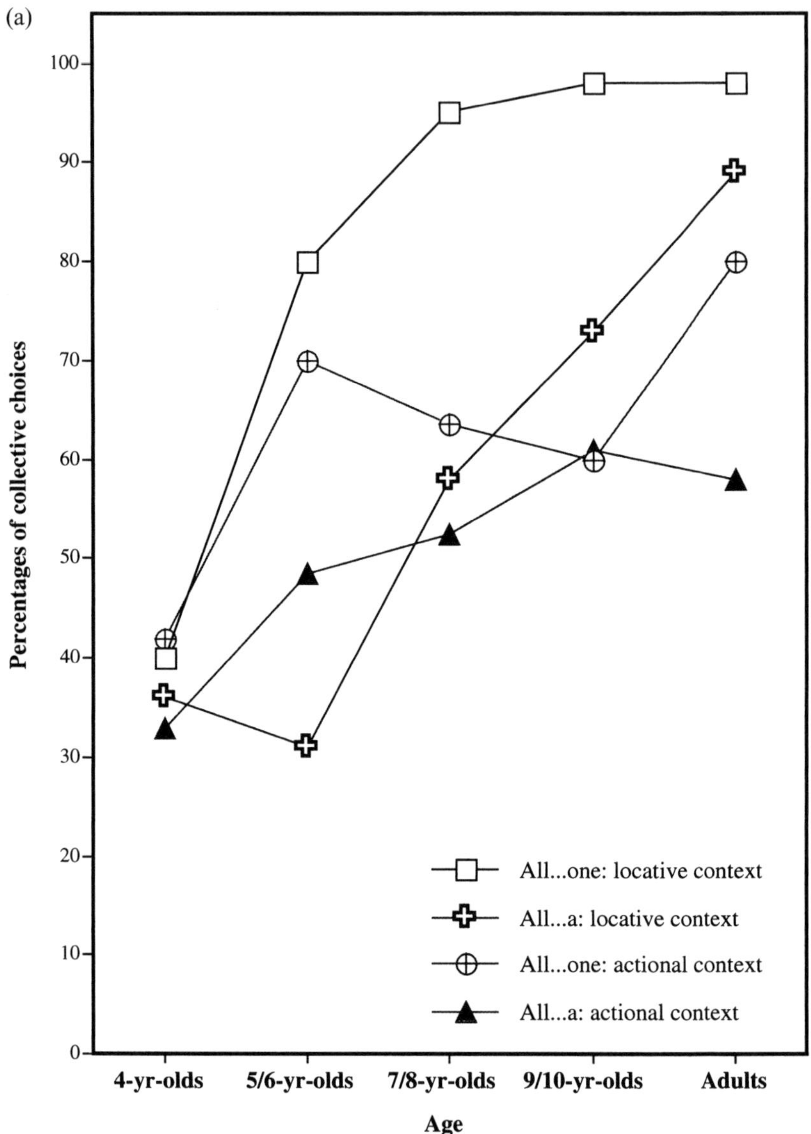

Fig. 11.6 Percentages of (a) collective picture choices and (b) distributive picture choices for English sentences; chance performance = 33.3%.

(b)

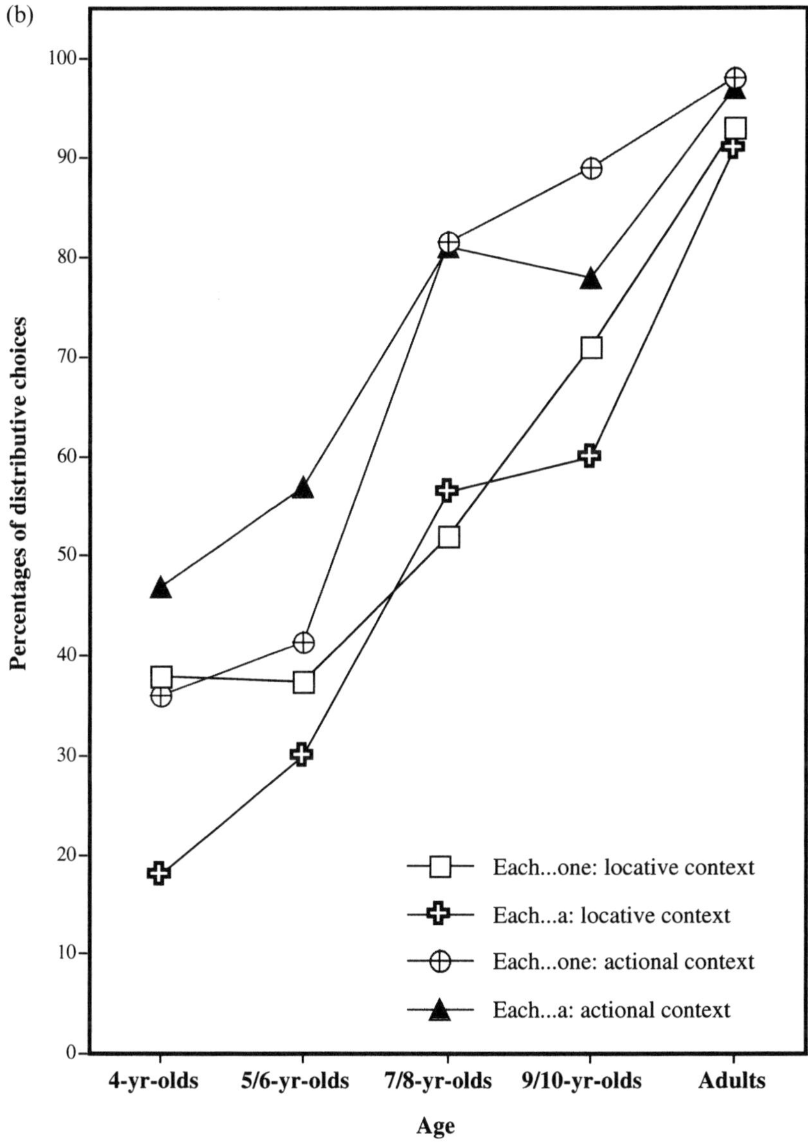
100
90
80
70
60
50
40
30
20
10
0
Percentages of distributive choices
4-yr-olds
5/6-yr-olds
7/8-yr-olds
9/10-yr-olds
Adults
Age
Each...one: locative context
Each...a: locative context
Each...one: actional context
Each...a: actional context

For sentences containing *each*, the presence of the numeral *one* in comparison to *a* had little impact on the frequency of distributive choices. It did however, affect the types of errors made. For sentences with *each* and the numeral *one*, subjects selected more collective than exhaustive pictures (28% versus 11% overall), indicating that *one* exerted a collective pull on children's responses. In contrast, collective picture selections were less common than exhaustive choices for *each* sentences with the indefinite article *a* (12% versus 28% overall). Indeed, the only case in the entire data set where a fair number of exhaustive errors were present was in the interpretation of the English sentences containing *each* with the indefinite article.

The English results show that, with age, there is a progressively stronger influence of the universal quantifier present on scope assignment. *Each* gradually becomes associated with a distributive interpretation, and *all* becomes increasingly biased towards a collective interpretation. Interestingly, *all* continues to be ambiguous, even for adults, especially in the actional context.[2] Children's interpretations of sentences were found to be jointly influenced by the universal quantifier present, the existential quantifier, and the choice of predicate. Sentences with the numeral *one* as "existential" quantifier tended towards a collective interpretation, relative to sentences with the indefinite article *a.* For sentences with the numeral *one*, context also appears to have influenced scope assignment. Children were biased towards interpreting *one* as meaning "the same one" for the locative events and as "just one" for the actional events. We suspect that *one* is more likely to be interpreted as 'the same one' in the locative context because an entity can only be in one container at a time (unless the containers are nested in each other). Given that the most plausible arrangement of objects in containers is for each object to be in "just one" container, *one* in the locative context appears to convey additional information, i.e. more specifically "the same one."

It is noteworthy that the results provide little evidence that children are prone to make the Piagetian type of quantifier-spreading error in this task. Nonetheless, Piagetian quantifier-spreading errors are common in class inclusion problems in children as old as 7 or 8 years of age so it is important to consider their source. We follow Bucci (1978) in suggesting that the Piagetian quantifier-spreading error is a consequence of performance factors rather than differences in underlying semantic competence. Such factors might include scope assignment based on real world knowledge, on the perceived plausibility of a situation, on task demands, or on guessing. Bucci argued that children frequently resort to a "scope-guessing" strategy in class inclusion tasks when they are unsure as to which noun phrase is affected by a universal quantifier. The scope-guessing strategy results in misinterpretations of sentences of the form "All the As are Bs" – children may guess that the sentence means that everything is both an A and a B, or that all the As are Bs and all the Bs are As. We agree with Bucci's suggestion that the Piagetian error likely disappears as a consequence of children becoming more familiar with and more expert in processing the linguistic cues that indicate the range of a universal quantifier.

4 Discussion and summary

The work presented argues for three important points regarding children's acquisition of the meaning of universal quantifiers. First, perfect one-to-one correspondence appears to be the canonical representation for *each*, and its counterparts in other languages, including the English quantifier *every*. The hypothesis that the canonical distributive representation is symmetric nicely accounts for the fact that young children are prone to make the Philip type of quantifier-spreading error. By associating *each* with one-to-one correspondence, children often fail to restrict the quantifier to the noun phrase it modifies.

Second, the crosslinguistic work provides solid evidence for the early availability of collective and distributive representations, albeit the evidence is stronger for Portuguese and Chinese than for English. The canonical semantic representations examined here are presumed to underlie linguistic universals (Ioup 1975) and seem to be likely candidates for a syntax of thought serving as a foundation for deductive reasoning across the life span (Braine 1994). Clearly the hypothesis about the availability of representations cannot be proven with data of the sort presented here. However, the conjecture that what is developing are the associations between collective and distributive interpretations and natural language quantifiers appears to be plausible.

Third, the results indicate that scope interpretation involves more than simply the universal quantifiers present in a sentence. There is not a simple one-to-one mapping between specific universal quantifiers and collective and distributive interpretations. Instead, complex assemblages of cues bias interpretations one way or another. In English, the quantifier *all* exhibits only a weak bias towards a collective interpretation, in contrast to the strong distributive bias of *each*. Also, the indefinite article as "existential" quantifier clearly plays a role in scope assignment. The English numeral *one* appears to have a collective-promoting effect on sentence interpretation in comparison to the indefinite article *a*. Concordance effects are evident for sentences with *all* and the numeral *one*, along with cue competition for sentences with *each* and *one.* Indeed, some of the language differences might be explained by the structural fact that the indefinite article and the numeral *one* arc the same word in many languages.

According to the cue competition framework of Bates and MacWhinney (e.g. Bates & MacWhinney 1987; MacWhinney 1987), the favored interpretation of a sentence is a function of what cues are present. Cues to quantifier scope might include usage of particular universal quantifiers, articles, and predicates, word order, and extralinguistic context, with the strength of individual cues determining the semantic range of the sentence. Children's interpretations of sentences might differ from adults as a consequence of variation in the strength of individual cues. In both the Mandarin and English studies, we have reported cue competition effects which are consistent with the predictions of the competition framework. It may take several years for children to develop flexible comprehension strategies which integrate the various cues to quantifier interpretation. We view age-related changes in sentence interpretation as resulting from children's increasing awareness of correlations between language-specific cues and collective and distributive representations.

NOTES

Portions of the English data were previously reported in Brooks & Braine (1996); some of the Chinese data appeared in Jia, Brooks, & Braine (1996). The authors thank the parents, teachers, and children at Little Red School House, The Jack and Jill School, and The City and Country School in New York City, The Cathedral School and Sacred Heart Elementary School in Pittsburgh, PA, Bem-me-quer and Arco-Iris schools in Recife, Brazil, and Zhong Guan Cun No.2 Elementary School, Bei Gong Men Elementary School and Jinhua Elementary School in Beijing, China, for their participation. We thank Stephen Levinson for helpful comments on the manuscript.

1 We used both actional and locative predicates in order to collect initial data on the role of predicate choice in quantifier interpretation. Our actional and locative predicates differ with respect to what inferences are supported by their corresponding collective interpretations. For the actional predicates, the collective pictures show a group performing an action collectively, for instance a group of men carrying one large box. For this scenario, if John is one of the men carrying the box, it does not follow that John is carrying a box (as he is only helping to do so). In contrast, our locative predicates support a different inference. For the collective scenario involving a group of flowers in one vase, if one of the flowers is red, it is true that the red flower is in a vase. In this chapter we do not attempt to address fully how predicate choice might influence the plausibility of quantifier interpretations.

2 As pointed out by S. Levinson (personal communication), it is possible that *all* is semantically general over collective and distributive interpretations, and is merely biased pragmatically towards the collective.

REFERENCES

Bates, E., & B. MacWhinney. 1987. Competition, variation, and language learning. In B. MacWhinney (ed.), *Mechanisms of language acquisition.* Hillsdale, NJ: Lawrence Erlbaum, 157–193.

Braine, M. D. S. 1978. On the relation between the natural logic of reasoning and standard logic. *Psychological Review* 85: 1–21.

1990. The "natural logic" approach to reasoning. In W. F. Overton (ed.), *Reasoning, necessity, and logic: developmental perspectives.* Hillsdale, NJ: Lawrence Erlbaum, 133–157.

1994. Mental logic and how to discover it. In J. Macnamara & G. E. Reyes (eds.), *The logical foundations of cognition.* Oxford: Oxford University Press, 241–263.

Braine, M. D. S., D. P. O'Brien, I. A. Noveck, M. C. Samuels, R. B. Lea, S. M. Fisch, & Y. Yang. 1995. Predicting intermediate and multiple conclusions in propositional logic inference problems: further evidence for a mental logic. *Journal of Experimental Psychology: General* 124: 263–292.

Braine, M. D. S., B. J. Reiser, & B. Rumain. 1984. Some empirical justification for a theory of natural propositional logic. In G. H. Bower (ed.), *The psychology of learning and motivation: advances in research and theory*, vol. 18. New York: Academic Press, 313–371.

Brooks, P. J., & M. D. S. Braine. 1996. What do children know about the universal quantifiers *all* and *each*? *Cognition* 60: 235–268.

Bucci, W. 1978. The interpretation of universal affirmative propositions: A developmental study. *Cognition* 6: 55–77.

Inhelder, B., & J. Piaget. 1958. *The growth of logical thinking from childhood to adolescence.* New York: Basic Books.

1964. *The early growth of logic in the child.* London: Routledge & Kegan Paul.

Ioup, G. 1975. Some universals for quantifier scope. *Syntax and Semantics* 4: 37–58.

Jia, X., P. J. Brooks, & M. D. S. Braine. 1996. A study of Chinese children's comprehension of universal quantifiers. In E. V. Clark (ed.), *The proceedings of the 27th Stanford Child Language Research Forum.* Stanford, CA: Center for the Study of Language and Information, 167–173.

MacWhinney, B. 1987. The competition model. In B. MacWhinney (ed.), *Mechanisms of language acquisition.* Hillsdale, NJ: Lawrence Erlbaum, 249–308.

Philip, W. 1991. Quantification over events in early universal quantification. Paper presented at the 16th Annual Boston University Conference on Language Development, Boston, October.

Philip, W., & S. Aurelio. 1991. Quantifier spreading: pilot study of preschoolers' "every." In T. Maxfield & B. Plunkett (eds.), *University of Massachusetts Occasional Papers: Special Edition: Papers in the Acquisition of WH.* Amherst, MA: GSLA Publications, 267–282.

Philip, W., & M. Takahashi. 1991. Quantifier spreading in the acquisition of "every." In T. Maxfield & B. Plunkett (eds.), *University of Massachusetts Occasional Papers: Special Edition: Papers in the Acquisition of WH.* Amherst, MA: GSLA, 283–301.

Vendler, Z. 1967. *Linguistics in philosophy.* Ithaca: Cornell University Press.

12 Children's weak interpretations of universally quantified questions

Kenneth F. Drozd

Aarhus University, Denmark, and Max Planck Institute for Psycholinguistics, Nijmegen, the Netherlands

Children's reasoning with universal quantifiers like *every* and *all* has been an important topic in developmental psychology and psycholinguistics since Piaget's class inclusion studies. One puzzle is why children make two particular kinds of unexpected responses when asked questions like *Is every boy riding an elephant?*

One type of error occurs when a child is presented with a picture like those shown in figures 12.1a and b and asked to judge whether every boy is riding an elephant in that context. The picture in figure 12.1a depicts an incomplete one-to-one matching context in which each of three boys is riding a different elephant, leaving one elephant unridden. Figure 12.1b depicts a many-to-one matching in which three boys are all riding one elephant, leaving two elephants unridden. Adults typically say *yes* on these tasks, but some children say *no*. When asked to explain, they point out the unridden elephant or elephants, in a way that suggests that they expected to see each of the elephants matched with a boy. Let us call this the "exhaustive pairing error."

The other type of error occurs when children are presented with a picture like that in figure 12.2 and asked the same question. Some children answer *yes* on this task, suggesting that they may fail to search exhaustively through an entire domain of objects, even when that domain is perceptually available.[1] Let us call this the "underexhaustive pairing error."

Why do children make these errors? Previous accounts all assume that children know the meaning of universal quantifiers but construct syntactic or semantic representations for universally quantified sentences which do not properly constrain how the domain of quantification is selected. As I will show, none of these accounts can explain the specific kinds of context-dependent interpretations which characterize these errors. I will argue instead for an alternative hypothesis, namely that children analyze universal quantifiers as weak quantifiers. The class of weak quantifiers, which includes *two*, *some*, and *many*, exhibits particular contextual dependencies and inferential properties which distinguish them from so-called "strong" quantifiers like *every*, *all*, and *most*. I support the Weak Quantifier Hypothesis (1) by showing how properties of both of the errors children

(a) One-to-One Match

(b) Many-to-One Match

Experimenter: Is every boy riding an elephant?
Adult Subject: Yes.
Child Subject: No, not this one.

Fig. 12.1 Exhaustive Pairing Task.

Experimenter: Is every boy riding an elephant?
Adult Subject: No.
Child Subject: Yes.

Fig. 12.2 Underexhaustive Pairing Task.

make follow from the inferential behaviour and context dependencies that are characteristic of weak quantification, and (2) by showing that this hypothesis explains why children's performance improves significantly under certain pragmatic conditions and not others.

1 More about the exhaustive pairing and underexhaustive pairing errors

What would an explanation of these errors need to account for? In this section, I summarize what we presently know about them.[2]

Table 12.1

Condition	Garage-Centered Strategy	Car-Centered Strategy	Exhaustive-Pairing-Only Strategy	Underexhaustive-Pairing-Only Strategy
Array and Question				
1. C C C G G G G				
a. Are all the cars in the garages?	No (Exhaustive pairing)	Yes (Correct)	No (Exhaustive pairing)	Yes (Correct)
b. Have all the garages got cars in them?	No (Correct)	Yes (Underexh. pairing)	No (Correct)	Yes (Underexh. pairing)
2. C C C C C G G G G				
a. Have all the garages got cars in them?	Yes (Correct)	No (Exhaustive pairing)	No (Exhaustive pairing)	Yes (Correct)
b. Are all the cars in the garages?	Yes (Underexh. pairing)	No (Correct)	No (Correct)	Yes (Underexh. pairing)

One set of developmental psychological studies has suggested that children's responses can be grouped according to four interpretive strategies, given in table 12.1 (Donaldson & Lloyd 1974; Freeman, Sinha, & Stedmon 1982; Stedmon & Freeman 1985; Freeman 1985; Freeman & Schreiner 1988). In these studies, children were asked quantified questions about two different arrays of actual (not pictured) objects represented by (1) and (2) in table 12.1. Here and throughout, each array of objects is represented by two rows of capital letters. Columns of two letters represent two related objects, e.g. a car C in a garage G. Objects which are not related to any other object appear in single-item columns.

The "garage-centered" and "car-centered" strategies (named for the objects used in the earliest studies by Donaldson and her colleagues) include exhaustive pairing errors, underexhaustive pairing errors and correct responses. Under the garage-centered strategy, a child who is asked if all the cars are in the garages will say *no* if one of the garages is empty (exhaustive pairing error) but *yes* if all the garages are occupied, even if one car is not matched with a garage (underexhaustive pairing error). Under the car-centered strategy, a child asked if all of the garages have cars in them will respond *no* if there is a free car (exhaustive pairing error) but *yes* if

Table 12.2

Conditions 1a and 1b	Conditions 2a and 2b
C C C Boat G G G G	C C C Boat C C G G G G

Table 12.3

Conditions 1a and 1b	Conditions 2a and 2b
C C C C G G G	C C C C G G G G G

there is a garage with no car in it (underexhaustive pairing error). The exhaustive-pairing-only strategy requires that all the cars be in a garage and all the garages be occupied by a car. The underexhaustive-pairing-only strategy treats unpaired cars or garages as irrelevant. Across studies, the garage-centered and exhaustive-pairing-only strategies occur most often, followed by the underexhaustive-pairing-only strategy and the car-centered strategy.

Contextual, pragmatic, and grammatical variation all seem to affect children's choice of strategy. Changes in the sizes or contents of the arrays or in how the arrays are presented have a significant effect. For example, placing a boat in the empty garages across conditions (as depicted in table 12.2) reduced the number of children making the exhaustive pairing error on Condition (1a) in table 12.1, and significantly increased the number of children giving correct responses across-the-board (Freeman 1985). This suggests that the presence of the boat lessened the salience of the extra garage for the children. However, these arrays also produced more underexhaustive-pairing-only strategists. This suggests that the presence of the boat may signal to some children that a particular relation is complete even when it is not.

In another study, children who had adopted the garage-centered strategy on the original conditions were given arrays in which it was the number of cars rather than the number of garages which were held invariant across contexts, as depicted in table 12.3. On these conditions, all four strategies were equally popular. When the number of garages was fixed, the children returned to the garage-centered strategy (Freeman *et al.* 1982:67). This outcome seems to suggest that children are particularly sensitive to invariant properties of landmark objects.

The order in which objects are presented to children may also make a difference. Freeman *et al.* (1982) and Freeman (1985) presented the garages first and then filled them with cars in a one-to-one manner, with extra cars placed to the side of the garages. This may have led the children to believe that the experimenter intended the cars and garages to be matched in a complete one-to-one correspondence, accounting for the large number of garage-centered strategists in their experiments.

Variation in how an experimenter talks about the arrays also appears to affect children's responses. For example, children could be influenced to adopt either the garage-centered or the car-centered strategy if one of the sets was treated as the discourse topic. Freeman *et al.* (1982:66) reported that, when told a story about cows, 89% of their subjects adopted a cow-centered strategy (corresponding to the car-centered strategy) but, when told a story about cowsheds burning down, 77% of the same children turned to a cowshed-strategy (corresponding to the garage-centered strategy).

Still other studies suggest that children are sensitive to the specific quantifier used in the question. Freeman & Schreiner (1988:348) reported that when the test question was quantified with *all*, 76% of their 6-year-old children adopted the garage-centered strategy, but when it was quantified with *every* or *every single*, 74% adopted the exhaustive-pairing-only strategy. Drozd & van Loosbroek (1998) reported that four- and five-year-old Dutch children made significantly more exhaustive-pairing errors with *every* than with *all* in a many-to-one context like in figure12.1b. This suggests that the use of *all* may lead a child to think in terms of whether a particular relation is completed or not, whereas *every* may promote an interpretation in terms of whether all of the objects in the picture are participating in the mentioned relation, an interpretation which is consistent with similar results reported by Brooks & Braine (1996; Brooks, Braine, Jia, & da Graca Dias, ch. 11 of this volume).

The studies I have just reviewed show that pragmatic, contextual, and grammatical variation affect children's overall choice of strategy. Other studies have focused more specifically on determining which conditions eliminate or reduce children's tendency to adopt the exhaustive-pairing only strategy (e.g. Philip 1995; Drozd 1995, 1996; Brinkmann, Drozd, & Krämer 1996; Crain, Thornton, Boster, Conway, Lillo-Martin, & Woodams 1996). Although experimental designs and data collection techniques differ from study to study, certain themes can be detected from the findings that will be important in helping us evaluate why children so often rely on this strategy. I summarize these as three generalizations. For ease of exposition, I refer from now on to the denotation of the noun or noun phrase occurring with the quantifier (e.g. the noun *boy* in *Every boy is riding an elephant*) as the (experimenter's intended) "domain of quantification" and the denotation of the direct object noun phrase (e.g. the noun phrase *an elephant* in the same sentence) as the "object set."

1. The first generalization is that the exhaustive-pairing-only strategy is – or somehow involves – a numerical strategy. Children often enumerate when they respond to universally quantified questions. Some responses indicate that they are enumerating the object set. For example, when they answer a question like *Is every mouse in a cup?*, they often point to each mouse–cup scene one at a time, mentioning each cup, e.g. *This cup, this cup, this cup, not this cup . . . no* (Philip & Aurelio 1991:277). Other responses suggest that children are enumerating scenes, e.g.:

EXPERIMENTER: *Is every boy riding an elephant?*
CHILD: *Here, here, here, not here* (pointing to the extra elephant).
(Drozd *et al.* 1996)

One might naturally expect children to enumerate a set in order to make sure that they have exhausted a particular domain of individuals. However, instead of using the intended domain of quantification as the basis for counting, children appear to be using the object set.

Children also show a distinct preference for numerical descriptions of the domain of quantification and/or the object set. For example, Crain *et al.* (1996) reported that children who incorrectly denied that every one of three skiers drank a cup of hot apple cider did so only to replace the universal quantifier in the question with the appropriate cardinal modifier, e.g. *No, THREE skiers drank a cup of hot apple cider*. Similarly, when Dutch children are asked *Is every boy riding an elephant?* (translated) in a many-to-one condition (12.1b), they often say *no*, only to replace the determiners with cardinal expressions, e.g. *No, (only) three*, *No, three on one*, or *No, on one* (Drozd *et al.* 1996). These results suggest that children either prefer numerically specific quantified descriptions or find universal quantifiers inappropriate on particular tasks.

The frequency of the exhaustive pairing error can be dramatically reduced if the object set is presented as a nonindividuated mass rather than as a collection of individuated objects. Brinkmann *et al.* (1996) reported that when Dutch children are asked *Did all the bad guys burn hay?* following a story, they made the exhaustive pairing error 30% of the time if the three bad guys each burned one separate pile of hay and one extra pile of hay was left over at the end of the story. However, the same children said *yes* correctly about 95% of the time if the three bad guys burned a portion of one large pile of hay and some hay was left over at the end of the story. This result may reflect children's use of a counting strategy. Children seem to have a strong tendency to treat discrete objects as countable entities (Shipley & Shepperson 1990), and may be unable to generalize their counting strategies to entities other than individuated entities before the age of 5 (Wynn 1990:160).

One may wonder if it is necessary to invoke "counting" to explain these observations. Perhaps children simply adopt a one-to-one correspondence strategy on the relevant tasks (e.g. Donaldson & McGarrigle 1973; Freeman *et al.* 1982; Takahashi 1991; Roeper & de Villiers 1993; Brooks & Braine 1996; Crain *et al.* 1996; Brooks *et al.*, ch. 11 of this volume). To instantiate this strategy, children might use the procedure of enumerating individuated objects or scenes but turn to other strategies when objects cannot easily be paired. Children may prefer cardinal descriptions (*No, three!*) on some tasks because such descriptions give the final tally of the one-to-one correspondence strategy.

If children's enumeration is simply the by-product of their use of a one-to-one correspondence strategy, we would expect to see the one-to-one strategy applied across the board. But this is not the case. The exhaustive pairing error occurs only when the universal quantifier is present and the object set outnumbers the domain of quantification, leaving one or more "extra" members of the object set (e.g. the unridden elephants in figures 12.1a and b – Drozd 1996). It does not occur when the universal quantifier is absent or when extra objects are removed from many-to-one match contexts like 12.1b, as I discuss directly below. Enumeration does not, then, seem to be simply a by-product of a more basic pragmatic strategy of making one-to-one pairings; it seems to signal some more specific cognitive operation.

2. The second generalization is that the exhaustive pairing error occurs with some kinds of contexts and question types far more than others. English and Dutch studies report error rates ranging from about 39% to 83% on tasks in which the child is presented with a context which includes an extra member of the object set, as in figures 12.1a and b above, and asked a universally quantified question like *Is every boy riding an elephant?* But the error either disappears or is severely reduced (to less than 12%) when the same question is asked of pictures like those in figures 12.3, 12.4 and 12.5, in which there are no extra objects (Drozd & Weissenborn 1996; Drozd 1996).

If we look just at those tasks in which there *are* extra objects, we find that children make the error in response to some questions but not others. Research on the exhaustive pairing error has focused almost exclusively on how children respond to universally quantified questions or statements. Philip (1995), in particular, reported a high rate of exhaustive pairing errors across a wide variety of such constructions, including passives (*Is an elephant being ridden by every boy?*), intransitives with prepositional adjuncts (*Is every cat sitting in a box?*), and ditransitives with and without object inversion (*Is every girl giving a Mom a present?*). The error is is also frequent if the universal quantifier appears in the direct object determiner position,

Fig. 12.3–12.5 Contexts without extra objects.

as in *Is a girl holding every balloon?* (Philip & Aurelio 1991; Drozd & Weissenborn 1996); it is also frequent, though less so, with simple intransitives as in *Is every boy waving?* (Takahashi 1991; Philip 1995).[3]

Strikingly, however, children respond like adults even when extra objects are present if the question includes not a universal quantifier but rather a definite plural subject, e.g. *the boys*, or a subject that is a "list of names," like *Jan, Bert, and Marco* (Drozd *et al.* 1996), or a subject with a cardinal modifier, e.g. *three boys* (Takahashi 1991).

This suggests that the source of the exhaustive pairing error is not a difficulty with plurality or with specifying distributive relations between two sets. Nor can the source be a child's fascination with the extra object(s) in the context. Rather, it is specifically the presence of a universal quantifier that triggers the error.

3. The third observation is that familiarizing a child with the intended domain of quantification before she is asked a question about it in a particular context is sufficient to reduce the rate of exhaustive pairing errors. Experimenters normally present the child first with a visual context in which the relevant objects are already related in the manner described in the test question, e.g. figure 12.1a or Condition 1 in table 12.1. Then they introduce

these objects verbally and present the test question. This is illustrated in examples 1 and 2 (related objects are represented in the same columns, as in table 12.1).

(1) Visual Context: pig pig pig
apple apple apple apple apple
Verbal Context and Question:
In this story, there are 3 pigs. Freddie, Porkie and Wilbur. Now they are in the yard. They've found apples. Every pig is eating an apple . . . Does this picture go with the story? (Philip 1995:29)

(2) Visual Context: chick chick chick
turtle turtle turtle turtle
Verbal Context and Question:
Wat zijn dit voor een beesten? ('What are these animals?') (Pointing)
Zijn het poezen? ('Are they cats?') (Answer: 'No')
En dit zijn zeker kuikentjes ('And these are surely chicks') (Pointing)
Kun je ieder kuikentje aanwijzen? ('Can you point to every chick?')
(Child points)
Staat ieder kuikentje op een schildpad? ('Is every chick standing on a turtle?') (Drozd *et al.* 1996)

In both of these examples, referents for the subject and object noun phrases are perceptually individuated in context and the child's attention is directed to the intended domain of quantification. In example 1, the cardinality and membership of this domain is made explicit in verbal context. In example 2, the child is asked to point out the objects in the intended domain of quantification. Under these circumstances, children make many exhaustive pairing errors (around 47%).

In contrast, the errors are drastically reduced when children are told a story which familiarizes them with the intended domain of quantification before they are asked to regard it as the actual domain of quantification for the universal quantifier in a test question. For example, Crain *et al.* (1996) presented fourteen children (ages 3–5) with a story in which a thirsty mom and her two thirsty daughters get something to drink after skiing. At a certain point in the story, the skiers are divided over their drink preferences. The following excerpt presents this situation:

(3)
MOM: Oh girls, that gave me a real fright. I almost banged into the arch. Let's go in now and get a drink (Mom and girls go over to drinks set out on a table). I'll have a cup of this nice hot apple cider. This will help calm me down (Mom takes a cup of cider).
GIRL 1: Oh, look at these sodas. I want this bottle of orange soda.
GIRL 2: I want this bottle of cola.
MOM: Girls, don't take a bottle of soda. You should have a cup of hot apple cider so you get nice and warm. You can have soda another time.

GIRL 1: OK. I'll take this cup, it's full to the top.
GIRL 2: I want a full cup too. Are any of these other cups of cider full? Oh, this one looks very full. I'll have this one. Mmm, it's good.

When the story ends, cups of hot apple cider outnumber the skiers. Kermit then presents the test question:

KERMIT: That was a hard story, but I think I know something that happened. Every skier drank a cup of hot apple cider.

In Crain *et al.*'s narrative (1996), the three individuals in the intended domain of quantification are presented first as a group of thirsty skiers who have different drink preferences. At the end of the story when the question is asked, all of the skiers are happy apple cider drinkers. Under these conditions, children respond incorrectly only 12% of the time (see Brinkmann *et al.* 1996 for a similar finding), and then only to replace the universal quantifier with an appropriate cardinal term.[4]

These data suggest that only particular kinds of information are useful to a child in establishing a domain of quantification. Explicitly mentioning a perceptually available set, or specifying the cardinality of that set when the members are portrayed as already engaged in the action described in the test question, is not enough to induce children to regard this set as the domain of quantification for the universal quantifier in the question. In contrast, presenting the intended domain of quantification in a story and talking about it *before* the relevant context is presented and the test question is asked does reduce the rate of error.

How should we account for the findings discussed under generalizations 1–3? Let us review some proposals.

2 Do children misapply universal quantifiers?

Various attempts have been made to explain how a child's exhaustive or underexhaustive pairing errors might result from a misapplication of universal quantification. All of these analyses begin with two assumptions. The first is that children in principle know how to quantify universally. That is, once a child has selected a particular domain of quantification, she can quantify the entire set, leaving no exceptions. Children's correct responses to questions with universal quantifiers given pictures like figures 12.3–12.5 have seemed to support this assumption (see also Smith 1980).

The second assumption is that when children make the exhaustive and underexhaustive pairing errors, they are indeed applying universal quantification but they are not appropriately constraining its domain of application. This failure to constrain the domain of application has been characterized in two ways: (1) children are asked to apply universal quantification under conditions in which the normal, constrained application of universal quantification is implausible or has no pragmatic support; (2) children fail to represent the structural connection between subject and predicate or quantifier and noun either semantically or syntactically. Let us examine each hypothesis separately.

2.1 *Hypothesis 1: children misapply universal quantification in implausible contexts*

On the first view, children make the exhaustive and underexhaustive pairing errors when the tasks do not provide a context in which a universally quantified question can be plausibly denied, an idea based on Wason (1965)[5] (Freeman *et al.* 1982; Crain *et al.* 1996). Freeman *et al.* (1982:64–66) propose that a question about "all the Xs" conventionally requests that a hearer "carry out an exhaustive search to check that no X is missing." If the hearer is to follow this convention, she must presuppose "that the size of the intended set [i.e. domain of quantification, kfd] is potentially larger than the contemporaneously present set of Xs" and "check the context for clues which might indicate the absence of one of the items." If no such clues are available, such a question cannot be plausibly denied.

Given this convention, tasks like those in figure 12.1a put the intentions of the experimenter and the expectations of the subject at odds. The experimenter intends the subject to regard the perceptually available set of boys as the domain of quantification, but the subject is looking for clues that will indicate whether a boy is missing or not. If the experimenter has provided no such clues, there is a "'context of plausible denial' effect" (Freeman *et al.* 1982:65): the subject will not be able to establish a boundary on the domain of quantification.

Under these conditions, a child is assumed to search for an alternative way to set the boundary. Freeman *et al.* propose that a child first uses salient contextual information to determine the experimenter's intended discourse topic, then uses the cardinality of the set picked out by the topic to specify the numerical boundary for the domain of quantification, and then universally quantifies up to that boundary (Freeman *et al.* 1982; Stedmon & Freeman 1985). Normally, it is the subject of the sentence that specifies the topic and the predicate that encodes the comment. But a child may override this convention if she has reason to believe that the speaker intends the topic to be something other than the subject. For example, though an experimenter may intend the cars to be the topic for the question *Are all the cars in the garages?*, when the child sees that it is garages rather than cars which are numerically invariant across trials, she may assume that the experimenter intends the garages to be the topic. The garage set, then, becomes “the natural set for checking that nothing is missing” (Freeman *et al.* 1982:65). The child will then use the number of garages to estimate the cardinality of the domain of quantification and universally quantify up to that boundary, thus making the exhaustive pairing error on Condition (1a) in table 12.1. Adults generally do not make the exhaustive pairing error because “real world knowledge is obviously called up in the subjects’ minds, and gives a rational basis for their replies.”

Crain *et al.* (1996) make a similar proposal: that a child makes the exhaustive pairing error in tasks like those in figure 12.1a because the experimenter has not given her any reason to think that the negation of the proposition in the question was ever a possibility, e.g. that some of the boys might *not* end up riding an elephant. Thus, tasks like those in figure 12.1a do not satisfy what these authors term the “Condition of Plausible Dissent.” Since there is no pragmatic support for the normal universal quantifier interpretation, children infer that the experimenter intends a question like *Is every boy riding an elephant?* to be a question about the numerical correspondence between boys and elephants (1996:116), so they apply universal quantification in a way that accommodates the extra elephant. Adults and older children do not make the exhaustive pairing error because “they have learned to see through misleading circumstances in which test sentences are presented” (1996:117).[6] This explains children’s improved performance on their “skiers” condition in (3). According to Crain *et al.*, children respond like adults in this condition because the skiers were described during the story as having different drink preferences. This introduced the child to the nonactualized possibility that not all of the skiers had ended up drinking hot apple cider, satisfying Plausible Dissent.

Crain *et al.* and Freeman *et al.* are certainly correct in assuming that pragmatic and contextual factors contribute to how a child interprets a universally quantified question. Moreover, it is possible that the tasks shown in figures 12.1a and b involve visual and/or verbal contexts which somehow violate plausibility conditions on universal quantifier interpretations. But a failure to satisfy plausibility conditions cannot completely explain the exhaustive pairing error. The same children who make the exhaustive pairing error on tasks like those in figures 12.1a and b respond like adults on conditions represented by the pictures in figures 12.3–12.5, even though these tasks should also create a “‘context of plausible denial’ effect” and fail to satisfy the Condition of Plausible Dissent. And other studies have shown that children interpret universally quantified questions like *Does every elephant have a trunk?* correctly when they are asked to rely on their own background knowledge for verification rather than a prepared context (Smith 1980), even though these tasks are, according to Freeman *et al.*’s and Crain *et al.*’s reasoning, presented in implausible contexts for universal quantification.

A second problem is that these accounts don't explain the body of facts described earlier. Neither account seems able to explain why exhaustive pairing errors disappear when cardinal or definite plural determiners replace universal quantifiers in the test sentence. Nor do they address why it is specifically the presence of the extra object which seems to trigger the exhaustive pairing error. Crain *et al.* do not deal with this issue at all. Freeman *et al.* claim that children will turn to the number of objects in the object set to establish the numerical boundary on the intended domain of quantification when they believe a speaker intends the topic to be other than the subject of the question. But the protocols in examples 1 and 2 *do* seem clearly to establish the referents of the subject as the topic – yet children still make errors. This challenges the proposal that children accommodate the presence of an extra object by making the object set the topic.

A third problem is that these accounts provide no evidence for the assumption that children are actually applying universal quantification like adults when they make the exhaustive and underexhaustive pairing errors. Crain *et al.* and Freeman *et al.* propose that children apply universal quantification on tasks such as in figure 12.1a and the conditions in table 12.1, because they succeed in finding a plausible context for a universal quantifier interpretation, although it is not the one intended by the experimenter. Crain *et al.* (1996:116) claim, without argument or discussion, that, given a task such as in figure 12.1, children infer that an "alternative interpretation" of the question was intended which "concerned the numerical correspondence between agents and objects." The most straightforward universal quantification interpretation of this correspondence would be a one-to-one correspondence, which, as I have already shown, does not underly the exhaustive pairing error. Another reading of Crain *et al.*'s claim is that children are attempting to match the numerical values of the intended domain of quantification and the object set. But such a strategy is unexpected if children are applying universal quantification, since universal quantifiers do not denote numerical relations (see below).

Freeman *et al.* propose that children who adopt the exhaustive pairing-only strategy, as in table 12.1, recognize that the set of garages rather than the set of cars is numerically invariant across trials and that this set provides a good basis for "checking that nothing is missing" from the set of cars. The assumption that children are paying attention to the cardinality of the sets involved is consistent with the observation made earlier that the exhaustive pairing strategy is or involves a numerical strategy. But it is not clear that children always use the object set to check that nothing is missing from the intended domain of quantification. Brinkmann *et al.*'s (1996) results from the "bad guys burning hay" experiment, reported above, would seem to be evidence against this analysis. Under Freeman *et al.*'s (1982) account, a numerically invariant object set should be used as the basis for establishing a plausible context for universal quantification regardless of whether it is portrayed as a single mass or as physically individuated objects. But children make significantly more exhaustive pairing errors when the object set is portrayed as physically individuated objects.

In conclusion, although experiments may violate plausibility conditions on the use of universally quantified questions, it seems unlikely that this is the whole explanation for exhaustive pairing and underexhaustive pairing errors. Moreover, it is not clear that children are actually applying universal quantification at all on conditions where there is no pragmatic support for it.

2.2 *Hypothesis 2: children fail to represent the structure of universally quantified sentences*

A second view of the exhaustive pairing error draws on the proposal of Inhelder & Piaget (1964) that children make errors with universally quantified sentences because they fail to understand class inclusion relations. Inhelder & Piaget discovered that up to age six or seven, children incorrectly say *no* to the question *Are all the circles blue?* if they can see blue objects other than circles. Adult speakers are assumed to understand this question as asking if all of the circles are *some* of the blue things, but children "assimilate" *all* to the predicate (1964:59). As a result, they understand the question as asking if all of the circles are all of the blue things.

A number of researchers have since tried to recast Inhelder & Piaget's assimilation analysis in terms of children's syntactic or semantic representations. This research has investigated how a child might universally quantify not only the denotation of the subject noun (the intended domain of quantification) but also the denotations of other constituents in the same sentence. Some researchers have proposed that exhaustive-pairing-only strategists somehow fail to represent subject–predicate structure at the semantic level, thus freeing a subject quantifier to apply also to constituents inside the predicate (Donaldson & McGarrigle 1973; Donaldson & Lloyd 1974; Bucci 1978). For example, Bucci (1978:75) proposed that children may interpret a sentence like *All the circles are blue* as unordered sets of substantive terms with no hierarchical organization – e.g. *all, circles, blue* – and allow the subject quantifier to apply to either one or both of the other two terms in the representation.

Other researchers have hypothesized that the exhaustive-pairing-only strategists do not establish an accurate semantic representation of the connection between (subject) quantifier and noun. Under one proposal, children interpret universal quantifiers as quantifying events rather than individuals (Philip 1995; Philip & Coopmans 1995). Philip argued, for example, that a child's semantic representation for *Every boy is riding an elephant* specifies that the sentence is true if every event in which either a boy or an elephant is a participant is an event in which a boy is riding an elephant. This account assumes that each boy and each elephant can be construed as representing an event as well as an individual. Thus, an extra unridden elephant will represent an event which is not a boy-riding-elephant event, and lead a child to make the exhaustive pairing error.

Still other researchers have hypothesized that children do not accurately represent the semantic contribution of the direct object. For example, Crain *et al.* suggest that the semantic interpretation of *an elephant* in the question *Is every boy riding an elephant?* involves a function which pairs an elephant with each boy in the domain of quantification. Children make the exhaustive pairing error on the task in figure 12.1a because, in order to accommodate the extra elephant, they choose the elephant set rather than the boy set as the basis for the pairing.

One strictly syntactic proposal made by Roeper & de Villiers (1991,1993) is that children fail to represent the syntactic connection between quantifier and noun. Roeper & de Villiers argued that children analyze universal quantifiers as sentential adverbs of quantification like *always*, a strategy which allows the quantifier to apply to either the subject noun or an (indefinite) direct object or both.

These analyses have been challenged on theoretical and/or methodological grounds (Drozd 1995, 1996; Philip 1995, 1996; Brinkmann *et al.* 1996; Crain *et al.* 1996). However, what I want to question here is the underlying assumption that children are in fact misapplying universal quantification when they make these errors. First, like the plausibility analyses, none of these analyses do justice to the body of facts reported earlier. For example, it is difficult to connect these analyses with the observation that the exhaustive-pairing-only strategy is or involves a numerical strategy, since they do not show any necessary connection between adverbial quantification, event quantification, or object assignment strategies and numerical interpretations. Moreover, none of these analyses tell us why children respond like adults when questions include cardinal or definite plural subjects rather than universally quantified subjects. Cardinal quantifiers in questions like *Are three boys riding an elephant?* are, in principle, susceptible to being interpreted as adverbial or event quantifiers or to interpretations where elephants rather than boys are used as the basis for pairing boys and elephants. But children don't make errors when they are asked these questions.

Further, there appears to be no independent evidence that the error involves the misapplication of universal quantification. The Piagetian conclusion that children are somehow quantifying the object set is seductive.

But the observation that the presence of an extra object, for example, influences how a child responds to a universally quantified question does not imply that the child is actually universally quantifying the set that the object belongs to.

The source of the problem here seems to be the analysis by Inhelder & Piaget which originally motivated this line of research. Inhelder & Piaget's proposal was that children somehow apply *all*, in *All the circles are blue*, to the predicate *blue*, producing an interpretation of the sentence resembling *All the circles are all (rather than some) of the blue things*. We immediately run into difficulties when we try to extend this analysis to other cases. For example, the most straightforward application of this analysis predicts that children will interpret *All the boys are riding an elephant* as either *All the boys are riding all the elephants* or *All the boys are all the elephant-riders*. But there is no evidence that children require that all the boys ride all the elephants or that the boy and elephant-rider sets be coextensive. Children never respond to the tasks in Figures 12.1a and b by saying *No, this boy's not riding all of them* or *No, this elephant just has one boy*.

Other less straightforward but possible assimilation analyses also seem to be ruled out. One option is that children are applying the quantifier only to the object set – e.g. *The boys are riding all the elephants* – rather than to both the intended domain of quantification and the object set. This correctly predicts the instances of the exhaustive and underexhaustive pairing errors on Conditions (1a), (1b), and (2a) in table 12.1. But it does not explain Brinkmann *et al.*'s (1996) findings regarding nonindividuated objects, discussed earlier. If children were quantifying the denotation of the direct object rather than the subject noun, we would expect them to interpret the question *Did all the bad guys burn hay?* as *Did the bad guys burn all (the) hay?*, regardless of the way the hay is portrayed. But Brinkmann *et al.* reported far fewer exhaustive pairing errors when there was one big pile as opposed to four individual piles of hay. This suggests that children are not quantifying over the direct object.

The Brinkmann *et al.* results also undermine Philip's event quantification analysis. According to Philip's account, any scene consisting of an object alone counts as an event whether it is portrayed as a mass or a physically individuated object. This means that children should make the exhaustive pairing error equally often under both conditions. But they do not.

A second option is that children are universally quantifying pairs, e.g. *Every pair of boys and elephants is such that the boy is riding the elephant*. Such an analysis is implied by Roeper and de Villiers' suggestion that children might quantify both subject and direct object. Although this option accounts for the underexhaustive pairing error, it incorrectly predicts that children will correctly answer *yes* on the task in figure 12.1a, since every boy–elephant pair is one where the boy is riding an elephant. Here, the extra elephant should be disregarded because it does not constitute a boy–elephant pair.

All of the analyses we have been looking at assume that when children make exhaustive pairing errors they are misapplying universal quantification. These analyses propose that children's universal quantifier interpretations are unconstrained because they fail to represent either subject–predicate structure or quantifier–noun structure adequately at either the syntactic or the semantic level. But there is little evidence that children are in fact misapplying universal quantification when they make these errors. If they are not, there may be no need to suspect faulty representations. Let us now turn to an explanation for their errors which locates the problem elsewhere.

3 Weak and strong quantification and the Weak Quantification Hypothesis

A better solution to the problem of exhaustive pairing and underexhaustive pairing errors can be provided by appealing to the distinction between weak and strong determiners. The universal quantifiers *every* and *all*, and their counterparts in other languages, occur in determiner position inside noun phrases. Natural languages typically contain a heterogeneous set of such "quantificational" determiners (i.e., quantifiers) such as *two, three, many, few, several,* and *most*. The distinction between strong and weak quantifiers has proven helpful in specifying the nature of natural-language quantifiers and determiner systems more generally (e.g. Barwise & Cooper 1981; Keenan 1987; Diesing 1992; Kamp & Reyle 1993; Partee 1995; Reinhart 1987, 1995). The class of strong quantifiers includes as prototypical members the universal quantifiers *all, every*, and *each*, and the proportional quantifier *most*. The class of weak quantifiers includes as prototypical members the numerals *one, two, three*, etc., and the vague quantifiers *few, some*, and *many*, which denote particular ranges of numerical values (Milsark 1977).[7] For example, *some* can be used to denote "a real quantity, greater than one but not especially large" (1977:23).

The Weak Quantification Hypothesis states that children interpret universal quantifiers as weak quantifiers. Quantifiers, like determiners more generally, can be classified according to which semantic inferences they give rise to, how their interpretations are affected by pragmatic and contextual information, and how the noun phrases they appear in are syntactically distributed. If the Weak Quantifier Hypothesis (WQH) is correct, then it should be possible to characterize children's exhaustive and underexhaustive pairing errors as the products of a weak quantification analysis of a universally quantified question. We should also expect this hypothesis to help us understand the three generalizations regarding the exhaustive pairing error which I discussed above. I now present evidence in favor of this hypothesis.

3.1 The contextual dependencies of weak quantifiers and the exhaustive pairing error

Many psychological studies of human quantificational reasoning have shown that the way speakers estimate the numerical value of vague weak quantifiers like *many* and *some* is affected by the meaning of other constituents in the sentences these words appear in. The interpretations of these quantifiers are thus dependent on their sentential context.

In particular, speakers make different estimates depending on the sizes of the objects, the particular perspective or field of vision, and the spatial situations mentioned in the sentence. For example, German speakers assign a smaller number to the German equivalent of *a few* when they hear *A few people are standing before a hut* than when they hear *A few people are standing before a building*. They also understand *several parcels* to denote fewer items when the parcels are said to be on a small table than when they are said to be on a large one. And they understand *a few cars* to be fewer when the cars are described as seen through a peephole than as seen through a window (Hörmann 1983).

Speakers' numerical judgments are also influenced by the identity of the weak quantifier. Moxey & Sanford (1993:29–30) report unpublished results by Moxey, Tuffield, & Temple showing that subjects assigned a larger number to *some* if it appeared in the noun phrase *some people standing in front of the fire station* than if it appeared in *some people standing in front of the cinema*, despite the relative similarity in the estimated sizes of the buildings in the background. However, subjects' numerical estimation for the weak quantifier *a few* did not vary across these conditions. Moxey & Sanford concluded that if there is a reason to expect a large number of people, only quantifiers denoting relatively large amounts, like *many* and *some*, will be assigned higher values than they would normally receive.

The interpretation of weakly quantified sentences is also influenced by a speaker's expectations of normal quantities. For example, speakers might consider the sentence *Many tourists visited the zoo today*, uttered on a rainy summer day which also happens to be a national holiday, to be true if they compare the number of tourists with the normal number of visitors to the zoo on rainy days (not many), but false if they compare it with the normal number of visitors on national holidays (quite a few; Keenan & Stavi 1986:258).

Expectations about a normal range of values for a weak quantifier in a subject noun phrase can be based on what is known about the denotation of the predicate. The following examples are taken from Westerståhl (1985).

(4) Many Scandinavians have won the Nobel prize in literature.
(5) Many winners of the Nobel prize in literature are Scandinavians.

Westerståhl argued that the preferred interpretation of example 4 is example 5. Under this interpretation, the value for *many* is derived by comparing the number of Scandinavian Nobel literature prize winners with the total number of Nobel literature prize winners (a ratio of 14 to 81, when Westerståhl wrote his paper). This proportion is then compared to the normal or expected frequency of Nobel literature prize winners from a single region. Since 14 of 81 constitutes a significantly higher percentage of prize winners than expected from one region, both examples 4 and 5 will be found true.

If we substitute universal quantifiers for weak quantifiers in these sentences, we arrive at different results. Universal quantifiers, like strong quantifiers more generally, specify no numerical value or range of values. In order to know how many *every*, *all*, or *most* is, one has to consult the cardinality of the denotation of the noun occurring with the quantifier (Reinhart 1995). Moreover, the interpretation of a universal quantifier is not susceptible to the same contextual dependencies as weak quantifiers. A sentence like *Every Scandinavian has won the Nobel prize in literature* is always interpreted unambiguously in terms of how many Scandinavians under discussion won the prize. The interpretation of this sentence as true or false involves no comparison of Scandinavians and expected normal frequencies of Nobel prize winners from a single region. And *Every tourist visited the zoo today* will be judged true only if every tourist under discussion visited the zoo on the day in question, regardless of whether it was a national holiday or a rainy day.

The WQH claims that children assign a weak-quantifier interpretation to universal quantifiers. This predicts that a child's interpretations of universal quantifiers can be affected by the meaning of other constituents in the sentence, or what the children know about the denotations of those constituents. For example, a child might be expected to interpret the question *Is every boy riding an elephant?* to be asking about every boy who ought to be riding an elephant or every boy whom the speaker intends to be riding an elephant given the situation.

This prediction seems intuitively to capture the exhaustive pairing error. As in Westerståhl's account of the preferred interpretation of example 4, children who make this error may arrive at a response to the question *Is every boy riding an elephant?* by first comparing the number of elephant-riding boys with what they consider to be the normal or expected frequency of elephant-riders given the situation shown in the picture. If children use the presence of the extra elephant in figure 12.1a to infer that the expected or normal frequency is four, they will say *no* to the question *Is every boy riding an elephant?* because the number of elephant-riding boys does not match their expectations. This is precisely what is expected under the WQH, but it is unexpected given standard interpretations of universally quantified sentences.

One might object to this explanation on grounds that even adult speakers do not always interpret universally quantified statements absolutely literally (Newstead & Griggs 1984; Moxey & Sanford 1993). For example, speakers often produce universally quantified statements like *all my friends hate me* as generalizations or exaggerations which are not really intended to exhaust the domain of quantification. Similarly, they allow *all* to mean *nearly all* on some logical tasks. For instance, Newstead & Griggs (1984) showed that when subjects perform logical transitive deductions (e.g. *If all A are B, and all B are C, then all A are C*), they allow *all* to permit exceptions as the number of premises increases. If adult speakers allow universal quantifiers to permit exceptions, why not assume children do so too, perhaps to a larger degree?

But these results with adults cannot account for the exhaustive pairing error. Adults who permit exceptions allow a domain of universal quantification to be compromised in one direction only – to a *subset* of the intended domain of quantification (*all* is understood to mean *nearly all*). In contrast, children who make the exhaustive pairing error allow universal quantifiers to specify *larger* quantities than those perceptually available, e.g. to encompass an unseen extra boy to ride the extra elephant.[8]

3.2 *The inferential behavior of weak quantifiers and the underexhaustive pairing error*

The WQH predicts that a child's semantic analysis of a universal quantifier will give rise to inferences characteristic of weak quantifiers. My claim in this section is that the underexhaustive pairing error is indeed the product of such an inference, namely the intersective inference.

In semantic terms, a quantifier in subject determiner position is called intersective if either the denotation of the subject noun or the intersection of the denotation of the subject noun and the denotation of the predicate (the predicate set) can be used to specify the domain of quantification for the quantifier without disturbing the truth conditions of the entire sentence. One diagnostic for deciding whether a determiner is intersective is whether placing it in the diagnostic biconditional sentence frame in example 6 results in a valid inference. In example 6, Det stands for determiner, N for the subject noun, and VP for the predicate verb phrase. The phrase "N who is/are VP" is the linguistic translation for the intersection of a subject denotation and a predicate set. As shown in example 7, *some* is intersective (as are all weak quantifiers).

(6) Intersectivity: Det N VP iff Det N who is/are VP is/are VP
(7) Some boys are riding an elephant iff some boys who are riding an elephant are riding an elephant.

By the same diagnostic, strong quantifiers are not intersective:

(8) *Every boy is riding an elephant iff every boy who is riding an elephant is riding an elephant.

Examples 6, 7, and 8 are biconditionals. Thus, we expect the left-hand clause logically to imply the right-hand clause and the right-hand clause logically to imply the left-hand clause. Example 8 is invalid because the right-hand clause does not logically imply the lefthand clause. Let's assume there is a context including a set of three boys. Two of them are riding an elephant and one of them is not. In this context, the right-hand clause *every boy who is riding an elephant is riding an elephant* is true but the left-hand clause *every boy is riding an elephant* is false – the implication does not go through. This suggests that knowing a property of every elephant-riding boy does not provide enough information to allow us to make a valid inference about every boy. This is because the set of elephant-riding boys may be only a subset of the set of boys.

The WQH predicts that a child's semantic analyses of universal quantifiers will give rise to intersective inferences. My suggestion is that underexhaustive pairing errors are the products of such inferences. If a child treated *every* as intersective on the underexhaustive pairing task in figure 12.2, we would expect her to allow the question *Is every boy riding an elephant?* to have as its truth-conditional equivalent, *Is every boy who is riding an elephant riding an elephant?* A child who made this inference would identify the set of boys who are already riding an elephant as the domain of quantification and ignore other boys as outside of that domain. And this is precisely what children seem to do when they make the underexhaustive-pairing error.

An apparent problem with this analysis is that now both the exhaustive and underexhaustive pairing errors are claimed to be products of weak quantification analyses.[9] This seems to predict incorrectly that both errors should be made by the same child. Why then do some children adopt an exhaustive-pairing-only strategy?

Although it is true that the WQH claims that both errors result from a child's weak-quantification analysis of a universal quantifier, this does not imply that both errors stem from exactly the same mechanism. The exhaustive pairing error occurs when a child's expectations of normal quantities interfere with her estimation of a domain of quantification. The underexhaustive pairing error is the product of logical inference. This allows each error to arise independently.

3.3 Weak quantification, numerical strategies, and familiar domains of quantification

Two questions still need to be explained under the WQH. First, why does a child's exhaustive pairing error seem to involve a numerical strategy? Second, why does it reduce the rate of error to familiarize a child with the intended domain of quantification before the child is asked to interpret a universally quantified question? Explaining these observations requires taking a look at how strong and weak quantifiers behave with respect to presuppositionality.

3.3.1 Presuppositional and cardinal interpretations of weak quantifiers

Weak quantifiers have both a cardinal or existential interpretation, exemplified by (9), and a presuppositional interpretation, exemplified by (10).

(9) There are three/some/many/few boys riding an elephant. (?The rest are having lunch.)

(10) Three/Some/Many/Few (of the) boys are riding an elephant. (The rest are having lunch.)

Under a cardinal interpretation, a weak quantifier simply asserts the cardinality of whatever set it applies to. In (9), the second sentence, *The rest are having lunch*, is odd because no set of boys larger than the set of elephant-riding boys is presupposed by the first assertion. In contrast, the presuppositional interpretation of a weak quantifier does not assert the existence or cardinality of its domain of quantification but rather presupposes it. Quantifiers intended to be interpreted in this way are commonly expressed with a partitive, when appropriate, e.g. *many of the*. In (10), the three, some, many, or few boys are understood as subsets of a larger set of boys under discussion. Hence, the second sentence is felicitous.

Cardinal interpretations can also be distinguished from presuppositional interpretations by using paraphrases of weakly quantified sentences. Weak cardinal quantifiers can occur in existential sentences like (9) and have semantically equivalent numerical paraphrases, e.g. *Many boys are riding an elephant* is semantically equivalent to *The number of elephant-riding boys is*

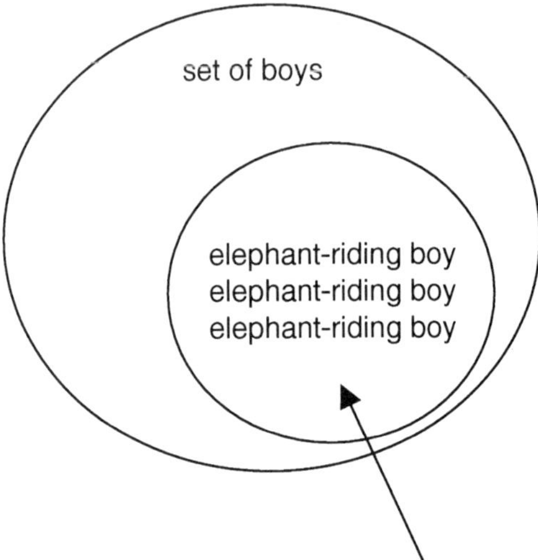

Fig. 12.6 Information needed to verify the cardinal interpretation of a weak quantifier like *many*.

many (Reinhart 1995; Kamp & Reyle 1993:454). Weak presuppositional quantifiers generally cannot appear in existential sentences, e.g. **There are many (of the) boys riding an elephant* (exact cardinals like *three* are one exception: Partee 1988), nor do they have numerical paraphrases, e.g. *Many of the boys are riding an elephant* cannot mean **The number of elephant-riding boys is many of them.*

Cardinal and presuppositional interpretations require different kinds of verification procedures. To find out whether *Many boys are riding an elephant* is true or not on the cardinal interpretation, we only need to find a set of elephant-riding boys and check if this set contains the minimal number that the speaker and hearer consider to be "many." This kind of procedure is diagrammed in figure 12.6. Figure 12.6 represents a subset relationship between a set of boys and a set of elephant-riding boys. The arrow indicates that verifying the cardinal interpretation of the sentence *Many boys are riding an elephant* only requires "activating" or examining the set of elephant-riding boys. Whether or not there are other boys is irrelevant to the interpetation.

To find out whether *Many boys are riding an elephant* is true on the presuppositional interpretation, the speaker is assumed to compare two sets, the set of elephant-riding boys and the presupposed set of boys, and to check whether the cardinality of the first set counts as "many" of the second set. This procedure is diagrammed in figure 12.7, where the additional arrow to the set of boys indicates that this set also needs to be activated for the presuppositional interpretation.

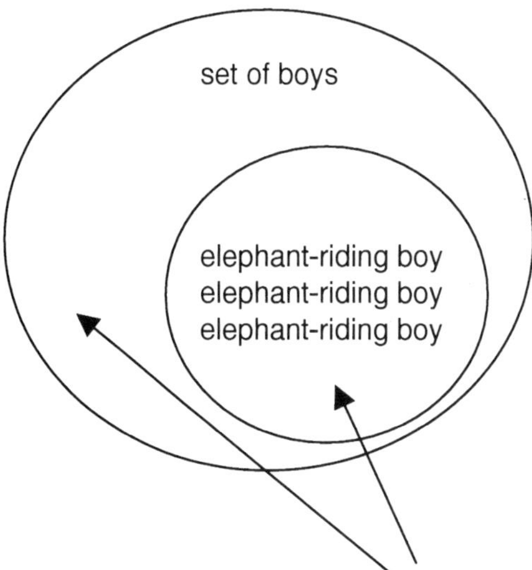

Fig. 12.7 Information needed to verify the presuppositional interpretation of a weak quantifier like *many*.

Strong quantifiers, in contrast to weak quantifiers, have only presuppositional interpretations. To find out whether *Most boys are riding an elephant* is true, we must compare the set of elephant-riding boys with a presupposed set of boys and check if the proportion of elephant-riding boys is what speaker and hearer both count as constituting "most" of the boys, e.g. more than half. This interpretation requires that the speaker knows at least approximately how many boys there actually are and compares the set of boys who are riding elephants to that set. Similarly, *Every boy is riding an elephant* is true if and only if the set of elephant-riding boys exhausts the presupposed set of boys under discussion. Strong quantifiers, like presuppositional weak quantifiers, do not appear in existential *there* sentences like (9), and they have no numerical paraphrases, such as **The number of elephant-riding boys is all/every*.

The interpretation of *Every boy is riding an elephant* is represented in figure 12.8. Here, the shaded area of the boy set must be found empty for the sentence to be true.[10]

The Weak Quantification Hypothesis claims that children assign weak quantifier interpretations to universal quantifiers. Since weak quantifiers can have either a presuppositional or a cardinal interpretation, children are free to interpret universally quantified questions as questions about the cardinality of a set rather than about the (inclusive) relationship between two sets. The WQH does not predict that children will never interpret universal quantifiers as presuppositional. Rather it claims that children analyze

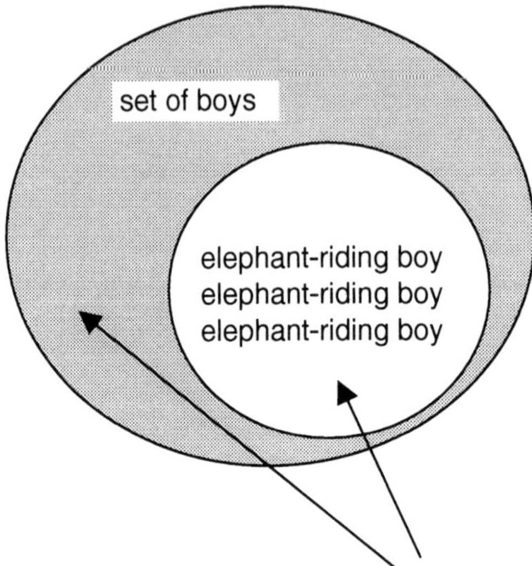

Fig. 12.8 Interpretation of *every*.

universal quantifiers as ambiguous between a presuppositional interpretation and a cardinal interpretation.

The WQH predicts that when a child is presented with the exhaustive pairing and underexhaustive pairing tasks in figures 12.1a and b and 12.2, she may interpret a question like *Is every boy riding an elephant?* to mean "Is the number of elephant-riding boys consistent with what speaker and hearer accept as 'every'?", where "every" retains its function as a universal quantifier over individuals.[11]

3.3.2 Numerical strategies If we assume that children assign weak quantifier interpretations to universal quantifiers, children's adoption of numerical strategies is understandable. One way to answer the question *Is every boy riding an elephant?* (in the tasks in figures 12.1a and b) under the cardinal interpretation would be to count the set of elephant-riding boys in the picture to check if there is an expected number of them. Since the number of elephant-riding boys is smaller than the number the child expects, she either points out that a boy is missing at a particular position (e.g. *there's no boy there*; *no boy* [pointing to elephant]*; nobody's riding that elephant*; *it takes a boy to ride an elephant and that elephant is empty; no boy is sitting there; only these* (*3 boys*) *are riding an elephant*) or points out the extra object where the boy was expected to appear (e.g. *that elephant is extra; one elephant has no boy by him*; *that elephant has no boy on it*). (These examples are based on Philip's – 1995:2 – list of actual child responses and my own lists of Dutch children's responses. In some cases, the original nouns and verbs have been replaced to fit the boy/elephant scenario.)

The important point here is that, in counting, a child reveals that she is not interpreting a question like *Is every boy riding an elephant?* as requiring a strong quantification analysis. Simply counting through the set of boys on elephants will provide a child with one set of objects, a set of elephant-riding boys. But to apply a strong quantificational analysis as an adult does in this situation, the child would have to think of two sets and compare them: a set of boys and a set of elephant-riding boys. It may never occur to a child who is presented with an exhaustive pairing task like fig. 12.1a and b that she should be distinguishing and comparing sets. A child who *is*, in principle, able to interpret the universal quantifier as a presuppositional quantifier may opt for a cardinal interpretation if she is not able to distinguish the two sets when they are presented as identical or coextensive, as in these tasks. This leads us to reconsider Crain *et al.*'s (1996) results.

3.3.3 Familiar domains of quantification Recall that familiarizing a child with the intended domain of quantification before the test question is asked drastically reduces the number of exhaustive pairing errors. Why should this be? I suggest that this information is useful to a child because it allows her to establish the presupposed set she needs to proceed with a presuppositional quantification analysis of the universally quantified question. In other words, it allows her to determine whether there are any counterexamples to the proposition embedded in the question.

In Crain *et al.*'s (1996) skiers story in example (3), the intended domain of quantification is first presented as a set of thirsty skiers. One might represent this information simply as a set of thirsty skiers, as in figure 12.9. At the end of the story, the same skiers are presented as a set of apple-cider drinkers, represented in figure 12.10.

When the question *Is every skier drinking a cup of hot apple cider?* is finally asked, the child has already been provided with two clearly distinct ways of regarding the set of skiers: as a set of (thirsty) skiers and as a set of apple-cider-drinking skiers. These are precisely the two sets the child needs to keep in mind to establish a strong quantification analysis of the test question. The child proceeds with a presuppositional interpretation of the quantifier by representing the set of skiers as the presupposed set and checking if the set of apple-cider-drinking skiers exhausts that set, as represented in figure 12.11.

It is now clear why children continue to make the exhaustive pairing error

Fig. 12.9 A set of thirsty skiers.

Fig. 12.10 A set of apple-cider-drinking skiers.

on tasks like those in examples (1) and (2). The verbal context in (1) is intended to direct a child to identify and presuppose a set of pigs as the intended domain of quantification. However, this verbal context gives a child no reason to distinguish a set of pigs from the pigs she may have already represented as apple-eating pigs when shown the visual context. The presence of one or two extra apples in the visual context may only focus the child more on the fact that the context depicts a set of apple-eating pigs. The identification of the apple-eating pigs is a necessary and sufficient condition for the cardinal interpretation of the test sentence. However, the set of apple-eating pigs constitutes only one of two representations of the pigs a child must have in mind in order to perform a presuppositional quantification analysis. Under these conditions, children proceed with a cardinal interpretation of the universal quantifier. A similar case can be made for (2). Importantly, the visual contexts in both examples support only a cardinal interpretation of a quantifier.

At this point, one might ask how the weak quantification analysis differs from the two pragmatic explanations of the exhaustive pairing error discussed earlier: Freeman *et al.*'s (1982) Plausible Denial explanation and

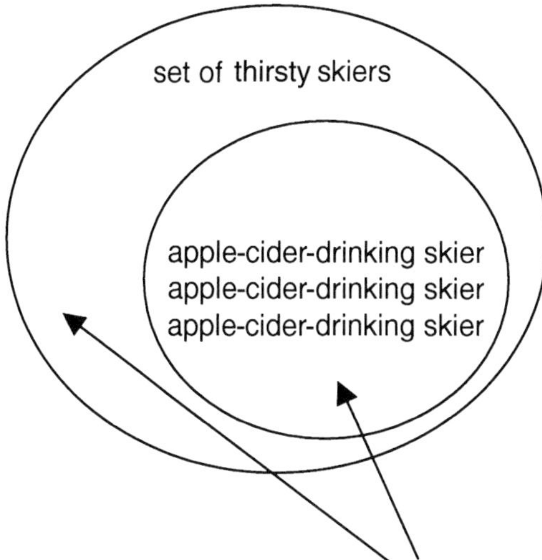

Fig. 12.11 Comparing the set of apple-cider-drinking skiers with the set of thirsty skiers.

Crain *et al.*'s (1996) Plausible Dissent explanation. All three explanations propose that children make the exhaustive pairing error because the context does not support the intended interpretation of the universally quantified sentence. Why not simply explain Crain *et al.*'s findings as the product of a Plausible Denial / Plausible Dissent analysis?

The WQH crucially goes beyond Freeman *et al.*'s and Crain *et al.*'s analyses by specifying the intuitive connection between the quantificational analysis the child actually comes up with and the properties of context which promote this analysis. According to the WQH, children interpret universal quantifiers as weak cardinal quantifiers in contexts like those in figures 12.1a and b and Condition 1 in table 12.1 because they find it difficult to distinguish the two sets they need to represent in order to proceed with a presuppositional interpretation of the universal quantifier. Children faced with such contexts will analyze the quantifier as a weak cardinal quantifier, whose interpretation is both supported by such contexts and requires no presuppositional commitments.

In contrast, Crain *et al.* and Freeman *et al.* locate the source of the errors at the level of speech acts. Crain *et al.*'s condition of Plausible Dissent is presented as a felicity condition on the presentation of statements and questions for truth-value judgments and is explicitly defined as "nonlinguistic" (Crain *et al.* 1996:114). Freeman *et al.* (1982:64) also explicitly define Plausible Denial as a condition on the conventions for asking universally quantified questions. What is crucially missing from these accounts is an adequate description of what quantificational analyses children actually use when plausibility conditions on universal quantification are not met. Both accounts propose that children continue to apply universal quantification even in contexts which make universal quantification implausible. But, as I have argued in detail above, this is unlikely.

4 Summary and discussion

In this chapter, I have argued that children interpret universal quantifiers as weak quantifiers. In particular, I have claimed that children analyze universal quantifiers as cardinal or existential quantifiers when they make the exhaustive and underexhaustive pairing errors, an analysis only available under the Weak Quantification Hypothesis. I supported this hypothesis by showing that children's interpretations of universally quantified sentences exhibit contextual dependencies and inferential behavior common to mature cardinal or existential interpretations of weakly quantified sentences. I also showed how this hypothesis helps to explain why children seem to adopt a numerical strategy to verify their incorrect responses, and why particular pragmatic conditions drastically reduce the rate of exhaustive pairing responses while others do not.

I argued against a number of accounts which claim that children misapply universal quantification in some fashion when they make the exhaustive and underexhaustive pairing errors. None of these accounts explains all of children's behaviors when they make these errors. Furthermore, they all claim that a child either applies universal quantification when it is infelicitous to do so or creates ungrammatical or inappropriate syntactic or semantic representations for universally quantified sentences. The Weak Quantifier Hypothesis suggests, counter to what Inhelder & Piaget (1964) originally claimed, that children do not misapply universal quantification to other constituents in a sentence, although they may not necessarily have the same semantic representations of universally quantified sentences as adults do. Consequently, existing proposals about the kinds of representations and verification procedures that underlie children's errors on questions with universal quantifiers are unlikely to be correct.

One question still left open is why a child might turn to a weak quantification analysis in the first place. One interesting possibility might be that children's understanding of linguistic quantification is based on their developing ability to represent numerical quantities and relations among these quantities. Spelke & Tsivkin (ch. 3 of this volume) speculate that young children may have two modular systems for representing number, which later merge to create a third system which underlies the mature verbal counting system. One preverbal system, present in both children and adults, represents exact numerosities of small sets of up to four elements (e.g. Gelman 1982; Wynn 1990; Gallistel & Gelman 1992). This system emerges early and provides the basis for simple arithmetic operations like subtraction and addition (Wynn 1992). The second preverbal system provides children with the means to represent larger numbers. This system provides inaccurate and unstable representations of larger numbers and specifies no limit on set size; it may also underlie the adult understanding of the relative sizes of larger sets. Spelke & Tsivkin suggest that a child may simultaneously be able to represent an array of two objects, for example, as an exact number by the small-number system but independently as an indeterminate number between *one* and *three* by the large-number system. Larger numerosities like *seven* may be unspecifiable by the small number system and be only approximately represented by the large-number system as somewhere between *six* and *eight*.

The principles underlying the mature verbal counting system may be provided by the preverbal number systems (Gallistel & Gelman 1992). In particular, Spelke & Tsivkin suggest that the verbal counting system may consist of a conjunction of the two modular preverbal systems. Like the small-number system it may include the ability both to represent small numbers and to support basic arithmetic operations, but like the large-number system it has no upper bound on set size and allows numerical comparisons across two sets. The language system may help children to learn the mature verbal system because it represents both small and large numerals in identical syntactic contexts.

This approach raises interesting possibilities regarding child and adult representations of linguistic quantification. In principle, any of the three number systems envisaged by Spelke & Tsivkin may support or be an integral part of the adult representation of the linguistic quantification system. In particular, the small-number system may be taken to underlie the adult representation of numerals describing small sets while the large-number system supports the adult representation of the vague weak quantifiers under their cardinal interpretations.

Children's preverbal number systems may initially serve as the basis for their understanding of both strong and weak quantification. Like adults, children may represent numerals describing small sets using the small-number system. But, unlike adults, children may initially represent both vague weak quantifiers and strong quantifiers in terms of the large-number system, perhaps because these quantifiers have no overt numerical specification. This would predict that children have some understanding that speakers use a universal quantifier when they intend to quantify an entire potentially large set, but that they will use a numerical strategy to verify a universally quantified sentence. It might also suggest that children find universal quantifiers inappropriate or infelicitous as descriptions of small sets whose cardinality can be grasped by the small-number system. This may explain why children often replace universal quantifiers with numerals on exhaustive pairing tasks with many-to-one contexts like that in figure 12.1b.

A second open question concerns how a child might learn the strong quantification system of her language. Importantly, the Weak Quantification Hypothesis does not predict that a child has to learn to how to use presuppositional quantification, nor does it claim that presuppositional interpretations are generally unavailable to a child. However, it does suggest that, to avoid making the (under)exhaustive pairing error, a child must learn that some quantifiers are "essentially" or "inherently" strong (Partee 1995), in the sense that they *require* presuppositional interpretations on each occasion of use, even under apparent conditions of presupposition failure.

The data suggest that a child may not represent a presupposed set or compare a presupposed and an actual set without an explicit clue from context. This hypothesis is consistent with the results of other studies which suggest that children may not use a particular strategy intended by the adult experimenter unless they are explicitly directed to do so (e.g. Flavell 1970; Sophian, Wood, & Vong 1995). For example, Sophian *et al.* reported that children aged three to five are much more likely to use the cardinality of one set to make numerical inferences about another set if they are directed to count the first set. The same kind of explicit direction may be needed for a child to represent a presupposed domain of quantification or to compare two sets, as required by a strong quantification analysis. A child will, presumably, come to distinguish between different kinds of quantifiers as she becomes more acquainted with using and interpreting quantified statements under various discourse conditions.

NOTES

1 Normal adults do not make errors on tasks like those in figures 12.1a and b and 12.2. However, exhaustive pairing errors have recently been reported for agrammatic aphasic adults on tasks similar to those in figures 12.1a and b (Avrutin and Philip 1998). Moreover, there is an obvious connection between (under)exhaustive pairing errors and the well-known "conversion error" reported in numerous studies of syllogistic reasoning by adults (e.g. Chapman & Chapman 1959; Revlis 1975; Revlin & Leirer 1980; Johnson-Laird 1983; Byrne

& Johnson-Laird 1993). Unfortunately, space prohibits a detailed discussion of these issues.

2 There is a massive literature on children's performance on other related Piagetian set-inclusion tasks in which a child is asked comparative questions like *Are there more apples or more fruit*? In this chapter, I restrict the discussion to children's behavior on the exhaustive pairing and underexhaustive pairing tasks.

3 Other results have been excluded because of significantly different error rates across experiments. For example, Philip (1995) reports a low exhaustive pairing error rate if the question includes a complex predicate nominal, e.g. *Is every boy an elephant-rider?*, whereas Crain *et al.* (1996) report a high error rate on similar questions, e.g. *Is every duck a skateboard-rider?*, even though the objects are displayed in a virtually identical manner. Further research is needed to determine the source(s) of these differences.

The percentage of children who responded like adults varies across experiments. Overall, about 12% of Philip's (1995) subjects gave adultlike responses across conditions and about 85% of Crain *et al.*'s (1996) subjects did. I do not discuss these children in this chapter.

4 Brinkmann *et al.* (1996) replicated the reduced error rate in a similar study with Dutch and German children. In this study, children were told stories illustrated with three pictures, the last of which resembles the exhaustive pairing task context in figure 12.1a. The rate of exhaustive pairing errors was about 23%, significantly less than in other studies, as well as less than when these authors tested the same children with the regular exhaustive pairing task.

5 Wason (1965) originally used the idea of plausible denial to explain response latencies in negation experiments. His notion is captured best, perhaps, by the following passage: "the ease or difficulty involved in denying a property of a class is a function of the formal characteristics of the contrast class of which the property is, explicitly or implicitly, predicated. The more this contrast class is perceived, or coded as subsidiary to the class of interest, the more readily can its property be abstracted and negated with respect to the class of interest" (1965:9).

6 The claims of Freeman *et al.* and Crain *et al.* are quite similar. Both claims assume that adult speakers (and older children) appeal to real-world knowledge to recover the expected interpretation of universally quantified questions in implausible contexts. Both claim that children regard contexts like those in figure 12.1a and Condition 1 in table 12.1 as plausible for a numerical analysis of a universally quantified sentence, and appeal to the object set to set the boundary on the intended domain of quantification. One difference is that while Freeman *et al.* propose that children use their inferences about the discourse topic in their procedure for determining the intended domain of quantification, Crain *et al.* propose that children don't worry about the intended domain of quantification but instead focus on how to accommodate the presence of the extra object in context.

7 In restricting the discussion to prototypical members, I avoid a number of well-known but poorly understood ambiguities among the class of weak quantifiers, some of which I mention below.

8 Another problem with the claim that universal quantifiers can receive a "fuzzy"

interpretation is that it is based on tasks involving extremely large numbers, or generalizations about extremely large sets. Newstead & Griggs (1984) asked subjects to rate the appropriateness of quantified statements with respect to nine different census statistics for a country with a population of 110,935 persons. For example, subjects were told that 34,873 people are under age 5 and 76,062 are over 5 and then asked if all, some, or no inhabitants are under 5. Each statistic compared different percentages of the total number from 50–50 to 100–0. Nearly half of the subjects (43%) rated statements with *all* as totally inappropriate even if only one exception was mentioned. The remaining subjects rated statements with *all* as only moderately appropriate when one or two exceptions were mentioned. In stark contrast, subjects rated statements with the weak quantifier *some* as highly appropriate if they mentioned between 5% and 70% of the total number. This is hardly evidence for a fuzzy interpretation of *all*. Nor does it seem likely that the same subjects would allow any exceptions for statements with *all* if the task were run with small-numbered sets.

9 Another apparent problem is that the right-hand sentence in (8) is a logical tautology – or true in every situation and therefore uninformative. What could a speaker gain by making such an inference? It can be shown that this is not a real problem. Unfortunately, my argument crucially refers to the difference between presuppositional and cardinal quantification, two notions I describe below. Therefore, I postpone a discussion of this point to note 10.

10 We can now return to the problem mentioned in note 9. The problem was that the right-hand sentence in the biconditional inference (8) is tautological and therefore uninformative. Hence, it is unclear what a speaker, even a child, might gain by making this inference. However, the sentence *Every boy who is riding an elephant is riding an elephant* is guaranteed to be tautological only when the universal quantifier is interpreted as strong. It need not be so when it is interpreted as weak, which is how I claim that children interpret it.

To understand this, notice that universal quantifiers, like all strong quantifiers, presuppose the domain of quantification they apply to. This means that the interpretation of the sentence *Every boy who is riding an elephant is riding an elephant* involves presupposing a set of elephant-riding boys and then asserting that the predicate holds of every boy in this set. What makes this sentence tautological is the fact that it asserts that a set which we have already presupposed to have a certain property has just this property. This will always be logically true, even if there are no elephant-riding boys around. If we replace *every* with the weak quantifier *many* on its cardinal interpretation, the diagnostic sentence is no longer tautological. In this case, *Many boys who are riding an elephant are riding an elephant* simply asserts that the number of boys who are riding an elephant counts as many. The truth of this statement is contingent on context and the perspectives of speaker and hearer. If speaker and hearer do not agree that the number of elephant-riding boys under discussion has a value within the range of "many," then the sentence can be false.

The WQH claims that children interpret universal quantifiers as weak quantifiers. This means that they can analyze universal quantifiers using cardinal interpretations. As I have just shown, these do not result in tautological statements when cast as in (8).

11 One interesting question I will not pursue in this chapter is whether children actu-

ally assign numerical values to strong quantifiers. One might expect that a child will assign a different range of numerical values to *every* than to *most*, just as speakers assign different ranges of numerical values to vague weak quantifiers like *some* and *many*. I leave this topic for further research. Another question is how weak presuppositional quantification differs from strong quantification, since both require the representation and comparison of two sets. This issue is complicated by the fact that the class of weak partitives – the prototypical example of weak presuppositional quantification – is heterogeneous both within and across languages. Unlike partitives with vague weak quantifiers (e.g. *many of the*), partitives with numerals like *three of the* are intersective (Partee 1988). And, in contrast to English, Dutch weak quantifiers like *enkele* 'some' can occur in *there*-existential sentences with partitive interpretations if the quantifier is stressed, e.g. *Er zijn ENKELE taalkundigen in de kroeg* 'There are SOME [partitive] linguists in the pub.'

Despite these complications, the interpretation of weak presuppositional quantifiers, like weak quantifiers more generally and unlike strong quantifiers, is clearly affected by pragmatic and contextual information (Moxey & Sanford 1993). Whether *many* is interpreted as presuppositional or cardinal, the number that counts as "many" will still be highly determined by contextual and pragmatic factors. As I showed earlier, the interpretation of universal quantifiers in particular does not exhibit this property. Weak presuppositional and strong quantifiers can also sometimes be distinguished by syntactic distribution. For example, although weak quantifiers may receive a partitive interpretation in *there* existential sentences in Dutch, strong determiners cannot occur in these sentences, e.g. **Er zijn de alle/de meeste taalkundigen in de kroeg* 'There are all/most linguists in the pub' (de Hoop 1990).

The analysis in the text also has interesting ramifications for theories of syntactic development. Some theories argue that cardinal quantifiers are represented syntactically as number phrases or complex noun phrases, while presuppositional quantifiers require an added layer of functional structure, such as a determiner phrase (e.g. Valois 1991). Other theories argue that noun phrases with cardinal quantifiers are interpreted as verb phrase constituents while noun phrases with presuppositional quantifiers are interpreted as constituents of a more complex inflectional phrase (Diesing 1992). Under either approach, children's difficulty with establishing presuppositional quantificational interpretations may be linked to their ability to represent functional projections in the syntax. This is consistent with the standard assumption in developmental syntactic research that the syntax of functional projections is more difficult for children than the syntax of lexical projections.

REFERENCES

Avrutin, S., & W. Philip. 1998. Quantification in agrammatic aphasia. In U. Sauerland & O. Percus (eds.). The interpretive tract: working papers in syntax and semantics. *MIT Working Papers in Linguistics*, 25, 63–72.

Barwise, J., & R. Cooper. 1981. Generalized quantifiers and natural language. *Linguistics and Philosophy* 4: 159–219.

Brinkmann, U., K. F. Drozd, & I. Krämer. 1996. Physical individuation as a prerequisite for children's symmetrical interpretations. In A. Stringfellow,

D. Cahana-Amitay, E. Hughes, & A. Zukowski (eds.), *Proceedings of the 20th Annual Boston University Conference on Language Development.* Somerville, MA: Cascadilla Press, 99–110.

Brooks, P. J., & M. D. S. Braine. 1996. What do children know about the universal quantifiers "all" and "each"? *Cognition* 60: 235–268.

Bucci, W. 1978a. The interpretation of universal affirmative propositions. *Cognition* 60: 55–77.

Byrne, R. M. J., & P. N. Johnson-Laird. 1993. *Deduction.* Hillsdale, NJ: Lawrence Erlbaum.

Chapman, L. J., & J. P. Chapman. 1959. Atmosphere effect reexamined. *Journal of Experimental Psychology* 58: 220–226.

Crain, S., R. Thornton, C. Boster, L. Conway, D. Lillo-Martin, & E. Woodams. 1996. Quantification without qualification. *Language Acquisition* 5: 83–153.

de Hoop, H. 1990. Case configuration and noun phrase interpretation. Unpublished doctoral dissertation, University of Groningen, The Netherlands.

Diesing, M. 1992. *Indefinites.* Cambridge, MA: MIT Press.

Donaldson, M., & P. Lloyd. 1974. Sentences and situations: children's judgements of match and mismatch. In F. Bresson (ed.), *Current problems in psycholinguistics.* Paris: Centre National de la Recherche Scientifique, 73–86.

Donaldson, M., & J. McGarrigle. 1973. Some clues to the nature of semantic development. *Journal of Child Language* 1: 185–194.

Drozd, K. F. 1995. On the sources of children's misinterpretations of quantified sentences. In W. Philip & F. Wijnen (eds.), *Amsterdam series in child language development.* Amsterdam: University of Amsterdam Department of General Linguistics, 173–213.

1996. Quantifier interpretation errors as errors of distributive scope. In A. Stringfellow, D. Cahana-Amitay, E. Hughes, & A. Zukowski (eds.), *Proceedings of the 20th Annual Boston Conference on Language Development.* Somerville, MA: Cascadilla Press, 177–188.

Drozd, K. F., I. Krämer, & E. van Loosbroek. 1996. Distributive scope as the source of children's quantifier errors. Unpublished ms., Max Planck Institute for Psycholinguistics, Nijmegen, The Netherlands.

Drozd, K. F., & E. van Loosbroek. 1998. Presuppositional quantification, Plausible Dissent, and role of pragmatic information in children's grammar of quantification. Unpublished ms., Max Planck Institute for Psycholinguistics, Nijmegen, The Netherlands.

Drozd, K. F., & J. Weissenborn. 1996. The acquisition of universal quantification in Dutch and German: a comparative study. Paper presented at the Acquisition of Scope Workshop, DGFS Conference, Freiburg, Germany.

Flavell, J. H. 1970. Developmental studies of mediated memory. In H. W. Reese & L. P. Lipsitt (eds.), *Advances in child development and behavior*, vol. 5. New York: Academic Press, 181–211.

Freeman, N. H.. 1985. Reasonable errors in basic reasoning. *Educational Psychology* 5: 239–249.

Freeman, N. H., & K. Schreiner. 1988. Complementary error patterns in collective and individuating judgements: their semantic basis in 6-year-olds. *British Journal of Developmental Psychology* 6: 341–350.

Freeman, N. H., C. G. Sinha, & J. A. Stedmon. 1982. All the cars – which cars? From word meaning to discourse analysis. In M. Beveridge (eds.), *Children thinking through language*. London: Edward Arnold, 52–74.

Gallistel, C. R., & R. Gelman. 1992. Preverbal and verbal counting and computation. *Cognition* 44: 43–74.

Gelman, R. 1982. Basic numerical abilities. In R. J. Sternberg (ed.), *Advances in the psychology of human intelligence*, vol. 1. Hillsdale, NJ: Lawrence Erlbaum, 181–205.

Hörmann, H. 1983. The calculating listener or how many are einige, mehrere, and ein paar (some, several, and a few)? In R. Bäurle, C. Schwarze, & A. von Stechow (eds.), *Meaning, use, and interpretation.* Berlin: Walter de Gruyter, 221–234.

Inhelder, B., & J. Piaget. 1964. *The early growth of logic in the child.* London: Routledge & Kegan Paul.

Johnson-Laird, P. N. 1983. *Mental models*. New York: Cambridge University Press.

Kamp, H., & U. Reyle. 1993. *From discourse to logic*. Dordrecht: Kluwer.

Keenan, E. L. 1987. A semantic definition of "Indefinite NP." In E. J. Reuland & A. G. B. ter Meulen (eds.), *The representation of indefiniteness.* Cambridge, MA: MIT Press, 286–317.

Keenan, E. L., & J. Stavi. 1986. A semantic characterization of natural language determiners. *Linguistics and Philosophy* 9: 253–326.

Milsark, G. 1977. Toward an explanation of certain peculiarities of the existential construction in English. *Linguistic Analysis* 3: 1–29.

Moxey, L. M., & A. J. Sanford. 1993. *Communicating quantities: a psychological perspective.* Hillsdale, NJ: Lawrence Erlbaum.

Newstead, S. E., & R. A. Griggs. 1984. Fuzzy quantifiers as an explanation of set inclusion performance. *Psychological Research* 46: 377–388.

Partee, B. H. 1988. Many quantifiers. In J. Powers & K. de Jong (eds.), *Proceedings of the 5th ESCOL*. Columbus: The Ohio State University.

1995. Quantificational structures and compositionality. In E. Bach, E. Jelinek, A. Kratzer, & B. H. Partee (eds.), *Quantification in natural languages*. Dordrecht: Kluwer, 541–602.

Philip, W. 1995. *Event quantification in the acquisition of universal quantification.* Amherst: GLSA Publications.

1996. The event quantificational account of symmetrical interpretation and a denial of implausible infelicity. In A. Stringfellow, D. Cahana-Amitay, E. Hughes, & A. Zukowski (eds.), *Proceedings of the 20th Annual Boston Conference on Language Development*. Somerville, MA: Cascadilla Press, 564–575.

Philip, W., & S. Aurelio. 1991. Quantifier spreading: pilot study of preschoolers' "every." In T. Maxwell & B. Plunkett (eds.), *University of Massachusetts Occasional Papers: Special Edition: Papers in the acquisition of WH.* Amherst, MA: GSLA Publications, 267–282.

Philip, W., & P. Coopmans. 1995. Symmetrical interpretation and scope ambiguity in the acquisition of universal quantification in Dutch and English. Unpublished ms., Research Institute for Language and Speech, Utrecht University, Utrecht, The Netherlands.

Reinhart, T. 1987. Specifier and operator binding. In E. J. Reuland & A. G. B. ter Meulen (eds.), *The representation of indefiniteness*. Cambridge, MA: MIT Press, 130–167.

1995. Interface strategies. OTS Working Papers, Research Institute for Language and Speech, Utrecht University, Utrecht, The Netherlands.

Revlin, R., & V. O. Leirer. 1980. Understanding quantified categorical expressions. *Memory and Cognition* 8: 447–458.

Revlis, R. 1975. Two models of syllogistic reasoning: feature selection and conversion. *Journal of Verbal Learning and Verbal Behavior* 14: 180–195.

Roeper T., & J. de Villiers. 1993. The emergence of bound variable structures. In E. Reuland & W. Abraham (eds.), *Knowledge and language*, vol. 1. Dordrecht: Kluwer, 105–140.

Shipley, E. F., & B. Shepperson. 1990. Countable entities: developmental changes. *Cognition* 34: 109–111.

Smith, C. L. 1980. Quantifiers and question answering in young children. *Journal of Experimental Child Psychology* 30: 191–205.

Sophian, C., A. M. Wood, & K. I. Vong. 1995. Making numbers count: the early development of numerical inferences. *Developmental Psychology* 31: 263–273.

Stedmon, J. A., & N. H. Freeman. 1985. When reference fails: analyses of the use and misuse of quantified expressions to make identifying reference. In J. Allwood & E. Hjelmquist (eds.), *Foregrounding background*. Nora, Sweden: Bokförlaget Nya Doxa, 185–208.

Takahashi, M. 1991. Children's interpretation of sentences containing *every*. In T. Maxfield & B. Plunkett (eds.), *University of Massachusetts Occasional Papers: Special Edition: Papers in the acquisition of WH*. Amherst: GLSA Publications, 303–329.

Valois, D. 1991. The internal structure of DP. Unpublished doctoral dissertation, University of California at Los Angeles.

Wason, P. C. 1965. The contexts of plausible denial. *Journal of Verbal Learning and Verbal Behavior* 4: 7–11.

Westerståhl, D. 1985. Logical constants in quantifier languages. *Linguistics and Philosophy* 8: 387–413.

Wynn, K. 1990. Children's understanding of counting. *Cognition* 36: 155–193.

Part 4

Relational concepts in form–function mapping

13 Emergent categories in first language acquisition

Eve V. Clark

Stanford University

Children start in on language in much the same way the world over. Their first fifty words tend to be very similar in content, as are their first word combinations (Slobin 1970; E. V. Clark 1979). But as children learn more about the specific language they are acquiring, the courses they follow diverge more and more (see Slobin 1985b, 1992). Early similarities have generally been attributed to children's reliance on conceptual categories such as agent, action, place, and so on, to provide the basis for meanings to be mapped onto their linguistic forms. Postulating a common cognitive basis for children beginning to use language can provide only part of the story: children also have to discover how their particular language encodes different notions and distinctions, and which of these distinctions have been grammaticalized. This they can only do by attending to the language adults address to them. Acquisition, then, must be a product of both cognitive and social influences.

On the cognitive side, investigators have assumed that all children start with some general, salient, conceptual categories; and that they search first for ways to convey these categories when they begin to attach meanings to words. Such categories are universal and should therefore surface in all early language use. Cognitive development, under this view, provides an opening wedge for getting in to language (Slobin 1985a). On the social side, caretakers (adults or older siblings) talk to young children and thereby provide the linguistic categories and grammatical distinctions pertinent to each language. Under this view, children's linguistic categories are shaped from the start by child-directed speech (Bowerman 1985b, 1989, 1996). Do universal conceptual categories play a role when children's earliest meanings are shaped by what they hear? Are all the meanings they express given by the input, the language of their community, or is there a general (universal) set of conceptual categories for which children will seek expression, whether or not they are all "given" in the surrounding language? Certain phenomena in early acquisition suggest that some conceptual categories may surface in children's speech even when they are not supported by the ambient language. These phenomena offer evidence for a set of general conceptual categories underlying language.

During acquisition, children sometimes try to express notions that do not receive any conventional expression in the language they are learning. In English, for instance, they may make use of different first-person pronoun forms (*I* and *me*, say) to express degree of agency, with one pronoun form used to express full control over an action contrasted with another used for minimal or no control. Or they may enlist different adjectival forms (formed with *-y* vs. *-ed*, for example) to contrast inherent properties with temporary ones. Or they may extend an inflection (the plural *-s*, say) to mark number agreement on adjectives. Degree of agency, inherence of properties, and agreement appear in a large number of the world's languages, but not in all; in particular, not in English. So children who try to express these notions in the course of acquiring English appear to be expressing conceptual distinctions that have not been grammaticalized and for which there are no conventional expressions in the input. Children may attempt to express such notions for as little as a couple of weeks, or for as long as several months. It is the expression of conceptual categories like these, that surface fleetingly in children's speech and then vanish again or evolve into something else, that constitute what I call *emergent categories*. They surface alongside more robust categories that also surface early in children's speech.

Robust categories are conceptual categories that do receive conventional expression in English, so once children have identified the relevant forms for their expression, they can continue to use them. These might include number (singular vs. plural marking on nouns and verbs), person marking (on verbs), or the expression of the notion of causative, lexical or periphrastic (also on verbs). These are all categories that receive conventional linguistic expression in English, that appear fairly early and that remain stable in children's language. Once the conventional forms have been acquired for a robust category, children do not have to make any drastic revisions in their analysis of the meaning being expressed. Robust categories are identified as such precisely because they appear early and are stable, and because children master their conventional expression, at least in part, relatively quickly. In short, robust categories in a language are those offered to children from the start and for which children readily identify the relevant conceptual categories as candidate meanings to map onto the relevant linguistic forms.

Emergent and robust categories together, within any one language, make up the set of categories for which children try to find linguistic expression early on in acquisition. Across languages, some categories turn out to be grammaticalized in language after language; others are grammaticalized in some languages, but not in others. But all of them can be given expression either because they have come to be grammaticalized and are therefore expressed, for instance, in noun or verb morphology, or because they can be conveyed in whatever expressions are available for encoding a specific conceptual domain (for instance, verbs for different kinds of motion in space). This suggests that such conceptual categories are privileged in that they reflect distinctions that are generally derivable from one or both of two main sources: the processing mechanisms that allow children to set up perceptual and conceptual categories in the first place and the language adults address to young children.

Emergent categories, then, will be just those categories that happen not to be given conventional expression *in a particular language*, even though they are accessible at the conceptual level. When children find no support for their expression in the surrounding language, they should abandon their emergent categories, re-analyze them as belonging together with some other category, or adapt them in some other way to fit whatever conventional forms are available for their (partial) expression. What is a robust category for the speakers of one language, therefore, may surface as an emergent category for the speakers of another, and vice versa. Emergent categories complement what we know from early robust categories in specific languages, and so offer us further insight into those categories that appear to be the most salient to young children for perceptual, conceptual, and processing reasons, and hence are commonly attested in the early stages of language acquisition.

I suggest that identifying children's emergent categories in specific languages will further our knowledge of which conceptual distinctions are likely to surface early on across languages. Emergent categories reveal part of the discovery process in acquisition and so can add to our knowledge in two ways: they offer further information about what should be counted as universal in language, and they add to what we know about children's analyses of the language people address to them. Emergent categories are one reflection of these factors in acquisition – on the one hand, the salience or universality of certain conceptual categories, and on the other, children's ability to link their analysis of linguistic forms to specific conceptual categories and domains.

In this chapter, I define "emergent category" and relate this notion to earlier claims about universals and a universal stock of conceptual categories underlying the grammatical categories found in the languages of the world. I then examine several candidate emergent categories or potential emergent categories that have been attested in the speech of children learning English. I conclude with some discussion of the light that emergent categories may cast on the process of acquisition.

1 Emergent categories, robust categories, and universals

Emergent categories reflect semantic conflations and distinctions of various sorts that seem to be made by children even when the language they are learning does not support them, or does so only partially, in its form classes, primary lexicalizations, or morphology. Where emergent categories are not supported in the adult language, they surface as short-lived categories, appearing only temporarily, often starting in the second year, when children assign a non-conventional meaning to whichever form or forms they have chosen to express such a category. As children analyze the language addressed to them in more detail, they may have to abandon their initial analysis and, with it, the emergent category; or they may conflate their emergent category with another; or they may split it into several smaller categories as they come to identify the conventional adult meanings of expressions available in the target language. Robust categories are categories that, for a specific language, are given consistent expression in syntactic form classes (e.g. nouns, verbs, adjectives), morphology, and the lexicon. They are supported, therefore, in the speech addressed to children, and this makes their linguistic realization more accessible in acquisition. Together, emergent and robust categories for any one language may form a continuum, with robust categories being given strong support in the form of conventional expressions for the relevant notions in the adult language, and with emergent categories receiving little or no support in the form of conventional linguistic expressions.

For children trying to find some way of talking about such categories, the general task appears to be the following: they start by attending to conceptual categories derived from their perceptual and conceptual experience. Around age 1;0, they begin looking for ways to communicate about some of these categories. From sometime in their first year, they also begin to engage in analysis and identification of linguistic categories in the speech addressed to them within the language community. This mapping of meanings and forms consists of identifying certain conceptual categories with possible meanings, and then linking these meanings to available linguistic forms. This account, though, is deceptively simple because, in fact, no language offers anything like a direct map of conceptual categories. As Slobin (1979:6) pointed out: "Language evokes ideas; it does not represent them. Linguistic expression is thus not a straightforward map of consciousness or thought. It is a highly selective and conventionally schematic map." Children have to learn just what the conventions are for expressing a particular notion (conceptual category) in a language, and, in learning the conventions, they learn which conceptual distinctions are represented systematically in that language.

Linguistic distinctions have to be discovered: they are not given *a priori*. Precisely because of this, children may start out looking for ways to express conceptual categories that do not necessarily receive linguistic expression in the target language. Their initial analysis of certain linguistic expressions may not match the adult meanings. Such mismatches may show up as emergent categories: systematic uses of linguistic expressions to mark conceptual distinctions that are not represented in adult linguistic usage. But since children are also very attentive to adult usage, which offers them the "highly selective and conventionally schematic map" of each domain for that particular language, they will eventually come to reanalyze the domain in question. In short, universal categories are filtered through the conventional schematic maps that link conceptual to linguistic categories.

Universals of language are generally assumed to be universals because they reflect a common origin in human perception, cognition, and processing capacities. Most universals are statistical in nature: they capture general tendencies and consistent patterns found across a large number of unrelated languages. This is consistent with the position that there is a continuum from robust to emergent categories for children acquiring a first language. The robust categories within any one target language will not necessarily be robust in every language, so what is robust in one language may surface as emergent in another. At the same time, within a particular language, the continuum from robust to emergent as a whole can offer evidence for a general set of universal categories across languages. The sum of emergent and robust categories should coincide across languages, and thereby allow us to establish in more detail what to count as universal. What actually surfaces as robust vs. emergent in a particular language will depend on how the grammatical and lexical systems of that language have evolved over time, and hence the particular ways in which adult speech shapes children's assumptions about how to link their linguistic and nonlinguistic categories.

Earlier research on a universal cognitive basis for language was influenced by a number of considerations. Some linguists argued for a set of universal semantic primitives, packaged with different patterns of conflation, in each language (e.g. Postal 1966; Bierwisch 1970). This allowed one to argue for a universal underlying semantics, even though there were large differences from one language to the next in how available forms and expressions divided up each conceptual domain. Other linguists focused on how particular grammatical distinctions were expressed, and argued that greater complexity of thought was reflected in added morphemes (e.g. Greenberg 1966). And still others focused on correlations among structures within languages and language families; they argued that how humans process linguistic information led to the consistent constructional patterns and clause orders observable in languages (e.g. Greenberg 1963; Lehmann 1972, 1973; Vennemann 1974; Keenan 1976). More recently, some of the proposals about a universal underlying conceptual structure have been re-examined, with emphasis, on the one hand, on the mental spaces that underlie much of linguistic organization (e.g. Fauconnier 1985), and, on the other, on the fundamental event-types that we try to represent in language (e.g. Jackendoff 1983; Talmy 1985; Langacker 1991). As Langacker (1991) pointed out, there are certain categories in experience that stand out against each other and appear particularly salient. He suggested that there were certain conceptual archetypes that underlie a basic set of linguistic constructs. Because these conceptual archetypes are salient, speakers of all languages will tend to look for some way to express them, and these conceptual categories may therefore "surface" as the prototypes of basic linguistic constructs.[1]

Some of these categories, salient as they are, do not receive direct linguistic expression in every language. Or they are not mapped in a unitary or coherent fashion. That is, even among the languages that do express these concepts, some may map them rather more consistently than others, in the sense that they opt for just one or a small number of conventional expressions to convey each distinction in a different syntactic guise; other languages may split up a particular concept over a number of different types of linguistic expression; and still others may group two or more distinctions together, and so offer no overt linguistic expression for certain of these distinctions, in either the lexicon or the grammatical system of the language. And in some languages, certain conceptual distinctions may receive no overt linguistic expression at all.

Children, however, often impose more order in their early attempts at mapping conceptual categories than their language actually licenses. When they do, we see evidence for emergent categories that are either not represented in the target language at all, or are not represented with such a straightforward or consistent mapping in the target language. Children's initial mappings may rely on underlying distinctions that are disguised to some degree by the range of conventional expressions for that conceptual category in the target language. These initial mappings offer critical information about the kinds of distinctions that they are trying to find expression for, and that therefore form part of a universal conceptual basis for human languages (e.g. H. H. Clark & Clark 1978). To discover which conceptual universals underlie language, therefore, we need to look at what children *do* and *don't* try to map onto linguistic expressions during the early stages of acquisition. My focus here is on candidate emergent categories, attempted mappings that are novel to a particular language, and hence on consistent early mappings that diverge from adult conventions of use.

Candidate universal categories are not necessarily readily identified in advance by the observer. In many languages, where there are conventional expressions that exactly map the relevant distinctions, such categories surface as robust. But in languages where there is no ready-made conventional mapping for some of the same categories, children's early attempts at a mapping *are* discernible, even if transitory. And in languages where the relevant distinctions are split up among several different types of expression, the nature of the pertinent category may be less obvious to adult speakers because of the range of expressions used, than to the young child who has taken a simpler approach to trying to express that category. In short, emergent categories stand out when children try to find expression for them in languages that have no conventional mapping for them, or that express them through a variety of different conventional expressions: "Emergent categories in acquisition tell us about the initial concepts children build on as they select grammatical devices to encode their meanings. In particular, emergent categories should offer information about universal conceptual categories that underlie languages, even though they are frequently obscured by language-specific conventions of expression" (E. V. Clark & Carpenter 1989a:24).

If emergent categories belong with other categories to which children try to assign linguistic expression early, this would explain why children attempt to give them some consistent linguistic expression even when their efforts receive little or no support from the speech around them. If we can identify such emergent categories, alongside the robust categories for particular languages, we will have made a start on identifying a universal set of conceptual categories that are generally given some linguistic form across languages. This would also allow us to reconcile the discrepancies among the sets of robust categories from one language to the next. When robust categories are complemented by emergent categories, the set of the universal categories should, ideally, be consistent across languages.

Children's early attempts to map such categories onto consistent linguistic forms suggest that they start out with some strong assumptions about the nature of the mappings that may hold between conceptual category and linguistic expression. But to what extent can certain kinds of mapping be overridden or modified in different languages? For example, across languages, verbs typically carry information about aspect, tense, and mood – nearly always in this order, with information about aspect closest to the verb stem, then tense, then mood (Bybee 1985). But there is also some variation: the verb itself may contain aspectual information as a part of its lexical meaning; information about mood may be expressed adverbially rather than as a verbal suffix, and so on. By adding what we can glean about emergent categories to the available crosslinguistic comparisons in acquisition (e.g.

Slobin 1973, 1985b, 1992), we will be able to paint a fuller picture of the cognitive basis on which children build their first language, and also be better placed to show how cognitive and social factors *jointly* shape children's acquisition of language.

2 Some candidate emergent categories

Children acquiring English present evidence for a number of emergent categories, categories for which there is no single, consistent grammatical expression. They try to map such categories onto linguistic forms, often choosing one specific form to mark the relevant distinction. Yet since the adult language either does not mark the distinction at all, or does not mark it conventionally in that way, children later give up their initial mappings in favor of whatever conventional options are available in the linguistic community. I now turn to some candidate emergent categories, identified on the basis of observations by myself and others of data from early acquisition. These candidate emergent categories offer support to the general argument that we need to look to such emergent categories as on a continuum with categories that are robust, for it is the categories on the continuum that are well represented across languages that seem to be strong candidates, in many cases, for grammaticalization. Robust categories, of course, receive consistent encoding in the input children hear, and this too will make them salient to young children (e.g. Choi & Bowerman 1991). But because it may be hard to distinguish whether the salience of a robust category stems from its consistent encoding in the input language, from its conceptual basis, or from the combination of the two, emergent categories offer important evidence: their salience can only stem from their conceptual basis since they receive at best minimal support, and at worst no support, in the language children hear.

I begin by considering children's over-extensions in early word uses, and show how these offer evidence for a primary classificatory system of objects based on the dimensionality of shapes. The same dimensionality surfaces in linguistic systems with noun or verb classifiers. I then take up, in turn, the notion of source, as in the source or origin of motion; inherent vs. temporary properties of objects; degrees of agency on the part of the doer; and eventive attribution, where the change effected by an action is attributed to the object affected. I conclude with further comments on the significance of emergent categories.

2.1 Classifiers and object categories

Many languages, especially in South-East Asia and in Central America, rely on extensive classifier systems, used to classify objects on various dimensions. The classifiers in South-East Asian languages such as Japanese, Mandarin, and Thai are numeral classifiers. These are combined with numerals and nouns when counting individual entities (Greenberg 1975). Such classifiers are also often used on their own for anaphoric reference. Some English analogues to noun classifiers are given in (1):

(1) a. 25 *sheets/leaves* of paper
    b. 4 *strings* of beads
    c. 9 *cups* of coffee

The terms *sheet*, *leaf*, *string*, and *cup* in (1) classify the entities involved. In English, these kinds of terms are common with mass nouns like *paper*, *coffee*, or *toast*, as well as with certain plural count nouns like *beads* or *grapes*. In South-East Asian languages, where there is no plural marking on the noun, classifiers are obligatory whenever the noun occurs with a numeral, as in the expressions in (2) where *flat-thing*, *long-thing*, *round-thing*, and *long-&-flexible-thing* represent the general meanings of some common classifier types (see further Berlin 1968; Friedrich 1970; Adams & Conklin 1973; Carpenter 1986; Craig 1986; Matsumoto 1993; Brown 1994):

(2) a. 7 flat-thing rug
    b. 16 long-thing pole
    c. 3 round-thing gourd
    d. 5 long-&-flexible-thing rope

In fact, most classifier systems contain classifiers for three basic shapes: *round* (extension in three dimensions, typically with spherical contour), *long* (extension in one dimension), and *flat* (extension in two dimensions). These, it has been suggested, are primary dimensions in classifier systems, and may be combined with one or more secondary dimensions such as rigid vs. flexible ("breakability"), relative size, empty vs. full (for containers), regular vs. irregular (overall shape), and vertical vs. horizontal (usually of long entities only). In some Amerindian languages such as Navajo, classifiers are attached to the verb complex and categorize the object being talked about (designated by another root in the verb complex); these classifiers on their own in the verb, like noun classifiers, can also be used anaphorically for entities mentioned previously.

The significance of primary dimensions in classifier systems for early language acquisition becomes apparent as soon as one looks at the kinds of over-extensions found in up to 40% of the first 100 words produced by young children. Over-extensions occur when children stretch their available words to refer to a more extended range than adult usage would license; such uses appear between age 1;0 and 2;6, sometimes lasting only a day or two, at other times several weeks; and they vanish as children acquire more

Table 13.1. *Over-extension types*

SHAPE		
mooi	moon	cakes, round marks on windows, writing on windows / in books, round shapes in books, tooling on leather covers, round post-marks, letter "O"
ticktock	watch	clock, all clocks & watches, gas-meter, firehose on spool, bathroom-scale with dial
baw	ball	apples, grapes, squash, bell-clapper, anything round
kotibaiz	bars of cot	large toy abacus, toast-rack, building with columned façade
tee	stick	cane, umbrella, ruler, old-fashioned razor, board of wood, all stick-like objects
kutija	box	matchbox, drawer, bedside table
mum	horse	cow, calf, pig, moose, all four-legged animals
SIZE, TEXTURE		
em	worm	flies, ants, all small insects, heads of timothy grass
pin	pin	crumbs, caterpillars
fly	fly	specks of dirt, dust, small insects, child's own toes, bread crumbs, toad
sizo	scissors	all metal objects
bow-wow	dog	toy dog, fur-piece with animal head, other fur-pieces
p'asaka	powder	dust, ashes

Source: E. V. Clark (1976)

appropriate words for the categories in question (E. V. Clark 1973, 1983). Their significance, though, lies in how children over-extend their early words. They typically do on the basis of similarity of shape. They pick out as possible referents for a word like *ball* objects that are small and round (three-dimensional); or, for a word like *stick*, objects that are long and thin (two-dimensional); or, for words like *cotty-bars*, objects matched on more complex combinations of primary and secondary dimensions (E. V. Clark 1976). Typical over-extensions like these are illustrated in table 13.1.

Such over-extensions suggest that young children are attentive to the dimensional properties of object-types, and use this information actively, not only when learning what counts as an instance of a particular category, but also when searching for the nearest appropriate-seeming term (in the absence of the conventional adult term). The higher-level classifications thus engendered pick out categories similar to those selected by the most widely used classifiers in a large variety of languages.

The spontaneous over-extensions observed in diary studies from a wide range of languages (E. V. Clark 1973) are paralleled by over-extensions elicited from 1- and 2-year-olds (e.g. Thomson & Chapman 1977). They are also supported by the extensive data on infants' preferred bases for sorting and for matching to sample: shape consistently takes precedence over size and color (e.g. Anglin 1977; E. V. Clark 1983; Baldwin 1989). In short, categorization based on the dimensional properties of objects appears to be fundamental to conceptual organization, and hence to the mapping of that information onto linguistic expressions. Yet, although very young children clearly make use of shape in learning word meanings and in learning how to make linguistic expressions refer, this does not in itself make classifiers easier to learn. That is, using the property of being round may long precede children's acquisition of the word *round* for this property (e.g. Bowerman 1985a:379). While children's early over-extensions reflect reliance on features of shape, classifiers with shape-based meanings are used to mark conventionalized higher-level categorizations that can be imposed on sets of entities. It takes time for children to learn the meanings of such classifiers as well as their syntax and range of uses (for Thai, see Carpenter 1991, and for Japanese, Matsumoto 1985, 1987). In summary, the same conceptual categories appear to underlie both the patterns of use in early over-extensions and the uses of classifier systems grammaticalized in many South-East Asian and Amerindian languages.

2.2 *Sources*

To what extent does space and the organization of objects located or moving in space offer a model for mental organization for spatial relations and other nonspatial domains? This question has been taken up in a variety of works on language and language acquisition (e.g. Anderson 1971; H. H. Clark 1973; Gruber 1976). The basic relation is that of motion and direction relative to a starting point and an ending point. The notion of source represents the starting point: "The source . . . is a relation linking a theme to a place and a direction. The place is the origin or starting point and the direction is 'away from' that place. The place and direction may, but need not, be associated with an explicit motion" (E. V. Clark & Carpenter 1989a:3). In adult English, spatial sources are typically marked by one of three prepositions – *from*, *out of*, and *off* – depending on the dimensionality of the source entity or the region of it that is taken as the source. (*Out of* marks a container as source and *off* a surface, while *from* does not specify.)

Around age 2, many children appear to identify a general category of source and link it to use of the locative preposition *from* in English. This leads them to make use of *from* in a variety of nonconventional ways – to mark agents of actions, possessors, and standards-of-comparison, for instance, with the preposition *from*, in addition to conventional uses with place and time (E. V. Clark & Carpenter 1989a). The range of source-types and their order of appearance in young children's spontaneous speech, documented in diary data and longitudinal transcripts, are illustrated in (3):[2]

(3) a. PLACES – Where that came from? (D, 2;1,28)
b. TIMES – and when I wake up from my nap (E, 2;2)
c. *AGENTS – This fall down from me.[3] (D, 2;2,3)
d. ?NATURAL FORCES – Look at that knocked down tree from the wind. (D, 2;11,12)
e. CAUSES – I not tired from my games. (A, 8)
f. *POSSESSORS – That's a finger from him. (S, 3;0,13)
g. *COMPARISON – This ear is longer from the other ear. (W, 3;1,15)
h. *CESSATION – I can't fix it from breaking. (D, 3;3,1).

Such uses – quite common between ages 2;6 and 4;0 – suggest that the children in question have an emergent category of *source* and that they have opted for a single means to mark its members, as shown in table 13.2.

Further evidence for the emergent higher-level category of source comes from a cross-sectional study in which we asked children aged 2;5 to 6;1 to imitate and repair grammatical and ungrammatical sentences containing *from*, *with*, and *by* (E. V. Clark & Carpenter 1989b). We focused in this study on locations and agents as sources, and assumed, following Slobin & Welsh (1973), that children interpret the utterances they hear in such tasks and, in imitating or repairing them, filter them through their own current linguistic system.[4] If they indeed have an emergent category of source around age 2;0, they should initially prefer *from* for places and agents, but as they get older, they should prefer *from* for places and *by* for agents. At all ages, they should prefer *with* for instruments. (In our study of spontaneous speech, children were very consistent in using *with* for this purpose.) These predictions were born out, both for children's imitations and their repairs. The younger children retained ungrammatical *from* with agents and also used *from* in place of *by*. Older children changed ungrammatical *from* to *by* and retained grammatical *by*, for agents. And children preferred and retained *with* for instruments at all ages.

Conventionally, the category of source has been divided up in English among a variety of forms and constructions, and children have to learn the full range of conventional options shown in (4), while gradually restricting their use of *from* for their earlier higher-level category of source.[5]

(4) a. He left **from Chicago**. (PLACE)
b. They stayed **from Tuesday** till Saturday. (TIME)
c. He was called **by his friend**. (AGENCY)
d. The cup got broken **because the baby dropped it**. (CAUSE)
e. The people died **from disease**. (CAUSE)
f. That one's different **from this**. (COMPARISON)
g. She stopped them **from climbing the tree**. (CESSATION).

Table 13.2. *Some* sources *in children's speech*

AGENTS and NATURAL FORCES

D (2;2,3, looking at pieces of sandwich he'd pushed off the edge of his plate): *These fall down from me.*

J (2;2, recounting a visit to the doctor): *I took my temperature from the doctor.*

C (3;0, talking about a character in a favorite book): *He's really scared from Tommy.*

Du (5;10,5, announcing his younger sister's finger-puppet show to his Fa): *Ken! Ken! Another puppet show! From Helen!*

Je (5;11, during a chase-game at a party, to the child who'd just caught her): *I was caught from you before.*

D (2;11,12, looking at a fallen tree after a storm): *Look at that knocked down tree from the wind.*

D (4;6,9, filling in a story that his Fa was about to continue reading to him): *Daddy, the pigs have been marooned from a flood.*

Sa (5;1): *Now the rainbow is getting higher from the rain.*

CAUSE, POSSESSION, and COMPARISON

D (2;6,12, recalling what he'd done three months earlier when his Mo left him with his GrMo while she fetched his Fa): *When gran'ma 'ancy was here, you go fetch Herb. (pause) Then I cried a bit from you go get him.*

S (2;8,7, explaining why his fire-engine was stuck on the roof of his toy garage): *That's fro – that's from I put a thing on it.*

W (3;3,25, explaining how to tell mean hawks from nice hawks): *Maybe from they – hawks eat sea-shells. Some hawks eat sea-shells.*

A (3;0): *I see boats from Mommy.*

S (3;0,13, looking at a picture of some people and a horse): *That's a finger from him.*

D (3;7,5, assigning roles in a game): *You can be a mum from two babies.*

W (4;1,15, to Fa): *D'you know there's two next-door neighbors from us?*

D (2;8,15, climbing into his car-seat): *This seat is getting too small from me.*

W (3;1,15, talking about a toy rabbit): *See, this ear is longer from the other ear.*

D (3;7,1, to Mo, comparing his height to hers): *. . . and you're the tallest from me.*

Source: E. V. Clark & Carpenter (1989a)

Causes in general are expressed using constructions with *because* and comparisons in general are expressed using constructions with *than* in English. Notice that the type of cause in (4e) is limited in English to use with nouns like *hunger*, *starvation*, or terms for various diseases; that the type in (4f) appears only with the adjective *different*, and that the type in (4g) appears only with a small set of verbs such as *stop*, *prevent*, and *forbid*. The adult domain for *from*, therefore, is much more limited than the range of uses to which children first put it in order to mark source.

At the same time, notice that each of the sub-types of source children identify in their emergent category is well represented in the languages of the world, even though few or no languages rely on a single means to mark every one of the sub-types attested in (3). What this suggests is that, in their early uses of *from*, children have identified a higher-level conceptual category of source and are trying to give it clear linguistic expression (Slobin 1985a). With time, though, they learn that this conceptual category is actually a collection of sub-kinds of source, conventionally expressed with different linguistic forms in the target language. These forms in turn may at times conceal or obscure the higher-level conceptual category (E. V. Clark & Carpenter 1989a, b).

2.3 *Inherent vs. temporary properties*

Some properties of objects are inherent and cannot normally be changed; they represent permanent characteristics (e.g. height, eye-color in humans; two- vs. four-leggedness in birds vs. mammals). Other properties are temporary, the consequence of some action or event (e.g. getting wet from rain; being tired, hungry, or cross; getting bruised or dirty). This general distinction between inherent or permanent properties and temporary or transitory ones is marked explicitly in some languages. In Spanish, for example, one use of the two copular verbs, *ser* and *estar*, captures the inherent vs. transitory nature of different properties. *Ser* is used in such utterances as *Jan is tall*, *The child's eyes are brown*, or *Eagles are large*, where the properties being predicated of each entity are inherent or permanent characteristics; while *estar* is required in utterances like *The sky was stormy this morning*, *The boy is tired*, or *The dog is outside*, where the properties predicated are temporary attributes, not inherent to the entities in question (e.g. Roldan 1974; De Mello 1979; Clements 1988). Spanish-speaking children appear to master this distinction for their uses of *ser* and *estar* with adjectives fairly early. By 3;6, they already produce the appropriate verb in an elicitation task 70% of the time. They use *ser* with adjectives for permanent characteristics (e.g. describing objects that differ in size, length, or color) and *estar* with adjectives for temporary ones (e.g. describing objects that are wet or dry, clean or dirty, whole or broken; Sera 1992).

This distinction between inherent and temporary appears to be one that children try to express even in languages that lack a specific grammaticalization for its expression. In English, for example, one child contrasted the adjectival suffix *-y* with the adjectival participle *-ed*, as in *crumby*, meaning "producing many crumbs," said of amarettini biscuits, vs. *crumbed*, meaning "[now] covered in crumbs," after he stepped on some crumbs on the floor (E. V. Clark, unpublished diary data). Some typical examples of the different adjective-types coined appear in table 13.3.

This child appeared to make consistent use of novel adjectives in *-y* where the property in question seemed characteristic of the entity. He

Table 13.3. *Inherent vs. temporary in innovative adjectives*

Inherent: adjectives in -y
D (2;6,9, talking about amarettini biscuits): *It isn't crumby?* [= full of crumbs]
D (2;6,27, seeing news on TV): *You wear gloves when it's snowy time.* [= when there's snow]
D (2;7,5, being driven home in the dark): *It's very nighty.* [= dark]
D (2;10,23, of the stone walls of a house in a ghost town): *There's a rocky house.* [= house made of rocks]
D (3;0,5, as parents parked in a parking lot): *It's a bit crowdy in here. There are lots of cars here.*

Temporary: adjectives in -ed
D (2;4,28, after watching Fa break up shredded wheat): *He was breaking them half'd . . .* [= in half]
D (2;6,7, looking at the rack in the dishwasher): *That fork is all . . . all BUTTERED.* [= covered in butter]
D (2;6,13, looking at pieces of veal Mo had just covered in flour and put on the counter): *These are floured.*
D (2;6,30, getting down from the table): *My foot is all crumbed.* [= bottom covered in crumbs]
D (2;8,9, wanting more water from the tap): *I want it a little bit fastened up. I want it to be a little bit fastened up.*

Source: E. V. Clark, unpublished diary data

appeared equally consistent in using adjectives in *-ed* in contexts where he had observed some action that resulted in acquisition of the property in question. That is, the property was a temporary one, conferred by or resulting from an action on the part of someone else. The overall pattern of use in this child's novel adjectives, when each context was analyzed, yielded the general pattern shown in table 13.4: where there was an action with an observable result, the child coined an adjective in *-ed* nearly 80% of the time; where no action was observed in relation to the pertinent property, he relied on *-y* nearly 80% of the time. Examination of these two adjectival forms in English shows that this distinction does not hold up in the conventional lexicon, and does not seem to underlie adult adjectival coinages. English, unlike Spanish, has not grammaticalized the distinction between inherent and temporary properties.

These data suggest that the distinction between inherent properties and properties conferred as the result of an action may be a fundamental one. It is sufficiently salient, in fact, for it to surface, albeit temporarily, as an emergent category in English, a language with no consistent grammaticalization of this distinction. The categories of temporary vs. permanent qualities or properties of objects are candidates for emergent categories. But a stronger determination of the status of these categories must wait for data from

Table 13.4. *Percentages of innovative adjectives with and without a prior observable action*

	-ed		*-y*	
Age	+ prior action	− prior action	+ prior action	− prior action
2;4 – 3;0	78	18	20	75
3;1 – 3;6	80	20	25	75
3;7 – 4;0	75	25	7	85

Note: where percentages do not sum to 100 for each adjective type, the remaining cases could not be categorized.

more children: so far, the proposal is based on detailed data from the diary study of one child.

2.4 *Degrees of agency*

Another candidate emergent category that appears during the acquisition of English is degree of agency. Young children appear to be sensitive early on to the extent to which people are the active doers of an action, or the more passive recipients affected by an action. In many languages, such a distinction is grammaticalized in the case system, with a contrast, for example, between nominative (for the doer) and dative case (for the recipient or undergoer) in the subject noun phrase. Modern English, having lost its case system, no longer marks this distinction for subjects.

Children learning English, however, appear to use different first person pronoun forms initially to mark degrees of agency or control, instead of using them to mark the grammatical distinction of subject vs. object. That is, instead of using *I* for first-person subjects and *me* for first-person objects in self-reference, young children (1;8 to 2;8) typically choose one pronoun form for self-reference, *me* or *my*, say, to mark actions where they are in control of the activity, and a different pronoun form (often *I*) where they have relatively little control over the activity (Budwig 1989). So where children are the ones carrying out the action, and hence in control, one hears utterances like *My cracked the eggs*, *Me jump*, *My taked it off*, or *My blew the candles out*. Where they are not in control, one hears instead utterances like *I like peas*, *I like Anna*, *I want my – the blocks*, or *I no want those* (Budwig 1989, 1995).[6] This preference for a contrast in the degree of control children express is illustrated in table 13.5, where the choices of pronoun form correlate with whether the child is in control of the action mentioned or not.

Table 13.5. *Percentage uses of* I *vs.* my

Pragmatic function	*I*	*my*
Child in control of action	19	81
Child not in control of action	63	37

Source: based on Budwig (1989:275)

Children appear to correlate verbs of one semantic type – telic actions often expressed with accomplishment verbs – with one of the pronoun forms they favor, and to use the other pronoun form with other verbs, typically verbs that are used to pick out non-telic events. But they also make use of different pronoun forms with the same verb to mark a difference in the degree of control involved: compare *My wear it* (the child in control) with *I wear it* (the child not in control). As Budwig (1989: 273) pointed out: "*I* tends to be used in utterances expressing children's internal states and intentions, utterances ranking low in agentivity. In contrast, *my* appears in clauses that often rank high in agentivity. In particular *my* appears in conjunction with highly kinetic verbs referring to telic actions." Children's early choices of pronoun forms, in other words, are not random and do not reflect some form of free variation. Rather, they offer further evidence that children distinguish event types and link them to the degree of agency (or control) the child is exercising.

In summary, at a point where children are just beginning to use pronouns for first-person reference (and are typically only using first-person pronoun forms, with no second- or third-person pronouns yet; see Deutsch *et al.*, ch. 10 of this volume), they assign different forms to mark degree of agency rather than the conventional grammaticalization of subject vs. object (*I* vs. *me*). In this instance, the emergent category will be replaced by the adult system, and the distinction children have attempted to grammaticalize will be submerged again. Yet in many languages, degree of agency is grammaticalized, often in the form of nominative vs. dative subjects.

2.5 *Eventive attribution*

In talking about events, speakers can choose constructions that avoid mention of any agent. In doing this, they may opt for an agentless passive, an impersonal, an unaccusative intransitive, a middle, or a reflexive, in order to indicate that they are talking about the object as the locus affected by the relevant action. Languages differ in which of these forms (and how many of them) are available, as well as in the exact shade of meaning conveyed by each one (Barber 1975; Berman 1979; Kemmer 1993). In general, these constructions tend to be distributed over the same cluster of semantic domains across languages, e.g. expressions of body-posture, grooming, cognition, and emotion, in addition to reciprocal and reflexive actions of various kinds (Kemmer 1993). In this, these constructions appear to carry the general meaning attributed to the middle voice in Indo-European (IE). Gonda (1975), for example, proposed that, historically, the middle was used "to indicate that something comes or happens to a person (or object), befalls him, takes place in the person of the subject so as to affect him, without any agent being mentioned, implied, or even known" (p. 49). Use of the middle in IE allowed speakers to talk about a change of state in the grammatical subject, with no regard to how the change was effected. That is, the middle allowed speakers to attribute what Gonda called "eventivity" to the object affected or changed by an action.

The eventive middle contrasts in meaning with both the active, where the agent is responsible for the change effected on an object, and the passive, where the object-affected is presented as being affected by someone's actions (even if the agent is not mentioned). The middle, though, attributes the change to the object affected by it, with no regard to any agency (see Fagan 1989). This characterization comes very close to what English-speaking children appear to be trying to do when, around the age of 2;6, they construct utterances with apparent middle forms that contrast with the corresponding active and passive forms also in their repertoires. The active counterparts of these middle constructions are transitive or causative verb forms with an agent and an object affected; early passive forms are either marked by the use of an auxiliary *be* or *get* (e.g. Budwig 1990) or by a demoted agent in a prepositional phrase (e.g. E. V. Clark & Carpenter 1989a), or both. For example, they start producing utterances like *It doesn't eat* (D 2;4,6, said of a small toy bell lying on his plate) or *This can't squeeze* (D 2;5,18, of a hard rubber toy). These uses of the verbs *eat* and *squeeze* contrast with active uses like *You can't eat it because I just ate it* (D 2;4,30) and *I'm squeezing it* (D 2;5,16, playing with a sandpie). They also appear to contrast with early uses of the passive, as in the successive use of passive and middle in *Look, look, this was broked* [of piece of paper torn from a brown bag] *and it broked from here* [touching the place] (D 2;7,1). Some typical middle forms from one child at this stage of acquisition are listed in table 13.6 (see also Bowerman 1974, 1990; Lord 1979; Berman 1982; Savasir & Gee 1982).[7]

Uses like these suggest that children may have an emergent category of middle to express eventive attribution where a change is presented as an attribute of the entity affected. However, untangling the precise set of contrasts for any one child is very complex. First, one must show that the child

Table 13.6. *Some typical middle verb uses*

D (2;4,6, at breakfast; balancing a small red bell on his spoon): *I not going to eat it. It doesn't eat. Only some food.*

D (2;5,18, holding a small toy lion made of hard rubber): *This can't squeeze.*

D (2;5,27, taking a block out of a pretend oven): *My block takes out of* [ə] *bakery.*

D (2;6,2, in the grocery store, shaking a carton of cream but hearing no noise): *Cream can't shake.*

D (2;7,0, after his Fa suggested he see how big a building he could build on his own): *I can't because it might knock down.*

D (2;8,11, as Mo was looking at some flowers in the garden): *That flower cuts.*

D (2;8,26, about his diaper which had been untaped): *Can that tape up?*

D (2;9,20, looking at the ruins of a castle): *Maybe it's a building building up.*

D (2;10,22, comparing the non-slip rubber mat in the bath to non-slip patches in the bath at home): *My one at home doesn't pick up.*

D (2;11,29, looking at a toy left out on the balcony): *How did it leave out there?*

D (3;3,15): *I poked my eye by mistake.*
Mo Is it okay?
D *No, it still pokes. It hurts.*

D (3;4,3, asked if he wanted some beans after he picked up then dropped a helping spoon): *No. I was just looking what they stirred like.*

D (3;4,25): *I went like that* (gesture of throwing toys) *and they didn't throw in.*

Source: E. V. Clark, unpublished diary data

contrasts the causative and passive forms with these emergent middle forms. Second, one must show that all the nonactive causative, nonpassive forms are consistently used to convey the eventive nature of the change in the object, with the action presented as an attribute of the object affected (Fagan 1989; Levin & Rappaport Hovav 1995). In adult English, the general meaning expressed by children's emergent eventive middles is instead conveyed by intransitive, passive, or reflexive forms, depending on the verb, in addition to middle forms. Reliance on the middle proper, as in *That shirt washes well*, is limited, largely because use of this form is restricted in various ways. First, it must normally co-occur with some form of adverb or particle qualifying the action or its outcome (e.g. *well*, *cleanly*, *down*, *outside*, etc.); second, the verb is usually in the simple present; and third, the middle is not used for talking about specific events, but rather for making generic claims and comments. Unlike conventional middle forms in English, children's emergent middles lack adverbs and appear with past as well as present tense inflections. That is, children's uses of middles are not initially restricted to the generic contexts of adult usage, but rather appear to form part of the broader emergent category of middle used for talking about eventivity – attributions of change to the objects affected, without regard to any agency.

In summary, the emergent category of middle or eventive forms suggests that children have identified this construction as a means for talking about events where the emphasis is on the attribution of the property embodied in the activity to the object affected. Middle verb forms at this point appear to contrast both with actives, where one starts with the agent responsible for the action and its effects, and with passives where one starts with the object undergoing the action (and may or may not specify who the agent was). Children acquiring English must eventually divide up this middle domain, assigning different parts of it to intransitive, agentless passives, and reflexives (Kemmer 1993). The middles that are retained must be formed from activity or accomplishment verbs and typically accompanied by adverbs or particles such as *well* or *outside* (Fagan 1989). The early construction of middle forms that do not follow the constraints placed on the middle construction in adult English suggests that, for children, this may be yet another emergent category in acquisition.

3 Conclusion

Children appear to look for consistent ways to mark certain distinctions – distinctions common in the repertoire of what is grammaticalized – across languages. In many cases, they appear to pick on a single lexical device or a single construction to express all instances of a category they have identified. This, in turn, leads to systematic errors in their usage prior to acquisition of the conventional expressions for those meanings in the target language. Where such emergent categories are mapped in a consistent way in a language, the input will offer children a straightforward route to mastery, so a particular category in some languages will result in practically errorless acquisition: this is a robust category, supported by the input children hear. In other languages, the same category may surface with extensive errors in the expressions produced by young children: this should occur, for example, where the target language subdivides that category and so spreads it over several different constructions. Or, where there is no support for that category at all in the input, it will surface via some apparently idiosyncratic distinction being drawn by the child who has co-opted some particular form to express the pertinent meaning; such uses will subside again and vanish as children come to realize that their language does not have any conventional expression for the distinction in question.

Although Slobin (ch. 14 of this volume) questions the idea that there is a fixed set of notions that get grammaticalized in closed classes across the world's languages, there is in fact a great deal of crosslinguistic research that tallies with many details of language acquisition. The interest of data on emergent categories lies in the evidence they provide in support of earlier findings. But emergent categories are a fleeting phenomenon, in part because children are so sensitive to the speech addressed to them and hence to the conventions of the language they are acquiring. As a result, such evidence has not, up to now, been appreciated for what it can add to our observations of robust categories in acquisition. The content of emergent categories in any one language, of course, may show up initially in many guises. It may be through an attempted grammaticalization that fails to match the adult system, as in the assignment of pronoun forms to express the presence or absence of control which must later be given up in favor of a different grammaticalization (subject vs. object). It may be through initial choice of a single form that must later be given up in favor of a range of different constructions and forms, as in the expression of the higher-level notion of source. Or, in some instances, the emergent category may have no consistent expression in the language, and so must be abandoned, as in the inherent vs. temporary attribution of properties in English. Still more difficult to detect would be cases where children assign a nonconventional meaning to a lexical item in order to express an emergent category.

This suggests that we need to look with more care at particular domains and at grammaticalized categories to track specific acquisitions and how they are related to the conventional expressions (lexical and constructional) favored across languages. Because emergent categories offer a further window on the general conceptual categories that underlie language and that are often grammaticalized, we should add this information to any account of what children are trying to do in the early stages of acquisition. The fact that children try to find expressions for certain categories that go unexpressed in some languages gives strong support to the view that there are notions so salient to young children that on occasion they will extend words, grammatical morphemes, and constructions for their expression in ways that are not licensed in any of the speech addressed to them.

To identify emergent categories in a language will require analyses of detailed diary data combined with cross-sectional studies of the candidate phenomena identified. It will also require careful attention to the set of contrasts relevant to a particular category that are present in children's data at each point in time. Children's language changes as they add new terms and new analyses of structure and function, so the order in which they produce particular forms and constructions, along with the contrasts made at each point in time, may be critical in discerning whether or not children have an emergent category. Detailed analyses like these will also help eliminate another possibility in some cases, the possibility that children are simply coming up with alternative (and equally salient) ways of analyzing the linguistic input they hear (e.g. Bowerman 1989, 1996). For instance, 1- and 2-year-olds talk about both location and possession from an early age. Slobin

(1985a) suggested that they start out with a higher-level category of location that includes possession (possessors are places that happen to be animate; see also E. V. Clark 1978). But Bowerman (1985b) argued that there is nothing to show that such "lumped categories" are more basic than the two narrower categories of location and possession: children could sometimes be focusing on one semantic relation, and sometimes on another. The issue is whether both categorizations are in fact available to very young children, or whether one is more basic and so acquired earlier than the other. Data on the emergent category of source, for example, suggest that the higher-level category provides the starting point, and the sub-kinds of source (and their possible linguistic expressions) are identified only later. Alternative categorizations can also result in what Bowerman (1982) has called "late errors," where children start to confuse terms that up to now they appear to have used in appropriate ways. These late errors typically involve what, up to that point, have been robust categories – forms picked up with few or no errors and used much as an adult would. In contrast, emergent categories typically involve early erroneous uses[8] and analyses that have no obvious counterparts in child-directed speech. Data from emergent categories, then, may serve to identify further the set of conceptual categories that children try to find expression for first.

Emergent categories can only be identified by correlating what children do during acquisition with the range of conventional options available, and with their patterning, across and within different languages. Only then can one see children trying to give a category linguistic expression in languages that happen not to contain a unified expression (or even any expression) for that particular conceptual distinction. But to do such analyses requires that one focus both on the range of erroneous uses in a domain and, simultaneously, on the range of conventional uses that children adopt, with few or no errors, in the same domain across languages. Errors point to possible emergent categories and allow us to identify those (emergent) categories that are so salient conceptually that children search for ways to express them, regardless of input. Systematic early errors plus early errorless acquisitions are evidence for those conceptual categories that all children bring to the task of acquiring a first language. Existing crosslinguistic generalizations based on robust categories, complemented by data from emergent categories, make it quite clear that children could indeed come to the learning task armed with prior ideas about potential grammatical categories.[9]

In summary, to study emergent categories, we need to document, day-by-day, young children's attempts at the expression of particular conceptual categories. In doing this, we also need to examine the sets of contrasts being established by individual children and the pragmatic functions these fill. Detailed scrutiny will also allow us to track the different routes children may follow in acquisition, and so account for the fact that not all children will necessarily attempt to express a specific emergent category in the same way (or even at all). What children do in acquisition always interacts with what they already know. Finally, daily observations will also allow us to find an account for what may be basic or not among alternative categorizations of a higher-level domain, and so determine whether some are basic and so stand at the entry level where children first assign linguistic expressions for them. In short, the identification and analysis of emergent categories offer insights into the role of language universals in early acquisition, a role illumined by children's own attempts to map conceptual categories that are salient to them, in early language use.

NOTES

Preparation of this chapter was supported in part by the Center for the Study of Language and Information, Stanford University. I am indebted to Kathie L. Carpenter and Dan I. Slobin for discussions of the notion of emergent category, and to Melissa Bowerman and Stephen Levinson for their helpful comments on an earlier version of this chapter.

1 "Certain recurrent and sharply differentiated aspects of our experience emerge as archetypes, which we normally use to structure our conceptions insofar as possible. Since language is a means by which we describe our experience, it is natural that such archetypes should be seized upon as the prototypical values of basic linguistic constructs" (Langacker 1991:294–295).

2 Types that would be ungrammatical for adult speakers are marked with an asterisk (*) and those often found unacceptable (perhaps depending on the dialect involved), by a question mark (?).

3 Children acquiring Dutch appear to make use of *van* 'from, of' for the same purpose in their early marking of nonsubject agents, and those acquiring Italian depend on *de*.

4 Even if children don't make much use of an expression in their spontaneous speech, it is often possible to study their systematic uses in tasks where they have to use the targeted forms. Since emergent categories may be hard to detect in data based on one hour of taping every two to three weeks, it is essential to find ways to track candidate emergent categories over time and in larger populations.

5 Some children make less consistent use of *from* for demoted agents (e.g. Bowerman 1990), but variations in preposition use probably depend on the order in which children acquire the various constructions conventionally used to mark each source-type when it appears in nonsubject position. For example, some children might initially omit all demoted agents, and later go straight to *by* to mark them. It is important to look at which forms children use at each stage, and how their overall system changes with the acquisition of new constructions. For further discussion, see E. V. Clark & Carpenter (1989a).

6 Why children tend to choose the form *me* for the expression of control is unclear. *My*, one could argue, is a natural candidate because it is also possessive, and so already carries some meaning consistent with the notion of control. The important

point, though, is that children assume there must be some contrast in meaning between such first-person pronoun pairs as *I* and *my* or *I* and *me* (E. V. Clark 1987, 1990).

7 Savasir & Gee (1982) also argue for the early emergence of the middle for eventivity in Turkish and Italian child data, as well as English. The utterance types are very similar to those noted here for children acquiring English. Their crosslinguistic observations offer additional evidence for the general salience of this category for young children.

8 The candidate cases of emergent categories documented here all seem to involve attempted expressions of particular conceptual categories between ages 2;0 and 3;0. It is possible that, as children get older, they become even more attentive to the forms of the speech around them, and so less likely to try to express a conceptual category for which there is no obvious conventional form in the language.

9 These prior ideas or conceptual categories are presumably built up as part of children's conceptual repertoire during their first year, before they start in on language. How this happens is not the issue here. If they are considered to be innate, we would need to specify just what that means: that the concepts themselves are built-in and need not develop; that the mechanisms for detecting similarity and difference in the construction of conceptual categories are part of the human endowment and so will arrive at the relevant conceptual categories given appropriate experience and exposure during development; and so on.

REFERENCES

Adams, K. L., & N. F. Conklin. 1973.Towards a theory of natural classification. In C. Corum, T. C. Smith-Stark, & A. Weiser (eds.), *Chicago Linguistic Society* 9: 1–10.

Anderson, J. M. 1971. *The grammar of case: towards a localistic theory*. Cambridge: Cambridge University Press.

Anglin, J. M. 1977. *Word, object, and conceptual development*. New York: Norton.

Baldwin, D. A. 1989. Priorities in children's expectations about object-label reference: form over color. *Child Development* 60: 1291–1306.

Barber, E. J. W. 1975. Voice beyond the passive. *Proceedings of the Berkeley Linguistics Society* 1: 16–24.

Berlin, B. 1968. *Tzeltal numeral classifiers*. The Hague: Mouton.

Berman, R. A.1979. Form and function: passives, middles, and impersonals in Modern Hebrew. *Proceedings of the Berkeley Linguistics Society* 5: 1–27.

1982. Verb-pattern alternation: the interface of morphology, syntax, and semantics in Hebrew child language. *Journal of Child Language* 9: 169–191.

Bierwisch, M. 1979. Semantics. In J. Lyons (ed.), *New horizons in linguistics*. Harmondsworth: Penguin Books, 166–184.

Bowerman, M. 1974. Learning the structure of causative verbs: a study in the relationship of cognitive, semantic, and syntactic development. *Papers and Reports on Child Language Development* 8: 142–178.

1982. Reorganizational processes in lexical and syntactic development. In E. Wanner & L. R. Gleitman (eds.), *Language acquisition: the state of the art*. Cambridge: Cambridge University Press, 319–346.

1985a. Beyond communicative adequacy: from piecemeal knowledge to an integrated system in the child's acquisition of language. In K. E. Nelson (ed.), *Children's language*, vol. 5. Hillsdale, NJ: Lawrence Erlbaum, 369–398.

1985b. What shapes children's grammars? In D. I. Slobin (ed.), *The crosslinguistic study of language acquisition*, vol. 2: *Theoretical issues.* Hillsdale, NJ: Lawrence Erlbaum, 1257–1319.

1989. Learning a semantic system: what role do cognitive predispositions play? In M. L. Rice & R. L. Schiefelbusch (eds.), *The teachability of language*. Baltimore, MD: Paul H. Brookes, 133–169.

1990. When a patient is the subject: sorting out passives, anticausatives, and middles in the acquisition of English. Paper presented at the conference on Voice, Santa Barbara, CA, March.

1996. The origins of children's spatial semantic categories: cognitive versus linguistic determinants. In J. J. Gumperz & S. C. Levinson (eds.), *Rethinking linguistic relativity*. Cambridge: Cambridge University Press, 145–176.

Brown, P. 1994. The INs and ONs of Tzeltal locative expressions: the semantics of state descriptions of location. *Linguistics* 32: 743–790.

Budwig, N. 1989. The linguistic marking of agentivity and control in child language. *Journal of Child Language* 16: 263–284.

1990. The linguistic marking of nonprototypical agency – an exploration in children's use of passives. *Linguistics* 28: 1221–1252.

1995. *A developmental–functional approach to child language*. Mahwah, NJ: Lawrence Erlbaum.

Bybee, J. L. 1985. *Morphology: a study of the relation between meaning and form*. Amsterdam/Philadelphia: John Benjamins.

Carpenter, K. L. 1986. Productivity and pragmatics of Thai classifiers. *Proceedings of the 12th Annual Meeting of the Berkeley Linguistics Society*. Berkeley, CA: Berkeley Linguistics Society, 14–25.

1991. Later rather than sooner: extralinguistic categories in the acquisition of Thai classifiers. *Journal of Child Language* 18: 93–113.

Choi, S., & M. Bowerman. 1991. Learning to express motion events in English and Korean: the influence of language-specific lexicalization patterns. *Cognition* 41: 83–121.

Clark, E. V. 1973. What's in a word? On the child's acquisition of semantics in his first language. In T. E. Moore (ed.), *Cognitive development and the acquisition of language*. New York: Academic Press, 65–110.

1976. Universal categories: on the semantics of classifiers and children's early word meanings. In A. Juilland (ed.), *Linguistic studies offered to Joseph Greenberg on the occasion of his sixtieth birthday*, vol. 3: *Syntax*. Saratoga, CA: Anma Libri, 449–462.

1978. Locationals: existential, locative, and possessive constructions. In J. H. Greenberg (ed.), *Universals of human language*, vol. 4: *Syntax*. Stanford, CA: Stanford University Press, 85–126.

1979. Building a vocabulary: words for objects, actions, and relations. In P. Fletcher & M. Garman (eds.), *Language acquisition*. Cambridge: Cambridge University Press, 149–160.

1983. Meanings and concepts. In J. H. Flavell & E. M. Markman (eds.), *Handbook of child psychology*, vol. 3: *Cognitive development.* New York: John Wiley, 787–840.

1987. The principle of contrast: a constraint on language acquisition. In B. MacWhinney (ed.), *Mechanisms of language acquisition*. Hillsdale, NJ: Lawrence Erlbaum, 1–33.

1990. On the pragmatics of contrast. *Journal of Child Language* 17: 417–431.

Clark, E. V., & K. L. Carpenter. 1989a. The notion of source in language acquisition. *Language* 65: 1–30.

1989b. On children's uses of "from," "by," and "with" in oblique noun phrases. *Journal of Child Language* 16: 349–364.

Clark, H. H. 1973. Space, time, semantics, and the child. In T. E. Moore (ed.), *Cognitive development and the acquisition of language*. New York: Academic Press, 27–63.

Clark, H. H., & E. V. Clark. 1978. Universals, relativity, and language processing. In J. H. Greenberg (ed.), *Universals of human language*, vol. 1: *Method and theory*. Stanford, CA: Stanford University Press, 225–277.

Clements, J. C. 1988. The semantics and pragmatics of the Spanish COPULA + ADJECTIVE construction. *Linguistics* 26: 779–822.

Craig, C. (ed.). 1986. *Noun classes and categorization*. Amsterdam/Philadelphia: John Benjamins.

De Mello, G. 1979. The semantic values of *ser* and *estar*. *Hispania* 62: 338–341.

Fagan, S. M. B. 1989. Constraints on middle formation. In J. Powers & K. de Jong (eds.), *Proceedings of ESCOL 1988*. Columbus, OH: Ohio State University, 130–141.

Fauconnier, G. 1985. *Mental spaces: aspects of meaning construction in natural language*. Cambridge, MA: Bradford/MIT Press.

Friedrich, P. 1970. Shape in grammar. *Language* 46: 370–407.

Gonda, J. 1975. *Selected studies*, vol. 1: *Indo-European linguistics*. Leiden: Brill.

Greenberg, J. H. 1963. Some universals of grammar with particular reference to the order of meaningful elements. In J. H. Greenberg (ed.), *Universals of language*. Cambridge, MA: MIT Press, 58–90.

1966. *Language universals*. The Hague: Mouton.

1975. Dynamic aspects of word order in the numeral classifier. In C. N. Li (ed.), *Word order and word order change*. Austin, TX: University of Texas Press, 27–45.

Gruber, J. S. 1976. *Lexical structures in syntax and semantics*. North-Holland Linguistic Series, 25. Amsterdam: North-Holland.

Jackendoff, R. S. 1983. *Semantics and cognition*. Cambridge, MA: MIT Press.

Keenan, E. L. 1976. Towards a universal definition of "subject." In C. N. Li (ed.), *Subject and topic*. New York: Academic Press, 303–333.

Kemmer, S. 1993. *The middle voice*. Amsterdam/Philadelphia: John Benjamins.

Langacker, R. W. 1991. *Foundations of cognitive grammar*, vol. 2: *Descriptive application*. Stanford, CA: Stanford University Press.

Lehmann, W. P. 1972. On converging theories in linguistics. *Language* 48: 266–275.

1973. A structural principle of language and its implications. *Language* 49: 47–66.

Levin, B., & M. Rappaport Hovav. 1995. *Unaccusativity: at the syntax–lexical semantics interface*. Linguistic Inquiry Monograph, 26. Cambridge, MA: MIT Press.

Lord, C. 1979. "Don't you fall me down!": children's generalizations regarding cause and transitivity. *Papers and Reports on Child Language Development* 17: 81–89.

Matsumoto, Y. 1985. Acquisition of some Japanese numeral classifiers: the search for convention. *Papers and Reports on Child Language Development* 24: 79–86.

1987. Order of acquisition in the lexicon: implications from Japanese numeral classifiers. In K. E. Nelson & A. van Kleeck (eds.), *Children's language*, vol. 6. Hillsdale, NJ: Lawrence Erlbaum, 229–260.

1993. Japanese numeral classifiers: a study of semantic categories and lexical organization. *Linguistics* 31: 667–713.

Postal, P. 1966. Review article: André Martinet, *Elements of general linguistics. Foundations of Language* 2: 151–186.

Roldan, M. 1974. Towards a semantic characterization of *ser* and *estar. Hispania* 57: 68–75.

Savasir, I., & J. Gee. 1982. The functional equivalents of the middle voice in child language. *Proceedings of the 8th Annual Meeting of the Berkeley Linguistics Society*. Berkeley, CA: Berkeley Linguistics Society, 607–616.

Sera, M. D. 1992. To be or to be: use and acquisition of the Spanish copulas. *Journal of Memory and Language* 31: 408–427.

Slobin, D. I. 1970. Universals of grammatical development in children. In G. B. Flores d'Arcais & W. J. M. Levelt (eds.), *Advances in psycholinguistics*. Amsterdam: North-Holland, 174–186.

1973. Cognitive prerequisites for the development of grammar. In C. A. Ferguson & D. I. Slobin (eds.), *Studies of child language development*. New York: Holt, Rinehart & Winston, 175–208.

1979. The role of language in language acquisition. Invited address, Fiftieth Annual Meeting of the Eastern Psychological Association, Philadelphia, April.

1985a. Crosslinguistic evidence for the Language-Making Capacity. In D. I. Slobin (ed.), *The crosslinguistic study of language acquisition*, vol. 2: *Theoretical issues*. Hillsdale, NJ: Lawrence Erlbaum, 1157–1256.

(ed.). 1985b. *The crosslinguistic study of language acquisition*, vols. 1 & 2. Hillsdale, NJ: Lawrence Erlbaum.

(ed.). 1992. *The crosslinguistic study of language acquisition*, vol. 3. Hillsdale, NJ: Lawrence Erlbaum.

Slobin, D. I., & C. A. Welsh. 1973. Elicited imitation as a research tool in developmental psycholinguistics. In C. A. Ferguson & D. I. Slobin (eds.), *Studies of child language development*. New York: Holt, Rinehart & Winston, 485–497.

Talmy, L. 1985. Lexicalization patterns: semantic structure in lexical form. In T. Shopen (ed.), *Language typology and syntactic description*, vol. 3: *Grammatical categories and the lexicon*. Cambridge: Cambridge University Press, 57–149.

Thomson, J. R., & R. S. Chapman. 1977. Who is "Daddy" revisited: the status of two-year-olds' over-extended words in use and comprehension. *Journal of Child Language* 4: 359–375.

Vennemann, T. 1974. Topics, subjects, and word order: from SXV to SVX via TVX. In J. M. Anderson & C. Jones (eds.), *Historical linguistics I: syntax, morphology, internal and comparative reconstruction*. Amsterdam: North-Holland, 339–376.

14 Form–function relations: how do children find out what they are?

Dan I. Slobin

University of California at Berkeley

Human languages, broadly speaking, provide two kinds of meaningful elements, using both to create grammatical constructions. On the one hand, there are morphemes that make reference to the objects and events of experience, and on the other, there are morphemes that relate these bits of experience to each other and to the discourse perspectives of the speaker. Linguistic theories of all stripes honor this duality, using such distinctions as "material content" vs. "relation" (Sapir 1921/1949), "lexical item" vs. "grammatical item" (Lyons 1968), or, most commonly, "content word" vs. "function word" (or, to include both free and bound morphemes, "functor"). Typically, the first class includes nouns and verbs, and usually also adjectives; the second class includes free morphemes such as conjunctions and prepositions, and bound morphemes, such as affixes marking such categories as number, case, tense, and so forth. It has generally been claimed that: (1) functors express a limited and universal set of meanings ("grammaticizable notions"), and (2) functor classes are small and closed, while content word classes are large and open. The first claim has led to proposals that the set of meanings is, in some sense, "prespecified" for language; the second has led to proposals that this collection of morphemes plays a critical role in both the acquisition and processing of language. Furthermore, many attempts have been made to relate these two "design features" of language:

- Theorists with a nativist bent – including both generative and cognitive linguists – equip the mind/brain with predispositions to relate particular types of meaning to grammatical elements and syntactic constructions. Such predispositions make it possible for the child to crack the code and for expert language-users to successfully parse sentences. (This position, for example, can be found in Bickerton 1981, Pinker 1984, and Slobin 1985.) On such accounts, the relations between the two design features – limited sets of meanings and limited sets of functors – are facts about the language module or language-making capacity, perhaps in relation to other modules or capacities, but not in need of developmental explanation.

- Theorists more concerned with language *use* – functionalists – point to recurrent diachronic processes that inevitably result in small, closed classes of grammatical morphemes with their characteristic meanings across languages. On these accounts, this design feature of language cannot be attributed to the mental structure of the individual alone.

Regardless of theoretical position, however, everyone agrees that grammaticizable notions are "special." Here I want to examine the consequences for acquisition theory that flow from taking grammaticizable notions as special in one way or another. If it is supposed that the mental lexicon consists of two classes of items, with two distinct kinds of meanings, then there are two separate semantic tasks for the learner. Further, if one class draws on prespecified meanings, its acquisition consists of procedures of look-up and elimination, while the acquisition of meanings in the other class requires some kind of more general learning abilities. I will propose, however, that such theorists – including myself – have erred in attributing the origins of structure to the mind of the child, rather than to the interpersonal communicative and cognitive processes that everywhere and always shape language in its peculiar expression of content and relation. As Sapir put it: "language struggles towards two poles of linguistic expression – material content and relation;" but he went on to add: "these poles tend to be connected by a long series of transitional concepts" (1921/1949:109). I will argue that the cline between the two poles, when properly understood, makes it unlikely that the child comes to the task of language acquisition prepared with the relevant distinctions – either semantic or syntactic – thereby challenging my own previous assumptions and those of both generative and cognitive linguists. But first, some necessary preliminaries.

1 Grammatically specified notions

It is clear from an examination of even a single language that grammatical morphemes and constructions encode specific types of notions. In English, for example, nouns can be marked for *plural*, relations of *possession*, and *definiteness*. In other languages, these particular notions may be left unmarked, while shape or substance of objects may be grammatically expressed. Looking across many languages, it is evident that there is a great deal of variation both in the categories that are grammaticized and in their boundaries. At the same time, however, it seems that the set of such notions is not vast.

This problem has been explored in depth by Leonard Talmy (1978, 1983, 1985, 1988). He has been struck by the finding that many notions seem to be excluded from grammatical expression. Thus no known language has grammatical morphemes indicating the color of an object referred to by a noun; nor are there verb inflections indicating whether an event occurred in the daytime or at night, or on a hot or a cold day. In his most extensive study, Talmy (1985) lists conceptual domains which are typically realized as verb inflections or particles, and contrasts this list with a collection of domains which are apparently not amenable to grammaticization.[1] For example, (1 a) lists domains that are typically expressed by grammatical elements associated with verbs (inflections, particles), whereas the domains listed in (1b) are apparently excluded from such expressions.[2]

(1a) **Grammaticizable domains typically marked on verbs**
tense (temporal relation to speech event)
aspect and phase (temporal distribution of an event)
causativity
valence/voice (e.g. active, passive)
mood (e.g. indicative, subjunctive, optative)
speech act type (e.g. declarative, interrogative, imperative)
personation (action on self vs. other)
person (1st, 2nd, etc.)
number of event participants (e.g. singular, dual, plural)
gender of participant
social/interpersonal status of interlocutors (e.g. intimate, formal)
speaker's evidence for making claim (e.g. direct experience, hearsay)
positive/negative status of an event's existence

(1b) **Conceptual domains *not* amenable to grammaticization as verbal inflection**
color of an event participant
symmetry of an event participant
relation to comparable events (e.g. "only," "even," "instead")
spatial setting (e.g. indoors, outside)
speaker's state of mind (e.g. bored, interested).

We are faced here with the first major question about grammaticizable notions: why are some conceptual domains apparently excluded from grammatical expression? Talmy goes on to raise a second major issue: within any particular grammaticizable domain, there are striking restrictions in the number and type of distinctions that are grammatically marked. He has explored this question most fully with regard to restrictions on the notions that can be *conflated* in a single grammatical morpheme. The most widely cited examples concern locative terms, and these will figure in some of the acquisition issues discussed later. For example, an English preposition like *through* indicates motion that proceeds in some medium (*through the grass/water/crowd*), but does not indicate the shape or contour of the path (e.g. zigzag, direct, circling), the nature of the medium, or the precise extent of the path. Another type of restriction suggests that grammar is concerned with *relative*, rather than quantified, distinctions.

For example, the deictic demonstratives *this* and *that* are neutral with regard to magnitude. One can just as well compare "*this* leaf and *that* leaf" as "*this* galaxy and *that* galaxy." Talmy (1988:171) summarizes across numerous examples to conclude that the notions excluded from grammatical expression "involve Euclidean-geometric concepts – e.g. fixed distance, size, contour, and angle – as well as quantified measure, and various particularities of a quantity: in sum, characteristics that are absolute or fixed." By contrast, grammaticizable notions are "topological, topology-like, or relativistic." He offers the following two lists. (For details, see the cited references.) I will call them *qualities* to distinguish them from *domains* such as those listed in (1a, b).

(2a) **Non-topological and non-grammaticizable qualities:** material, motion, medium, precise or quantified space or time

(b) **Topological/topology-like and grammaticizable qualities:** point, linear extent, locatedness, within, region, side, partition, singularity, plurality, same, different, "adjacency" of points, one-to-one correspondence, pattern of distribution

Finally, Talmy (1988) notes a series of restrictions that impose a limited schematization of semantic content for any grammatically specified notion. These restrictions apply to both nouns and verbs. For example, Talmy introduces the term "plexity" to characterize the distinction of number. Thus a "uniplex" noun becomes "multiplex" by pluralization (e.g. *bird/birds*) and a uniplex verb can become multiplex by verbal inflection and/or auxiliary (e.g. *sigh/keep sighing*). Talmy calls these *categories of grammatically specified notions*. In the course of a lengthy analysis (Talmy 1988:173–192), he lists the following types of distinction:

(3) **Categories of grammatically specified notions**
dimension (continuous/discrete)
plexity (uniplex/multiplex)
boundedness (unbounded/bounded)
dividedness (particulate/continuous)
disposition (combinations of the above)
extension (point, bounded extent, unbounded extent)
distribution (one-way non-resettable, one-way resettable, full-cycle, multiplex, steady-state, gradient)
axiality (relation to border)
perspectival mode (long-range/close-up; moving/static)
level of synthesis (Gestalt/componential)
level of exemplarity (full complement / single exemplar)

Putting together the various parts of Talmy's analysis – *domains*, *qualities*, and *categories* of grammaticizable notions – we can more precisely characterize the meanings of grammatical morphemes. To take just one example, consider the sentence ***The** boy-**s were** runn-**ing in-to the*** *house.* The grammatical elements in boldface point to particular domains and categories within those domains, while the lexical items *boy*, *run*, and *house* provide the items of content that are related by the grammatical frame. The article *the*, together with the plural *-s*, categorizes the *disposition* of the actors as *multiplex* and *particulate* (as opposed to *Boys were running*, where the absence of the article categorizes the actors as *multiplex* and *continuous*). The plural past-tense *were* categorizes the reported event in the domains of *tense* (*past*) and *number* (*plural*), while the progressive *-ing* categorizes *aspect* (*progressive*). The form *in-to* schematizes *path* and *ground of movement* as directed across a border into an extent. The quality of the path is topological: simply movement across a partition to within a region. (The two uses of *the* also situate the sentence in a discourse context of presupposed information – that is, the speaker assumes that the listener has specific referents in mind for *boys* and *house.* Talmy's analysis does not include the pragmatic functions of grammatical morphemes. The interpersonal domain must also figure heavily in any account of the origins and functions of these items.)

To return to the guiding question: why should precisely *these* types of notions receive grammatical expression across the languages of the world? Talmy offers two kinds of accounts. One is presented in cognitive terms: "The grammatical specifications in a sentence . . . provide a conceptual framework or, imagistically, a skeletal structure or scaffolding, for the conceptual material that is lexically specified" (1988:166). That is, the grammatical elements – functors and syntactic construction types – provide a schematization of experience. The cognitive argument is that this particular schematization is a consequence of schematization at a nonlinguistic conceptual level. For example, Talmy (1978, 1983, 1988) proposes parallels between structuring in visual perception and in language. Landau & Jackendoff make a similar proposal, tying the limited set of locative prepositions to a "submodule" of the brain specialized for object location: "Our hypothesis is that there are so few prepositions because the class of spatial relations available to be expressed in language – the notions prepositions can mean – is extremely limited" (1993:224).

Such parallels between cognitive domains, however, do not explain the linguistic division of labor between content words and functors, nor all of the peculiarities of grammaticizable notions. For Talmy, and other linguists, the division of labor is apparently taken as given, as is the set of grammaticizable notions. Talmy refers to "an innate inventory of concepts available for serving a structuring function in language" (1985:197). Such innate knowledge, of course, would facilitate the acquisition task. Bickerton includes a version of the inventory in his bioprogram, equipping the acquisition mechanism with "a very short list of semantic primes" that serve the child as "grammatically-markable semantic features" (1981:205).

Whether or not the "inventory" is innate, it has been assumed to play a key role in the child's entry into the linguistic system. In 1979 I presented Talmy's analysis as part of the child's "initial assumptions" about grammar. And in later work on "operating principles" for acquisition, I suggested "that such notions must constitute a privileged set for the child, and that they are embodied in the child's conceptions of 'prototypical events' that are mapped onto the first grammatical forms universally" (Slobin 1985:1173f.). The proposal was that the division between the two classes of grammatical morphemes reflected a cognitive division between concrete and relational concepts, and that the relational concepts were, to some extent, already in place at the beginning of grammatical acquisition (whether on the basis of an "innate list" or arising from prior cognitive development). A similar position was taken by Pinker, in his proposal that "the child can extract . . . the potentially grammatically relevant semantic features of the sentence participants (their number, person, sex, etc.) and of the proposition as a whole (tense, aspect, modality, etc.)" (1984:30). He, too, was agnostic about the prelinguistic origins of such features: "the theory is, of course, mute as to whether these cognitive distinctions are themselves innate or learned, as long as the child is capable of making them" (1984:363). The position continues in *Learnability and cognition*, with a clear statement of the learning task (Pinker 1989:254f.):

> Consider the target in the learning of an inflection, namely, a list of features . . . The features are drawn from a finite universal set of possible grammaticizable features. Each one has a conceptual or perceptual correlate: the child can determine, for example, whether the referent of a noun in a particular context is singular or plural, human or nonhuman. When attempting to learn a given inflection from its use in a given utterance, the child samples a subset of features with their currently true values from the universal pool.

The purpose of these proposals was to clear the way for "operating principles" or "procedures" to work out inflectional paradigms and other form–function mappings. However, such procedures also run into the problem that the set of grammaticizable features, although limited, is still large; and many of the features are not relevant to the particular language being acquired. The solution here was to appeal to a preestablished ranking of notions with regard to their applicability to grammar. With the addition of an innate "accessibility hierarchy" (Talmy 1988:197) or a "weighting of hypotheses" based on "cognitive saliency" (Pinker 1984:170), the child is spared the task of initially scanning the entire inventory of grammaticizable notions.[3]

In my work on operating principles, I called upon cognitive and processing variables to account for differences in the accessibility of grammaticizable notions, rather than building the hierarchy into a grammar module. My solution was to attempt to ground the accessibility hierarchy in the child's cognitive development. On this account, the first notions to receive grammatical marking in a child's speech are those that correspond to the child's conceptions of "prototypical events." For example, I proposed that the salience of hands-on action on objects – the "Manipulative Activity Scene" – provided the starting point for the acquisition of such forms as accusative or ergative inflections. Much empirical work remains to be done before we can specify the range of such starting points. I expect that some will be universal, whereas others will show crosslinguistic variation. Pioneering research, such as the work of Bowerman, Choi (Choi & Bowerman 1991; Bowerman 1993, 1994, 1996a, b), Clark (ch. 13 of this volume), and others, places the conceptual origins of grammaticizable notions in domains of cognitive development, tempered by the semantic organization inherent in the exposure language.

It is important, however, to distinguish between the course of development of grammaticizable notions *in the child* and explanations for their existence *as linguistic phenomena*. On closer inspection, crosslinguistic diversity in patterns of grammaticization points to adult communicative practices as the most plausible source of form–function mappings in human languages, rather than prototypical events in infant cognition. The following sections of the chapter explore the roles of grammaticizable notions in ontogeny and diachrony, drawing on recent findings in cognitive linguistics and grammatic(al)ization theory.

2 The learning task

This historical and theoretical introduction sets the stage for defining the task that the child faces in determining the meanings of grammatical morphemes. The standard definition of the task assumes the following linguistic conditions to be true:

Condition 1: there is a distinct and identifiable collection of grammatical morphemes, arranged in small, closed classes.

Condition 2: these morphemes map onto a universal, limited set of semantic entities (grammaticizable notions).

Condition 3: grammaticizable notions are arranged in a universal accessibility hierarchy.

According to standard accounts, acquisition occurs on the basis of assumptions about biology and cognition:

Assumption 1: conditions 1, 2, and 3 exist because of the structure of the mind/brain (in modules for aspects of language, perhaps in conjunction with other modules).

Assumption 2: the role of linguistic input is to allow the relevant mental capacities to organize themselves in terms of the exposure language.

Assumption 3: the child learns the meaning of a grammatical form by isolating and identifying a particular stretch of speech as instantiating a grammatical form and attempting to map it onto a relevant grammaticizable notion.

I propose that Conditions 1, 2, and 3 are only partly true, and that therefore Assumption 1 must be seriously modified or abandoned. Assumption 2 remains, but with a shift of emphasis to structures inhering in the exposure language. Assumption 3 must be seriously modified – and this is the challenge to learning theory posed by my reanalysis.

3 Synchronic evidence for modifying the linguistic conditions on learnability

3.1 What is a grammatical morpheme?

Prototypical grammatical morphemes are affixed to content words, are general in meaning, phonologically reduced, and not etymologically transparent. Familiar examples are elements like plural markers on nouns and tense/aspect inflections on verbs. Another obvious type of grammatical morpheme is represented by "little words" like prepositions and auxiliaries, which consist of small sets of items occurring in syntactically fixed positions. But there are also items that are not so obvious. Consider several examples that demonstrate the lack of clear boundaries of syntactic categories defined as "functors," "grammatical morphemes," or "closed-class elements."

3.1.1. English modals and equivalents English has a grammatical class of modal auxiliaries that fit in the frame, SUBJECT MODAL VERB, such as *You* ***should/must/can/might*** *. . . go.* This is a prototypical small, closed class: *can, could, shall, should, will, would, may, might, must.* The forms do not function as normal verbs; rather, they have a number of grammatical peculiarities – e.g. they don't have normal past tenses (**you shoulded go*) or person inflections (**he shoulds go*), they can take a contracted negative clitic (*shouldn't*), and they "move" under certain syntactic conditions (e.g. *Should you go?*). However, there are other items that can occur in the same slot, such as *You* ***hafta / needa*** *. . . go.* These function as normal verbs – e.g. PAST: *You* ***had*** *to go; PERSON: you* ***hafta****, he* ***hasta****;* QUESTION*:* ***Do*** *you* ***hafta*** *go?;* NEGATIVE *You* ***don't*** *hafta go.* Nevertheless, they, too, are part of a small, closed, and specialized set, with phonological reduction in some contexts.

Therefore some linguists refer to them as "quasi-modals." Nonverbs can also fall in the specialized slot of modals and quasi-modals, but with other syntactic constraints. Consider *You* ***better*** *go*, which (in American English) has no obvious past tense or question form. It is negated like an auxiliary, but only in the uncontracted form (compare *you should not go /you better not go; but you shouldn't go /you *bettern't go*). Looking across contexts of use, *better* is another sort of specialized "modal-like" element in American English. If you are a child learning this dialect, you can identify a set of full auxiliaries on syntactic grounds, and find that it maps onto a restricted set of grammaticized meanings in the domain of modality. This knowledge is adequate for the *comprehension* of modals; however, when you are concerned with speech *production*, and access the set of modal notions from your mental set of grammaticizable notions in this domain, you find that there is, indeed, a small closed set – but that it does not have a clear or unitary syntactic definition. The slot in declarative sentences that is reserved for expressing categories within the grammaticizable domain of modality can be filled with a heterogeneous collection of modal auxiliaries, semi-modals, and an adjective/adverb *better* that does not act like a normal adjective or adverb in this function. The semantic and syntactic tasks do not seem to run in parallel as neatly as in the textbook cases, which take only well-defined grammatical morphemes into account in their expositions.

This is, in fact, a widespread problem in acquisition – only coming to light when we consider production, rather than comprehension. Consider several more examples of the fuzziness of the category "grammatical morpheme" or "closed-class element."

3.1.2 Spanish modal verbs and auxiliaries In Spanish the equivalents of English modal verbs do not have syntactic peculiarities. That is, they function just like normal, full verbs, using the standard paradigms for person/number and tense/aspect. Yet they, too, are a small closed set, performing similar functions. The set, however, can only be defined on semantic grounds, listing those verbs – such as *poder* 'can,' *deber* 'should,' and the like – that perform a modal function. For example, *puedo ir* 'I.can go,' *debo ir* 'I.should go' have the same morphosyntactic characteristics as constructions with nonmodal verbs. Lacking the peculiar morphosyntactic definition of English modals, however, the corresponding Spanish verbs are a small closed set *within the "open" class*. (I will argue that, in fact, the "open class" of verbs is better conceived of as a collection of closed classes.) There is also a small class of about twenty-four "semi-auxiliaries" (Green 1982) which have restricted meanings in particular semantic/syntactic contexts. These are verbs that can function both as main verbs and semi-auxiliaries – again, making it difficult to draw a clear boundary around "grammatical morphemes." In their grammatical function, such verbs have restricted meanings in comparison to their uses as fully lexical verbs. For example, the verb *llevar* 'carry,' in construction with a participle, takes on an auxiliary aspectual meaning: *Juan **lleva** entendido que X* 'Juan **carries** understood that X' predicates an established state of understanding in Juan that X; *la diferencia **viene** motivada por X* 'the difference **comes** motivated by X' means that the difference can be accounted for by X. Green notes that some of the twenty-four semi-auxiliaries are more specialized and limited in their functions than others. He observes that a semantic examination of these verbs "strongly favours a gradient analysis . . . At one extreme of the gradience would be verbs like *haber* [have] which have lost virtually all trace of lexical meaning, and at the other, verbs like *mostrarse* [show.self] and *notarse* [note] which have lost virtually none of theirs" (p. 127). A critical feature is thus the "fullness" versus "abstractness" of lexical meaning of an item. This is not a criterion that a child could use to identify an item as belonging to either the lexical class or the grammatical class. Looked at in diachronic perspective, some are more "grammaticized" than others (as I will discuss later in more detail). Some may remain on the borderline between lexical and grammatical item for centuries, and may never become fully grammaticized.

The Spanish "modal" and "semi-auxiliary" verbs attract our interest because their semantic and discourse functions parallel the more highly grammaticized auxiliaries of English. This leads one to wonder whether Spanish-speaking children are using their prespecified "grammatical acquisition device" or their more general "lexical acquisition device" in learning such forms.

Many more examples could be adduced, underlining the point that there is no clear dividing line between "content words" and "functors." Rather, there is a continuum with clearly lexical items on one end (nouns like *computer*, *couch*, *zebra*, verbs like *tackle*, *broil*, *sneeze*) and grammatical inflections on the other (such as English progressive *-ing*, Turkish accusative *-I*, Warlpiri ergative *-ngku*). In between, there are lexical items that play more or less specialized roles, sometimes on their way to becoming grammatical morphemes over time. What, then, is a grammatical morpheme? It depends on the purposes of the analysis. In any event, it would be difficult to preprogram the child with an adequate definition.

3.2 *What is a closed-class item?*

One way of getting the child started in the task of grammatical form–function mapping has been to equip the language acquisition device with a special detector for members of the "closed class." The terminology is deceptive here, however. Obviously, the child cannot define a class as "closed" before having acquired all of its members and finding that there are no more to acquire. Therefore this can't be part of early acquisition. Lila Gleitman and her associates have proposed an acoustic rather than a semantic or syntactic cue to closed-class membership (Gleitman & Wanner 1982; Landau & Gleitman 1985; Gleitman, Landau, & Wanner 1988). On this model, the child eventually comes to pay attention to elements in the speech stream that are unstressed or otherwise perceptually non-salient. They propose that "the distinction between open and closed class may play a role in the child's discovery of linguistic structure. This is because, though this distinction may be discovered through a physical property (i.e. stress), it is well correlated with syntactic analyses the child will have to recognize to recover the structure of sentences" (Gleitman & Wanner 1982:23). However, this analysis obliterates both the syntactic and semantic characteristics of closed classes, as well as their statistical distribution. That is, grammatical morphemes are high-frequency elements, occurring in fixed syntactic positions. The child must be sensitive to these factors, along with prosodic features. An acoustic definition of the class leads Gleitman and her associates to define stressed grammatical inflections, paradoxically, as open class. For example, when discussing the fact that grammatical morphemes are acquired earlier in Turkish than in many other languages, they argue: "According to Slobin, the relevant inflectional items in Turkish . . . are a full syllable long, are stressed, do not deform the surrounding words phonetically, and do not cliticize. Thus these items are OPEN CLASS, not CLOSED CLASS, under phonological definitions of this partitioning of the morphological stock" (Gleitman *et al.*, 1988:158). On this account, agglutinative languages like Turkish and Japanese have no closed-class morphemes, thus exempting children acquiring such languages from the learning task defined in §2. This solution clearly throws out the baby with the bath water.

In other formulations, Gleitman and her associates rely on the traditional definition of the two classes. Landau & Gleitman (1985:44ff.) define the closed class on *distributional* grounds alone, including such items as auxiliaries, prepositions, and determiners, which are full syllables and can receive stress. On this model, the child must have some means of identifying members of these grammatical categories. The only possible cues are meaning, syntactic position, and statistical distribution – the traditional cues used in all models of language acquisition. Thus there is no evident definition of "closed-class morpheme" that can give the child a solution to the learning task.[4] Gleitman's solution, at best, suggests that some kind of "prosodic bootstrapping" might help children learning particular types of languages to identify particular types of grammatical morphemes. But this leaves open the question of how grammatical morphemes in general are discovered, and how they are mapped onto linguistically relevant notions.

The original motivation behind the definition of "closed" classes comes from the observation that some types of words are rarely added to a language; as a consequence, it is unlikely that speakers will encounter new instances of such words during their lifetimes. Languages are most free in adding new nouns over time, as new artifacts are created and new phenomena are categorized and labeled. It is my impression that verbs are hardly ever invented "out of whole cloth," as nouns are; rather, they tend to be derived from nouns by morphological or phrasal means – e.g. *to xerox*, *to skateboard*, *to privatize*, *to test drive*, *to do a number.*

The verb lexicon of a language can be subdivided into many limited, fairly closed classes that provide the language's analysis and categorization of a given conceptual domain. Consider, for example, the set of English verbs of manner of talking (*shout*, *scream*, *whisper*, *mumble*, *mutter* . . .), posture (*sit*, *stand*, *lie*, *crouch* . . .), or cooking (*bake*, *fry*, *roast*, *boil* . . .). Within such a subclass it is possible to find systematic sets of semantic components in quite the same fashion as componential analyses of grammatical morphemes. A good example is the domain of object destruction, which is quite elaborated in the English verb lexicon. We make distinctions of the nature of the object to be destroyed (e.g. *break*, *tear*, *smash*), force dynamics (e.g. *tear* vs. *rip*), the degree of destruction or deformation (e.g. *cut* vs. *shred*), the texture or constituency of the object (e.g. *crumple*, *crumble*, *shatter*), and so forth. In learning this "closed-class" set of verbs, the English-speaking child has acquired a language-specific set of linguistically relevant notions, and will not go on learning more and more such verbs throughout life. This process is, in principle, no different than the acquisition of a "closed-class" set such as the English spatial prepositions.

Organization of the verbal lexicon into classes also has profound syntactic consequences As Beth Levin (1993) has documented in detail in her recent book, *English verb classes and alternations*, "verbs in English and other languages fall into classes on the basis of shared components of meaning" (p. 11), and the members of a class "have common syntactic as well as semantic properties" (p. 7). This pioneering attempt to characterize the "open class" of verbs as a collection of linguistically definable subclasses poses another type of challenge to theories that postulate a special psycholinguistic module devoted to the acquisition and processing of the "closed class."

3.3 *What makes a notion grammaticizable?*

The other side of the coin is to equip the child with grammaticizable notions that can be mapped onto the specialized morphemes of the "closed class," however defined. When we look across languages, though, we find that the same notions are often also used to delimit the meanings of *content* words – members of the open class – depending on the language and the type of analysis chosen. Simply identifying a notion as grammaticizable does not allow the child to determine *whether* it is actually grammaticized in the exposure language or *how* it is grammaticized. (That is, crosslinguistic diversity precludes a preestablished table of correspondences between grammatical forms and semantic meanings, as in Pinker 1984.) Again, there are many possible examples. I will consider three types of problem: (1) morphemes that are called closed class, or grammatical, in one language, compared with similar morphemes that are called open class or lexical in another; (2) languages in which variants of the very same lexical item can function as either closed or open class; and (3) pairs of languages in which the same type of conceptual material is lexicalized in one and grammaticized in the other. The dichotomy between two types of learning mechanisms becomes questionable in the light of all three phenomena.

3.3.1 Mandarin and English classifiers First, it is useful to consider one language from the point of view of grammaticized categories in other types of languages. For example, a Mandarin perspective on English brings our covert *classifier* system into focus. In Mandarin, as in many languages (cf. Craig 1986), when objects are counted or otherwise pointed to linguistically it is necessary to use a classifier morpheme along with the noun making object reference. Classifiers are considered grammatical morphemes in Mandarin because they constitute a small set with categorial meanings and are obligatory in certain contexts. One says, for example, *yi* ***qún*** *yáng* 'one **flock** sheep,' *nèi* ***duī*** *lāxī* 'that **pile** garbage,' *zhěng* ***chuàn*** *zhūzi* 'whole **string** pearl.' Li & Thompson (1981:105) say that Mandarin has "several dozen classifiers" and Erbaugh (1986:406) reports that adults tend almost always to use the single general classifier *gè* rather than one of the special classifiers. It is apparent that there is a syntactic slot for a classifier, but that it rarely is occupied by a form that has specific meaning. Is this really any different from English, with regard to grammaticizable notions? In most cases, it is sufficient in English to use a numeral or demonstrative, without indicating class membership, and to use a plural morpheme for numbers greater than one; in Mandarin, in most cases, it is sufficient to use a numeral or demonstrative, with an empty classifier, and no noun marking for number. When it *is* necessary to classify in addition to counting or demonstrating, English has a set of classifiers quite analogous to Mandarin, as is evident in the translations above: *flock*, *pile*, *string*. In fact, there is no other way to refer to such collections or pluralities in English. The English-speaking child must learn words like these – and *grain*, *piece*, *sheet*, *slice*, *stack*, *cup*, *bowl*, *drop*, etc. just as the Mandarin-speaking child must learn classifiers that translate as 'slice,' 'animal,' 'row,' 'sheet,' 'pot,' 'grain,' etc. Yet Chinese classifiers, by tradition, strike us as "grammatical" in a way that English measure terms do not. From the point of view of learning theory, though, it is not evident that the Chinese child is faced with a grammatical task, played off in a prespecified component of the language module, while the American child has to learn a very similar system using a quite different set of linguistic and cognitive resources.

3.3.2 Mayan motion verbs and directionals Mayan languages typically have a small, closed class of directional suffixes that can be used on verbs, stative predicates, and nonverbal predicates of various types, such as adjectives. For example, in Jakaltek (Craig 1993) there are ten directional suffixes, such as *-(a)y* 'down' and *-toj* 'away from.' Consider an example in which these two forms are affixed to a caused motion verb (1993:23):

(4)	*sirnih-**ay-toj***	*sb'a*	*naj*	*sat*	*pahaw*	*b'et*	*wichen*
	A3.E3.threw-**DIR-DIR**	E3.REFL	NCL/he	E3.in.front	cliff	into	gully[5]

'he threw himself down over the cliff into the gully.'

The first word, *sirnih-ay-toj*, affixes two directionals to a verb meaning 'throw,' similar to English verb particles. The directionals have all of the defining features of closed-class morphemes: there is a small, phonologically reduced set of bound morphemes, with schematic and generalized meanings. However, each of these suffixes corresponds to a full verb of motion, and such verbs are clearly open class by standard definitions. Craig presents the following parallels (1993:23):

Motion verbs		Directionals	
toyi	'to go'	*-toj*	'away from'
tita	'come!'	*-tij*	'toward'
ahi	'to ascend'	*-(a)h*	'up'
ayi	'to descend'	*-(a)y*	'down'
oki	'enter'	*-(o/e/i)k*	'in'
eli	'to exit'	*-(e/i)l*	'out'
ek'i	'to pass'	*-(e/i)k'*	'passing through'
paxi	'to return'	*-pax*	'back, again'
hani	'to remain, to stay'	*-kan*	'remaining, still'
kanh	'to rise, to burst'	*-kanh*	'up, suddenly'

It would be strange to postulate two different learning mechanisms for these two sets of obviously related items. In fact, both sets are small and closed, and both have the familiar semantic characteristics of grammaticizable notions. Clearly, the directionals are grammaticized forms of the verbs. And just as clearly – within the "open class" – these ten motion verbs constitute a small, closed class. Indeed, as I will argue later, the verb class seems to consist of a number of small, closed sets, thus blurring further the distinction between "open" and "closed" classes.

3.3.3 Motion in English and Korean Soonja Choi and Melissa Bowerman, in an important paper (1991; also see chapter 16 of this volume), compare how children learn to express motion events in English and Korean. The details of the analysis cannot be explored here. What is significant for the present argument is the fact that meaning elements that are expressed by grammatical morphemes in English (verb particles) are expressed by verbs in Korean. Choi & Bowerman examine children's acquisition of expressions for *path of movement* in English verb particles and Korean path verbs. Note, however, that this is a comparison of closed-class (English) and open-class (Korean) elements. Yet, a common developmental story can be told. This crosslinguistic comparison presents the same pattern as the intralinguistic pattern in the Mayan languages – namely, the expression of comparable locative notions in small, closed sets, as either "content words" or "functor morphemes." Compare the set of Korean path verbs with the set of English particles:

Korean	English
olla 'ascend'	*up*
naylye 'descend'	*down*
tule 'enter'	*in*
na 'exit'	*out*
cina 'pass'	*past, by*
ttala 'move.along'	*along*
thonghay 'move.through'	*through*
kalocille 'cross'	*across*
tulle 'move.via'	*along, through*

It is not evident that the task of learning a small, closed set of path *verbs* is qualitatively different from the task of learning a small, closed set of verb *particles* expressing path – though these two tasks would be assigned to two different modules or types of acquisition mechanisms on the standard account.

3.4 How are grammaticizable notions organized?

Up to this point I have treated grammaticizable notions as a universally specified collection, applicable across languages. However, it has become more and more evident in research since the late 1980s or so that there is considerable crosslinguistic variation in the meanings of closed-class categories, including both functors and small, closed verb classes. Melissa

Bowerman has been a pioneer in arguing that "the way in which languages organize meaning . . . [is] an integral part of their structure" (1985:1313), with consequences for patterns of acquisition. Her work has demonstrated that children can be guided by language-specific form–meaning relations – perhaps from the earliest phases of acquisition – in establishing categories appropriate to the exposure language (Choi & Bowerman 1991; Bowerman 1994, 1996a, b; Bowerman, de León, & Choi 1995). This work has stimulated others to find similar patterns (e.g. Slobin 1991, 1996; Berman & Slobin 1994; Choi 1997). Crosslinguistic variation in types of "conceptual packaging" in a semantic domain poses another serious challenge to learning models, because there is no set of prelinguistic categories that can be directly mapped onto the meanings of linguistic elements. (See Bowerman 1996a for a recent and cogent exposition of this problem in the domain of spatial concepts and language.) Four types of problems must be faced by learning theories: (1) languages differ in how finely they divide up a conceptual continuum and in where they place cuts for grammatical purposes; (2) languages differ in the combinations of semantic components that are packaged into grammatical morphemes in common conceptual domains; (3) languages differ in the overall division of a semantic domain into linguistically relevant categories; (4) the array of concepts relevant to a particular domain is distributed across several types of linguistic elements in any given language, and the patterns of distribution also vary across languages. I will give examples of these four problem types.

3.4.1 Dividing a continuum into linguistically relevant categories Izchak Schlesinger has long argued for a distinction between cognitive and semantic levels of categorization (1982, 1988). In a broad crosslinguistic study he offers evidence for the proposal that "conceptually, the instrumental and comitative are really only two extreme points on what is a conceptual continuum" (1979:308). This continuum is marked by a single preposition in English –*with*– as shown in the following ten sentences that Schlesinger used in his study:

1. The pantomimist gave a show with the clown.
2. The engineer built the machine with an assistant.
3. The general captured the hill with a squad of paratroopers.
4. The acrobat performed an act with an elephant.
5. The blind man crossed the street with his dog.
6. The officer caught the smuggler with a police dog.
7. The prisoner won the appeal with a highly paid lawyer.
8. The Nobel Prize winner found the solution with a computer.
9. The sportsman hunted deer with a rifle.
10. The hoodlum broke the window with a stone.

English speakers were asked to rank these sentences on a continuum from the meaning of "together" (as in "He went to the movie with his friend") to the meaning of "by means of" (as in "He cut the meat with a knife"). The respondents agreed, at a high level of statistical significance, on the ranking given above. Schlesinger then presented these sentences to speakers of languages that use distinct grammatical forms for parts of this continuum. Speakers of twelve different languages divided the continuum at different points and agreed in treating it as a continuum.[6] In general, wherever they may have made a division they did not violate the ranking. For example, sentences 1–8 received the same form in Iraqi Arabic, while 9–10 received a different form; Swahili, by contrast, required a separate form for 7–10. Schlesinger concludes that "the finding that languages differ widely in their cut off points runs counter to the hypothesis that the instrumental and comitative are two disparate categories in our cognitive structures . . . [Rather], there seems to be a continuum in our cognitive system, which each language segments in its own way" (1979:313).

More recently, Bowerman & Pederson (1992) report a similar pattern in the spatial domain. They found that it was possible to rank pictured situations of locative relations between two objects on a continuum from *containment* to *support*, with differences between languages in their division of the continuum. Thus, even if the child were equipped with predefined conceptual continua, it would not be evident how many linguistically relevant cuts to make on a continuum, or even whether it is divisible at all, since some languages use a single term for an entire continuum such as *comitative–instrumental* (e.g. English *with*) or *containment–support* (e.g. Spanish *en*).

3.4.2 Packaging components into linguistically relevant categories

Languages differ in terms of the "granularity" of their division of conceptual material into linguistically relevant categories. For example, one language may have a simple *continuative* aspect for any temporally unbounded situation, while others may subdivide this aspect to distinguish between *habitual* and *iterative* events, or between *progressive* events and *states.* Further, events can be cross-classified on different dimensions: one language may mark such distinctions only in the past, for example, while another might mark them in other tenses as well. It is the hope of cognitive linguists such as Jackendoff (1983, 1987, 1990) that there is a universal set of conceptual components underlying crosslinguistic diversity in the semantics of lexical items. I share this hope, but even if the child had a definitive set of such components, the task of packaging them into the linguistically relevant categories of the particular exposure language would remain. In some learning theories such packages are given in advance, as in

Pinker's (1984:41) table of correspondences between grammatical and conceptual categories. On closer inspection, however, considerable diversity remains to be accounted for.

As one example, consider the grammatical category *accusative*, which appears in various languages in the form of case affixes or particles associated with nouns, or as verb affixes, or as special construction types. In Pinker's table, "Accusative" is linked with "Patient of transitive action."[7] However, in many languages this semantic category is subdivided – and in different ways. That is, it is not a unitary notion, nor does it lie on a one-dimensional continuum with other case categories, because the subdivisions cut across different types of categories. Here are just a few examples of the many possibilities:

Some factors influencing choice of grammatical marking of patient:
definite patient only (Turkish case inflection)
masculine animate vs. other, whole vs. partial patient, singular vs. plural patient, affirmative vs. negative clause (Russian case inflections)
whole vs. partial patient, completed vs. non-completed action (Finnish case inflections)
direct physical action on patient only (Mandarin particle)
patient marking (direct and indirect conflated) in present tense only (Georgian)
one marker for patient, goal, recipient, beneficiary (English personal pronouns)

This is just a very brief and simplified list, but it makes it clear that the notion of "patient," or "direct object," conflates with various other notions from language to language, including such categories as tense, aspect, definiteness, nature of effect, and so forth. It may well be that some packagings are more accessible to the child than others, and that children across languages begin with similar notions of patient (e.g. the prototypical event of direct physical manipulation proposed in my "Manipulative Activity Scene" [Slobin 1985]). This is, of course, an empirical question. But however children may break into the mapping of such grammaticizable notions, our learning theories will have to account for the selective fine tuning required for arriving at language-specific patterns of grammaticization. That is, regardless of a child's starting point in grammaticizing a particular notion, a developmental account is needed because the endpoints vary so much across languages.

3.4.3 Carving up a conceptual domain into grammaticized categories The work of Melissa Bowerman and Soonja Choi is perhaps the clearest example of how languages not only place cuts at different points on a continuum, or conflate different categories in particular grammatical forms –

but, more broadly, differ in structuring entire conceptual domains. This work has been presented in detail in a number of places (see references to Bowerman and to Choi in §3.4). The domain in question is spatial location and movement of various types, comparing English and Korean. Consider the domain of locative placement – that is, caused movement of an object from or to a location. It is evident that each of the two languages has a different overall conceptual organization of what it is important to mark linguistically in this domain. For example, English is concerned with relations of containment and support – whether one object is *in* or *on* another, whether an object is taken *off* or *out* in relation to another. Korean, by contrast, is concerned with the type of surface contact between two objects – tight or loose containment, contact or attachment with a surface. For example, where English uses the same term for putting an apple *in* a bowl or a tape cassette *in* its case, Korean uses two terms, indicating loose vs. tight fit. On the other hand, where English uses two terms to differentiate between putting a cassette *in* a case and a lid *on* a jar, Korean uses one, because these are both instances of tight fit. Working across entire semantic domains in several languages, Bowerman finds distinctly different arrays and combinations of conceptual features employed in the overall structuring of a domain for purposes of linguistic expression, concluding that children "must work out the meanings of the forms by observing how they are distributed across contexts in fluent speech" (1996a:425).

3.4.4 Distributing a concept across linguistic elements The child not only has to keep track of the distribution of forms across contexts, but also the distribution of concepts across forms. Up to this point we have primarily considered individual forms, such as verbs, affixes, prepositions, and particles. But, in fact, most linguistic elements are only interpretable in relation to other co-occurring elements. To take a trivial example, an English personal pronoun, taken out of context, only indicates the global thematic relations of subject or object, and the object forms – *me, us, him, her, them* – do not distinguish such roles as patient, recipient, or goal. However, the forms are not ambiguous in context. The *me* of *she loves me* is not the same *me*, conceptually, as the *me* of *she sent me a letter* or *she approached me.* In English, these concepts are distinguishable in combination with verb semantics and construction type. In any given utterance, the meaning of the closed-class element, *me*, does not reside in that element alone.

Chris Sinha & Tania Kuteva (1995) have explored this issue in detail with regard to the semantics of locative particles in several types of languages, introducing the useful term, *distributed spatial semantics*. To begin with, spatial relational meaning is expressed in English by a variety of word types, both lexical and grammatical: prepositions (*in*), adverbs (*inwards*), verbs (*enter*), nouns (*inside*), adjectives (*inner*). Sinha & Kuteva also point out that construction types can distinguish aspects of spatial meaning, as in the following Dutch example, where the meaning of a locative particle, *in*, varies with its position in constructions with verbs of motion:

(6) a. *Mieke loopt **in** het bos.*
'Mieke walks **in** the woods.'
b. *Mieke loopt het bos **in**.*
'Mieke walks **into** the woods.'

Thus spatial relational meaning is *distributed* over different form classes and constructions.

Distributed spatial semantics can also have consequences for learning the meanings of closed-class elements, depending on their overall functional load in the language. English has a relatively large set of differentiated locative prepositions (at least forty). These forms can often distinguish between paths and figure–ground relationships on their own, with no further information provided by the verb. For example, using a neutral non-path verb such as *put*, English can differentiate *placement* from *insertion* by choice of particle: *put the book **on / in** the box.* In a language like Spanish, where path is expressed by means of verb selection, there is a small collection of prepositions, each with a wider and more general range of meanings, such as *en* 'in, on,' *a* 'at, to,' *de* 'from, of,' *por* 'through, via, along, by means of.' Distinctions such as *placement* versus *insertion* must therefore be carried by the verb: ***poner** el libro **en** la caja* '**place** the book ***en*** the box,' ***meter** el libro **en** la caja* '**insert** the book ***en*** the box.' In both types of languages, sentences such as these require understanding of the meanings of all of the lexical items in order to build up the appropriate mental image of the event. However, because parts of the overall semantic content are differentially distributed across linguistic elements, the acquisition tasks differ. Although English and Spanish prepositions appear to be syntactically comparable closed-class items, they play distinctly different roles in the overall structure and use of the language.

Similarly, although English and Spanish motion verbs are "open-class," they are distinctly different kinds of "open-class sets," in that Spanish presents a small, closed class of path verbs which play a central role in describing motion events. The following set is typical of the Romance languages in general (and is comparable to the set of Korean path verbs in §3.3.3).

advance, approach, arrive – recede, depart
ascend, climb – descend, fall
enter – exit
pass, cross,
come, return

Therefore I disagree with the proposal by Landau and Jackendoff that spatial verbs are qualitatively different from spatial prepositions: "We agree with Talmy (1983) that crosslinguistic investigation should focus on closed-class elements (whether verb markers, prepositions, postpositions, etc.) that express spatial relationships" (1993:238). This claim must be relativized to the overall typology of the language under consideration. One cannot "leave spatial verbs untouched" if one wishes to understand the patterning and acquisition of grammaticizable notions in a verb-framed language.

3.5 Summary

Let us briefly summarize the answers to the questions posed in the preceding four subsections before moving on to the diachronic evidence.

3.5.1 What is a grammatical morpheme? There is a cline of linguistic elements from fully lexical content words to fully specialized grammatical morphemes, but there is no obvious place to draw a line between lexical and grammatical items.[8]

3.5.2 What is a closed-class item? The lexicon is made up of a number of classes, ranging from almost entirely open (prototypically nouns) to almost entirely closed (prototypically grammatical morphemes such as clitics and inflections).

3.5.3 What makes a notion grammaticizable? At present there is no useful answer to this question beyond an empirically based list of the notions that receive grammatical expression in the languages of the world. The same notions are found repeatedly in the analysis of both lexical and grammatical items, as has been noted frequently by linguists working in various traditions (e.g. Lyons 1968:438). A modern statement of this position can be found in Pinker's (1989) analysis of the acquisition of argument structure. He suggests that a single "Grammatically Relevant Subsystem" of concepts (derived from Jackendoff and Talmy) provides the "privileged semantic machinery" (p. 166) needed *both* to specify the meanings of closed-class morphemes and to organize verbs into subclasses that are sensitive to various types of lexical rules and patterns of syntactic alternation.

3.5.4 How are grammaticizable notions organized? There is great diversity across languages in the level of granularity, the number and positions of cuts on semantic continua, the types of semantic components employed, and the balance between different parts of the linguistic system in expressing grammaticizable notions. This diversity has not yet been sufficiently systematized to make claims about its conceptual or developmental underpinnings. At the present state of our knowledge, it is premature to attribute a particular organization of grammaticizable notions to the child at the beginning of language acquisition (*pace* Slobin 1985). It would seem more plausible to endow the child with sufficient flexibility to discern and master the particular organization of the exposure language.

4 Diachronic evidence for modifying the linguistic conditions on learnability

All of the dominant accounts of learnability attempt to relate the structure of the mind with the structure of language, as if these were the only two factors to consider. When the social factor is considered, it is only as a source of data: the "input" language, perhaps with some attention to the interactive speech contexts in which the input is situated. Accordingly, when there is not enough information in the input to account for the structure of language, it must be sought in the individual mind. The end result is always some kind of nativism, whether of syntactic form, semantic content, or some interaction between form and content, perhaps with various cognitive prerequisites added in. This argument has been re-stated thousands of times since Chomsky first proposed it in the 1960s. Of the many formulations, the following representative summary by Jackendoff (1987:87) is useful in clearly revealing the limited options that flow from this conception of the problem:

> The claim, then, is that some aspects of our language capacity are not a result of learning from environmental evidence. Aside from divine intervention, the only other way we know of to get them into the mind is biologically: genetic information determining brain architecture, which in turn determines the form of possible computations. In other words, certain aspects of the structure of language are *inherited.*
>
> This conclusion, which I will call the *innateness hypothesis*, provides a potential solution to the paradox of language acquisition by appealing to evolution. The child alone does not have enough time to acquire all the aspects of language that linguists are struggling to discover. But evolution has had more time at its disposal to develop this structure than linguists will ever have . . .

Note a jump in the argument: it begins by discussing "some aspects of our language *capacity*," but ends up with the claim that "certain aspects of the *structure* of language are inherited" (emphasis added). There can be no disagreement that aspects of the capacity to acquire and use language are inherited: this is a general truth about species-specific behavior. But the *structure* of language arises in *two* diachronic processes: biological evolution and ever-changing processes of communicative interaction. The structure of language could not have arisen in the genetically determined brain architecture of an individual ancestor alone, because language arises only in communication between individuals. That is, after all, what language is for. As soon as we free ourselves of this confusion of levels of analysis – the individual and the social – many of the puzzles of language structure appear to have solutions beyond divine intervention or genetic determinism. The traditional attempt to account for linguistic structure is rather like trying to locate the law of supply and demand in the minds of the individual producer and consumer, or the shape of a honeycomb in the genetic structure of the individual bee.

Since the late 1970s there has been a rapidly growing interest in the *historical*, rather than the evolutionary processes that shape language – particularly with regard to the ways in which languages acquire and modify grammatical elements and constructions. A field calling itself "grammaticization" or "grammaticalization" (see note 1) has revived longstanding interest in language change, using a wealth of new typological, historical, and psycholinguistic data and theory.[9] As I have suggested, this field helps to explain the nature and origins of grammaticizable notions.

A central phenomenon of language change was already identified at the beginning of the last century by the French linguist Antoine Meillet. In 1912, in a paper titled "L'évolution des formes grammaticales," he introduced the term *grammaticalization* to designate the process by which a word develops into a grammatical morpheme ("le passage d'un mot autonome au rôle d'élément grammatical"). This process provides an explanation of why it is impossible to draw a line between lexical and grammatical items, as well as why grammatical morphemes have their peculiarly restricted and universal semantics. Hopper & Traugott (1993:7) define a cline of linguistic elements from a "lexical area" to a "grammatical area," with no firm boundaries between the categories:

> content item > grammatical word > clitic > inflectional affix

Diachronically "a given form typically moves from a point on the left of the cline to a point further on the right" (1993:7).

The literature is full of examples of the lexical origins of grammatical items. Familiar English examples are the development of the verb *go* from a full verb of motion to a reduced future marker *gonna*, and the development of modals from verbs of cognition and ability – e.g. *can* originally meant 'know how to,' *may* and *might* developed from a verb meaning 'have the (physical) power to.' The English contracted negative, *n't*, began in Old English as an emphatic form, *ne-a-wiht* 'not-ever-anything,' used to reinforce another negative form, *ne*. By the time of Middle English it had contracted to *nat* and eventually replaced the nonemphatic *ne*, becoming the new nonemphatic negative and finally contracting (Traugott 1972:146f.). This is the typical progress along the cline from full, stressed form with a more specific meaning, to reduced, unstressed form with a more general meaning. When such processes are traced out in full, the nature of grammatical morphemes – unstressed and general in meaning – is no longer mysterious. Here I will explore only one set of diachronic patterns in some detail, because it is relevant to several of the basic synchronic problems discussed in the previous section.

4.1 Origins and extensions of accusative markers

In the long history of Mandarin Chinese it is possible to see the entire developmental path from a lexical item to a grammatical morpheme (Lord 1982, with examples from Li & Thompson 1974, 1976). In the fifth century BC the verb *bǎ* was a full lexical verb meaning 'take hold of.' Much later, in the time of the Tang dynasty (seventh–ninth centuries AD), it appears in serial-verb constructions, opening the way to reanalysis and eventual grammaticization. For example, the following sentence is open to two different interpretations:

(8) *Zuì bǎ zhū-gēn-zǐ xì kàn*
drunk *bǎ* dogwood careful look

In the expected serial-verb interpretation the sentence means:

(a) 'While drunk, (I) *took* the dogwood and carefully looked at it.'

However, a verb meaning 'take' can also be interpreted, in this context, as simply reinforcing the act of examining something that has been taken or held:

(b) 'While drunk, (I) carefully looked at the dogwood.'

On this interpretation, *bǎ* has become a sort of object marker. Such possibilities of alternate interpretations open the way to the reanalyses that result in grammaticization. Sentence (8) "invites" a hearer to consider a single act – looking carefully, rather than two acts – taking and then looking carefully. This kind of "conversational implicature" (Grice 1975) or "pragmatic inferencing" (Hopper & Traugott 1993) can set a full verb like *bǎ* off on the course towards becoming a grammatical marker. And, indeed, that is what has happened in this case. In modern Mandarin, *bǎ* no longer has all of the syntactic properties of a full verb: it can't take an aspect marker and can no longer occur as the predicate of a simple sentence meaning "take" (Li & Thompson, 1981:464ff.). Now it functions as an objective casemarker in the frame, SUBJECT *bǎ* DIRECT.OBJECT VERB, as in:

(9) *nǐ bǎ jiǔ màn-màn-de hē*
you *bǎ* wine slowly drink
'You drink the wine slowly!'

However, the *bǎ*-construction is still not a full objective or *accusative* casemarker. The process of grammaticization is long, and traces of the original meaning of a lexical item linger on to influence or restrict its grammatical function. The construction can only be appropriately used with a *definite* direct object, that is, to indicate a referent that the speaker believes the hearer knows about. And, most interestingly, it is further restricted to situations in which something happens to the object – in Li & Thompson's terms (1981:468), "how an entity is handled or dealt with." It cannot mark objects of verbs of emotion, like 'love' and 'miss,' or verbs of cognition, like 'understand' or 'see,' because these verbs do not imply manipulation or handling of the object. It may come to mark such objects at some future time, like accusative casemarkers in languages like German and Russian, but at present it still retains traces of its semantic origin.

Lord describes almost identical grammaticization processes in several West African languages of the Benue-Kwa group. In Akan and Ga, a verb that meant 'take, hold, possess, use' no longer occurs as a verb in simple sentences and does not inflect for tense/aspect. It is now an invariant, noninflecting morpheme that functions as a casemarking preposition but only when referring to physical manipulation and only in affirmative sentences (that is, manipulation that is actually realized). However, in a related language, Idoma, the corresponding morpheme has become a prefix and, although still restricted to affirmative clauses, can also mark the objects of experience, such as 'she *prefix*-tree saw.' Lord cites a parallel development in the Native American language, Chickasaw, which seems to be at an earlier stage in the process of using a verb meaning 'take' to mark instruments and objects that are moved by an agent.

None of the many language-specific variants of the "accusative" or "direct object" or "patient" category could be part of a child's initial assumptions about the "grammaticizable notion" underlying the object marker in any particular Asian, African, or Amerindian language. Clearly, the child must be guided by the patterns of the exposure language. To be sure, all of these examples are consistent with a collection of "grammatically relevant notions" – definiteness, negation, manipulability, agent vs. experiencer – but there are too many different packagings of such semantic and pragmatic characteristics to build in all of the possibilities in advance or rank them in terms of "naturalness" or "accessibility."

At the same time, there is something intriguing about the fact that a verb like 'take' can repeatedly develop into an object marker in languages that have nothing in common geographically or typologically. In earlier work

(Slobin 1981, 1985) I suggested that children might begin to relate an accusative or an ergative casemarker, depending on the typology of the exposure language, to a notion of "prototypical direct manipulation," that is, "the experiential gestalt of a basic causal event in which an agent carries out a physical and perceptible change of state in a patient by means of direct body contact or with an instrument under the agent's control" (1985:1175). Verbs like 'take' clearly fit this definition. Can we conclude, then, that this is a privileged grammaticizable notion (§§ 3.3, 3.5.3)? It is important here to distinguish between what is salient to the cognition and life experience of a 2-year-old and the processes that drive grammaticization in the discourse of adult speakers of a language. The "Manipulative Activity Scene" is central to a 2-year-old's interaction with the world, and grammatical markers that regularly occur in conjunction with such events may well come to be associated with the notion of manipulation or direct effect on an object. But adult speakers of Tang Dynasty Chinese, Akan, Ga, or Chickasaw do not set out to grammaticize manipulation or effect. Rather, they use a verb like 'take' in constructions that allow it to be interpreted as a marker of manipulation, and, over time, such verbs follow the familiar cline described by Hopper & Traugott. The processes, then, are quite different, though superficially similar.[10] In order to fill out the picture, it is necessary to understand the psycholinguistic forces that move a linguistic element along that cline.

Diachronic paths of accusative development such as these raise critical questions for the Conditions and Assumptions of §2. Each step in the long evolution can be motivated by semantic and discourse factors – but at which point does the form mark a "true grammaticizable notion," and at which point is it a "true grammatical morpheme"? Which of the many "accusatives" in all of these language histories is the one to put on Pinker's innate chart of form/function correspondences? Which of these various historically attested grammatical morphemes corresponds to "core notions" like manipulation or purpose or goal?

4.2 *Psycholinguistic forces responsible for restrictions on grammaticizable notions*

Grammaticization paths such as those just sketched out take place, to begin with, in the processes of communication. Therefore they are shaped by the online demands on the speaker to be maximally clear within pragmatic constraints and maximally efficient within economy constraints, and by online capacities of the listener to segment, analyze, and interpret the message. Experimental and theoretical psycholinguists have learned much about these processes, in a literature far too large to cite or review here. It is clear that pressures of expressivity, economy, and clarity are always in competition, keeping language always changing in shifting states of balancing equilibrium (e.g. Slobin 1977; Hawkins 1983, 1994; Bybee 1985; Bates & MacWhinney 1987; MacWhinney & Bates 1989). Several psycholinguistic processes seem to account for the peculiar semantic limitations on grammaticizable notions that Talmy and others have discussed.

4.2.1 Frequency of use and generality of meaning Bybee (1985; Bybee, Perkins, & Pagliuca 1994) has explained much of grammaticization in terms of the fact that lexical items that are used with high frequency also have general meanings. For example, motion verbs such as *crawl, limp, hobble, creep, slither, wriggle* are applicable to describing a small number of situations and are, accordingly, not very frequent. By contrast, generalized motion verbs like *come* and *go* do not have such restrictions; they are applicable to a wide range of contexts and are used frequently. Generality of meaning and frequency of use go hand in hand – both in the "open" and "closed" classes. For example, compare highly frequent English prepositions like *in* and *on* with less frequent and more specialized prepositions such as *alongside, underneath, in back of* (American), *throughout*. The latter require more detailed attention to the geometry of the objects involved, and are therefore applicable to more limited contexts.

4.2.2 Frequency of use and reduction of form It is also a commonplace that any motor program that is called upon frequently is reduced and automatized. Zipf (1935) demonstrated the strong tendency for the length of a word to be negatively correlated with its frequency. Note that the more specialized prepositions just listed are also much longer than *in* and *on*. They are also more etymologically transparent – that is, they still have recognizable lexical components, including nouns (*side, back*) and more frequent prepositions (*in, of*, etc.). It is no surprise that as lexical items move along the grammaticization cline they become phonologically reduced and bound to associated content words.

4.2.3 Frequency of use and online accessibility In order for a speaker to express any notion in language, it is necessary to make a rapid decision with regard to the appropriate means of expression of that notion. Elements that are highly frequent and general – both content words and grammatical forms – must be easily accessible to online processing for both speaker and listener. Again, the same processing demands apply to content words and grammatical forms alike. Eve Clark (1978) has observed that early in English child language development the most frequent verbs are *go, put, get, do*, and *make*. She reports similar findings for Finnish, French,

Japanese, and Korean. This pattern probably reflects the high frequency of such verbs in adult speech, but the fact of their early frequency also bears on the issue of ability to choose the appropriate element online. In Clark's examples, when a child says *Do it!* it might apply to unrolling some tape, taking out a toy, or building a tower. *Make* + NOUN can mean *write*, *draw*, *move*, *cut out*, and so forth. *Do* and *make* place low demands on online access. In order to say *write* or *draw* or *cut out* the speaker must decide what kind of act of construction is involved, and determine the distinctions that are lexicalized in the language (for example, in some languages a single verb means both 'write' and 'draw').

These same sorts of "light" verbs appear as the sources of grammatical morphemes, as the examples of 'go' and 'take' discussed earlier. Hopper & Traugott (1993:87) present this as a general fact of grammaticization:

> As we have noted in previous chapters, the lexical meanings subject to grammaticalization are usually quite general. For example, verbs which grammaticalize, whether to case markers or to complementizers, tend to be superordinate terms (also known as "hyponyms") in lexical fields, for example, *say*, *move*, *go*. They are typically not selected from more specialized terms such as *whisper*, *chortle*, *assert*, *squirm*, *writhe*. Likewise, if a nominal from a taxonomic field grammaticalizes into a numeral classifier, it is likely to be selected from the following taxonomic levels: beginner (e.g. *creature*, *plant*), life form (e.g. *mammal*, *bush*), and generic (e.g. *dog*, *rose*), but not from specific (e.g. *spaniel*, *hybrid tea*), or varietal (e.g. *Cocker*, *Peace*) (Adams & Conklin, 1973). In other words, the lexical items that grammaticalize are typically what are known as "basic words."

Again, it is an illusion that child language development and grammaticization are due to the same sorts of processes. Children use basic verbs early on because they are easy to learn: they do not place high demands on lexical choice; they are frequent; they are used across a wide range of situations; they are short. But basic verbs appear at the beginnings of grammaticization clines because, when they are used in a conversational context, they contrast with the more specific verbs that *could* be used in that context, thereby signaling to the hearer that those more specific meanings were not intended. This opens the way for the kinds of pragmatic inferencing and reanalysis that lie at the heart of grammaticization.

Given these facts, it is evident that the special character of grammaticizable notions has its origin, in part, in the lexical items from which grammatical markers are prone to develop. That is, the "open class" is already organized into general and specialized terms – and this division can be accounted for by quite ordinary psycholinguistic and communicative processes. There is no need to postulate a special "grammar module" as responsible for these facts about the meanings of frequent lexical items. Why are such words prone to grammaticize? Because of their generality they are both highly frequent and likely to be used in contexts in which the speaker does not intend to communicate a specialized meaning. If I say, for example, "While drunk, I *grasped* the dogwood" or "*seized* the dogwood," the choice of a specialized verb of taking or holding suggests to the hearer that I wish to focus on the manner of taking or holding. This is simply an application of Grice's second maxim of Quantity: "Do not make your contribution more informative than is required" (Grice 1975). The hearer may well assume that I used a specialized verb because I intended to draw attention to the manner of acting. If, however, I use a more general verb like 'take,' the hearer will assume that I have followed the first maxim of Quantity, "Make your contribution as informative as is required (for the current purposes of the exchange)," and will not attend to the manner of taking the dogwood. In fact, following this maxim, the hearer might arrive at the interpretation given earlier in example (8b) – that is, backgrounding the fact of taking entirely and focusing on the act of looking, which is, after all, what may be relevant in this communicative situation. In such situations, the way has been opened for the grammaticization of 'take' as an object marker.

4.2.4. Frequency of use and schematization of a domain If a small set of linguistic items ends up being used frequently to reference divisions within a semantic domain, pressures towards easy lexical access will inevitably move the system towards a schematic representation of that domain, selecting a set of parameters or features for sorting instances. The most familiar example of schematization is an inflectional paradigm, in which slots are filled in for such features as person and number, or case and gender, and so forth. But schematization is also evident in linguistic systems which might appear to be more lexical than grammatical. A good example is Levinson's (1994) analysis of the Tzeltal use of body-part terminology to locate an object in relation to a ground. In English we have suggestions of such a system in grammaticized expressions like *in back of the house* and lexicalized descriptions such as *the foot of the mountain.* In Tzeltal, as in many Mesoamerican languages, body-part terms are used systematically to specify the grounds involved in locative relations. One says, for example, that an object is at the 'ear' (= corner) of a table or at the 'butt' (= bottom) of a bottle (P. Brown 1994:750). Levinson shows that choice of body-part term is based on a precise geometric schematization of objects. For example, the base of an arc defines the 'butt' of an object, including the large end of a pear, the bottom of a bowl, and the point where a stem is attached to a leaf. If an object has two surfaces, the flatter, less-featured surface will be labeled 'back' and the opposing surface will be 'belly' if concave or convex and 'face' if flat. In order to use the system in Levinson's analysis, the speaker must carry out a series of algorithms, such as finding the orthogonal axis, finding the direction of the subsidiary arc, and finding junctures between surfaces. He proposes that, using such calculations of the intrinsic shape of an object, speakers know how to use the body-part terms with regard to any particular object. Thus, Tzeltal words like 'butt,' 'ear,' 'belly,' and 'neck' are as fully grammaticized as English prepositions. They constitute a small, closed set, with schematized representations of those features of their spatial characteristics that are used in the language to specify locative relations of particular types. Because body-part terms must be used to designate parts of any object in the world – doors, tables, computers, chili beans – speakers must be able to decide easily which term to apply to which part or surface of an object. Such a system cannot simply leave the speaker to pick a body-part term and search for a possible metaphorical extension; nor can it leave the speaker to use all possible body parts. Out of several hundred such terms, the language uses about twenty to label parts of inanimate objects. In order to apply this small set to all possible objects, there is no choice but to develop a way of schematizing their meanings within a structured semantic domain.[11]

4.3 A functionalist account of the classes of grammaticizable and non-grammaticizable notions

If a domain is to be divided up such that each of the subcategories can be rapidly accessed online, by speaker and hearer, there cannot be too many divisions in the domain, nor can the deciding factors be infrequent or idiosyncratic. Typically, as forms become highly grammaticized, they divide up a domain exhaustively into a very small number of options: *singular* vs. *plural* (with possible additions of *dual*), *perfective* vs. *imperfective*, the six cases and three genders of Russian. Markers such as these are obligatory, which means they must be accessed in almost every utterance. The facts of language processing work against ambiguities of online access. The notions that evolve into such very small and obligatory sets must (1) unambiguously divide the domain, and (2) use criteria that are generally relevant to that domain. Thus it is no mystery that grammatical inflections do not indicate color or rate or ambient temperature: these are not aspects of experience that are universally applicable or memorable with regard to all of the event types that we talk about. That is, they are not aspects that are relevant to how we interpret and store events IN GENERAL. In order, for example, to grammaticize a temperature marker or a color marker, it would be necessary, first, to have a speech community in which lexical items of temperature or color occurred frequently in discourse, and in which there were a few general terms that marked readily agreed-upon distinctions, such as *cold* –

cool – warm – hot, or *black – white – red – yellow – blue/green*. Such scenarios are unlikely for several reasons. For one, these distinctions are not relevant to most of human discourse. The things that we care to communicate about, by and large, are true on cool and warm days; the things we act upon are important regardless of their color. Because we don't tend to store such information in memory, such a language would place terrible burdens on deciding which linguistic form to use in referring to a situation. For example, if I wanted to tell you a juicy bit of gossip, I would have to remember whether the reported event (or the time of my hearing about it) occurred on a warm or cool day. Or when a newscaster reports a bomb explosion in the Paris Metro, he would have to know the color of the bomb, or the Metro, or the explosion. We do not grammaticize such notions because we do not think or talk in such terms.

"Lower" on grammaticization clines there are relatively small sets that provide options. For example, as discussed in §3.1.1, English has a small set of modal auxiliaries, supplemented by quasi-modals and some less clearly grammaticized terms. Most of the time modality can simply be left unmarked. The "zero option" means that it is not necessary to decide about the modality of every utterance. A similar function is provided by the general classifier *gè* in Mandarin. When a speaker does choose to mark modality in English or to classify a noun in Mandarin, a small set of terms is provided, with more flexibility in their applicability. Erbaugh (1986) finds about twenty-two classifiers in ordinary speech in Mandarin, and she reports that the same object occurs with different classifiers in discourse; e.g. different speakers viewing the same film referred to a goat with the classifiers *yī-zhī* 'one.animal,' *yì-tóu* 'one.head,' and *yì-tíao* 'one.long.thing.' The choices in a set like the Mandarin classifiers do not unambiguously divide up a domain, but they are still semantically relevant to the nouns that are marked.

Relevance, however, does not have to be part of a *universal* human "semantic space." There is nothing in the nature of our cognitive and linguistic systems that precludes grammaticization of idiosyncratic information if it assumes sufficient social or cultural relevance to be regularly communicable. For example, social structure is repeatedly grammaticized in choices of personal pronouns and verb inflections. Although a European speaker would find it hard to decide whether each person addressed is older or younger than the speaker, this is obligatory in Korean, and children learn to pay attention to this feature. English speakers in France might find it hard to decide if an interlocutor falls into the *tu* or the *vous* category, and, as Roger Brown and Albert Gilman (1960) have shown, the criteria for choosing one of the two pronoun types have changed historically and vary between European countries. The languages of the world grammaticize an array of social categories of rank, status, relative age, servitude, and the like. These are sociocultural facts, and could not possibly be part of the child's innate linguistic categories or prelinguistic sensorimotor concepts. Yet they are grammaticized in those societies where they are relevant, and are marked with a small number of forms that are frequent and decidable online. The reason why languages have no grammatical markers for quantified categories of "fixed distance, size, contour, and angle" (Talmy 1988:171) is simply because human beings do not regularly code, store, and report their experience in these terms – not because these categories are *a priori* excluded from the grammar module. I would suggest, then, that anything that is important and salient enough for people to want to refer to it routinely and automatically most of the time, and across a wide range of situations, *can* come to be grammatically marked, within the constraints of online processing briefly alluded to earlier.

I believe that similar arguments could be made with regard to each of the "conceptual domains *not* accessible to grammaticization" listed by Talmy and others (as in (1b)). These arguments would draw on the factors of across-the-board relevance to human experience and communication, online decision making, and the availability of high-frequency and general lexical items that could start off paths of grammaticization in those domains. I leave it to the reader to try to find examples or counterexamples.

5 Challenges to learning theory

5.1 The conditions and assumptions of the learning task

In §2 I listed three linguistic Conditions and three psychological Assumptions underlying standard definitions of the task of learning to use grammatical morphemes. It is time to return to that starting point.

5.1.1 The conditions

Condition 1: there is a distinct and identifiable collection of grammatical morphemes, arranged in small, closed classes. It turns out that there is a cline of linguistic elements, arising naturally over time, and that the "distinct and identifiable collection of grammatical morphemes" only defines the endpoint of that cline. However, looking at an entire language, one can only rank elements on various dimensions, both formal and functional. There are, to be sure, many small, closed and semi-closed sets of items – but they are not all grammatical morphemes. Thus the language does not present itself to the learner as a neat set of little packages labeled as "grammatical" and "lexical."

Condition 2: these morphemes map onto a universal, limited set of semantic entities (grammaticizable notions). The further one moves to the right on the cline, the more true is this condition. And there are regular diachronic progressions of particular types of meanings towards the highly grammaticized pole of the cline.

Condition 3: grammaticizable notions are arranged in a universal accessibility hierarchy. If "accessible" means either "learnable" or "more frequent in human languages," we lack the data to evaluate this condition. If "accessible" means that some notions are more likely to grammaticize than others, the claim can be filled out with more and more data, and the patterns are amenable to explanation in terms of such interacting factors as online processing, pragmatic inference, and syntactic reanalysis.

5.1.2 *The assumptions*

Assumption 1: Conditions 1, 2, and 3 exist because of the structure of the mind/brain (in modules for aspects of language, perhaps in conjunction with other modules). There is a great deal of evidence that the Conditions exist because of conditions on the processing, social use, and learning of form–function relations. Such evidence greatly reduces the role of *a priori* specification of grammatical structures and their specialized meanings.

Assumption 2: the role of linguistic input is to allow the relevant mental capacities to organize themselves in terms of the exposure language. This, of course, remains true – but relativized to the definition of "relevant mental capacities." Linguistic diversity in the domains considered here precludes a simple selection between prespecified alignments of formal and semantic categories. The role of linguistic input is to guide the child towards discovery and construction of the form–function relations inherent in the exposure language. That is, input is not a "trigger" but a "nutrient."

Assumption 3: the child learns the meaning of a grammatical form by isolating and identifying a particular stretch of speech as instantiating a grammatical form and attempting to map it onto a relevant grammaticizable notion. This formulation is built upon *a priori* definitions of "grammatical form" and "relevant grammaticizable notion" – the very concepts that demand reanalysis. The result of that reanalysis is, of course, the challenge to learning theory.

5.2 *Towards a solution*

It is not (and cannot be) the goal of this chapter to answer these challenges by presenting The Adequate Learning Theory. At best, a reorientation might serve to head us towards different kinds of solutions. Once we have established a social-historical, rather than an individual-mind source of grammaticized notions and their means of expression, we can abandon the search for an innate form–function module and follow Annette Karmiloff-

Smith (1992) "beyond modularity." That is, we can take a *developmental* approach to the structuring of grammaticizable notions in the child. A major theme that emerges from the reanalysis is the proposal that the same learning mechanisms apply across the lexicon, including "content words" and "functors." To be sure, the child requires specialized mechanisms of perception (auditory for speech, visual for sign), storage, and analysis of linguistic material. And the architecture of syntax is certainly determined by quite different processes than those involved in learning the kinds of form–function mappings considered here. The reanalysis of the learning task places "grammaticizable notions" in the more general domain of concept formation.

5.2.1 The problem of constraints on hypotheses: what is "economy"? Regardless of the revision of the task definition, the child will always be faced with a large set of possible form–function mappings. My very brief overview of a few problems to do with the grammatical marking of semantic and pragmatic categories makes it evident that the child could be prey to many false starts and dead-end attempts. This fact alone has led to the proliferation of "constraints," "predispositions," "parameter settings," "operating principles," and the like in the theoretical literature of recent decades. But there are no obvious constraints on the constraints, because we have no plausible metric of what makes a task "too hard" for a child learner. We know that children do acquire the manifold and subtle complexities of language. And we realize that this is a hard task for conscious, problem-solving adults (even linguists). Therefore we try to make the task "easier" for children by providing bootstraps that they can use to pull themselves up (an unclear metaphor at best). The list of grammaticizable notions was intended to provide an aid – intended to prevent the child from making too many false hypotheses. But, I would propose, we really have no way of knowing how many false hypotheses it takes to overburden the vastly complex human brain, or how quickly and efficiently they can be revised or dismissed. It is unsettling to realize how many of our theories are aimed at the simplistic criterion of "economy," when we have no rational measure of that economy.

5.2.2 What is "reasonable"? Having voiced these qualms about the soundness of our endeavor, I will return to the attempt to give the child some guidelines for the task. Our theories are haunted by the risk that children might think that everything might be relevant to everything. Our data, however, suggest that children are more "reasonable" than that. As developmental psychologists have pointed out, children are at work constructing "intuitive theories" of domains of experience (e.g. Keil 1989, 1994; Gopnik

& Meltzoff 1996). Hypotheses about the meanings of linguistic forms occur in the context of such general theorizing, which provides the child with "reasonable" factors to consider when encountering, say, verbs of motion or locative particles or casemarkers. Recall the diachronic processes of grammaticization (and, I would add, the processes of forming small sets of specialized verbs). The only available items are those which occur again and again in talking about a great range of experiences. They occur so frequently because they are applicable so generally. Therefore it should be no surprise that children find these notions salient. For example, the factors that apply to many instances of moving and placing objects include the force-dynamic and motoric aspects of picking up an object, moving it, and placing it in another location. It is "reasonable" for grammatical items and small verb sets dealing with these actions to be sensitive to such factors as characteristics of figure and ground objects, direction of movement, and relation of the two objects at the end point of the action (e.g. tight fit, located near the bottom of another object, etc.).[12] The color of the objects or the time of day are not *relevant* to this type of scene, given the kind of social world in which we live at present. In part, then, children are reasonable because languages are reasonable. It has been assumed in the literature that it is odd that systems of grammatical meaning, and children acquiring such systems, seem to be indifferent to "non-grammaticizable" notions such as those listed by Talmy. However, if we look carefully at the communicative contexts in which language is used – both on the diachronic and ontogenetic planes – the situation seems much less odd. I suggest that the same factors that keep certain notions from becoming grammaticized also keep children from postulating them as the meanings of grammatical forms.

There are several parts to this argument. One part is social-pragmatic, as has been eloquently and elegantly advanced by Tomasello (e.g. 1992, 1995, ch. 5 of this volume). That is, the child is at work figuring out adults' intentions, aided both by social knowledge and by the cooperative communicative behavior of adults. Another factor is what might be called "the texture of experience." For example, particular colors do not occur frequently in association with the linguistic encoding of particular event types. The child is not likely to encounter one set of object placement events that consistently occur with red objects and another with black ones. Even a simple model of statistical sampling, not to mention a connectionist network, would quickly drop color as a determining factor in choice of linguistic form. And a third factor can be found in the nature of form–function mappings themselves. It has long been noted by linguists that grammatical morphemes are placed in association with the content words with which they have the most conceptual affinity – e.g. tense is marked on verbs rather than nouns, shape classifiers are placed in relation to object nouns or verbs of handling, and so forth. A classic formulation of this principle was offered by the German linguist Behaghel (1932:4): "What belongs together mentally is placed close together syntactically."[13] Bybee (1985) has refined the principle, showing not only that particular notions are relevant to verb stems, but that grammatical morphemes reflecting such notions are ordered in a reasonable way, with those meanings that are most relevant to the meaning of the stem occurring closest to the stem, and often phonologically fusing with the stem. Bybee's analysis is part of a series of discoveries of the "iconicity" of form–function mappings in language (e.g. Haiman 1985a, b). To the extent that the arrangement of linguistic items is a "diagram" or "icon" of the arrangement of mental items, the child may be aided by "iconic bootstrapping." There are many examples of iconicity in children's early grammars, across languages, summarized in Slobin (1985). Putting these various sorts of factors together – social-pragmatic, environmental, linguistic – reduces the need to posit *a priori* constraints on form–function relations.

5.2.3 Typological bootstrapping In the process of concept formation, children build up and revise "explanatory systems" that are relevant to classes of phenomena. As the child develops a successful explanatory structure for part of the exposure language, other parts become more accessible – that is, a coherent theory of the language begins to emerge. This is true, in part, because the language really *is* a fairly coherent system – as a result of constant balancing out of competing forces. Over time, each language acquires a typological character resulting from the particular interplay of forces in its history. (There is a small number of language types, but this is not because there is a small number of innate parameter settings; rather, there is a small number of solutions to the kinds of competing forces which shape language in use.) At the risk of overburdening the child's shoe-rack, I propose yet another kind of bootstrapping: *typological bootstrapping.* For example, Korean uses verbs to express paths of motion, while English uses particles; and each language uses particular semantic features in categorizing location and movement. As a Korean child learns more linguistic constructions describing motion events, the lexicalization patterns and grammaticized notions of the language become an established pattern. She comes to expect that paths will be lexicalized in verb stems, that caused-motion verbs are sensitive to properties of the objects involved, and so forth. The English-speaking child comes to expect verb particles to structure domains in terms of locative and temporal relations, and finds that certain locative and temporal notions occur again and again. That is, to some extent, the language structures itself as it is learned. Certain patterns of semantic and formal organization become more and more familiar, and, to use an old term, habits are established. This is possible because of the fact that languages naturally develop into coherent systems of various types. As elements of a system are learned, they come to interrelate because of inherent typological factors. In Karmiloff-Smith's (1992) terms, "representational redescription" occurs – in this case aided by the systematicity inherent in the language that is being learned.

An intriguing consequence of typological bootstrapping is that children come to formulate experience for linguistic expression in quite different ways, depending on the type of language they are learning. I have suggested that each type of language fosters its own modes of "thinking for speaking" (Slobin 1991b, 1996). Because of the systematic crosslinguistic diversity in selection and patterning of grammaticizable notions, different patterns of online mental organization result. In crosslinguistic work on narrative development, Ruth Berman and I (Berman & Slobin 1994) have identified a number of ways in which children come to structure discourse in terms of the typological characteristics of the particular language. By school age, children have acquired typologically distinct ways of describing events and constructing connected texts. From this point of view, grammaticizable notions have a role in structuring language-specific mental spaces, rather than being there at the beginning, waiting for an input language to turn them on.

I am aware that this formulation still leaves open the mechanisms that a child might use to detect and "representationally redescribe" the systematicity of the exposure language. Various sorts of "operating principles" and "procedures" will be needed in order to give substance to the formulation. However, the very fact that form–function relations become systematically patterned in the course of acquiring a particular language points to an important learning mechanism. As suggested above, in the course of development the child comes to attend to particular types of meanings and to expect them to be expressed by particular types of forms. Such a combination of thinking for speaking and typological bootstrapping seems to guarantee that language-specific form–function patterns will be established and maintained by learners.

5.2.4 In my end is my beginning Allow me to end on a retrospective note. Since the 1960s our linguistic, psychological, and philosophical disciplines have sought to replicate themselves in the mind/brain of the child. The modules that are postulated often have names that evoke suspicion: they are the names of our own academic fields (linguistics, mathematics, physics, biology) or subfields (closed-class morphemes, grammaticizable notions). Could God or evolution have anticipated the academic and intellectual organization of late twentieth-century America? At the beginning of my career I was skeptical of building academia into the child. Later I found it attractive to "help" the child by removing some problems from the learning task. Now – partly to my surprise – I find myself thinking things that I said long ago (Slobin 1966:87ff.):

[According to Chomsky] the reason that human languages utilize such strikingly universal grammatical relations and formal devices is . . . due to the fact that these universal characteristics are themselves part of the innate structure of man . . . I would rather think of the child as learning [a category such as the Russian animate accusative] through feedback than to have him waiting for confirmation of dozens of such categories from his mother's expansions. It seems to me more reasonable to suppose that it is language that plays a role in drawing the child's attention to the possibility of dividing nouns on the basis of animacy; or verbs on the basis of duration, or determinacy, or validity; or pronouns on the basis of social status, and the like.

NOTES

I have benefited from many long discussions of these topics with Melissa Bowerman, and she will find her influence obvious in the revisions of my earlier position. I also owe much to Joan Bybee, Alison Gopnik, Len Talmy, David Wilkins, the many colleagues in Nijmegen who have provided stimulation and (re-)education, and the participants in the 1995 conference on "Language acquisition and conceptual development." Thanks also to Paul Bloom, Steve Levinson, Marianne Mithun, Izchak Schlesinger, Elizabeth Traugott, and Tania Kuteva for valuable correspondence on topics raised here. A longer version of this chapter has been published as "The origins of grammaticizable notions: beyond the individual mind" (Slobin 1997).

1 At present there are two roughly synonymous terms in the literature: "grammaticization" and "grammaticalization." I prefer the former, shorter form, but nothing hangs on the difference. Theorists working within the same overall theoretical framework have not agreed. It seems that American researchers prefer "grammaticization" (e.g. Wallace Chafe, Marianne Mithun, Joan Bybee, and her associates), while those of European origin prefer "grammaticalization" (e.g. Elizabeth Traugott, Paul Hopper, Bernd Heine, and his associates).

2 This is a partial listing, extracted from Talmy (1985:126–138). The domains listed in (1a) can be expressed by bound morphemes (inflections), suggesting that they are more highly grammaticized than other domains that Talmy lists as being realized as satellites to the verb. The important distinction for present purposes is between (1a) and (1b). For details, see Talmy (1985).

3 Various investigators have proposed that the hierarchy corresponds to the frequency of occurrence of grammaticized notions in the languages of the world (e.g. Pinker 1984:171; Bowerman 1985:1306). This suggestion has at least two major problems: (1) we lack an adequate sample of the world's existing languages, and can never have a full sample of all of the languages that have been used by human beings; (2) on this hypothesis, languages using "rare" forms should pose problems of acquisition and processing – but there is no evidence for such problems. (For discussion of these issues, see the longer version of this chapter [Slobin 1997].)

4 There is also a long tradition in aphasiology that has sought to find a neurological basis for grammatical morphology in syndromes of telegraphic speech. The classical claim has been that closed-class items are lost, thus proving that they reside in a distinct module. However, by now there is ample evidence against the view that agrammatism is simply an impairment of linguistic structure. Grammatical morphology is often preserved in judgments of grammaticality and in tasks that reduce online time pressure; crosslinguistic studies of aphasia show differential loss of grammatical morphemes, depending on both their "functional load" in the language and their acoustic salience (e.g. Bates & Wulfeck 1989). All of these findings remove any basis for a neurological definition of the closed class as a linguistic subsystem. What remains is a congeries of factors which lie outside the various attempts to distinguish the two classes on linguistic grounds, including "the sonorance hierarchy, the status of an affix with respect to derivational or inflectional morphology, the lexical status of a root or stem, the salience of a lexical item, attentional and control processes" (Caplan 1992:340).

5 Abbreviations: A = Absolutive, DIR = Directional, E = Ergative, NCL = Nominal classifier, REFL = Reflexive.

6 The languages were Slovak, Serbo-Croatian, Iraqi Arabic, Polish, Luo, Akan, Alur, Finnish, Swahili, Japanese, Korean, and Tamil. This ordering of languages reflects the division point on the continuum, from mainly comitative to mainly instrumental. For example, Slovak uses a distinct instrumental only for sentence 10 ("with a stone"), whereas Tamil uses a special comitative form only for sentences I and 2 ("with the clown," "with an assistant").

7 Pinker attempts to deal with the typology of Nominative/Accusative and Ergative/Absolutive languages by linking "Patient of transitive action" with "Accusative or Absolutive," and "Agent of transitive action" with "Nominative or Ergative." This leaves the child with the problem of determining the typology of the exposure language, with problems such as those spelled out by Van Valin (1992) for ergative languages.

8 Note that the existence of clines wreaks havoc with parameter-setting theories, which rely on discrete categories and principles that are applicable throughout a language.

9 Two recent overviews, both with the title *Grammaticalization*, have been provided by Heine, Claudi, & Hünnemeyer (1991) and Hopper & Traugott (1993). An early and insightful approach was developed by Bybee (1985), elaborated in successive papers with various collaborators, and most recently presented as *The evolution of grammar* (Bybee, Perkins, & Pagliuca 1994). Two volumes of conference papers, *Approaches to grammaticalization*, have been edited by Traugott & Heine (1991) and published in the John Benjamins Series, "Typological Studies in Language," which includes many books dealing with diachronic linguistic issues. The journal *Language Variation and Change* is a forum for diachronic research using statistical methods. The closely related field of "typology and universals" places diachronic issues in a synchronic framework; see textbooks by Comrie (1981) and Croft (1990), and the new journal, *Linguistic Typology*, of the recently established Association for Linguistic Typology.

10 For a similar argument against equating processes of ontogeny and grammaticization, see my discussion of the development of the English *perfect* (Slobin 1994).

11 Levinson proposes that the schematization is given by the visual system, thus raising a problem for modularity theories: "According to modularity arguments, linguistic processes should have no access to strictly visual processes. Although the present facts are not decisive, together with other observations they favor models where there is shared linguistic and visual access to the underlying processes of volumetric shape analysis" (1994:791).

12 What was, in retrospect, not "reasonable" was my Platonic hope that all children would start with the same semantic notions – the "Basic Child Grammar" of Slobin (1985).

13 "Das oberste Gesetz ist dieses, daß das geistig eng Zusammengehörige auch eng zusammengestellt wird."

REFERENCES

Adams, K. L., & N. F. Conklin. 1973. Toward a theory of natural classification. In C. Corum, T. C. Smith-Stark, & A. Weiser (eds.), *Chicago Linguistic Society* 9: 1–10.

Bates, E., & B. MacWhinney. 1987. Competition, variation, and language learning. In B. MacWhinney (ed.), *Mechanisms of language acquisition.* Hillsdale, NJ: Lawrence Erlbaum, 157–193.

Bates, E., & B. Wulfeck. 1989. Crosslinguistic studies of aphasia. In E. Bates & B. MacWhinney (eds.), *The crosslinguistic study of sentence processing.* Cambridge: Cambridge University Press, 328–374.

Behaghel, O. 1932. *Deutsche syntax: eine geschichtliche Darstellung*, vol. 4: *Wortstellung. Periodenbau.* Heidelberg: Carl Winter.

Berman, R. A., & D. I. Slobin (eds.). 1994. *Relating events in narrative: a crosslinguistic developmental study.* Hillsdale, NJ: Lawrence Erlbaum.

Bickerton, D. 1981. *Roots of language.* Ann Arbor, MI: Karoma Publishers.

Bowerman, M. 1985. What shapes children's grammars? In D. I. Slobin (ed.), *The crosslinguistic study of language acquisition*, vol. 2: *Theoretical issues.* Hillsdale, NJ: Lawrence Erlbaum, 1257–1319.

1993. Typological perspectives in language acquisition: do crosslinguistic patterns predict development? In E. V. Clark (ed.), *The proceedings of the 25th Annual Child Language Research Forum.* Stanford, CA: Center for the Study of Language and Information, 7–15.

1994. From universal to language-specific in early grammatical development. *Philosophical Transactions of the Royal Society of London B* 346: 37–45.

1996a. Learning how to structure space for language: a crosslinguistic perspective. In P. Bloom, M. A. Peterson, L. Nadel, & M. F. Garrett (eds.), *Language and space.* Cambridge, MA: MIT Press, 385–436.

1996b. The origins of children's spatial semantic categories: cognitive versus linguistic determinants. In J. J. Gumperz & S. C. Levinson (eds.), *Rethinking linguistic relativity*. Cambridge: Cambridge University Press, 145–176.

Bowerman, M., L. de León, & S. Choi. 1995. Verbs, particles, and spatial semantics: learning to talk about spatial actions in typologically different languages. In E. V. Clark (ed.), *The proceedings of the 27th Annual Child Language Research Forum.* Stanford, CA: Center for the Study of Language and Information, 101–110.

Bowerman, M., & E. Pederson. 1992. Crosslinguistic perspectives on topological spatial relationships. Paper presented at the annual meeting of the American Anthropological Association, San Francisco, CA, December.

Brown, P. 1994. The INs and ONs of Tzeltal locative expressions: the semantics of static descriptions of location. *Linguistics* 32: 743–790.

Brown, R., & A. Gilman. 1960. The pronouns of power and solidarity. In T. Sebeok (ed.), *Aspects of style in language.* Cambridge, MA: MIT Press, 253–277.

Bybee, J. L. 1985. *Morphology: a study of the relation between meaning and form.* Amsterdam/ Philadelphia: John Benjamins.

Bybee, J. L., R. Perkins, & W. Pagliuca. 1994. *The evolution of grammar: tense, aspect, and modality in the languages of the world.* Chicago: University of Chicago Press.

Caplan, D. 1992. *Language: structure, processing, and disorders.* Cambridge, MA: MIT Press.

Choi, S. 1997. Language-specific input and early semantic development: evidence from children learning Korean. In D. I. Slobin (ed.), *The crosslinguistic study of language acquisition*, vol. 5: *Expanding the contexts.* Mahwah, NJ: Lawrence Erlbaum, 41–133.

Choi, S., & M. Bowerman. 1991. Learning to express motion events in English and Korean: the influence of language-specific lexicalization patterns. *Cognition* 41: 83–121.

Clark, E. V. 1978. Discovering what words can do. In D. Farkas, W. M. Jacobsen, & K. W. Todrys (eds.), *Papers from the parasession on the lexicon.* Chicago: Chicago Linguistic Society, 34–57.

Comrie, B. 1981. *Language universals and linguistic typology: syntax and morphology.* Chicago: University of Chicago Press.

Craig, C. (ed.). 1986. *Noun classes and categorization.* Amsterdam/Philadelphia: John Benjamins.

Craig, C. G. 1993. Jakaltek directionals: their meaning and discourse function. *Languages of the World* 7: 23–36.

Croft, W. 1990. *Typology and universals.* Cambridge: Cambridge University Press.

Erbaugh, M. S. 1986. Taking stock: the development of Chinese noun classifiers historically and in young children. In Craig 1986: 399–436.

Gleitman, L. R., H. Gleitman, B. Landau, & E. Wanner. 1988. Where learning begins: initial representations for language learning. In F. J. Newmeyer (ed.), *Linguistics: the Cambridge survey*, vol. 3: *Language: psychological and biological aspects*. Cambridge: Cambridge University Press, 150–193.

Gleitman, L. R., & E. Wanner. 1982. Language acquisition: the state of the state of the art. In E. Wanner & L. R. Gleitman (eds.), *Language acquisition: the state of the art.* Cambridge: Cambridge University Press, 3–48.

Gopnik, A., & A. N. Meltzoff. 1996. *Words, thoughts, and theories.* Cambridge, MA: MIT Press.

Green, J. N. 1982. The status of the Romance auxiliaries of voice. In N. Vincent & M. Harris (eds.), *Studies in the Romance verb.* London/Canberra: Croom Helm, 97–138.

Grice, H. P. 1975. Logic and conversation. In P. Cole & J. L. Morgan (eds.), *Syntax and semantics*, vol. 3: *Speech acts.* New York: Academic Press, 41–58.

Haiman, J. (ed.). 1985a. *Iconicity in syntax.* Amsterdam/Philadelphia: John Benjamins.

1985b. *Natural syntax: iconicity and erosion.* Cambridge: Cambridge University Press.

Hawkins, J. A. 1983. *Word order universals.* New York: Academic Press.

1988. Explaining language universals. In J. A. Hawkins (ed.), *Explaining language universals.* Oxford: Blackwell, 3–28.

1994. *A performance theory of order and constituency.* Cambridge: Cambridge University Press.

Heine, B., U. Claudi, & F. Hünnemeyer. 1991. *Grammaticalization: a conceptual framework.* Chicago: University of Chicago Press.

Hopper, P. J., & E. C. Traugott. 1993. *Grammaticalization.* Cambridge: Cambridge University Press.

Jackendoff, R.S. 1983. *Semantics and cognition.* Cambridge, MA: MIT Press.

1987. *Consciousness and the computational mind.* Cambridge, MA: MIT Press.

1990. *Semantic structures.* Cambridge, MA: MIT Press.

Karmiloff-Smith, A. 1992. *Beyond modularity: a developmental perspective on cognitive science*. Cambridge, MA: MIT Press.

Keil, F. C. 1989. *Concepts, kinds, and cognitive development.* Cambridge, MA: Bradford Books.

1994. Explanation, association, and the acquisition of word meaning. *Lingua* 92: 169–196.

Landau, B., & L. R. Gleitman. 1985. *Language and experience: evidence from the blind child.* Cambridge, MA: Harvard University Press.

Landau, B., & R. Jackendoff. 1993. "What" and "where" in spatial language and spatial cognition. *Behavioral and Brain Sciences* 16: 217–265.

Levin, B. 1993. *English verb classes and alternations: a preliminary investigation.* Chicago: University of Chicago Press.

Levinson, S. C. 1994. Vision, shape and linguistic description: Tzeltal body-part terminology and object description. *Linguistics* 32: 791–855.

Li, C., & S. Thompson. 1974. Coverbs in Mandarin Chinese: verbs or prepositions? *Journal of Chinese Linguistics* 2: 257–278.

1976. Development of the causative in Mandarin Chinese: interaction of diachronic processes. In M. Shibatani (ed.), *Syntax and semantics*, vol. 6: *The grammar of causative constructions.* New York: Academic Press, 477–492.

1981. A *functional reference grammar of Mandarin Chinese.* Berkeley/Los Angeles: University of California Press.

Lord, C. 1982. The development of object markers in serial verb languages. In P. J. Hopper & S. A. Thompson (eds.), *Syntax and semantics*, vol. 15: *Studies in transitivity.* New York: Academic Press, 277–299.

Lyons, J. 1968. *Introduction to theoretical linguistics.* Cambridge: Cambridge University Press.

MacWhinney, B., & E. Bates. (eds.). 1989. *The crosslinguistic study of sentence processing.* Cambridge: Cambridge University Press.

Meillet, A. 1912. L'évolution des formes grammaticales. *Scientia (Rivista di scienza)*, 12. Reprinted in Meillet, A. [1982]. *Linguistique historique et linguistique générale.* Geneva: Slatkine / Paris: Champion, 130–148.

Pinker, S. 1984. *Language learnability and language development.* Cambridge, MA: Harvard University Press.

1989. *Learnability and cognition: the acquisition of argument structure.* Cambridge, MA: MIT Press.

Sapir, E. 1921/1949. *Language: an introduction to the study of speech.* New York: Harcourt, Brace and World.

Schlesinger, I. M. 1979. Cognitive and linguistic structures: the case of the instrumental. *Journal of Linguistics* 15: 307–324.

1982. *Steps to language: toward a theory of language acquisition.* Hillsdale, NJ: Lawrence Erlbaum.

1988. The origin of relational categories. In Y. Levy, I. M. Schlesinger, & M. D. S. Braine (eds.), *Categories and processes in language acquisition.* Hillsdale, NJ: Lawrence Erlbaum, 121–178.

Sinha, C., & T. Kuteva. 1995. Distributed spatial semantics. *Nordic Journal of Linguistics* 18: 167–199.

Slobin, D. I. 1966. Comments on "Developmental psycholinguistics": a discussion of McNeill's presentation. In F. Smith & G. A. Miller (eds.), *The genesis of language: a psycholinguistic approach.* Cambridge, MA: MIT Press, 85–91.

1977. Language change in childhood and in history. In J. Macnamara (ed.), *Language learning and thought.* New York: Academic Press, 185–214.

1981. The origins of grammatical encoding of events. In W. Deutsch (ed.), *The child's construction of language.* London: Academic Press, 185–200.

1985. Crosslinguistic evidence for the Language-Making Capacity. In D. I. Slobin (ed.), *The crosslinguistic study of language acquisition*, vol. 2: *Theoretical issues.* Hillsdale, NJ: Lawrence Erlbaum, 1157–1256.

1991. Learning to think for speaking: native language, cognition, and rhetorical style. *Pragmatics* 1: 7–25.

1994. Talking perfectly: discourse origins of the present perfect. In W. Pagliuca (ed.), *Perspectives on grammaticalization.* Philadelphia/Amsterdam: John Benjamins, 199–233.

1996. From "thought and language" to "thinking for speaking." In J. J. Gumperz & S. C. Levinson (eds.), *Rethinking linguistic relativity.* Cambridge: Cambridge University Press, 70–86.

1997. The origins of grammaticizable notions: beyond the individual mind. In D. I. Slobin (ed.), *The crosslinguistic study of language acquisition*, vol. 5: *Expanding the contexts.* Mahwah, NJ: Lawrence Erlbaum, 265–323.

Talmy, L. 1978. The relation of grammar to cognition – a synopsis. In D. Waltz (ed.), *Proceedings of TINLAP-2 (Theoretical Issues in Language Processing).* New York: Association for Computing Machinery, 1-11.

1983. How language structures space. In H. Pick & L. Acredolo (eds.), *Spatial orientation: theory, research, and application.* New York: Plenum Press, 181–238.

1985. Lexicalization patterns: semantic structure in lexical form. In T. Shopen (ed.), *Language typology and semantic description*, vol. 3: *Grammatical categories and the lexicon.* Cambridge: Cambridge University Press, 36–149.

1988. The relation of grammar to cognition. In B. Rudzka-Ostyn (ed.), *Topics in cognitive linguistics.* Amsterdam/Philadelphia: John Benjamins, 166–205.

Tomasello, M. 1992. The social bases of language acquisition. *Social Development* 1: 67–87.

1995. Pragmatic contexts for early verb learning. In M. Tomasello & W. E. Merriman (eds.), *Beyond names for things: young children's acquisition of verbs.* Hillsdale, NJ/Hove: Lawrence Erlbaum, 115–146.

Traugott, E. C. 1972. *The history of English syntax.* New York: Holt, Rinehart & Winston.

Traugott, E. C., & B. Heine. (eds.). 1991. *Approaches to grammaticalization*, vol. 1*: Focus on theoretical and methodological issues*; vol. 2: *Focus on types of grammatical markers.* Amsterdam/Philadelphia: John Benjamins.

Van Valin, R. D., Jr. 1992. An overview of ergative phenomena and their implications for language acquisition. In D. I. Slobin (ed.), *The crosslinguistic study of language acquisition*, vol. 3. Hillsdale, NJ: Lawrence Erlbaum, 15–38.

Zipf, G. K. 1935. *The psycho-biology of language*. Boston: Houghton Mifflin.

15 Cognitive–conceptual development and the acquisition of grammatical morphemes: the development of time concepts and verb tense

Heike Behrens

Max Planck Institute for Evolutionary Anthropology, Leipzig (Germany)

The influence of cognitive and conceptual development on language development has been studied most extensively for the acquisition of the lexicon. There is, for example, a large body of research describing the acquisition of object names, and also of temporal adverbials like *before* and *after*. Relational terms like verbs, which not only encode semantic content but also establish a grammatical and logical relationship between their arguments, have only recently been explored in greater depth (see Merriman & Tomasello 1995 for a discussion of this negligence). Even less research has been carried out on the relationship between conceptual development and *grammatical* development. One of the few exceptions is work on the acquisition of temporal morphology. This has been seen as an ideal testing ground because there are clearly a number of cognitive prerequisites for encoding temporally remote events – most saliently, the ability to remember them.

This chapter starts out by discussing two approaches which claim that cognitive or conceptual development are the driving forces behind language development. It will be argued that neither of them can explain grammatical development as we see it in crosslinguistic data on the acquisition of tense and aspect marking. A third approach to the acquisition of grammatical morphemes is thus needed – one that takes into account the different and additional requirements placed on the acquisition process by the semantic and morphosyntactic structure of the specific language being learned.

In order to specify the learner's task more closely, and to distinguish between the various approaches in the literature, several levels of representation will be differentiated, ranging from more general cognitive abilities to more specific linguistic properties (see figure 15.1). On the cognitive level, the child has to have some language-independent temporal representations, e.g. some memory of events which happened earlier, and some anticipa-

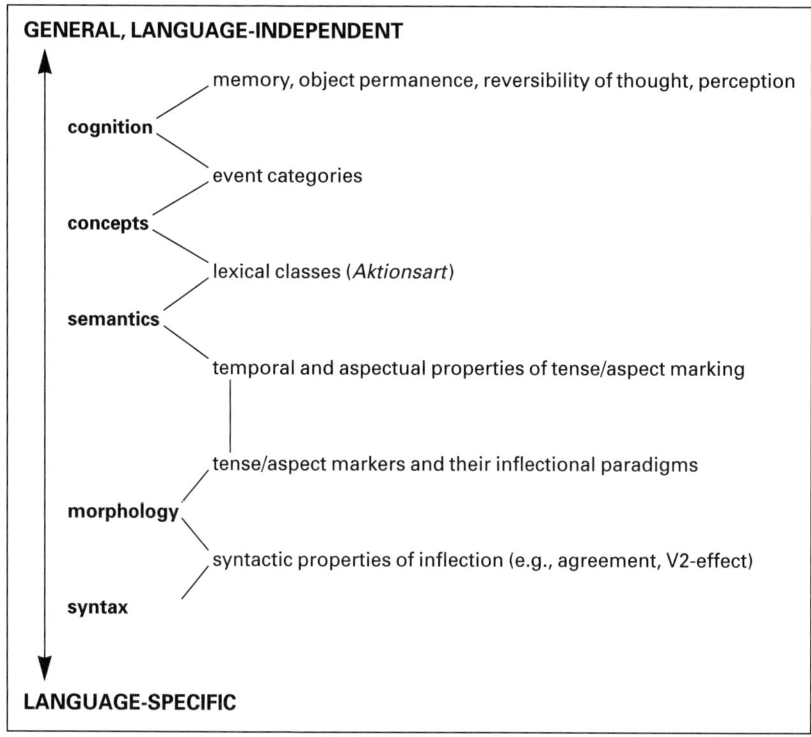

Fig. 15.1 Levels of representation.

tions of future events. These could be based on knowledge about recurrent action routines (so-called "scripts"); scripts allow the child to anticipate future events on the basis of the steps that have already happened. Representations of this kind are not linguistic notions as such. When it comes to language acquisition, children have to figure out which concepts are encoded by the semantic system of the language they are learning. For instance, they first have to learn to categorize their perceptions into event types (see Tomasello, ch. 5 of this volume), and then to identify the lexical and morphological means to encode them.

Properties of event types are encoded by both lexical elements and inflectional markers. For example, argument structure patterns can be predicted to a large extent on the basis of the general conceptual and semantic properties of the verb (see Levin & Rapaport Hovav 1995). Lexical verb classes (so-called *Aktionsarten*) match certain event types by virtue of semantic properties like telicity and durativity. However, languages differ in how they assign verbs to *Aktionsarten* (see Rispoli 1990, 1991). For example, English makes a lexical distinction between the state of wearing clothes (1) and the resultative activity of putting on clothes (2), whereas both meanings can be expressed by a single verb, *hak-*, in Japanese (3).

(1) *I am wearing pants.*

(2) *I am putting on pants*

(3) *Watashi wa pantsu haiteru.*
'I am wearing pants' and 'I am putting on pants.' (Rispoli 1990:377)

On the next level, verbs are combined with tense and aspect markers. Usually verbs of a particular lexical class have a similar temporal or aspectual reading when combined with a particular marker, but again, these readings may vary across languages. For example, like English, Japanese has a progressive marker: *tei*. But unlike English *-ing*, this marker has two different meanings depending on the *Aktionsart* of the verb it is applied to: with activity verbs like *run* it means action in progress, while with achievement verbs like *fall* it encodes not the process, as in English *has been falling*, but the resultant state; see (4).

(4) *hon-ga* *oti-teiru*
book-SUBJ fall-ASP[1]
'A book has fallen (and it is there).' (Shirai 1993:194)

The assignment of conceptual distinctions to tense and aspect morphology varies across languages. English and German, for example, share a similar tense system: both languages use a simple past tense and a present perfect to encode the general concept of "pastness." In English, this formal contrast corresponds to a full-fledged functional contrast, where past tense refers to completed past events and present perfect to events with relevance to the present (see Klein 1992 for a detailed discussion). German, however, is in the process of losing its simple past tense and it makes no such distinction: for main verbs, simple past and present perfect are widely, though not completely, interchangeable (Ehrich 1992; Grewendorf 1995). Thus, German and English have the same morphological contrast between the simple past and present perfect constructions, but this morphological contrast encodes different semantic contrasts.

Tense morphology can, moreover, interact with purely formal factors in syntax. Consider, for example, German and Dutch. In these languages, finite forms (those marked for tense and for person and number agreement) appear in verb-second position (5, 6), and nonfinite forms occur in final position (6). This difference in verb placement is a syntactic requirement which is independent of the temporal content of verb morphology; that is, the syntactic separation of the components of the predicate affects past, future, and simultaneous reference in the same way.

(5) *ich sah*$_{Vfin}$ *Hans.*
'I saw Hans.'

(6) *ich werde*$_{Vfin}$ *Hans sehen*$_{Vnon\text{-}fin}$
'I will see Hans.'

This brief discussion of levels of representations shows that, when going from language-independent to language-specific properties, domains map to some extent neatly from one level to the next. Language acquisition researchers have proposed that language learners exploit such mappings, taking their knowledge of one domain (e.g. event types or lexical verb classes) and using it to acquire knowledge of another (e.g. verb morphology).

Evidence of such an overlap between levels of representation has been found for the acquisition of tense and aspect marking. Crosslinguistic studies show surprisingly similar results: in most languages, first tense and aspect morphemes are acquired in the first "wave" of grammatical development around age 2. Crucially, there is a strong correlation between early tense marking and the *Aktionsart*, or lexical semantics, of the verb itself: present tense and progressive aspect occur predominantly with activity verbs (e.g. *I am running*), whereas past tense and perfective aspect occur with resultative verbs (e.g. *it broke*).

How to account for this correlation? Is it due to cognitive constraints, does it result from an underlying universal semantic or conceptual organization, or can it be explained by reference to the child's analysis of the form–function patterns of the input language? Researchers have proposed each of these levels as a starting point for language acquisition. In the following sections, I will first discuss the extent to which cognitive development licenses and constrains the acquisition of tense and aspect morphology, a position encompassed by what is often called the Cognition Hypothesis about language acquisition (section 1.1). Next I will discuss whether there are semantic predispositions which function as starting points for early grammatical acquisition. The Semantic Predisposition Hypothesis, presented in section 1.2, assumes that children draw on universally favored preexisting concepts in identifying the form–function relationships of their language. Thirdly, I will present evidence for whether children can derive semantic and conceptual distinctions from language itself by observing and abstracting the distributional patterns in the speech they hear. In this perspective, children home in on language-particular form–function patterns from the start (Language Specificity Hypothesis, to be discussed in section 1.3).

1 Three hypotheses about the acquisiton of tense-aspect morphology

In the following, these three hypotheses will be reviewed and their validity tested with data from the acquisition of the German tense system. The discussion is based on acquisition data from seven German children between the ages of 1;0 and 4;0 (see Behrens 1993b for details). The data from Hilde, Günther, and Eva were collected by Clara and William Stern (cf. Stern & Stern 1928); the data from Julia, Daniel, and Mathias were collected by Harald Clahsen (cf. Clahsen 1982); and the data from Simone were collected by Max Miller (cf. Miller 1976).[2] With the exception of Günther, a holistic learner, all the children started out with a preinflectional period in which they predominantly used uninflected infinitives or stems, plus some unanalyzed finite forms. At around age 2 (between ages 1;10 and 2;1, depending on the child), the children started to use finite forms productively, as measured by the criterion of productive contrast (Bates & Rankin 1979): use of more than one form of a verb (e.g. infinitive, present tense forms, and/or past participles) in a semantically adequate way. Some two to three months after that, the children acquired the auxiliary system and produced present perfect constructions (cf. Behrens 1993b for a detailed discussion).

Since the hypotheses to be tested concern the mechanisms used in the acquisition of the first tense distinctions, all examples presented here come from the phase either before the onset of productive inflection (Phase 1), or from the first three months after the first occurrence of productive tense marking (the onset of Phase 2).

1.1 The Cognition Hypothesis

Two aspects of the relationship between cognitive and linguistic development will be discussed: the role of cognition as a determinant of linguistic development, and the temporal relationship between the emergence of cognitive abilities and the acquisition of related linguistic markers.

1.1.1 Cognitive development as determinant of language development

The Cognition Hypothesis (cf. Cromer 1974:234) for language development was inspired primarily by Jean Piaget's constructionist theory of development. According to Piaget, thought processes are ontogenetically prior to and developmentally prerequisite for language development (cf. Cromer 1988:223). Since cognitive development lays the foundation for linguistic development, children seek to express concepts which are built up prelinguistically: "Schemata that are built up during the sensori-motor period have structural properties that make language acquisition possible" (Cromer 1988:228). Cognitive development is commonly seen as a necessary, but not a sufficient, condition for language development, since other factors like semantic or formal complexity may influence the course of acquisition as well (cf. Cromer 1988; Slobin 1973).

In testing the Cognition Hypothesis, the crucial question is: to what extent does cognitive development constrain and determine language development? Under the Cognition Hypothesis it is assumed that (1) children can only talk about concepts they already have developed and (2) the structural complexity of children's language does not exceed their cognitive abilities (Johnston 1985:963; cf. also Cromer 1974:246, who states that "Our cognitive abilities at different stages of development make certain meanings *available* for expression").

With respect to temporality, Piaget's developmental theory states that young children are egocentric and live in the here-and-now. They are initially unable to decenter, i.e. to abstract spatially or temporally from their present perspective and see events from another viewpoint (cf. Piaget 1946). In a number of language-independent experiments Piaget established the course of development of temporal concepts leading from the initial egocentric stage to the so-called *operational time concept*, which children reach at about age 8. By then, children are not only able to talk about events in inverted order (requiring reversibility of thought), but also to integrate the order of events with their duration (cf. Butterworth 1980 for discussion). When children have reached the operational time concept, they master the physical definition of time, which specifies time as a relation between distance and velocity. Knowledge of this kind is needed, for example, to work out whether we have enough time to cross the street before the next car comes.

Several studies of temporal encoding in child language have found a correlation between stages in cognitive development and stages in language development (Cromer 1968; Ferreiro 1971; Ferreiro & Sinclair 1971; Bronckart & Sinclair 1973; see also Smith 1980 for review). For example, Ferreiro found that children in the preoperational period are unable to talk about events in inverted order (Ferreiro 1971; Ferreiro & Sinclair 1971).

A number of studies of the acquisition of tense marking drew on the primacy of cognitive development to explain children's early use of verb tense. Early past-tense markers are predominantly applied to resultative verbs like *break* and *fall* (Cromer 1968; Bronckart & Sinclair 1973; Bloom, Lifter, & Hafitz 1980; McShane & Whittaker 1988; Bloom & Harner 1989; see Slobin 1985 and Weist 1986 for a summary). In some of these studies, no past marking of state or activity verbs was observed at all in the earliest phases of development (e.g. Antinucci & Miller 1976). In their analysis of longitudinal Italian and English data, Antinucci & Miller (1976) found that the children used past-tense markers only when the event encoded resulted in a present state. Italian children initially used past participles syntactically like adjectives, i.e. as if they encoded the present state of an object (172f.). Similarly, the children learning English applied their first past-tense markings only to resultative verbs and scenes with a clear end state. Antinucci & Miller conclude that early past-tense marking "has more of an aspectual than a temporal value" (1976:183): according to them, children encode the temporal contour of the event (= aspect) rather than a deictic tense relation between the event and the present moment. Only after age 2;1 did children begin to use the past tense with state and activity verbs as well as with resultative verbs. Antinucci & Miller (181f.) argued that this is so because young children have not yet developed a representation of the past which is independent of the immediate context. Resultative events with a visible end state would, according to Antinucci & Miller (183ff.), help children to build up representations of past events and allow them to map these representations onto linguistic markers.

These results have given rise to the "Aspect before Tense Hypothesis," which predicts that first past-tense marking is restricted to resultative events which happened in the immediate past. In this view, tense distinctions are redundant, providing only information that is already contained in the verb semantics (see Bloom, Lifter, & Hafitz 1980; Bloom & Harner 1989). The hypothesis could therefore more appropriately be called the "*Aktionsart* before Tense Hypothesis" (Li 1990).

To test whether cognitive development can account for the observed restriction in children's use of tense markers, let us have a look at the time course of development of first expressions of temporal concepts and their first encoding with tense and aspect morphology.

1.1.2 The time course of acquisition The proposal that the inability to encode tense reflects children's deficient time concepts becomes questionable when we look at the time course of acquisition. The postulated relationship should hold only if exactly the same cognitive mechanisms are required for Piaget's language-independent tests of the development of time concepts and for particular tense markers. Is this the case? Tense encodes the deictic relationship between the time of the utterance and the time of the event referred to. Thus, tense expresses temporal order relations by presenting an event as prior or posterior to, or as simultaneous with, the moment of speech. This does not seem to depend on reversibility of thought or the integration of time, distance, and velocity – all abilities entailed by Piaget's operational time concept. Consequently, there is no reason to assume that the mastery of Piaget's operational time concept and its associated cognitive abilities is a *necessary* condition for appropriate tense use (see also Bronckart & Sinclair 1973).

Recent studies have in any event shown that many of Piaget's original results, and especially the age at which cognitive abilities can be attributed to the child, have to be reassessed. For example, Weist (1989, 1996) points out that all cognitive abilities necessary for making deictic temporal reference are available to the child at a much younger age than Piaget believed, long before the emergence of grammatical tense or aspect marking (see also Behrens 1993b for discussion).

The asynchrony between the mastery of the requisite cognitive abilities and language learning is obvious in children's spontaneous, albeit unmarked, references to prior events, which begin to appear in the preinflectional period. For example, in encoding state changes, children refer to both past and future events (7). Examples (7a, b) show that young children are sensitive to the temporal boundedness of (change-of-state) events. And they occasionally use the same verb particles and adverbs for future reference when they want a state change to come about (7c). This contrast in use indicates that children use their tense forms in a semantically flexible way, not merely to mark a fixed association between event type and linguistic marker.

(7)	**Encoding of change-of-state**
(a) EVA 1;3,13	[A lightbulb stops swinging. Eva comments:] *alle* 'finished / all gone.'
(b) HIL 1;6;24	"Hilde expands her earlier uses of *fettich* [= *fertig* 'all done, finished'] from situations where she is finished on the potty to when she has finished her bottle."
(c) GÜN 1;4,6	[His mother massages his gums to soothe his tooth pain. G. pushes her finger away and says:] *alle* 'finished' [= 'I want it to be over'].

The examples under (8) show that children can recall past events and thus have built up representations of past events.

(8)	**Recall of past events**
(a) EVA 1;11,0	[In bed, Eva spontaneously remembers an event which took place about 10–14 days ago. The three siblings had assembled all their shoes and had a little stick to knock on heels and soles. Eva recollects:] *Schuster pielen, kloppe kloppe machen* 'play shoemaker, knock knock make.'
(b) GÜN 1;8,10	"In the afternoon Günther played very happily with Hilde in the playground, for the first time, actually . . . The children played ball and horse. When father came home at 7:30 in the evening (the game had been over at about 5 p.m.) and asked "what did you play with Hilde today?," Günther answered right away *bai* [=Ball] 'ball.' "

These examples illustrate that young children's temporal horizon, i.e. the time period they can conceptually cover (Friedman 1978), extends well beyond the immediate past or future. Evidence of this kind challenges the usefulness of models which presuppose that there is a close parallel in the development of cognitive and linguistic abilities. Consonant with this, evidence has accumulated (to be discussed in section 1.2) that the use of early tense markers is not, in fact, as constrained as had been thought.

1.1.3 Summary and conclusions The assumption of a unidirectional and determinative relationship between cognitive and language development as it was conceived in the Piagetian tradition seems no longer tenable. First, there is no logical connection between tense marking and certain Piagetian notions; for example, for encoding simple deictic contrasts the reversibility of thought is not necessary. From a methodological perspective, these findings underline the need for caution in trying to correlate cognitive abilities with particular linguistic markers. Are the cognitive abilities true prerequisites for the mastery of these linguistic markers? Conversely, are the selected linguistic markers the only ones through which a particular language-independent cognitive skill could be manifested? Second, there is no evidence for synchronization in the emergence of temporal markers and their supposedly prerequisite cognitive skills: children are able to decenter from the here-and-now and to remember past events long before they acquire the tense markers that allow them to encode these meanings. Because of this temporal discrepancy, there is no reason to assume that cognitive development is responsible for the correlation observed in many studies between past-tense marking and resultative verbs.

Results like those just discussed have stimulated researchers to search for noncognitive explanations for the observed course of acquisition. As another "helping hand" for entering the linguistic system, Slobin (1985) suggested the existence of semantic predispositions.

1.2 Semantic Predisposition Hypothesis

According to Slobin (1985), the strong correlation between tense marking and verb semantics is due to semantic principles that are available to the child before language learning, and thus facilitate the decoding of the form–function patterns of the target language. Slobin argued that children show an inclination towards particularly salient Scenes and Perspectives which provide a starting point for learning about grammatical morphemes. These Scenes and Perspectives provide an initial Semantic Space "without at first biasing the child to any particular language" (Slobin 1985:1184). The learning task is simplified because children start out with some knowledge of meanings that are privileged for encoding in language, and only have to look for the morphemes to encode them with. Let us refer to this approach as the "Semantic Predisposition Hypothesis." Under this hypothesis, children go through a stage determined by universal semantic distinctions before they acquire the specific semantic distinctions of the target language. If we recall the levels of representation presented in figure 15.1, the difference between the Cognition Hypothesis and the Semantic Predisposition Hypothesis is that under the Cognition Hypothesis, linguistic development is paced and constrained by general cognitive development, whereas under the Semantic Predisposition Hypothesis, the acquisition of grammatical markers is governed by pre-existing conceptual distinctions that are privileged for language.

With respect to temporal reference, the Semantic Predisposition Hypothesis tries to account for the same facts as the Cognition Hypothesis. This is because both hypotheses are based on the crosslinguistic acquisition data available at the time, which showed that early tense marking is closely linked to the *Aktionsart* of the verb. Counterevidence to the Semantic Predisposition Hypothesis therefore also counts as additional evidence against the Cognition Hypothesis.

The motivation for the Semantic Predisposition Hypothesis is different, however: instead of claiming that the correlation between pastness markers and *Aktionsart* is due to children's cognitive immaturity with respect to the operational time concept – a claim that cannot be maintained in the face of evidence of the kind presented in section 1.1 – Slobin's account emphasizes processing factors. Slobin argued that resultative events constitute prototypical scenes in that "they regularly occur as part of frequent and salient activities and perceptions, and thereby become the organizing points for later elaboration of the use of functors" (Slobin 1985:1175), in this case past-tense markers: "Whenever there is an acoustically salient past-tense or perfect marking on the verb, its first use by the child seems to be to comment on an immediately completed event that results in a visible change of state of some object" (1985:1181).

The Semantic Predisposition Hypothesis thus makes two predictions: that there is a strong correlation between early past-tense marking and resultative verbs, and that this correlation is restricted to the encoding of the visible post-state of resultative events. To test these predictions, I analyzed my German subjects' past-tense forms from the first three months after the productive acquisition of inflection, paying special attention not only to the most frequent patterns, but also to the semantic range of past-tense usage. The proposed narrow semantic constraints on early tense marking were not corroborated: the children used pastness markers across a wider range of verbs than had been predicted. For example, although the majority of early verbs marked for pastness are indeed resultative (see Behrens 1993b:166–167), the German children also used activity verbs in the past, as illustrated in (9):

(9) **Past participles of activity verbs**

(a) EVA 1;11,0 [Eva accompanies her mother to the kitchen and remembers the following, which had taken place 15 minutes before:]
bissl zucker e tonte eva egeben [= gegeben]
'a little bit of sugar has Toni [to] Eva given$_{\text{participle}}$.'

(b) EVA 1;11,0 [A couple of hours after the event, her mother asks Eva "What did mommy do?" While pointing to her behind, Eva answers:]
Mutter ehaun [= gehauen] – *dis*
'mother spanked$_{\text{participle}}$ – this.'

There is a clear developmental trend for children to talk about past activities more frequently in later stages. In Simone's data, there are only twelve instances of past participle or *Perfekt* up to age 1;11, four of which are activity verbs. After age 2, past participles and *Perfekt* forms become more frequent, and while proportions vary due to the topics talked about in the recording session, past activity verbs represent 11%–45% of the total in the period from age 2;0 to age 2;6 (cf. Behrens 1993b:166). State verbs with preterite or *Perfekt* marking occur late (10) and remain rather infrequent throughout the phase studied here. The infrequency of state verbs may be due to the fact that there are generally fewer stative verbs than activity or telic verbs.

(10) **Past participles of state verbs**

(a) SIM 2;10,4 *was'n da angeklebt?*
'what's glued-onto$_{\text{participle}}$ there?'

(b) SIM 2;11,18 *ja, ich hab . . . die pritz – auch eine spritze gehabt*
yes, I have an injection needle – also an injection needle had$_{\text{participle}}$
'yes, I also have had an injection needle.'

However, the late occurrence of state verbs in the past cannot be seen as evidence for the inability to represent past situations altogether. The clearest counterevidence comes from the early emergence of the copula in the past tense. Since the copula is semantically empty, its tensed form can *only* express tense, not aspect (11).

(11) **Copula preterite**

(a) HIL 2;1,27 *ba waden* [= ba (= Spaziergang) waren]
'we were for a walk.'

(b) SIM 2;2,20 *eine fliege war das*
'a fly was that.'

The German data show that the preference for past resultative verbs is a quantitative, not qualitative or constraint-based fact of acquisition; that is, the observed correlation is probabilistic, not absolute (see also Bloom, Lifter, & Hafitz 1980; Weist, Wysocka, Witkowska-Stadnik, Buczowska, & Konieczna 1984; Shirai 1991; Li & Bowerman 1998).

In a next step, I tested whether the children's use of resultative verbs in the past refers only to visible resultant post-states of events, as predicted by Slobin. As it turned out, there are several classes of counterexamples.

1.2.1 Nonresultative use of telic verbs These are utterances with telic verbs in the past which describe events that do not result "in a visible change of state of some object." In some cases the event results in the disappearance of the reference object such that there is no visible resultant post-state (12). In other cases, a telic verb is negated. These sentences do not refer to resultant states, because no change of state has taken place (13). In still other cases telic verbs are used in pretense play activities where the reference is hypothetical and no object changes state (14).

(12) **Disappearance of reference object**

(a) HIL 2;1,19 [Hilde's parents went away on a trip. The next morning, the nurse takes Hilde through the parents' bedroom. Hilde notices her mother's absence, but thinks her father is still asleep:]
Mama weg gelauft, Papa läft tatei
'Mom ran/gone$_{participle}$ away, Daddy sleeps.'

(b) JUL 2;4,21 [Karin is looking for a pair of scissors and asks Julia whether she knows where Anke put them:]
das mitnomm
'that taken-with$_{participle}$.'

(13) **Negation**

(a) JUL 2;4,21 [Julia thought she had spilled something, but does not find any stains:]
da nich kleckert [= gekleckert]
'there not spilled$_{participle}$.'

(b) JUL 2;5,28 *hier nich reinemalt*
'here not painted$_{participle}$.'

(14) **Pretense activities**

GÜN 2;5,4 [Günther expresses his dislike of a torn picture in a picture book:]
das ä häfflich [= häßlich]. *Bein ehaus ehitten* [= geschnitten]. *haushehmen* [= rausnehmen]!
'That's ugly. Leg cut$_{participle}$ out. Take [it] out!'
[Mother: "Can you take it out?" Günther pretends to do so and comments:]
hausehehm [= herausgenommen] 'out-taken$_{participle}$.'

These utterances do seem to refer to resultative events, but – contrary to Slobin's prediction – the post-state is invisible or hypothetical. Children's early uses of pastness markers thus cover events beyond those referring only to immediate post-states of events. The evidence becomes more conclusive in the next group of examples, where children refer to remote events.

1.2.2 Reference to remote past events The events referred to in (15) are cases of genuine remote past reference without any visible post-state to suggest a resultative reading. Example (c) even gives evidence for Eva's ability to reason causally about a past activity.

(15)

(a) JUL 2;4,21 [Julia talks about her absent father, who had a headache:]
in kopf wehtan
'in head hurt$_{\text{participle}}$.'

(b) HIL 2;0,18 "Yesterday Hilde came with a wooden egg that her aunt had given to her in Berlin. Hilde told me in a doubtful tone
'*Mama, Tante ßenkt* [= geschenkt]?'
'Mom, aunt given$_{\text{participle}}$?'"

(c) EVA 2;1,23 [Eva's mother praises her because earlier that day she had drunk from a cup, which she usually rejects, instead of from her beloved baby-bottle. Eva replies:]
Eva fasche paput macht hat – Eva tasse tunken
[= Eva Flasche kaputt gemacht hat – Eva Tasse getrunken]
'Eva bottle broken made has – Eva cup drunk$_{\text{participle}}$.'
'Because Eva has broken the bottle, Eva drank from a cup.'

The next group of examples shows that not all instances of early past-tense marking have a resultative reading, and that even among those that do, not all are used aspectually to encode the temporal contour of events. Rather, some past-tense markers are used deictically to encode a temporal contrast with other forms.

1.2.3 Contrast of early past-tense marking with other tenses

(16)

(a) HIL 2;0,3 "When Hilde saw an empty bottle, which she had finished about 15 minutes earlier, she said *Fasche tunken* [= Flasche getrunken] 'bottle drunk'; but when she wants the bottle, she calls *Fasche tinken* [= Flasche trinken] 'bottle drink$_{\text{infinitive}}$.' In the morning, when we come to her bed, she sometimes says *gut lafen* [= gut geschlafen] 'slept well' (I usually ask her *Hast Du gut geschlafen* 'Did you sleep well?'), but when the doll or her father sleeps, she says *läft* [= schläft] 'sleeps.'"

(b) HIL 2;2,14 [Hilde unties a ribbon at her bed and comments:]
aufdemacht [= aufgemacht]
'open.made$_{\text{participle}}$'
[Then she demands:]
wiederzumachen
'make.closed.again$_{\text{infinitive}}$'

(c) GÜN 2;5,4 [Günther asks for permission to drink something:]
tinken, ja? [= trinken, ja?]
'drink$_{\text{infinitive}}$ yes?'
[Immediately after that he puts down the empty glass and says:]
aus etinken [= ausgetrunken]
'out-drunk$_{\text{participle}}$.'

(d) GÜN 2;5,4 "Günther's language becomes richer in participles, often used in contrast to an infinitive. We often hear *Ewaden, ewesen* 'been,'[3] *ausetinken* [= ausgetrunken] 'drunk' and many others."

The contrast of early past participles with infinitives and present tense forms in the examples in (16) shows that children immediately start to encode temporal contrasts by making a past/nonpast distinction. They thus encode a resultative event, but also use these forms in a deictically appropriate way, as was also shown in (15). Further evidence for early tense marking – in contrast to aspect marking – comes from languages which have both tense and aspect morphemes (Toivainen 1980; Weist *et al.* 1984; Stephany 1985; Smoczyńska 1995; see section 1.3).

1.2.4 Reference to future events The flexibility of children's use of early tense markers is also attested by examples in which the child projects a resultant state in the future (17).

(17) SIM 2;2,4 *gleich mone ausgetrunk*
'soon Mone [will have] drunk.out$_{\text{participle}}$.'

In addition to the above-mentioned cases of activity verbs (9) and copula preterites (11), examples (12) through (17) show that the child's linguistic system at the onset of productive inflection is more versatile than predicted by the Semantic Predisposition Hypothesis. Children are able to encode not only nonresultative events in the past, but also resultative events which did not happen in the immediate past and did not leave visible resultant post-states, and hypothetical or future events.

1.2.5 Summary and conclusions This section reviewed an approach which tries to explain the dominance of resultative events in early tense marking in terms of a preexisting semantic organization, and it tested predictions made by this hypothesis against data from German child language. The German data are congruent with previously reported crosslinguistic findings in that the majority of the verbs which are first marked for past reference are resultative. However, on closer inspection of the range of use of these tensed forms, it turns out that the preference is quantitative, and cannot be attributed to a qualitative constraint. The children use tense marking in a variety of target-like ways and observe subtle distributional patterns of the input language (to be further discussed in section 1.3).

Instead of semantic predispositions, there could be another reason for the observed conformity of tense marking and *Aktionsart* in the German data. In the linguistic literature, most of the supposedly universal conceptual distinctions are based on those that figure importantly in Indo-European languages, including German. It is therefore not surprising that the German acquisition data conform to these "universal" conceptualization patterns. But the Semantic Predisposition Hypothesis predicts that German children will use past-tense markers in only a very restricted subset of possible uses. The data above show that although this subset indeed captures the most frequent relations encoded by German children, learners do use past tenses across a wider semantic range.

Studies of other languages provide similar evidence against a purely aspectual reading of early tense markers, showing that there is a quantitative trend towards perfective aspect marking, but not a qualitative cognitive or conceptual inability to encode pastness (e.g. Stephany 1985 [Greek] and Toivainen 1980 [Finnish]). In fact, even the children originally studied by Antinucci & Miller (1976) did not, it turns out, conform as well as had been thought to the "Aspect-before-tense hypothesis": in reanalyzing their data, Fantuzzi (1996) found that the past tense was used with verb types other than resultatives.

Further counterevidence comes from languages like Polish, in which tense and aspect markers emerge at the same time. Children use perfective aspect to refer to past events, but they also use past tense with state and activity verbs (Weist *et al.* 1984; Smoczyńska 1995). Given the properties of Polish verb morphology, it is impossible to acquire aspect without tense, because in most cases verbs must be marked for both (Smoczyńska 1995; for related evidence for the simultaneous emergence of tense and aspect see Toivainen 1980 for Finnish; Bancroft 1985; Sachs 1983; and Smith 1980 for English).[4]

To put the Semantic Predisposition Hypothesis properly to the test, the acquisition of languages with distinctly different tense and/or aspect systems should be studied. For example, Comrie (1985) observes that some Bantu languages encode up to five remoteness distinctions by different tense markers, thus distinguishing events which happened only recently from those which happened longer ago. If past-tense marking is indeed guided by the universal conceptualization of resultativity, the Bantu distinctions based on the qualitatively different concept of temporal distality should be overridden.

The claim made in this and the previous sections is not that children's tense system is already perfect in all its subtleties at age 2, but that it is much broader and more versatile than claimed by the constraint-based hypotheses. Already at this early stage, children start to explore the range of usage of tense markers permissible in German. Recently, Slobin himself has argued against the assumption of a restricted set of universal and pre-existing semantic notions (Slobin, ch. 14 of this volume; 1997). In the next section, the data will be discussed with respect to evidence for a language-specific rather than universal course of development.

1.3 Language Specificity Hypothesis

Two aspects of the influence of language-specific properties on the acquisition process will be considered: the role of the morphological and syntactic system in the acquisition of tense markers, and the proposal that language itself might influence the acquisition and development of conceptual and cognitive distinctions.

The Language Specificity Hypothesis emphasizes the child's productive analysis of the form–function patterns of the target language (Bowerman 1985; Choi & Bowerman 1991; Gopnik & Choi 1995). On the semantic level, this hypothesis predicts that early child language should not clash with the target language distinctions. This prediction is borne out in the German data: tense-marked forms are generally used correctly.

Clearer evidence for language-specificity can be found in the acquisition of morphosyntactic properties associated with verb inflection. There are considerable differences even among closely related languages in the clustering of morphological and syntactic factors. For example, although all Germanic languages have analytic predicates consisting of auxiliaries and main verb forms, they do not all separate these syntactically as German does (cf. examples 5 and 6 above). If children conform to language-specific morphosyntactic patterns from early on, they must have derived them from the linguistic input.

When we look at the distributional factors, the German data provide strong evidence for children's close orientation to the input language: all the children adhere closely to the distribution of tenses across verb categories displayed in the adult language. For example, in adult German, *Perfekt* is the predominant tense used with main verbs to encode pastness. Like adults, children hardly ever use the preterite with main verbs, but it is the default past-tense form for copula and modal verbs for children and adults alike. Children acquire preterite copulas at about the same time as their first past participles (cf. Behrens 1993b:206–214). This suggests that they are able to mark deictic tense and not only perfective aspect, because – as noted earlier – the copula is semantically empty and so the preterite copula only encodes pastness.

Also relevant is that children immediately place finite and nonfinite forms in their appropriate syntactic slots (cf. Behrens 1993b). German children thus not only acquire the appropriate form–function mapping with respect to the meaning of particular tense morphemes, but also pick up the syntactic distribution of the inflected verb forms. These results show that from the onset of productive verb morphology, German children are sensitive to the *cluster* of morphological, syntactic, and semantic distinctions specific to German. This cannot be explained by reference to children's reliance on semantically privileged notions; rather, it shows that, from early on, children detect the language-specific form–function patterns of tense morphology and discover how these patterns are syntactically distributed. Additional support for language specificity in the acquisition of the German tense system comes from domains not discussed here (see Behrens 1993b), e.g. the observance of language-specific distribution patterns in references to simultaneous and future events.

Related evidence pointing to the influence of language-specific processing comes from bilingual acquisition data (see also Slobin 1973 and 1985). If acquisition were constrained by cognitive prerequisites, these constraints should affect both languages. However, Schlyter (1990) found different courses of acquisition of German and French in German–French bilingual children: in the earliest phase of grammatical development, the bilinguals used German infinitives to refer to immediate future events but French past participles to talk about the immediate past. Since these two languages are in the same mind, differences in their acquisition cannot be due to cognitive or conceptual constraints. Rather, the children combine aspects of the two languages by encoding the temporal notions with the forms which have the most salient formal properties and clearest form–function relationships. Similar results were obtained in a study of a Spanish–English bilingual child by Krasinski (1995). Both Schlyter and Krasinski find that children do adhere to some of the semantic constraints proposed in the literature, but only if the language being learned already shows a high degree of conformity to these constraints. Significantly, the frequency, regularity, and saliency of the tense markers determined which marker children singled out in each of their two languages.

Supportive evidence comes from Gathercole (1986) in a study of the acquisition of the English present perfect in Scottish and American children. Scottish children acquired this construction earlier than their American counterparts, which Gathercole attributes to the greater frequency of this construction in the input. The role of frequency in form–function patterns is emphasized by Shirai & Andersen (1995) as well. These authors argue that first- and second-language learners acquire the most prototypical meanings of tense and aspect markers through observing the distributional patterns in the input language (see also Andersen & Shirai 1994; Li & Bowerman 1998). Interesting evidence pointing in this direction also comes from Aksu-Koç (1988), who studied the acquisition of the evidential mood in Turkish. This semantic distinction is not typically grammaticized and so is unlikely to be part of a universal semantic repertoire for grammatical morphemes, but Turkish children still learn it, presumably on the basis of language-specific form–meaning mappings in the speech they hear (1988:202).

Further evidence for the importance of language-specific factors is that, depending on the morphological system of the target language, not all children go through an initial phase of using verbs without temporal marking. Children acquiring Finnish or Polish, for example, cannot extract from the input an uninflected "citation" form of the verb comparable to the infinitive or stem in German. In consequence, they acquire morphological distinctions right away, never evidencing a "telegraphic," zero-morphology, and semantically neutral stage (see Smoczyńska 1995 on Polish and Toivainen 1980 on Finnish).

Findings like these have motivated a shift of attention by some acquisition researchers. Instead of concentrating on the most frequent patterns found in each individual language as well as crosslinguistically in order to identify potentially universal conceptualizations, some researchers now focus on differences between languages to determine whether the conceptualizations marked in children's language are a product of the child's productive analyses of the input patterns. The most conclusive evidence for this approach to date comes from the crosslinguistic study of the encoding of spatial relations in child language. Evidence from typologically different languages suggests that children acquire strikingly different semantic categories of space very early (Choi & Bowerman 1991; Bowerman 1994; Bowerman and Choi, ch. 16 of this volume; Brown, ch. 17 of this volume; de León, ch. 18 of this volume). That is, children learning different languages do not all encode the same spatial concepts; rather, even 2-year-olds acquire the spatial distinctions that are relevant in their input language, even though these distinctions may be irrelevant in other languages. There is thus some evidence that language itself is responsible for conceptualization (cf. Slobin 1991, 1997, ch. 14 of this volume).

The findings on spatial semantic development suggest that the reason prior crosslinguistic research on the acquisition of temporal reference has shown such uniform results is that the effect of crosslinguistic differences has not been studied in the same detail for tense systems (but see Rispoli 1990, 1991; Li & Bowerman 1998). But it seems plausible that also in the domain of time concepts, language itself may lead the conceptualization process. For example, many time concepts can only be mediated through language itself (Nelson 1991; see also Johnston 1985; Cromer 1988). According to Nelson (1991:307–309), time is an abstract entity which cannot be discovered like concrete objects or visible spatial constellations. Rather, temporal concepts – e.g. calendrical notions like *today*, *December*, or *1998* – are cultural constructions of reality, conveyed through language.

There has as yet been no investigation of whether the development of time concepts is affected by the acquisition of verb tense, but there is some evidence that more general aspects of cognitive development may be influenced by the acquisition of the verb category itself. Gopnik & Choi (1995) studied the acquisition of nouns vs. verbs in English and Korean, motivated by the observation that American mothers use more object terms with their children, whereas Korean mothers use more verbs and other relational terms. Contrary to the prevalent view that relational terms like verbs are acquired later than object terms like nouns (Gentner 1978), Korean children used verbs and other relational terms very early and correctly. This difference in the order of occurrence and distribution of word categories was associated with a difference in the cognitive domain: whereas English children did better in language-independent, but noun-related object-categorization tasks, Korean children did better in language-independent, but verb-related means–ends task (Gopnik & Choi 1995: 77). These results suggest that a particular linguistic structure may influence the focus of our perception of the world and enhance our cognitive abilities (Slobin 1991).

1.3.1 Summary and conclusions In this section, the role of language-specific form–function mappings in the acquisition process was addressed. When we look at the formal properties of grammatical morphemes, we find that the number and kind of temporal and aspectual distinctions made in early child language reflect the patterns of the input language. That is, the morphosyntactic properties acquired by German children during the earliest stages of productive tense morphology reflect a language-specific cluster of properties. These findings support the view that the correlations found in child language are due to children's extraction of form–function patterns in their input language rather than to preexisting universal conceptualizations.

2 Summary

This chapter has discussed the relationship between the development of temporal concepts and the use of tense markers in German child language. First, the impact of cognitive development on language development was addressed. The first studies of the acquisition of temporal marking proposed that the emergence of tense and aspect markers, and changes in their use, are guided and paced by newly developed cognitive abilities to represent events nonlinguistically, to remember remote events, and to decenter in time. Results from studies of the acquisition of tense marking challenge this claim, however. For example, the emergence of past-tense markers or temporial adverbials does not go hand in hand with the first evidence of memory for past events. Rather, there can be a considerable time lag between the first nonlinguistic evidence that certain time concepts are available and their formal encoding by linguistic means. Time is, moreover, an abstract notion, so many temporal notions are not subject to immediate perception or to some kind of "autonomous" cognitive development. Thus, cognitive and linguistic development are intertwined in more than one way.

Second, the role of semantic predispositions was investigated. Is early acquisition guided by universally privileged semantic distinctions? The literature on the acquisition of temporal reference has suggested a uniform mapping whereby present tense and imperfective or progressive aspect morphology are associated with activity verbs, whereas past tense and perfective aspect morphology are associated with resultative verbs. This correspondence has been explained as a constraint based on conceptual pre-wiring (semantic predispositions: Slobin 1985). Although this tendency can also be observed in the German acquisition data, my analyses suggest it is due not to semantic biases that predate any linguistic experience, but rather to children's productive analyses of the form–function patterns of the language being learned. Language-specific development becomes obvious in cases where children correctly use tense forms in contexts which go beyond a simple "*tense = Aktionsart*" match, while at the same time attending to specifically German co-occurrence patterns. For example, spoken adult German has a language-specific division of labor between past tense and present perfect; this division differs from that found for the morphologically equivalent English forms. German children have to learn which pastness marker (past tense vs. *Perfekt*) goes with which verb category (main verbs, modal verbs, auxiliaries), even though these two pastness markers typically do not encode a semantic contrast, but can be used interchangeably. English-speaking children, on the other hand, have to pay attention to the semantic contrast encoded by the formal distinction between simple past and present perfect. In doing so, they are guided by frequency patterns (Gathercole 1986).

The German data presented here allow us to narrow down the time window in which language-specific learning takes place. By the time tense marking becomes productive, children learning German are not semantically or conceptually constrained in the ways predicted by either the Cognition Hypothesis or the Semantic Predisposition Hypothesis. If children do rely on innate semantic predispositions to categorize events or build hypotheses about the potential meanings of temporal markers, this influence must be over by the time their temporal morphology becomes productive. This finding is consistent with a growing body of evidence in the domains of both temporal and spatial reference that children tune in to the properties of their language in this early stage of acquisition (cf. Li & Bowerman 1998; Bowerman and Choi, ch. 16 of this volume; de León, ch. 18 of this volume).

Currently we do not have a very clear idea of which mechanisms and language processing abilities enable children to analyze and use language productively (but see Bowerman & Choi, ch. 16 of this volume). More comparative research which studies a wider range of languages while paying close attention to their differences is necessary (cf. Berman & Slobin 1994). Also needed is more research on learning mechanisms, e.g. children's ability to perform probabilistic abstractions (cf. Menn 1996; Smith, ch. 4 of this volume). In recent years, important research has been carried out on the development of language segmentation abilities in the period before language production begins. There is evidence that by age one, children are able to identify and segment phonological, prosodic, and also basic constructional information of the input language (see the papers in Morgan & Demuth 1995). Given that it takes children an additional six to twelve months before they start to combine morphemes, learners have a long period at their disposal for extracting and analyzing the morphological, syntactic, and lexical properties of the target language. Closer investigation of this period may shed more light on how children address the acquisition task.

NOTES

Parts of this chapter are based on a larger study of the acquisition of tense markers in German (Behrens 1993b) and the data have been partially reported in Behrens (1993a). The chapter was written during a stay at the University of California, Berkeley, while I was on a research grant from the Deutsche Forschungsgemeinschaft (Be 1513/2–1). I would like to thank my colleagues at the Max Planck Institute for Psycholinguistics and University of California, Berkeley, as well as the other contributors to this volume for valuable suggestions. I especially thank Melissa Bowerman for her thorough comments on the manuscript version of this chapter.

1 SUBJ: Subject; ASP: aspect.
2 The Stern and the Clahsen data are part of the CHILDES database (cf. MacWhinney & Snow 1990).
3 In this example, Günther constructs two versions of the past participle of the verb *sein* 'to be,' namely *ewesen* and *ewaden*. *Ewesen* models the correct form *gewesen* (the omission of initial consonants is frequent in Günther's speech), whereas *ewaden* is his own formation, probably modelled after the past-tense plural form *waren* 'were.'
4 From a linguistic perspective, recent theories of tense do away with the aspect *or* tense bias, stating that all tense or aspect markers have both aspectual *and* temporal properties (Ehrich 1992; Lehmann 1992; Klein 1994). The question of whether early child language encodes tense or aspect can thus be resolved by assuming that children encode both properties.

REFERENCES

Aksu-Koç, A. 1988. *The acquisition of aspect and modality: the case of past reference in Turkish*. Cambridge: Cambridge University Press.

Andersen, R. W., & Y. Shirai. 1994. Discourse motivation for some cognitive acquisition principles. *Studies in Second Language Acquisition* 16: 133–156.

Antinucci, F., & R. Miller. 1976. How children talk about what happened. *Journal of Child Language* 3: 167–189.

Bancroft, D. M. R. 1985. The development of temporal reference: a study of children's language. Unpublished doctoral dissertation, University of Nottingham.

Bates, E., & J. Rankin. 1979. Morphological development in Italian: connotation and denotation. *Journal of Child Language* 6: 29–52.

Behrens, H. 1993a. The relationship between conceptual and linguistic development: the early encoding of past reference by German children. In K. Beals, G. Cooke, D. Kathman, S. Kita, K.-E. McCullough, & D. Testen (eds.), *Chicago Linguistic Society 29*, vol. 2: *What we think, what we mean, and how we say it: Papers from the parasession on the correspondence of conceptual, semantic and grammatical representations*. Chicago: Chicago Linguistic Society, 63–75.

1993b. Temporal reference in German child language: form and function of early verb use. Unpublished doctoral dissertation, University of Amsterdam.

Berman, R. A., & D. I. Slobin (eds.). 1994. *Relating events in narrative: a crosslinguistic developmental study*. Hillsdale, NJ: Lawrence Erlbaum.

Bloom, L., & L. Harner. 1989. On the developmental contour of child language: a reply to Smith and Weist. *Journal of Child Language* 16: 207–216.

Bloom, L., K. Lifter, & J. Hafitz. 1980. Semantics of verbs and the development of verb inflection in child language. *Language* 56: 386–412.

Bowerman, M. 1985. What shapes children's grammars? In D. I. Slobin (ed.), *The crosslinguistic study of language acquisition*, Vol. 2: *Theoretical issues*. Hillsdale, NJ: Lawrence Erlbaum, 1257–1319.

1994. From universal to language-specific in early grammatical development. *Philosophical Transactions of the Royal Society of London B*, 346: 37–45.

Bronckart, J.-P., & H. Sinclair. 1973. Time, tense and aspect. *Cognition* 2: 107–130.

Butterworth, G. 1980. A discussion of some issues raised by Piaget's concept of childhood egocentrism. In M.V. Cox (ed.), *Are young children egocentric?* New York: St. Martin's Press, 17–40.

Choi, S., & M. Bowerman. 1991. Learning to express motion events in English and Korean: the influence of language-specific lexicalization patterns. *Cognition* 41: 83–121.

Clahsen, H. 1982. *Spracherwerb in der Kindheit: Eine Untersuchung zur Entwicklung der Syntax bei Kleinkindern.* Tübingen: Narr.

Comrie, B. 1985. *Tense*. Cambridge: Cambridge University Press.

Cromer, R. F. 1968. The development of temporal reference during the acquisition of language. Unpublished doctoral dissertation, Harvard University.

1974. The development of language and cognition: the cognition hypothesis. In B. Foss (ed.), *New perspectives in child development*. Harmondsworth: Penguin, 184–253.

1988. The cognition hypothesis revisited. In F. S. Kessel (ed.), *The development of language and language researchers: essays in honour of Roger Brown*. Hillsdale, NJ: Lawrence Erlbaum, 223–248.

Ehrich, V. 1992. *Hier und Jetzt: Studien zur lokalen und temporalen Deixis im Deutschen.* Tübingen: Niemeyer.

Fantuzzi, C. 1996. The emergence of temporal reference in language acquisition: tense, aspect, and argument structure. Unpublished doctoral dissertation, University of California at Los Angeles.

Ferreiro, E. 1971. *Les relations temporelles dans le langage de l'enfant.* Geneva: Droz.

Ferreiro, E., & H. Sinclair. 1971. Temporal relationships in language. *International Journal of Psychology* 6: 39–47.

Friedman, W. J. 1978. Development of time concepts in children. In H. W. Reese & L. P. Lipsitt (eds.), *Advances in child development and behavior*, vol. 12. New York: Academic Press, 267–298.

Gathercole, V. C. 1986. The acquisition of the present perfect: examining differences in the speech of Scottish and American children. *Journal of Child Language* 13: 537–560.

Gentner, D. 1978. On relational meaning: the acquisition of verb meaning. *Child Development* 49: 988–998.

Gopnik, A., & S. Choi. 1995. Names, relational words, and cognitive development in English and Korean speakers: nouns are not always learned before verbs. In M. Tomasello & W. E. Merriman (eds.), *Beyond names for things: young children's acquisition of verbs*. Hillsdale, NJ/Hove: Lawrence Erlbaum, 63–80.

Grewendorf, G. 1995. Präsens und Perfekt im Deutschen. *Zeitschrift für Sprachwissenschaft* 14: 72–90.

Johnston, J. R. 1985. Cognitive prerequisites: the evidence from children learning English. In D. I. Slobin (ed.), *The crosslinguistic study of language acquisition*, vol. 2: *Theoretical issues*. Hillsdale, NJ: Lawrence Erlbaum, 961–1004.

Klein, W. 1992. The present perfect puzzle. *Language* 68: 525–552.

1994. *Time in language.* London: Routledge.

Krasinski, E. 1995. The development of past marking in a bilingual child and the punctual–nonpunctual distinction. *First Language* 15: 239–276.

Lehmann, V. 1992. Grammatische Zeitkonzepte und ihre Erklärung. *Kognitionswissenschaft* 2: 156–170.

Levin, B., & M. Rapaport Hovav. 1995. *Unaccusativity: at the syntax – lexical semantics interface*. Cambridge, MA: MIT Press.

Li, P. 1990. Aspect and Aktionsart in child Mandarin. Unpublished doctoral dissertation, University of Leiden.

Li, P., & M. Bowerman. 1998. The acquisition of lexical and grammatical aspect in Chinese. *First Language* 18: 311–350.

MacWhinney, B., & C. Snow. 1990. The Child Language Data Exchange System: an update. *Journal of Child Language* 17: 457–472.

McShane, J. M., & S. Whittaker. 1988. The encodings of tense and aspect by three- to five-year-old children. *Journal of Experimental Child Psychology* 45: 52–70.

Menn, L. 1996. Evidence children use: learnability and the acquisition of grammatical morphemes. Paper presented at the 22nd Annual Meeting of the Berkeley Linguistics Society, Berkeley, February.

Merriman, W. E., & M. Tomasello. 1995. Introduction: verbs are words too. In W. Tomasello & E. Merriman (eds.), *Beyond names for things: young children's acquisition of verbs*. Hillsdale, NJ/Hove: Lawrence Erlbaum, 1–18.

Miller, M. 1976. *Zur Logik der frühkindlichen Sprachentwicklung: Empirische Untersuchungen und Theoriediskussion*. Stuttgart: Klett.

Morgan, J. L., & K. Demuth (eds.). 1996. *Signal to syntax: bootstrapping from speech to grammar in early acquisition*. Hillsdale, NJ: Lawrence Erlbaum.

Nelson, K. 1991. The matter of time: interdependencies between language and thought in development. In S. A. Gelman & J. P. Byrnes (eds.), *Perspectives on language and thought: interrelations in development*. Cambridge: Cambridge University Press, 278–318.

Piaget, J. 1946. *Le développement de la notion du temps chez l'enfant*. Paris: Presses Universitaires de France.

Rispoli, M. 1990. Lexical assignability and perspective switch: the acquisition of verb subcategorization for aspectual inflections. *Journal of Child Language* 17: 375–392.

1991. The acquisition of verb subcategorization in a functionalist framework. *First Language* 11: 41–63.

Sachs, J. 1983. Talking about the there and then: the emergence of displaced reference in parent–child discourse. In K. E. Nelson (ed.), *Children's language*, vol. 4. Hillsdale, NJ: Lawrence Erlbaum, 1–28.

Schlyter, S. 1990. The acquisition of tense and aspect. In J. M. Meisel (ed.), *Two first languages: early grammatical development in bilingual children*. Dordrecht: Foris, 87–121.

Shirai, Y. 1991. Primacy of aspect in language acquisition: simplified input and prototype. Unpublished doctoral dissertation, University of California at Los Angeles.

1993. Inherent aspect and the acquisition of tense–aspect morphology in Japanese. In H. Nakajima & Y. Otsu (eds.), *Argument structure: its syntax and acquisition*. Tokyo: Kaitakusha, 185–211.

Shirai, Y., & R. W. Andersen. 1995. The acquisition of tense–aspect morphology: a prototype account. *Language* 71: 743–762.

Slobin, D. I. 1973. Cognitive prerequisites for the development of grammar. In C. A. Ferguson & D. I. Slobin (eds.), *Studies of child language development*. New York: Holt, Rinehart & Winston, 175–208.

1985. Crosslinguistic evidence for the Language-Making Capacity. In D. I. Slobin (ed.), *The crosslinguistic study of language acquisition*, vol. 2: *Theoretical issues*. Hillsdale, NJ: Lawrence Erlbaum, 1157–1249.

1991. Learning to think for speaking: native language, cognition, and rhetorical style. *Pragmatics* 1: 7–25.

1997. The origins of grammaticizable notions: beyond the individual mind. In D. I. Slobin (ed.), *The crosslinguistic study of language acquisition*, vol. 5: *Expanding the contexts*. Mahwah, NJ: Lawrence Erlbaum, 265–323.

Smith, C. S. 1980. The acquisition of time talk: relations between child and adult grammar. *Journal of Child Language* 7: 263–278.

Smoczyńska, M. 1995. The acquisition of Polish verb morphology. Paper presented to the Colloquium on Developmental Psychology, University of California, Berkeley, September.

Stephany, U. 1985. *Aspekt, Tempus und Modalität: zur Entwicklung der Verbalgrammatik in der neugriechischen Kindersprache.* Tübingen: Narr.

Stern, C., & W. Stern. 1928. *Die Kindersprache*, 4th edn. Leipzig: Barth (reprint: Darmstadt: Wissenschaftliche Buchgesellschaft, 1987).

Toivainen, J. 1980. *Inflectional affixes used by Finnish-speaking children aged 1–3 years*. Helsinki: Suomalaisen Kirjallisuuden Seura.

Weist, R. M. 1986. Tense and aspect: temporal systems in child language. In P. Fletcher & M. Garman (eds.), *Language acquisition*, 2nd edn. Cambridge: Cambridge University Press, 356–374.

1996. Constraints on the acquisition of tense and aspect. Paper presented at the 7th International Congress for the Study of Child Language, Istanbul, July.

Weist, R. M., H. Wysocka, K. Witkowska-Stadnik, E. Buczowska, & E. Konieczna. 1984. The defective tense hypothesis: on the emergence of tense and aspect in child Polish. *Journal of Child Language* 11: 347–374.

16 Shaping meanings for language: universal and language-specific in the acquisition of spatial semantic categories

Melissa Bowerman and Soonja Choi

Max Planck Institute for Psycholinguistics, Nijmegen, The Netherlands and San Diego State University

Opening a box a toddler says *open*; seeing a toy car in it she says *car*; taking the car out she says *out*; putting it on the floor she says *down*. In the world at large these little remarks do not command much attention. But to people interested in how children learn to talk, the first steps into language raise fascinating and difficult questions. In this chapter, we are concerned with the central puzzle of where children's early word meanings come from. Are they introduced through language? Do they reflect concepts that arise spontaneously through infants' perceptual and cognitive development? Do language and cognition interact to produce early word meanings, and, if so, how?

The idea that children learn how to structure meanings through exposure to language is usually associated with Whorf (1956). Whorf stressed that languages differ in the way they partition the world, and he proposed that in learning the semantic categories of their language, children also acquire a world view, a way of interpreting their experiences. Inspired by Whorf, Roger Brown also emphasized the role of the linguistic input in children's concept formation, arguing that a new word can be a "lure to cognition" (R. Brown 1958:206–7) – a recurrent signal that "serves to attract relevant experiences, to sum them over time into a conception governing the use of the word" (1965: 311).

During the cognitive revolution of the 1960s and 1970s, the idea that language could spur young children to form new concepts was abandoned for the view that children's first words label concepts that originate nonlinguistically. There was much motivation for this shift. Piaget (e.g. 1954) had demonstrated that babies start to build up a basic understanding of their world well before they learn to talk. Work on semantic structure was beginning to show that the meanings associated with linguistic forms are more uniform than had earlier been supposed, constrained perhaps by both deepseated perceptual and cognitive biases in how humans view the world, and learners' sensitivity to clusterings of the attributes of referents in the real world (Berlin & Kay 1969; Rosch 1973; E. V. Clark 1976; Rosch, Mervis, Gray, Johnson, & Boyes-Braem 1976; Allan 1979). Far from being arbitrary, the semantic categories of language appeared to reflect just the sorts of concepts that are nonlinguistically salient to human beings.

As this way of thinking took hold, it seemed increasingly implausible that children look to language for clues to how to structure their early word meanings. More likely was that they bring their own concepts with them to the language-learning task and try to figure out how to encode them. In an influential statement of this position, Nelson (1974: 268) argued that traditional models of concept formation posed the basic question backwards: instead of asking "how does the child form a concept to fit the word?", we should be asking "how does the child match words to his concepts?"

The wave of crosslinguistic work on language acquisition in the 1970s was consistent with this new emphasis on cognitive priority. This work showed that children's first utterances all around the world revolve around a restricted set of meanings to do with agents moving their bodies or acting on objects, with possession and attribution, and with the existence, location, disappearance, and recurrence of objects (Bowerman 1973; R. Brown 1973; Slobin 1970, 1973). These crosslinguistic similarities could be accounted for by assuming that the meanings arise from nonlinguistic cognitive processes common to all children. In a seminal statement of this position, Slobin (1973) argued that the meanings expressed by language arise in children on a nonlinguistic basis in a fairly constant order and at a fairly constant rate, regardless of the language being learned. Once a given meaning emerges, the child will look for a linguistic device (e.g. word, inflection, word order pattern) to express it with.

The assumption that children know the meanings to be mapped ahead of time is still evident in much present-day work on semantic development, although many researchers have gone back to the question of how a child fits a concept to a word (as opposed to finding a word for a concept to be communicated). The question is now often inspired by interest in "Quine's problem" (Quine 1960): the indeterminacy for a learner of what an observed instance of a word refers to. Since it is unlikely that a newly encountered word will usually encode just that aspect of a situation a child happens to be thinking about, learners must have ways of homing in on the meaning the adult has in mind. Proposals about how they accomplish this vary (e.g. Gleitman 1990; Markman 1990; P. Bloom 1994, ch. 6 of this volume; Tomasello 1995, ch. 5 of this volume), but most presuppose that the needed concept is already available. The child is characterized as needing to *identify* the concept from among a set of plausible possibilities, not actually to *construct* it.

In this chapter we will argue for a more interactive view of how children's early word meanings arise. We suggest that early semantic development involves a pervasive interaction between nonlinguistic conceptual development and the semantic categories of the input language, not just a one-way mapping from preexisting concepts. The domain we investigate is space. It may seem surprising to argue for sensitivity to language-specific semantic structure in this domain: spatial words are typically cited as prime evidence for the claim that first words label nonlinguistic concepts. We do not, of course, dispute that children bring much nonlinguistic knowledge about space to the language acquisition task, and we assume that this knowledge contributes importantly to their word learning. But recent research reveals that languages vary surprisingly in their semantic structuring of space. We will show that different semantic patterns in the linguistic input influence the meanings of children's spatial words from as early as the one-word stage of development.

To forestall a misunderstanding that arises easily, let us clarify here the intended scope of our claim. The problem we are investigating is how children learn to *talk* about space. To use words like adults, children must gain productive control over the semantic categories associated with them. Do these categories, once mastered, influence how learners *think* about space nonlinguistically, e.g. how they perceive, mentally represent, judge, remember, or draw inferences about spatial situations (the Whorfian Linguistic Determinism hypothesis)? Or do they play a role *only* in language behavior ("Thinking for speaking," Slobin 1991)? This question can only be answered by studies that compare language with language-independent studies of cognition (as has been done, for example, by Lucy 1992; Levinson 1996; and Lucy & Gaskins, ch. 9 of this volume). The work we discuss in this chapter asks how children master the structuring of meaning in their native language, not whether they use the semantic categories for nonlinguistic cognitive purposes. The mastery of a language-specific semantic system must be recognized as an important cognitive problem-solving task in its own right – one of the most critical, in fact, to confront the growing child.

In the following, we first summarize evidence for the view that young children map spatial words directly onto spatial concepts they have already formed on the basis of their nonlinguistic development. We then illustrate the problem of variation in how languages categorize spatial meanings. Next we show that children learning different languages begin to home in on language-specific meanings for early spatial words from as early as 18 months – sometimes even before they are producing the words. Finally, we consider some learning mechanisms that may help resolve a seeming paradox: that there is robust evidence for the influence of *both* nonlinguistic spatial conceptualization *and* the semantic categories of the input language on spatial semantic development.

1 Evidence for the role of nonlinguistic spatial development in the acquisition of spatial words

One of the cornerstones of the assumption that children map spatial words to prelinguistically available meanings is evidence that they know a great deal about space before they begin to talk about it (Piaget & Inhelder 1956; Gibson & Spelke 1983; see Bowerman 1996a for a review). For example, within the first few days or months of life, infants can distinguish between scenes and categorize them on the basis of spatial information such as left–right (Behl-Chadha & Eimas 1995) and above–below (Antell & Caron 1985; Quinn 1994). By a few months of age babies know that moving objects must follow a continuous trajectory and cannot pass through one another (Spelke, Breinlinger, Macomber, & Jacobson 1992), that objects deposited in midair should fall (Needham & Baillargeon 1993), and that containers must have bottoms (Baillargeon 1995). Clearly, children do not wait for language to instruct them on how to represent and interpret spatial relationships in concrete situations.

A second compelling source of evidence for the role of nonlinguistic spatial cognition is that spatial words emerge over a long period of time in a relatively consistent order, both within children learning the same language and across children learning different languages. In particular, words for functional and topological notions of containment (*in*), contiguity and support (*on*) and occlusion (*under*) emerge first, then words for notions of proximity (*next to*, *beside*, *between*), and finally words for projective relationships (*in front of*, *behind*). This sequence is consistent with the order of emergence of spatial concepts as established by Piaget & Inhelder (1956) with the use of nonlinguistic tests. A straightforward hypothesis that accounts for this correspondence is that as new spatial concepts mature nonlinguistically, children discover the forms that are used to express them in their local language (Johnston & Slobin 1979; Johnston 1985; see also Sinha, Thorseng, Hayashi, & Plunkett 1994).

Evidence that children's nonlinguistic spatial understanding plays a critical role also comes from differences in the way words are used by learners and adults. Some words are initially *underextended* relative to their range in adult speech. For example, *behind* and *in front of* are at first used only for things located behind or in front of the child's own body, with apparent intended meanings such as "inaccessible and/or hidden" vs. "visible" (Johnston 1984). Other words are typically *overextended*: e.g. *open* is used not only for manipulations with doors, windows, and containers, but also for taking a piece out of a jigsaw puzzle, pulling Frisbees apart, and turning on an electric typewriter (Bowerman 1978; E. V. Clark 1993). Deviations from adult usage have suggested that the concepts guiding the learner's early generalizations are the child's own, rather than modeled directly on adult usage (see Bowerman 1978, 1980; Clark, ch. 13 of this volume; Smiley & Huttenlocher 1995 on the reasoning behind this assumption). Widespread patterns of under- and overextension have often been interpreted as pointing to *universal* child conceptualizations (Slobin 1985; Clark, ch. 13 of this volume).

Consistent with the idea that early spatial words are mapped to preestablished spatial concepts, generalization often takes place very rapidly. For example, Smiley & Huttenlocher (1995) found that as early as the single-word period, children generalize words like *up*, *down*, *out*, *off*, and *open* to a wide variety of events that are similar in trajectory of movement or salient outcome state, abstracted across entities of different kinds. Similarly, McCune-Nicolich (1981) found that *up*, *down*, *back*, and *open*, along with a few other relational words, come in abruptly, generalize rapidly, and are less likely to be imitated than other words. Rapid generalization has suggested that children's use of the words is guided by knowledge that is already in place at the time the words are acquired.

Taken together, these studies show persuasively that nonlinguistic spatial development supports the acquisition of spatial language and provides many of the guidelines children follow in extending spatial morphemes to novel situations. But they do not demonstrate the stronger supposition that the meanings of children's early spatial words reflect nonlinguistic concepts directly. For example, the maturation of spatial understanding might make possible the acquisition of spatial words of a certain general type (e.g. words for topological relations) without necessarily prespecifying the shape of the associated categories. And we could expect rapid generalization of early spatial words not only if children rely on their preexisting spatial concepts, but also if they are capable of learning something about the categories of their language in comprehension, before production begins.

2 Crosslinguistic variation in spatial semantic organization

An important foundation for the "nonlinguistic concepts" view of spatial semantic development has been the assumption that although the *forms* of spatial morphemes differ across languages, their *meanings* are closely similar (e.g. Slobin 1973). Similarity could be expected because these meanings are presumably worked on by biological and environmental constraints (e.g. upright posture, front–back asymmetry, gravity) that affect people in the same way everywhere (H. H. Clark 1973). But recent work shows that there is more crosslinguistic variation in spatial semantic structuring than had been supposed (e.g. Brugman 1984; Talmy 1985; Lakoff 1987; MacLaury 1989; Choi & Bowerman 1991; P. Brown 1994; Levinson 1994, 1996; Ameka 1995; Bowerman 1996a, b; Wilkins & Hill 1996). Spatial situations can clearly be construed in different ways, and languages provide different conventionalized "takes" on how to do it. Differences affect many aspects of spatial encoding (see Bowerman 1996a for an overview). In this chapter, we will be concerned with differences in the kinds of meanings children express with their very first spatial morphemes, which typically revolve around notions of containment, support, attachment, motion up and down the vertical axis, and opening and closing.

In English, children express such meanings from the one-word stage on with particles like *up*, *down*, *in*, *out*, *on*, and *off*, and a few verbs like *open* and *close* (L. Bloom 1973:70; R. Brown 1973:328ff.; Nelson 1974; Bowerman 1978, 1980; McCune-Nicolich 1981; Gopnik & Meltzoff 1986). The meanings of these little words seem so straightforward that it is easy to suppose they reflect an inevitable conceptual parsing of the world. But although all languages provide ways to talk about the situations for which English speakers use these words, they do not necessarily have morphemes with translation-equivalent meanings. In some cases languages focus on surprisingly different properties for calculating whether situations qualify as instances of the same or different semantic categories of space. In other cases languages agree on the overall topology of the semantic space to be partitioned, but differ dramatically in how they work out the boundaries between neighboring categories. Let us consider an example of each type. The first has to do with the motion of one object with respect to another, and the second with static spatial relations. In discussing these examples we follow Talmy's (1985) terminology: the entity whose motion or location is at issue is the Figure, the entity with respect to which the Figure moves or is located is the Ground, and the course or trajectory the Figure follows with respect to the Ground is the Path.

2.1 Motion along a Path

Figure 16.1 illustrates some differences between English and Korean in the categorization of actions of placing one object in contact with another. In English the critical words are particles or prepositions, while in Korean they are verbs. This is because English and Korean differ typologically in their characteristic way of expressing Path: English is a "satellite-framed" language,[1] while Korean is a "verb-framed" language (see Talmy 1985, 1991, on the typological distinction, and Choi & Bowerman 1991 for a detailed comparison of English and Korean).

As figure 16.1a shows, English makes a fundamental distinction between putting a Figure into contact with an external (i.e. flat or convex) surface of a Ground object, which then typically supports it ([*put*] ***on***), and putting a Figure into some sort of enclosure or container ([*put*] ***in***) (figure 16.1a). This cleavage is absent in Korean. As figure 16.1b shows, the Korean Path verb *kkita* cuts across the "on-in" contrast, picking out a spatial category for which English has no morpheme: actions in which two objects with complementary shapes are brought into an interlocking, tight-fitting relationship. In some cases the Figure interlocks with an external flat or convex surface of the Ground (e.g. one Lego piece stacked on another, top on a pen, ring on a finger; [*put*] ***on*** in English). In other cases the Figure ends up tightly contained in the Ground (e.g. piece in jigsaw puzzle; [*put*] ***in*** in English). In still other cases – such as buttoning a button and closing a tightly latching drawer – the action could be called neither *on* nor *in* in English. The "interlocking" property that unites all the *"kkita"* actions plays no role in the semantic system of English.

Because of the presence of the *kkita* category, Korean makes a systematic distinction quite foreign to English between putting things into *tight* containers (e.g. piece into jigsaw puzzle: *kkita*) and putting things into *loose* containers (e.g. book into bag: *nehta* 'put loosely in or around'; this latter category comprises not just the "loose" subset of English "put in" relations, but also relations of loose encirclement and envelopment, e.g. loose-fitting ring on pole). The existence of *kkita* is similarly responsible for a systematic distinction between surface-contact relations that feature *interlocking* surfaces (e.g. Lego pieces: *kkita*) and those with *noninterlocking* surfaces (all called [*put*] *on* in English). Relative to English, Korean subdivides "noninterlocking" surface relations quite finely (see figure 16.1b); for example, there is a verb for depositing things on roughly horizontal surfaces (e.g. cup on table: *nohta*), a verb for joining flat or conceptualized-as-if-flat surfaces (e.g. magnet on refrigerator: *pwuchita*), and a set of verbs for putting clothing on various parts of the body (e.g. on head: *ssuta*; on trunk: *ipta*; on feet: *sinta*).

A difference between English and Korean that is not apparent from figure 16.1 is that English Path forms are indifferent to whether the motion of the Figure is *caused* or *spontaneous* (or in many cases even to whether there is motion at all), while Korean Path forms are sensitive to this distinction. Note, for instance, that English uses the same Path form for both *put it* **on** *(the table)* – caused motion – and *climb* ***on*** *(the table)* – spontaneous motion; and similarly for both *put it* ***in*** *(the bathtub)* and *get* ***in*** *(the bathtub)*. But Korean uses different Path verbs for caused and spontaneous motion, and – strikingly from the standpoint of English – the categories associated with these verbs do not necessarily coincide. For example,

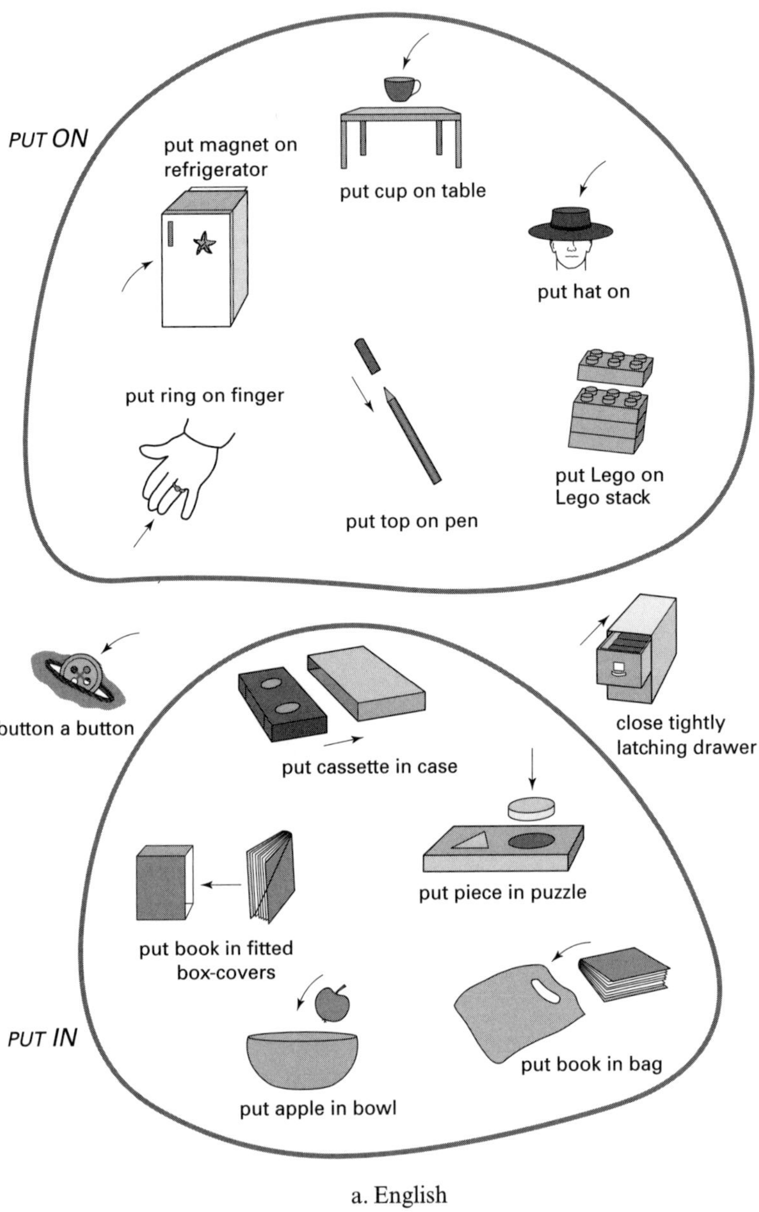

a. English

Fig. 16.1 Categorization of some object placements in English and Korean.

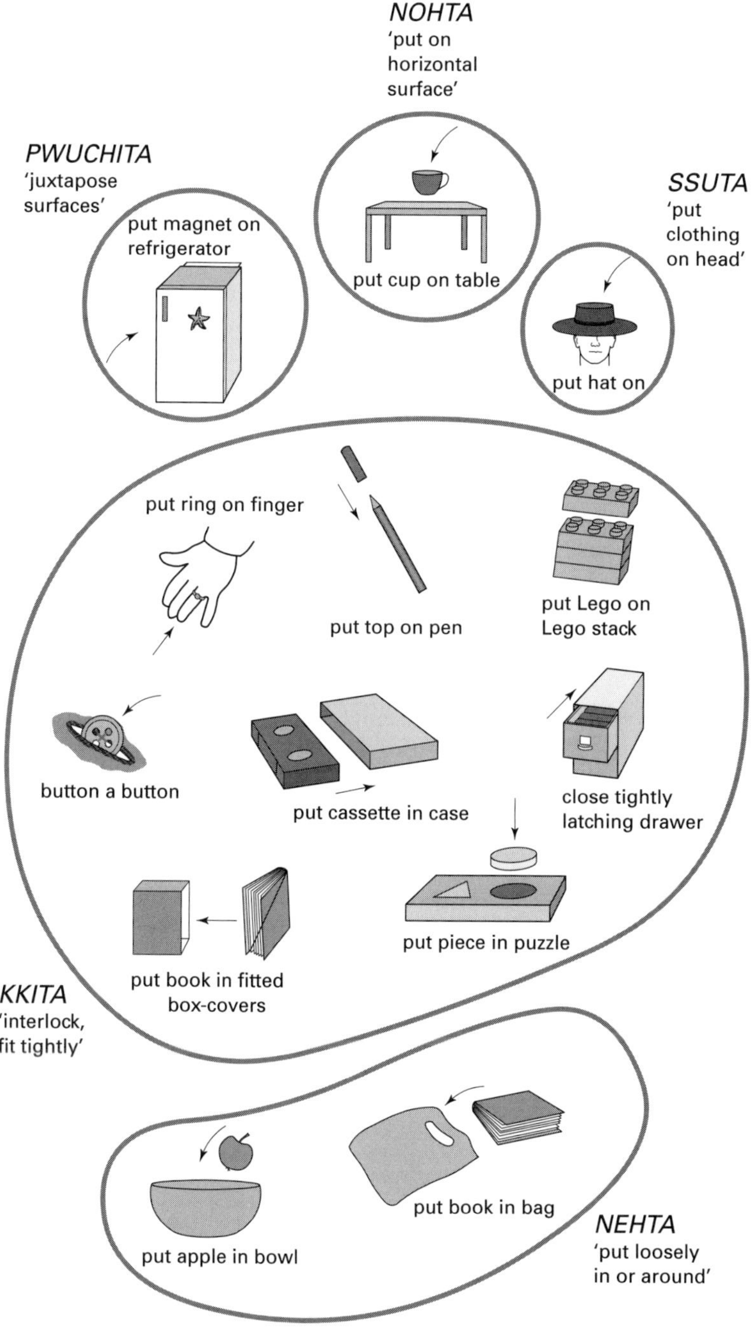
NOHTA
'put on
horizontal
surface'
put cup on table
PWUCHITA
'juxtapose
surfaces'
put magnet on
refrigerator
SSUTA
'put
clothing
on head'
put hat on
put ring on finger
put top on pen
put Lego on
Lego stack
button a button
put cassette in case
close tightly
latching drawer
put piece in puzzle
put book in fitted
box-covers
KKITA
'interlock,
fit tightly'
put book in bag
put apple in bowl
NEHTA
'put loosely
in or around'

b. Korean

corresponding to the transitive verb *kkita* 'interlock, fit tightly' there is no intransitive verb meaning 'move (physically) into an interlocking, tight-fitting relationship' (e.g. crawl into a narrow hole).[2] Similarly, corresponding to *nehta* 'put loosely in or around' there is no intransitive verb meaning 'move into a relationship of loose containment or encirclement' (e.g. get in the bathtub). There is only an intransitive verb *tulta* 'move/be in,' which – like English *in* – is indifferent to the tight-fit/loose-fit distinction. Thus, children learning English must establish a uniform set of Path categories that abstract away from how the motion came about, while children learning Korean must distinguish meticulously between caused and spontaneous motion and master two sets of Path categories that often do not coincide.

2.2 *Static spatial relationships*

Continuing to focus on the kinds of situations covered by the English prepositions *on* and *in*, let us have a look at *static* spatial relations. In a crosslinguistic study, Bowerman & Pederson (1992, in preparation) investigated how speakers of thirty-eight languages from twenty-five different language families described situations of containment, support, encirclement, attachment, adhesion, piercing, hanging, and so on. Consider as examples the six spatial situations shown in figure 16.2.[3] No language provided a distinct spatial term for all six. But which situations were grouped and which were distinguished varied across languages. Some of the attested patterns, as schematized in figure 16.2, were these:

1. One term for situations (a)–(e) and another for (f). This is a common pattern, followed by languages as diverse as English, Hebrew, Hungarian, and Mopan Mayan. In English, (a)–(e) are covered by *(be) on*, and (f) by *(be) in*.
2. One term for (a) and another for (f). Neither term is used for (b)–(e); these situations are covered instead by a general locative word or inflection – also applicable to (a) and (f) – that indicates only that there is *some* spatial relationship between the Figure and the Ground, normally understood as the most canonical one for the objects in question. This pattern, also common, is found for example in Japanese and Korean, in which the terms used to encode situations (*a*) and (*f*) are nominals: e.g. Japanese *ue* 'upper region, top, above,' and *naka* 'interior region.'
3. One term for (a)–(b), another for (c)–(e), and still another for (f). This pattern is rare in the languages Bowerman & Pederson looked at, occurring only in Dutch (German is similar but not identical). The three Dutch terms, all prepositions, are *op* (for a–b), *aan* (c–e), and *in* (f). *Op* and *aan* are both usually translated as *on* in English. The difference between them for situations like those shown in figure 16.2 has to do

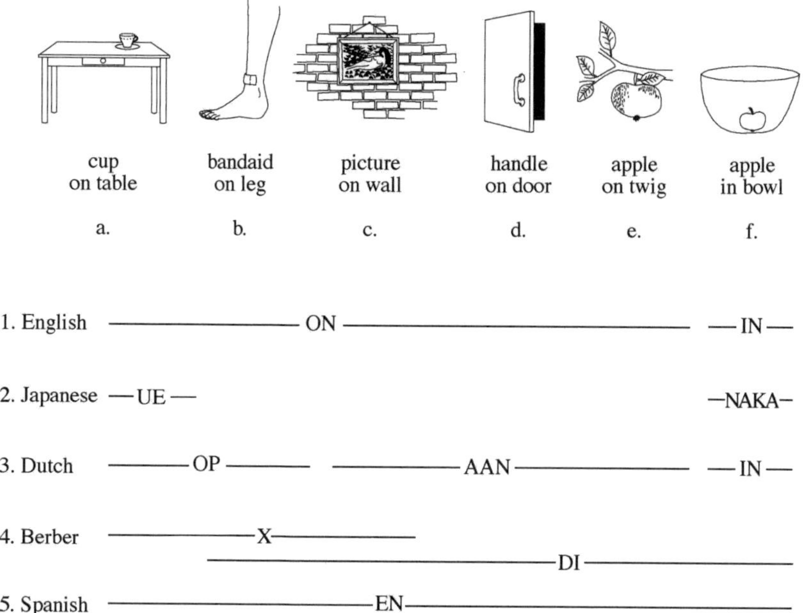

Fig. 16.2 Some crosslinguistic differences in categorizing static spatial relationships.

with the force dynamics of the situation (Bowerman 1996b). If the Figure is conceptualized as acted on by a salient force, usually gravity, that must be counteracted if the Figure is to stay in contact with the Ground, *aan* is selected (e.g. picture on wall). But if the Figure is seen as resting comfortably on the Ground with no "pull" towards separation, *op* is chosen (e.g. cup on table, bandaid on leg).

4. One term for (a)–(c) and another for (b)–(f). A language of this type is Berber, with the prepositions *x* and *di* (roughly 'on' and 'in'); similar but not identical is Finnish, with the locative case endings *-lla* and *-ssa* (again, roughly 'on' and 'in'). What is new and surprising here is the extension of an 'in'-type morpheme to many situations that English categorizes as 'on' relations; note also that there is some overlap in the range of the 'on'–'in' terms.
5. One term for the whole range from (a) to (f), e.g. the Spanish preposition *en*, normally translated in English as either *in* or *on*. (Spanish speakers can, if they desire, be more explicit, distinguishing (a) as *encima (de)* 'on top (of)' and (f) as *dentro (de)* 'inside (of).')

Despite all this variation, the languages Bowerman & Pederson investigated did not categorize spatial situations in arbitrarily different ways. All of them appeared to be constrained by an underlying gradient – an implicational hierarchy – that orders spatial situations in the way shown in figure 16.2 (the hierarchy includes additional situation types not shown here). Thus, there was variation in how many spatial terms a language used to cover the situations, and in where the territory of one term left off and that of the next began, but if a term was used for more than one segment of the gradient, it covered *adjacent* segments. In no language did Bowerman and Pederson find a term used, for instance, for (a) "cup on table" and (e) "apple on twig" but not (c) "picture on wall."

What accounts for this systematicity? Many properties of the spatial situations ordered by the gradient vary simultaneously, so it is difficult to characterize the ordering principle in simple terms. But as a rough approximation, read from left to right, the gradient seems to capture how easily a configuration can be construed as similar to a situation of support from below – as in (a) "cup on table". Thus, in (c) "picture on wall," the Ground object, the wall, offers support from the side rather than from below, but it is still a surface. In (e) "apple on twig," the Ground has dwindled to a point and the support is from above. There is nothing that dictates that a language must use an 'on'-type morpheme for either of these situations, but *if* it does so, it is more likely to use it for (c) than for (e), and if it uses it for (e), it will also use it for (c).

Read the other way, from right to left, the gradient captures how easily a configuration can be construed as similar to a prototypical situation of containment – as in (f) "apple in bowl". An apple on a twig (e) is of course not literally contained in the twig, but it is attached to it. A language can apparently choose to treat attachment to an exterior surface or point as a kind of "incorporation" more akin to containment, as in (f), than to mere juxtaposition, as in (a). Being tightly attached through an organic relationship or screws, as in (e) "apple on twig" and (d) "handle on door," is apparently easier to construe this way than being attached, for example, through adhesion, as in (b) "bandaid on leg." So if a language uses an 'in'-type morpheme for (b), it will also use it for (d) and (e). Notice that situations like (b)–(e) – congruent with their intermediate position on the hierarchy – are indeterminant: languages can treat them as similar to *either* support from below *or* containment, or as like neither or like both.

Support and containment are often cited as two of the most fundamental and early-maturing spatial concepts – responsible for the early acquisition of *in* and *on* and similar words in other languages (R. Brown 1973; Johnston & Slobin 1979). In section 2.1 we saw that although the support–containment distinction is indeed important in classifying actions of object placement in English, other distinctions take precedence in Korean. In this section, we have seen that prototypical situations of support and containment anchor an implicit gradient of static spatial situation types.[4] But what a language *counts* as (sufficiently like) support or (sufficiently like) containment is not given by the structure of reality or our perception of it, but is determined instead to a large extent by language-specific conventions for how to construe spatial scenes. Such conventions must of course be learned. Learning could, however, be facilitated if children are implicitly guided in their generalizations by a sense of similarity among spatial situations that is congruent with the hierarchy illustrated in figure 16.2. We come back to this possibility in section 4.

3 How early are language-specific spatial semantic categories acquired?

What does crosslinguistic variation in spatial semantics mean for the question of where the meanings of children's early spatial words come from? Do children perhaps share an initial organization of semantic concepts of space and diverge only later in the direction of the input language (as Slobin 1985 argues more generally for "grammaticizable" notions such as those associated with prepositions)? Alternatively, do children's early spatial categories differ from the beginning in accordance with the structuring of space in the input language? To explore these questions, we have carried out studies comparing early spatial semantic categorization among children learning English, Korean, Dutch, and Tzotzil Mayan (Choi & Bowerman 1991; Bowerman 1994, 1996a, b; Bowerman, de León, & Choi 1995). These studies have employed a variety of techniques, including analysis and comparison of spontaneous speech data from children from about 1 to 3 years of age, elicited production with children and adults, and tests of comprehension down to 18 months of age using the "preferential looking" paradigm.

3.1 Early spontaneous speech

In one study, we examined the spontaneous speech of children learning English and Korean between the ages of about 1 and 3 through analysis of longitudinal data (Choi & Bowerman 1991). Both sets of children began to talk about space between 14 and 16 months, and to use spatial words productively (i.e., for novel as well as familiar situations) between about 16 and 20 months. They talked about similar events, including putting on and taking off clothing; opening and closing containers; putting things in and taking them out; joining and separating Legos and other toys; climbing up on and down off laps and furniture; going in and out of buildings, bathtubs, and other "containers"; being picked up and put down; and standing up and sitting down. These similarities presumably reflect the shared interests of young children. For our purposes, the critical question is whether learners of English and Korean semantically *categorized* these events in the same way, as inferred from the range of situations to which they applied their spatial words.

The words they used were of course different. As expected, our English speakers started out with particles like *up*, *down*, *on*, *off*, *in*, *out*, and *back*, and a few verbs like *open* and *close*. The Korean children used exclusively verbs (recall that Korean encodes motion along a Path with verbs; it lacks a system of Path markers equivalent to English particles and prepositions). Despite form-class differences, we can meaningfully compare the range of events for which each word was used. If the children had mapped the words to a shared set of spatial concepts arising from built-in perceptual biases or universal stages of nonlinguistic spatial cognition, they should use them to pick out similar sets of events. We would then find words over- or underextended from the adult perspective, given that the Path categories of adult English and Korean differ in many ways. But we can indeed expect over- and underextensions – recall that deviations from adult norms have been taken as prime evidence that early spatial words express nonlinguistic concepts.[5]

Our most important finding was that from their first productive uses of spatial words, the children categorized spatial events language-specifically – there was no evidence that they relied on the same set of basic spatial concepts.[6] In both their routine and novel uses, our English-speaking subjects concentrated on notions of containment (*in* and *out*), support and surface contact, especially attachment (*on* and *off*), and vertical motion (*up* and *down*). The children's initial use of these particles was mostly restricted to motion, so in this respect they made a selection from the range of uses modeled in adult speech (cf. also Smiley & Huttenlocher 1995). But within these limits they soon generalized the words across an English-style range of uses.

For instance, by 18–19 months they used spatial particles freely for both spontaneous and caused motion along a path (e.g. *in* for both getting into a bathtub and putting a picture into a wallet; *up* both when trying to climb onto a chair and as a request to be picked up). They respected the important English distinction between containment and contact-and-support, and they used *in* and *out* freely for both tight and loose containment (e.g. putting a book into a fitted case [tight] and a toy into a bag [loose]), and *on* and *off* for a variety of surface contact relations (e.g. taking Lego pieces apart [tight] and getting off a chair or taking off clothing [loose]). Viewed from the perspective offered by children learning another language, their overextensions were minor, suggesting difficulty in establishing the boundaries of categories that in overall contour were already language-specific, e.g. *in* for putting a pingpong ball between the knees (an enclosure of sorts), and *off* for pulling two Lego pieces apart (removal from surface contact).

The children learning Korean differed from those learning English in several important respects. First, like adults, they distinguished scrupulously between caused and spontaneous motions along a path (e.g. they applied the transitive verb *nehta* 'put loosely in or around' to putting toys in a box, but never to climbing into a bathtub). They made no general distinction between "containment" and "contact and support," but followed instead the crosscutting Korean distinction between "interlocking, tight-fit" relations and "loose" relations. Thus, they used *kkita* 'interlock, fit tightly,' and its opposite *ppayta* 'remove from an interlocking relation,' for relations of both containment and contact-and-support, as long as there was a tight fit (e.g. *kkita* for both putting a peg doll *into* a perfectly fitting niche-seat and stacking Lego pieces *on top of* each other). For "loose" relations of containment and contact-and-support they used a variety of words more or less appropriately; e.g. *nehta* 'put loosely in or around' and its opposite *kkenayta* 'remove from loosely in or around' for putting toys into a box or bag and taking them out and for putting loose rings onto a pole and taking them off; *nohta* 'put on horizontal surface' for putting things down on table or floor; and three different clothing verbs: *ssuta* 'put clothing on head,' *ipta* '. . . on trunk,' and *sinta* '. . . on feet.'

The errors of the Korean learners, like those of the English learners, suggested difficulty in establishing the boundaries of categories that in broad outline were already language-specific. For example, *kkita* 'interlock, fit tightly' was used for sticking a fork into an apple and for attaching a metal fish to the magnetized beak of a toy duck. Both events are clearly similar to events that can be described as *kkita*, but for adults they fall outside the category, the fork example because the two objects did not have complementary shapes *before* the action took place (the holes in the apple were created by the action), and the magnet example because the surfaces, although tightly attached to each other, are flat and do not interlock.

Children learning Tzotzil are similar to those learning English and Korean in the kinds of situations they talk about at the one- and two-word stage, but their spatial words also pick out language-specific categories (Bowerman, de León, & Choi 1995; see de León, ch. 18 of this volume, on categories of motion "up" and "down"). For example, one of their favorite early words is the verb *xoj*, which they use, like adults, for actions that cause an elongated object to end up encircled by a ring- or tube-shaped object (e.g. putting a ring *on* a pole or a pole *through* a ring, putting an arm *into* a sleeve or a leg *into* a trouser-leg, putting a coil of rope *over* a peg). Children exposed to English and Korean use no word for a comparable category:

those learning English divide *xoj* events up between *in* (e.g. pole in ring) and *on* (e.g. ring on pole, clothing on), while those learning Korean parcel them out among *kkita* 'interlock, fit tightly' (e.g. tightly-fitting ring on pole or pole in ring), *nehta* 'put loosely in or around' (e.g. loose ring on pole or pole in ring), and the various clothing verbs.

To summarize, spontaneous speech data suggest that language-specific learning gets under way by at least the second half of the second year of life. Despite certain under- and overextensions, the overall use of spatial words from the one-word stage on reflects the major semantic distinctions and grouping principles of the target language.

3.2 *Elicited production of words for "separating" and "joining" objects*

Spontaneous speech gives a good overview of the early stages of semantic development, and offers valuable evidence on how children conceptualize events they are interested in. But comparisons of spontaneous utterances are somewhat indirect, since the specific events children choose to talk about differ. To allow more direct comparisons, we designed an elicited production study that examined how child and adult speakers of English, Korean, and Dutch describe a standardized set of manipulations of small objects (Bowerman & Choi 1994; Bowerman 1996a; Choi 1997).

The actions we used involved both familiar and novel objects, and covered a broad range of "joining" and "separating" events, e.g. putting objects into containers of different kinds – both tight and loose – and taking them out; putting objects down onto surfaces; attaching and detaching things in various ways (bandaid, train cars joined with hooks or magnets, suction cup, rubber band, lid on pan, Legos, Pop-beads, buttons); opening and closing; hanging and "unhanging"; and donning and doffing clothing.

For each language, we tested forty speakers individually, ten each in the age ranges 2;0 to 2;5, 2;6 to 2;11, 3;0 to 3;6, and ten adults. In a play-like situation we elicited descriptions by presenting the subject with the relevant objects – e.g. a wooden jigsaw puzzle with one piece separate, or a ring poised over a pole – and almost but not quite performing the action, pausing to say things like "What should I do? Tell me what to do." This technique worked well: even in the youngest age group, 87% of the responses were attempts to label the action. Responses from the English and Dutch speakers typically involved Path particles (e.g. *Put it in!* or just *In!*), while those from the Korean speakers were verbs (e.g. *Kki-e*! [stem of *kkita* 'interlock, fit tightly']-MODAL).

We explored speakers' classification systems by evaluating which actions they used the same expressions for, and which ones they distinguished. The logic is similar to that applied to data collected in sorting tasks: actions labeled in the same way are like stimuli sorted into the same pile; actions labeled in different ways are like stimuli sorted into different piles. The data can be arranged in similarity matrices (for all actions taken pairwise, is the same expression used? different expressions?), which can then be analyzed with any technique suitable for similarity data, such as multidimensional scaling or cluster analysis.

Comparison of the various age groups both within and across languages showed that the children of every age group classified space significantly more like *adult* speakers of their own language than like *same-age* children learning the other languages. They did not classify exactly like the adults; for example, they used fewer words and extended some words more broadly. But there was no evidence for a uniform set of starting spatial categories across children learning different languages. By at least 2;0 to 2;5, the children clearly classified in a language-specific way.

As an example, figure 16.3 shows how the youngest learners of English and Korean classified a subset of the "joining" actions. (For more detail, see figures 3 and 4 in Bowerman 1996a.) We include here only actions for which at least four of the ten children in each group used the word shown (the actual number is indicated next to the name of the action), and no other response was as frequent. Notice how consistently the English children made the by-now familiar distinction between containment and surface-contact relations (*put in*, *put on*). Their Korean counterparts were attentive instead to the distinction between interlocking relations (*kkita*) and various "looser" kinds of joinings, including putting clothing onto different body parts.

3.3 Comprehension of language-specific spatial categories before age 2

In still further work, we returned to younger children. Our investigation of spontaneous speech (section 3.1) had suggested that children develop sensitivity to language-specific spatial categories before their second birthday. Our elicited production study (3.2) showed language sensitivity with more systematic data, but the task was too demanding for children under about 2 years. To test younger children in a more controlled way, we turned to the preferential-looking paradigm that was pioneered for use with language by Golinkoff, Hirsh-Pasek, Cauley, & Gordon (1987) and further adapted by Naigles (1990).[7] This technique is minimally demanding. It requires the child only to look at two scenes shown simultaneously while listening to an auditory input that "matches" (describes) just one of the scenes. Several studies have shown that if children understand the auditory input, they will look longer at the matching scene. We adapted the technique to our purposes with a crosslingu-

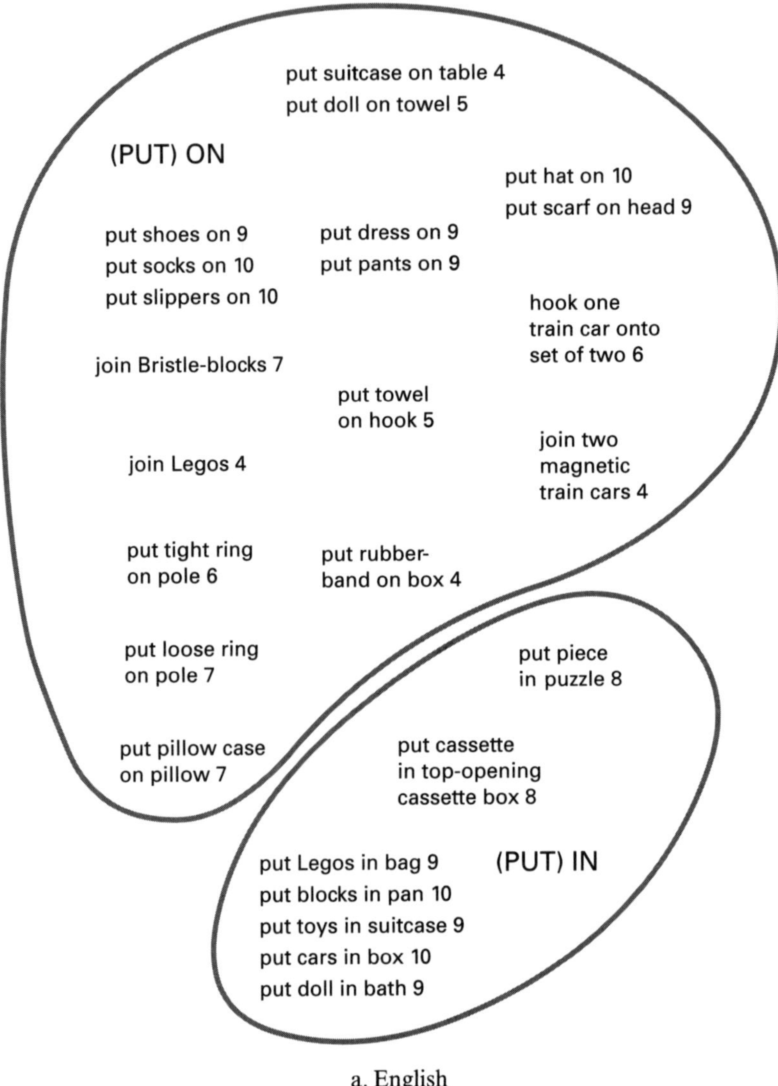

a. English

Fig. 16.3 Categorization of joining actions by children age 2;0–2;5 learning English and Korean.

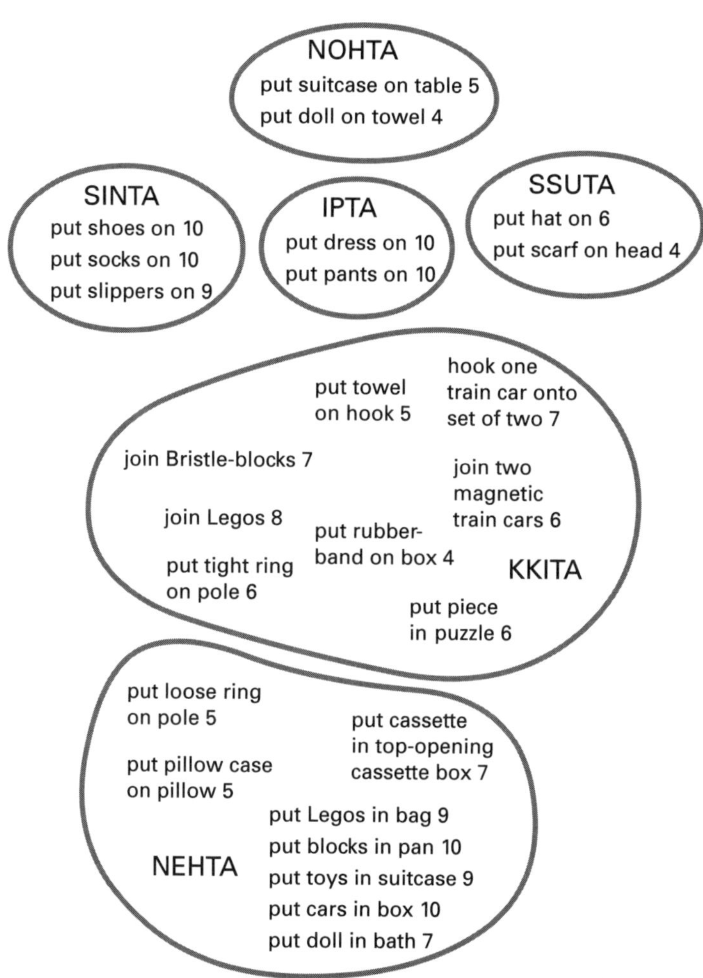
NOHTA
put suitcase on table 5
put doll on towel 4
SINTA
put shoes on 10
put socks on 10
put slippers on 9
IPTA
put dress on 10
put pants on 10
SSUTA
put hat on 6
put scarf on head 4
put towel on hook 5
hook one train car onto set of two 7
join Bristle-blocks 7
join two magnetic train cars 6
join Legos 8
put rubber-band on box 4
put tight ring on pole 6
KKITA
put piece in puzzle 6
put loose ring on pole 5
put cassette in top-opening cassette box 7
put pillow case on pillow 5
put Legos in bag 9
put blocks in pan 10
NEHTA
put toys in suitcase 9
put cars in box 10
put doll in bath 7

b. Korean

istic design that allowed us to explore the comprehension of two overlapping semantic categories: *(put) in* for learners of English, and *kkita* 'interlock, fit tightly,' for learners of Korean (Choi, McDonough, Bowerman, & Mandler 1999).

Our subjects were thirty children between 18 and 23 months, twenty learning English and ten learning Korean. According to parental report, only six of the English learners and two of the Korean learners were producing the target word for their language, so the majority did not yet use the word. The child sat on a parent's lap in front of two TV monitors mounted side by side, with a loudspeaker between them through which the auditory input could be presented. The child's gaze behavior during the experiment was videotaped for offline coding and analysis.

The experiment was made up of four pairs of videotaped actions designed to test whether the children understood the properties of events that are relevant to the two target words: containment for (*put*) *in* and tight fit or interlocking for *kkita* (see figure 16.4). In the first and the third pairs, Pegs and Books, the matching scene was the same for both languages: the Figure ended up both contained by the Ground and in a tight-fitting relationship with it, so the action qualified as an instance of both (*put*) *in* and *kkita.* We will call these "conflated pairs," since the properties of "containment" and "tight fit" were combined in the same scene. For Pegs, the matching scene was "putting pegs tightly into holes in a wooden block" and the nonmatching scene was "putting pegs on top of a solid block." For Books, the matching scene was "putting books tightly into fitted box-covers" and the nonmatching scene was "stacking books on top of each other."

In the second and fourth pairs, Legos and Rings, the properties of containment and tight fit were split up and assigned to different scenes, so the matching scenes were different for the two languages. We refer to these as "split pairs." In the Legos pair, the two scenes were "putting Lego pieces into a large plastic container" (containment; this was the match for English) and "adding a Lego piece to the top of a stack of Lego pieces" (tight fit, the match for Korean). In the Rings pair, the scenes were "putting plastic rings into a basket" (containment, the match for English) and "putting rings onto tapered plastic poles" (tight fit, the match for Korean).[8]

If the English-speaking children understand *in*, they should look longer at scenes showing "containment" regardless of whether it is tight or loose. And if Korean-speaking children understand *kkita*, they should look longer at scenes showing a tight-fitting relation regardless of whether the fit involves containment or surface attachment. This means that on the conflated pairs, the two sets of children should look at the same scene (e.g. "putting books into fitted box-covers") but for different reasons – the English group because it depicts "containment," and the Korean group

Scene 1 Scene 2

Pair 1 (Conflated pair): **Pegs**

PUT PEGS IN TIGHT-FITTING HOLES

IN/KKITA[1]

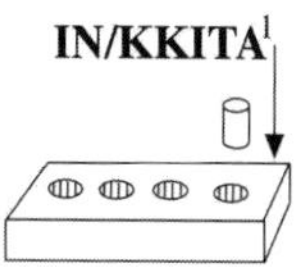

PUT PEGS ON SOLID BLOCK

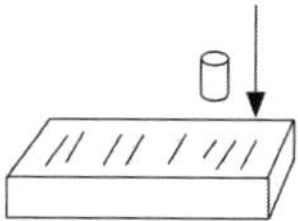

Pair 2 (Split pair): **Legos**

PUT LEGOS IN BOX

IN

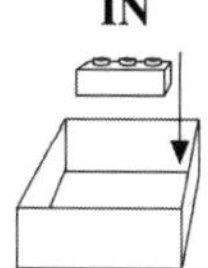

PUT LEGOS ON ANOTHER LEGO

KKITA

Pair 3 (Conflated pair): **Books**

PUT BOOKS IN FITTED BOX-COVERS

IN/KKITA

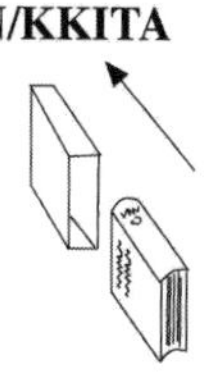

PUT BOOKS ON PILE OF BOOKS

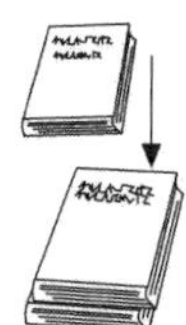

Pair 4 (Split pair): **Rings**

PUT RINGS IN BIG BASKET

IN

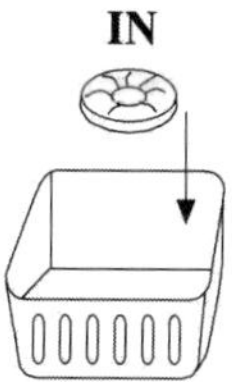

PUT RINGS TIGHTLY ON POLE

KKITA

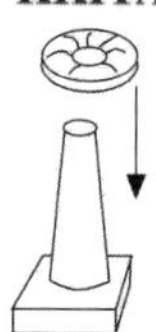

[1] The target word is shown above the scene that matches the word's meaning.

Fig. 16.4 Four pairs of scenes used to test comprehension of English *put in* and Korean *kkita* in Choi, McDonough, Mandler, & Bowerman (1999).

because it depicts "tight fit." Which property children were attending to on the conflated pairs is revealed by their gaze direction on the split pairs.

For each of the four pairs, five trials were administered. First, two familiarization trials introduced each scene of the pair individually. Then a control trial presented both scenes simultaneously. The familiarization and control trials were accompanied by an audio that encouraged the child to look at the scenes, but did not contain the target word. The purpose of the control trial was to get a baseline measure of the child's relative interest in the two scenes in the absence of the target word. Then came two identical test trials. These again showed both scenes together, but now with the addition of the target word, embedded in a sentence like "Where's she putting it *IN*?" (English) or "Eti-ey *KKI*-e?" (roughly, "Where's [she] tight-fitting it?"; Korean). A ring of flickering lights brought the child's gaze back to the midpoint between trials. The parent wore opaque glasses to prevent inadvertent cuing.

During the test trials, the children from both language groups looked significantly longer overall at the matching scenes than at the nonmatching scenes. This finding is not in itself conclusive, since the children might have preferred the matching scenes for purely nonlinguistic reasons (although recall that the matching scenes for the two languages were different on the two split pairs). To control for this possibility, we investigated whether the children's preference for the matching scene over the nonmatching scene was significantly greater when they heard the target word (test trials) than when they did not (control trial). It was. On the control trials the children showed no overall preference for either the matching or the nonmatching scene, so we can conclude that their overall preference for the matching scenes on the test trials was indeed due to the presence of the target word.

In summary, this study shows that between 18 and 23 months, children learning English and Korean already understand *in* and *kkita* – words that pick out overlapping sets of referents in adult speech – in language-specific ways. English learners know that "containment" is relevant for *in* but "tight fit" is not, while Korean learners know that "tight fit" is relevant for *kkita* but "containment" is not. Since most of the children were not yet producing the target word for their language, we conclude that sensitivity to language-specific spatial categories begins to develop in comprehension even before production begins.

This is an important finding, since it shows how we can reconcile two observations that otherwise seem to conflict. (1) From the moment spatial words first appear in children's spontaneous speech, they are often generalized rapidly to a wide range of referents. As noted earlier, this has been taken as strong evidence that children rely initially on their own spatial concepts, not those introduced by the input language. (2) Children extend their spatial words to language-specific categories from the beginning of productive use (as discussed in section 3.1). Rapid generalization along language-specific lines is not paradoxical if children are able to get a sense of the contours of the categories in comprehension before production begins.

4 How does spatial semantic learning take place?

Taken together, the studies we have discussed show that children are sensitive to language-specific principles of semantic categorization from their earliest productive uses of spatial words, and that this sensitivity begins to develop even before production begins. Spatial semantic development is, then, far more responsive to the properties of the input language than has been supposed.[9] This outcome is particularly striking because, of all semantic domains, space is the one that has been cited most often in arguments for the critical role of children's autonomous concepts in early lexical development.

Evidence for early language specificity does not, of course, mean that children have no ideas of their own about spatial classification. The children we investigated, like those studied by others, used their early spatial words for a somewhat different range of situations than they heard them applied to; that is, they made systematic selections from among the uses modeled, and they extended words to situations for which adults would not use them. Clearly they were not merely passively awaiting the imprint of the input language.

What account of the acquisition process will do justice to both overall language specificity and evidence for language-independent spatial conceptualizations? We suggest that the story goes something like this.

Children construct spatial semantic categories over time on the basis of the way they hear words used in the input, and, in doing so, they draw on perceptual sensitivities and conceptual biases they bring with them to the task. Language input helps the learner decide which kinds of similarities and differences among referent situations are important for purposes of selecting a word, but the sensitivity to these properties must of course ultimately be supplied by the child. Some properties are undoubtedly more accessible or salient to learners than others, and categories that depend on these will, all else being equal, be learned earlier and with fewer errors than categories that depend on properties that are cognitively or perceptually more obscure (see also Clark, ch. 13 of this volume). Where the relevant properties are not obvious, because they are either low in salience or maturationally not yet available, children will make errors, either underextending or overextending words according to principles that are more readily available to them.

Throughout this process, learners' built-in sensitivities to space are in constant interaction with a variety of characteristics of the language input. These include, for instance, the *frequency* with which given words are used (e.g. relevant spatial properties with relatively low initial salience might still be identified relatively quickly if the child has frequent learning opportunities), the *consistency* of the range of referents for which the words are used (e.g. polysemy in a word's meaning might mislead the child and promote overextensions), the *number of words* that populate a given corner of semantic space (e.g. many words may help the child draw boundaries between categories, few may encourage overextensions), and the *degree of overlap* in the referents for which different words are used (low overlap may facilitate learning, high overlap – different words applied to the same referents on different occasions – may slow it down). We will illustrate some of these influences shortly.

This view of the process of acquiring spatial words can be placed within the framework of usage-based approaches to language that stress the *dynamic* properties of linguistic knowledge – i.e. the critical role played by input factors like type and token frequency and competition among forms in the input, and by learner capacities like the ability to induce categories and schemas and to restructure them continually in response to both changes in the input and pressure exerted by the growth of other categories in the learner's system (e.g. Bybee 1985, 1991; MacWhinney 1987). The view is also in accord with Slobin's (ch. 14 of this volume) emphasis on the competing forces that shape language in use, and on children's growing sensitivity to the specific properties that characterize the local language ("typological bootstrapping"); and with Smith's (ch. 4 of this volume) claim that basic and domain-general processes of attentional learning can give rise to "smart," seemingly domain-specific attentional biases. It is also compatible with computational approaches to modeling the acquisition of word meaning, especially those designed to be sensitive to crosslinguistic differences (e.g. Regier 1995, 1996, 1997).

4.1 Evidence for category-shaping processes

In our data, especially from the elicited production study described in section 3.2, there is ample evidence for the dynamic shaping of children's spatial semantic categories by properties of the input language acting in concert with children's inherent biases. Consider the domain of "separating objects."

Among the overextensions often cited to support the claim that children map spatial words to their own concepts, it is striking that many have to do with "separation." Recall, for instance the use of *open* in English for actions like separating Frisbees (Bowerman 1978; E. V. Clark 1993; see section 1). Related is the use of several different words for separation across a similar range of contexts (Griffiths & Atkinson 1978; McCune & Vihman 1997), and the blending of words, such as Hildegarde's [ʔau], later [ʔaux], which was apparently derived both from German *auf* 'open' (among other meanings) and *aus* 'out,' and from English *off* and *out*, and was used for acts of separation as diverse as clothing removal and opening a tin box (Leopold 1939, as discussed by McCune & Vihman 1997). McCune & Vihman suggest that "separation" (along with "attachment") is a common early relational meaning that children will express even if the adult language lacks a well-suited word.

In our studies of spontaneous speech from children learning English, Korean, and Tzotzil Mayan, and our elicited production study with children learning English, Korean, and Dutch, we found a tendency for children to underdifferentiate spatial events relative to the adult target language, and this was indeed especially marked in the domain of "separation": in all the languages, children discriminated acts of separation less finely and accurately in their choice of words than acts of joining (Bowerman 1996a; Bowerman *et al.* 1995). But – critical for present purposes – the children did not overextend words for "separation" indiscriminately. Which words they overextended, and exactly how they used them, depended on how "separation" was semantically structured in the input language. Let us consider three examples.

4.1.1 Example 1: polysemy Our first example concerns the use of *out* and *off*, and their translation equivalents *uit* and *af*, by children learning English and Dutch (Bowerman 1996a). The youngest English-speaking children (age 2;0–2;5) in our elicited production study (see section 3.2) used *out* systematically for actions like those shown in (1) below and *off* for actions like those in (2). In contrast, Dutch children of the same age overextended *uit* 'out' massively, applying it to all the actions in both (1) and (2):

1. taking Legos out of a bag; a cassette out of a case; a doll and a toy boat out of a bathtub; cars out of a box; blocks out of a pan . . .
2. taking the lid off a pan; the top off a pen; a ring off a pole; a pillowcase off a pillow; a rubber-band off a box; taking off a dress, underpants, undershirt, shoes, socks, hat . . .

Why should the two groups of children differ in this way? A look at the use of the words by adults provides a clue. In adult speech, these words mark a systematic split between "removal from containment" (*out*, *uit*) and "removal from surface contact," including encirclement and envelopment (*off*, *af*). But in Dutch there is an important class of exceptions: *uit* is used instead of the expected *af* for taking enveloping clothing items off the body, e.g. *trek je schoen, sok, trui, jas* UIT 'take your shoe, sock, sweater, jacket OUT [=off].'

When this incursion of *uit* into what is normally the territory of *af* – "removal from surface contact" – is brought to their attention, Dutch adults are surprised: they recognize that the foot after all comes out of the shoe, not the shoe out of the foot. *Uit* seems to be polysemous, with the clothing use stored as a separate, idiosyncratic sense. But for children in the early stages of language development, this polysemy creates a special learning problem. They have no *a priori* way of knowing that the use of *uit* for removing clothing (a high-frequency and salient event in their lives) is special – at odds with the more canonical uses of *uit*. So they try to construct a meaning that encompasses both. The only meaning consistent with both the canonical use and the idiosyncratic clothing use is "removal" itself – which immediately sanctions the extension of *uit* to all acts of removal, including taking objects off surfaces.

This example shows that while children are prone to overextend words for separation, whether they actually do so with a particular word is influenced by details of the word's use in the linguistic input. If adults distinguish consistently between removal from containment and removal from surface contact, children can do so too. But if there is "noise" in the input – in this case a misleading polysemy in a word's meaning – children may have trouble homing in on the relevant categorization principle.[10]

4.1.2 Example 2: "spacing" of words But what about English-speaking children's overextensions of *open* – do these perhaps show that they have the same broad "separation" category as Dutch children, but just happen to encode it with *open* instead of *out*? Careful inspection of the data argues against this. The overextension of *open* – like the overextension of Dutch *uit* – is also conditioned by the semantic categories of the input language.

In our elicited production study, the learners of English often overextended *open* to actions for which the adults never used it (e.g. taking a shoe off, separating two Lego pieces). (This was also true of the children learning Dutch; the word for 'open' has the same form and a similar extension in the two adult languages.) There was only one such error in the elicited Korean data (*yelta* 'open,' used for unhooking two train cars), and we have found none in our spontaneous Korean data. To understand why there is this difference, compare the way actions of 'opening' are encoded in English vs. Korean (figure 16.5).

Korean breaks down the domain of English *open* into many categories, distinguishing opening doors and boxes, opening things that separate symmetrically (a mouth or a clamshell), opening paper things that involve tearing (an envelope), opening things that spread out flat (a book, hand, or

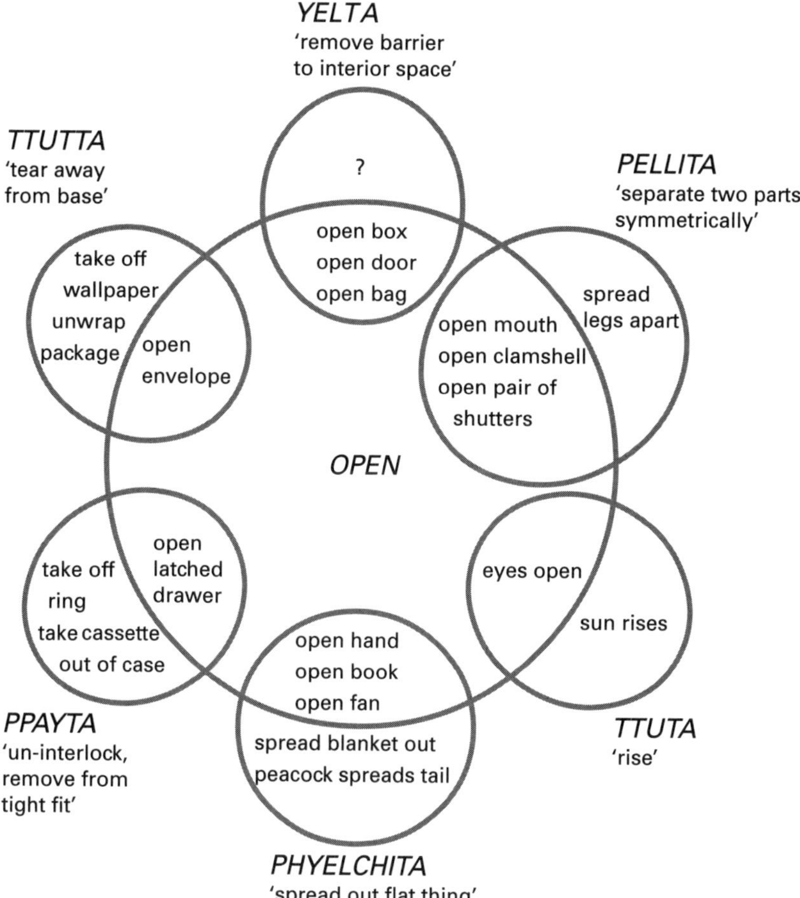

Fig. 16.5 Categorization of "opening" in English and Korean.

fan), and so on. How might this affect learners? A possible answer is suggested by an ingeniously simple experiment conducted by Landau & Shipley (in press) to test the effect on classification of the "spacing" of the words in the linguistic input.

These researchers placed two novel objects – the "standards" – in front of 2- and 3-year-old subjects. In the Same Label condition they gave both standards the same name ("This is a blicket . . . And this is a blicket"). In the Different Label condition they gave them different names ("This is a blicket . . . And this is a steb"). Then they showed, one by one, four test objects that were intermediate in shape along a continuum between the first and the second standards, and asked about each one, "Is this a blicket?" In the Same Label condition, the children accepted the label at ceiling for all the test objects. But in the Different Label condition, there was a sharp dropoff in acceptance as the test object grew less like the first standard and more like the second standard. Landau & Shipley conclude that the presence of two identical labels can induce children to "fill in" the gap between even very different exemplars, "probably guided by the assumption that members lying on the hypothetical similarity line between standards are also members of the category." Conversely, the presence of different labels induces children to set up a boundary somewhere on the hypothetical similarity line between the first and second exemplars.

Applying these findings to the problem of 'open,' children learning English or Dutch are clearly in the Same Label condition: they are invited by the application of *open* to many different kinds of actions to fill in the gaps along a potential generalization gradient and create a very broad category. In doing so, they overshoot the mark. In contrast, children learning Korean are in the Different Label condition: at every turn they hear different verbs applied to actions to which they might have been inclined to generalize *yelta* 'open' (the "opening" verb they learn earliest and use appropriately for opening doors and containers). The impulse to generalize is checked before it can blossom.

4.1.3 Example 3: core members of a category Although the Korean children in our elicited production study did not overextend *yelta* 'open,' they did overuse another word for separation: *ppayta* 'remove from an interlocking, tight-fit relation.' (Like overextensions of *open* by children learning English and Dutch, this may be encouraged by the broad range of the overextended word in adult speech: *ppayta* was used by at least one adult subject for twenty-four out of the thirty-six "separation" actions in our experiment.) We should ask, then, whether Korean children's *ppayta* category has the same shape as the overextended *open* category of children learning English and Dutch – if so, this could suggest the imprint of a nonlinguistic concept available to all children independently of language.

But although *open* and *ppayta* are often applied to similar situations, the two categories revolve around different cores in children's speech (Bowerman 1996a). For children learning English and Dutch, the core (the earliest and by far the most frequent and consistent) use of *open* is for actions of opening containers of various sorts. The word is only incidentally used for other acts of separation like separating Pop-beads or Lego pieces (*out/uit* or *off* are more frequent). In a different branch of overextensions, *open* is also used occasionally for actions in which there is no separation but something is made accessible, such as turning on TVs, electric lights, and water faucets. This latter use is motivated by a key feature of canonical acts of opening: when something is opened, something is often made accessible (Bowerman 1978). Korean children do not use *ppayta* for "making something accessible." Its core use, by children and adults alike, is for separating things that are stuck tightly together, like Lego pieces. "Making accessible" plays no role in these core uses, and children do not spontaneously supply the extension. (See Choi 1997 for an analogous analysis of different core meanings for English *on* and Korean *kkita* 'interlock, fit tightly'.)

As these three examples illustrate, children learning different languages may all have a tendency to overextend words for separation, but the focal point and exact extensions of their resulting categories are influenced by the contours of each word's category – and neighboring categories – in the adult linguistic input. What at first sight may seem like a universal child category resolves, on closer inspection, into a family of related, but different categories, each one shaped by thc particular features of the input language.

4.2 *What are spatial semantic categories constructed out of?*

Up to now, we have skirted the critical problem of characterizing what we referred to as "perceptual sensitivities and conceptual biases" for space – the raw material out of which children construct the meanings of spatial words. This is a difficult issue for investigators of all theoretical persuasions.

One common proposal, which accords with the emphasis in the current literature on "constraints" in word learning, is that children come equipped with a set of domain-specific semantic primitives for space (e.g. Landau & Jackendoff 1993). In this view, learning involves figuring out how these primitives should be combined. Although we agree with the spirit of this proposal that children do not waste time on crazy possibilities and must have some sense of what properties of situations are likely to matter, there are a number of difficulties with crediting the child with a ready-made assembly kit of primitives, as discussed by Carey (1982), Choi & Bowerman (1991), Bowerman (1996a), Levinson (ch. 19 of this volume), and Slobin (ch. 14 of this volume).

A more fruitful approach, we believe, may be to conceive of the conceptual prerequisites to semantic learning not in terms of discrete components but in terms of *gradients* of perceived similarity between situations of different types.[11] We have already drawn informally on the notion of similarity gradients in discussing the possible relevance of Landau & Shipley's (in press) study of novel object naming to overgeneralizations of *open*. And in section 2.2 we mentioned one candidate similarity gradient for space: the continuum revealed by Bowerman & Pederson's (1992, in preparation) study of 'in' and 'on'-type words.

If children understand similarities and differences among static spatial situations in a way that is consistent with Bowerman & Pederson's gradient, they could be expected to generalize spatial words in systematic ways. For example, on hearing the same form applied to both "cup on table" and "handle on door" (see, for instance, Pattern 1 in figure 16.2 [this amounts to the "Same Label" condition]), children could "fill in the gap" to predict that this form can also be used for "bandaid on leg" and "picture on wall." The information that the form is not fussy about the orientation of the Ground object could be inferred directly from the input (horizontal table, vertical door), but the information that the form is also not fussy about the way the Figure is attached to a (nonhorizontal) Ground would be supplied indirectly: both adhesion and hanging against something fall *between* support from below and fixed attachment (e.g. with screws) on the gradient. If, on the other hand, children hear one form for "cup on table" and another for "handle on door" (cf. Pattern 3: Dutch *op* vs. *aan* ["Different Label" condition]), the impetus to generalize will be checked. More evidence will be needed before learners know what to do with pictures on walls (is it more like a cup on a table or a handle on door?), and they will have to pay close attention to details of orientation and attachment.

There is some limited evidence for this scenario from an elicited production study of how young learners of Dutch and English describe static spatial relationships (Bowerman 1993; Gentner 1996; Bowerman & Gentner, in preparation). English-speaking children aged 2;6 to 3;6 used *on* extensively for both familiar and novel situations similar to (a)–(e) in figure 16.2. Same-age Dutch children, in contrast, used only *op* frequently, and mostly only for familiar situations. *Aan* was rare. For situations like (b)–(e), the Dutch children often failed to produce a preposition at all. English-speaking children's experience of the "wide-span" preposition *on* seems to have fostered a sense of a large, tolerant category. In contrast, Dutch-speaking children's exposure to two, more restricted words in this corner of semantic space seems to have generated uncertainty about where one category leaves off and the next begins.

More research is clearly needed to determine whether it is sensible to credit children with an *a priori* shared sense of similarity gradients for space, and, if so, how such gradients can best be characterized. Also in need of study is whether some ways of partitioning a gradient are inherently easier for children than others.[12] But research along these lines may ultimately yield a better picture than is currently available of children's conceptual predispositions for spatial categorization.

5 Conclusions

In this chapter we have shown that the structuring of spatial categories differs strikingly across languages, and that children are sensitive to language-specific categorization principles from their earliest productive uses of spatial forms, and at least in some cases in comprehension even before production begins. This sensitivity does not, we stressed, mean that children are passive in the learning process. Learners clearly have an extensive practical understanding of space long before language acquisition begins, and they apply this knowledge actively to the task of figuring out what spatial words mean. In some cases they generalize too narrowly, restricting their use of a form to a subset of its everyday uses in adult speech. In other cases they generalize too broadly, using a form for spatial situations an adult would never apply it to. Both kinds of extension patterns testify to the influence of language-independent sources of spatial conceptualization.

In the past, deviations from adult speech have been interpreted as evidence that early spatial words are mapped directly to concepts of space that arise universally though nonlinguistic cognitive development. But crosslinguistic comparisons show that children's extension patterns do not converge on a uniform set of categories, as they should if this hypothesis were correct. Some non-adultlike extension patterns look at first glance very similar across languages, but closer inspection shows that they have clearly been influenced by the categories of the input language.

Nonlinguistic perceptual and conceptual predispositions for space do not, then, shape children's semantic categories directly, but only in interaction with the semantic structure of the language being acquired. Much remains to be learned about this interaction, but progress can be made, we have suggested, by viewing the process within a framework that stresses the usage-based, dynamic properties of language.

NOTES

We are grateful to Steve Levinson and Dan Slobin for their comments on an earlier draft of this chapter.

1 In English, Path satellites (which are spatial particles) overlap to some extent with prepositions, and in certain cases they fall together to produce a "merged form" that has properties of both (Talmy 1985:105).

2 *Kkita* can be used as an intransitive verb, but then it expresses an abstract sense of entering, as in joining a group or breaking into a queue.

3 Each example shown in figure 16.2 can be seen as representative of a larger class of situation types: (a) SUPPORT FROM BELOW (e.g. cup on table, pen on desk); (b) "CLINGY" ATTACHMENT (adhesion or surface tension, e.g. bandaid on leg, rain drops on window); (c) HANGING OVER/AGAINST (e.g. picture on wall, coat on bannister); (d) FIXED ATTACHMENT (handle on door, telephone on

wall); (e) POINT-TO-POINT ATTACHMENT (e.g. apple on twig, balloon on string); and (f) FULL INCLUSION (e.g. apple in bowl, rabbit in cage). With certain exceptions, spatial configurations falling into each of these situation types were encoded with the same spatial words within each language.

4 Even seemingly uncontroversial examples like (a) "cup on table" and (f) "apple in bowl" in figure 16.2 are not classified straightforwardly in terms of "support" and "containment" in all languages. For example, many languages (especially those following Pattern 2 above, like Japanese and Korean) use the same word for objects both "on" a supporting surface, as in (a), and "above" it (so contact and support are not critical). Australian languages often use the same term for both "being in," as in (f), and "being under" (Wilkins & Evans 1995). And Tzeltal Maya breaks down both "support" and "containment" quite finely: for example, "being in" a container is encoded with different morphemes depending on the shape of the container (P. Brown 1994).

5 Overextensions were important in our analysis, as were appropriate uses of words for novel situations. This is because if children do not yet use spatial words productively, they might *appear* to follow language-specific principles of categorization when they are actually simply repeating what they have frequently heard adults say in particular situations. Only when children go beyond what they have heard is it possible to make inferences about the principles guiding their word extensions.

6 Productivity was sometimes preceded by a period of restricted use, e.g. one English-speaking child initially said *out* only for going outdoors; another said *off* only for taking clothes off the body (see Choi & Bowerman 1991). These uses were idiosyncratic – different for different children.

7 Our lab is modeled on that of Letty Naigles. We would like to thank her for her generous help in setting it up.

8 Each action was performed three times in succession. All scenes showed only the actor's hands and arms to avoid unnecessary distractions, and within each pair care was taken to equate colors, rhythm with which the actions were performed, and other factors that might influence overall salience. For half the children the side on which the matching screen was positioned was left, right, right, left across the four pairs, and for the other half it was right, left, left, right.

9 But this evidence for language sensitivity is congruent with other studies showing a very early influence of experience with a particular language, e.g. on infants' discrimination and categorization of speech sounds (Streeter 1976; Werker & Tees 1984; Kuhl, Williams, Lacerda, Stevens, & Lindblom 1992), on their preference for one stress pattern over another (Jusczyk, Cutler, & Redanz 1993), and on their relative emphasis on nouns vs. verbs (Choi & Gopnik 1995).

10 See Regier (1997) for a replication of English and Dutch children's learning patterns, using computational modeling in which the input to the "learner" reflected the above reasoning.

11 We use the term "perceived" here for lack of a better term. But we do not mean to suggest that only "perceptual" similarity, strictly defined, counts towards learners' construal of two situations as similar. For children as well as for adults, implicit similarity judgments are likely to be affected by "conceptual" considerations as well, such as – for spatial relations – assumptions about why an object stays in place and does not fall.

12 Bowerman & Gentner (in preparation) explore the hypothesis that ease might be predicted by the frequency with which a particular partitioning is adopted by languages of the world. This hypothesis is based on the assumption that both ease of acquisition and frequency across languages will reflect the "naturalness" of a particular classification scheme for human beings.

REFERENCES

Allan, K. 1979. Classifiers. *Language* 53: 285–311.

Ameka, F. 1995. The linguistic construction of space in Ewe. *Cognitive Linguistics* 6: 139–181.

Antell, S. E. G. & A. J. Caron. 1985. Neonatal perception of spatial relationships. *Infant Behavior and Development* 8:15–23.

Baillargeon, R. 1995. A model of physical reasoning in infancy. In C. Rovee-Collier & L.P. Lipsitt (eds.), *Advances in Infancy Research* 9: 305–371.

Behl-Chadha, G., & P. D. Eimas. 1995. Infant categorization of left–right spatial relations. *British Journal of Developmental Psychology* 13: 69–79.

Berlin, B., & P. Kay. 1969. *Basic color terms*. Berkeley: University of California Press.

Bloom, L. 1973. *One word at a time: the use of single word utterances before syntax*. The Hague: Mouton.

Bloom, P. 1994. Overview: controversies in language acquisition. In P. Bloom (ed.), *Language acquisition: core readings*. Cambridge, MA: MIT Press, 5–48.

Bowerman, M. 1973. *Early syntactic development: a cross-linguistic study with special reference to Finnish*. Cambridge: Cambridge University Press.

1978. The acquisition of word meaning: an investigation into some current conflicts. In N. Waterson & C. Snow (eds.), *The development of communication*. New York: John Wiley, 263–287.

1980. The structure and origin of semantic categories in the language-learning child. In M. L. Foster & S. H. Brandes (eds.), *Symbol as sense: new approaches to the analysis of meaning*. New York: Academic Press, 277–299.

1993. Typological perspectives on language acquisition: do crosslinguistic patterns predict development? In E. V. Clark (ed.), *The proceedings of the 25th Annual Child Language Research Forum*. Stanford, CA: Center for the Study of Language and Information, 7–15.

1994. From universal to language-specific in early grammatical development. *Philosophical Transactions of the Royal Society of London B* 346: 37–45.

1996a. Learning how to structure space for language: a crosslinguistic perspective. In P. Bloom, M. A. Peterson, L. Nadel, & M. F. Garrett (eds.), *Language and space*. Cambridge, MA: MIT Press, 385–436.

1996b. The origins of children's spatial semantic categories: cognitive versus linguistic determinants. In J. J. Gumperz & S. C. Levinson (eds.), *Rethinking linguistic relativity*. Cambridge: Cambridge University Press, 145–176.

Bowerman, M., & S. Choi. 1994. Linguistic and nonlinguistic determinants of spatial semantic development. Paper presented at the Boston University Conference on Language Development, Boston, MA, January.

Bowerman, M., L. de León, & S. Choi. 1995. Verbs, particles, and spatial semantics: learning to talk about spatial actions in typologically different languages. In E. V. Clark (ed.), *The proceedings of the 27th Annual Child Language Research*

Forum. Stanford, CA: Center for the Study of Language and Information, 101–110.

Bowerman, M., & D. Gentner. In preparation. Are some ways to partition space more natural than others? Learning to categorize 'in' and 'on' relations in Dutch and English.

Bowerman, M., & E. Pederson. 1992. Cross-linguistic perspectives on topological spatial relationships. Paper presented at the annual meeting of the American Anthropological Association, San Francisco, CA, December.

In preparation. Cross-linguistic perspectives on topological spatial relationships.

Brown, P. 1994. The INs and ONs of Tzeltal locative expressions: the semantics of static descriptions of location. *Linguistics* 32: 743–790.

Brown, R. 1958. *Words and things*. New York: Free Press.

1965. *Social psychology*. New York: Free Press.

1973. *A first language: the early stages*. Cambridge, MA: Harvard University Press.

Brugman, C. 1984. Metaphor in the elaboration of grammatical categories in Mixtec. Unpublished manuscript, Linguistics Department, University of California, Berkeley.

Bybee, J. L. 1985. *Morphology: a study of the relation between meaning and form*. Amsterdam/Philadelphia: John Benjamins.

1991. Natural morphology: the organization of paradigms and language acquisition. In T. Heubner & C. A. Ferguson (ed.), *Crosscurrents in second language and linguistic theories*. Amsterdam/Philadelphia: John Benjamins, 67–91.

Carey, S. 1982. Semantic development: the state of the art. In E. Wanner & L. R. Gleitman (ed.), *Language acquisition: the state of the art*. Cambridge: Cambridge University Press, 347–389.

Choi, S. 1997. Language-specific input and early semantic development: evidence from children learning Korean. In D. I. Slobin (ed.), *The crosslinguistic study of language acquisition*, vol. 5: *Expanding the contexts*. Mahwah, NJ: Lawrence Erlbaum, 111–133.

Choi, S., & M. Bowerman. 1991. Learning to express motion events in English and Korean: the influence of language-specific lexicalization patterns. *Cognition* 41: 83–121.

Choi, S., & A. Gopnik. 1995. Early acquisition of verbs in Korean: a cross-linguistic study. *Journal of Child Language* 22: 497–529.

Choi, S., L. McDonough, M. Bowerman, & J. Mandler. 1999. Early sensitivity to language-specific spatial categories in English and Korean. *Cognitive Development* 14: 241–268.

Clark, E. V. 1976. Universal categories: on the semantics of classifiers and children's early word meanings. In A. Juilland (ed.), *Linguistic studies offered to Joseph Greenberg on the occasion of his sixtieth birthday*, vol. 3: *Syntax*. Saratoga, CA: Anna Libri, 449–462.

1993. *The lexicon in acquisition*. Cambridge: Cambridge University Press.

Clark, H. H. 1973. Space, time, semantics, and the child. In T. E. Moore (ed.), *Cognitive development and the acquisition of language*. New York: Academic Press, 27–63.

Gentner, D. 1982. Why nouns are learned before verbs: linguistic relativity versus natural partitioning. In S. A. Kuczaj II (ed.), *Language development*, vol. 2: *Language, thought, and culture*. Hillsdale, NJ: Lawrence Erlbaum, 301–334.

1996. Crosslinguistic differences in the lexicalization of spatial relations, and effects on acquisition. Paper presented at the 7th International Congress for the Study of Child Language, Istanbul, July.

Gibson, E. J., & E. S. Spelke. 1983. The development of perception. In J. H. Flavell & E. M. Markman (eds.), *Mussen handbook of child psychology*, vol. 3: *Cognitive development*. New York: John Wiley, 1–76.

Gleitman, L. R. 1990. The structural sources of verb meanings. *Language Acquisition* 1: 3–55.

Golinkoff, R. M., K. Hirsh-Pasek, K. M. Cauley, & L. Gordon. 1987. The eyes have it: lexical and syntactic comprehension in a new paradigm. *Journal of Child Language* 14: 23–45.

Gopnik, A., & A. N. Meltzoff. 1986. Words, plans, things, and locations: interactions between semantic and cognitive development in the one-word stage. In S. A. Kuczaj II & M. D. Barrett (eds.), *The development of word meaning*. New York: Springer, 199–223.

Griffiths, P., & M. Atkinson. 1978. A "door" to verbs. In N. Waterson & C. Snow (eds.), *The development of communication*. New York: John Wiley.

Johnston, J.R. 1984. Acquisition of locative meanings: *behind* and *in front of*. *Journal of Child Language* 11: 407–422.

1985. Cognitive prerequisites: the evidence from children learning English. In D. I. Slobin (ed.), *The crosslinguistic study of language acquisition*, vol. 2: *Theoretical issues*. Hillsdale, NJ: Lawrence Erlbaum, 961–1004.

Johnston, J. R., & D. I. Slobin. 1979. The development of locative expressions in English, Italian, Serbo-Croatian and Turkish. *Journal of Child Language* 6: 529–545.

Jusczyk, P. W., A. Cutler, & N. J. Redanz. 1993. Infants' preference for the predominant stress patterns of English words. *Child Development* 64: 675–687.

Kuhl, P., K. A. Williams, F. Lacerda, K. N. Stevens, & B. Lindblom. 1992. Linguistic experience alters phonetic perception in infants by 6 months of age. *Science* 255: 606–608.

Lakoff, G. 1987. *Women, fire, and dangerous things: what categories reveal about the mind*. Chicago: University of Chicago Press.

Landau, B., & R. Jackendoff. 1993. "What" and "where" in spatial language and spatial cognition. *Behavioral and Brain Sciences* 16: 217–238.

Landau, B., & E. Shipley. In press. Object naming and category boundaries. *Developmental Science*.

Leopold, W. 1939. *Speech development of a bilingual child*, vol. 1. Evanston, IL: Northwestern University Press.

Levinson, S. C. 1994. Vision, shape and linguistic description: Tzeltal body-part terminology and object description. *Linguistics* 32: 791–855.

1996. Frames of reference and Molyneux's question: crosslinguistic evidence. In P. Bloom, M. A. Peterson, L. Nadel, & M. F. Garrett (eds.), *Language and space*. Cambridge, MA: MIT Press, 109–169.

Lucy, J. A. 1992. *Grammatical categories and cognition: a case study of the linguistic relativity hypothesis*. Cambridge: Cambridge University Press.

MacLaury, R. E. 1989. Zapotec body-part locatives: prototypes and metaphoric extensions. *International Journal of American Linguistics* 55: 119–154.

MacWhinney, B. 1987. The competition model. In B. MacWhinney (ed.), *Mechanisms of language acquisition*. Hillsdale, NJ: Lawrence Erlbaum, 249–308.

Markman, E. M. 1990. Constraints children place on word meanings. *Cognitive Science* 14: 57–77.

McCune, L., & M. Vihman. 1997. The transition to reference in infancy, ms.

McCune-Nicolich, L. 1981. The cognitive bases of relational words in the single-word period. *Journal of Child Language* 8: 15–34.

Naigles, L. 1990. Children use syntax to learn verb meanings. *Journal of Child Language* 17: 357–374.

Needham, A., & R. Baillargeon. 1993. Intuitions about support in 4.5-month-old infants. *Cognition* 47: 121–148.

Nelson, K. 1974. Concept, word, and sentence: interrelations in acquisition and development. *Psychological Review* 81: 267–285.

Piaget, J. 1954. *The construction of reality in the child*. New York: Basic Books.

Piaget, J., & B. Inhelder. 1956 [1948]. *The child's conception of space*. London: Routledge & Kegan Paul.

Quine, W. V. O. 1960. *Word and object*. Cambridge, MA: MIT Press.

Quinn, P. C. 1994. The categorization of above and below spatial relations by young infants. *Child Development* 65: 58–69.

Regier, T. 1995. A model of the human capacity for categorizing spatial relations. *Cognitive Linguistics* 6: 63–88.

1996. *The human semantic potential: spatial language and constrained connectionism*. Cambridge, MA: MIT Press.

1997. Constraints on the learning of spatial terms: a computational investigation. In R. L. Goldstone, P. G. Schyns, & D. L. Medin (eds.), *Psychology of learning and motivation*, vol. 36. San Diego, CA: Academic Press, 171–217.

Rosch, E. 1973. On the internal structure of perceptual and semantic categories. In T. E. Moore (ed.), *Cognitive development and the acquisition of language*. New York: Academic Press, 111–114.

Rosch, E., C. B. Mervis, W. D. Gray, D. M. Johnson, & P. Boyes-Braem. 1976. Basic objects in natural categories. *Cognitive Psychology* 8: 382–439.

Sinha, C., L.A. Thorseng, M. Hayashi, & K. Plunkett. 1994. Comparative spatial semantics and language acquisition: evidence from Danish, English, and Japanese. *Journal of Semantics* 11: 253–287.

Slobin, D. I. 1970. Universals of grammatical development in children. In G. B. Flores D'Arcais & W. J. M. Levelt (eds.), *Advances in psycholinguistics*. Amsterdam: North-Holland, 174–186.

1973. Cognitive prerequisites for the development of grammar. In C. A. Ferguson & D. I. Slobin (eds.), *Studies of child language development*. New York: Holt, Rinehart & Winston, 175–208.

1985. Crosslinguistic evidence for the Language-Making Capacity. In D. I. Slobin (ed.), *The crosslinguistic study of language acquisition*, vol. 2: *Theoretical issues*. Hillsdale, NJ: Lawrence Erlbaum, 1157–1249.

1991. Learning to think for speaking: native language, cognition, and rhetorical style. *Pragmatics* 1: 7–25.

Smiley, P., & J. Huttenlocher. 1995. Conceptual development and the child's early words for events, objects, and persons. In M. Tomasello & W. E. Merriman (eds.), *Beyond names for things: young children's acquisition of verbs.* Hillsdale, NJ/Hove: Lawrence Erlbaum, 21–61.

Spelke, E. S., K. Breinlinger, J. Macomber, & K. Jacobson. 1992. Origins of knowledge. *Psychological Review* 99: 605–632.

Streeter, L. A. 1976. Language perception of two-month-old infants shows effects of both innate mechanism and experience. *Nature* 259: 39–41.

Talmy, L. 1983. How language structures space. In H. Pick & L. Acredolo (eds.), *Spatial orientation: theory, research, and application.* New York: Plenum Press, 181–238.

1985. Lexicalization patterns: semantic structure in lexical form. In T. Shopen (ed.), *Language typology and syntactic description*, vol. 3: *Grammatical categories and the lexicon.* Cambridge: Cambridge University Press, 36–149.

1991. Path to realization: a typology of event conflation. In *Proceedings of the 17th Annual Meeting of the Berkeley Linguistics Society.* Berkeley, CA: Berkeley Linguistics Society, 480–519.

Tomasello, M. 1995. Pragmatic contexts for early verb learning. In M. Tomasello & W. E. Merriman (eds.), *Beyond names for things: young children's acquisition of verbs.* Hillsdale, NJ/Hove: Lawrence Erlbaum, 115–146.

Werker, J. F., & R. C. Tees. 1984. Cross-language speech perception: evidence for perceptual reorganization during the first year of life. *Infant Behavior and Development* 7: 49–63.

Whorf, B. L. 1956. *Language, thought, and reality: selected writings of Benjamin Lee Whorf* (ed. J. B. Carroll). Cambridge, MA: MIT Press.

Wilkins, D. P, & N. R. D. Evans. 1995. "Inside" and "down" in Australian languages. In H. Hendriks & J. McQueen (eds.), *Max Planck Institute for Psycholinguistics Annual Report* 16. Nijmegen: Max Planck Institute for Psycholinguists, 99–102.

Wilkins, D. P., & D. Hill. 1995. When GO means COME: questioning the basicness of basic motion verbs. *Cognitive Linguistics* 6: 209–259.

17 Learning to talk about motion UP and DOWN in Tzeltal: is there a language-specific bias for verb learning?

Penelope Brown

Max Planck Institute for Psycholinguistics, Nijmegen, The Netherlands

1 Introduction

This chapter discusses a case of language-specific semantics, and proposes a language-specific learning process to account for how children acquire the relevant expressions. The language-specific semantics is that of the vocabulary involved in the "uphill/downhill" system of spatial description in the Mayan language Tzeltal. Tenejapan speakers of Tzeltal[1] speak as if the whole world tilted down northwards; thus one can speak of the "uphill" end of a table, for example, using the general South/North slope of the land as a frame of reference for describing spatial relations on the horizontal. I will focus on that subpart of the system which has an element of verticality: the verbs, directional adverbs, and nouns of this system, which are used both for spatial relations arrayed along a vertical axis *and* for those arrayed along a horizontal axis derived from the overall slope of the land. The vocabulary at issue is set out in table 17.1; for convenience I will refer to this as the UP/DOWN vocabulary of Tzeltal, but it must be borne in mind that the role of the vertical axis is precisely what is being treated as problematic in this discussion. I will relate the acquisition of this system to currently controversial issues in the language acquisition literature: the strategies children adopt for learning words, the possible biases they begin the task with, and the role of universal semantic features like "vertical" in this process.

Spatial language and cognition have provided a key focus for theories of word learning in recent years. Work in linguistic theory (Talmy 1985), in language acquisition (Slobin 1985), and in developmental psychology (Piaget & Inhelder 1967) has converged on the position that there is a universal set of basic spatial concepts, and that in the spatial domain cognitive development precedes, and provides the basis for, language development. However, the accumulation of crosslinguistic evidence by Bowerman, Choi, de León, and others[2] of children's very early language-specific spatial meanings has made a convincing case for the necessity to rethink our theories of how children approach the word learning task. In particular, it casts doubt on two major lines of theorizing about how children learn spatial word meanings. The first is that children's early hypotheses are guided by a universally given set of precomposed, "natural" prelinguistic concepts (H. H. Clark 1973, Slobin 1985). Until recently there was a consensus that such prelinguistic concepts provide ready-made semantic units, at least in the domain of spatial language.[3] Many theorists have been unable to see how children can learn word meanings without substantial preconceptions about the semantic content. There is still much disagreement about the degree to which children need a privileged set of universal notions to start them off on the language-learning task, vs. the extent to which (and indeed, how) the process of learning the words of a language and their appropriate contexts of use can actually help children build the concepts they encode. (See Levinson, ch. 19 of this volume, for a discussion of the levels of difficulty imposed by such a task.)

A second, related, theoretical debate concerns the nature of children's initial hypotheses about the meaning of a new word: what sorts of biases do learners bring to the task? As a solution to Quine's problem of the indeterminacy of reference,[4] many biases – presumptions about meaning – have been attributed to the language-learning child for the learning of concrete nouns.[5] Some theorists have tried to extend this approach to verb learning. One such suggestion has been that children in general have a strategy of starting with simpler (more general, "light") verb meanings, going on to learn more complex (specific) meanings by adding restricting features (E. V. Clark 1973, 1993).[6] Others have extended the idea of pregiven biases for noun learning to postulate that children may have predispositions that they apply specifically to the task of verb learning (e.g. Golinkoff, Hirsh-Pasek, Mervis, Frawley, & Parillo 1995). Difficulties with these hypotheses have prompted other theorists to reject the idea of word learning biases altogether, and to emphasize the crucial role of context, interaction, and the ascription of communicative intent in how children learn word meanings (Tomasello 1992, ch. 5 of this volume; Tomasello & Merriman 1995).

In this chapter I bring data from another language to bear on these questions. I will discuss how children learn the Tzeltal spatial vocabulary for UP/DOWN relations. I argue that:

1. Tzeltal children do *not* necessarily start with a putatively universal, perceptually based vertical meaning for these nouns and verbs. From their earliest uses of the UP/DOWN vocabulary, children use the words with language-specific landslope meanings as well as with vertical meanings. Rather than verticality, a sense of "place" is the semantic core to the meanings children attribute to these words.
2. The word learning biases proposed in the literature are not applicable to

Tzeltal children's learning of this vocabulary. Those proposed for nouns would not help with Tzeltal UP/DOWN nouns (which denote relations, not concrete objects), while those for verbs (e.g. light verbs in children's one- and two-word stages) would wrongly predict which verbs children learn first in this language. Tzeltal children generally learn semantically specific verbs first, and initially stick to very specific meanings for the UP/DOWN verbs they learn.

The proposal put forward here is that the highly specific nature of Tzeltal verbs influences the children's hypotheses about what kinds of meanings verbs can have. This suggests that a different kind of bias from those discussed above may be adopted by the children: a language-specific bias towards verb specificity, induced on the basis of verbs they have already learned. Two seemingly contradictory observations about children's early meanings for the spatial verbs of Tzeltal motivate this proposal. On the one hand, Tzeltal children's UP/DOWN vocabulary shows early sensitivity to the semantic structure of the language they are learning: the meanings they associate with these verbs and relational nouns are from the first attached to the slope of the land, and to particular places; there is no evidence of an initial preference for the vertical meaning. On the other hand, children's meanings for the verbs remain for a long time too specific, and errors of interpretation/production (using and understanding the verbs to mean 'ascend/descend' with respect to the *local* slope of land rather than the *overall* (South/North) slope of land direction) are evident in some children as late as age 7 or 8.

The Tzeltal data presented here complement those of de León (ch. 18 of this volume) for the closely related language Tzotzil. De León focuses on the language-specific nature of Tzotzil children's first descriptions of events involving vertical paths, and the relatively late emergence of intransitive motion verbs and directionals encoding UP/DOWN paths. My examination of Tzeltal starts from the beginning of children's acquisition of intransitive motion verbs around the age of 2, and summarizes the language-specific nature of their acquisition of the UP/DOWN system in general. I then draw on these findings, as well as those of de León (1994) for the Tzotzil Absolute system, to speculate about the consequences of the semantic structure of languages of this Mayan type for children's initial relational word learning hypotheses.

2 UP and DOWN in Tzeltal

2.1 *The Tzeltal UP/DOWN system*

The spatial vocabulary of Tzeltal is dominated by an Absolute system of spatial reckoning, that is, a system whose coordinates are extrinsic to the

Table 17.1. *Vertical location and UP/DOWN motion in Tzeltal*

	MOTION		STASIS		POSITION
	verb	directional	relational noun: unpossessed	relational noun: possessed	verb root
UP	*mo* 'ascend'	*moel* 'ascending'	*ajk'ol*, or *kajal* 'uphill'	*y-ajk'ol* 'its-above-side' *s-ba* 'its top or uphill side'	*kaj* 'be above' *toy** 'be high up' etc.
DOWN	*ko* 'descend'	*koel* 'descending'	*alan* 'downhill'	*y-anil* 'its underneath or downhill side' *y-e'tal* 'its downhill side'	*pek'* 'be low down' *toy** 'be deep down,' etc.

Note: **toy* means either 'high up' or 'deep down,' i.e. far from some reference level (usually ground level).

spatial scene, as in the familiar cardinal (North/South/East/West) systems (see Levinson, ch. 19 of this volume). In the Tzeltal system, an "uphill/downhill" coordinate abstracted from the lay of the land is used to reckon spatial relationships on the horizontal in both small-scale and long-distance space (Brown & Levinson 1993a; Levinson, ch. 19 of this volume). In some respects the system is a bit like a cardinal direction system, with UP equated roughly with South, DOWN with North.[7] This system is used in lieu of a projective Front/Back/Left/Right system, which does not exist in this language.[8] The spatial vocabulary dedicated to this Absolute system (which is what I am referring to as the UP/DOWN vocabulary) is encoded in noun and verb roots, and is given in table 17.1. It includes the Motion + Path conflating intransitive verb roots[9] *mo/ko* (roughly translatable as 'ascend/descend,' i.e. 'move in a South/North direction'), their transitivized counterparts (*mo-tes/ko-tes* 'make ascend/descend'), and directional adverbials transparently derived from them (*moel/koel* 'up(hill)wards/down(hill)wards'). It also includes relational nouns denoting 'uphill/downhill' regions, which may be either unpossessed (and hence only implicitly relational) or possessed and hence explicitly relational ('uphill/downhill in relation to X'). This same vocabulary applies to spatial relations on the vertical axis. The system also has an axis transverse to the South/North UP/DOWN one, undifferentiated at the two ends; both directions along this axis are labelled *jelawel* 'acrossways' and motion along it *jelaw* 'going across.'[10] Using this system, one speaks of a Figure (the object being located) as being 'uphill/downhill/across' in relation to a Ground (the reference point). (See figure 17.1.)

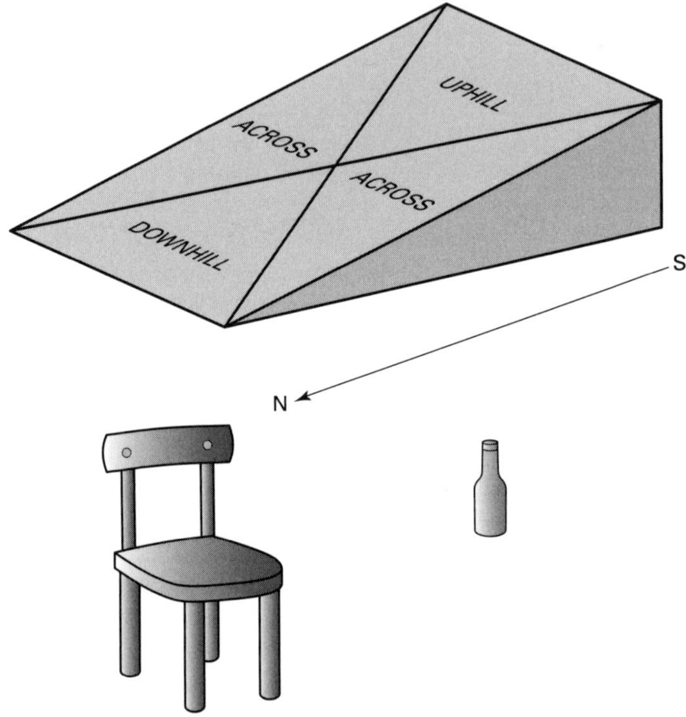

Fig. 17.1 Tzeltal uphill/downhill system.

Such a system poses interesting problems to the learner. To use an Absolute system in an adult-like way requires some fairly complex cognitive abilities: in Piagetian terms the system is Euclidean, utilizing precise fixed angles and precise geometric constructions like "a specific angle around a fixed direction." Since horizontal spatial relations beyond those of immediate proximity are routinely encoded using this system, it requires speakers to maintain absolute orientation at all times, so that they always know where "uphill" and "downhill" are, even at night and in unfamiliar places (Brown & Levinson 1993a; Levinson 1996).

To this cognitive complexity we must add the semantic complexity of the UP/DOWN vocabulary of Tzeltal, which resides in the variety of meanings it can have in context. Since the vertical axis in Tzeltal semantics is confounded with the Absolute system of spatial reference, when people say the Tzeltal equivalent of "Go up" or "It's descending" or "X is uphillwards of Y" they can mean either vertically or horizontally along a coordinate abstracted from the lay of the land, roughly South/North.[11] To make things even more difficult, there is a third source of ambiguity: the UP/DOWN axis may also be abstracted from the *local* slope of land even when it deviates from a South/North direction. In both the Absolute and the local uses, the spatial relations referred to may actually be on the horizontal, with Figure and Ground on the same level, even though they are based conceptually on the slope of the land. There is thus a three-way ambiguity in the frame of reference underlying use of these spatial terms: UP/DOWN with respect to (1) the vertical, (2) the conceptually abstract overall downhill slope of land from South to North, and (3) the local slope of land (which may deviate from the overall South/North slope).

Learning spatial language involves two distinct tasks: learning the relational categories and the language's labels for them, and learning the frames of reference for calculating spatial relations employed in the language community (Levinson 1996). But the Tzeltal child is simply presented with language in use: she hears motion verbs used in contexts like 'Descend!' (from a tree, a bed, the uphillwards [i.e. southwards] house, etc.), 'He ascended' (into the bus, to the uphillwards (southern) fields, etc.), 'She descended from San Cristobal,' 'The rain is descending' [i.e. coming from the south], 'Bring me the machete standing uphillwards [south] of the door,' 'It [a puzzle piece] goes in downhillwards, in the downhillwards (i.e. northwards) hole.' From utterances like these, paired with their contexts, the child must abstract a sense of "up/down" which can apply equally to spatial relations which are vertical or which are arrayed along the axis corresponding to the slope of the land, whether or not the objects being talked about are on a slope or on the horizontal.[12]

The Tzeltal child also has to learn to differentiate these overlapping distinctions from the meanings of other intransitive Motion+Path verbs, in particular to distinguish path types on the horizontal which differ only in their anchoring frame of reference: path towards/away from the speaker ("come/go"), as opposed to path oriented along the "uphill/downhill" axis ("ascend/descend") or at right angles to it ("go across"). As these distinctions go well beyond the sorts of meanings predicted for basic motion verbs crosslinguistically (Talmy 1985), this is another potential source of difficulty for these verbs.

This raises interesting questions for language acquisition. Which of the uses of UP/DOWN do Tzeltal children acquire first? Do they go for verticality or for lay-of-the-land, and, if lay-of-the-land, is it local or long-distance? Is there any evidence of pressure on their early word-meanings from a universal prelinguistic concept of verticality? If there is in fact a salient prelinguistic concept of "upness" (Bloom 1973) or Vertical Motion (Nelson 1974), Tzeltal requires children to extend it to the lay of the land and to the horizontal.

How is this ambiguity handled, and, in particular, how does the Absolute system develop for use on the horizontal, in relation to meanings clearly involving verticality? How long does it take children to develop the full adult-like Absolute system?

In this chapter I begin to try to answer these questions, and to account for children's early meanings for the Tzeltal intransitive path verbs and relational nouns whose core semantics includes reference to a vertical axis. The data are drawn from a longitudinal corpus of natural language production from children aged 1;6 to 4;6 in five Tzeltal families, as well as from elicited production and comprehension tasks performed by these and other children between the ages of 4;0 and 12;0.[13]

3 Children's learning of the UP/DOWN vocabulary

3.1 *Natural production data*

The vocabulary with which the Absolute system is constructed (given in table 17.1) begins to appear in children's speech at around the age of 2;0 (two years, zero months), in some cases when the child is still in the one- or two-word stage.[14] This vocabulary is not very frequent in children's speech (nor indeed is it frequent in adult input to children),[15] and it remains restricted to specific local contexts at first – 'ascend/descend' to a set of particular places – as the examples in table 17.2 illustrate. From the start these places are spatially related to their reference points either *vertically* (the terms being used in collocation with verbs of falling, or in contexts of climbing into trees, up onto furniture, etc., as shown in table 17.3) or *horizontally* (landslope; e.g. used for movement between houses, movement of toy cars on the flat patio, movement in relation to the household layout, as in table 17.2). The children are thus apparently willing to postulate language-specific meanings for verbs from the beginning: in this case, meanings for Motion+Path verbs distinguishing four "kinds of motion" along the ground on the basis of directionality, with motion towards/away from speaker ("come/go") distinguished from motion in relation to certain ("uphill/downhill") places. This supports the conclusion of Choi & Bowerman (1991) that there is no shared starting point for children's meanings of such path-conflating verbs across languages.

The relational nouns *ajk'ol/alan* 'up(hill)/down(hill)' also appear in Tzeltal children's speech at around age 2;0, and are used at first to label places (e.g. 'downhill' = where the family cornfields are) and to identify persons as associated with specific "uphill/downhill" places ('granny downhill').

Between the ages of 2 and 3 children's usage of these UP/DOWN terms

Table 17.2. *Examples of "ascend/descend" verbs and directionals in their* landslope *senses (pooled data from six children) Criteria: clear meaning in context; not a repeat of prior utterance. Verb stems and directionals are shown in italics.*

Name & age	Example	Context
Lus 2;0	*mo*em bel. 'It has ascended away.'	re a toy car just mentioned as "going to San Cristobal" (she is playing with another child with toy cars on the flat patio)
Xaw 2;3	*ko ko* xi ini. 'Descend, descend it says here.'	as she wheels toy along floor
Xan 2;4	ya *ko*on. 'I'm descending.'	announcing intention to go to downhill house
Xan 2;4	kuchoj bel i alali ya *mo* bel. 'The doll was carried away, (she) ascends away.'	up slope towards other house
Pet 2;4	kinam a *mo* bel. 'My wife ascend(ed) away.'	claiming that his imaginary wife has gone "uphillwards"
Pet 2;5	*ko* tal, ilaik, *ko* la 'wil li'i. 'It came down, look, it came down here.'	re a toy down the hillside
Pet 2;5	*ko*an bel. 'Descend away.'	to house below
Xan 2;5	ya x*mo*on ek . . . *ko*ixix tal. 'I'll go up too. . . . They have come down.'	between lower (North) and upper (South) house
Nik 2;6	*mo* tal ja' ini. 'This has ascended here.'	a toy car
Pet 2;6	*ko*on ta *alan*. 'I descend to downhill.'	i.e. to the downhill house
Xaw 2;8	e *ko*on. je *mo*. 'I descend. (I) ascend.'	between houses
Mal 2;8	ya x*mo*onix bel jo'tik a. 'We are ascending away now.'	to other house
Xaw 2;9	ya x*mo*onix bel a. 'I'm now ascending away there.'	to other house
Xan 2;9	ya x*ko*onix bel a . . . jo, banti *mo*on tal. 'I'm going up away. Hm, where do I ascend coming.'	up/down local slope
Mal 2;9	jich *ko*onix tukeli. 'Thus I've descended by myself.'	to other house
Xaw 2;11	ya j*ko* bel. 'I descend awayward.'	to other house
Nik 2;11	ma k'an *ko*ix tal. '(He) doesn't want to come down.'	from other house

Table 17.2 (*cont.*)

Name & age	Example	Context
Lus 3;0	ya x*mo*ix bel te Nikoe. 'Nik is going up away [to his house].'	Nik's house is uphillwards (South) from where she is.
Lus 3;1	ya laj *mo* bel ta karo ek i. 'He's ascending away in the car.'	re her cousin in toy car
Nik 3;1	x*ko* yuch', . . . *mo*ix bel. 'He came down to drink, . . . he has gone up.'	between houses (kitchen downhill from sleeping house)
Lus 3;2	ja' i li' xtal *koel* ta karetera. 'It's that it's coming downhill here on the road.'	car on road
Xaw 3;2	*ko* xan tale. '(She) descended again.'	from upper house to lower
Xan 3;4	ya sujt *koel* stukel. 'He's going back down alone.'	to other house
Lus 3;6	ya to *mo* xan bel. 'I'm going up away again.'	to other house
Lus 3;6	ya x*mo* bel ta k'altik ya'tik. 'She's ascending away to the fields now.'	re mother going up to cornfields
Lus 3;6	ma me xtalat, sujtan me te *koel* ine. 'Don't come (here), return to down there.'	telling her playmate to go to a place downhillwards from where they are
Lus 3;8	ay la yich'bet *moel* ye i a'karo. 'He took your car up.'	her cousin took toy car uphill to his house
Lus 3;8	*mo*an bel te' a ini . . . *mo*an bel Nik. 'Go on up there . . . go on up, Nik.'	towards his other house
Nik 3;9	ma me tal *koel* ya'tik, *mo* bel ta jnatik ya'tik ch'in Antun i . . . 'He (Antun) didn't come down now, he ascended away to our house.'	contrasting the respective locations of two houses
Nik 4;2	ya kich' *moel* ta jmel. 'I'll take it upwards, for good.'	claiming a toy he wants to take home to house

very closely matches that in the input they hear; I have found no examples in this period of clearly novel usage, nor of errors. This is in contrast to the children's first verbs at the one-word stage, which are occasionally overgeneralized.[16] The relative infrequency in the children's speech of 'ascend/descend,' especially in its landslope sense, means that we cannot be certain from this early production data how flexibly children use them – whether, for example, they have simply memorized a list of contexts or placename collocations for which *mo*/*ko* are used to describe motion, or have really generalized to an axis based on the land slope.

Table 17.3. *Examples of "ascend/descend" verbs and directionals in their* vertical *senses (pooled data from five children). Criteria: clear meaning in context; not a repeat of prior utterance. Verb stems and directionals are shown in italics*

Name & age	Example	Context
Xan 2;0	ch'ay *koel*, ma 'tam. 'It fell down, don't pick it up (ball).'	from 2;0 to 2;5 she always uses *koel* with falling verbs and with nothing else at this stage; no contrast with *moel*
Xan 2;3	*mo*on. 'I ascend.'	up onto chair
Lus 2;6	*kojtes* yakan i. 'Lower its foot' [lit. 'make it descend'].	re camera tripod, the legs of which "ascend" and "descend"
Lus 2;7	*moix* tal. '(They) have ascended coming.'	toy animals up onto table into toy corral
Pet 2;7	*mo*ik laj ta te', . . . *mo*on ta te', *ko*on tal. 'They ascended the tree, . . . I climb the tree, I descend.'	up/down into trees
Pet 2;7	*mo*otik ta karo, xi. 'We ascend (in)to the car, he said.'	up/down into car
Xan 2;8	ya to *kojtes* alali. 'I'll lower my doll.' *kojtes*ben tal. 'Lower it (doll off back) for me.'	i.e. I'll untie it and let it down off my back; untie it and take it down for me
Mal 2;9	ay binti *mo* bel ta 'ni'. 'There's something (that) ascended away (in)to your nose.'	to her cousin, commenting on something in her nose
Nik 2;11	ile' *ko*ix tal. ma jk'an *ko*ix tal. 'Look (she) descended. I don't want to descend.'	re getting down out of toy car
Lus 3;2	*mo*ix muti. 'The chicken ascended.'	into tree
Lus 3;3	*mo* laj tal ta te' eki, . . . ban tzaka *koel*. 'It ascended (in)to the tree . . . go grab it down.'	chicken, up/down into trees
Xan 3;3	li' *mo* xan tal, *koel* xan ma x*ko*. 'Here it ascended coming, down again it doesn't descend.'	toy car up/down hill of sand
Xan 3;3	*mo*emon ta regla jo'tik. 'We have ascended (on)to the boards.'	she and her playmate having climbed onto pile of stacked boards
Xan 3;3	ay skoral ek, la xluch *koel* ye ini yala xulub. 'He has a corral too, he has lowered his little horns [as if to fight with them].'	toy cow she has put into a toy corral
Lus 3;6	*mo*an tal i anton, ya jkuchat bel. 'Come ascend X'an, I'll carry you away.'	up into large toy wooden car they can climb into

Table 17.3 (*cont.*)

Name & age	Example	Context
Lus 3;6	ja' yala ch'ujt li' ni, tzisbil *koel* li' ini. 'It's its little stomach here, sewn downwards here.'	re sewing on her doll's skirt, which goes downwards across the stomach.
Lus 3;8	*mo* ta jtzek, tal *mo*ok ta jtzek. 'It ascended my skirt, it came to ascend my skirt.'	a bug climbing upwards on her skirt
Lus 3;10	ya *moo*n ta yutil k'an *moo*n ta yut ek. 'I ascend into (the toy car), he wants to ascend in(to it) too.'	toy car they can climb into
Lus 3;11	ya jpet tal *koel* me'tik; maili i. 'I'll carry (her) down, Mrs.; wait.'	telling researcher she'll carry her cousin from her bed to researcher

Table 17.4. *Summary of production, ages 2–4, for Absolute vocabulary*

First appearance of terms: x
Productive use, in contrast sets, with no "errors": yy
n = 3

	verbs ('ascend/descend')	directionals ('ascending/ descending')	unpossessed nouns ('uphill/downhill')	possessed nouns ('its-uphill,' 'its-downhill,' 'above it,' 'below it' [ABS]
2;0–2;5	x	x	x	
2;6–3;0	yy	yy	yy	
3;1–3;6				x
3;7–4;0				yy

Table 17.4 summarizes the natural production data from three of the children for UP/DOWN verbs and nouns. The children appear to have mastered the semantic contrasts of the terms in the Absolute system by age 3, by which time there is evidence that they are not just imitating the input, but are using the terms for novel situations. They have acquired the syntax of possessed nouns by at least 3;6, and are using the vocabulary explicitly relationally by this time, in at least some contexts (saying things like "F [a Figure object] is uphillwards of G [a Ground object or reference point]" or "F is moving uphillwards in relation to G"). By age 3;6 to 4;0, all three children produce the requisite vocabulary in contrast sets, in different contexts,

in different grammatical constructions (using it with different aspectual, causative, or subjunctive affixes), in both possessed and unpossessed forms, and in some novel (not modelled by an adult) contexts (see tables 17.2 and 17.3 for examples).

In order to produce such novel utterances the children must have the rudiments of an Absolute system of spatial reference: they must be able to use the lay of the land to establish a vector in a fixed direction with differentiated "up" and "down" ends as the basis for deciding where an object is in relation to the Ground object. The children's production data analyzed so far is compatible with use of the local slope of land to establish the Absolute axis; I don't yet have clear evidence from children's natural production that they have abstracted an overall (South to North) slope of land axis for the system. They can, however, by at least age 4;0, accurately point to *ajk'ol* 'uphill' and *alan* 'downhill' across considerable distances and not necessarily coinciding with the local slope, showing that their geographical knowledge already provides the basis for an abstract geographical Absolute system, at least from their home base. Their use of the system is thus to a limited extent "productive": by about 3;6 children can use this system to relate objects and events spatially to places and people familiar to them, amounting (as an approximation) to some twenty or thirty fixed places (their own households and those of their relations, the fields of their family and those of other families who work with their family, the school, medical clinic, shop, etc.). Just when this extends to *any* place is still unclear; children undoubtedly differ in this respect.

The data show that Tzeltal children do not make semantic overgeneralizations on the basis of putatively universal spatial notions like vertical UP/DOWN. They do not generalize the UP/DOWN path vocabulary to events where vertical motion is involved in the event but is not overtly lexicalized in the adult language (e.g. to the contexts of posture changes, lifting, and carrying, as is also demonstrated by de León for Tzotzil; 1994, ch. 18 of this volume). The child's first meanings for the UP/DOWN path vocabulary are language-specific, characteristically Tzeltalan. In addition to vertical uses, landslope UP/DOWN is a feature of their early uses for *mo*/*ko*, this landslope UP/DOWN being a language-specific notion, and for them, even a household-specific notion at first.[17] This is even more emphatically the case for the nouns: *ajk'ol*/*alan* 'uphill/downhill' are used by these children *only* in their landslope senses, although the input includes some vertical uses.[18] (See examples in table 17.5.) The core semantics for both nouns and verbs is built perhaps at first around concepts of place; for the nouns *ajk'ol*/*alan* these can be quite far-away places (e.g. the hot country fields where the family grows corn), while for the verbs *mo*/*ko* they are at first quite locally restricted places (particular houses in the local compound, for example, to

Table 17.5. *Examples of "uphill/downhill/across" relational nouns in their landslope senses (pooled data from five children). Relational nouns are shown in italics*

Name & age	Example	Context
Xan 2;2	pet *kajal.* 'Downhill Xpet.'	identifying Xpet as the person asked about in previous utterance
Xan 2;2	*kajal.* '(To) downhill.'	reply to question about where she wants to go
Xan 2;3	baem na jtatik *alan.* 'Gone (to) house (of) downhill-sir' (i.e. her grandfather)	reply to question about where her father has gone
Xan 2;3	bajt *alan.* 'Gone downhill.'	reply to question: where's father?
Lus 2;6	xkatal *jejch.* 'Sideways Xkatal.'	reference to dog named Xkatal who lives across slope of land
Mik 2;6	bajt *kajal.* 'Gone (to) uphill'	re house of his grandmother, uphill/South of his own house
Xaw 2;6	jnn, talon ek i *jejch* i. 'Hm, I come too (to) the side.'	to kitchen house, across the slope from their two other houses
Pet 2;9	ay ta *alan* . . . ay ta *jejch* . . . *alan* to xan. 'It's to downhill, . . . to the side. More downhillwards.'	toy on patio
Pet 2;11	sjojk'o kichan ta *jejch.* 'My cousin to-the-side asked.'	identifying person
Xan 3;0	mach'a wixtikil, macha ay i li' ta *ajk'ol* i. 'Which sister, who is it here to uphill?'	querying identity of person
Xaw 3;1	li' ta *alan* i. 'It's here to downhill.'	at the other house
Lus 3;1	bajtix ta a'tel ek' i me'tik ta *alan.* 'Downhill Mrs. has gone to work.'	identifying person as 'downhill Mrs.,' not where 'Mrs.' is working
Lus 3;1	ja' i jNik li' ta *kajal* i. 'It's the Nik here uphill.'	identifying which Nik is referred to
Xaw 3;1	ja' i li' ta *alan* i . . . a ta *jejch.* 'It's here to downhill, . . . to the side.'	where she's left something
Lus 3;2	ja'i lum ta *kajal* lum ta snaik Nike, lum lum ta sna *kajal* Nike. 'It's there uphill, there at Nik's house, there at Nik's uphill house.'	identifying where X happened
Lus 3;2	ta y*ajk'ol*e li' talotik xan wojei. 'To its uphill [uphill = south side of house] here we came again yesterday.'	describing her and her playmate's movements circumnavigating the house
Lus 3;6	. . . ya ka'y xan tza'nel jo'tik lum a ine ta y*anil* retrina. '. . . we're going again for a shit there below [downhillwards of] the latrine.'	downhillwards of the latrine is on the same level as the latrine, but north of it.

Table 17.5 (*cont.*)

Name & age	Example	Context
Lus 3;6	. . . la stamike i keremetik ta *jejch.* '. . . the acrossways boys found it.'	identifying which boys – the ones who live acrossways
Lus 3;6	te xa'wak' ta y*anil* a, y*anil* a'basoe. 'Put it there at its-underneath (of) your cup.'	telling sibling to put something vertically underneath her cup
Lus 3;8	. . . lum y*ajk'ol* na lumine. '. . . over above the house over there.'	i.e. uphillwards (south) of the house over there
Lus 3;8	ju' baemon me ta julel ta y*ajk'ol* na Albina jo'tik i. 'Hm, we went for shots (to the clinic) above Alvina's house.'	i.e. uphillwards (south) of it
Lus 3;9	la nutz chitame i lum ta *jejch.* 'He chased a pig there at across.'	identifying where the pig was chased: at a place across the lay of the land
Lus 3;11	lum ay ta *yanil* mantarinae. 'There it is below (downhillwards of) the mandarin tree.'	reference to lost ball
Lus 3;11	taojbe me ta y*anil* tuwa men me'. 'It's been found below the waterpipe.'	downhillwards of the waterpipe
Lus 4;1	li' me ta y*anil* ini tajuntik li' ta *ajk'ol* a kili. 'Here below our uncle, here uphill I saw it.'	reporting event she saw downhill from uncle's house and uphill from her own
Lus 4;3	yu' ma jichuk a jelawon ta *ajk'ol* li' ta sna mejun a'wil ini xi. ' ". . . I crossed above Aunt's house here," she said.'	i.e. south of Aunt's house

which one "ascends" or "descends" if they are arrayed along the South/North axis, or "goes across" if they are situated across the lay of the land from each other). Only gradually are the places associated with *mo/ko* and *ajk'ol/alan* combined with increasing geographical knowledge so that a general landslope direction abstracted from the idiosyncrasies of local spatial layouts enters the semantics of these words.

The place-linked specificity of the child's Absolute system lasts for a long time, although the number of places related in the system gradually increases. Children do generalize across contexts; *mo/ko* usage is not restricted to exactly what is heard in the input, but extends to the motion of movable (and therefore sometimes novel) objects into trees, onto beds or other furniture, up onto the roof, to and from particular houses or other landmarks. By about the age of 3;6, children use *mo/ko* productively for certain kinds of motions: talking about motion from house to house in the local arena, and about movement to and from certain named places. (See examples in table 17.2.) The *molko* verbs seem at first to be restricted to animates (including cars and toy cars), although this is not the case for adults. The use of these verbs by age 4, in explicit contrast sets that include the "acrossways" terms (distinguishing "uphill/downhill/across"), confirms the language-specific nature of the terms as forming an Absolute system based on the lay of the land.[19]

3.2 Data from interactional "space games"

In children's natural production the use of the UP/DOWN vocabulary for small-scale spatial relations (saying, for example, X is 'uphill' or 'downhill' of Y, of moveable objects on a tabletop) is rare, since it is rarely necessary to be so explicit. In an attempt to establish the degree of productivity of children's Absolute system, I therefore engaged a group of older children, aged 4 to 12, in interactional tasks designed to prompt such usage. These "Farm Animal games" are played by two players visually screened from each other, one of whom (the Director) describes a spatial array of toy farm animals set out on a table in front of him; from his instructions the other player (the Matcher), has to reproduce the array with an identical set of farm animal toys on another table.[20] In these games, adults routinely use the Absolute system to distinguish spatial relations, and some children of 4 are able to follow the instructions for placement in terms of Absolute (South/North) 'uphill/downhill,' albeit with some difficulty:

(1) (CL, a girl of 4;1, is the Matcher; the Director is MN, her father):

MN: *jo', ta yolil ta meru yolil. jitza to koel alan teb li' ta stojol yajk'ol te' i.*
'Yeah, at the middle [between the two toy trees], at the real middle. Pull it [toy pig] downhillwards, downhillwards downhill a bit, here at the front of the uphill-side of the tree.'

CL: *aj li'i.*
'Oh here.'

MN: *te' a mene. eso.*
'There. That's it.'

In *production* of the same novel tasks, when a child operates as the Director, we find adult-like usage (for example, 'Put the cow uphillwards of the horse, facing acrossways') in one child by 5;8, and in four others between the ages of 7 and 8.[21] Some of the children in this production task are using the system indoors, without visual access to the lay of the land, and using the abstract South/North slope as the reference axis. The production of Absolute spatial relators is fluent, accurate, and productive in this task (although we still get some errors in interpretation due to the local slope/overall slope ambiguity). The existence of local slope misunderstandings in Farm Animal games even at age 7–8 suggests that for some children the meanings for the intransitive verbs *molko* stay for a long time *too* specific, not having yet been generalized to the overall South/North slope of land. Alternatively, the children may have all the correct meanings but misapply the pragmatic rules governing when the words should be understood as referring to overall slope instead of local slope.

There is thus good evidence for productivity of the Absolute system, even in novel tabletop tasks, by the age of 7–8. This is not to say that the children's mastery is equivalent to that of adults at this point. There are several thresholds for which we have not yet pinned down the point at which children attain adult competence. These are:

1. How "productive" is the uphill/downhill system in children of 2–3? For example, can they talk about 'granny-uphill' as 'granny-downhill' if they are currently located above her, on the local or Absolute slope? Can they choose between 'ascend' and 'descend' to refer to going to her house, depending on where they are? Or is there, instead, a rigid one-to-one correspondence between places or persons and their corresponding location-specifier, as if it were a name?
2. At what point can the children use or understand the words according to the Absolute system even when this is in conflict with the visual scene (for example, describing one object as higher than another, meaning to its South, even when it is actually lower in terms of local positioning)?
3. When can children use this system in all the situations in which adults do, keeping constant track ("dead-reckoning") of where uphill (South) / downhill (North) are, even in unfamiliar places, at night, etc.?

These questions are currently under investigation. But what is clear at this point is that Tzeltal children do master this system, with at least a limited degree of productivity, at an early age, by at least 4;0. They are capable of using it projectively to describe small-scale spatial layouts in novel situations (i.e. not a context their normal life provides) by at least 7 or 8, in some cases even younger.

4 Discussion

Children's mastery of the Tzeltal Absolute system (perhaps in a restricted way) by age 4 presents puzzles on two counts: the semantic complexity of the vocabulary, and the cognitive complexity of the frame of reference it involves. On the semantic side, we need to explain both the children's early willingness to entertain language-specific meanings for the path-incorporating motion verbs and the associated directionals and nominals, and the slowness with which they abstract from their initially place-linked meanings to a more general landslope meaning. On the cognitive side, children's early learning of the Tzeltal Absolute system in a language-specific manner raises the possibility that exposure to linguistic categories in appropriate nonlinguistic contexts may induce precociously early development of cognitive categories which, without exposure to such a language, would not be expected at that stage of development. This is because a proper mastery of this system (using fixed angles to calculate spatial relationships on the horizontal) presupposes Piaget's Euclidean stage of spatial cognition. On Piagetian grounds one would not expect children to have early use of an Absolute (Euclidean) system; the relevant Euclidean conceptual development occurs in the Western children tested by Piaget and his colleagues around the ages of 8 or 9 (see Piaget, Inhelder, & Szeminska 1960; Brown & Levinson in press). Thus even the limited productivity of children's UP/DOWN system by age 4, and certainly children's ability to use it for calculating spatial relations in a novel task prior to age 8, are very suggestive for the possibility that language affects cognitive development.[22]

Turning to the semantic complexity issue, I will propose an explanation for the characteristics of Tzeltal children's early spatial verbs based on the verb semantics of the language itself.

4.1 The verb specificity hypothesis

An important typological property of Tzeltal is the highly specific semantics of verb roots; transitive and "positional" roots[23] tend to be restricted to very limited sets of activities, and they distinguish events partly on the nature of the arguments they can take. There are, for example, many different verbs for eating depending on the characteristics of what you eat, and many different verbs for holding or carrying something depending on its shape and how you carry it (see figure 17.2). The same applies to verbs of position, cutting, breaking, insertion, extraction, and many others. These are basic-level verbs in Tzeltal, in the sense of Rosch (1978): that is, they are the unmarked way to label such events. We may contrast, for example, the basic-level English verb *eat* as opposed to its hyponym *munch*, with the Tzeltal verb *tun* 'eat in general' and its hyponym *ti'* 'eat meat.' In Tzeltal it is the 'eat meat' verb, and its cohorts 'eat crunchy things,' etc., which are basic-level verbs in terms of frequency and unmarkedness. Unlike most basic-level verbs in Indo-European languages, the Tzeltal verbs are like classifiers for kinds of activities, specific in terms of the nominal arguments they can take.[24]

These kinds of verbs are prominent in children's vocabularies at the one-word stage (see examples in table 17.6).[25] Perhaps the tendency to verb specificity in Tzeltal has an effect on the child's further hypotheses about verb meanings, and, in particular, about the meanings of motion verbs. Figure 17.3 illustrates the specific semantics of Tzeltal Path+Motion verbs;

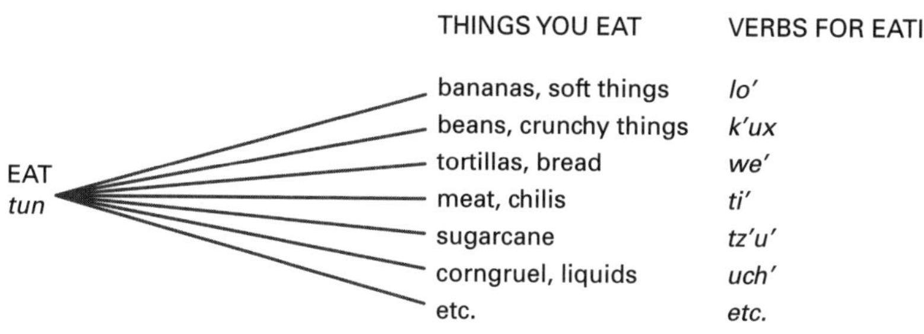

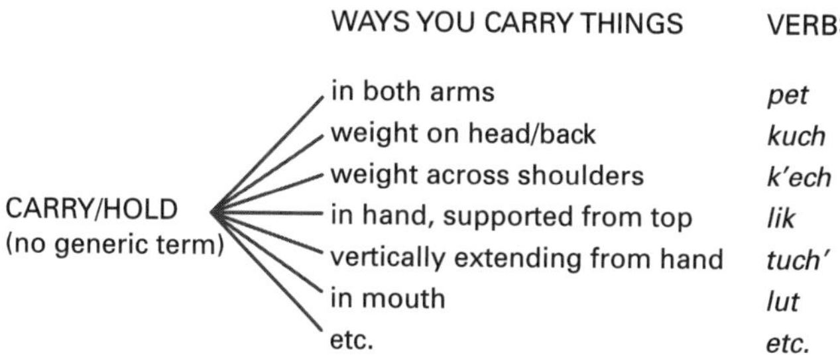

Fig. 17.2 Semantic specificity in Tzeltal verbs.

we can see how a Tzeltal child might extrapolate, from the specificity of verb meanings she has already learned, to an analogous specificity in the meanings of *mo/ko/jelaw* 'ascend/descend/go across.' That is, on analogy with the semantic specificity of transitive and positional verbs, it is perhaps a reasonable hypothesis for Tzeltal children that motion too comes in different "kinds," depending on the characteristics of the path and goal. A presumption of specificity might lead children to choose very specific meanings for the verbs 'ascend' and 'descend,' such as 'go to particular places,' as illustrated in figure 17.4. Children might then resist generalization to different contexts unless they hear evidence in the input that such new contexts are places to which one "ascends" or "descends." Adhering to such a policy means that it can take a long time before what these contexts have in common – the fact that they are arrayed along an uphill/downhill axis, or vertically – forms the basis for abstracting a more general meaning not attached to particular places but to the relative location of places along such an axis. It takes an even longer time before cumulative geographical knowledge allows children to form an even more abstract concept of the overall slope of the land falling from South to North: this occurs sometime

Table 17.6. *First thirty-five verbs used in data samples from two Tzeltal children at the one- to two-word stage, listed in order of emergence. Boldface indicates "heavy" verbs restricted to specific arguments, nonboldface indicates "light" verbs. Criteria: used at least twice; not a repeat of prior utterance; not a frozen formula; meaning clear in context.*

Mik (1;5–2;0) MLU [mean length of utterance] about 1	Xan (1;3–2;2) MLU 1 to 1.43
ba 'go, gone'	**we'** 'eat [tortillas, corn-based foods]'
la' 'come!'	**chu'** 'suckle [breast]'
we' 'eat [tortillas, corn-based foods]'	ay 'exist, be located'
ak' 'give'	**boj** 'cut [with knife/machete]'
tzak 'take, grasp [in hand]'	**k'ux** 'eat [beans, crunchy things]'
jach 'get/stand up'	(ma) na' 'don't know'
chu' 'suckle [breast]'	ba 'go, gone'
tza' 'shit'	jun 'accompany'
poj 'take away, steal'	**pet** 'carry [in arms]'
ay 'exist, be located'	ch'ay koel 'fall down'
tek' 'step on something [2-footed]'	**tam** 'pick up, gather [thing dropped or fallen on ground]'
muk 'cover over [with cloth]'	**lo'** 'eat [fruit, soft things]'
tak' '(I) can('t)'	**chik'** 'insert [wood into fire]'
way 'sleep'	ta 'reach/find it'
ajch' 'get wet'	xi' '(I) fear (it)'
pet 'carry [in arms]'	way 'sleep'
k'an 'want'	**tij** 'play [radio, tape recorder]'
chux 'pee'	ak' 'give'
pix 'wrap [in cloth]'	laj 'die, finish'
mes 'sweep [with broom]'	k'opoj 'speak'
k-il 'I see'	tal 'come'
chuk 'tie [rope-like thing]'	**poch'** 'peel [skin off fruit or animal]'
lo' 'eat [fruit, soft things]'	kux 'hurt'
pas 'do, make'	och 'enter'
laj 'finish'	**juch'** 'grind [corn]'
pach 'be positioned [bowl-shaped object, upright]'	**tz'us** 'close [door]'
tz'ap 'insert [stick-like thing tightly]'	k'ej 'put away'
och 'enter'	lok' 'exit'
kay 'open [hinged thing, door]'	**til** 'burn [flame, flashlight]'
tal 'come'	**tek'** 'stand [on two legs]'
kux 'hurt'	k'an 'want'
xi' '(I) fear (it)'	il 'see'
ch'ay 'fall'	**puk'** 'mix [corngruel with hand]'
pok' 'wash [outside surface, hands]'	**xet'** 'break [flexible flat thing]'
lap 'put on [clothes on body]'	**tuy** 'cut [meat, acrossways]'

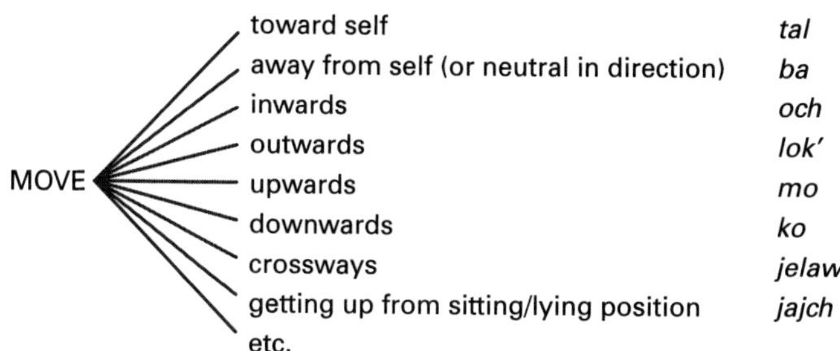

Fig. 17.3 Semantic specificity in Tzeltal motion verbs.

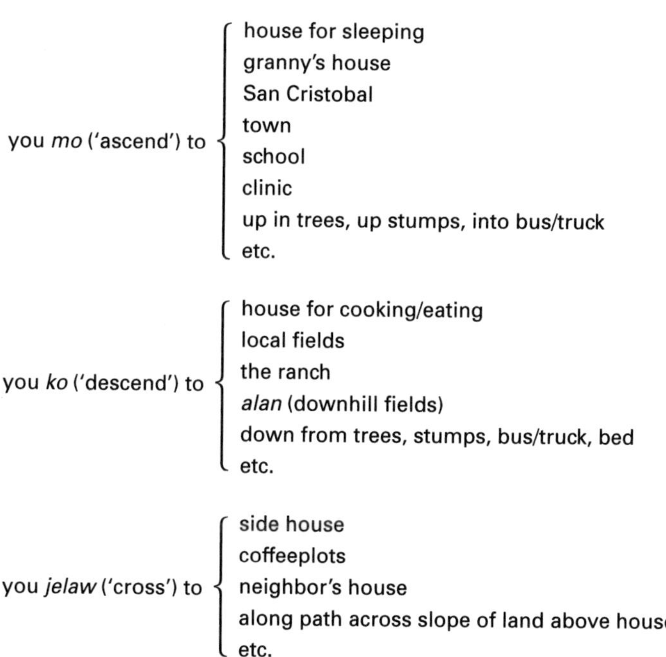

Fig. 17.4 Child's UP/DOWN verb meanings: motion via path comes in different "kinds."

between the ages of 5 and 8, judging by the data from our Farm Animal games.

The argument here is similar to a proposal made by Carey (1978) for the semantics of the English word *tall* (see also Keil & Carroll 1980.) Carey argued that children's immature meanings for relational words of this sort in English are probably best captured by a "missing features plus haphazard examples" theory, with *tall* at first closely linked to specific instances of use, its meaning not necessarily integrated in terms of features across different instances (e.g. *tall* for buildings being based on different criteria than *tall* for people). My proposal is that a propensity to construct word meanings in this fashion might be favored or disfavored by general properties of the language's semantic structure (see also Bowerman, de León & Choi 1995; Choi & Bowerman 1991).

Such a semantic specificity bias would make for conservative learners, thus helping Tzeltal children to get the language-specific meanings early by disinclining them to overgeneralize verb meanings. The mechanism by which such a bias comes to affect Tzeltal children's hypotheses about what verbs can mean could be a simple associative mechanism such as that proposed by Linda Smith, ch. 4 of this volume. At present this is just a hypothesis; further evidence – for example experiments with novel-verb learning – would be required to confirm that Tzeltal children do indeed operate with such a verb-learning bias. Other evidence could come from children's early "errors" in assigning word meanings, e.g. associating words with meanings that are more restricted than is warranted by adult usage.[26]

Such a bias does not necessarily develop by the one-word stage, since it would require some exposure to and use of the language. It is thus distinct from the specificity of children's "holophrastic" early word meanings, where the word "means" or indexes the whole context of its use; such meanings are (for some children, and some words) a feature of the early one-word stage (Barrett 1982; Tomasello & Brooks 1999). In Tzeltal children's acquisition of the Absolute system vocabulary, the shift from context-dependent meanings to an increasingly abstract symbolic meaning (beyond place-specificity to local slope, and beyond local slope to South/North land slope) is a more drawn-out process. The symbolic basis for South/North land slope UP/DOWN relies on children's geographical knowledge, which gradually increases in the preschool years. Nonetheless, there is evidence that the core uses of the terms are related for the child – that they are not simply attached to a list of arbitrary places. For example, children of 2–3 can point to places they describe in "uphill/downhill" terms, and a sense of their landslope spatial relations is visually apparent in the open valley of this community, as well as kinetically apparent in the effort required to go there (easy downhill, hard uphill; children are often required to walk downhill, but are carried uphill). Certainly by age 4, by the time children are using the system explicitly and productively in a relational way for small movable objects, even on flat terrain (e.g. 'the ball is downhillwards of the water tap'), it is clear that they have meanings for 'up/downhillwards' that are generalized at least to the local land slope. The verb specificity hypothesis would help them acquire such meanings, and predispose them to limit the meanings to the local land slope for an extended time.

Such a bias would of course be only part of the story of how Tzeltal children learn the meanings of *mo/ko/jelaw* 'ascend/descend/go across.' They do, of course, have to attend to the contexts of use, infer the intentions of speakers when they use these verbs, and abstract what is common across different instances of *mo*, in contrast to *ko*, in contrast to *jelaw*. They could be helped by the consistent semantic relationship between these verbs and the corresponding nouns in the same frame: people regularly say things like *ko bel ta alan* 'He descended away to downhill.' The fact that children at first use the "uphill/downhill" nouns like place names, and only gradually acquire their relational usages ("up/down in relation to X"), is likely to be closely tied to the place-linked specificity of path verbs. Children are perhaps helped in formulating an uphill/downhill axis and locating places along it by very consistent input (motion to certain places is routinely described with "ascend/descend" verbs, rather than the more general "go"), as well as by adults' accurate pointing in collocation with Absolute usage. The semantic structure of the language, and the hypothesized verb-specificity bias it engenders in Tzeltal children, would thus work in conjunction with many context-dependent cues to the system.

4.2 *Semantic specificity in typological perspective*

The hypothesis I have proposed concerns semantic specificity within the Tzeltal class of verbs. Such specificity is a typological feature of Mayan (and, indeed, of many other Mesoamerican) languages. There are two additional typological features of Tzeltal – and of Mayan languages in general – that are relevant to this hypothesis. The first is that spatial relations are encoded in nouns and verbs in Tzeltal, rather than in the prepositions, postpositions, or case markers of more familiar languages. There is only one all-purpose preposition in Tzeltal. Spatial relations involving an UP/DOWN contrast are, as we have seen, conveyed by verbs meaning things like 'to be high up,' 'to be low down,' 'to ascend' or 'to descend,' by adverbials that are transparently derived from verb roots and mean 'upwards' or 'downwards,' and by possessed nouns meaning things like 'its-top/uphillward-side' and 'its-underneath/downhillward-side.' Spatial meanings encoded in verbs and nouns ("content words") present a very different problem to a child than spatial meanings encoded in grammatical morphemes ("functors") like prepositions or case markers. Spatial relations encoded in nouns and verbs (in "open classes," or – more accurately for Tzeltal – in closed subsets of open classes) are more context-specific, tied more closely to content, to particular activities and things, while functors, to the extent to which they are grammaticalized, have abstracted from the contextual specificity a spatial core which then applies across many different kinds of contexts.[27] Having the functional load of spatial reference carried by nouns and verbs is one source, then, of specificity in Tzeltal spatial language.

The second relevant typological characteristic of the language concerns the distribution of information in an utterance. In Tzeltal, the semantic division of labor between verbs and nouns is rather different from that in Indo-European languages. In the latter, nouns tend to encode specific properties of objects, and verbs to denote relations between objects while remaining agnostic as to the properties of objects whose relations they denote (Gentner 1978, 1982, ch. 8 of this volume). In the Mayan languages, many basic-level verb roots[28] encode properties of the objects to which they can apply (e.g. *pach* 'be positioned [bowl-shaped object canonically upright]'; see de León, ch. 18 of this volume, for examples). Inanimate noun roots, by contrast, are often unspecified as to the form of their referents, denoting only the material they are composed of (e.g. "wood-stuff," "banana-stuff," "coffee-stuff;" see Lucy 1992; Gaskins & Lucy, ch. 9 of this volume).

These differences between Mayan and Indo-European languages suggest that languages may actually differ broadly in terms of which word classes are characterized by specific and which by more general kinds of meanings. Suppose we could operationalize a measure of specificity across word classes – simplistically, this might be thought of in terms of number of features, or in terms of meaning inclusion (the meanings of general words being included in those of their more specific hyponyms). We could then compare word classes with a tendency to highly differentiated meanings to those with a tendency to general meanings by calculating the average number of features involved in their meanings. A notional cline of specificity in word classes is illustrated in figure 17.5: for a language like English such a cline might have common nouns at the most specific end, followed by verbs and adjectives, and with prepositions and other grammatical morphemes at the most general end. But a cline for Tzeltal would have transitive and positional verb roots towards the specific end, followed by intransitive verbs, then common nouns, and with the one all-purpose preposition at the most general end.[29] This sort of broad typological difference in the semantic organization of languages has implications for theories of spatial language; for example, it undermines proposed cognitive explanations (e.g. Talmy 1985; Landau & Jackendoff 1993) for the supposedly

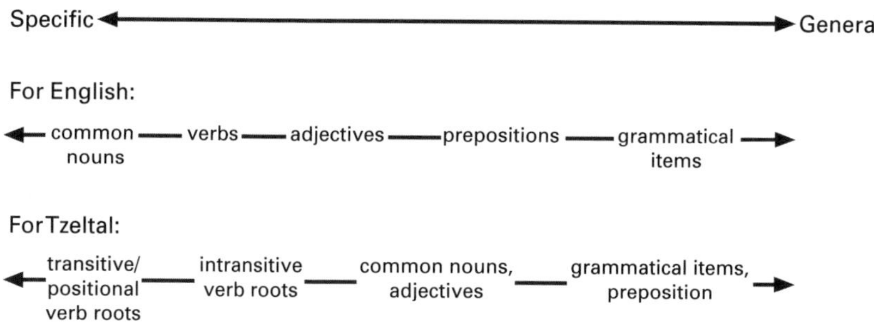

Fig. 17.5 Comparing specificity of meaning across word classes, across languages.

semantically bleached character of spatial morphemes. (See Slobin, ch. 14 of this volume, for additional arguments against such cognitive explanations.)

My proposal for a verb specificity bias in Tzeltal appears to run in the opposite direction to E. V. Clark's 1973 hypothesis based on Indo-European language data: that children begin with a preference for general word meanings, which they later modify by adding in more specific features. Although Clark (1993) no longer holds to her 1973 hypothesis, there are still current proposals, based on the high frequency of light verbs in children's early speech, that children tend to start with "light" semantically bleached verbs and that these play an important role in the acquisition of syntax (e.g. Hollebrandse & van Hout 1994 for Dutch; Ninio 1999 for English and Hebrew). There is no evidence in Tzeltal children's speech of a tendency for early verbs to be "light": while a handful of light verbs do exist and are frequent in Tzeltal (e.g. *ak'* 'give,' *pas* 'do/make,' *ay* 'exist,' *ich'* 'get'), in children's early vocabularies these are vastly outnumbered by specific verbs (see table 17.6). More importantly, there is no evidence that Tzeltal children use light verbs as general-purpose verbs in lieu of more specific ones: from the start, a child wanting her belt retied will say things like "Tie it for me," using a specific verb, rather than expressing such a request with a general verb as in: "Do my belt up for me" (Brown 1998b).

5 Conclusion

The Tzeltal data on "uphill/downhill" acquisition reviewed here have a number of implications for theories of language acquisition and cognitive development.

First, proposed universal prelinguistic concepts like "vertical" do not seem to be providing ready-made semantic units which children start with in learning the Tzeltal Absolute vocabulary. Rather, learning the words in context *provides* the concepts, by a process of induction across instances of use, instances which include both vertical contexts and landslope contexts for the same words. Both the concepts and the predispositions for verb learning that I have proposed are induced from the language itself, and are language-specific. Whatever the role of putative universal semantic primes may be in providing children with a starting point for learning word meanings in general (and that role is a hotly debated issue), they are not providing in any direct way a repertoire of privileged meanings onto which Tzeltal children map the spatial words of their language. The Tzeltal findings support the views of Tomasello and others on the importance of context in children's developing word meanings.

A second point arising from the Tzeltal data is that languages can vary in which word class generally carries the referential load, and that this has important implications for children's learning of their first language. In English, nominal arguments pick out their referents directly; in Tzeltal, the information necessary to pick out the referent is very largely encoded in the verb, at least for the transitive verbs like *ti'* 'eat meat' and the positional verbs like *pach* 'be positioned [bowl-shaped object canonically upright]' discussed above. On the assumption that at least part of what children are doing when they begin to use language is learning how to refer, if the referential load of the language they are exposed to is mainly carried in verbs, then, *pace* Gentner & Boroditsky (ch. 8 of this volume), it doesn't seem surprising that verbs are what children tend to learn first. This may explain the early prominence of verbs in children's corpora in languages like Tzeltal, Tzotzil, and perhaps also Korean (see Choi 1997; Brown 1998b; de León 1999a, b, ch. 18 of this volume; contrast Gentner & Boroditsky, ch. 8 of this volume).

The proposal that the semantic structure of previously learned words might influence children's hypotheses about what words can mean is not new. It is articulated in the work of Bowerman and her colleagues,[30] who document children's early sensitivity to the semantic structure of their language, finding that the very earliest uses of words reflect their language-specific meanings. My proposal adds the claim that very general lexicalization properties of the language (e.g. what semantic features are likely to be lexicalized in verbs as opposed to nouns) may sensitize children to what the semantic weight of different word classes is likely to be, providing a basis for language-specific hypotheses about possible word meanings which may extend throughout the preschool years. The proposal developed here is that the language Tzeltal children hear provides many different verb labels for a given domain of activity, and thereby affects the hypotheses they bring to bear on what new verbs can mean. This argument is also in harmony with Slobin's proposal (ch. 14 of this volume) of "typological bootstrapping." We are now beginning to have detailed longitudinal data from children learning languages with a semantic structure radically different from those predominantly studied by students of child language development.[31] We will thus soon be in a position to test such hypotheses more directly.

NOTES

I am grateful to Melissa Bowerman, Wolfgang Klein, Lourdes de León, Stephen Levinson, and David Wilkins, for critical comments on earlier versions of this chapter.

1 The community of this study is the remote rural hamlet of Majosik', in the Tzeltal-speaking *municipio* of Tenejapa, Chiapas, Mexico. There are some 150,000 speakers of Tzeltal in Chiapas, and perhaps an equivalent number of speakers of Tzotzil in the closely related Tzotzil communities (see de León, ch. 18 of this volume). An "uphill/downhill" system of spatial description is found in many Mayan communities throughout this mountainous region.

2 For example, Bowerman (1989, 1996a, b), Choi & Bowerman (1991), Bowerman, de León, & Choi (1995), Bowerman & Choi (ch. 16 of this volume), de León (ch. 18 of this volume).

3 For example, the early acquisition of the prepositions corresponding to IN and ON in English and related languages has been attributed to the universal early availability of the topological concepts of containment and support; similarly, the early acquisition of UP and DOWN was attributed to the perceptually given salience of the vertical dimension (Bloom 1973; Nelson 1974; Miller & Johnson-Laird 1976; Johnston & Slobin 1979; E. V. Clark 1980).

4 See Carey, ch. 7 of this volume.

5 For example the Mutual Exclusivity Principle, the Whole Object Constraint, the Shape Bias. For a recent summary of these "developmental lexical principles" see Golinkoff, Mervis, & Hirsh-Pasek 1994.

6 We can compare "general" and "specific" verbs in a given semantic domain (e.g. "eating verbs") in terms of meaning inclusion, with the former (e.g. "eat, in general") being a proper subset of the latter ("eat meat," "eat tortillas," etc.) in terms of componential features (E. V. Clark 1973, Gentner 1978).

7 Although I use the South/North contrast to clarify one sense of the "uphill/downhill" terms, Tenejapans themselves do not think in terms of North/South/East/West and most of them do not know the Spanish cardinal terms.

8 It does not exist for the monolingual speakers of the present study. Speakers who are bilingual in Tzeltal and Spanish may adopt (part of) a Front/Back/Left/Right system from Spanish.

9 These verbs are used only for change of location, not for posture changes, and only for spontaneous motion (a causative suffix is required to indicate caused motion), just as in Tzotzil. See Talmy (1985) for lexicalization patterns of motion verbs; see also de León (1994 and ch. 18 of this volume) for Tzotzil.

10 As this chapter concentrates on the acquisition of UP/DOWN spatial relations, vocabulary acquisition for this transverse axis will not be considered here. See, however, Brown & Levinson (in press).

11 The overall slope is South/North in Tenejapa, but it varies in different communities; the neighboring Tzotzil community of Zinacantan, for example, slopes down to the West and their system is correspondingly shifted 90°.

12 I am at present not taking a stand as to whether the multiple meanings discussed here are at the lexical level (the terms being polysemous) or at the utterance level (the terms being semantically general across the three different bases for establishing an UP/DOWN distinction, with pragmatic rules providing an interpretation in context). The clear semantic relationship among the three uses of these terms (vertical, local land slope, South/North land slope) argues for monosemous meanings for the UP/DOWN terms, with "higher/lower" as the core semantic feature; things may be higher/lower at any angle from the horizontal. The fact that there are other Mayan communities with analogous systems based on different geographical features (the direction of sunrise/sunset, or the flow of a river, for example) suggests a metaphorical process common to them all.

13 The data were collected over the course of three years of regular six-weekly visits to children in the five extended households. It comprises more than 600 hours of videotaped and/or audiotaped natural interaction, supplemented by more structured sessions with children up to age 12. This is work in progress: data are still being collected and analyzed.

14 Children in this society seem to be somewhat late talkers; of the five focal children in my study, all were still in the one- to two-word stage at age two. This is likely to be related to childrearing practices: in this community babies and small children are talked to very little, and are not treated as interlocutors until they are walking (Brown 1998c).

15 For example, a sample of two hours' input to an 18-month-old girl yielded only three instances of the "ascend/descend" verbs. This low frequency is partly due to the fact that, in Tzeltal, spatial language is encoded in nouns and verbs, rather than in semantically bleached (and hence appropriate for many different kinds of contexts) grammatical particles. It is also doubtless due to the "here and now" character of talk with small children, where deictics, pointing, and other nonexplicit forms are normally contextually appropriate. This may account for the relative absence of this vocabulary at the one-word stage, as was also found by de León (ch. 18 of this volume) for Tzotzil children. The more frequent motion verb 'go' is, in fact, present in Tzeltal children's productions at the one-word stage, and the 'come/go' verbs precede 'ascend/descend' in acquisition, but they do not seem to be overgeneralized to situations where motion is appropriately described with 'ascend/descend.'

16 For example *balch'oj* 'tip over sideways [of a cylinder-shaped object]' being used for a toy of any shape tipping over in any direction, including end-over-end.

17 It is household-specific in the sense that it depends on the orientation of their household compound and the local slope of the land where it is set: some households are oriented South/North, others on a local slope at some other angle. In both cases, children of this age use the local slope and arrangement of houses to establish their Absolute axis.

18 For example, one child's mother says: *ixtal kalantik i a'wala tzek i* (lit: 'Come let's "down[hill]" your little skirt,' meaning 'Let's pull your skirt down [to its proper level].' (This is actually a verbal use of the noun *alan* 'downhill.')

19 This point was first demonstrated for the Tzotzil Absolute system by de León (1994).

20 The task was designed by members of the Cognitive Anthropology Research Group at the Max Planck Institute for Psycholinguistics, Nijmegen; see their Space Stimuli Kit 1.2, June 1993.

21 This task has been carried out to date with a total of twenty children (ranging from age 4;1 to 10) acting as Matcher, and ten children (from age 5;7 to 12) acting as Director. Here I am reporting only on the six games for which the data are fully processed.

22 Further work needs to be done to establish whether language really is affecting cognitive development in this case. First one must ascertain what exactly in the Tzeltal Absolute system is the analogue of Piaget's Euclidean thinking. Secondly, one must rule out the possibility that children are getting the right answer for the wrong reasons – for example, using the local slope of land as a reference line, as in Piaget's table edge task, against which to line up a spatial array visually. In addition, both cognitive testing and more controlled linguistic testing of a larger group of Tzeltal children would be necessary. These are tasks for future research.

23 Positionals are a large class of roots in Mayan languages with distinct derivational morphology, often combining semantic features of shape, position, configuration; they are important in predicating location (Brown 1994; Haviland 1994a, b; see also de León, ch. 18 of this volume). These comprise perhaps a third of the verbal lexicon, on analogy with Tzotzil (Haviland 1994a).

24 See Brown (1994), Brown & Levinson (1993a), for analyses of the semantics of these verbs in Tzeltal; see Haviland 1994a for Tzotzil. See also Choi & Bowerman 1991 for similar semantics of early verbs in Korean.

25 For further details about Tzeltal children's first verbs see Brown (1997, 1998a, b, c. See also de León (ch. 18 of this volume), for Tzotzil.

26 For example, Suzanne Gaskins (p.c.) reports an American child's misunderstanding of *upstairs* to mean 'place where we sleep' (an error only discovered when the family moved to a house where they slept downstairs). Similarly, Choi & Bowerman (1991:107) report a Korean child's initial misunderstanding of a verb meaning 'cause to go up' to mean 'put away where object belongs,' an error which they attribute to the child's recently having learned many verbs that do incorporate features of the Ground.

27 See Slobin, ch. 14 of this volume, for a related argument. See also Landau & Jackendoff (1993).

28 Roots are the semantic packages in Mayan languages relevant for this comparison; not the syntactic categories N and V. Roots may freely combine with derivational morphology to change syntactic category (e.g. from N to V and vice versa), but the semantic specificity of the root is retained.

29 I owe the current formulation of this argument to discussion with Wolfgang Klein (p.c.). Gentner (1988) has also argued that English verbs are intermediate between nouns and prepositions, on a scale ranging from prepositions and other "closed-class" items at the most linguistically determined end to concrete (basic-level) nouns and names for individuals at the most cognitively/perceptually determined end.

30 For example: "Korean children . . . are not prompted to analyze out Path as an

abstract component of motion events as strongly as are learners of English, and this may account for their delay in acquiring those Path verbs that do express Path in relatively pure form. Instead, they are encouraged to classify motion events on the basis of Path meanings admixed with causativity and properties of the Figure and Ground" (Choi & Bowerman 1991: 114).

31 Longitudinal work on Korean has perhaps been the first to prompt language acquisition researchers to reappraise theories based primarily on Indo-European semantic structures (see Choi 1997). Among longitudinal studies on the "exotic" languages of largely illiterate, unindustrialized societies, the Mayan languages are especially well represented (K'iche' [Pye 1992], Yucatec [Pfeiler & Martín Briceño 1997], Tzotzil [de León 1994, 1997, 1999a, b, ch. 18 of this volume], and Tzeltal (Stross 1969; Brown 1993; 1997, 1998a, b, c; Brown & Levinson, in press), making a potential for detailed crosslinguistic analysis within this language family.

REFERENCES

Barrett, M. 1982. The holophrastic hypothesis: conceptual and empirical issues. *Cognition* 11: 47–76.

Bloom, L. 1973. *One word at a time: the use of single word utterances before syntax*. The Hague: Mouton.

Bowerman, M. 1989. Learning a semantic system: what role do cognitive predispositions play? In M. L. Rice & R. L. Schiefelbusch (eds.), *The teachability of language*. Baltimore, MD: Paul H. Brookes, 133-169.

1996a. The origins of children's spatial semantic categories: cognitive vs. linguistic determinants. In J. J. Gumperz & S. C. Levinson (eds.),*Rethinking linguistic relativity*. Cambridge: Cambridge University Press, 145–176.

1996b. Learning how to structure space for language: a crosslinguistic perspective. In P. Bloom, M. A. Peterson, L. Nadel, & M. F. Garrett (eds.), *Language and space*. Cambridge, MA: MIT Press, 385–436.

Bowerman, M., L. de León, & S. Choi. 1995. Verbs, particles, and spatial semantics: learning to talk about spatial actions in typologically different languages. In E. V. Clark (ed.), *The proceedings of the 27th Annual Child Language Research Forum*. Stanford, CA: Center for the Study of Language and Information, 101–110.

Brown, P. 1993. The role of shape in the acquisition of Tzeltal (Mayan) locatives. In E. V. Clark (ed.), *The proceedings of the 25th Annual Child Language Research Forum*. Stanford, CA: Center for the Study of Language and Information, 211–220.

1994. The INS and ONS of Tzeltal locative expressions: the semantics of static descriptions of location. *Linguistics* 32:743–790.

1997. Isolating the CVC root in Tzeltal Mayan: a study of children's first verbs. In E. V. Clark (ed.), *The proceedings of the 28th Annual Child Language Research Forum*. Stanford, CA: Center for the Study of Language and Information, 41–52.

1998a. Early Tzeltal verbs: argument structure and argument representation. In E. V. Clark (ed.), *The proceedings of the 29th Annual Child Language Research Forum*. Stanford, CA: Center for the Study of Language and Information, 129–140.

1998b. Children's first verbs in Tzeltal: evidence for an early verb category. *Linguistics* 36: 715–753.

1998c. Conversational structure and language acquisition: the role of repetition in Tzeltal adult and child speech. *Journal of Linguistic Anthropology* 8: 1–25.

Brown, P., & S. C. Levinson. 1993a. "Uphill" and "downhill" in Tzeltal. *Journal of Linguistic Anthropology* 3: 46–74.

1993b. Shaping the world: semantic distinctions of shape and orientation in Tzeltal roots. Paper presented at the annual meeting of the American Anthropological Association, Washington, DC.

In press. Frames of spatial reference and their acquisition in Tenejapan Tzeltal. In L. Nucci, G. Saxe, & E. Turiel (eds.), *Culture, thought, and development*. Mahwah, NJ: Lawrence Erlbaum.

Carey, S. 1978. The child as word learner. In M. Halle, J. Bresnan, & G. A. Miller (eds.), *Linguistic theory and psychological reality*. Cambridge, MA: MIT Press, 264–293.

Choi, S. 1997. Language-specific input and early semantic development: evidence from children learning Korean. In D. I. Slobin (ed.), *The crosslinguistic study of language acquisition*, vol. 5: *Expanding the contexts*. Mahwah, NJ: Lawrence Erlbaum, 41–133.

Choi, S., & M. Bowerman. 1991. Learning to express motion events in English and Korean: the influence of language-specific lexicalization patterns. *Cognition* 41: 83–121.

Clark, E. V. 1973. What's in a word? On the child's acquisition of semantics in his first language. In T. E. Moore (ed.), *Cognitive development and the acquisition of language*. New York: Academic Press, 65–110.

1980. Here's the *top*: nonlinguistic strategies in the acquisition of orientational terms. *Child Development* 51: 329–338.

1993. *The lexicon in acquisition*. Cambridge: Cambridge University Press.

Clark, H. H. 1973. Space, time, semantics, and the child. In T. E. Moore (ed.), *Cognitive development and the acquisition of language*. New York: Academic Press, 27–63.

de León, L. 1994. Exploration in the acquisition of geocentric location by Tzotzil children. *Linguistics* 32: 857–884.

1997. Vertical path in Tzotzil (Mayan) early acquisition: linguistic vs. cognitive determinants. In E. V. Clark (ed.), *The proceedings of the 28th Annual Child Language Research Forum*. Stanford, CA: Center for the Study of Language and Information, 183–197.

1999a. Verb roots and caregiver speech in early Tzotzil acquisition. In B. A. Fox, D. Jurafsky, & L. A. Michaelis (eds.), *Cognition and function in language*. Stanford, CA: Center for the Study of Language and Information, 99–119.

1999b. Verbs in Tzotzil early syntactic development. *International Journal of Bilingualism* 3: 219–240.

Gentner, D. 1978. On relational meaning: the acquisition of verb meaning. *Child Development* 49: 988–998.

1982. Why nouns are learned before verbs: linguistic relativity versus natural partitioning. In S. A. Kuczaj II (ed.), *Language development*, vol. 2: *Language, thought, and culture*. Hillsdale, NJ: Lawrence Erlbaum, 301–334.

1988. Cognitive and linguistic determinism: object reference and relational reference. Paper presented at the Boston Child Language Conference, Boston, MA, November.

Golinkoff, R. M., K. Hirsh-Pasek, C. B. Mervis, W. B. Frawley, & M.Parillo. 1995. Lexical principles can be extended to the acquisition of verbs. In M. Tomasello & W. E. Merriman 1995, 185–222.

Golinkoff, R. M., C. B. Mervis, & K. Hirsh-Pasek. 1994. Early object labels: the case for lexical principles. *Journal of Child Language* 21: 185–215.

Haviland, J. B. 1994a. "Te xa setel xulem" (The buzzards were circling): categories of verbal roots in (Zinacantec) Tzotzil. *Linguistics* 32: 691–742.

1994b. Verbs and shapes in (Zinacantec) Tzotzil: the case of "insert." *Función* (University of Guadalajara) 15–16: 83–117.

Hollebrandse, B., & A. van Hout. 1994. Light verb learning in Dutch. In *Papers from the Dutch–German Colloquium on Language Acquisition.* Amsterdam Series in Child Language Development, 3. Groningen: University of Groningen.

Johnston, J. R., & D. I. Slobin. 1979. The development of locative expressions in English, Italian, Serbo-Croatian and Turkish. *Journal of Child Language* 6: 529–545.

Keil, F., & J. J. Carroll. 1980. The child's acquisition of "tall": implications for an alternative view of semantic development. *Papers and Reports on Child Language Development* 19: 21–28.

Landau, B., & R. Jackendoff. 1993. "What" and "where" in spatial language and spatial cognition. *Behavioral and Brain Sciences* 16: 217–238.

Levinson, S. C. 1996. Frames of reference and Molyneux's question: crosslinguistic evidence. In P. Bloom, M. A. Peterson, L. Nadel, & M. F. Garrett (eds.), *Language and space*. Cambridge, MA: MIT Press, 109–169.

Lucy, J. 1992. *Grammatical categories and cognition: a case study of the linguistic relativity hypothesis*. Cambridge: Cambridge University Press.

Miller, G. A., & P. N. Johnson-Laird. 1976. *Language and perception*. Cambridge, MA: Harvard University Press.

Nelson, K. 1974. Concept, word, and sentence: interrelations in acquisition and development. *Psychological Review* 81: 267–285.

1996. *Language in cognitive development: the emergence of the mediated mind.* Cambridge: Cambridge University Press.

Ninio, A. 1999. Pathbreaking verbs in syntactic development and the question of prototypical transitivity. *Journal of Child Language* 26: 619–653.

Pfeiler, B., & E. Martín Briceño. 1997. Early verb inflection in Yucatec Maya. *Papers and Studies in Contrastive Linguistics* 33: 117–125.

Piaget, J., & B. Inhelder. 1967 [1948]. *The child's conception of space*. New York: Norton.

Piaget, J., B. Inhelder, & A. Szeminska. 1960. *The child's conception of geometry*. London: Routledge & Kegan Paul.

Pye, C. 1992. The acquisition of K'iche' Maya. In D. I. Slobin (ed.), *The crosslinguistic study of language acquisition*, vol. 3. Hillsdale, NJ: Lawrence Erlbaum, 221–308.

Rosch, E. 1978. Principles of categorization. In E. Rosch & B. B. Lloyd (eds.), *Cognition and categorization*. Hillsdale, NJ: Lawrence Erlbaum, 28–46.

Slobin, D. I. 1985. Crosslinguistic evidence for the Language-Making Capacity. In

D. I. Slobin (ed.), *The crosslinguistic study of language acquisition*, vol. 2: *Theoretical issues.* Hillsdale, NJ: Lawrence Erlbaum, 1157–1249.

Stross, B. 1969. Language acquisition by Tenejapa Tzeltal children. Unpublished doctoral dissertation, University of California at Berkeley.

Talmy, L. 1985. Lexicalization patterns: semantic structure in lexical form. In T. Shopen (ed.), *Language typology and syntactic description*, vol. 3: *Grammatical categories and the lexicon*. Cambridge: Cambridge University Press, 36–149.

Tomasello, M. 1992. *First verbs: a case study of early grammatical development*. Cambridge: Cambridge University Press.

Tomasello, M., & P. J. Brooks. 1999. Early syntactic development: a construction grammar approach. In M. Barrett (ed.), *The development of language*. Hove: Psychology Press, 161–190.

Tomasello, M., & W. E. Merriman (eds.). 1995. *Beyond names for things: young children's acquisition of verbs.* Hillsdale, NJ/Hove: Lawrence Erlbaum.

18 Finding the richest path: language and cognition in the acquisition of verticality in Tzotzil (Mayan)

Lourdes de León

CIESAS-Sureste (Center for Research and Higher Studies in Social Anthropology), San Cristobal de las Casas, Chiapas, Mexico

1 Introduction

Up and *down* are among the earliest words used by English-speaking children: already at the one-word stage they are extended to many events involving motion on the vertical axis. The early use and rapid generalization of these words have been attributed to children's reliance on spatial concepts that have already been established in nonlinguistic cognition. By hypothesis, children map the words directly to preexisting notions of vertical motion UP and DOWN (Bloom 1973; H. H. Clark 1973; Nelson 1974; McCune-Nicolich 1981; see Choi & Bowerman 1991, for discussion).

Tzotzil[1] provides the verbs *muy* 'ascend,' *yal* 'descend,' and the directional forms *muyel* 'upward' and *yalel* 'downward.' But when Lupa, a 19-month-old Tzotzil Mayan girl, talks about vertical motion she does not use them. When she wants to be picked up she uses the verbs

pet! 'hold in arms,' or
kuch! 'hold on back,'

depending on whether she just wants to be held for a short time in her mother's arms or to sleep or rest on her mother's back. In a similar situation English-speaking children of the same age typically say *up!* When Lupa wants her mother to adopt a lower position so as to nurse her she tells her

kej! 'kneel,'

and when she wants her playmate to sit down beside her she uses the Baby Talk verb

pepex! 'sit down.'

In these situations English-speaking children of her age routinely say *down!*

If English-speaking children's choice of *up* and *down* in such situations is driven by their analysis of the events as involving vertical motion, and their understanding that these words encode vertical motion, why does Lupa not use the equivalent Tzotzil words?

The present chapter suggests that the expression of vertical path *per se* is not an early concern for Tzotzil children. It evaluates the acquisition of path in relation to spatial cognitive determinants, the typological properties of the language being learned, and the language-specific meanings of spatial words. The research is based on a longitudinal study of three Tzotzil children, with supplementary data from a fourth child.

I will start with a brief review of research on the development of spatial language and previous crosslinguistic findings regarding the acquisition of path. Tzotzil's resources for expressing path will be sketched briefly. This is followed by a section on how vertical motion is expressed in early one- and two-word utterances in Tzotzil. The Tzotzil data will be used to evaluate the possible influence of a nonlinguistic notion of vertical motion against typological and language-specific determinants of language acquisition.

2 Cognition and language in the acquisition of path

Since the early seventies, theorists who approach language acquisition from a *cognitive* perspective have postulated that universal cognitive biases are at work in the acquisition of spatial language. According to this view, spatial notions such as containment, support, contact, and vertical motion are established first, and guide the acquisition of words like *in*, *on*, *up*, and *down* (E. V. Clark 1973a, b; H. H. Clark 1973; Johnston & Slobin 1979; Slobin 1985; Sinha, Thorseng, Hayashi, & Plunkett 1994). Of the basic spatial notions, verticality and an associated notion of gravity have been proposed as candidate semantic primitives, associated with innate perceptual processing mechanisms (H. H. Clark 1973).

More recently, theorists taking a more *language-oriented* approach have asked how allegedly universal spatial concepts are reflected in language, and how they interact with language-specific patterns in the course of acquisition. In particular, they have begun to investigate typological features of the language being learned, such as where and how in the grammar spatial notions are encoded – e.g. in closed-class or open-class morphemes? In relatively "pure" form or conflated [combined] with information about the identity of moving or located objects and their reference points? – and to ask how such differences affect the acquisition of spatial language. For typologically minded acquisition researchers, Talmy's (1985, 1991) typology of the way languages lexicalize meanings to do with motion and path has provided a useful starting point.

According to Talmy, "motion events" can be analyzed as involving a moving object (the *Figure*), a reference object (the *Ground*), and the trajectory of the figure with respect to the ground (the *Path*). Additional information about manner or cause may also be given. Path is lexicalized differently across languages. In "verb-framed" languages, it is typically encoded in the main verb of a clause, along with the fact of motion; cf. Spanish *subir* 'ascend,' *bajar* 'descend,' *entrar* 'enter,' *salir* 'exit.' Information about the manner or cause of the motion, if provided, is encoded in a separate adverbial, e.g. *salir corriendo* 'exit running.' In "satellite-framed" languages, in contrast, path is characteristically encoded with closed-class forms such as affixes on the verb or particles; cf. English *up*, *down*, *in*, *out*, *on*, and *off*. The main verb expresses the fact of motion along with information about manner or cause, as in English *run in*, *fly up*, *jump off*.

In a pioneering study, Choi & Bowerman (1991) compared the development of path in children acquiring a verb-framed language – Korean – and a satellite-framed language – English. They showed that the typological difference in where the two languages encode path was associated with differences in children's expression of paths; that is, nonlinguistic spatial concepts of, say, motion "up" or "down" the vertical axis, or of "containment," do not override language-specific ways of lexicalizing such concepts. In particular, Choi & Bowerman found that English-speaking children use path particles like *up*, *down*, and *in* from early on for vertical motion and containment, abstracted away from the particulars of the figure and ground objects. Korean children, in contrast, first learn semantically specific verbs that conflate information about path with information about figure and ground; only later do they learn path verbs comparable to 'ascend,' 'descend,' and 'enter,' and they do not overgeneralize verbs for vertical motion to motions that are conventionally expressed with semantically more specific verbs. In further crosslinguistic work with children learning English, Japanese, and Danish, Sinha *et al.* (1994:82) concluded that words expressing vertical motion will be among the earliest spatial forms learned provided that they are encoded with closed-class "basic morphemes" (although see Slobin, ch. 14 of this volume, for a critique of the open- and closed-class distinction). Recent typological investigations thus challenge the primacy of nonlinguistic spatial cognition, and show that language-specific patterns influence the child from the beginning (Bowerman 1989, 1993, 1996a, b; Berman & Slobin 1994; Choi & Gopnik 1995; de León 1995, 1996, 1997, 1999b; Bowerman, de León, & Choi 1995; Gopnik & Choi 1995).

Table 18.1. *Semantically specific path verbs in Tzotzil*

Insertion	*tik'*	'insert loosely'
	xoj	'put pole in ring/ring on pole'
	paj	'insert with force'
Extraction	*tas*	'take out of container'
	mas	'take off of liquid'
	botz'	'pull out/off'
Gravity	*p'aj*	'fall vertically from height' (e.g. off cliff, table)
	lom	'topple over,' of vertical figure (e.g. tree, lamp-post)
	jach'	'slip and fall on base' (e.g. person on mud, ice)
	jin	'fall over / roll down' (e.g. chair, pot, pile of rocks)

3 Tzotzil language-specific patterns and the cognitive predictions

Tzotzil does not fall neatly into Talmy's typology, but combines features of both verb-framed and satellite-framed languages (Bowerman *et al.* 1995; de León 1996, 1997), as follows.

(1) In common with "verb-framed languages" Tzotzil has many everyday verbs that conflate path with fact-of-motion. These include a small set of high-frequency intransitive verbs with meanings like 'ascend,' 'descend,' 'enter,' 'exit,' and 'pass.'[2] They also include a large inventory of verb roots that combine path with features such as the shape, geometry, and nature of the attachment or contact between figure and ground (see table 18.1). These latter verbs crosscut categories like containment, support, and attachment,[3] which has led Haviland (1992, 1994a, b) and Brown (1994) to reject notions like these as prelinguistic guides to the acquisition of Tzotzil and the closely related language Tzeltal. In the following, I will call these "semantically specific" path verbs. Semantically specific path verbs of particular relevance for the domain of vertical motion are the "falling" verbs shown in table 18.1.

(2) But Tzotzil also has many characteristics of a "satellite-framed language." In addition to encoding path in verbs, it encodes abstract path notions with directional forms that are historically derived from intransitive motion verbs.[4] These are shown in table 18.2, along with the intransitive verbs from which they are derived.

Table 18.2. *English path particles and Tzotzil motion verbs and directionals (*Intr.: *Intransitive verb;* Tr.: *Transitive verb)*

English	Tzotzil			
	intr.	tr.	directional	gloss
in	*och*	*otes*	*ochel*	'enter'
out	*lok'*	*lok'es, lok'*	*lok'el*	'exit, off, remove'
up	*muy*	*muyes*	*muyel*	'ascend'
down	*yal*	*yales*	*yalel*	'descend'

Although directionals are not grammatically obligatory, they combine freely with virtually any predicate (Haviland 1991). For instance, much like English path particles they combine with verbs expressing manner or cause in a pattern characteristic of satellite-framed languages, as shown in the following examples:[5]

pit' ochel 'jump in'
jip lok'el 'throw out'
xuj muyel 'push up'

Directionals can also occur with path-conflating verbs, redundantly adding a path meaning similar to the one conveyed by the main verb. Thus, in the next two examples both the verb and the directional encode path involving a topological relation, while in the subsequent two examples both the verb and the directional encode vertical path:

botz' lok'el 'pull.off removing'
tik' ochel 'insert.loosely in'
p'aj yalel 'fall.from.height down'
sol yalel 'fall.down down' (of clothing, e.g. pants, skirt).

Directionals can also combine with stative predicates:

tz'ukul yalel 'falling head down' (be upside-down downwards)
latzal muyel 'stacked up' (having been stacked up, e.g. stack of bricks).

From a typological perspective, then, Mayan directionals share the following semantic and functional features with Germanic path particles:

- they convey abstract notions of trajectory which are systematically encoded by many languages (topological space, vertical axis, etc.; Talmy 1985; Slobin, ch. 14 of this volume);
- they combine with manner or cause verbs in a similar way to satellites (Talmy 1985);
- they are prosodically salient and, due to frequent argument elision in Tzotzil, they often occur in utterance-final position, especially in speech addressed to children.[6]

Given the rich linguistic resources with which Tzotzil encodes path, where will young Tzotzil learners begin? Will they start with the lexical items that belong to a closed class and denote pure path (i.e., with intransitive path verbs or directionals), or will they choose semantically more specific verbs from larger, open-class inventories? On the basis of the existing cognitive and language-typological literature, there are strong grounds for predicting that intransitive path verbs and directionals should predominate. In what follows, I will evaluate the following hypotheses:

1. *Verticality will be expressed very early.* Guided by nonlinguistic spatial notions of verticality and gravity, Tzotzil children might be expected to talk about vertical motion from a very young age.

2. *General motion verbs and/or directionals expressing motion "up" or "down" should appear before semantically specific verbs.* To express the notion of vertical motion, Tzotzil children have the option of using either general motion verbs meaning 'ascend' and 'descend' and directionals meaning 'up' and 'down,' or semantically more specific verbs such as *p'aj* 'fall from height.' Children learning better-studied languages have been observed to show a preference for general-purpose verbs like – in English – *do*, *make*, *get*, and *go*, and for directionals like *up* and *down* (E. V. Clark 1993:29–30). On these grounds we would expect Tzotzil children to choose general verbs and/or directionals for vertical motion and apply them freely across different kinds of contexts. However, this prediction must be tentative, since Choi & Bowerman (1991) observed that the Korean children they studied used semantically specific verbs for events involving vertical motion before they learned the more general verbs for the meanings 'ascend,' 'descend,' 'make-ascend,' and 'make-descend.'

3. *Closed-class forms for spatial notions will be learned earlier than open-class forms.* It has been observed that closed-class forms encoding a given spatial meaning are acquired earlier than open-class forms for the same meaning; among the first spatial closed-class forms to be learned are words for containment, support, and verticality (Sinha *et al.* 1994). Since such notions are encoded by members of both the closed set of Tzotzil intransitive motion verbs and the closed class of directionals, these forms would be expected to appear very early, not only on grounds of their semantic generality (cf. hypothesis 2) but also on grounds that they are closed-class.

4. *What will be learned first is what is sentence-final and stressed.* Children learning Germanic languages have been hypothesized to acquire particles at an early age because they are stressed and often sentence-final, both properties that increase perceptual salience and facilitate acquisition more generally (Slobin 1973; see Bowerman *et al.* 1995:104 for discussion). Tzotzil directionals are perceptually more salient than the verbs they combine with because they receive the main stress of the verb phrase and

often occur sentence-finally. So this is yet another reason for predicting that Tzotzil directionals will be acquired early.[7]

Let us now test these hypotheses against our longitudinal data.

4 Expression of vertical path in four Tzotzil children

The data come from a longitudinal study of two girls (Lupa and Mal), and two boys (Xun and Palas). Lupa's data were collected by video- and audio-taping during weekly three-hour visits over a period of six months when she was 19–25 months old. At the beginning of this period she was producing only one-word utterances; word combinations appeared in the twenty-fourth month. The examples reported here come from a total of around fifty hours of analyzed material.

Data from Mal come from an ongoing study spanning the period from 18 months – when she entered the one-word stage – to 24 months. The investigator is Mal's godmother (as well as Lupa's), and has studied her through periodic in-home visits since the child's birth. The data from this child total about thirty hours of analyzed audiotaped and videotaped material, in addition to personal notes and in-home observations.

Data from Xun and Palas are based on monthly one-hour audio recordings over a period of two years, starting when they were 2 years old and were already producing combinations of three or more words. Videotaped recordings were also made every two to three months. Of these two children I will rely mostly on Xun; data from Palas are used to supplement findings.

Our three main subjects, Lupa, Mal, and Xun, are first children and first grandchildren. They spend more time with adult caregivers and less with younger children than many other Zinacantec youngsters, although they are in constant interaction with cousins and young neighbors. Palas is the fourth child in his family and lives in a compound with six other children, his parents, aunts, uncles, and grandparents.

The data come exclusively from the researcher's notes and recordings. Materials from all the children were transcribed by the researcher and her assistant in consultation with the parents.

4.1 Findings

4.1.1 Overview of early verbs In striking conflict with our hypotheses based on the previous literature, none of our four subjects used directionals before path verbs.[8] From the one-word stage, they produced verb roots, successfully segmenting out the Mayan CVC (consonant-vowel-consonant) bases and pronouncing them in isolation without person or aspect affixes (de Léon 1999a).[9] In a further departure from expectations, they showed a general preference for semantically specific verbs like *p'aj* 'fall vertically from height' and *xoj* 'put pole in ring / ring on pole' over "pure" path verbs such as 'ascend' and 'descend.' They did develop a few pure path verbs at this early stage, including *bat* 'go,' *la* 'come' (imperative form), *och* 'enter,' *lok'*, 'exit,' and *lok'es* 'take out,' but the verbs of greatest interest to us for present purposes – *muy* 'ascend' and *yal* 'descend' – appeared only later, after utterances several words long were common, and they were used very infrequently compared to the earlier-appearing motion verbs.

The Tzotzil children talked about many everyday events involving vertical motion, such as picking up, kneeling down, and falling. But of these events, they initially expressed only falling with verbs that explicitly encode motion and path, albeit admixed with additional semantic information. They made their desire to be picked up known with various "holding" verbs, starting with *kuch* 'support on back,' used as a request to be put on the caregiver's back, followed by *pet* 'hold in arms.' They expressed posture changes and the vertical displacement of entities with so-called "positional" verbs,[10] which include both posture verb roots such as *chot* 'sit,' *kot* 'stand on all fours,' and *nuj* 'face down / upside down' and verb roots having to do with where or how on the vertical axis an object is supported (e.g. *pak'* 'on ground,' *kaj* 'on high surface,' *jok'* 'hanging.' These Tzotzil verb roots of holding, posture, and support do not in themselves encode either motion or path, although a listener can of course infer that motion along a certain path may be involved in initiating situations of holding, posture change, and vertical positioning. In contrast, the English phrasal verbs that are used in comparable situations, such as *pick up*, *sit / lie / kneel down*, *sit / stand up*, and *put up / down*, are composed of a manner component and a satellite that explicitly indicates the relevant direction on the vertical axis. In their preference for semantically specific verbs of falling and for verbs of holding, posture, and support/disposition, the Tzotzil children pattern like the Korean children studied by Choi & Bowerman (1991): in both cases the children home in on verbs specific to events of certain types rather than referring to these events, as English-speaking children do, with words that capture overarching notions of vertical motion "upward" or "downward."[11]

4.1.2 Verbs of ascending and descending Lupa did not use the verb root *muy* 'ascend' until she was relatively old – 25 months and already in the stage of early word combinations. She initially used it to mean both 'ascend' and 'descend' in a vertical line in the restricted context of a child climbing up and sliding down corn bags. Mal also started to use *muy* 'ascend' at 25 months after she was already combining three or more words. Unlike Lupa, Mal generalized it quickly across several contexts, using it productively, e.g. to point out someone climbing up a ladder, when climbing up on a table, and when a boy climbed up on a car roof. However, she used it less frequently than many other verbs that she applied to situations involving directed motion.

Our other two subjects, Xun and Palas, were already producing the verb *yal* 'descend' when they were first observed; they used it to mean 'go downhill.' This use is consistent with one of the meanings of the adult Tzotzil verbs *yal* 'descend / go downhill' and *muy* 'ascend / go uphill.' For these two boys, reference to the local slope of the domestic space seemed to dominate over reference to motion on the vertical axis, such as climbing on a table. Of course, at first observation these boys were already well into word combination (Xun's mean length of utterance was 4.3 morphemes and Palas' was 3.5), so we don't know whether at an earlier stage they might have started out using *yal* 'descend' to refer to motion on a vertical axis, either in a restricted way, like Lupa's *muy* 'ascend,' or generalized across contexts, like Mal's *muy* 'ascend.'

When the verbs *muy* 'ascend' and *yal* 'descend' appeared in the speech of the Tzotzil children, I observed no (over)generalizations to any and all situations involving vertical motion; e.g. the children never use *muy* 'ascend' or *muyes* 'make ascend' as a request to be lifted or to comment on a posture change like sitting up. In contrast, English-speaking children of the same age (16–24 months, period of one-word utterances and early word combinations) quickly generalize the path particles *up* and *down* to all changes of location involving vertical motion, including but not limited to picking up and posture changes (Choi & Bowerman 1991). Table 18.3 illustrates these differences with examples of utterances produced by children learning English and Tzotzil in similar contexts. (The utterances were produced just before, during, or after the events indicated.)

4.1.3 "Falling" verbs: early attention to the effects of gravity Tzotzil has a large collection of verbs for falling events. These encode not only a notion of "effect of gravity" but also a manner component. Among the more frequent in adult speech are *p'aj* 'fall from height,' said of objects falling from a high surface such as a table, cliff, or roof, and *lom* 'topple over,' said of the falling over of vertically oriented objects such as trees, lamp posts, sticks, or a drunken man. *Jach'* 'slip and fall' is applied to animate beings that fall while in motion, while *jin* 'fall over / roll down' is applied to objects that fall from a canonical position, such as a chair, pot, bicycle, or even a pile of rocks. Several of these verbs appear earlier than the pure vertical motion verbs in the speech of our four subjects.

P'aj 'fall from height' is among the first verb roots produced by our two youngest subjects at the one-word stage, suggesting a very early awareness

Table 18.3. *Examples of English and Tzotzil utterances used in similar contexts involving motion, change of location, or change of posture on the vertical axis*

Context	English[a]	Tzotzil[b]
Standing up	*up* (e.g. in crib, car)	*va'al* 'stand upright' (e.g. in corral, on ground) *kot* 'stand on all fours'
Asking adult to lift child up	*up*	*pet* 'hold in arms' *kuch* 'hold on back'
Climbing on raised surface	*up* (e.g. on high chair, counter)	*luch* 'perch on top' (e.g. on tree, bags of corn)
Putting object on raised surface (e.g. table)	*up*	*kaj* 'be located on a raised surface' *pach* 'be located on surface, of bowl'
Putting object on pile of objects	*up*	*busul* 'be on piles'
Asking adult to sit down or kneel down	*down*	*chot* 'sit' *kej* 'kneel'
Setting objects on floor, ground	*down*	*pak'* 'be located on ground carelessly' *vuch* 'be located, of object on sitting base, mouth up' (e.g. bottle)
Describing a person or animal with head down	*down* (looking at doll floating head down in tub)	*nuj* 'be face down / upside down' (describing a child or doll that has her face down) *patal* 'be lying stretched, face down' (describing animal lying face down)

Notes:

[a] English examples are from Bowerman's daughters C and E, as presented in Choi & Bowerman (1991:101–102). Ages in months: 16 to 21. Only those utterances that matched in context with the Tzotzil utterances are included here.

[b] Examples from Tzotzil come from the author's case studies of Lupa in the period of one-word utterances and early word combinations (19–25 months), and Xun in the stage of early word combinations (25–30 months).

of the effects of gravity. The subsequent acquisition of the other "falling" verbs varies from child to child, but it is clear that once *p'aj* 'fall from height' appears, the children already have a sense of the semantic category, and further semantic contrasts emerge within a few months in accordance with the way this semantic domain is organized in Tzotzil. Tables 18.4, 18.5, and 18.6 show the developmental progression of "falling" verbs in Lupa, Xun, and Mal, along with verbs to be discussed in the next section.

4.1.4 Verbs of posture and support The late acquisition of the pure vertical motion verbs *muy* 'ascend,' and *yal* 'descend,' contrasts strikingly with

Table 18.4. *Lupa's early falling, posture, and support verbs*

Age in months	19	20	21	22	23	24	25
FALLING							
'fall from height'	*p'aj*						
'topple over'					*lom*		
'slip and fall'						*jach'*	
POSTURE							
'sit'	*pepex*			*chotol*			
'kneel'	*kej*						
'face down'	*nuj*				*nujp'ij*		
'standing up'		*va'al*					
'standing on all fours'			*kotol*				*xkotet*
'face up'					*javk'uj*		
'flipped over'					*valk'uj*		
'lying face down'							*patal*
SUPPORT							
'on high surface'	*kaj*						
'on ground'			*pak'al*				
'hanging'	*jok'*						
'perched'		*luchul*					
'piled up'				*busul*			
'bowl on surface'						*pach*	
'on base, mouth up'							*vuch*
'hold on back'		*kuch*					
'hold in arms'							*pet*

the early profusion of verbs denoting the posture or support of entities. As noted, these verbs do not, in themselves, encode path or motion, but they were often used to request or comment on changes of posture or location on the vertical axis. The development of verbs of posture and support is shown – along with the falling verbs – in table 18.4 for Lupa, 18.5 for Xun, and 18.6 for Mal. Included in the "support" category in these tables are not only positional roots like *nuj* 'face down / upside down' but also "holding" verbs like *pet* 'hold in arms.' (Empty boxes indicate no production of new forms in that particular month but maintenance of the previously acquired forms, unless otherwise indicated.)

Lupa's positionals lacked inflections, but, as indicated, they incipiently show the derivational morphology (suffixes on the CVC roots) characteristic of positionals. Xun also had some derivational morphology but this is not shown in his table. At the time of the study Mal was still in the one-word stage, with a lexicon of under fifty words. She did not display as wide

Table 18.5. *Xun's early falling, posture, and support verbs*

Age in months	25	26	27	28	29	30
FALLING						
'fall from height'	*p'aj*					
'topple over'						
'slip and fall'					*jach'*	
POSTURE						
'stand on all fours'			*kot*			
'sit'	*pepex*	*chot*				
'stand upright'			*va'*			
'face up'						*jav*
SUPPORT						
'stack'		*latz*				
'on ground'				*pak'*		
'on high surface'				*kaj*		
'hanging'				*jok'*		
'perched'						*noch'*
'hold on back'				*kuch*		
'hold in arms'		*pet*				

Table 18.6. *Mal's early falling, posture, and support verbs*

Age in months	18	19	20	21	22	23	24
FALLING							
'fall from height'	*p'aj*						
'fall over/roll down'				*jin*			
'slip and fall'					*jach'*		
POSTURE							
'sit'		*pepex*					
'face down'					*nuj*		
'stand on all fours'				*kot*			*kotol*
'face up'					*javk'uj*		
SUPPORT							
'on high surface'							*kaj*
'hanging'							*jok'*
'on base/mouth up'							*vuch*
'hold on back'	*kuch*						
'hold in arms'				*pet*			

a range of lexical contrasts in her positional verbs as Lupa and Xun did, but she already had a set of positional roots with contrasting meanings such as 'sit' vs. 'stand on all fours,' and '(be) face down' vs. '(be) face up.' Her most frequent verbs at this stage were *pepex* 'sit,' *kaj* '(be) on high surface,' and *kuch* 'support / hold on back.' She used this latter verb when she wanted to be lifted up and held by a caregiver. She used *kaj* '(be) on high surface' quite frequently and productively to contrast objects located on a high surface (table, board over fire, roof) with objects located on the ground.

Some uses of positional verbs by Lupa in the period of one-word utterances and early word combinations are shown in table 18.7. (The utterances were produced just before, during, or after the events indicated.) A close look at these uses, and at the inventory of Lupa's, Xun's, and Mal's early posture and support verb roots shown in tables 18.4, 18.5, and 18.6, reveals an early attention by Tzotzil learners to canonical position, fine anatomical contrasts, and the shape and geometry of figure and ground, and these meaning distinctions are consistent with the semantic categories of adult Tzotzil.

For example, the early use of posture verbs by these children shows sensitivity to the main axes of objects and their canonical orientations. This sensitivity may be driven by an early visual orientation to a main axis (Landau & Jackendoff 1993; Landau 1996), but such a nonlinguistic predisposition is not in itself enough: it cannot account for the way our subjects further discriminated according to the precise semantics of Tzotzil positional verbs. From the very beginning, they used posture verbs appropriately to draw distinctions between lying 'face up,' 'mouth up,' 'belly down,' 'down with stretched limbs,' 'on one's side,' and so on. In addition to early attention to posture and orientation, the children showed awareness of where and how an object is located on the vertical axis (e.g. on the ground vs. on a raised surface, hanging, perched, etc.). Here again the children paid close attention to just those distinctions that are central to Tzotzil positional verb semantics.

To summarize, the Tzotzil children acquired semantically specific path verbs before they acquired either general verbs for expressing motion along a vertical path or their associated directionals, and they referred to many events involving vertical motion with positional verbs that encode fine details of the posture and static vertical location of objects, but not their motion or path. Once the children learned the general verbs meaning 'ascend' and 'descend' they did not generalize them across a wide range of situations involving vertical motion, and in this they contrast sharply with English-speaking children, who use *up* and *down* from a young age for essentially any event involving an upward or downward motion. These patterns

Table 18.7. *Contexts of use of posture and location verbs by Lupa*

Verb	Context
Posture	
pepex (Baby Talk) 'sit down' (19)	asking people to sit beside her, describing people and dolls sitting
chotol 'be in sitting position' (22)	describing people and dolls sitting
va'al 'be in standing position' (20)	after standing up two spools of thread, after standing doll
nuj 'be face down / upside down' (20)	describing a child's posture on ground, and doll facing down
valk'uj 'flip over' (23)	describing a child's sudden change of posture
javk'uj 'be located with belly up' (23)	describing a child's sudden change of posture, a doll lying face up
patal 'be lying stretched out, face down' (25)	describing dog, cat, toy, lying face down with stretched limbs
Location	
(i) High/low placement	
kaj 'be located on raised surface' (19)	asking for ring, bag to be placed on table
pak'al 'be lying on ground, carelessly' (21)	describing objects lying on the ground such as cloth, bag, coin
(ii) Canonical orientation	
pach 'be located on surface, of bowl' (24)	asking for bowl of soup or beans to be placed on table
vuchul 'be located, of object sitting on base, mouth up' (e.g. bottle, jar) (25)	describing a container of powdered soap, a clay pot standing on ground
(iii) Form of attachment	
luchul 'be perched on top' (20)	describing person/object perched on top of base: e.g. bird on tree, girl on top of piles of corn bags, two spools on top of each other
jok' 'hang' (19)	asking for help in hanging a cloth from a branch, and a balloon from a ceiling lamp
(iv) Arrangement	
busul 'be piled up' (22)	describing multiple objects piled up on a surface: beans, stones, small toys

Note: Numbers in parentheses refer to age in months.

clearly reveal the power of language-specific determinants over purely cognitive ones to guide the acquisition of spatial words and shape semantic categories in the domain of vertical motion; cultural factors may, however, play a role as well.[12]

5 Discussion

Let us now return to the hypotheses that were posed earlier in this chapter.

1. *Verticality will be expressed very early.* Tzotzil children do show an early awareness of gravity and of change of posture and location on the vertical axis, but they do not express verticality *per se* at an early stage. Their earliest forms encoding verticality are for events involving nonvolitional downward motion, i.e. falling. These forms do not express downward motion in "pure" form, but conflate it with distinctions both of manner (e.g. slipping) and of figure and ground (e.g. figure is vertically oriented; figure falls off a raised ground). Volitional motion upward and downward is not expressed until much later. Many events involving upward or downward motion are communicated with verbs that do not in themselves encode either motion or path, but instead pick out situations of holding, being in a certain posture, or being located up high or on the ground.

2. *General motion verbs and/or directionals expressing motion "up" or "down" should appear before semantically specific verbs.* This hypothesis is clearly refuted by the data. Tzotzil children do not express vertical path with "pure" motion verbs or directionals until long after they have acquired a rich repertoire of semantically specific verbs. This finding is consistent with both Choi & Bowerman's (1991) finding that verbs meaning 'ascend' and 'descend' are acquired late by Korean children, and with Bowerman *et al.*'s (1995) finding, based on a developmental crosslinguistic study of the expression of topological spatial actions, that Tzotzil children do not use the directional form meaning 'in' before they acquire a set of semantically more specific path verbs for topological actions. In general, then, Tzotzil learners show an early preference for semantically "*rich*" as opposed to "*lean*" path markers – i.e. for forms that encode path along with a variety of other semantic distinctions rather than path alone (Bowerman *et al.* 1995; de León 1996, 1997; see also Brown, ch. 17 of this volume, for evidence that children learning Tzeltal Mayan also show an early preference for semantically rich – i.e. specific – verb roots).

This is quite a striking finding. Recall that although Tzotzil has many path-conflating verbs, it also offers the option of combining directionals meaning 'up,' 'down,' 'in,' etc., with manner verbs in a way quite analogous to the characteristic pattern of satellite-framed languages like English. (In contrast, this is not an option available to Korean children.) It has often been assumed that the early acquisition and frequent use of path particles by children learning English is due to a combination of the cognitive accessibility of path meanings and the perceptual salience of the particles, which are stressed and often utterance-final. But the present findings cast doubt on these assumptions: given the choice between, e.g. *(p'aj) yalel* '(fall from height) down' and *p'aj* 'fall from height,' Tzotzil children bypass the directionals of their language and home in instead on semantically more specific verbs.

3. *Closed-class forms for spatial notions will be learned earlier than open-class forms.* This hypothesis is clearly not supported. Tzotzil directionals constitute a closed class, smaller than the set of verbs from which they are derived (i.e. some of the verbs of the larger set do not yield directionals), but they are acquired rather late, well after their verb counterparts. And this is true not only of directionals that express vertical paths, as shown in the present study, but also of those that express topological paths (de León 1996). In general, the bias of Tzotzil learners towards *semantically rich path markers* seems to override any bias they might have for closed-class forms.[13]

4. *What will be learned first is what is sentence-final and stressed.* This hypothesis also fails to find support in the Tzotzil data: directionals are ordinarily both sentence-final and stressed, but they are not produced until relatively late – at the multi-word utterance stage. The Tzotzil children's preference for semantically "rich" – i.e. specific – forms over directionals thus goes counter not only to the predicted priority of closed-class forms, but also to the predicted dominance of perceptually favored forms. (See also Brown 1996a, who argues that the early production of verb roots by children learning Tzeltal, Tzotzil's sister language, may be driven by semantic rather than prosodic factors.)

This chapter has examined the roles of language and cognition in the way children talk about vertical path in Tzotzil. In earlier crosslinguistic work, my colleagues and I had found that the acquisition of words for motions that result in a topological relation such as containment is influenced both by an early cognitive preoccupation with topological relations and by the specific way in which these spatial meanings are semantically structured in the language being learned (Bowerman *et al.* 1995; de León 1996). A comparable cognitive bias seems to motivate children to express the effects of gravity from a very young age (cf. the early acquisition of verbs for nonvolitional events of falling), but there is no evidence for a more general drive to express upward and downward motion *per se*; e.g. the children were relatively slow to talk about volitional motion "up" or "down" the vertical axis. Verticality does seem to be an early preoccupation in and of itself, but only in connection with the static location of entities on the vertical axis (e.g.

high, low, hanging . . .), and their orientation with respect to verticality (e.g. lying down, standing . . .). This preoccupation is consistent with the semantics of the Tzotzil posture and location verbs, which clearly guide these Mayan youngsters from the very beginning.

The early use of different kinds of "falling" verbs reveals a bias for expressing path conflated with information about manner and about the figure and ground objects. This bias was also apparent in our earlier studies of the expression of topological relations, and it characterizes not only Tzotzil but also Korean children; it contrasts sharply with the approach of children learning English, who orient from the beginning towards path forms that abstract away from manner, figure, and ground. The many similarities in the way the early verbs of Tzotzil and Korean children semantically package meanings to do with motion, path, verticality, and topology may reveal the influence of typological factors on semantic development. And this suggests that the interaction between cognition and semantic development is more subtle than has long been thought: rather than exerting its influence directly on the acquisition of word meaning, cognition may interact with the typological patterns with which languages lexicalize meaning, along the lines of the "typological bootstrapping" hypothesis put forward in this volume by Slobin.

NOTES

Research for this study was supported by NSF Grant # SBR-9222394, awarded to the author together with John B. Haviland. I thank Stephen Levinson and Melissa Bowerman for a most rewarding conference. I am grateful to Melissa Bowerman, Penny Brown, John B. Haviland, and Stephen Levinson for their careful reading of an earlier version and their valuable comments. I also acknowledge inspiration and feedback from Melissa Bowerman, Soonja Choi, and Dan Slobin. Any misconceptions or errors are entirely my own responsibility. Special thanks go to my *compadre* Xun, who also served as my faithful assistant, and to my beloved goddaughters Lupa and Mal. A shorter version of this chapter appears in de León (1997a).

1 Tzotzil is a Mayan language spoken in the highlands of Chiapas by about 300,000 speakers. It is a morphologically ergative VOS language with relatively few lexical roots but with a high degree of morphological word derivation. Data for this study were obtained in the hamlet of Nabenchauk, Zinacantan. For a grammatical description of Tzotzil see Haviland (1981) and Aissen (1987).

2 Tzotzil verbs denoting UP and DOWN refer also to motion on a slope and to East (abstractly UP) and West (abstractly DOWN) (de León 1994, 1995). The closely related language Tzeltal has a similar system, although in this case UP is associated with South and DOWN with North (see Brown & Levinson 1993; and Brown, ch. 17 of this volume, who terms the geocentric system of spatial reference "Absolute"). According to Brown (this volume), the vertical axis and inclined plane meanings are not clearly distinct senses in Tzeltal, but Tzotzil speakers do distinguish between them: when they are using the UP/DOWN verbs

to refer to motion up or down a slope, they normally also use the relational nouns *ak'ol* 'uphill' or *'olon* 'downhill.' Tzotzil children acquire the Absolute (East/West) frame of reference by around age 9 (de León 1994, 1995); it apparently evolves developmentally from a frame of reference that is anchored to the local slope of the land.

3 A good example is the root *xoj*, roughly, 'impale,' which is used for putting both a ring-like figure 'onto' a pole-like ground and a pole-like figure 'into' a ring-like ground. This verb is used, for instance, to refer to putting a bead on a string and a coil on a peg ('ring on pole'), and for inserting limbs into sleeves or trouser legs, head into sweater neck, and threading a needle ('pole in ring').

4 Directionals result from a grammaticalization process common across Mayan languages, where members of closed classes of "bleached" motion verbs denote schematic trajectories, and combine freely with any verb. The degree of grammaticalization of such motion verbs varies across the family, but the resulting forms consistently encode schematic path meanings (Haviland 1991, 1993; Craig 1993; Zavala 1993). For example, Pye (1992:234) says that directionals in K'iche' Mayan "are semantically similar to adverbial particles of location or motion (up, down, away) found in English and other Germanic languages."

5 In combination with manner verbs, many Tzotzil directionals express "boundary-crossing" (path across a border), a feature of path satellites more generally, as proposed by Slobin & Hoiting (1994). In general, verb-framed languages seem to allow manner-of-motion verbs as main verbs as long as there is no border crossing. Thus we have in Spanish *corrió a/hasta la casa* 'he ran to the house,' but *entró corriendo a/en la casa* 'he entered to/in the house, running'), with an adverbial form of *correr* 'run.' According to Dan Slobin (p.c.) what is at issue is whether one focuses on arrival at a location or on the path across the boundary. I am indebted to him for drawing this point to my attention.

6 These forms are frequent in adult speech to children, especially the deictics 'hither/thither,' 'up/down,' and topological directionals. In a sample of 100 utterances to a 2-year-old there were about 25 directionals, including *tik'o ochel* 'insert in' (asking child to put key in lock), *tik'o yalel* 'insert downwards' (asking child to insert peach through a hole in a broken brick), *nit'o muyel* 'pull upwards' (asking child to roll up godmother's socks), *meso ech'el* 'sweep away' (asking child to sweep away dust), and *ilok' tal* 'it has exited hither' (talking about a mouse running out of the house towards the speaker and child).

7 In K'iche' Mayan, directionals are among the earliest forms acquired, according to Pye; Pye (1992:261) proposes that this is due to their high perceptual saliency.

8 The deictic directional *tal* 'come' is an exception: it appears in the data relatively early. However, it does not seem to be productive at this stage, but appears only in amalgams with a small number of verbs.

9 This pattern differs from that shown by children learning K'iche' Mayan, who often isolate syllables consisting of the final consonant of the verb root plus a suffix (Pye 1983). However, it is consistent with the pattern observed by Brown (1996a) for her Tzeltal Mayan child subjects. Brown (1996b) attributes her subjects' ability to home in on the CVC root mainly to discourse factors; in particular, Tzeltal adults often repeat the verb. A look at the Tzotzil input to children younger than 2 suggests that, although conversational factors may

play a role, there may be other factors at work as well. Long before children can interact conversationally, they are exposed to child-directed speech in which the root is often produced in the relatively transparent utterance-final position, or in syntactic frames that remain constant while the root varies (de León 1998, 1999a).

10 Positional roots are an important class of verb roots with a specific derivational morphology in Mayan languages, where they play a central role in conveying location. They range over several notional domains, encoding shape, geometry, position and collocation, surface, material, and visual appearance (Haviland 1994a:727). In Tzotzil they constitute about 30% of the verbal raw material (Haviland 1992, 1994a, b). See Brown (1994) on Tzeltal positional roots.

11 An obvious objection to the claim that the spatial semantic categories of children learning Tzotzil and Korean are more specific than those of children learning English is that children learning English perhaps also initially use *up* and *down* for specific events without (implicitly) recognizing that these events share "upward" or "downward" motion; e.g. *up* could be represented in the child's lexicon as a set of independent homonyms meaning 'pick up,' 'stand up,' 'put up,' etc. In this case the semantic categories of learners of English and Tzotzil would look very similar. Choi & Bowerman (1991) explicitly consider what they term the "homonym" hypothesis and reject it, arguing among other things that "once particular spatial words emerge in [English-speaking] children's speech they often spread rapidly to new uses, which supports the intuition that [these uses] are interrelated" (113). A second objection might be that English-speaking children often hear the words *up* and *down* in connection with changes of posture and position, while Tzotzil-speaking children do not encounter pure path forms like the directionals *muyel* 'up' and *yalel* 'down' in these contexts. In fact, however, adult Tzotzil speakers often use *muyel* and *yalel* in combination with posture or holding verbs, e.g. a mother might ask someone to lower or raise her child to her for nursing by saying *peto yalel*/*muyel* 'hold it down/up.'

12 To judge from examples in Choi & Bowerman (1991), there is a high frequency of actions involving motion or change of location on the vertical axis in the everyday lives of middle-class American children. These actions are associated with the design of the domestic space, e.g. the use of high chairs, high tables, car seats, and playground equipment. Life in Tzotzil domestic space is spent closer to the ground: women kneel on the ground instead of sitting on chairs, and they spend a lot of time in this position while they weave, cook, spin, and so on. Young children's main options for vertical position are to be on their mother's backs, on the ground or a mat, or sitting on a very low chair.

13 Slobin (ch. 14 of this volume) has challenged the assumption that there is a strict dichotomy between open and closed classes, arguing that open- / closedness should be seen instead as a relative, i.e. graded notion. In line with this proposal, he suggests that verbs in a language often form subsets that are relatively "closed": e.g. languages may easily add new manner verbs, but they do not easily add new path-conflating verbs to the set with forms comparable to 'enter,' 'exit,' 'ascend,' and 'descend.' Many, though not all, of the Tzotzil children's early verbs come from sets that in Slobin's sense are relatively closed: these include, for instance, the verbs of holding, posture, and support. Possibly, then, hypotheses about the rela-

tive ease of learning open- versus closed-class forms could be refined and made more cogent by conceptualizing the distinction in more relative terms.

REFERENCES

Aissen, J. A. 1987. *Tzotzil clause structure*. Boston: D. Reidel.

Berman, R. A., & D. I. Slobin. 1994. *Relating events in narrative: a crosslinguistic developmental study*. Hillsdale, NJ: Lawrence Erlbaum.

Bloom, L. 1973. *One word at a time: the use of single word utterances before syntax*. The Hague: Mouton.

Bowerman, M. 1989. Learning a semantic system: what role do cognitive predispositions play? In M. L. Rice & R. L. Schiefelbusch (eds.), *The teachability of language*. Baltimore, MD: Paul H. Brookes, 133–169.

1993. Typological perspectives on language acquisition: do crosslinguistic patterns predict development? In E. V. Clark (ed.), *The proceedings of the 25th Annual Child Language Research Forum*. Stanford, CA: Center for the Study of Language and Information, 7–15.

1996a. The origins of children's spatial semantic categories: cognitive versus linguistic determinants. In J. J. Gumperz & S. C. Levinson (eds.), *Rethinking linguistic relativity*. Cambridge: Cambridge University Press, 145–176.

1996b. Learning how to structure space for language: a crosslinguistic perspective. In P. Bloom, M. A. Peterson, L. Nadel, & M. F. Garrett (eds.), *Language and space*. Cambridge, MA: MIT Press, 385–436.

Bowerman, M., L. de León, & S. Choi. 1995. Verbs, particles, and spatial semantics: learning to talk about spatial actions in typologically different languages. In E. V. Clark (ed.), *The proceedings of the 27th Annual Child Language Research Forum*. Stanford, CA: Center for the Study of Language and Information, 101–110.

Brown, P. 1994. The INs and ONs of Tzeltal locative expressions: the semantics of static descriptions of location. *Linguistics* 32: 743–790.

1996a. Isolating the CVC root in Tzeltal Mayan: a study of children's first verbs. In E. Clark (ed.), *The proceedings of the 28th Annual Child Language Research Forum*. Stanford, CA: Center for the Study of Language and Information, 41–52.

1996b. The conversational context for language acquisition: a Tzeltal (Mayan) case study. Keynote address at the 1996 International Pragmatics Association meetings, Mexico City, July.

Brown, P., & S. Levinson. 1993. "Uphill" and "Downhill" in Tzeltal. *Journal of Linguistic Anthropology* 3: 46–74.

Choi, S., & M. Bowerman. 1991. Learning to express motion events in English and Korean: the influence of language-specific lexicalization patterns. *Cognition* 41: 83–121.

Choi, S., & A. Gopnik. 1995. Early acquisition of verbs in Korean: a cross-linguistic study. *Journal of Child Language* 22: 497–529.

Clark, E. V. 1973a. Nonlinguistic strategies and the acquisition of word meanings. *Cognition* 2: 161–182.

1973b. What's in a word? On the child's acquisition of semantics in his first language. In T. E. Moore (ed.), *Cognitive development and the acquisition of language*. New York: Academic Press, 65–110.

1993. *The lexicon in acquisition*. Cambridge: Cambridge University Press.
Clark, H. H. 1973. Space, time, semantics, and the child. In T. E. Moore (ed.), *Cognitive development and the acquisition of language*. New York: Academic Press, 27–63.
Craig, C. G. 1993. Jakaltek directionals: their meaning and discourse function. *Languages of the World* 7: 23–36.
de León, L. 1994. Exploration in the acquisition of geocentric location by Tzotzil children. *Linguistics* 32: 857–884.
1995. The development of geocentric location in young speakers of Guugu Yimithirr. *Working Paper 33*. Nijmegen, The Netherlands: Cognitive Anthropology Research Group, Max Planck Institute for Psycholinguistics.
1996. The expression of motion in early Tzotzil (Mayan): the role of cognitive versus linguistic factors. Paper presented at the 7th International Congress for the Study of Child Language, Istanbul, July.
1997. Vertical path in Tzotzil (Mayan) acquisition: cognitive vs. linguistic determinants. In E. V. Clark (ed.), *The proceedings of the 28th Annnual Child Language Research Forum*. Stanford, CA: Center for the Study of Language and Information, 183–197.
1998. Raices verbales tempranas en tzotzil: *input* materno vs. restricciones cognoscitivas. *Función* (University of Guadalajara) 17–18: 147–174.
1999a. Verb roots and caregiver speech in early Tzotzil acquisition. In B. A. Fox, D. Jurafsky, & L. A. Michaelis (eds.), *Cognition and function in language*. Stanford, CA: Stanford University Center for Language and Information 99–119.
1999b. Verbs in Tzotzil early syntactic development. *International Journal of Bilingualism* 3: 219–240.
Gopnik, A., & S. Choi. 1995. Names, relational words, and cognitive development in English and Korean speakers: nouns are not always learned before verbs. In M. Tomasello & W. E. Merriman (eds.), *Beyond names for things: young children's acquisition of verbs*. Hillsdale, NJ/Hove: Lawrence Erlbaum, 63–80.
Haviland, J. B. 1981. *Sk'op Sotz'leb. El tzotzil de San Lorenzo Zinacantán*. Mexico: Universidad Nacional Autonama de Mexico. (English translation in http:www.zapata.org)
1991. The grammaticalization of motion and time in Tzotzil. Working Paper 2. Nijmegen, The Netherlands: Cognitive Anthropology Research Group, Max Planck Institute for Psycholinguistics.
1992. Seated and settled: Tzotzil verbs of the body. *Zeitschrift für Phonetik, Sprachwissenschaft und Kommunikationsforschung* 45: 534–561.
1993. The syntax of Tzotzil auxiliaries and directionals: the grammaticalization of "motion." In *Proceedings of the 19th Annual Meeting of the Berkeley Linguistics Society*. Berkeley, CA: Berkeley Linguistics Society 35–49.
1994a. "Te xu setel xulem" (The buzzards were circling): categories of verbal roots in (Zinacantec) Tzotzil. *Linguistics* 32: 691–742.
1994b. Verbs and shapes in (Zinacantec) Tzotzil: the case of "insert." *Función* (University of Guadalajara) 15–16:83–117.
Johnston, J., & D. I. Slobin. 1979. The development of locative expressions in English, Italian, Serbo-Croatian and Turkish. *Journal of Child Language* 6: 529–545.

Landau, B. 1996. Multiple representations of objects in languages and language learners. In P. Bloom, M. A. Peterson, L. Nadel, & M. F. Garrett (eds.), *Language and space*. Cambridge, MA: MIT Press, 317–363.

Landau, B., & R. Jackendoff. 1993. "What" and "where" in spatial language and spatial cognition. *Behavioral and Brain Sciences* 16: 217–265.

McCune-Nicolich, L. 1981. The cognitive bases of relational words in the single-word period. *Journal of Child Language* 8: 15–34.

Nelson, K. 1974. Concept, word, and sentence: interrelations in acquisition and development. *Psychological Review* 81: 267–285.

Pye, C. 1983. Mayan telegraphese: intonational determinants of inflectional development in Quiché Mayan. *Language* 59: 583–604.

1992. The acquisition of K'iche' Maya. In D. I. Slobin (ed.), *The crosslinguistic study of language acquisition*, vol. 3. Hillsdale, NJ: Lawrence Erlbaum, 221–308.

Sinha, C., L. A. Thorseng, M. Hayashi, & K. Plunkett. 1994. Comparative spatial semantics and language acquisition: evidence from Danish, English and Japanese. *Journal of Semantics* 11: 253–287.

Slobin, D. I. 1973. Cognitive prerequisites for the development of grammar. In C. A. Ferguson & D. I. Slobin (eds.), *Studies of child language development*. New York: Holt, Rinehart & Winston, 175–208.

1985. Crosslinguistic evidence for the Language-Making Capacity. In D. I. Slobin (ed.), *The crosslinguistic study of language acquisition*, vol. 2: *Theoretical issues*. Hillsdale, NJ: Lawrence Erlbaum, 1157–1249.

Slobin, D. I., & N. Hoiting. 1994. Reference to movement in spoken and signed languages: typological considerations. In *Proceedings of the 20th Annual Meeting of the Berkeley Linguistics Society*. Berkeley, CA: Berkeley Linguistics Society 487–505.

Talmy, L. 1985. Lexicalization patterns: semantic structure in lexical form. In T. Shopen (ed.), *Language typology and syntactic description*, vol. 3: *Grammatical categories and the lexicon*. Cambridge: Cambridge University Press, 57–149.

1991. Path to realization: a typology of event conflation. In *Proceedings of the 17th Annual Meeting of the Berkeley Linguistics Society*. Berkeley, CA: Berkeley Linguistics Society, 480–519.

Zavala, R. 1993. Clause integration with verbs of motion in Mayan languages. Unpublished MA thesis, University of Oregon.

19 Covariation between spatial language and cognition, and its implications for language learning

Stephen C. Levinson

Max Planck Institute for Psycholinguistics, Nijmegen, The Netherlands

1 Word learning: the scope of the problem

Much of this volume is concerned with the problem of how children learn the meanings of words, or more exactly morphemes of various kinds. The answers may depend on many factors of course: different kinds of morphemes may be, indeed must be, learnt in different ways, the ways themselves may be opened up by conceptual development within the child over time, and so on. However, we can (not without some danger) abstract away from these divergent factors and ask general questions about the scope of the "induction" or "mapping" problem.

Now in the chapters that immediately precede, those by Bowerman & Choi, de León, and Brown, an issue is raised that has significant bearing on the dimensions of the "mapping problem." What these chapters show is that, in a number of spatial domains, the kinds of categories that need to be associated with the meanings of words can vary rather drastically across languages, and moreover that, at least by the beginning of systematic speech, there is no evidence of a uniform initial state of the learning machine, i.e. little evidence that children are *presuming* certain kinds of natural categories, later discarding them in favor of the local idiosyncrasies. Nor does this picture change when one starts to plumb comprehension before the age of complex utterance production. In short, the semantic categories look almost as variable as the phonological strings onto which they must be mapped.

In this chapter, my central purpose is to lay out some additional facts about adult mental life that seem to compound the problems radically: they seem to raise the stakes against the child's possibilities of success still higher. The essential finding that I will lay out is that not only, on a crosscultural basis, do we find sound-systems changing, and meaning-systems in radical diversity, but also we find that the adult cognitive operations that underly or support those meanings seem to covary with the linguistic system. Why this should radically alter the picture needs some explanation.

First, I need a pair of linguistic examples that may demonstrate different kinds of semantic variation across languages. Suppose we translate the English description (a) below into Tzeltal (b), the Mayan language further described in Brown's paper (ch. 17 of this volume).[1]

(1) (a) ENGLISH
Put the bowl behind the box

(b) TZELTAL

pach-an-a	*bojch*	*ta*	*y-anil*	*te*	*karton-e*
bowl+put-CAUSE-IMP	gourd+bowl	at	its-down	the	cardboard-DEIC

The first word of the Tzeltal example is the imperative of the causative of the root *pach*, which means (roughly) 'place a bowl-shaped vessel upright on a surface.' This is one kind of semantic variation we may find across languages: familiar distinctions turning up in unfamiliar places, here bowl-shaped (or hemispherical) being a verbal rather than a nominal component. Similarly, the word *bojch* denotes not a bowl in general, but one made from a half of a spherical gourd (compare English *bowl*, which is indifferent to the material from which it is made). These kinds of crosslinguistic contrast suggest that what we may find when we look across languages are repackagings or distinct lexicalizations of the same or at least similar semantic parameters. Now consider *karton*, a Spanish loan, which in Tzeltal is semantically general across 'cardboard' rather than 'box'; this is a Mayan pattern whereby the basic nominal (other than names for humans, beasts and artifacts) denotes a substance rather than a thing (Lucy 1992). Similarly *lo'bal* 'banana stuff' denotes the tree, the leaves, the roots as well as the fruit (for the cognitive consequences of this Mayan pattern, see Lucy & Gaskins, ch. 9 of this volume). This is arguably somewhat different from a mere shuffling of semantic features, since we have no colloquial notion of "banana essence" or "stuff manufactured by banana genotype"; but in any case it shows that nouns are not necessarily basically words for things – which might seem to be an essential assumption a child must make at the initial stages of language-learning (see Gentner & Boroditsky, ch. 8 of this volume). Finally, consider how English *behind* is rendered into Tzeltal *ta yanil*: although these terms may on an occasion of use have descriptive equivalence, these are actually not in the same intensional ballpark at all. English *behind* is ambiguous (between what I will call an intrinsic and relative – or "deictic" – coordinate system), but is here used in the "deictic" or relative way, so that the utterance means that the box is between the speaker and the bowl. Tzeltal has no term equivalent to either of these meanings of English *behind.* Tzeltal *ta yanil* 'at its down(hill)' (also ambiguous) here means something quite different, which may be specified in our concepts (not theirs) as lying in the quadrant bisected by the line North 010° – it is a cardinal direction term, which they think of in terms of a world essentially tilted North(-north-east)wards. These cardinal direction parameters (uphill, downhill, across) show up in a systematic range of vocabulary from motion verbs to words for edges. Clearly, we can't find any such semantic parameters built on the assumption of a tilted world showing up in English. This is a different kind of semantic variation across languages, and this chapter is about the cognitive consequences of such semantic variation.

Now we are prepared to think about these different kinds of semantic variation more abstractly (indeed, I shall here propose a way of thinking that is far *too* abstract, returning later to correct the picture). A precondition to mapping words (or other morphemes) onto meanings is of course to isolate the phonological words (or other morphemes). Current research shows that babies are beginning to learn the fundamental algorithms here a year or more before they speak (Cutler 1995). Language-specific factors are involved not only at the level of phoneme inventories, stress, and syllable identification, but also at the level of finding roots obscured by derivational and inflectional morphemes, secondary phonological processes, etc. Meaning may also be involved, but in the limited sense of finding units that "have meaning," a precondition to asking *what* meaning they have (Lyons 1968:412). That second question is the mapping problem.

We can imagine three distinct levels, or degrees, of ascending complexity in the mapping problem.

1.1 Degree 1.0 Mapping Problem: mapping known phonological entities onto known semantic or conceptual entities (or mapping language-specific phonological units onto language-independent semantic units)

Once the word-forms[2] (or major meaning-bearing morphemes) have been isolated, the easiest kind of mapping would be from words to *preexisting conceptual bundles*, i.e. concepts identified independently of language, on nonlinguistic grounds. Fodor (1975) is an influential proponent of such a view.[3]

As Quine (1960) pointed out in his celebrated conundrum of the indeterminacy of radical translation, even here, at the simplest level of form–meaning mapping, the mapping problem becomes fundamentally problematic: *rabbit* accompanied by glimpse of scurrying rabbit could mean 'scurry,' 'white fluff,' or whatever. The problem seems quite insoluble without powerful general heuristics of some kind. But the more specific the heuristics the more they threaten to compound the problem, for they will then be inconsistent with one another. Consider for example the oft-proposed heuristic designed for learning nominals: let there be a bias towards object-naming, so that the child may assume that 3D constancies of size and shape map onto nominals (see Gentner & Boroditsky's chapter, this volume; see also Bloom (ch. 6), where count nouns are presumed to map to individuals). Such a heuristic will then hinder rather than help with the learning of abstract or relational nominals (like *birthday*, *night*, or *brother*), and interfere with the learning of predicates (again see Gentner & Boroditsky, this volume, and Gleitman 1990 for parallel suggestions about Degree 1 verb heuristics). Clearly a prior form–class identification will help; and one might hope for language-independent patterns, e.g. at least a distinction between function-morphemes and content-morphemes, but even here things look language-specific (see Slobin, ch. 14 of this volume). These problems are well rehearsed in other chapters in this volume (see, e.g., ch. 7 by Carey and ch. 2 by Gopnik).

We can think of the Degree 1 mapping problem as constructing the set of ordered pairs for each correct association between a phonological word and a semantic concept, where the latter are preexisting conceptual bundles. Then we can get a measure of the size of the "design space" (Dennett 1995) or *problem space* for the child under Degree 1 assumptions: she must select the correct pairings from all the possible pairings, that is, from the Cartesian product of the set of lexemes/morphemes A and the set of meanings/concepts B.

1.2 Degree 2.0 Mapping Problem: mapping known phonological entities onto unknown semantic entities (or mapping language-specific word-forms onto language-specific word meanings, in turn constructed from universal concepts)

It is easy to see that Degree 1 assumptions may underplay the scope of the problem. Even between closely related languages, we cannot expect exactly the same bundling of semantic notions even in basic lexical items and morphemes. Thus Indo-European spatial prepositions tend to encode similar notions; but we are not surprised to find the range of English *on* split into German *auf* and *an* or Dutch *aan*, *om*, and *op* (see Bowerman 1996 on the acquisition of such terms). Once outside the language family, we can be sure to find not only subdivisions of semantic space but also new cross-cutting parameters (see Bowerman & Choi, ch. 16 of this volume). Thus the semantic bundles that the child will find in its first language cannot be predicted in advance.[4] (If they could, what would conceptual development be about anyway? See Carey, this volume.)

We are often blind to the cultural foundations of our basic vocabulary: English *brother* seems a word that would have pertinence in most children's universes, but few languages have lexical items that denote just that. Tzeltal *ijtz'in*, for example, denotes the younger male sibling of a male or the younger female or male sibling of a female, or cousins of specific kinds, and there are distinct words for older siblings.[5] The chapters that precede in this section clearly establish that many words that are learnt early have this culture-specific quality. They confirm that the problem facing the child trying to map word-forms to meanings is actually of a higher order than Degree 1. Rather than map words to preexisting meanings, the child must construct the meaning. Where the child does this construction by selecting from a reassuring, finite set of universal underlying atomic concepts, we have a Degree 2 level of difficulty.

Now the mapping problem begins to look extremely difficult: the problem space is now much greater than at the Degree 1 level. Indeed it is beginning to look vast. We can glimpse the size of the problem space by supposing (as a radical idealization) that a possible cultural concept is any combination or permutation of the set of universal concepts B. Then under Degree 2 assumptions the *problem space* for the child (i.e. the set of all possible pairings of word-forms and possible meanings) is the Cartesian product of A and all the combinations and permutations of B (of some maximum length) out of which vast array of possible mappings the child must select just the small set of actual ones.[6]

Perhaps not all words are as problematic as this – Gentner & Boroditsky (this volume) argue that relational nominals and predicates have a linguistic relativity of this sort, but other nominals may allow a way into a language by offering a Degree 1 transparency. But nevertheless it is clear that amongst the early words a child masters are indeed words of Degree 2 complexity.

1.3 Degree 3.0 Mapping Problem: mapping L-specific word-forms onto L-specific word meanings, given non-universal working concepts

Degree 2 mapping problems look staggeringly difficult. Yet children succeed. Perhaps they succeed at something even harder: Degree 3 mapping problems. Under a Degree 3 mapping problem, the kinds of semantic units mapped onto words are not simply a combination of a set of universal concepts B; instead they are combinations of culture-specific concepts – the set B cannot be taken to be identical for all languages and cultures. This degree of problem would arise if there is no guaranteed commonality between adult everyday working nonlinguistic concepts and the infants' naturally attainable concepts (concepts based on innate predispositions or shared terrestrial fate).[7] Then what seems salient to the child may not be at all what the adult has in mind.

We've already met an example of the kind of fundamental linguistic variation which might constitute a Degree 3 problem, namely the difference between English *behind* and Tzeltal *ta yanil*. Adults in these two speech communities (say, Boulder and Tenejapa) don't have the choice to use the other system – their linguistic systems provide them no easy way to speak in the other manner. Nor, as I shall show below, is the other way of *thinking* easily accessible to them. This is because the two systems, while using fundamentally different coordinate systems, offer roughly equivalent functionality. Of course, this doesn't rule out the possibility that at some yet further, deeper level of decomposition, the two coordinate systems use the same universal primitives; but it does make the point that this universal level is not the level of workaday concepts.[8] It is the higher composite level of everyday concepts which the child can tap into, not only through the observation of language but also through many other kinds of observed behavior; but the child has no privileged access to that culturally variable level by virtue of matching innate predispositions.

In case there is still unclarity about the distinction between Degree 2 and Degree 3 problems, consider it another way. Degree 1 problems involve finding correspondences between just two levels – the word-forms and the innate concepts corresponding directly to the meanings. Degree 2 problems consist of mappings between three levels: word-forms, word meanings, and the universal semantic primes from which they are formed. Degree 3 problems consist of mappings between four levels: word-forms, word meanings, semantic parameters, and the universal conceptual primes (if any) underlying the culture-specific semantic parameters. The more intermediate levels there are between universal concepts and language-specific word-forms, the more the child actually has to construct in the way of entities to be mapped one upon the other, and the more different possible mapping relations arise.

The learning challenge raised by Degree 3 problems differs from that raised by Degree 2 problems in both quantitative and qualitative ways. Firstly, the problem space – the set of possible meanings the child may construct – is now either infinite (if there are no conceptual primes), or at least truly vast (if there are, as we may assume). The vastness of the problem space can be assessed along the following lines: the set B of culture-relative workaday adult concepts forms one conceptual level, a level of composite concepts or semantic parameters which are themselves recombined to make semantic units (word meanings). For example, Tzeltal *yanil* might have a meaning specified in terms of a quadrant bisected at a fixed bearing – our N 010°, but their parallel lines on a notional inclined plane. So far this seems just like a Degree 2 problem. But these B-level concepts are culture-relative, and are attainable, let us suppose, just because they are in turn combinations and permutations of elements of set C, a large universal inventory of atomic concepts from which those macro-concepts at level B are constructed. Then the problem space (i.e. the set of possible pairings of word-forms A and meanings B, ultimately strings at level C) is vastly increased because B is not a fixed inventory of meanings. And from that utterly vast space of possibilities, the child must select just the correct assignment of meaning to each and every morpheme.

Why care about the size of the problem space? Sure, in really small spaces, one might hit on the right answer by chance, and a few clues will reduce the chance to certainty. But once it is really large (as it already is in Degree 2, and arguably even in Degree 1, problems), does it matter *how* large it is? Well, consider two points. First, one can search even large spaces efficiently with simple algorithms (witness the game of "Twenty Questions"), but really vast spaces are another matter. When the filing cabinet gets too large, it's quicker to rewrite the document than to try to find it: construction is a better strategy than search. At that point, Fodor's imagined stock of innate meanings will be a hindrance rather than a help. A second point is that as the search space becomes vaster, the heuristics must get better. This is the paradox of linguistic relativity: cultural variation is not, as commonly thought, in opposition to nativism – the more variation (and thus the greater the problem space), the more we would need in the way of pregiven heuristics and constraints to find correct solutions to the mapping problem, as Sperber (1996) has pointed out.

Secondly, the difficulty is qualitative. Consider the Gricean theory of meaning (Grice 1957): S says something X intending addressee A to figure out that S intended X to have a specific mental effect E on A, by virtue of *a shared mentality* that makes it salient that S might mean E by X. Some such picture seems to be assumed by those who emphasize the shared intentional and attentional structure lying behind language acquisition (see Tomasello, ch. 5 of this volume). But suppose there is no such shared mentality – how can communication get off the ground? Only if A can build a model of what S thinks A would find salient. This is the fundamental difficulty posed by Degree 3 problems: the child must somehow discern the conceptual parameters that the adult is using to construct the semantic distinctions that show up bundled in morphemes.

Problems of Degree 3 kind may seem insoluble in principle, since no heuristics are likely to be workable in an infinite or utterly vast problem space. But as a matter of fact it seems that children do attain concepts of a culture-specific kind, which are not just trivial combinations of concepts that are culture-independent. I will spell out some examples of adult concepts of this kind below, and the chapter by Brown provides some corresponding information about child acquisition of such concepts in the same culture. We will then return at the end of this chapter to consider just *how* such concepts may be learnable after all. Meanwhile we should note that presumably not *all* linguistic meanings are of this kind: perhaps there are

Degree 1, Degree 2, and Degree 3 problems in different areas of the vocabulary (again, see Gentner & Boroditsky, this volume).

In the child language literature it has for long been thought that the target problem was of Degree 1 difficulty. Many of the heuristics proposed by, e.g., Markman (1989, 1992), Gleitman (1990), and others, are aimed at this target, which is already extremely challenging. However, as many chapters in this volume suggest (see e.g. Bowerman & Choi, Gaskins & Lucy, Gentner & Boroditsky, de León, Brown), the problem – at least in part – actually appears to be of at least Degree 2 difficulty. The particular focus of this chapter is to suggest that even that underestimates the problem, which may even be of Degree 3 difficulty: for I will produce evidence that adult nonlinguistic cognition varies, not randomly, but in line with the coding of the adult language. This does radically change the picture: instead of children having to find meanings in a cognitive space which can be presumed to be shared between themselves and adults, children actually have to construct progressively an adult-like cognitive space in which the conceptual parameters which will enter word meanings must be discovered.

2 Cultural variation in spatial frames of reference

2.1 Variation in language

I turn now to sketch the finding that adult cognition may vary in line with the language spoken. Our data come from the crosscultural study of spatial cognition. As made clear by Spelke & Tviskin in ch. 3 of this volume, there is in human spatial cognition a strong background of common mammalian inheritance in spatial abilities. For this reason, *spatial conception is one of the areas in which we might* ***least*** *expect to find significant variation across cultures*. Indeed, there is no shortage of pronouncements in the linguistics and psycholinguistics literature to the effect that the kinds of spatial notion we find in our own languages are more or less inevitable, due either to our common biological inheritance or our shared terrestrial existence, or both (see e.g. H. H. Clark 1973; Miller & Johnson-Laird 1976).

After working in about twenty fieldsites around the world, our research group at the Max Planck Institute for Psycholinguistics has come to the conclusion that this picture simply is not right (see, e.g., Pederson, Danziger, Wilkins, Levinson, Kita, & Senft 1998). There is substantial variation in the semantic parameters employed in languages for spatial description, even if the variation can often be seen to be restricted within certain types. I will report now on one of these dimensions of variation, namely variation in coordinate systems, or "frames of reference" as they are called in the psychological literature (see Levinson 1996a).

I shall restrict myself to discussing the specification of angles on the horizontal, that is, how languages specify the location of one thing, the Figure or object to be located, as positioned at a specific angle or direction from another, the Ground or landmark object. (Amongst the many other kinds of spatial concept therefore ignored here are, for example, the so-called topological notions like "at," as well as deictic notions like "there," where no angular specification is given, which therefore lie outside the scope of these remarks.)

Finding angles on the horizontal is a non-trivial task: there simply is no overwhelming force on the horizontal as there is gravity on the vertical – we have to invent or construct coordinate systems and apply them. In a tradition that goes back at least to Kant (1768), it has been assumed that languages will inevitably make central the egocentric, person-based coordinates of the kind exemplified in our "left/right/front/back" terms. This turns out not to be the case. Instead, languages make differential use of three quite different strategies for solving the problem of specifying angles on the horizontal, which we will call the Intrinsic, the Relative, and the Absolute frames of reference. In the Intrinsic frame of reference, designated facets of the Ground object are used to specify an angle, which in turn can be used to specify a search domain in which the Figure will be found, as in "The ball is in front of the chair" (see figure 19.1, top). In the Relative frame of reference, the body planes of the viewer can be utilized to extract a coordinate system, such that one can say, e.g., "The ball is to the right of the chair" (figure 19.1, middle). In the Absolute frame of reference, fixed bearings based ultimately on such things as celestial, meteorological, or landscape constancies can be used to specify that, e.g., "The ball is north of the chair" (figure 19.1 bottom).

These systems may seem familiar enough, but the familiarity can be misleading. Note for example that *north of the chair* is not a locution we would normally use, because, for one thing, most English speakers will not at any one moment (especially inside a house) know where North is. For another, we reserve all such locutions for geographical, not table-top or intimate, space. Secondly, each of these frames of reference is a large genus, with many language-specific distinct species. For example, there are Intrinsic systems that are anything but familiar; thus, whereas for us the "front" of a television or a book or a building is defined in terms of the functional properties of those objects, for speakers of Tzeltal the "face" of an object is defined by strict geometry (see Levinson 1994). Similarly, our Relative system could be different: whereas for us a man hiding behind a tree from us could be said to be "behind the tree," for a Hausa speaker he would be "in front" of it (Hill 1982); and in conditions where we would say the man is "to the left of the tree," other languages may prefer "to the right of the tree,"

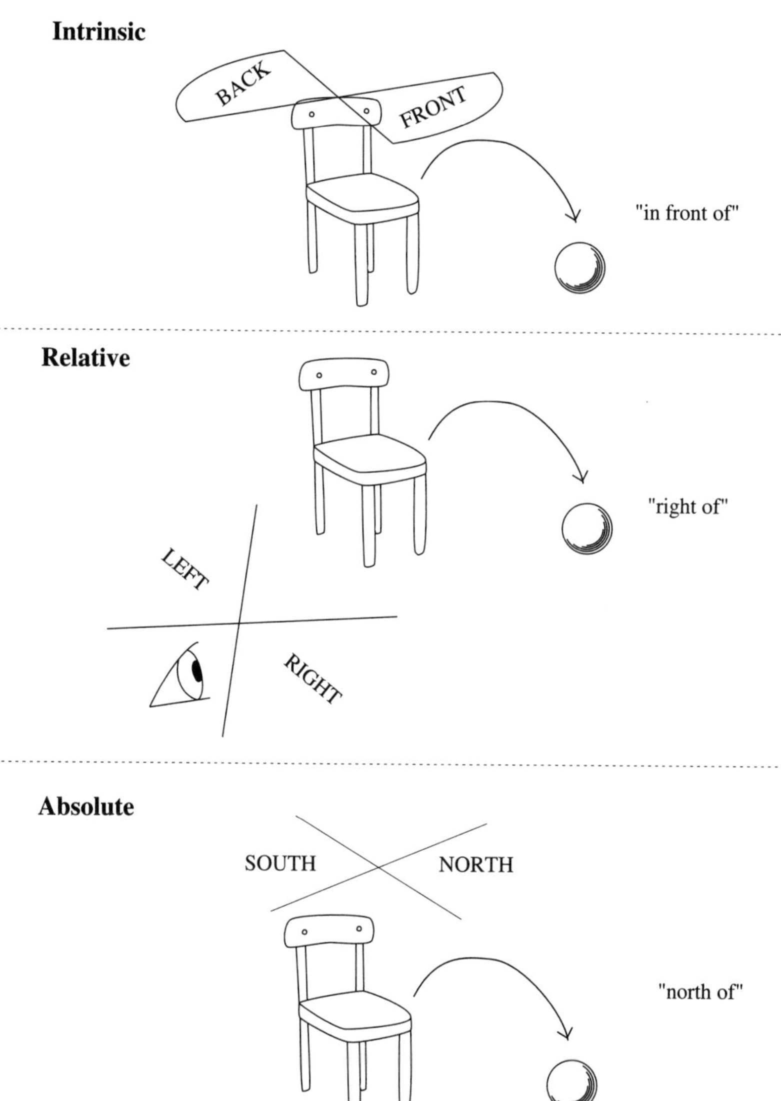

Fig. 19.1 Sketch typology of linguistic coordinate systems (horizontal plane, stasis).

having mapped a left and right upon the tree. Finally, Absolute systems are again various: many have abstract bearing systems askew from our North/South/East/West (see e.g. Haviland 1979; Levinson 1992a, 1996b), others use bearings derived from the stars, the winds, or landscape features like drainage systems, which may form no quadrant. Yet other systems, like the Austronesian ones, may mix landmark axes (whose directions therefore vary with travel) with true fixed-bearing systems (based, e.g., upon monsoons; see Levinson 1992b, 1996b for references). Thus each of these types is actually a great family of systems, the members of which can be radically different from one another.

But the main point here is simply that *not all languages use all three systems.* There are languages that use almost exclusively only Intrinsic or only Absolute coordinates (see, respectively, Danziger 1996 and Levinson 1992a). Many languages use a combination of all three systems, or just two of them; in fact the only combination that doesn't seem to occur is Relative without Intrinsic. This variation in the basic set of coordinate systems available in a language is a fundamental dimension of semantic variation at the most abstract level, and was scarcely to be expected given the current trends of thinking in the cognitive sciences. As already indicated, most languages can be expected to differ further in the way these major types are instantiated (a) in terms of their conceptual anchors (e.g. whether a fixed bearing is determined by notional inclined planes or monsoons), (b) as a set of semantic categories (and of course formal categories too), and (c) in terms of mapping rules for deriving secondary coordinate systems of various kinds (see Levinson 1996a, b for discussion) – but this variation, important as it is, is at a different level of detail. The surprise value of the findings is the high-level variation in the fundamental kinds of coordinate system employed.

2.2 *Variation in adult cognition in line with language*

An interesting observation is that the distinct underlying frames of reference employed in semantic systems require different cognitive underpinnings. This is self-evident in the case of cardinal directions: if at this moment you cannot accurately point to North, let alone to where you were born, you simply don't have the necessary "dead-reckoning" system constantly operating in your conceptual background. "Dead-reckoning" implies knowing where you are by virtue of knowing how far in each direction you have traveled: it allows you to estimate straight-line directions and distances to a range of familiar locations. The properties of such a system are non-trivial. Gallistel (1990) provides an outline of the mathematical routines required. Many species, from ants, to bees, to birds, are thought to have these routines hard-wired. But the extreme cultural variability in human populations (see Levinson 1996c) makes it probable that in those cultures where humans are good dead-reckoners, they are so by virtue of learnt "software." In fact, the crosscultural evidence we have seems to show that these abilities correlate with language: languages that primarily provide absolute coordinate systems for spatial description require constant dead-reckoning; consequently their speakers can consistently point to a range of locations from a novel place, while speakers of languages which predominantly use relative coordinates are highly inconsistent or inaccurate or both (Levinson 1996c). Thus speaking a language that requires absolute specifications forces a constant background computation of direction.[9]

The possibility is then raised that semantic differences in this area run more than skin-deep. Against this background it is interesting to ask what are the cognitive implications of linguistic specializations in this area – e.g. what happens to the way we *think* about space if we are speakers of a language which uses only (or at least primarily) Absolute and not Relative frames of reference, or vice versa? Is there, despite the linguistic variation (and despite the fact that one might need *additional* computations to speak in terms of fixed bearings), just one basic human way to think about spatial arrays? Or, to put it another way, do the language-specific semantic notions employed in the language one speaks match the conceptual notions one uses to, e.g., solve nonlinguistic spatial problems?

To explore these issues empirically, we can exploit properties of each of these frames of reference, in particular the fact that these three different coordinate systems have different properties under rotation. Using the Relative system, the speaker rotates "left" and "right" with himself: thus if X was "left" of Y on a table, and the speaker goes around to the other side, X will now be "right" of Y. But using the Absolute system, the speaker's rotation has no effect on spatial description: if X was north of Y it remains so, regardless of speaker position or rotation. On the other hand, if the array – e.g. ball X to the "left" and "north" of chair Y – rotates while the speaker remains constant, both Absolute and Relative designations must change; however Intrinsic designations (e.g. "The ball is at the chair's front") are invariant to such external coordinates – the coordinate system is based within the assemblage.

Thus we can with relative ease devise *nonlinguistic* tasks that will reveal which kind of coordinate systems subjects utilize to solve them. So now we can explore the question: if a language L provides for a particular kind of array just one natural frame of reference, is this frame of reference also the one employed by speakers of that language when performing *nonlinguistic* tasks on similar kinds of array?

Let me illustrate with a very simple nonlinguistic task, utilized to distinguish whether subjects coded for recall memory using an Absolute or a Relative frame of reference (if they used neither, they failed the task, in the sense that they produced random or arbitrary results). Subjects were shown three toy animals in a row, asked to memorize them, and after a short delay turned around 180°, led over to another table, and asked to make the same assemblage again. If they preserved the left–right direction and ordering of the animals under rotation, they were clearly using body-centered or Relative coordinates, while if they preserved the, say, northwards orientation and North–South ordering of the row, they were clearly using some kind of coordinate system locked to the larger environment or to abstract bearings (like "North"). Figure 19.2 illustrates the task diagrammatically.

On the basis of many informal observations, we made the simple prediction that if a language provides only or primarily an Absolute frame of reference for the description of such arrays, then speakers of that language *when performing nonlinguistic tasks* would also employ the same frame of reference; and conversely we expected speakers of languages favoring the Relative frame of reference to employ that same coordinate system in their nonlinguistic memory. The results are broadly in line with the predictions. For example, just comparing two contrasting speech communities – Tzeltal-speaking Tenejapans, who utilize an Absolute system in language to describe arrays of such a kind, and Dutch-speaking subjects, who of course use a Relative linguistic system like English – one obtains the results illustrated in figure 19.3. The abscissa here is an index of "Absolute" responses: the more trials performed using Absolute coordinates the higher the score, the more performed using Relative ones the lower the score. As is immediately evident, the Dutch were consistent Relative encoders on this memory task, while the Tenejapans were Absolute encoders. In short, subjects appear to memorize spatial arrays using a coding system isomorphic with the language they speak.

We have carried out as a research group parallel examinations in a large range of languages (see e.g. Levinson & Nagy 1997; Pederson *et al.* 1998). What we find is that where languages rely primarily on an Absolute or a Relative frame of reference for the description of arrays of a similar sort, then we obtain just the same kind of results as we have just reported for the Tenejapans on the one hand and the Dutch on the other. Thus there appears to be a robust tendency for the mental coding of arrays to follow the pattern in the subject's language.

A single task is only a diagnostic. But in many of these fieldsites we have been able to run a whole battery of tasks. The idea here was to see whether the effects are only "skin-deep" as it were, or whether if we give subjects tasks involving differing cognitive capacities – recall, recognition, pattern

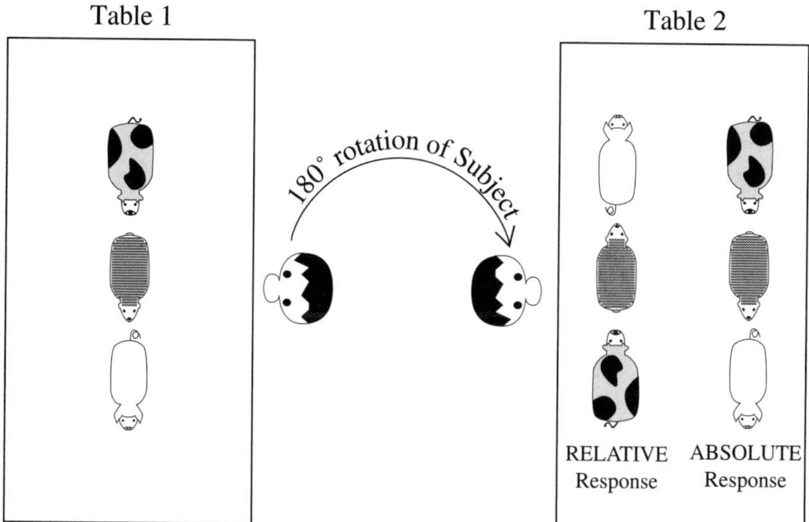

Fig. 19.2 Animals in a row.

matching, inference – they nevertheless persist in preferring the frame of reference enshrined in and encouraged by their language. For example, in Tenejapa Penelope Brown and myself have conducted a series of tasks involving propositional coding of spatial arrays for recall, recognition, and inference. In the inference task (designed by E. Pederson), the subject sees a spatial "premise" of a kind that might be coded "blue cylinder to the left of yellow cube," or conversely "blue cylinder to the north of yellow cube." He or she is then rotated 180°, and sees a second spatial "premise," which might be coded as, say, "yellow cube to the left of red cone" or "yellow cube to the south of red cone." The subject is then rotated back to the starting position and asked to draw the nonverbal conclusion from the two premises by arranging the red cone with respect to the blue cylinder. Absolute coders do it one way, Relative coders another (work it out – or see Levinson 1996a). In addition to these kinds of tasks which clearly require a coordinate system but which require no precise metric retention, we also carried out tasks which would seem to require visual memory for metric distances and angles. For example, we asked subjects to memorize a heap of objects, and then after rotation to recall and rebuild the assemblage: Dutch subjects

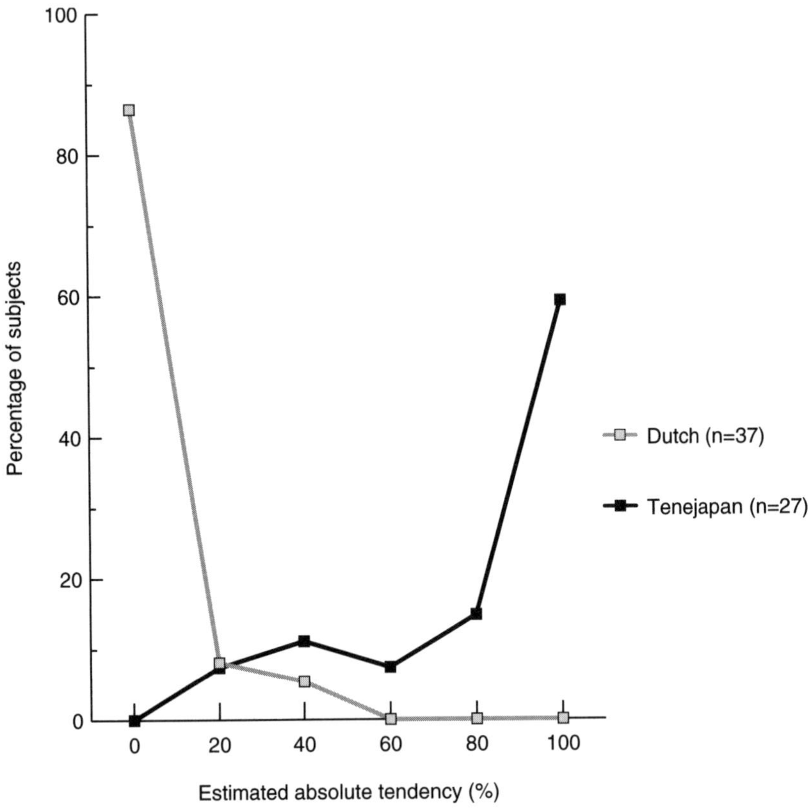

Fig. 19.3 Graph of Tzeltal vs. Dutch animals in a row data.

recall the array as seen from the original vantage point, Tenejapans remake the array as if they had seen it from the other side (i.e. they appear to make a mental rotation; see Levinson 1996a). Finally, we have observed unselfconscious gesturing accompanying speech. Where the gesturer speaks a language preferring Absolute coordinates, as in Tenejapan Tzeltal, regardless of rotation the speaker uses absolute coordinates when gesturing, i.e. points in the correct direction to the places or events described (even when, if less consistently, this was a virtual event like a movie stimulus); in contrast Dutch speakers when rotated also rotate their coordinates with them. In short, if one finds a clear preference for one coordinate system in the semantics, one turtle supporting linguistic behavior as it were, then it is turtles all the way down!

This consistent behavior across a range of tasks or behaviors is fundamentally interesting. It appears to show that the coordinate system predominant in the subject's language comes to work its way into a number of distinct kinds of representational systems, so that we end up with an isomorphism across semantic representations, nonlinguistic propositional representations, imagistic representations, and even kinesthetic ones. Indeed, it is probably this which makes it possible to speak about what we remember, see, or feel (see Levinson 1996a).

These are the sorts of findings that seem to substantiate the view that the kind of problem facing the child learning a language is more formidable than had been imagined. Instead of being able to assume that an adult will share the same fundamental "take" on a scene, with a consequent likely mapping of words to things or relations, the possibility arises that adult conceptual classifications will be initially quite unfathomable. Two table settings opposite one another with fork on left and knife on right may appear to be the same array from the perspective of the diners in a Relative perspective, and appear systematically opposed (or contrary) representations from the perspective of Absolute diners (after all, one fork points, say, west and is north of the knife while the other points east and is south of the knife). If there is a fundamental mismatch in child and adult cognition, how does the child even begin to make the first tentative steps towards cracking the local linguistic code?[10]

3 Solving the impossible

At the beginning of this chapter, I outlined a ranking of learning problems from what I called Degree 1 to Degree 3, according to the size of the problem space within which the child must find the solution. The adult language and cognition data I have now described suggest that the child really does face Degree 3 problems in some areas of the vocabulary.

Now the suspicion must arise that all this amounts to a *reductio ad absurdum*: there must be something wrong with this depiction. If the Degree 1 Mapping Problem, the Quinean conundrum, is already so difficult, then apparent demonstrations that the child's problem is actually Degree 2, let alone Degree 3, can be discounted: if these demonstrations were correct, language would be unlearnable. Ergo, there must be some flaw in those demonstrations. After all, even powerful heuristics and constraints may not be enough to help one find an atom in a haystack. What use would be innate domain-specific theories, special constraints on expected word meanings, etc., if the problem space is impossibly vast?

In a sense, this is indeed correct: namely, the problem is underdescribed. There are at least two fundamental heuristics that lie outside the mapping space problem as described. Firstly, even the Degree 1 problem presupposes that the child has a theory of meaning, perhaps along the lines sketched by Grice (1957). Grice's theory of meaning situates meaning-recognition within the sphere of intention-recognition, and brings the interactional context of joint focus of intention, mutual salience, etc., to bear on the problem (see e.g. Schiffer 1972). It is easily empirically demonstrable that such contexts allow determinate solutions to infinite mapping problems (see e.g. Schelling 1960; H. H. Clark 1996), thus beating the mathematical odds (see Levinson 1995a): if you and I will both get $1,000 if we think of the same number without communication, we can easily achieve this "telepathy." These issues are addressed by Tomasello (1995:116, and ch. 5 of this volume). Now, I have suggested that the infant might be in a state of cognitive mismatch with the adult, because the adult is thinking along lines consonant with the language he or she masters, yet to be learnt by the infant. This of course makes it harder to achieve "telepathy." On the other hand, the very fact that the adult's *thinking* is isomorphic to the categories of the language provides a whole barrage of nonlinguistic, behavioral clues to the nature of those categories. For example, many Absolute speakers arrange their world in such a way that environmental constancies reflect fixed bearings: windbreaks always to the East, or hearths to the South, in just the same way that Relative speakers arrange their environments so that forks are left of knives, cars drive consistently on the left or right, knobs turn things on clockwise, etc. Adult cognitive isomorphism to language presents the child with countless behavioral clues to the underlying cognition.[11]

Secondly, there is a temporal succession within the mapping problem that is often omitted in discussions. Once the child has cracked *some* word meanings, a pattern for a specific language begins to reveal itself, allowing the assimilation of accumulative clues which reinforce language-specific mapping solutions (see Choi & Bowerman 1991:107; Brown, ch. 17 of this volume). The importance of the temporal succession of word learning is underlined by the demonstration by Linda Smith in this volume (ch. 4) that even quite simple connectionist or associationist models of the learning process will exploit such emerging patterns. Temporal succession might provide a solution in another way: the child might progress in orderly sequence from Degree 1 to Degree 2 to Degree 3 solutions. This could happen in two ways: (1) she might initially think all words have Degree 1 solutions, only later learning that some have Degree 2 solutions, and yet later revising her opinion and noting that some even have Degree 3 solutions; alternatively, (2), the child might be able to detect differences in the size of the problem spaces associated with different words (e.g. perhaps she can tell that some words are inscrutable) – then she might assign Degree 1 solutions only to Degree 1 words, using them first, and only later have a shot at Degree 2 words, aiming for Degree 2 solutions, and so on. This is essentially Gentner & Boroditsky's view (ch. 8 of this volume), who suggest children learn concrete nouns first, verbs second.

It is worth mentioning a third set of powerful heuristics, often omitted from discussions of this kind (but see E. V. Clark 1993 on the principle of contrast, and Merriman, Marazita, & Jarvis 1995:151ff. for a survey of other suggestions). These are pragmatic principles which appear to govern the structure of a vocabulary field, so that, e.g., alternate terms may be assumed to contrast in one of a small number of ways, partially guessable by the formal properties of the expressions (Levinson 1995b). Such heuristics may be readily learned and transferred from one learning task to another.

While these three kinds of heuristic or additional information significantly restrict the kinds of hypotheses that might be entertained by the child, one must concede that they do not alone show how Degree 2 or 3 problems could in principle be solved. But what they do show is that the discussion of the problem in these terms is not sufficient, is perhaps even a misleading way to think, and that there may be any number of further restricting heuristics that have so far been neglected in the analysis of the child's learning problem. For this reason, I do not think that there is any good implausibility argument to the effect that the child cannot really be successfully navigating Degree 2 or Degree 3 problem spaces.

The findings announced in the chapters by Bowerman & Choi, de León, and Brown all point clearly towards the conclusion that the problem space for the child is at least of the Degree 2 kind, and there are hints (perhaps especially clear in the chapters by Brown and de León) that it is actually of Degree 3. Direct corroboration that the problem is indeed of the Degree 3 kind comes not only from our work reported above on adult cognition, but also from the work of Gaskins & Lucy (ch. 9 of this volume), which includes studies of middle childhood.

The Gaskins & Lucy chapter suggests another interesting possibility. Perhaps children construe Degree 3 problems as if they were Degree 2 problems: that is, they map directly from the deep conceptual primes to the word meanings without going through a level of culture-relative composite semantic parameters. This would be a bit like treating every instance of the number 20 as a long sequence of 1s, 11111111111111111111 (corresponding, e.g., to all my fingers and toes), rather than as a multiple of 10s. You can still do simple arithmetic if you haven't grasped the decimal system, it's just hard work. Only in middle childhood, so such an account might go, do children remap the system from three levels (as in Degree 2 problems) into four (as in Degree 3 problems), incorporating a level of everyday macro-concepts. It is only at such a point that they *think* like adults think, and can come to acquire the more complex parts of lexical semantics (for a review of such later reorganizations of previously acquired semantic and morphosyntactic structures, see Bowerman 1982).

Indeed, a number of the spatial concepts discussed here are not acquired early, and in various ways fail to meet the criteria outlined by Landau & Gleitman (1985:178) for "natural" or innate categories. Such "natural" categories should be learned early, alternative construals should hardly arise, they should be universal in the core vocabulary, and they should be learnable under poor input conditions. For example, Relative concepts like "front," "back," "left," "right" are not universal. Nor are they learnt early: Relative as opposed to Intrinsic "front" is mastered only by 3% of English-speaking children up to 4;4 (Johnston & Slobin 1979), and of course problems with "left" and "right" are notorious (as Piaget pointed out, Relative "left," as in "ball left of tree," is not fully mastered till as late as age 11). By these criteria, it is the Intrinsic concepts ("front," "back," "between," etc.) that the English-speaking children find relatively "natural." But we do *not* find this same picture across languages – that is part of the message of the chapters by de León and Brown (this volume): e.g. Absolute semantic concepts may proceed Intrinsic ones. This crosscultural variability in what is most easily accessible to the child suggests that many linguistic categories are simply not *natural* in any straightforward sense at all: they have to be learnt from instances of usage. Sure, they may be built out of underlying "natural" concepts, and moreover the range of variation may be limited. But the point is that languages *construct* concepts that otherwise might not have been. And that is precisely the added cognitive value of language: it provides "un-natural concepts," complex conceptual wholes which connect across natural capacities (see Dennett 1991; Spelke & Tviskin, ch. 3 of this volume), and which can be processed as units in working memory, thus vastly increasing the power of our mental computations (Levinson 1997). This picture is radically opposed to the standard line in child language research, which assumes that language rests directly on the fundaments of preexisting categories – that is, that the learning problems are of Degree 1. On the new view, when a child learns a language she is undergoing a cognitive revolution, learning to construct new macro-concepts. These macro-concepts which are part of our cultural baggage are precisely the contribution of language to our thinking. Language invades our thinking because languages are good to think with.

NOTES

I am most grateful for comments by Penelope Brown and Melissa Bowerman on a draft of this chapter.

1 There are certain artificialities about this translation – e.g. one rarely gets two expressed NPs in a Tzeltal sentence, one or the other being anaphorically elided. But this does not, I think, have any bearing on the point being made here.

2 I'll talk henceforth in terms of "words" despite the perilous ambiguities between word-form, lexeme, type vs. token meanings, etc., and despite the fact that what we are really interested in is morphemes, simply in the interests of a colloquial style.

3 Thus Fodor (1980:151): "A theory of the conceptual plasticity of organisms must be a theory of how the environment selects among the innately specified concepts. It is not a theory of how you acquire concepts, but a theory of how the environment determines which parts of the conceptual mechanism in principle available to you are in fact exploited."

4 For a brief, trenchant philosophical critique of Fodor's position, see Putnam 1988:ch. 1.

5 For an insightful analysis of the apparently similar but in fact very different sibling terms in Japanese and Korean, see Matsumoto (1995:30–31). And Deutsch, Wagner, Burchardt, Schulz, & Nakath (ch. 10 of this volume) gives another exotic case in our own nurseries.

6 We can, indeed I would argue we must (Levinson 1997), interpolate a semantic level S between the concepts B and the morphemes A. We might hope that units of S will map one-to-one onto morphemes A, and therefore that this extra level does not increase the size of the problem space; but see discussion of Degree 3 problems.

7 Of course, we may assume that children only have access to a subset of adult concepts; the question here is whether adult cognition is fundamentally shifted from such "natural concepts" in everyday thinking.

8 Another example may help to distinguish proximate culture-specific semantic dimensions from their ultimate underlying conceptual foundations. Take the meaning of the word *December*; it is the twelfth month (of roughly thirty days) in our year. Compare the Tzeltal *tz'un*; it is the eighteenth month (of exactly twenty days) of their year; *December* and *tz'un*; overlap referentially, but the concepts aren't at all the same. It would be fatuous to claim that both December and *tz'un* are somehow preexisting concepts, waiting to be named (but see Fodor 1983); even the underlying concepts on which they immediately rest are distinct, since our number system is to base 10 and theirs to base 20, and their year is five days shorter than ours. Still, deep down, the notion of day and number are shared, and out of these ingredients we can derive different number systems and calendrical cycles. But clearly the meaning of the word *tz'un* is a whole complex cultural concept, built on other cultural concepts, that in turn may be built on conceptual bedrock.

9 To be useful locutions in conversation, there has to be an automaticity to comprehension (I once seriously risked an off-road vehicle in quicksand because my Australian aboriginal navigator said "Quick swerve North!" and it simply took me too long to compute the response). Less obvious, perhaps, is that people who don't routinely use Relative left/right tend to take a long time to figure out which is their left side (the Imperial Russian armies are said to have been drilled with straw tied to their left legs).

10 I have here downplayed what other scholars might have played up: namely that on the account given there are only three major types of spatial frame of reference that the child must choose between. Could this be a kind of parameter switch, inbuilt, which the child only has to learn to set? I would rather look at it

differently. Perhaps these three types of frame of reference are innately given to us, perhaps in connection with different cognitive and perceptual modalities (see Levinson 1996a); but they are only huge classes of possible geometric solutions. The local system is still always one of an indefinite array of possibilities. Talk of parameter setting will not solve the learning problem, although constraints on variation do of course restrict the problem space.

11 Would these cultural reflexes alone be sufficient for the child to build culture-specific concepts, without language input? I think this is unlikely to any significant degree. The reason is that it is communication which provides the focus of attention on the exact intentional background to behaviors (see H. H. Clark 1996; Tomasello, ch. 5 of this volume): learning a word is like a parlor miming-game – a coordination problem involving a signal whose issuance carries a warrant that there are just enough clues to find the correct solution. It is interesting to note that alien observers (e.g. anthropologists) have often failed to realize that the community they were living in utilized an Absolute frame of reference.

REFERENCES

Bowerman, M. 1982. Reorganizational processes in lexical and syntactic development. In E. Wanner & L. R. Gleitman, (eds.), *Language acquisition: the state of the art*. Cambridge: Cambridge University Press, 319–346.

1996. Learning how to structure space for language: a crosslinguistic perspective. In P. Bloom, M. A. Peterson, L. Nadel, & M. F. Garrett (eds.), *Language and space*. Cambridge, MA: MIT Press, 385–436.

Brown, P., & S. Levinson. 1993. "Uphill" and "downhill" in Tzeltal. *Journal of Linguistic Anthropology* 3: 46–74.

Choi, S., & M. Bowerman. 1991. Learning to express motion events in English and Korean: the influence of language-specific lexicalization patterns. *Cognition* 41: 83–121.

Clark, E. V. 1993. *The lexicon in acquisition*. Cambridge: Cambridge University Press.

Clark, H. H. 1973. Space, time, semantics, and the child. In T. E. Moore (ed.), *Cognitive development and the acquisition of language*. New York: Academic Press, 27–63.

1996. *Using language*. Cambridge: Cambridge University Press.

Cutler, A. 1995. Universal and language-specific in the development of speech. *Biology International* 33: 50–53.

Danziger, E. 1996. Parts and their counter-parts: social and spatial relationships in Mopan Maya. *Man* 2: 67–82.

Dennett, D. 1991. *Consciousness explained*. Boston: Little, Brown.

1995. *Darwin's dangerous idea*. New York: Simon & Schuster.

Fodor, J. A. 1975. *The language of thought*. New York: Thomas Y. Crowell.

1980. Fixation of belief and concept acquisition. In M. Piatelli-Palmarini (ed.), *Language and learning: the debate between Jean Piaget and Noam Chomsky*. London: Routledge & Kegan Paul, 143–162.

1983. *The modularity of mind: an essay on faculty psychology*. Cambridge, MA: MIT Press.

Gallistel, C. R. 1990. *The organization of learning*. Cambridge, MA: MIT Press.

Gleitman, L. R. 1990. The structural sources of verb meanings. *Language Acquisition* 1: 3–55.

Grice, H. P. 1957. Meaning. *Philosophical Review* 67: 377–388.

Haviland, J. B. 1979. Guugu Yimidhirr. In R. M. W. Dixon & B. Blake (eds.), *Handbook of Australian languages*, vol. 1. Canberra: Australian National University Press, 27–182.

Hill, C. 1982. Up/down, front/back, left/right: a contrastive study of Hausa and English. In J. Weissenborn & W. Klein (eds.), *Here and there: cross-linguistic studies on deixis and demonstration*. Amsterdam: John Benjamins, 11–42.

Johnston, J. R., & D. I. Slobin. 1979. The development of locative expressions in English, Italian, Serbo-Croatian and Turkish. *Journal of Child Language* 6: 529–545.

Kant, E. 1768. Von dem ersten Grunde des Unterschiedes der Gegenden im Raume. Translated as: "On the first ground of the distinction of regions in space." In J. van Cleve & R. E. Frederick (eds.), 1991, *The philosophy of right and left: incongruent counterparts and the nature of space*. Dordrecht: Kluwer, 27–34.

Landau, B., & L. R. Gleitman. 1985. *Language and experience: evidence from the blind child*. Cambridge, MA: Harvard University Press.

Levinson, S. C. 1992a. Primer for the field investigation of spatial description and conception. *Pragmatics* 2: 5–47.

1992b. Language and cognition: the cognitive consequences of spatial description in Guugu Yimithirr. *Working Paper 13*. Nijmegen, The Netherlands: Cognitive Anthropology Research Group, Max Planck Institute for Psycholinguistics.

1994. Deixis. In R. E. Asher (ed.), *Encyclopedia of language and linguistics*, vol. 2. Oxford: Pergamon Press, 853–857.

1995a. Interactional biases in human thinking. In E. Goody (ed.), *Social intelligence and interaction*. Cambridge: Cambridge University Press, 221–260.

1995b. Three levels of meaning. In F. Palmer (ed.), *Grammar and meaning. Festschrift for John Lyons*. Cambridge: Cambridge University Press, 90–115.

1996a. Frames of reference and Molyneux's question: crosslinguistic evidence. In P. Bloom, M. A. Peterson, L. Nadel, & M. F. Garrett (eds.), *Language and space*. Cambridge, MA: MIT Press, 109–169.

1996b. Language and space. *Annual Review of Anthropology* 25: 353–382.

1996c. The role of language in everyday human navigation. *Working Paper 38*. Nijmegen, The Netherlands: Cognitive Anthropology Research Group, Max Planck Institute for Psycholinguistics.

1997. From outer to inner space: linguistic categories and nonlinguistic thinking. In J. Nuyts & E. Pederson (eds.), *Language and conceptualization*. Cambridge: Cambridge University Press, 13–45.

Levinson, S. C., & L. Nagy. 1997. Look at your southern leg: a statistical approach to cross-cultural field studies of language and spatial orientation. Unpublished ms., Max Planck Institute for Psycholinguistics, Nijmegen, The Netherlands.

Lucy, J. 1992. *Grammatical categories and cognition: a case study of the linguistic relativity hypothesis*. Cambridge: Cambridge University Press.

Lyons, J. 1968. *Introduction to theoretical linguistics*. Cambridge: Cambridge University Press.

Markman, E. 1989. *Categorization and naming in children: problems of induction*. Cambridge, MA: Bradford/MIT Press.

1992. Constraints on word learning: speculations about their nature, origins, and word specificity. In M. Gunnar & M. Maratsos (eds.), *Modularity and constraints in language and cognition*. Hillsdale, NJ: Lawrence Erlbaum, 59–102.

Matsumoto, Y. 1995. The conversational condition on Horn scales. *Linguistics and Philosophy*, 18: 21–60.

Merriman, W., J. Marazita, & L. Jarvis. 1995. Children's disposition to map new words onto new referents. In M. Tomasello & W. Merriman (eds.), *Beyond names for things: young children's acquisition of verbs*. Hillsdale, NJ/Hove: Lawrence Erlbaum, 147–185.

Miller, G. A., & P. N. Johnson-Laird. 1976. *Language and perception*. Cambridge, MA: Harvard University Press.

Pederson, E., E. Danziger, D. Wilkins, S. Levinson, S. Kita, & G. Senft. 1998. Semantic typology and spatial conceptualization. *Language* 74: 557–589.

Putnam, H. 1988. *Representation and reality*. Cambridge, MA: MIT Press.

Quine, W. V. O. 1960. *Word and object*. Cambridge, MA: MIT. Press.

Schelling, T. 1960. *The strategy of conflict*. Cambridge, MA: Harvard University Press.

Schiffer, S. R. 1972. *Meaning*. Oxford: Basil Blackwell.

Sperber, D. 1996. *Explaining culture: a naturalistic approach*. Oxford: Basil Blackwell.

Tomasello, M. 1995. Pragmatic contexts for early verb learning. In M. Tomasello & W. E. Merriman (eds.), *Beyond names for things: young children's acquisition of verbs*. Hillsdale, NJ/Hove: Lawrence Erlbaum, 115–146.

Author index

Subject index